BOOK OF MORMON STUDENT MANUAL

RELIGION 121–122

Published by
The Church of Jesus Christ of Latter-day Saints
Salt Lake City, Utah

Cover art
Christ in the Land Bountiful by Simon Dewey, © 2003 IRI

Comments and corrections are appreciated.
Please send them, including errors, to

Seminaries and Institutes of Religion Curriculum
50 E North Temple Street, Floor 8
Salt Lake City UT 84150-2722 USA
E-mail: ces-manuals@ldschurch.org

Please list your complete name, address, ward, and stake.
Be sure to give the title of the manual. Then offer your comments.

Contents

CHAPTER

Introduction 1

1 The Keystone of Our Religion 4

2 1 Nephi 1–5 12

3 1 Nephi 6–11 19

4 1 Nephi 12–15 26

5 1 Nephi 16–18 34

6 1 Nephi 19–22 42

7 2 Nephi 1–3 49

8 2 Nephi 4–8 58

9 2 Nephi 9–10 65

10 2 Nephi 11–16 72

11 2 Nephi 17–24 81

12 2 Nephi 25–27 92

13 2 Nephi 28–30 101

14 2 Nephi 31–33 107

15 Jacob 1–4 113

16 Jacob 5–7 122

17 Enos–Words of Mormon 130

18 Mosiah 1–3 136

19 Mosiah 4–8 142

20 Mosiah 9–17 149

21 Mosiah 18–24 156

22 Mosiah 25–29 163

23 Alma 1–4 170

24 Alma 5–7 178

25 Alma 8–12 184

26 Alma 13–16 191

27 Alma 17–22 198

28 Alma 23–29 205

29 Alma 30–31 213

30 Alma 32–35 222

31 Alma 36–39 232

32 Alma 40–42 242

33 Alma 43–51 248

34 Alma 52–63 256

35 Helaman 1–4 262

36 Helaman 5–9 268

37 Helaman 10–12 274

38 Helaman 13–16 281

39 3 Nephi 1–7 288

40 3 Nephi 8–11 295

41 3 Nephi 12–14 302

42 3 Nephi 15–17 312

43 3 Nephi 18–19 317

44 3 Nephi 20–22 323

45 3 Nephi 23–26 331

46 3 Nephi 27–30 337

47 4 Nephi 341

48 Mormon 1–6 348

49 Mormon 7–9 354

50 Ether 1–5 361

51 Ether 6–10 369

52 Ether 11–15 375

53 Moroni 1–6 382

54 Moroni 7 388

55 Moroni 8–9 395

56 Moroni 10 401

APPENDIX

Book of Mormon Plates and Records 407

Nephite Record Keepers 408

The Witnesses of the Book of Mormon Plates 409

Possible Route Taken by Lehi's Family 410

Book of Mormon Pages and Time Periods 411

The Stick of Judah and the Stick of Joseph 412

Flashbacks from Omni through Mosiah 413

The Cycle of Righteousness and Wickedness 414

Brief History of the Scattering of Israel 415

The Gathering of Israel 416

SUBJECT INDEX 417

The Book of Mormon testifies of Jesus Christ and teaches us how to become His disciples. The Prophet Joseph Smith (1805–44) affirmed that "a man would get nearer to God by abiding by its precepts, than by any other book" (*History of the Church,* 4:461; Book of Mormon introduction). As you study the Book of Mormon and are prayerful, the Holy Ghost continually bears witness to your heart and mind of the Savior's divine role as the Redeemer of mankind.

The Book of Mormon exerts a powerful influence on the hearts of those who receive it and ponder its message. Elder Parley P. Pratt (1807–57), an early convert of the Restoration and an eventual member of the Quorum of the Twelve Apostles, related the following regarding the first time he read the Book of Mormon:

"I opened it with eagerness, and read its title page. I then read the testimony of several witnesses in relation to the manner of its being found and translated. After this I commenced its contents by course. I read all day; eating was a burden, I had no desire for food; sleep was a burden when the night came, for I preferred reading to sleep.

"As I read, the spirit of the Lord was upon me, and I knew and comprehended that the book was true" (*Autobiography of Parley P. Pratt,* ed. Parley P. Pratt Jr. [1938], 37).

Modern prophets have continually emphasized the need for every Latter-day Saint to read and reread the Book of Mormon. President Gordon B. Hinckley (1910–2008) declared, "I promise you that if each of you will [read the Book of Mormon], regardless of how many times you previously may have read the Book of Mormon, there will come into your lives and into your homes an added measure of the Spirit of the Lord, a strengthened resolution to walk in obedience to His commandments, and a stronger testimony of the living reality of the Son of God" ("A Testimony Vibrant and True," *Ensign,* Aug. 2005, 6).

President Boyd K. Packer, President of the Quorum of the Twelve Apostles, shared how he learned that studying the Book of Mormon leads to personal revelation:

"I found [the Book of Mormon] to be plain and precious. . . .

"I learned that anyone, anywhere, could read in the Book of Mormon and receive inspiration.

"Some insights came after reading a second, even a third time and seemed to be 'likened' to what I faced in everyday life" (in Conference Report, Apr. 2005, 6; or *Ensign,* May 2005, 7).

Inspiration, as President Packer testified, will come as you consistently read from the Book of Mormon.

The Purpose of This Manual

This student manual supplements your reading and study of the Book of Mormon and should not replace it. The manual contains a compilation of prophetic insights and inspired counsel to assist you as you seek direction to "liken all scriptures" unto yourself (1 Nephi 19:23 📖). Evaluate your learning habits and determine how this manual best complements your personal reading and study of the Book of Mormon. Possible study options may include (1) referring to the manual while you read, (2) reading the manual after you have read several chapters in the Book of Mormon, or (3) reviewing the manual before you read the scriptures to strengthen your comprehension of the assigned chapters.

How This Manual Is Organized

The student manual contains 56 chapters covering the entire Book of Mormon. Each chapter has five parts: Introduction, Commentary, study questions (in callout boxes), Points to Ponder, and Suggested Assignments.

Introduction

A brief introduction at the beginning of each chapter places the story in context, identifies themes, and identifies a few of the doctrines and principles found in the scripture block.

Commentary

The commentary section clarifies doctrines and principles found in the scripture block. A careful reading of the commentary allows you to further identify and analyze the inspired messages of the Book of Mormon prophets. You will see how prophets in our day liken the truths in the scriptures to modern conditions and prevalent worldly situations.

The commentary also frequently quotes from correlated Church publications, including *True to the Faith: A Gospel Reference* (2004), *For the Strength of Youth: Fulfilling Our Duty to God* (2001), Guide to the Scriptures (available on the Internet at www.scriptures.lds.org), and the Topical Guide and Bible Dictionary.

Study Questions

Throughout the commentary section you will find study questions in shaded boxes like the one below. These questions will help you search and understand particular verses.

MOSIAH 18:21–29

What did Alma teach his people to do to "walk uprightly before God"? (v. 29).

Points to Ponder

The Points to Ponder section will help you reflect deeply on some items from your reading. Elder Russell M. Nelson of the Quorum of the Twelve

Apostles affirmed that pondering the scriptures will bring valuable results: "As you ponder and pray about doctrines and principles, the Holy Ghost will speak to your mind and your heart. From events portrayed in the scriptures, new insights will come and principles relevant to your situation will distill upon your heart" (in Conference Report, Oct. 2000, 19; or *Ensign,* Nov. 2000, 18). You may wish to have a scripture journal or separate notebook to record responses to some of these questions and impressions from your reading.

Suggested Assignments

At the end of every chapter are additional assignments that encourage personal application of truths from the scriptures. Some of these assignments may be incorporated into your class by your teacher if you are enrolled in a Book of Mormon religion or institute course. Please note that these assignments are suggestions and should be adapted according to your individual needs and direction from the Holy Ghost.

Information for Those with Disabilities

Alternative formats of this student manual may be available at www.ldsces.org. If you have difficulty using this manual due to a disability, please contact your instructor for additional resources.

Scripture Mastery

This manual contains a scripture mastery icon 📖, which designates scripture mastery passages. During seminary, students are asked to become familiar with 100 scriptures identified as being doctrinally significant. Each time one of the 100 scripture mastery verses is listed, you will see the 📖 symbol identifying it.

Introduction

The Prophet Joseph Smith (1805–44) stated, "I told the brethren that the Book of Mormon was the most correct of any book on earth, and the keystone of our religion, and a man would get nearer to God by abiding by its precepts, than by any other book" (*History of the Church,* 4:461; Book of Mormon introduction).

Elder Jeffrey R. Holland of the Quorum of the Twelve Apostles wrote that the Book of Mormon "should be considered the most remarkable and important religious text to be revealed since the writings of the New Testament were compiled nearly two millennia ago. Indeed, in its role of restoring plain and precious biblical truths that had been lost, while adding scores of new truths about Jesus Christ and preparing the way for the complete restoration of his gospel and the triumphant day of his millennial return, the Book of Mormon may be considered the most remarkable and important religious text ever given to the world" (*Christ and the New Covenant* [1997], 9–10).

As you begin your study of the Book of Mormon, look for the great truths it contains. Specifically, the Book of Mormon testifies of Jesus Christ's divinity and the reality of His Atonement. Furthermore, the Book of Mormon reaffirms God's covenant with the house of Israel and demonstrates the need for us to make and keep sacred covenants. By prayerfully studying this volume of scripture, you will gain depth and power in your testimony of the gospel of Jesus Christ and its Restoration to the earth in the latter days.

Commentary

Title Page

• The Book of Mormon title page begins: "The Book of Mormon, an account written by the hand of Mormon upon plates taken from the plates of Nephi." This is followed by two paragraphs, believed to be authored by the Book of Mormon prophet Moroni, son of Mormon. The Prophet Joseph Smith explained that "the title-page of the Book of Mormon is a literal translation, taken from the very last leaf, on the left hand side of the collection or book of plates, which contained the record which has been translated, the language of the whole running the same as all Hebrew writing in general [that is, from right to left]; and that said title page is not by any means a modern composition, either of mine or of any other man who has lived or does live in this generation" (*History of the Church,* 1:71).

"To Come Forth in Due Time"

• The first paragraph of the Book of Mormon title page declares that the sacred record will "come forth in due time." President Ezra Taft Benson (1899–1994) testified that the timing of the coming forth of the Book of Mormon shows its significance in the Restoration of the gospel:

"A . . . powerful testimony to the importance of the Book of Mormon is to note where the Lord placed its coming forth in the timetable of the unfolding Restoration. The only thing that preceded it was the First Vision. In that marvelous manifestation, the Prophet Joseph Smith learned the true nature of God and that God had a work for him to do. The coming forth of the Book of Mormon was the next thing to follow.

"Think of that in terms of what it implies. The coming forth of the Book of Mormon preceded the restoration of the priesthood. It was published just a few days before the Church was organized. The Saints were given the Book of Mormon to read before they were given the revelations outlining such great doctrines as the three degrees of glory, celestial marriage, or work for the dead. It came before priesthood quorums and Church organization. Doesn't this tell us something about how the Lord views this sacred work?" (in Conference Report, Oct. 1986, 3; or *Ensign,* Nov. 1986, 4).

• Elder L. Tom Perry of the Quorum of the Twelve Apostles explained that the Book of Mormon was written for our day: "The major writers of the Book of Mormon fully understood that their writings were primarily for the people of a future generation rather than for the people of their own generation. Moroni wrote to our generation, 'I speak unto you as if ye were present' (Mormon 8:35)" (in Conference Report, Oct. 2005, 5; or *Ensign,* Nov. 2005, 6–7).

• Speaking of our need to apply the Book of Mormon in our lives, President Ezra Taft Benson declared: "If they saw our day and chose those things which would be of greatest worth to us, is not that how we should study the Book of Mormon? We should constantly ask ourselves, 'Why did the Lord inspire Mormon (or Moroni or Alma) to include that in his record? What lesson can I learn from that to help me live in this day and age?'" (in Conference Report, Oct. 1986, 5; or *Ensign,* Nov. 1986, 6).

Elder Perry also suggested an important practice when reading the Book of Mormon: "Each time we read the book we should probably ask ourselves: 'Why did these writers choose these particular stories or events to include in the record? What value are they for us today?'" (in Conference Report, Oct. 2005, 5; or *Ensign,* Nov. 2005, 8).

Interpretation by the Gift of God
• The gold plates themselves contained a promise that they would be interpreted "by the gift and power of God" (Book of Mormon title page). Elder Russell M. Nelson of the Quorum of the Twelve Apostles shared some remarkable information about the Book of Mormon's translation:

"The details of this miraculous method of translation are still not fully known. Yet we do have a few precious insights. . . .

"Emma Smith, who acted as an earlier scribe for Joseph, gave this account in 1856:

"'When my husband was translating the Book of Mormon, I wrote a part of it, as he dictated each sentence, word for word, and when he came to proper names he could not pronounce, or long words, he spelled them out, and while I was writing them, if I made any mistake in spelling, he would stop me and correct my spelling although it was impossible for him to see how I was writing them down at the time. Even

the word *Sarah* he could not pronounce at first, but had to spell it, and I would pronounce it for him.

"'When he stopped for any purpose at any time he would, when he commenced again, begin where he left off without any hesitation, and one time while he was translating he stopped suddenly, pale as a sheet, and said, "Emma, did Jerusalem have walls around it?" When I answered, "Yes," he replied, "Oh! [I didn't know]. I was afraid I had been deceived." He had such a limited knowledge of history at that time that he did not even know that Jerusalem was surrounded by walls.' (Edmund C. Briggs, 'A Visit to Nauvoo in 1856,' *Journal of History,* Jan. 1916, p. 454). . . .

"Although the Prophet would polish his skills over the years, Emma acknowledged that Joseph possessed only rudimentary literacy at the time he translated the gold plates:

"'Joseph Smith . . . could neither write nor dictate a coherent and well-worded letter; let alone dictating a book like the Book of Mormon. And, though I was an active participant in the scenes that transpired, it is marvelous to me, "a marvel and a wonder," as much so as to any one else.' (Ibid)" ("A Treasured Testament," *Ensign,* July 1993, 62–63).

The Book of Mormon Affirms God's Covenant with Israel
• In addition to testifying of Jesus Christ, the Book of Mormon demonstrates that God remembers His covenant with the house of Israel. The Guide to the Scriptures describes the house of Israel, its scattering, and its gathering:

"The Lord gave the name Israel to Jacob, the son of Isaac and grandson of Abraham in the Old Testament (Gen. 32:28; 35:10). The name Israel can refer to Jacob himself, his descendants, or to the kingdom those descendants once possessed in Old Testament times. . . .

"*The twelve tribes of Israel:* Abraham's grandson Jacob, whose name was changed to Israel, had twelve sons. Their descendants have become known as the twelve tribes of Israel or the children of Israel. . . .

"The scattering of Israel: The Lord scattered and afflicted the twelve tribes of Israel because of their unrighteousness and rebellion. However, the Lord also used this scattering of his chosen people among the nations of the world to bless those nations. . . .

"The gathering of Israel: The house of Israel shall be gathered together in the last days before the coming of Christ (A of F 1:10). The Lord gathers his people Israel when they accept him and keep his commandments" (Guide to the Scriptures, "Israel").

• Members of The Church of Jesus Christ of Latter-day Saints are the portion of the house of Israel that has been gathered to the knowledge of their fathers and to the covenants of the Lord. The Lord has declared, "For ye are the children of Israel, and of the seed of Abraham" (D&C 103:17).

• Concerning the Book of Mormon's role in the gathering of Israel in the last days, Elder Bruce R. McConkie (1915–85) of the Quorum of the Twelve Apostles wrote: "As far as the gathering of Israel is concerned, the Book of Mormon is the most important book that ever has been or ever will be written. It is the book that gathers Israel and that reveals, in plainness and perfection, the doctrine of the gathering of the chosen seed. It is the book, given of God, to prove the truth and divinity of his great latter-day work. It contains the fulness of the everlasting gospel and carries with it the evidence of its own divinity. Every person who is truly converted knows by the revelations of the Holy Ghost to the spirit within him that the Book of Mormon is the mind and will and voice of the Lord to the world today. It is the Book of Mormon that causes people to believe the gospel and join the Church, and, as we have heretofore seen, it is the power that brings to pass the gathering of Israel. If there were no Book of Mormon, from a practical standpoint, the gathering of the Lord's people in the last days would come to a standstill. The lost sheep of Israel hear the voice of their Shepherd as it is found in that book and, heeding that voice, come into the true sheepfold. There is no way of overstating the importance of this book of Nephite scripture in the salvation of men in the last days" (*A New Witness for the Articles of Faith* [1985], 554).

Convincing Jew and Gentile "That Jesus Is the Christ"

• According to the title page, the purpose of the Book of Mormon is to bring Jew and Gentile to the conviction that "Jesus is the Christ, the Eternal God, manifesting himself unto all nations." The Book of Mormon subtitle, Another Testament of Jesus Christ, emphasizes its paramount purpose. President Boyd K. Packer, President of the Quorum of the Twelve Apostles, explained the significance of the subtitle:

"By recent decision of the Brethren the Book of Mormon will henceforth bear the title 'The Book of Mormon,' with the subtitle 'Another Testament of Jesus Christ.'

"The stick or record of Judah—the Old Testament and the New Testament—and the stick or record of Ephraim—the Book of Mormon, which is another testament of Jesus Christ—are now woven together in such a way that as you pore over one you are drawn to the other; as you learn from one you are enlightened by the other. They are indeed one in our hands. Ezekiel's prophecy now stands fulfilled" (in Conference Report, Oct. 1982, 75; or *Ensign,* Nov. 1982, 53).

• President Ezra Taft Benson explained the meaning of the word *testament:* "'Do we remember the new covenant, even the Book of Mormon?' [see D&C 84:57]. In the Bible we have the Old Testament and the New Testament. The word *testament* is the English rendering of a Greek word that can also be translated as *covenant.* Is this what the Lord meant when He called the Book of Mormon the 'new covenant'? It is indeed another testament or witness of Jesus. This is one of the reasons why we have recently added the words 'Another Testament of Jesus Christ' to the title of the Book of Mormon" (in Conference Report, Oct. 1986, 4; or *Ensign,* Nov. 1986, 4).

• Elder Russell M. Nelson of the Quorum of the Twelve Apostles counseled: "When you read the Book of Mormon, concentrate on the principal figure in the book—from its first chapter to the last—the Lord Jesus Christ, Son of the Living God" (in Conference Report, Oct. 1999, 87; or *Ensign,* Nov. 1999, 69).

Elder Jeffrey R. Holland gave further explanation:

"[The Lord] has offered us one last covenant, given us one last testament, as part of his final outreach to fallen man. He has offered us one last written witness of his love and his mercy extended for the final time. . . . That testament and culminating witness, that 'new covenant' offered to the children of men but once more, is the message of the Book of Mormon.

Del Parson, © 1996 IRI

"No record teaches more of God's promise to those in the last days. Those promises focus on his Only Begotten Son, on 'the merits, and mercy, and grace of the Holy Messiah . . . [who] shall make intercession for all the children of men; and they that believe in him shall be saved' [2 Nephi 2:8–9].

"The task of the children of God in these concluding days of the world's history is to proceed with 'unshaken faith in him, relying wholly upon the merits of him who is mighty to save,' to 'press forward with a steadfastness in Christ, having a perfect brightness of hope, and a love of God and of all men[,] . . . feasting upon the word of Christ, and endur[ing] to the end. This is the way; and there is none other way nor name given under heaven whereby man can be saved in the kingdom of God' [2 Nephi 31:19–21].

"No other book helps us do this so well. No other book was ever divinely produced and protected solely for that purpose. No other book has ever been written with such a full view of the future dispensation to which that record would eventually come. . . .

". . . In its message of faith in Christ, hope in Christ, and charity in Christ, the Book of Mormon is God's 'new covenant' to his children—for the last time" (*Christ and the New Covenant,* 8–10).

BOOK OF MORMON TITLE PAGE
What facts recorded on the title page testify of the miraculous nature of the book?

How the Book of Mormon Is the Keystone

• The Prophet Joseph Smith identified the Book of Mormon as the "keystone of our religion" (*History of the Church,* 4:461; Book of Mormon introduction). President Ezra Taft Benson explained the role of a keystone as follows:

"A keystone is the central stone in an arch. It holds all the other stones in place, and if removed, the arch crumbles.

"There are three ways in which the Book of Mormon is the keystone of our religion. It is the keystone in our witness of Christ. It is the keystone of our doctrine. It is the keystone of testimony" (in Conference Report, Oct. 1986, 4; or *Ensign,* Nov. 1986, 5).

• President James E. Faust (1920–2007) of the First Presidency expanded the idea of the Book of Mormon as our doctrinal keystone:

"The Book of Mormon is a keystone because it establishes and ties together eternal principles and precepts, rounding out basic doctrines of salvation. It is the crowning gem in the diadem of our holy scriptures.

"It is a keystone for other reasons also. In the promise of Moroni . . . —namely, that God will manifest the truth of the Book of Mormon to every sincere inquirer having faith in Christ—we have a key link in a self-locking chain.

"A confirming testimony of the Book of Mormon convinces 'that Jesus is the Christ, the Eternal God' and also spiritually verifies the divine calling of Joseph Smith and that he did see the Father and the Son. With that firmly in place, it logically follows that one can also receive a verification that the Doctrine and Covenants and the Pearl of Great Price are true companion scriptures to the Bible and the Book of Mormon.

"All of this confirms the Restoration of the gospel of Jesus Christ and the divine mission of The Church of Jesus Christ of Latter-day Saints, led by a living prophet enjoying continuous revelation. From these basic verities, an understanding can flow of other saving principles of the fulness of the gospel" ("The Keystone of Our Religion," *Ensign*, Jan. 2004, 3–4).

"Nearer to God by Abiding by Its Precepts"

• On Sunday, November 28, 1841, the Prophet Joseph Smith spent the day in council with the Twelve Apostles at the house of President Young. While talking with them on a variety of subjects, he declared that "a man would get nearer to God by abiding by its [the Book of Mormon] precepts, than by any other book" (*History of the Church,* 4:461; Book of Mormon introduction).

• President Ezra Taft Benson taught that the Book of Mormon helps us discern truth from error:

"We . . . should know the Book of Mormon better than any other book. Not only should we know what history and faith-promoting stories it contains, but we should understand its teachings. If we really do our homework and approach the Book of Mormon doctrinally, we can expose the errors and find the truths to combat many of the current false theories and philosophies of men.

"I have noted within the Church a difference in discernment, insight, conviction, and spirit between those who know and love the Book of Mormon and those who do not. That book is a great sifter" ("Jesus Christ—Gifts and Expectations," *Ensign,* Dec. 1988, 4).

• President Marion G. Romney (1897–1988) of the First Presidency related how study from the Book of Mormon preserved his spiritual safety: "A few years ago as I began to practice law, members of my family

were a little uneasy. They were afraid I would lose my faith. I wanted to practice law, but I had an even greater desire to keep my testimony, and so I decided upon a little procedure which I recommend to you. For thirty minutes each morning before I began the day's work I read from the Book of Mormon—I read also from all the other standard works of the Church, but I am talking now about the Book of Mormon—and in just a few minutes a day I read the Book of Mormon through, every year, for nine years. I know that it kept me in harmony, so far as I did keep in harmony, with the Spirit of the Lord" (in Conference Report, Apr. 1949, 36).

The Reader Determines What Is Learned

• Reading the Book of Mormon has the potential to bring marvelous blessings. There is, however, a great responsibility that rests with the reader. Elder Dallin H. Oaks of the Quorum of the Twelve Apostles spoke about one's need to read with the properly positioned heart and attitude: "What we get from a book, especially a sacred text, is mostly dependent on what we take to its reading—in desire and readiness to learn, and in attunement to the light communicated by the Spirit of the Lord" (in Conference Report, Apr. 2006, 78; or *Ensign,* May 2006, 77).

Receiving a Personal Testimony of the Book of Mormon

• The last prophet to engrave on the record of the Nephites was Moroni, Mormon's son. As a prophet of God, Moroni gave a formula whereby readers may receive a personal witness from the Holy Ghost that the Book of Mormon is sacred scripture. This promise, given to all who sincerely read the Book of Mormon and desire to know of its truthfulness, is found in Moroni 10:3–5. 📖

• A sincere reader may not immediately gain a testimony when reading the Book of Mormon. Further, some people may not recognize the testimony that is growing as they study and pray over this tremendous text. But the promise of Moroni will come. President Boyd K. Packer, President of the Quorum of the Twelve Apostles, shared his personal experience and counsel for those seeking a testimony:

"When I first read the Book of Mormon from cover to cover, I read the promise that if I 'would ask God, the Eternal Father, in the name of Christ, if [the things I had read were] true; and if [I would] ask with a sincere heart, with real intent, having faith in Christ, he [would] manifest the truth of it unto [me], by the power of the Holy Ghost' (Moroni 10:4). I tried to follow those instructions as I understood them.

"If I expected a glorious manifestation to come at once as an overpowering experience, it did not happen. Nevertheless, it felt good, and I began to believe. . . .

"My experience has been that a testimony does not burst upon us suddenly. Rather, it grows, as Alma said, from a seed of faith. 'It will strengthen your faith: for ye will say I know that this is a good seed; for behold it sprouteth and beginneth to grow' (Alma 32:30). If you nourish it, it will grow; and if you do not nourish it, it will wither (see Alma 32:37–41).

"Do not be disappointed if you have read and reread and yet have not received a powerful witness. You may be somewhat like the disciples spoken of in the Book of Mormon who were filled with the power of God in great glory 'and they knew it not' (3 Nephi 9:20).

"Do the best you can. Think of this verse: 'See that all these things are done in wisdom and order; for it is not requisite that a man should run faster than he has strength. And again, it is expedient that he should be diligent, that thereby he might win the prize; therefore, all things must be done in order' (Mosiah 4:27)" (in Conference Report, Apr. 2005, 6–7; or *Ensign,* May 2005, 6, 8).

Moroni 10:3–5 📖

Reread Moroni's promise. How will you apply this promise as you study the Book of Mormon?

External Evidences of the Book of Mormon

• Some students of the Book of Mormon are interested in geographical, textual, or archaeological evidences of the book's ancient origin. While these are often fascinating and helpful, it must be remembered that these kinds of discoveries do not constitute the substance and truth of the Book of Mormon. President Gordon B. Hinckley (1910–2008) counseled against relying solely on these discoveries for our testimony of the Book of Mormon: "The evidence for its truth, for its validity in a world that is prone to demand evidence, lies not in archaeology or anthropology, though these may be helpful to some. It lies not in word research or historical analysis, though these may be confirmatory. The evidence for its truth and validity lies within the covers of the book itself. The test of its truth lies in reading it. It is a book of God. Reasonable people may sincerely question its origin; but those who have read it prayerfully have come to know by a power beyond their natural senses that it is true, that it contains the word of God, that it outlines saving truths of the everlasting gospel, that it 'came forth by the gift and power of God . . . to the convincing of the Jew and Gentile that Jesus is the Christ' (Book of Mormon title page)" ("Four Cornerstones of Faith," *Ensign,* Feb. 2004, 6).

Blessings of the Book of Mormon

• President Gordon B. Hinckley explained how the Book of Mormon can keep members of the Church spiritually sound:

"[The Book of Mormon] so clearly illustrates the fact that when men and nations walk in the fear of God and in obedience to His commandments, they prosper and grow, but when they disregard Him and His word, there comes a decay that, unless arrested by righteousness, leads to impotence and death. . . .

"Without reservation I promise you that if each of you will [read the Book of Mormon], . . . there will come into your lives and into your homes an added measure of the Spirit of the Lord, a strengthened resolution to walk in obedience to His commandments, and a stronger testimony of the living reality of the Son of God" ("A Testimony Vibrant and True," *Ensign,* Aug. 2005, 4–6).

• President James E. Faust related an experience shared by Elder F. Burton Howard of the Seventy that demonstrates the converting power of the Book of Mormon:

"Sister Celia Cruz Ayala of the Puerto Rico San Juan Mission decided to give the Book of Mormon to a friend. She wrapped it in attractive paper and set out to deliver her present.

"On the way she was attacked by a bandit who stole her purse and with it the wrapped copy of the Book of Mormon. A few days later she received this letter:

"'Mrs. Cruz:

"'Forgive me, forgive me. You will never know how sorry I am for attacking you. But because of it, my life has changed and will continue to change. That book [the Book of Mormon] has helped me in my life. The dream of that man of God has shaken me. . . . I am returning your five pesos for I can't spend them. I want you to know that you seemed to have a radiance about you. That light seemed to stop me [from harming you, so] I ran away instead.

"'I want you to know that you will see me again, but when you do, you won't recognize me, for I will be your brother. . . . Here, where I live, I have to find the Lord and go to the church you belong to.

"'The message you wrote in that book brought tears to my eyes. Since Wednesday night I have not been able to stop reading it. I have prayed and asked God to forgive me, [and] I ask you to forgive me. . . . I thought your wrapped gift was something I could sell. [Instead,] it has made me want to make my life over. Forgive me, forgive me, I beg you.

"'Your absent friend.'

"Such is the conversion power of the Book of Mormon" (in Conference Report, Apr. 1996, 58; or *Ensign,* May 1996, 42).

Book of Mormon Plates and Records

• Refer to the chart "Book of Mormon Plates and Records" in the appendix (p. 407). It shows the individual records written by the different prophets and which plates contained which record.

Nephite Record Keepers

• Refer to the chart "Nephite Record Keepers" in the appendix (p. 408). It shows the individual writers and the books each one wrote.

Witnesses to the Truth of the Book of Mormon

• Elder Bruce R. McConkie explained that the Lord will always provide witnesses of the divinity of His work:

"Whenever the Lord has established a dispensation by revealing his gospel and by conferring priesthood and keys upon men, he has acted in accordance with the *law of witnesses* which he himself ordained. This law is: 'In the mouth of two or three witnesses shall every word be established.' (2 Cor. 13:1; Deut. 17:6; 19:15; Matt. 18:15–16. . . .)

"Never does one man stand alone in establishing a new dispensation of revealed truth, or in carrying the burden of such a message and warning to the world. In every dispensation, from Adam to the present, two or more witnesses have always joined their testimonies, thus leaving their hearers without excuse in the day of judgment should the testimony be rejected" (*Mormon Doctrine,* 2nd ed. [1966], 436).

• President Heber J. Grant (1856–1945) emphasized the importance of the witnesses to the Book of Mormon: "I do not believe that in any court of justice in the world if a man was being tried for murder and twelve reputable citizens testified of their knowledge of the circumstances leading to the murder, and there was no one who could testify against what they said, there would be a failure to convict the man. We have the testimony of Joseph Smith and the testimony of three witnesses to the effect that God gave them a knowledge regarding the Book of Mormon, that an angel of God declared from heaven that the book had been translated by the gift and power of God. These men were Oliver Cowdery, David Whitmer and Martin Harris. They left the Church, but to the day of their death they maintained their testimony regarding the declaration of the angel, and that they were commanded to bear witness of the divinity of this book, and they did so. Eight men, some of whom were excommunicated from the Church, maintained their testimony that they had seen and handled the plates from which the Book of Mormon was translated, and they remained true to that testimony to the day of their death. The disbelief of all the world does not prove that those men did not tell the truth, because there are no witnesses on the other side" (in Conference Report, Apr. 1929, 128). (Refer to "The Witnesses of the Book of Mormon Plates" in the appendix, p. 409.)

- Despite the experience of seeing and handling the gold plates in June 1829, some of the witnesses did not remain true to The Church of Jesus Christ of Latter-day Saints. President James E. Faust explained: "Knowledge comes through faith. In our day and time we must come to know the truthfulness of what was on the golden plates without seeing them. They are not available for us to see and handle as they were for the Three Witnesses and for the Eight Witnesses. Some of those who actually saw and handled the golden plates did not remain faithful to the Church. Seeing an angel would be a great experience, but it is far greater to come to a knowledge of the divinity of the Savior through faith and the witness of the Spirit [see John 20:29]" (in Conference Report, Apr. 2002, 57; or *Ensign,* May 2002, 48).

> ### WITNESSES
> *What is the difference between the experience recorded by the Three Witnesses and the experience recorded by the Eight Witnesses?*

The Witnesses of the Book of Mormon Plates

- Refer to "The Witnesses of the Book of Mormon Plates" in the appendix (p. 409). It lists the Three Witnesses and the Eight Witnesses with their birth dates, birth places, ages when each was shown the plates, occupations, information on baptisms, and death dates and places.

Points to Ponder

- In what ways is the Book of Mormon another testament of Jesus Christ?

- How does studying the Book of Mormon help us to "condemn not the things of God"? (Book of Mormon title page).

- Why should every Church member be able to bear witness that the Book of Mormon is the word of God?

Suggested Assignments

- Write a short summary of what you feel are the purposes of the Book of Mormon. Compare your list with the purposes listed by Moroni on the title page of the Book of Mormon.

- Analyze the promise in Moroni 10:3–5 and determine what you need to do to gain or strengthen your testimony of the Book of Mormon.

Introduction

In 1995 the First Presidency and the Quorum of the Twelve Apostles described the family as "central to the Creator's plan for the eternal destiny of His children." They declared that "happiness in family life is most likely to be achieved when founded upon the teachings of the Lord Jesus Christ" ("The Family: A Proclamation to the World," *Ensign,* Nov. 1995, 102). Nephi wrote about the family of Lehi and Sariah, his parents. These "goodly parents" (1 Nephi 1:1) sought to raise and guide their family with the Lord's teachings, even during challenging times. Father Lehi experienced visions of heaven as well as attempts on his life. Family members found safety in fleeing from Jerusalem, only to be sent back on the dangerous and difficult assignment to retrieve the brass plates. Faithful sons supported their parents and followed the Lord while other sons rebelled. As you read these early Book of Mormon chapters, observe this family's efforts to follow the Lord and see how their example can direct you to do the same.

Commentary

The First Book of Nephi: His Reign and Ministry

• The heading to 1 Nephi is a summary of the book and is part of the original text. All headings in the Book of Mormon are part of the original record given to the Prophet Joseph Smith, including the inserts preceding individual chapters (for example, see Mosiah 9 and Alma 21). The brief summaries at the head of each chapter are later additions to help the reader better understand the chapter.

• As compiler of the Book of Mormon, Mormon faced difficult challenges in determining what to include in the abridged record. At least two directives guided his selections. First, the Lord told Mormon to "write the things which have been commanded" (3 Nephi 26:12). Second, Mormon saw our day and the conditions that would exist (see Mormon 8:34–35). We understand, then, that when Mormon made editorial decisions, these two factors were his governing concerns.

It may be instructive to compare the length of books in the Book of Mormon and the time periods they covered. Refer to the chart "Book of Mormon Pages and Time Periods" in the appendix (p. 411).

1 Nephi 1:1. Many Afflictions, Yet Highly Favored

• Nephi wrote of "many afflictions" yet also acknowledged many blessings from the Lord. His record recounts numerous trials he and others of his family endured while staying faithful and grateful to the Lord. Nephi felt highly favored because he had come to a great knowledge of the goodness of God (see 1 Nephi 2:16), and relying on His strength became Nephi's support (see 2 Nephi 4:19–26). The understanding of God's plan gave context to the afflictions Nephi experienced (see Boyd K. Packer, "Conversation with Teachers" [an evening with President Boyd K. Packer, Feb. 29, 2008], 7, www.ldsces.org).

In contrast, we also see that Laman and Lemuel, as well as many others in the Book of Mormon, required frequent afflictions to remind them of the Lord's blessings. This principle is sadly reaffirmed by the prophet Mormon: "And thus we see that except the Lord doth chasten his people with many afflictions, yea, except he doth visit them with death and with terror, and with famine and with all manner of pestilence, they will not remember him" (Helaman 12:3).

1 Nephi 1:2. "The Language of the Egyptians"

• Verse 2 of 1 Nephi 1 indicates that Lehi and Nephi used "the language of the Egyptians" to record their history onto gold plates. Four hundred and seventy years later, King Benjamin taught his sons "the language of the Egyptians," which was not only the language of the gold plates but the language of the brass plates as well (Mosiah 1:1–4). The term "reformed Egyptian" only appears in the Book of Mormon in Mormon 9:32. Reformed Egyptian appears to be a term that reflects a variation in the language used by Lehi and Nephi. In Mormon 9:32–33 Moroni indicated that by his day, approximately a thousand years from the time of Lehi and Nephi, both the Egyptian and Hebrew had been altered from that used by Lehi and Nephi.

1 Nephi 1:4. Prophets Warn the People

• Babylonian world domination took control of the kingdom of Judah about 605 B.C. when Jehoiakim was king of Judah. Jehoiakim attempted a revolt against Babylon. Babylonian forces put Jerusalem under siege. Jehoiakim was either killed or captured. Zedekiah, the uncle of Jehoiakim, was appointed by Babylon to the throne. It was a time of great wickedness among the people of Judah—immorality and corruption were rampant. This is the setting of Lehi's day. Shortly after Lehi's departure from the area, Zedekiah attempted another revolt against Babylon, resulting in a much greater destruction of Jerusalem in about 587 B.C. Many people were killed, and most of the rest of the Jews were taken captive into Babylon for the next 70 years. This fulfilled Lehi's prophecies to Judah that if they did not repent they would be destroyed.

Del Parson, © IRI

• Nephi said that "many prophets" came among the people. We know Jeremiah, Obadiah, Nahum, Habakkuk, and Zephaniah were all contemporary prophets who testified in the kingdom of Judah. Jeremiah 35:15 includes a similar comment about numerous prophets being sent by the Lord to warn the people (see also 2 Chronicles 36:15–16).

1 Nephi 1:16–17. Two Sets of Records

• Nephi wrote his record about 30 years after Lehi's family left Jerusalem and journeyed to the promised land (see 1 Nephi 19:1–5; 2 Nephi 5:28–31). The record begins with an abridgment of his father's record,

comprising 1 Nephi 1–8. Mormon's abridgment of Lehi's record was in the lost 116 manuscript pages. It was a translation from a portion of the plates called the "Book of Lehi" (see D&C 10 heading; 10:42, footnote *a*; commentary for 1 Nephi 19:1–6 on p. 42).

1 Nephi 1:20. "Tender Mercies of the Lord"

• Elder David A. Bednar of the Quorum of the Twelve Apostles described the "tender mercies of the Lord":

"I testify that the tender mercies of the Lord are real and that they do not occur randomly or merely by coincidence. Often the Lord's timing of His tender mercies helps us to both discern and acknowledge them.

". . . The Lord's tender mercies are the very personal and individualized blessings, strength, protection, assurances, guidance, loving-kindness, consolation, support, and spiritual gifts which we receive from and because of and through the Lord Jesus Christ. Truly the Lord suits 'his mercies according to the conditions of the children of men' (D&C 46:15).

". . . One of the ways whereby the Savior comes to each of us is through His abundant and tender mercies. For instance, as you and I face challenges and tests in our lives, the gift of faith and an appropriate sense of personal confidence that reaches beyond our own capacity are two examples of the tender mercies of the Lord. Repentance and forgiveness of sins and peace of conscience are examples of the tender mercies of the Lord. And the persistence and the fortitude that enable us to press forward with cheerfulness through physical limitations and spiritual difficulties are examples of the tender mercies of the Lord" (in Conference Report, Apr. 2005, 105; or *Ensign,* May 2005, 99–100).

From 1 Nephi 1:20 we learn that through the rest of his writings Nephi is intent on showing us how the Lord will deliver the righteous. Watch for this repeating theme throughout 1 Nephi.

1 Nephi 3:15. "As the Lord Liveth"

• Elder Bruce R. McConkie (1915–85) of the Quorum of the Twelve Apostles gave this explanation: "Nephi made God his partner. If he failed to get the plates, it meant God had failed. And because God does not fail, it was incumbent upon Nephi to get the plates or lay down his life in the attempt" (in Conference Report, Apr. 1982, 49–50; or *Ensign,* May 1982, 33).

1 Nephi 2:5–10. Lehi Traveled from Jerusalem to the Shores of the Red Sea

• The distance from Jerusalem to the Red Sea is approximately 180 miles through hot, barren country infested anciently by many marauders. Lehi and his family "traveled three days" beyond this point (see 1 Nephi 2:5–6). This meant at least a 12- to 14-day trip one way from Jerusalem to their temporary home in the valley of Lemuel. (Refer to the map "Possible Route Taken by Lehi's Family" in the appendix, p. 410.)

Scott Snow, © 1981 IRI

1 Nephi 2:6–10. Showing Gratitude to the Lord

• Lehi's appreciation for the Lord's guidance and protection is demonstrated by his first act after pitching his tent: "He built an altar of stones, and made an offering unto the Lord, and gave thanks unto the Lord our God" (1 Nephi 2:7). This is the first of several instances in the Book of Mormon where faithful followers of Christ offered sacrifices and burnt offerings to express thanks to God (see 1 Nephi 7:22; Mosiah 2:3–4).

Lehi followed the offering by teaching his sons the importance of staying firm in keeping the Lord's commandments. Sincere expressions of gratitude and obedience to Heavenly Father are necessary for all His children if they are to please Him. The Lord taught, "And in nothing doth man offend God, or against none is his wrath kindled, save those who confess not his hand in all things, and obey not his commandments" (D&C 59:21).

Elder M. Russell Ballard of the Quorum of the Twelve Apostles counseled us to make sure our prayers are filled with humility and thankfulness: "I often hear people say 'I told the Lord' this or 'I told the Lord' that. Be careful not to 'tell' Him but, rather, to humbly seek and ask your Heavenly Father for guidance and direction. Prayer should be yearning and filled with gratitude" ("Be Strong in the Lord, and in the Power of His Might" [CES fireside for young adults, Mar. 3, 2002], 3, www.ldsces.org).

1 Nephi 2:11–15. Murmuring

• One reason Satan encourages murmuring is to prevent us from following living prophets, inspired leaders, and parents. Elder H. Ross Workman of the Seventy explained that "murmuring consists of three steps, each leading to the next in a descending path to disobedience." First, when people murmur they begin to question. They question "first in their own minds and then [plant] questions in the minds of others." Second, those who murmur begin to "rationalize and excuse themselves from doing what they [have] been instructed to do. . . . Thus, they [make] an excuse for disobedience." Their excuses lead to the third step: "Slothfulness in following the commandment."

"The Lord has spoken against this attitude in our day: 'But he that doeth not anything until he is commanded, and receiveth a commandment with doubtful heart, and keepeth it with slothfulness, the same is damned' (D&C 58:29). . . .

"I invite you to focus on the commandment from living prophets that bothers you the most. Do you question whether the commandment is applicable to you? Do you find ready excuses why you cannot now comply with the commandment? Do you feel frustrated or irritated with those who remind you of the commandment? Are you slothful in keeping it? Beware of the deception of the adversary. Beware of murmuring" (in Conference Report, Oct. 2001, 104–6; or *Ensign,* Nov. 2001, 85–86).

> **1 NEPHI 2:16**
> *Although Nephi did not murmur, what evidence does this verse provide that leaving Jerusalem may have also been a challenge for him?*

1 Nephi 2:20. Keep the Commandments and Prosper

• Elder Russell M. Nelson of the Quorum of the Twelve Apostles observed that the scriptures promise "thirty-four times—that people will prosper in the land only if they obey the commandments of God" (in Conference Report, Apr. 1985, 15; or *Ensign,* May 1985, 13). In the scriptures, the meaning of the word *prosperity* may also have other meanings not restricted to financial benefits. Further, prospering doesn't mean that life will be free from trials. Lehi and his faithful family members kept the commandments, but they still suffered many afflictions (see 1 Nephi 15:5; 18:15–17; 2 Nephi 2:1–2).

President Joseph F. Smith (1838–1918) taught that a person who keeps the commandments will be sustained and prospered by the Lord: "The man who stays with the kingdom of God, the man who is true to this people, the man who keeps himself pure and unspotted from the world, is the man that God will accept, that God will uphold, that he will sustain, and that will prosper in the land, whether he be in the enjoyment of his liberty or be confined in prison cells, it makes no difference where he is, he will come out all right" (*Gospel Doctrine,* 5th ed. [1939], 257).

1 Nephi 3:7. 📖 "I Will Go and Do"

• Commenting on 1 Nephi 3:7, Elder Russell M. Nelson taught, "I have learned not to put question marks but to use exclamation points when calls are issued through inspired channels of priesthood government" (in Conference Report, Apr. 1984, 76–77; or *Ensign,* May 1984, 52).

• Elder Donald L. Staheli of the Seventy quoted President Ezra Taft Benson (1899–1994) in order to teach about the power that comes through obedience:

"Regardless of our age and stage in life, daily obedience to gospel principles is the only sure way to eternal happiness. President Ezra Taft Benson put it most poignantly when he said, 'When obedience ceases to be an irritant and becomes our quest, in that moment God will endow us with power'" (in Conference Report, Apr. 1998, 108; or *Ensign,* May 1998, 82).

• President Henry B. Eyring of the First Presidency acknowledged the need for prayer and faith to obey the Lord's commandments:

"Whoever we are, however difficult our circumstances, we can know that what our Father commands we do to qualify for the blessings of eternal life will not be beyond us. . . .

"We may have to pray with faith to know what we are to do and we must pray with a determination to obey, but we can know what to do and be sure that the way has been prepared for us by the Lord" ("The Family" [CES fireside for young adults, Nov. 5, 1995], 1, www.ldsces.org).

> **1 NEPHI 3:19–20; 5:11–14**
> *What did the brass plates contain that made them so important to Lehi's family and descendants?*

1 Nephi 4:6. "Led by the Spirit"

• Sometimes it takes courage to be led by the Spirit. There will be times when the world's logic and reasoning will suggest a course of action that is contrary to the Lord's teaching. Elder John H. Groberg of the Seventy challenged us:

"Be willing to take reasonable risks. We live in an age of reason, logic, facts, and figures. These can be useful if kept in subjection to faith in the Lord, Jesus Christ. But if they ever take precedence over faith in Him, then they are not useful and can be very harmful. I have found in my life that most of the good decisions I have made may not have been made if they were based solely on logic or reason. . . .

". . . Nephi was determined to do what God wanted him to do even with logic to the contrary. The scriptures tell us in 1 Nephi 4:6 that he went forth not knowing beforehand what he should do but knowing he should obey God and get the plates. . . .

"I suspect had he listened only to reason, Nephi and his brethren would still be waiting outside the walls of Jerusalem. I sometimes wonder if by our listening to reason and logic too much, and not trusting God enough, we may find ourselves waiting outside the walls of His holy city" ("Trust in the Lord" [CES fireside for young adults, May 1, 1994], 3, www.ldsces.org).

1 Nephi 4:10. Nephi Commanded to Kill Laban

• What justification is there for a righteous man like Nephi to take the life of another person? The Prophet Joseph Smith (1805–44) taught that it is the Lord who sets the standard of right and wrong: "God said, 'Thou shalt not kill;' at another time He said 'Thou shalt utterly destroy.' This is the principle on which the government of heaven is conducted—by revelation adapted to the circumstances in which the children of the kingdom are placed. Whatever God requires is right, no matter what it is, although we may not see the reason thereof till long after the events transpire. If we seek first the kingdom of God, all good things will be added. So with Solomon: first he asked wisdom, and God gave it him, and with it every desire of his heart, even things which might be considered abominable to all who understand the order of heaven only in part, but which in reality were right because God gave and sanctioned by special revelation" (*History of the Church,* 5:135).

• Some people have incorrectly felt that the Spirit of the Lord has prompted them to do something contrary to what the Lord has already commanded, such as was the case with Nephi. Today we need not worry that the Lord might prompt us to do something that runs contrary to current commandments. President Harold B. Lee (1899–1973) has taught us who the Lord will give such promptings to: "When there is to be anything different from that which the Lord has told us already, He will reveal it to His prophet and no one else" (*Stand Ye in Holy Places* [1974], 159).

• It should be remembered that the Lord gave Laban at least two chances to part with the brass plates without requiring his life. Laban was a liar, a robber, and he had at least twice sought to murder. Stealing and attempted murder could both be punishable by death (see Exodus 21:14; 22:2; Deuteronomy 24:7). The Lord wanted Lehi and his descendants to have the scriptural record even if "one man should perish" (1 Nephi 4:13) for it to happen. The brass plates blessed not only the

Nephite and Mulekite nations, but they led to some of the written portions of the gold plates as well (such as Isaiah quotations and the allegory of Zenos). The Book of Mormon has blessed and will bless the lives of millions of people and nations. Ultimately, all this was at stake when Nephi stood over Laban and followed the voice of the Spirit.

1 Nephi 4:30–37. The Integrity of One's Word

• When Zoram realized that he was with Nephi and not with his master Laban, "he began to tremble, and was about to flee" (1 Nephi 4:30). His fears ceased, however, when Nephi promised the servant that he would not be harmed and could be a free man if he went to the wilderness with Lehi's sons. When Zoram returned an oath that he would stay with Nephi and his brothers, their "fears did cease concerning him" (v. 37). Both Zoram and Nephi illustrate the potential power of a person's integrity.

• Elder Richard G. Scott of the Quorum of the Twelve Apostles observed the need for integrity as a foundation for spiritual strength: "The bedrock of character is integrity. Worthy character will strengthen your capacity to respond obediently to the direction of the Spirit. Righteous character is what you are becoming. It is more important than what you own, what you have learned, or what goals you have accomplished. It allows you to be trusted. Righteous character provides the foundation of spiritual strength.

It enables you in times of trial and testing to make difficult, extremely important decisions correctly even when they seem overpowering" (in Conference Report, Apr. 2003, 80; or *Ensign,* May 2003, 77).

1 Nephi 4:33. Oath Making

• The Book of Mormon contains a number of instances where oaths were taken. Oath making was taken very seriously in Nephi's day and culture. "The principle on which an oath is held to be binding is incidentally laid down in [Hebrews 6:16] as an ultimate appeal to divine authority to ratify an assertion. There the Almighty is represented as promising or denouncing with an oath, *i.e.* doing so in the most positive and solemn manner. On the same principle, that oath has always been held most binding which appealed to the highest authority, both as regards individuals and communities. As a consequence of this principle, appeals to God's name on the one hand, and to heathen deities on the other, are treated in Scripture as tests of allegiance" (William Smith, ed., *A Dictionary of the Bible* [n.d.], "Oath," 467; see also commentary for 1 Nephi 4:30–37 on p. 16).

• One scholar explained the power of oath making in ancient times:

"What astonishes the western reader is the miraculous effect of Nephi's oath on Zoram, who upon hearing a few conventional words promptly becomes tractable, while as for the brothers, as soon as Zoram 'made an oath unto us that he would tarry with us from that time forth . . . our fears did cease concerning him.' (1 Ne. 4:35, 37.)

"The reaction of both parties make sense when one realizes that the oath is the one thing that is most sacred and inviolable among the desert people and their descendants: 'Hardly will an Arab break his oath, even if his life be in jeopardy,' for 'there is nothing stronger, and nothing more sacred than the oath among the nomads,' and even the city Arabs, if it be exacted under special conditions. 'The taking of an oath is a holy thing with the Bedouins,' says one authority. 'Wo to him who swears falsely; his social standing will be damaged and his reputation ruined. No one will receive his testimony, and he must also pay a money fine.'

"But not every oath will do. To be most binding and solemn an oath should be by the *life* of something, even if it be but a blade of grass. The only oath more awful than that 'by my life' or (less commonly) 'by the life of my head' is the *wa hayat Allah* 'by the life of God,' or 'as the Lord Liveth,' the exact Arabic equivalent of the ancient Hebrew *hai Elohim.* Today it is glibly employed by the city riff raff, but anciently it was an awful thing, as it still is among the desert people. 'I confirmed my answer in the Bedouin wise,' says [Charles M.] Doughty. 'By his life . . . he said, . . . "Well, swear by the life of Ullah" (God)! . . . I answered and thus even the nomads use, in a greater occasion, but they say *by the life of thee* in a little matter.' Among both Arabs and Jews, says [Samuel] Rosenblatt, 'an oath without God's name is no oath,' while 'both in Jewish and Mohammedan societies oaths by "the life of God" are frequent.'

"So we see that the only way that Nephi could possibly have pacified the struggling Zoram in an instant was to utter the one oath that no man would dream of breaking, the most solemn of all oaths to the Semite: 'As the Lord liveth, and as I live!' (1 Ne. 4:32.)" (Hugh Nibley, *An Approach to the Book of Mormon,* 2nd ed. [1964], 104–5).

---

1 NEPHI 5:9–10, 17
What did Lehi do when he received the sacred record, and how did it affect him? How could this example improve your scripture study?

---

1 Nephi 5:10–22. The Plates of Brass

• The plates of brass were a volume of ancient scripture. They were valuable to Lehi's family and the future inhabitants in the Americas just as the Bible and latter-day scriptures are to us. Elder Bruce R. McConkie used Book of Mormon scriptures to describe the plates of brass and their importance. He explained that the plates of brass "were 'the record of the Jews' (1 Ne. 3:3), a record of many of the prophecies from the beginning down to and including part of those spoken by Jeremiah. On them was the law of Moses, the five books of Moses, and the genealogy of the Nephite forbears. (1 Ne. 3:3, 20; 4:15–16; 5:11–14.)

"There was more on them than there is in the Old Testament as we now have it. (1 Ne. 13:23.) The prophecies of Zenock, Neum, Zenos, Joseph the son of Jacob, and probably many other prophets were preserved by them, and many of these writings foretold matters pertaining to the Nephites. (1 Ne. 19:10, 21; 2 Ne. 4:2, 15; 3 Ne. 10:17.)

"The value of the Brass Plates to the Nephites cannot be overestimated. By means of them they were able to preserve the language (1 Ne. 3:19), most of the civilization, and the religious knowledge of the people from whence they came. (1 Ne. 22:30.) By way of contrast, the Mulekites, who were led out of Jerusalem

some 11 years after Lehi's departure, and who had no record equivalent to the Brass Plates, soon dwindled in apostasy and unbelief and lost their language, civilization, and religion. (Omni 14–18.)

"From prophet to prophet and generation to generation the Brass Plates were handed down and preserved by the Nephites. (Mosiah 1:16; 28:20; 3 Ne. 1:2.) At some future date the Lord has promised to bring them forth, undimmed by time and retaining their original brightness, and the scriptural accounts recorded on them are to 'go forth unto every nation, kindred, tongue, and people.' (Alma 37:3–5; 1 Ne. 5:18–19.)" (*Mormon Doctrine,* 2nd ed. [1966], 103).

Points to Ponder

- Why do you think Laman and Lemuel murmured? (see 1 Nephi 2:11–13). Why did Nephi support his father? (see vv. 16, 19). What determines whether you are a murmurer or a supporter of the Lord's servants?

- What evidence is there that Nephi had great faith? How do you think he obtained such faith?

Suggested Assignments

- Consider the sacrifices Lehi's family made to obtain the brass plates. Compare this to the sacrifices required to bring forth the Book of Mormon in our day (see D&C 135:6). Discuss with a friend or family member the value of the scriptures and what you are willing to do to utilize these precious records.

Introduction

Nephi wrote to persuade men to come unto Jesus Christ (see 1 Nephi 6:3–4). While studying 1 Nephi 6–11, seek to understand how Nephi's writings fulfill this purpose. In particular, note how the vision of the tree of life testifies of the love of God and the mission of the Savior. Nephi received this vision as a result of his righteous desires and willingness to be obedient. As you align your desires and actions with the will of the Lord like Nephi, you can also receive personal revelation "by the power of the Holy Ghost" (1 Nephi 10:19).

© 1987 Greg K. Olsen

Commentary

1 Nephi 6:4. "The Fulness of Mine Intent"

• Nephi's motive for writing was to bring people to Jesus Christ so they could be saved. President Ezra Taft Benson (1899–1994) explained how the Book of Mormon accomplishes this important purpose: "The

Book of Mormon brings men to Christ. . . . It tells in a plain manner of Christ and His gospel. It testifies of His divinity and of the necessity for a Redeemer and the need of our putting trust in Him. It bears witness of the Fall and the Atonement and the first principles of the gospel, including our need of a broken heart and a contrite spirit and a spiritual rebirth. It proclaims we must endure to the end in righteousness and live the moral life of a Saint" ("We Add Our Witness," *Ensign,* Mar. 1989, 5).

• President Benson explained that the phrase "the God of Abraham, the God of Isaac, and the God of Jacob," refers to the Savior: "We must keep in mind who Jesus was before He was born. He was the Creator of all things, the great Jehovah, the Lamb slain before the foundation of the world, the God of Abraham, Isaac, and Jacob. He was and is the Holy One of Israel" ("Five Marks of the Divinity of Jesus Christ," *Ensign,* Dec. 2001, 10).

1 Nephi 7:1. "Raise Up Seed unto the Lord"

• The sons and daughters of Lehi and Ishmael would marry and rear children "unto the Lord in the land of promise" (1 Nephi 7:1). Righteous families are an integral part of the Lord's divine purposes. The First Presidency and the Quorum of the Twelve Apostles proclaimed that "marriage between a man and a woman is ordained of God and that the family is central to the Creator's plan for the eternal destiny of His children. . . .

"The first commandment that God gave to Adam and Eve pertained to their potential for parenthood as husband and wife. We declare that God's commandment for His children to multiply and replenish the earth remains in force" ("The Family: A Proclamation to the World," *Ensign,* Nov. 1995, 102).

• President Boyd K. Packer, President of the Quorum of the Twelve Apostles, testified that joy comes from following the divine pattern for parenthood:

"Our destiny is so established that man can only find complete fulfillment and fill the divine purpose for his creation with a woman to whom he is legally and lawfully married. The union of man and woman begets babies that are conceived and cross that frail footpath into mortality.

"This divine pattern was planned and the gospel designed from 'before the world was' (D&C 49:17). The plan provides for us to come to the world into a mortal body. It is 'the great plan of happiness' (Alma 42:8). We did not design it. If we follow the pattern, happiness and joy will follow" (*Children of God* [BYU Women's Conference, May 5, 2006], 5–6).

1 Nephi 7:2. Ishmael Is of Ephraim

• The Book of Mormon is sometimes referred to as the "stick of Joseph" (Ezekiel 37:19) or the "stick of Ephraim" (D&C 27:5). Lehi was a descendant of Manasseh (see Alma 10:3) and Ishmael was a descendant of Ephraim. The prophecies of Jacob (see Genesis 48:16; 49:22) were fulfilled as Ishmael (Ephraim) came to the American continent with Lehi (Manasseh).

Elder Erastus Snow (1818–88) of the Quorum of the Twelve Apostles discussed the importance of Ishmael's lineage: "Whoever has read the Book of Mormon carefully will have learned that the remnants of the house of Joseph dwelt upon the American continent; and that Lehi learned by searching the records of his fathers that were written upon the plates of brass, that he was of the lineage of Manasseh. The Prophet Joseph informed us that the record of Lehi was contained on the 116 pages that were first translated and subsequently stolen, and of which an abridgment is given us in the first Book of Nephi, which is the record of Nephi individually, he himself being of the lineage of Manasseh; but that Ishmael was of the lineage of Ephraim, and that his sons married into Lehi's family, and Lehi's sons married Ishmael's daughters, thus fulfilling the words of Jacob upon Ephraim and Manasseh in the 48th chapter of Genesis, which says: 'And let my name be named on them, and the name of my fathers Abraham and Isaac; and let them grow into a multitude in the midst of the land.' Thus these descendants of Manasseh and Ephraim grew together upon this American continent" (in Daniel H. Ludlow, *A Companion to Your Study of the Book of Mormon* [1976], 199).

• Refer to the chart "The Stick of Judah and the Stick of Joseph" in the appendix (p. 412).

> ### 1 NEPHI 7:10–12
> *What spiritual experiences did Laman and Lemuel forget? How can we keep from forgetting what we should remember?*

1 Nephi 7:14. A Result of Rejecting the Prophets

• Nephi explained that the Jews in Jerusalem in his day rejected God; as a result, the Spirit of the Lord would no longer be with them. If the Lord's people reject His prophets, the prophets are taken out of their midst and tragedy follows (see 1 Nephi 3:17–18; Helaman 13:24–27). "When the Spirit ceaseth to strive with man then cometh speedy destruction" (2 Nephi 26:11). Such was the case in Noah's day (see Moses 8:17), with the Nephites (see Mormon 5:16), and with the Jaredites (see Ether 15:19). The same warning has been given in the latter days (see D&C 1:33).

1 Nephi 7:15. "Ye Have Choice"

• Laman and those influenced by him were not captives on the journey toward the land of promise. Nephi answered their desire to return to Jerusalem by declaring a fundamental doctrine, "Ye have choice" (1 Nephi 7:15). As President Thomas S. Monson stated, "Each of us has the responsibility to choose. You may ask, 'Are decisions really that important?' I say to you, decisions determine destiny. You can't make eternal decisions without eternal consequences" ("Pathways to Perfection," *Ensign,* May 2002, 100).

Nephi warned his brothers and those who wanted to go with them that they would perish if they returned to Jerusalem. Blinded by hardheartedness and disobedience, those rebelling against Lehi and Nephi failed to perceive the truth of Lehi's prophecies concerning the destruction that awaited Jerusalem. According to the Bible, soon after Lehi's colony left, the city was surrounded by the Babylonians, "there was no bread for the people of the land," the "city was broken up," and Zedekiah's army was scattered (see 2 Kings 25:1–7). If Laman and Lemuel had returned to Jerusalem, they would have suffered captivity or death. Because they chose to follow Lehi and Nephi, they enjoyed the fruit and honey of the land of Bountiful while preparing for an inheritance in the land of promise (see 1 Nephi 17:3–6).

1 Nephi 7:17–19. Delivered from Bonds

• Elder Gene R. Cook of the Seventy pointed out that, like Nephi, we can be delivered from our own bonds by the prayer of faith: "Note that they [Nephi, Alma, and Amulek] did not have faith in their own strength; they trusted in the Lord and relied on his strength. It is faith in Christ that will deliver us from our own bonds; it is increasing our faith in Christ that will give us added power in prayer" (*Receiving Answers to Our Prayers* [1996], 18).

1 Nephi 8:4–35. Vision of the Tree of Life

• The following chart identifies some of what Nephi learned about his father's dream:

Symbol from Lehi's Dream (1 Nephi 8)	Interpretation Given to Nephi (1 Nephi 11–12)
The tree with white fruit (see vv. 10–11)	The love of God, which He showed by giving His Son to be our Savior (see 11:21–25; called "the tree of life" in 15:22)
The river of filthy water (see v. 13; 12:16)	The depths of hell into which the wicked fall (see 12:16; called "filthiness" in 15:27)
The rod of iron (see v. 19)	The word of God, which leads to the tree of life (see 11:25)
The mist of darkness (see v. 23)	The temptations of the devil, which blind people so they lose their way and cannot find the tree (see 12:17)
The great and spacious building in the air (see v. 26)	The pride and vain imaginations of the world (see 11:36; 12:18)
People who start on the path to the tree but are lost in the mist (see vv. 21–23)	Nephi saw the following kinds of people in the dream:
People who make it to the tree (and taste the fruit) by holding onto the rod but fall away when they are mocked (see vv. 24–25, 28)	• Multitudes who heard Jesus but "cast him out" (11:28) • People who crucified Jesus even after He healed the sick and cast out devils (see 11:31–33) • Multitudes who gathered together in a large and spacious building to fight against the Twelve Apostles of the Lamb (see 11:34–36)
People who desire the great and spacious building more than the tree (see vv. 26–27, 31–33)	• Nephites and Lamanites who were gathered together to battle and were slaughtered in war (see 12:1–4, 13–15) • Nephites who, because of pride, were destroyed by the Lamanites and dwindled in unbelief (see 12:19–23)
People who held onto the rod and partook of the fruit; they ignored the mockers and did not fall away (see vv. 30, 33)	Those who partake of the greatest of all of God's gifts—eternal life (see 15:36)

1 Nephi 8:10–12; 11:8–25. The Tree of Life as a Symbol of Jesus Christ and His Atonement

• Elder Jeffrey R. Holland of the Quorum of the Twelve Apostles taught that the tree of life represents the Savior and His Atonement: "The Spirit made explicit that the Tree of Life and its precious fruit are symbols of Christ's redemption" (*Christ and the New Covenant: The Messianic Message of the Book of Mormon* [1997], 160).

Elder Neal A. Maxwell (1926–2004) of the Quorum of the Twelve Apostles further emphasized that partaking of the love of God means partaking of the blessings of the Atonement. The tree of life is a symbol of God's love and Christ's Atonement: "The tree of life . . . is the love of God (see 1 Nephi 11:25). The love of God for His children is most profoundly expressed in His gift of Jesus as our Redeemer: 'God so loved the world, that he gave his only begotten Son' (John 3:16). To partake of the love of God is to partake of Jesus' Atonement and the emancipations and joys which it can bring" (in Conference Report, Oct. 1999, 6; or *Ensign,* Nov. 1999, 8).

1 Nephi 8:20. The "Strait and Narrow Path"

• Jesus Christ taught that He is the only path or "the way" that will lead to the Father (see John 14:6). Elder Lowell M. Snow of the Seventy testified of the constant direction the Savior provides:

"Life is full of many intersecting roads and trails. There are so many paths to follow, so many voices calling out 'lo, here' or 'lo, there' [Joseph Smith—History 1:5]. There is such a variety and volume of media flooding our personal space, most of it intent on herding us down a path that is broad and traveled by many.

"When pondering which of these voices to listen to or which road among the many is right, have you ever asked yourself, as Joseph Smith did: 'What is to be done? Who of all these [voices and roads is] right; or, are they all wrong together? If any one of them be right, which is it, and how shall I know it?' [Joseph Smith—History 1:10].

"My witness to you is that Jesus Christ continues to mark the path, lead the way, and define every point on our journey. His path is strait and narrow and leads toward 'light and life and endless day' [*Hymns,* no. 195]" (in Conference Report, Oct. 2005, 100; or *Ensign,* Nov. 2005, 96).

1 Nephi 8:23–33. Are We Holding Fast to the Rod of Iron?

• Elder David A. Bednar of the Quorum of the Twelve Apostles explained what it means to hold fast to the rod of iron:

"Let me suggest that holding fast to the iron rod entails the prayerful and consistent use of all three of the ways of obtaining living water that we have discussed tonight [reading, studying, and searching].

". . . The regular use of all three methods produces a more constant flow of living water and is in large measure what it means to hold fast to the rod of iron. . . .

"Are you and I daily reading, studying, and searching the scriptures in a way that enables us to hold fast to the rod of iron . . . ?" ("A Reservoir of Living Water" [CES fireside for young adults, Feb. 4, 2007], 10–11, www.ldsces.org).

• Elder Joseph B. Wirthlin (1917–2008) of the Quorum of the Twelve Apostles explained not only the importance of "holding fast" to the rod but also explained how to get back if we lose our hold: "You must hold firmly to the rod of iron through the mists and darkness, the hardships and trials of life. If you relax your grip and slip from the path, the iron rod might become lost in the darkness for a time until you repent and regain your grasp of it" (in Conference Report, Oct. 1989, 93; or *Ensign,* Nov. 1989, 74).

> ### *1 NEPHI 8:24*
> *What words and phrases describe an individual's faithfulness to the word of God?*

1 Nephi 8:26–27. "Great and Spacious Building"

• The great and spacious building stands in opposition to the Savior, who is the tree of life. Elder Glenn L. Pace of the Seventy contrasted the standards of God with the behaviors of the people in the great and spacious building:

"To those of you who are inching your way closer and closer to that great and spacious building, let me make it completely clear that the people in that building have absolutely nothing to offer except instant, short-term gratification inescapably connected to long-term sorrow and suffering. The commandments you observe were not given by a dispassionate God to prevent you from having fun, but by a loving Father in Heaven who wants you to be happy while you are living on this earth as well as in the hereafter.

"Compare the blessings of living the Word of Wisdom to those available to you if you choose to party with those in the great and spacious building. Compare the joy of intelligent humor and wit to drunken, silly, crude, loud laughter. Compare our faithful young women who still have a blush in their cheeks with those who, having long lost their blush, try to persuade you to join them in their loss. Compare lifting people up to putting people down. Compare the ability to receive personal revelation and direction in your life to being tossed to and fro with every wind of doctrine. Compare holding the priesthood of God with anything you see going on in that great and spacious building" (in Conference Report, Oct. 1987, 49–50; or *Ensign,* Nov. 1987, 40).

• Elder L. Tom Perry of the Quorum of the Twelve Apostles warned that preoccupation with material possessions is a behavior typical of those people in the great and spacious building: "The current cries we hear coming from the great and spacious building tempt us to compete for ownership in the things of this world. We think we need a larger home, with a three-car garage and a recreational vehicle parked next to it. We long for designer clothes, extra TV sets (all with [DVDs]), the latest model computers, and the newest car. Often these items are purchased with borrowed money without giving any thought to providing for our future needs. The result of all this instant gratification is overloaded bankruptcy courts and families that are far too preoccupied with their financial burdens" (in Conference Report, Oct. 1995, 45; or *Ensign,* Nov. 1995, 35).

• In Lehi's vision, the scorners and mockers ridiculed those who were partaking of the fruit—those who love God and want to serve Him. Elder Neal A. Maxwell reminded us to hold up the shield of faith when scorners can be seen and heard from the great and spacious building: "Let us expect that many will regard us indifferently. Others will see us as quaint or misled. Let us bear the pointing fingers which, ironically, belong to those finally who, being bored,

© Clark Kelley Price

find the 'great and spacious building' to be a stale and cramped third-class hotel (see 1 Nephi 8:31–33). Let us revile not the revilers and heed them not (see D&C 31:9). Instead, let us use our energy to hold up the shield of faith to quench the incoming fiery darts" (in Conference Report, Oct. 2003, 108; or *Ensign,* Nov. 2003, 102).

1 Nephi 8:37. "Feelings of a Tender Parent"

• Elder Robert D. Hales of the Quorum of the Twelve Apostles taught that parents can follow Lehi's example when dealing with wayward children: "We too must have the faith to teach our children and bid them to keep the commandments. We should not let their choices weaken our faith. Our worthiness will not be measured according to their righteousness. Lehi did not lose the blessing of feasting at the tree of life because Laman and Lemuel refused to partake of its fruit. Sometimes as parents we feel we have failed when our children make mistakes or stray. Parents are never failures when they do their best to love, teach, pray, and care for their children. Their faith, prayers, and efforts will be consecrated to the good of their children" (in Conference Report, Apr. 2004, 90; or *Ensign,* May 2004, 88).

1 Nephi 9:1–5. "A Wise Purpose"

• Although Nephi had already begun a record of the secular history of his people, the Lord inspired him to make a second record containing the religious history of his people. The following list clarifies the differences and similarities between the two accounts:

1. Verses 1–5 in 1 Nephi 9 are an account taken directly from the small plates.

2. When Nephi used the term *these* he was referring to the small plates.

3. When Nephi used the term *those* or *other* he was referring to the large plates.

4. The large plates were first made about 590 B.C.

5. The small plates were made 20 years later, about 570 B.C.

6. Nephi's explanation of why the Lord commanded him to make a second record (the small plates) is in 1 Nephi 9:5.

7. The large plates cover a period from 570 B.C.–A.D. 385 and cover the account of kings, wars, and history.

8. The small plates cover a period from 570–130 B.C. and give an account of the Nephite ministry.

Although Nephi did not know the reason for the duplicate record, he trusted that it was "for a wise purpose" (1 Nephi 9:5) that was known to the Lord (see commentary for Words of Mormon 1:7 on p. 134).

• Elder Marvin J. Ashton (1915–94) of the Quorum of the Twelve Apostles observed that we can obey as Nephi did, even when we do not understand the reason: "Sometimes when we are asked to be obedient, we do not know why, except the Lord has commanded. Nephi followed instructions even though he didn't fully understand the wise purpose. His obedience resulted in blessings to mankind all over the world. By not obeying our present-day leaders, we plant our seeds in stony places and may forfeit the harvest" (in Conference Report, Oct. 1978, 76; or *Ensign,* Nov. 1978, 51).

1 Nephi 9:6. "The Lord Knoweth All Things"

• Elder Neal A. Maxwell testified that there is no limit to God's knowledge:

"Some have sincere faith in the existence of a God but not necessarily in a revealing and omniscient God. Other sincere individuals question God's omniscience, wondering, even though respectfully, whether even God can know the future. But an omniscient and revealing God can at any present moment disclose things future. This is possible because 'in the presence of God, . . . all things for their glory are manifest, past, present, and future, and are continually before the Lord' (D&C 130:7). Thus God 'knoweth all things, for all things are present before [his] eyes' (D&C 38:2). He

told Moses, 'There is no God beside me, and all things are present with me, for I know them all' (Moses 1:6).

"No qualifiers on the scope of God's knowledge appear in holy writ. Instead, we read: 'O how great the holiness of our God! For he knoweth all things, and there is not anything save he knows it.' (2 Nephi 9:20.)" (*If Thou Endure It Well* [1996], 46).

1 Nephi 10:11–14. Scattering and Gathering of Israel

• Elder Bruce R. McConkie (1915–85) of the Quorum of the Twelve Apostles explained why Israel was scattered and what some of the considerations are in the gathering of Israel:

"Why was Israel scattered? The answer is clear; it is plain; of it there is no doubt. Our Israelite forebears were scattered because they rejected the gospel, defiled the priesthood, forsook the church, and departed from the kingdom. They were scattered because they turned from the Lord, worshipped false gods, and walked in all the ways of the heathen nations. . . . Israel was scattered for apostasy. The Lord in his wrath, because of their wickedness and rebellion, scattered them among the heathen in all the nations of the earth.

"What, then, is involved in the gathering of Israel? The gathering of Israel consists in believing and accepting and living in harmony with all that the Lord once offered his ancient chosen people. It consists of having faith in the Lord Jesus Christ, of repenting, of being baptized and receiving the gift of the Holy Ghost, and of keeping the commandments of God. It consists of believing the gospel, joining the Church, and coming into the kingdom. It consists of receiving the holy priesthood, being endowed in holy places with power from on high, and receiving all the blessings of Abraham, Isaac, and Jacob, through the ordinance of celestial marriage. And it may also consist of assembling to an appointed place or land of worship.

"Having this concept of the scattering and gathering of the chosen seed, we are able to understand the prophetic word relative thereto" (*A New Witness for the Articles of Faith* [1985], 515).

• For more information on the scattering of Israel, refer to "Brief History of the Scattering of Israel" in the appendix (p. 415). For more information on the gathering of Israel, refer to "The Gathering of Israel" in the appendix (p. 416).

1 Nephi 10:17–19. Learn by the Power of the Holy Ghost

• Elder Russell M. Nelson of the Quorum of the Twelve Apostles emphasized our need to learn gospel truths by the power of the Holy Ghost: "Living the Lord's standards requires that we cultivate the gift of the Holy Ghost. That gift helps us understand doctrine and apply it personally. Because truth that is given by revelation can be understood only by revelation, our studies need to be prayerful" (in Conference Report, Oct. 2000, 19; or *Ensign,* Nov. 2000, 17).

• Elder David A. Bednar of the Quorum of the Twelve Apostles explained that we must avoid anything that offends the Spirit:

"The Spirit of the Lord usually communicates with us in ways that are quiet, delicate, and subtle. . . .

"The standard is clear. If something we think, see, hear, or do distances us from the Holy Ghost, then we should stop thinking, seeing, hearing, or doing that thing. If that which is intended to entertain, for example, alienates us from the Holy Spirit, then certainly that type of entertainment is not for us. Because the Spirit cannot abide that which is vulgar, crude, or immodest, then clearly such things are not for us. Because we estrange the Spirit of the Lord when we engage in activities we know we should shun, then such things definitely are not for us" (in Conference Report, Apr. 2006, 29–30; or *Ensign,* May 2006, 29–30).

> **1 NEPHI 10:17–19; 11:1–8**
> *What principles for receiving revelation can you identify from Nephi's experience?*

1 Nephi 11:16, 26. The Condescension of God

• *Condescension* means a voluntary descent from rank or dignity. Elder Gerald N. Lund, formerly of the Seventy, commented on how well this word describes the coming of the Savior into mortality:

"Here was Jesus—a member of the Godhead, the Firstborn of the Father, the Creator, Jehovah of the Old Testament—now leaving His divine and holy station; divesting Himself of all that glory and majesty and entering the body of a tiny infant; helpless, completely dependent on His mother and earthly father. That He should not come to the finest of earthly palaces and be . . . showered with jewels but should come to a lowly stable is astonishing. Little wonder that the angel should say to Nephi, 'Behold the condescension of God!' " (*Jesus Christ, Key to the Plan of Salvation* [1991], 16).

Points to Ponder

• Think of the many individuals presented in Lehi's vision of the tree of life. How can you emulate those who reached the tree, partook of it, and remained faithful?

• How has scripture study and following the words of the prophets helped you stay on the strait and narrow path, despite the mists of darkness?

• What steps could you take to more "diligently seek" to understand the "mysteries of God . . . by the power of the Holy Ghost"? (1 Nephi 10:19).

Suggested Assignments

Jerry Thompson, © 1987 IRI

• Lehi's dream contains intricate symbolism. Draw a diagram that includes the elements of Lehi's dream to help you visualize the relationship of the various symbols.

• Only those who held fast to the iron rod partook of the fruit of the tree. Outline a personal plan for daily scripture study to help you draw closer to the Savior and more fully receive the blessings of the Atonement.

• Nephi was shown Jehovah's condescension into mortality. Read the accounts of the Savior's birth found in Matthew 1–2; Luke 1–2; and John 1:1–13. Record in your journal or scriptures new insights you discover about this event.

Introduction

President Boyd K. Packer, President of the Quorum of the Twelve Apostles, spoke of Heavenly Father's desire to give us the righteous desires of our hearts: "No message appears in scripture more times, in more ways than 'Ask, and ye shall receive'" (in Conference Report, Oct. 1991, 26; or *Ensign,* Nov. 1991, 21). Nephi applied the invitation to ask for the "things that [his] father had seen, and believing that the Lord was able to make them known" (1 Nephi 11:1). Nephi's righteous desires were rewarded, for he not only recorded information that was similar to what we have recorded about Lehi's vision, but he recorded a panoramic vision of this world to the end of time (see 1 Nephi 14:18–30). This vision was similar to the vision of John in the New Testament book of Revelation. As you study Nephi's vision, look for specific prophecies that have been or will be fulfilled in the events of history—especially important are the effects of the Apostasy, the eventual Restoration of the gospel, and the ultimate triumph of good.

Commentary

1 Nephi 12:11. "Made White in the Blood of the Lamb"

• White is a symbol for cleanliness, righteousness, and holiness. Being completely clean is necessary to be like the Savior. To have white garments symbolizes that a person is clothed in purity, or that purity is a characteristic of that individual. Such cleanliness is made possible only through the atoning sacrifice of Jesus Christ, in which His blood was shed for our sins.

• President John Taylor (1808–87) spoke of the necessity of going beyond simply being members of the Lord's Church if we are to be sufficiently worthy to stand before our Father in Heaven: "There is something that goes a little further than we think about sometimes; and that is, while we profess to be followers of the Lord, while we profess to have received the Gospel and to be governed by it, a profession will amount to nothing unless we have washed our robes and made them white in the blood of the Lamb. It is not enough for us to be connected with the Zion of God, for the Zion of God must consist of men that are pure in heart and pure in life and spotless before God, at least that is what we have got to arrive at. We are not there yet, but we must

get there before we shall be prepared to inherit glory and exaltation; therefore a form of godliness will amount to but little with any of us. . . . It is not enough for us to embrace the Gospel . . . and be associated with the people of God, attend our meetings and partake of the Sacrament of the Lord's supper, and endeavor to move along without much blame of any kind attached to us; for notwithstanding all this, if our hearts are not right, if we are not pure in heart before God, if we have not pure hearts and pure consciences, fearing God and keeping His commandments, we shall not, unless we repent, participate in these blessings about which I have spoken, and of which the Prophets bear testimony" (*Teachings of Presidents of the Church: John Taylor* [2001], 114–15).

1 Nephi 12–14. Overview

• The following chart helps us visualize significant events leading to the establishment of God's kingdom on earth:

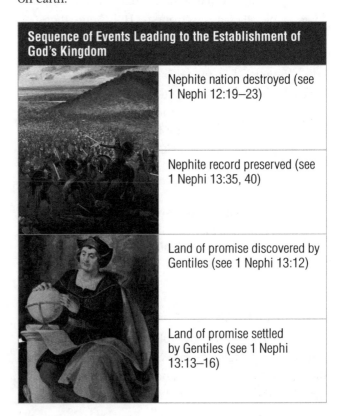

Sequence of Events Leading to the Establishment of God's Kingdom	
	Nephite nation destroyed (see 1 Nephi 12:19–23)
	Nephite record preserved (see 1 Nephi 13:35, 40)
	Land of promise discovered by Gentiles (see 1 Nephi 13:12)
	Land of promise settled by Gentiles (see 1 Nephi 13:13–16)

Sequence of Events Leading to the Establishment of God's Kingdom	
	An international war in the land of promise (Revolutionary War; see 1 Nephi 13:16–19)
	Gentiles who hearken to the Lord may be "numbered among the house of Israel" (Restoration of the gospel; see 1 Nephi 14:1–2)
	New scripture comes forth (see 1 Nephi 13:35–40; 14:7)
	Christ's Church restored (see 1 Nephi 14:10–17)

1 Nephi 13:1–9. The Great and Abominable Church

• "In relation to the kingdom of God, the devil always sets up his kingdom at the very same time in opposition to God" (Joseph Smith, in *History of the Church,* 6:364).

• Elder Bruce R. McConkie (1915–85) of the Quorum of the Twelve Apostles defined the great and abominable church: "The titles *church of the devil* and *great and abominable church* are used to identify all . . . organizations of whatever name or nature—whether political, philosophical, educational, economic, social, fraternal, civic, or religious—which are designed to take men on a course that leads away from God and his laws and thus from salvation in the kingdom of God" (*Mormon Doctrine,* 2nd ed. [1966], 137–38).

• One commentator explained that the great and abominable church consists of more than one entity:

"Actually, no single known historical church, denomination, or set of believers meets all the requirements for the great and abominable church: it must have formed among the Gentiles; it must have edited and controlled the distribution of the scriptures; it must have slain the Saints of God, including the Apostles and prophets; it must be in league with civil governments and use their police power to enforce its religious views; it must have dominion over all the earth; it must pursue great wealth and sexual immorality; and it must last until close to the end of the world. No single denomination or system of beliefs fits the entire description. Rather, the role of Babylon has been played by many different agencies, ideologies, and churches in many different times. . . .

"Can we, then, identify the historical agency that acted as the great and abominable church in earliest Christianity? Such an agent would have had its origins in the second half of the first century and would have done much of its work by the middle of the second century.

"This period might be called the blind spot in Christian history, for it is here that the fewest primary historical sources have been preserved. We have good sources for New Testament Christianity; then the lights go out, so to speak, and we hear the muffled sounds of a great struggle. When the lights come on again a hundred or so years later, we find that someone has rearranged all the furniture and Christianity has become something very different from what it was in the beginning" (Stephen E. Robinson, "Warring against the Saints of God," *Ensign,* Jan. 1988, 38–39).

---

1 NEPHI 13:4–9
List several general characteristics associated with the great and abominable church. How can recognizing these help you avoid deception?

---

1 Nephi 13:12. "A Man among the Gentiles"

• President Ezra Taft Benson (1899–1994) identified this man among the Gentiles as Christopher Columbus:

"God inspired 'a man among the Gentiles' (1 Nephi 13:12) who, by the Spirit of God was led to rediscover the land of America and bring this rich new land to the attention of the people in Europe. That man, of course, was Christopher Columbus, who testified that he was inspired in what he did.

"'Our Lord,' said Columbus, 'unlocked my mind, sent me upon the sea, and gave me fire for the deed. Those who heard of my enterprise called it foolish, mocked me, and laughed. But who can doubt but that the Holy Ghost inspired me?' (Jacob Wasserman, *Columbus, Don Quixote of the Seas,* pp. 19–20.)" (*The Teachings of Ezra Taft Benson* [1988], 577).

• President Gordon B. Hinckley (1910–2008) revered Columbus as being inspired of the Lord: "A host of critics have spoken out against [Christopher Columbus]. I do not dispute that there were others who came to this Western Hemisphere before him. But it was he who in faith lighted a lamp to look for a new way to China and who in the process discovered America. His was an awesome undertaking—to sail west across the unknown seas farther than any before him of his generation. He it was who, in spite of the terror of the unknown and the complaints and near mutiny of his crew, sailed on with frequent prayers to the Almighty for guidance. In his reports to the sovereigns of Spain, Columbus repeatedly asserted that his voyage was for the glory of God and the spread of the Christian faith. Properly do we honor him for his unyielding strength in the face of uncertainty and danger" (in Conference Report, Oct. 1992, 73–74; or *Ensign,* Nov. 1992, 52).

1 Nephi 13:12–19. The Lord's Hand in the History of the United States of America

• President Joseph F. Smith (1838–1918) linked the establishment of the United States of America with the Restoration of the gospel: "This great American nation the Almighty raised up by the power of his omnipotent hand, that it might be possible in the latter days for the kingdom of God to be established in the earth. If the Lord had not prepared the way by laying the foundations of this glorious nation, it would have been

impossible (under the stringent laws and bigotry of the monarchical governments of the world) to have laid the foundations for the coming of his great kingdom. The Lord has done this" (*Gospel Doctrine,* 5th ed. [1939], 409).

• Elder Robert D. Hales of the Quorum of the Twelve Apostles spoke of how God inspired the founders of America to establish a new nation with religious freedom for all in preparation for the Restoration of the gospel: "Over a century later [after the discovery of America] such religious feeling guided founders of a new nation on the American continent. Under God's hand they secured religious freedom for every citizen with an inspired Bill of Rights. Fourteen years later, on December 23, 1805, the Prophet Joseph Smith was born. The preparation was nearing its completion for the Restoration" (in Conference Report, Oct. 2005, 94; or *Ensign,* Nov. 2005, 90).

---

1 NEPHI 13:20–29

Nephi mentioned a book with parts taken out. What is the book? What are some of the things that were removed? Why were they removed?

---

1 Nephi 13:20–29. Plain and Precious Truths Removed from the Bible

• Elder Jeffrey R. Holland of the Quorum of the Twelve Apostles explained the meaning of "plain and precious": "Elements . . . missing from the Bible were both 'plain and most precious.' They were plain in their simplicity and clarity, being easy to 'the understanding of . . . men'; they were precious in their purity and profound worth, their saving significance and eternal importance to the children of God" (*Christ and the New Covenant* [1997], 5).

• One educator suggested the following explanation for changes in the scriptures:

"Apparently the original manuscripts of the Bible disappeared very early. This seems particularly true of the New Testament. Sir Frederic Kenyon, one of the greatest textual scholars of the early twentieth century, commented thus: 'The originals of the several books have long ago disappeared. They must have perished in the very infancy of the Church; for no allusion is ever made to them by any Christian writer.' Kenyon's statement is particularly important to us because it means that for centuries there has not been an original Bible manuscript to guide the reader. Even in the early decades of the original Christian church, the original texts seem to have been absent. . . .

"The angel [in 1 Nephi 13:21–29] makes it clear that he is not talking about subtle accidents of hand and eye, resulting in a few misplaced letters or words—the unplanned errors of copyists. He pointedly ascribes these changes to the planned editorial work of designing men [see 1 Nephi 13:27–28]. . . .

"As we read the words of the angel, we discover that the world never has had a complete Bible, for it was massively—even cataclysmically—corrupted *before* it was distributed. Of course, in addition to the major willful corruption of the Bible in the early Christian era, the manuscripts have also continued to suffer the gradual and relatively mild changes, due to errors of hand and eye, that the scholars talk about. Thus there have been two processes at work: (1) a major, sudden, and deliberate editorial corruption of the text and (2) a gradual promulgation of variants that has occurred as a natural consequence of copying and translation" (Robert J. Matthews, *A Bible! A Bible!* [1990], 74–75).

Joseph Smith taught that "many important points touching the salvation of man, had been taken from the Bible, or lost before it was compiled" (*History of the Church,* 1:245). He also said that the Bible was correct as "it came from the pen of the original writers," but that "ignorant translators, careless transcribers, or designing and corrupt priests have committed many errors" (*History of the Church,* 6:57.)

1 Nephi 13:32–40. Plain and Precious Things Restored

• President James E. Faust (1920–2007) of the First Presidency spoke of how the standard works of the Church have been the principal means of restoring lost truths:

"The Apostle John saw in vision the time when an angel would come to the earth as part of the Restoration of the gospel. That angel was Moroni, who appeared to the Prophet Joseph Smith. He directed Joseph to the place where golden plates containing ancient writings were deposited. Joseph Smith then translated these plates by the gift and power of God, and the Book of Mormon was published. This is a record of two groups of people who lived centuries ago on the American continent. Little was known about them before the coming forth of the Book of Mormon. But more importantly, the Book of Mormon is another testament of Christ. It restored precious truths concerning the Fall, the Atonement, the Resurrection, and life after death.

"Prior to the Restoration, the heavens had been closed for centuries. But with prophets and apostles upon the earth once more, the heavens were opened once again with visions and revelations. Many of the revelations that came to the Prophet Joseph Smith were written down in a book that came to be known as the Doctrine and Covenants. This contains further insights about principles and ordinances and is a valuable source concerning the structure of the priesthood. In addition, we have another canon of scripture called the Pearl of Great Price. It contains the book of Moses, which came by revelation to the Prophet Joseph Smith, and the book of Abraham, which he translated from a purchased Egyptian scroll. From these we learn not only a great deal more about Moses, Abraham, Enoch, and other prophets but also many more details about the Creation. We learn that the gospel of Jesus Christ was taught to all of the prophets from the beginning—even from the time of Adam" (in Conference Report, Apr. 2006, 68; or *Ensign,* May 2006, 67–68).

• The Joseph Smith Translation of the Bible also helps restore many plain and precious truths. The Joseph Smith Translation is "a revision or translation of the King James Version of the Bible in English, which the Prophet Joseph Smith began in June 1830. He was commanded by God to make the translation and regarded it as part of his calling as a prophet. . . .

"The Joseph Smith Translation has restored some of the plain and precious things that have been lost from the Bible (1 Nephi 13). Although it is not the official Bible of the Church, this translation does offer many interesting insights and is very valuable in understanding the Bible. It is also a witness for the divine calling and ministry of the Prophet Joseph Smith" (Guide to the Scriptures, "Joseph Smith Translation"; see also 2 Nephi 3:11; *History of the Church,* 1:238).

With continuing revelation in the Lord's Church, the process of bringing the plain and precious doctrines and principles of the gospel to people throughout the world is an ongoing process. The conference reports and other inspired writings from the Lord's apostles and prophets are vital for gospel understanding of the plain and precious truths.

1 Nephi 14:7. "A Great and a Marvelous Work"

• The scriptures describe the Restoration of the gospel and the organization of the Church as "a great and a marvelous work" (1 Nephi 14:7; 3 Nephi 21:9). In this context, the word *great* means significant and meaningful, while *marvelous* means wonderful and incomprehensible. *Work* speaks of an act or accomplishment that is everlasting.

Elder Jeffrey R. Holland of the Quorum of the Twelve Apostles explained that the significance of the Church is two-fold: "This church, the great institutional body of Christ, is a marvelous work and a wonder not only because of what it does for the faithful but also because of what the faithful do for it. Your lives are at the very heart of that marvel. You are evidence of the wonder of it all" (in Conference Report, Oct. 1994, 42; or *Ensign,* Nov. 1994, 32).

> ### 1 NEPHI 14:10–14
> *What did Nephi prophesy regarding latter-day Church members?*

1 Nephi 14:14. Armed with Righteousness and Power

• Elder Neal A. Maxwell (1926–2004) of the Quorum of the Twelve Apostles explained that righteousness will be the power of the Lord's people: "So let us look at ourselves. For the Church, the scriptures suggest both an accelerated sifting and accelerated spiritual numerical growth—with all this preceding the time when the people of God will be 'armed with righteousness'—not weapons—and when the Lord's glory will be poured out upon them (1 Nephi 14:14; see also 1 Peter 4:17; D&C 112:25). The Lord is determined to have a tried, pure, and proven people (see D&C 100:16; 101:4; 136:31), and 'there is nothing that the Lord thy God shall take in his heart to do but what he will do it' (Abraham 3:17)" (in Conference Report, Apr. 1988, 8; or *Ensign,* May 1988, 8).

• Elder Maxwell further explained that honoring our covenants is vital to the reception of this promise: "Church members have a special rendezvous to keep, brothers and sisters. Nephi saw it. One future day, he said, Jesus' covenant people, 'scattered upon all the face of the earth,' will be 'armed with righteousness and with the power of God in great glory' (1 Nephi 14:14). This will happen, but only after more members become more saintly and more consecrated in conduct" (in Conference Report, Oct. 1991, 43; or *Ensign,* Nov. 1991, 32).

1 Nephi 14:18–30. The Record of John the Revelator

• Verses 18–30 in 1 Nephi 14 refer to the book of Revelation, the last book in the New Testament, written by the Apostle John. Nephi saw the events of our day but was not allowed to write them because it was John's responsibility. Verse 26 could have reference to the portion of the Book of Mormon that was sealed.

(For further information about the sealed portion, see 2 Nephi 27:7; 3 Nephi 26:7–11; Ether 4:7.)

1 Nephi 15:2–11. "Hard in Their Hearts"

• Elder Dallin H. Oaks of the Quorum of the Twelve Apostles discussed how a hard heart limits our spirituality:

"Nephi attempted to teach his brothers that they could know the meaning of their father's prophetic utterances, 'which were hard to be understood, save a man should inquire of the Lord' (1 Ne. 15:3). Nephi told them if they did not harden their hearts and would keep the commandments and inquire of the Lord in faith, 'surely these things shall be made known unto you' (1 Ne. 15:11).

"If we harden our hearts, reject continuing revelation, and limit our learning to what we can obtain by study and reason on the precise language of the present canon of scriptures, our understanding will be limited to what Alma called 'the lesser portion of the word' (Alma 12:11). If we seek and accept revelation and inspiration to enlarge our understanding of the scriptures, we will realize a fulfillment of Nephi's inspired promise that those who diligently seek will have 'the mysteries of God . . . unfolded unto them, by the power of the Holy Ghost' (1 Ne. 10:19)" ("Scripture Reading and Revelation," *Ensign,* Jan. 1995, 7).

• The Prophet Joseph Smith explained that not only could Laman and Lemuel know the things Nephi and his father knew, but that this principle applies to us as well: "Could we all come together with one heart and one mind in perfect faith the veil might as well be rent today as next week, or any other time" (*Teachings of the Prophet Joseph Smith,* sel. Joseph Fielding Smith [1976], 9).

"God hath not revealed anything to Joseph, but what He will make known unto the Twelve, and even the least Saint may know all things as fast as he is able to bear them" (*History of the Church,* 3:380).

1 Nephi 15:12–13. Jews and Gentiles

• We frequently read about the Jews and Gentiles in the Book of Mormon. Sometimes it is difficult to understand whom the text is speaking to. Elder Bruce R. McConkie of the Quorum of the Twelve Apostles provided help with this challenge: "Both Lehi and Nephi divide all men into two camps, Jews and Gentiles. The Jews were either the nationals of the kingdom of Judah or their descendants; all others were considered to be Gentiles. Thus, we are the Gentiles of whom this scripture speaks; we are the ones who have received the fulness of the gospel; and we shall take it to the Lamanites, who are Jews, because their fathers came from Jerusalem and from the kingdom of Judah" (*A New Witness for the Articles of Faith* [1985], 556).

Elder McConkie also identified one gentile who would greatly assist in the Restoration: "Joseph Smith . . . was the Gentile by whose hand the Book of Mormon came forth, and the members of The Church of Jesus Christ of Latter-day Saints . . . are the Gentiles who carry salvation to the Lamanites and to the Jews" (*The Millennial Messiah* [1982], 233).

1 Nephi 15:13–16. Latter-day Restoration of the Gospel

• President Gordon B. Hinckley declared the impact of the Restoration in history: "My brethren and sisters, do you realize what we have? Do you recognize our place in the great drama of human history? This is the focal point of all that has gone before. This is the season of restitution. These are the days of restoration. This is the time when men from over the earth come to the mountain of the Lord's house to seek and learn of His ways and to walk in His paths. This is the summation of all of the centuries of time since the birth of Christ to this present and wonderful day" (in Conference Report, Oct. 1999, 94; or *Ensign,* Nov. 1999, 74).

1 Nephi 15:12–20. The Gathering of Israel

• For more information on the gathering of Israel, refer to "The Gathering of Israel" in the appendix (p. 416).

1 Nephi 15:24. The Word of God and Fiery Darts

• President Ezra Taft Benson spoke of the blessing of having the word of God in our possession. It will not only lead us to great blessings, but gives us the strength to stand firm in the face of temptation: "In his dream, Lehi saw an iron rod which led through the mists of darkness. He saw that if people would hold fast to that rod, they could avoid the rivers of filthiness, stay away from the forbidden paths, stop from wandering in the strange roads that lead to destruction. Later his son Nephi clearly explained the symbolism of the iron rod. When Laman and Lemuel asked, 'What meaneth the rod of iron?' Nephi answered, 'It was the word of God; and [note this promise] *whoso would hearken unto the word of God, and would hold fast unto it, they would never perish; neither could the temptations and the fiery darts of the adversary overpower them unto blindness, to lead them away to destruction.'* (1 Ne. 15:23–24; italics added.) Not only will the word of God lead us to the fruit which is desirable above all others, but in the word of God and through it we can find the power to resist temptation, the power to thwart the work of Satan and his emissaries" ("The Power of the Word," *Ensign,* May 1986, 80).

1 Nephi 15:32–35. "Judged of Their Works"

• Elder Dallin H. Oaks spoke of how our works define who we are. What we become through our works constitutes the judgment we will receive:

"Many Bible and modern scriptures speak of a final judgment at which all persons will be rewarded according to their deeds or works or the desires of their hearts. But other scriptures enlarge upon this by referring to our being judged by the *condition* we have achieved.

"The prophet Nephi describes the Final Judgment in terms of what we *have become:* 'And if their works have been filthiness they must needs *be* filthy; and if they *be* filthy it must needs be that they cannot dwell in the kingdom of God' (1 Nephi 15:33; italics added). Moroni declares, 'He that *is* filthy shall be filthy still; and he that *is* righteous shall be righteous still' (Mormon 9:14; italics added; see also Revelation 22:11–12; 2 Nephi 9:16; D&C 88:35). The same would be true of 'selfish' or 'disobedient' or any other personal attribute inconsistent with the requirements of God. Referring to the 'state' of the wicked in the Final Judgment, Alma explains that if we are condemned by our words, our works, and our thoughts, 'we shall not be found spotless; . . . and in this awful state we shall not dare to look up to our God' (Alma 12:14).

"From such teachings we conclude that the Final Judgment is not just an evaluation of a sum total of good and evil acts—what we have *done.* It is an acknowledgment of the final effect of our acts and thoughts—what we have *become.* It is not enough for anyone just to go through the motions. The commandments, ordinances, and covenants of the gospel are not a list of deposits required to be made in some heavenly account. The gospel of Jesus Christ is a plan that shows us how to become what our Heavenly Father desires us to become" (in Conference Report, Oct. 2000, 41; or *Ensign,* Nov. 2000, 32).

1 Nephi 15:34–35. The Final State of Souls

• A clear distinction exists between good and evil, light and darkness, the kingdom of God and the kingdom of the devil. Hell is the place prepared for the filthy who follow Satan, while the righteous who have followed God enjoy the peace and glory of His kingdom. But how can the *final state* of all people be divided into just two groups—those who "dwell in the kingdom of God" or those who will be "cast out"? (1 Nephi 15:35).

The key to answering this question is found in Doctrine and Covenants 76:43, which summarizes the work of Jesus Christ as follows: "[He] glorifies the Father, and saves all the works of his hands, except those sons of perdition who deny the Son after the Father has revealed him." Thus, the final state will include the grouping of saved individuals and unsaved individuals, or sons of perdition. Saved individuals will include those who are allowed to enter a degree of glory. Doctrine and Covenants 76 names three degrees of glory—celestial, terrestrial, and telestial—with information about the individuals who are worthy of each place in God's kingdom. Thus, salvation within the kingdom of God occurs in all three degrees of glory, while those who do not qualify are sons of perdition.

Points to Ponder

- How can you use Nephi's example of inquiring of the Lord to make inspiration and revelation a more important part of your life?

- In what ways did the Lord prepare for the Restoration of the gospel in this dispensation?

- How would you define the term "fiery darts of the adversary"? What specific fiery darts afflict your life? What do you need to do to better withstand the fiery darts that inhibit your spiritual growth?

Suggested Assignments

- Write a short essay on one of the following questions:

  1. In what ways are you progressing toward the tree of life?

  2. What does the "great and abominable church" represent?

  3. How does 1 Nephi 13 relate to the eighth article of faith?

Introduction

Have you ever wondered why people respond differently to the same set of circumstances? Such was the case with Lehi's family. During their trials, some of the family members looked to God and trusted in Him while others complained, lacked faith, and rebelled. Our response to circumstances should produce growth and greater faith rather than an attitude of complaining and rebellion. As you read 1 Nephi 16–18, examine the challenges these people faced and how the Lord was able to help Lehi's family when they were faithful. Notice the suffering caused by rebelliousness and disobedience. Look for examples of how to be faithful during difficult circumstances by comparing the challenges in your life to the experiences of Lehi's family.

Commentary

1 Nephi 16:2. "The Guilty Taketh the Truth to Be Hard"

• Nephi declared truth to his disobedient brothers in an effort to help them turn their hearts to God. Those who offend the Spirit through wickedness often take offense when given inspired correction or chastisement. Elder Neal A. Maxwell (1926–2004) of the Quorum of the Twelve Apostles explained why we should accept the Lord's correction even if it is painful: "God is not only there in the mildest expressions of His presence, but also in those seemingly harsh expressions. For example, when truth 'cutteth . . . to the very center' (1 Nephi 16:2), this may signal that spiritual surgery is underway, painfully severing pride from the soul" (in Conference Report, Oct. 1987, 37; or *Ensign,* Nov. 1987, 31).

1 Nephi 16:7–8. The Importance of Marriage

• After reading about the marriages between Lehi's and Ishmael's families, we are told that Lehi had fulfilled all the commandments the Lord had given him (see 1 Nephi 16:8). Marriage is central to the Lord's plans for His children. The First Presidency and the Quorum of the Twelve Apostles declared the Lord's view on marriage: "The family is ordained of God. Marriage between man and woman is essential to His eternal plan. Children are entitled to birth within the bonds of matrimony, and to be reared by a father and a mother who honor marital vows with complete fidelity. Happiness in family life is most likely to be achieved when founded upon the teachings of the Lord Jesus Christ" ("The Family: A Proclamation to the World," *Ensign,* Nov. 1995, 102).

1 Nephi 16:10, 26–29. The Liahona

• Elder David A. Bednar of the Quorum of the Twelve Apostles explained the purpose of the Liahona and compared it to the Holy Spirit in our day:

"The Liahona was prepared by the Lord and given to Lehi and his family after they left Jerusalem and were traveling in the wilderness (see Alma 37:38; D&C 17:1). This compass or director pointed the way that Lehi and his caravan should go (see 1 Nephi 16:10), even 'a straight course to the promised land' (Alma 37:44). The pointers in the Liahona operated 'according to the faith and diligence and heed' (1 Nephi 16:28) of the travelers and failed to work when family members were contentious, rude, slothful, or forgetful (see 1 Nephi 18:12, 21; Alma 37:41, 43).

"The compass also provided a means whereby Lehi and his family could obtain greater 'understanding concerning the ways of the Lord' (1 Nephi 16:29). Thus, the primary purposes of the Liahona were to provide both direction and instruction during a long and demanding journey. The director was a physical instrument that served as an outward indicator of their inner spiritual standing before God. It worked according to the principles of faith and diligence.

"Just as Lehi was blessed in ancient times, each of us in this day has been given a spiritual compass that can direct and instruct us during our mortal journey. The Holy Ghost was conferred upon you and me as we came out of the world and into the Savior's Church through baptism and confirmation. By the authority of the holy priesthood we were confirmed as members of the Church and admonished to seek for the constant companionship of 'the Spirit of truth; whom the world cannot receive, because it seeth him not, neither knoweth him: but ye know him; for he dwelleth with you, and shall be in you' (John 14:17).

"As we each press forward along the pathway of life, we receive direction from the Holy Ghost just as Lehi was directed through the Liahona. 'For behold, again I say unto you that if ye will enter in by the way, and receive the Holy Ghost, it will show unto you all things what ye should do' (2 Nephi 32:5).

"The Holy Ghost operates in our lives precisely as the Liahona did for Lehi and his family, according to our faith and diligence and heed" (in Conference Report, Apr. 2006, 31; or *Ensign,* May 2006, 30–31).

---

1 NEPHI 16:29

What are the "small means" referred to in this scripture? What spiritual small means have made a difference in your life?

---

1 Nephi 16:18. A Bow "Made of Fine Steel"

• One commentator explained the use of steel in the Book of Mormon: "The overall question of the use of metals by Book of Mormon cultures is an important topic that deserves detailed attention [see John Sorenson, *An Ancient American Setting for the Book of Mormon* (1985), 277–88]. . . . There are five explicit references to metal weapons and armor in the Book of Mormon. Two are references to Near East weapons: 'the blade [of Laban's sword] was of the most precious steel' (1 Nephi 4:9), and Nephi's bow was made of 'fine steel' (1 Nephi 16:18). The existence of steel (that is, carburized iron) weapons in the Near East in the early sixth century B.C. has been clearly demonstrated. Robert Maddin writes, 'To sum up, by the beginning of the seventh century B.C. at the latest, the blacksmiths of the eastern Mediterranean had mastered two of the processes that make iron a useful material for tools and weapons: carburizing and quenching' ["How the Iron Age Began," *Scientific American,* Oct. 1977: 131]" (William J. Hamblin and A. Brent Merrill, "Swords in the Book of Mormon," in *Warfare in the Book of Mormon,* ed. Stephen D. Ricks and William J. Hamblin [1990], 345–46).

1 Nephi 16:21–25. The Broken Bow Experience

• Elder Neal A. Maxwell shared how great lessons often come after difficulties: "Nephi's broken bow doubtless brought to him some irritation, but not immobilizing bitterness. After all, he was just trying to feed the extended family, so why should he have to contend as well with a broken bow? Yet out of that episode came a great teaching moment. Irritation often precedes instruction" (*If Thou Endure It Well* [1996], 128).

• Elder Richard G. Scott of the Quorum of the Twelve Apostles taught that adversity can help stimulate necessary growth in our lives:

"May I share some suggestions with you who face . . . the testing that a wise Heavenly Father determines is needed even when you are living a worthy, righteous life and are obedient to His commandments.

"Just when all seems to be going right, challenges often come in multiple doses applied simultaneously.

When those trials are not consequences of your disobedience, they are evidence that the Lord feels you are prepared to grow more (see Proverbs 3:11–12). He therefore gives you experiences that stimulate growth, understanding, and compassion which polish you for your everlasting benefit. To get you from where you are to where He wants you to be requires a lot of stretching, and that generally entails discomfort and pain" (in Conference Report, Oct. 1995, 18; or *Ensign,* Nov. 1995, 16–17).

• The loss of Nephi's bow raised doubts in Lehi's colony, causing some to turn from God and focus on the negative. Elder Robert D. Hales of the Quorum of the Twelve Apostles counseled us to turn to the Lord when we face trials: "I have come to understand how useless it is to dwell on the *whys, what ifs,* and *if onlys* for which there likely will be given no answers in mortality. To receive the Lord's comfort, we must exercise faith. The questions Why me? Why our family? Why now? are usually unanswerable questions. These questions detract from our spirituality and can destroy our faith. We need to spend our time and energy building our faith by turning to the Lord and asking for strength to overcome the pains and trials of this world and to endure to the end for greater understanding" (in Conference Report, Oct. 1998, 16; or *Ensign,* Nov. 1998, 14–15).

• Murmuring and complaining seemed to have become second nature for Laman and Lemuel Even Lehi had become discouraged enough that he murmured. Elder Marion D. Hanks of the Presidency of the Seventy emphasized Nephi's great character in how he approached this crisis:

"What to do? Nephi says he made a bow and an arrow out of some available wood, got a sling and stones and, 'I said unto my Father, "Whither shall I go to obtain food?"' It is a simple thing, isn't it? . . . This means that Nephi went to his father and said, 'Dad, the Lord has blessed you. You are his servant. I need to know where to go to get food. Dad, you ask him, will you?' Oh, he could have gone to his own knees. He could have taken over.

"I count this one of the really significant lessons of life in the book, and, I repeat, the pages are full of them. A son who had strength enough, and humility enough, and manliness enough to go to his wavering superior and say, 'You ask God, will you?' because somehow he knew this is how you make men strong, that wise confidence in men builds them. Lehi asked God and God told him, and Lehi's leadership was restored" (*Steps to Learning,* Brigham Young University Speeches of the Year [May 4, 1960], 7).

© Gary Smith

1 Nephi 16:23. Nephi's Confidence in Lehi

• Nephi showed great humility by going to his father even after Lehi had murmured; Nephi still honored him. President Ezra Taft Benson (1899–1994) told of an experience that illustrates the principle of seeking counsel from our fathers, even though they may not be perfect:

"Some time ago, a young man came to my office requesting a blessing. He was about eighteen years of age and had some problems. There were no serious moral problems, but he was mixed up in his thinking and worried. He requested a blessing.

"I said to him, 'Have you ever asked your father to give you a blessing? Your father is a member of the Church, I assume?'

"He said, 'Yes, he is an elder, a rather inactive elder.'

"When I asked, 'Do you love your father?' he replied, 'Yes, Brother Benson, he is a good man. I love him.' He then said, 'He doesn't attend to his priesthood duties as he should. He doesn't go to church regularly, I don't know that he is a tithe payer, but he is a good man, a good provider, a kind man.'

"I said, 'How would you like to talk to him at an opportune time and ask him if he would be willing to give you a father's blessing?'

"'Oh,' he said, 'I think that would frighten him.'

"I then said, 'Are you willing to try it? I will be praying for you.'

"He said, 'All right; on that basis, I will.'

"A few days later he came back. He said, 'Brother Benson, that's the sweetest thing that has happened in our family.' He could hardly control his feelings as he told me what had happened. He said, 'When the opportunity was right, I mentioned it to Father, and he replied, "Son, do you really want me to give you a blessing?" I told him, "Yes, Dad, I would like you to."' Then he said, 'Brother Benson, he gave me one of the most beautiful blessings you could ever ask for. Mother sat there crying all during the blessing. When he got through there was a bond of appreciation and gratitude and love between us that we have never had in our home'" (in Conference Report, Oct. 1977, 45–46; or *Ensign,* Nov. 1977, 31–32).

1 Nephi 16:34. "The Place Which Was Called *Nahom*"

• The Hebrew meaning of *nahom* might be "consolation," from the verb *nahom,* which means to "be sorry, console oneself" (see 1 Nephi 16:34*b*). An *Ensign* news article described an archaeological find that revealed the name *Nahom* in the Arabian Peninsula:

"A group of Latter-day Saint researchers recently found evidence linking a site in Yemen, on the southwest corner of the Arabian peninsula, to a name associated with Lehi's journey as recorded in the Book of Mormon.

"Warren Aston, Lynn Hilton, and Gregory Witt located a stone altar that professional archaeologists dated to at least 700 B.C. This altar contains an inscription confirming 'Nahom' as an actual place that existed in the peninsula before the time of Lehi" ("News of the Church," *Ensign,* Feb. 2001, 79).

1 Nephi 17:4. Why Did It Take Eight Years to Make This Journey?

• In Alma 37:39–43 Alma informed us that Lehi's family "did not travel a direct course" or "did not progress in their journey" because on so many occasions the Liahona ceased to work. It ceased because many of them did not exercise faith, and they transgressed the laws of God. This would explain why a journey that would have been of much shorter duration took so long. (Refer to the map "Possible Route Taken by Lehi's Family" in the appendix, p. 410.)

1 Nephi 17:6. Twelve Conditions That Existed in the Land of Bountiful

• Lehi's family "exceedingly rejoiced when [they] came to the seashore" at Bountiful (1 Nephi 17:6). Bountiful must have been a fertile area. Following are 12 conditions that existed in the land of Bountiful (identified in Warren P. and Michaela Knoth Aston, *In the Footsteps of Lehi: New Evidence for Lehi's Journey across Arabia to Bountiful* [1994], 28–29):

1. Fresh water available year round
2. "Much fruit and also wild honey" (1 Nephi 17:5–6; 18:6)
3. Fertile ground in both the general area (17:5, 8) and the specific location (17:6) where Lehi's family camped
4. Reasonable access from the interior desert to the coast
5. A mountain prominent enough to justify Nephi's reference to "the mount" and close enough that he could go there to "pray oft" (18:3; see also 17:7)
6. Cliffs from which Nephi's brothers could have thrown him "into the depths of the sea" (17:48)

7. Shoreline (17:5) suitable for the construction and launching of a ship (18:8)

8. Ore and flint for Nephi's tools (17:9–11, 16)

9. Enough large timber to build a seaworthy ship (18:1–2, 6)

10. Suitable winds and ocean currents to take the ship out into the ocean (18:8–9)

11. No population residing in the area

12. "Nearly eastward" of Nahom (17:1; see also 16:34)

Possible Route Taken by Lehi's Family

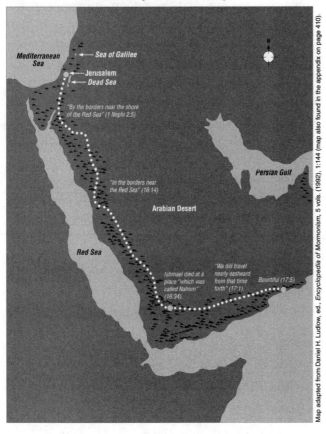

Map adapted from Daniel H. Ludlow, ed., *Encyclopedia of Mormonism*, 5 vols. (1992), 1:144 (map also found in the appendix on page 410).

1 Nephi 17:7–19. Nephi's Faith Was Manifest by His Action

• Nephi's response to the Lord's command to build a ship gives us insight into his remarkable faith. Other prophets have also been overwhelmed at times by tasks commanded by the Lord. Moses felt inadequate when called to lead the children of Israel (see Exodus 4:1–5). Enoch felt he was slow of speech and wondered why the Lord called him (see Moses 6:31). Nephi might have been overwhelmed with the thought of building an ocean-going vessel. Instead, his response displayed great faith: "Whither shall I go that I may find ore to molten, that I may make tools to construct the ship . . . ?" (1 Nephi 17:9). Nephi's confidence did not likely come from any previous ship-building experience. Rather, his confidence stemmed from tremendous faith in God.

Ship-building images by Jerry Thompson, © IRI

1 Nephi 17:23–34. Exodus of the Children of Israel from Egypt

• Nephi viewed his family's wilderness experience as a type or parallel to ancient Israel's wanderings in the wilderness (see 1 Nephi 17:13, 23, 30, 41–42). One writer discussed the witness the Book of Mormon provides regarding the exodus led by Moses: "The so-called higher critics of the Bible have raised the question as to whether or not the miracles of the exodus of Israel under Moses actually happened as they are recorded in the Old Testament. (See Exodus 14:19–20, 26–31; 16:4, 15; 17:5–6; Numbers 21:6–9.) However, the Book of Mormon substantiates the actuality of these miraculous events. (1 Nephi 17:23, 26, 28, 29, 30, 41.) Inasmuch as Nephi's knowledge of these miracles came from the authentic account on the brass plates of Laban (1 Nephi 5:11), Latter-day Saints should have no question concerning the reliability of the biblical account. Once again the Book of Mormon serves as a witness to its companion scripture, the Bible" (Daniel H. Ludlow, *A Companion to Your Study of the Book of Mormon* [1976], 115).

1 NEPHI 17:19–46

In what ways did Nephi use the story of Israel's exodus to teach Laman and Lemuel? What are some events in your life that testify of God's mercy?

1 Nephi 17:45. Sensitivity to Spiritual Communication

• Why were Laman and Lemuel unable to understand the Lord's will, even after seeing an angel? Why couldn't they receive a spiritual confirmation of their journey as their younger brother Nephi did? (see 1 Nephi 2:16). Nephi identified the cause of their spiritual insensitivity as being "swift to do iniquity" (1 Nephi 17:45). President James E. Faust (1920–2007) of the First Presidency compared a person's worthiness of receiving the Spirit to receiving a signal on a cell phone:

"Cellular phones are used for much of the communication in our time. Occasionally, however, we find dead spots where the signal coming to a cell phone fails. This can happen when the cell phone user is in a tunnel or a canyon or when there is other interference.

"So it is with divine communication. The still, small voice, though still and small, is very powerful. It 'whispereth through and pierceth all things' [D&C 85:6]. . . . Perhaps something in our lives prevents us from hearing the message because we are 'past feeling' [1 Nephi 17:45]. We often put ourselves in spiritual dead spots—places and situations that block out divine messages. Some of these dead spots include anger, pornography, transgression, selfishness, and other situations that offend the Spirit" (in Conference Report, Apr. 2004, 67–68; or *Ensign,* May 2004, 67).

• President Boyd K. Packer, President of the Quorum of the Twelve Apostles, described spiritual communication:

"The Holy Ghost speaks with a voice that you *feel* more than you *hear.* It is described as a 'still small voice' [D&C 85:6]. And while we speak of 'listening' to the whisperings of the Spirit, most often one describes a spiritual prompting by saying, 'I had a *feeling. . . .'*

"Revelation comes as words we *feel* more than *hear.* Nephi told his wayward brothers, who were visited by an angel, 'Ye were past *feeling,* that ye could not *feel* his words.' [1 Nephi 17:45; italics added]" (in Conference Report, Oct. 1994, 77; or *Ensign,* Nov. 1994, 60).

• Laman and Lemuel were "past feeling" and could not "feel" the words of the Holy Ghost (1 Nephi 17:45). Elder Joseph B. Wirthlin (1917–2008) of the Quorum of the Twelve Apostles explained that spiritual insensitivity isn't just a problem for those with serious sin:

"I fear that some members of the Lord's Church 'live far beneath our privileges' with regard to the gift of the Holy Ghost. Some are distracted by the things of the world that block out the influence of the Holy Ghost, preventing them from recognizing spiritual promptings. This is a noisy and busy world that we live in. Remember that being busy is not necessarily being spiritual. If we are not careful, the things of this world can crowd out the things of the Spirit.

"Some are spiritually deadened and past feeling because of their choices to commit sin. Others simply hover in spiritual complacency with no desire to rise above themselves and commune with the Infinite. If they would open their hearts to the refining influence of this unspeakable gift of the Holy Ghost, a glorious new spiritual dimension would come to light. Their eyes would gaze upon a vista scarcely imaginable. They could know for themselves things of the Spirit that are choice, precious, and capable of enlarging the soul, expanding the mind, and filling the heart with inexpressible joy" (in Conference Report, Apr. 2003, 27; or *Ensign,* May 2003, 27).

1 NEPHI 17:45

Examine this verse and identify different ways the Lord may speak at different times.

1 Nephi 18:9. Dancing and Singing

• Some may erroneously conclude from 1 Nephi 18:9 that the Lord does not approve of dancing or singing. Nephi said twice that they erred when their dancing and singing led them "to speak with much rudeness" (1 Nephi 18:9). The word *rude* refers to being harsh, vulgar, or coarse. The Lord has stated that He approves of proper dancing and singing (see Psalm 149:1–4; D&C 136:28). Note from these scriptures that we may praise the Lord through dancing and singing. Satan can use dancing or music, however, as a means of corruption and loss of the Spirit. This is why Church leaders caution us about the kinds of music we listen to and how we dance. The First Presidency has counseled:

"Choose carefully the music you listen to. Pay attention to how you feel when you are listening. Don't listen to music that drives away the Spirit, encourages immorality, glorifies violence, [or] uses foul or offensive language. . . .

"Dancing can be fun and can provide an opportunity to meet new people. However, it too can be misused. When dancing, avoid full body contact with your partner. Do not use positions or moves that are suggestive of sexual behavior. Plan and attend dances where dress, grooming, lighting, lyrics, and music contribute to a wholesome atmosphere where the Spirit of the Lord may be present" (*For the Strength of Youth: Fulfilling Our Duty to God* [2001], 20–21).

1 Nephi 18:25. Horses

• There was controversy regarding horses in the Western Hemisphere before Columbus arrived. However, modern archaeological discoveries have shed new light on the subject: "'Fossil remains of true horses, differing but very slightly from the smaller and inferior breeds of those now existing, are found abundantly in deposits of the most recent geological age, in almost every part of America, from Escholz Bay in the north to Patagonia in the South. In that continent however, they became quite extinct, and no horses, either wild or domesticated, existed there at the time of the Spanish conquest, which is the most remarkable as, when introduced from Europe the horses that ran wild proved by their rapid multiplication in the plains of South America and Texas that the climate, food, and other circumstances were highly favorable for their existence. The former great abundance of Equidae in America, their complete extinction, and their perfect acclimatization when reintroduced by man, form curious but as yet unsolved problems in geographical distribution.' (*New Americanized Encyclopedia,* Vol. 5, p. 3197.)" (Joy M. Osborn, *The Book of Mormon—The Stick of Joseph,* 2nd ed. [2001], 164).

Points to Ponder

• What qualities made Nephi someone the Lord could depend on?

• Why would asking your parents for counsel strengthen your relationship with them and with the Lord?

• Why is it dangerous to ignore or become "past feeling" to the promptings of the Holy Ghost?

Suggested Assignments

• Write a paragraph describing the purpose of the Liahona and the principles it worked by.

• Identify a doctrine or principle found in each of the following references:

1 Nephi 16:28 _____

_____.

1 Nephi 17:13–14 _____

_____.

1 Nephi 17:45–46 _____

_____.

1 Nephi 18:15–16 _____

_____.

• Compare Nephi's previous experience of deliverance in 1 Nephi 7:16–18 with 1 Nephi 18:11–20. Then answer the following questions:

1. Even though this is the same righteous person with the same faith, why do you think Nephi was delivered immediately the first time and not until after four days on the second occasion?

2. What had to happen in 1 Nephi 18 before Nephi was delivered?

Introduction

As he studied the brass plates, Nephi encountered many prophecies concerning the mission of Jesus Christ. Among these were the writings of Isaiah, Zenos, Zenock, and Neum. Nephi read these prophecies to his people. He also included a portion of them on the small plates hoping to persuade his people and future readers to believe in the Redeemer (see 1 Nephi 19:18, 23–24).

As you study 1 Nephi 19–22, look for evidence of the Lord's great love for His children. Nephi recorded prophecies that demonstrate that scattered Israel would eventually be restored to the fulness of the gospel and gathered together. Furthermore, Nephi taught that even though great wickedness will cover the earth during the last days, "the righteous need not fear" (1 Nephi 22:17) because the Lord's protective hand will be upon them. Never in the course of history has the Lord forgotten His people, nor will He forget them now, for He has "graven [them] upon the palms of [His] hands" (1 Nephi 21:16).

Commentary

1 Nephi 19:1–6. Two Sets of Plates

• Nephi wrote about the two sets of plates he made (see 1 Nephi 9). The large plates of Nephi contained a detailed account of his people. The small plates of Nephi were a sacred religious record. In 1 Nephi 19:1–6, "first plates" and "other plates" refers to the large plates of Nephi; "these plates" refers to the small plates of Nephi (see commentary for Words of Mormon on p. 134).

Bill Hill, © 1982 IRI

1 Nephi 19:7–9. The World Shall Judge Him to Be a Thing of Naught

• Nephi recorded that Jesus Christ was smitten because people of His day judged Him "to be a thing of naught." The Savior was unimportant to them. He was deemed to be "good for nothing, but to be . . . trodden under foot of men" (Matthew 5:13). Elder Neal A. Maxwell (1926–2004) of the Quorum of the Twelve Apostles noted how men today often follow the same fateful thinking: "For many moderns, sad to say, the query 'What think ye of Christ?' (Matthew 22:42) would be answered, 'I really don't think of Him at all!'" (in Conference Report, Oct. 1995, 27; or *Ensign,* Nov. 1995, 22–23).

• On another occasion Elder Maxwell taught that regardless of what the world says, we must stand fast in our testimony of the Savior: "At the center of the Father's plan is Jesus Christ, mankind's Redeemer. Yet, as foreseen, many judge Jesus 'to be a thing of naught' (1 Nephi 19:9), or 'consider him' merely 'a man' (Mosiah 3:9). Whether others deny or delimit Jesus, for us He is our Lord and Savior! Comparatively, brothers and sisters, it matters very little what people think of us, but it matters very much what we think of Him. It matters very little, too, who others say we are; what matters is who we say Jesus is" (in Conference Report, Apr. 1984, 27; or *Ensign,* May 1984, 21).

1 Nephi 19:10–16. Zenock, Neum, and Zenos

• Nephi quoted from Zenock, Neum, and Zenos. These were prophets of Old Testament times whose detailed prophecies of Jesus Christ were recorded on the brass plates; therefore we know they lived before 600 B.C. They spoke plainly about the life and ministry of the Messiah and the destiny of the house of Israel (see also Helaman 8:19–20). Without the Book of Mormon, we would know nothing about these three prophets or their witnesses of Christ.

1 NEPHI 19:11

While not all physical calamities are a result of divine punishment, what appears to be the purpose of the natural disasters spoken of?

1 Nephi 19:21–24. 📖 Likening the Scriptures unto Ourselves

• Nephi read the scriptures to his people and "did liken all scriptures unto [them]" (v. 23 📖). How do we liken the scriptures unto ourselves for "profit and learning"? (v. 23 📖). Questions like the following ones can help us profitably apply the scriptures to our lives:

What significance does this particular event or principle have for me today? For example: What does the rebellion of Laman and Lemuel teach me? What can I learn about faithfulness from Nephi's obedience?

If I were in this particular situation or faced with this challenge or question, how would I react? What flaws or strengths would I find in my own character? Am I like Lehi's family members who murmured in the wilderness, or am I like Nephi and Sam? Do I complain when things get difficult, or do I trust in God no matter what the circumstances?

What do I learn about God and His dealings with His children from this event? As I study the lives of men and women in the scriptures, what do I learn about the things that please or displease God? Why was this particular concept, principle, or event included in the scriptures?

1 Nephi 20–21. Introduction to the Writings of Isaiah

• Why did Nephi include Isaiah 48–49 (1 Nephi 20–21) at this point in his record? We find an answer to this question in 1 Nephi 19:21: "And [the Lord] surely did show unto the prophets of old [including Isaiah] all things concerning them [the Jews in Jerusalem]; and also he did show unto many concerning us [the Nephites in America]."

Overview of 1 Nephi, Chapters 20–21

The prophets (including Isaiah) were shown "them," referring to the Jews.
The prophets (including Isaiah) were shown "us," referring to the Nephites.
1 Nephi 20 (Isaiah 48) is about "them"—the Jews in Jerusalem. 1 Nephi 21 (Isaiah 49) is about "us"—the Nephites in America.
The Lord showed the Jews to Isaiah—1 Nephi 20 (Isaiah 48). The Lord showed the Nephites to Isaiah—1 Nephi 21 (Isaiah 49).

• Why did Nephi include other writings of Isaiah throughout his record (particularly 2 Nephi 12–25)?

Nephi began the first of his Isaiah citations with these words: "Hear ye the words of the prophet, ye who are a remnant of the house of Israel, a branch who have been broken off; hear ye the words of the prophet, which were written unto all the house of Israel, and liken them unto yourselves, *that ye may have hope* as well as your brethren from whom ye have been broken off; for after this manner has the prophet written" (1 Nephi 19:24; italics added).

Isaiah's writings testify that Jesus Christ is the only true source of hope for men and women living in a fallen world. Consequently, Nephi cited hundreds of verses Isaiah wrote that testify of the Savior. One scholar noted that "of the 425 separate verses of Isaiah which are quoted in the Book of Mormon, 391 say something about the attributes or mission of Jesus Christ" (Monte S. Nyman, *"Great Are the Words of Isaiah"* [1980], 7).

Moreover, Nephi recognized that Isaiah's testimony was similar to his own, as both had seen the Lord. Nephi explained:

"And now I, Nephi, write more of the words of Isaiah, for my soul delighteth in his words. For I will liken his words unto my people, and I will send them forth unto all my children, for he verily saw my Redeemer, even as I have seen him.

"And my brother, Jacob, also has seen him as I have seen him; wherefore, I will send their words forth unto my children to prove unto them that my words are true. Wherefore, by the words of three, God hath said, I will establish my word. Nevertheless, God sendeth more witnesses, and he proveth all his words" (2 Nephi 11:2–3).

The greatest validation of Isaiah's writings came from the Savior Himself. While ministering to the Nephites, Jesus declared:

"And now, behold, I say unto you, that ye ought to search these things. Yea, a commandment I give unto you that ye search these things diligently; for great are the words of Isaiah.

"For surely he spake as touching all things concerning my people which are of the house of Israel; therefore it must needs be that he must speak also to the Gentiles.

"And *all things that he spake have been and shall be,* even according to the words which he spake" (3 Nephi 23:1–3; italics added).

• What happened during Isaiah's lifetime, and why are his prophecies still being fulfilled today?

Isaiah prophesied from approximately 740–701 B.C. During his lifetime the kingdoms of Israel and Judah rose in prosperity and struggled with idolatry. The unrighteousness of the people led to spiritual weakness and political peril. In a short period of time, Israel and Judah became weak vassal states cowering under the mighty Assyrian empire. In fact, the scattering of Israel began during Isaiah's lifetime, as many Israelites from the northern kingdom of Israel were carried away captive by the Assyrians.

Isaiah repeatedly warned of the consequences of wickedness and foretold the calamities that would fall upon the house of Israel as a result, including the scattering of Israel from their lands of inheritance and the loss of the blessings of the covenant. He also testified repeatedly that Israel's only hope could come from redemption through the Messiah. Many of Isaiah's prophecies concern the coming of the Savior to the earth, both in the meridian of time and at the millennial day. Furthermore, he gave specific details concerning the latter-day gathering of Israel and the restoration of the gospel covenant.

• Why is Isaiah difficult to understand?

As Nephi selected passages from Isaiah for his record, he knew that many readers would struggle to understand them. Even many of the people in Nephi's day could not grasp their meaning. He mentioned three specific reasons for this difficulty:

1. They did not know "the manner of prophesying among the Jews" (2 Nephi 25:1).
2. They were not "filled with the spirit of prophecy" (v. 4).
3. They were not "taught after the manner of the things of the Jews" (v. 5).

In addition to the reasons Nephi gave, other difficulties exist for modern readers:

1. Most of Isaiah's writings are in poetic form. The beauty and depth of poetry in one language does not easily translate into other languages.
2. Many of Isaiah's prophecies are dualistic in nature. Consequently, the prophecies can be fulfilled in many circumstances at different times in history.
3. Isaiah used extensive symbolism. Many of the objects and events he referred to were contemporary to his day and are difficult for us to understand today.

In summary, just as Jesus taught profound truths through parables that concealed their meaning from those not prepared to understand, Isaiah spoke in a manner that required more of his listeners than casual consideration.

• What can help readers understand Isaiah's words?

Three basic guidelines assist anyone who wishes to understand what Isaiah wrote:

1. Study other scripture. The scriptures themselves offer many insights into the meaning of Isaiah's writings. The Bible Dictionary states, "The reader today has no greater written commentary and guide to understanding Isaiah than the Book of Mormon and the Doctrine and Covenants" ("Isaiah," 707). Not only do these books of scripture interpret passages of Isaiah, they contain doctrines and prophecies that shed light on Isaiah's words. These modern scriptures fill in details that are not as evident in the Bible.

2. Seek the spirit of prophecy. As Nephi mentioned, those who were not "filled with the spirit of prophecy" (2 Nephi 25:1) in his day could not understand the meaning of Isaiah's writings. The same is true today. Each serious student of Isaiah must seek revelation through the Holy Ghost to enlighten their mind and to help them read the words by the same Spirit in which they were written—in the testimony of Jesus Christ (see Revelation 19:10).

© 1989 Greg K. Olsen

3. Study diligently. Elder Bruce R. McConkie (1915–85) of the Quorum of the Twelve Apostles encouraged Latter-day Saints to devote themselves to serious study of Isaiah: "Read, ponder, and pray—verse by verse, thought by thought, passage by passage, chapter by chapter! As Isaiah himself asks: 'Whom shall he teach knowledge? and whom shall he make to understand doctrine?' His answer: 'them that are weaned from the milk, and drawn from the breasts. For precept must be upon precept, precept upon precept; line upon line, line upon line; here a little, and there a little.' (Isa. 28:9–10.)" ("Ten Keys to Understanding Isaiah," *Ensign,* Oct. 1973, 83).

1 Nephi 20:1–2. "They Call Themselves of the Holy City"

• In 1 Nephi 20:1–2, the prophet Isaiah chastised the house of Israel for claiming to follow the Lord without keeping His commandments. They felt that because they were His covenant people and lived in the holy city of Jerusalem, God would always protect them. Isaiah taught that it is not where you live but how you live that is important (see vv. 18–22).

1 Nephi 20:10. "Furnace of Affliction"

• Intense heat refines metal and removes impurities. Elder Dallin H. Oaks of the Quorum of the Twelve Apostles observed that affliction can likewise refine and purify each of us: "Most of us experience some measure of what the scriptures call 'the furnace of affliction' (Isaiah 48:10; 1 Nephi 20:10). Some are submerged in service to a disadvantaged family member. Others suffer the death of a loved one or the loss or postponement of a righteous goal like marriage or childbearing. Still others struggle with personal impairments or with feelings of rejection, inadequacy, or depression. Through the justice and mercy of a loving Father in Heaven, the refinement and sanctification possible through such experiences can help us achieve what God desires us to become" (in Conference Report, Oct. 2000, 43; or *Ensign,* Nov. 2000, 33–34).

• Elder Robert D. Hales of the Quorum of the Twelve Apostles described the personal sanctification he experienced following three major surgeries:

"In the past two years, I have waited upon the Lord for mortal lessons to be taught me through periods of physical pain, mental anguish, and pondering. I learned that constant, intense pain is a great consecrating purifier that humbles us and draws us closer to God's Spirit. If we listen and obey, we will be guided by His Spirit and do His will in our daily endeavors.

"There were times when I have asked a few direct questions in my prayers, such as, 'What lessons dost Thou want me to learn from these experiences?'

"As I studied the scriptures during this critical period of my life, the veil was thin and answers were given to me as they were recorded in lives of others who had gone through even more severe trials.

"'My son, peace be unto thy soul; thine adversity and thine afflictions shall be but a small moment;

"'And then, if thou endure it well, God shall exalt thee on high' (D&C 121:7–8).

"Dark moments of depression were quickly dispelled by the light of the gospel as the Spirit brought peace and comfort with assurances that all would be well.

"On a few occasions I told the Lord that I had surely learned the lessons to be taught and that it wouldn't be necessary for me to endure any more suffering. Such entreaties seemed to be of no avail, for it was made clear to me that this purifying process of testing was to be endured in the Lord's time and in the Lord's own way" (in Conference Report, Oct. 2000, 3–4; or *Ensign,* Nov. 2000, 6).

1 Nephi 20:14, 20. Babylon

• As with other great ancient empires, Babylon's ascendancy to wealth and glory was accompanied by moral decay, wickedness, and iniquity. Babylon's corruption was so extensive that the very name became a symbol for worldliness, spiritual wickedness, and Satan's kingdom.

Paul Gustave Dore

God decreed that the Medes should completely destroy Babylon in its wickedness (see Isaiah 13:17–22). Under the rule of Cyrus the Great, an alliance of Medes and Persians dammed the mighty Euphrates River and marched through the riverbed and under the walls of Babylon to capture the city and overthrow the empire around 538 B.C. When Isaiah spoke of Babylon, he referred to both the actual empire as well as spiritual Babylon. Isaiah foresaw the graphic destruction of the Babylon of his day as a result of the great wickedness of its people. Consequently, he used the term *Babylon* in his prophecies to typify the spiritual condition of the latter days and the judgment that would come upon the world at the Second Coming of Jesus Christ (see D&C 1:16).

The Doctrine and Covenants clarifies Isaiah's exhortation to "go ye forth of Babylon" (1 Nephi 20:20). Those who "bear the vessels of the Lord" must be clean, leaving the wickedness of the "spiritual Babylon" behind them (D&C 38:42; 133:5, 14).

1 Nephi 21:13–16. Can a Woman Forget Her Child?

• Just as it seems impossible for a woman to forget a nursing baby, Elder Jeffrey R. Holland of the Quorum of the Twelve Apostles explained that it would be even more impossible for the Savior to forget us: "This poetic passage provides yet another reminder of Christ's saving role, that of protective, redeeming parent to Zion's children. He comforts his people and shows mercy when they are afflicted, as any loving father or mother would toward a child, but, as Nephi here reminds us through Isaiah, much more than any mortal father and mother could do. Although a mother may forget her sucking child (as unlikely as any parent might think that could be), Christ will not forget the children he has redeemed or the covenant he has made with them for salvation in Zion. The painful reminders of that watch care and covenant are the marks of the Roman nails graven upon the palms of his hands, a sign to his disciples in the Old World, his Nephite congregation in the New World, and to us in latter-day Zion that he is the Savior of the world and was wounded in the house of his friends" (*Christ and the New Covenant* [1997], 84).

1 Nephi 21:23. Nursing Fathers and Mothers

• Nephi explained that the Lord would raise up a gentile nation to nurse scattered Israel (see 1 Nephi 22:6–9). As part of the fulfillment of this prophecy, the gospel was restored in the United States of America, a gentile nation (see D&C 109:60). The gospel is the Lord's "standard to the people" (1 Nephi 21:22), restoring the new and everlasting covenant to the children of men (see D&C 66:2) and feeding the need of a spiritually famished Israel (see Amos 8:11–13) scattered throughout the world. The analogy of the Restoration of the gospel is that of a "feast of fat things" taken to the world to nurse them to spiritual health (see D&C 58:6–11).

1 Nephi 22:4. "The Isles of the Sea"

• A scholar explained the meaning of "the isles of the sea": "Nephi not only refers to the isles of the sea as the location of other remnants of the house of Israel, but he also indicates that he and his people were then living upon an 'isle of the sea' when he quite clearly is referring to the great land mass known as the American continent. (2 Nephi 10:20–21.)" (Daniel H. Ludlow, *A Companion to Your Study of the Book of Mormon* [1976], 121).

• For more information on the scattering of Israel, refer to "Brief History of the Scattering of Israel" in the appendix (p. 415).

1 Nephi 22:6–9. "A Mighty Nation" and "a Marvelous Work"

• The phrase "the Lord God will raise up a mighty nation among the Gentiles" (1 Nephi 22:7) refers to the United States of America in 1776. The First Amendment to the Constitution of the United States included a proclamation of freedom of religion. These amendments were ratified on December 15, 1791. The Constitution of the United States was where freedom of religion first took root in the modern world.

• In 1 Nephi 22:8, Nephi referred to "a marvelous work among the Gentiles" in the latter days. This great work includes the Restoration of the gospel of Jesus Christ and the priesthood keys necessary to bring the covenants of God to "all the kindreds of the earth" (v. 9).

The events in verse 7 had to precede those in verse 8. The world was typically full of countries with forced state religions. For the gospel to be restored, it required a country that both legally professed and practiced freedom of religion. Joseph Smith was born in December 1805, just 14 years after the ratification of the amendments to the Constitution.

1 Nephi 22:6–12. The Gathering of Israel

• For more information on the gathering of Israel, refer to "The Gathering of Israel" in the appendix (p. 416).

1 Nephi 22:10–12. "Make Bare His Arm"

• Nephi spoke of God making "bare his arm in the eyes of all the nations" (1 Nephi 22:11). Isaiah used a similar phrase (Isaiah 52:10). An arm is a symbol of power. The metaphor that God will make "bare his arm" means that God will show his power to the entire world.

> ### *1 Nephi 22:13–17*
> *What is one reason Satan's host will not prevail over the people of God? What else will keep the righteous from being overpowered?*

1 Nephi 22:17, 22. "The Righteous Need Not Fear"

• While Nephi recorded that "the righteous need not fear" (1 Nephi 22:17, 22) because the Lord's protective hand will be over them during the calamities of the last days, the wicked have no promise of protection from these events. Elder Bruce R. McConkie taught: "We do not say that all of the Saints will be spared and saved from the coming day of desolation. But we do say there is no promise of safety and no promise of security except for those who love the Lord and who are seeking to do all that he commands" (in Conference Report, Apr. 1979, 133; or *Ensign,* May 1979, 93).

1 Nephi 22:24. "Calves of the Stall"

• President Joseph Fielding Smith (1876–1972) taught that children who will be raised during the Millennium "shall grow up 'as calves of the stall' unto righteousness, that is, without sin or the temptations which are so prevalent today" (*The Way to Perfection* [1970], 299).

• Contemplate the difference between a calf that is raised out on the range or in the mountains and one that is raised in a barn. The calf on the range is subject to all the forces of nature: inclement weather, predatory animals, and occasional scarcity of food and water. On the other hand, the calf raised in the barn or in a stall is protected from poor weather and predatory animals. Likewise, food and water are regularly provided. Nephi taught that "the time cometh speedily that the righteous must be led up as calves of the stall" (1 Nephi 22:24).

One commentator said: "Those who are left after the judgment of the Second Coming will be able to raise up their children as calves are raised in a stall. The calf is protected from the elements, and his environment is controlled (Malachi 4:2; 1 Nephi 22:24). The children in the Millennium will similarly 'grow up without sin unto salvation' (D&C 45:58). The telestial element will be removed, and with Satan being bound (Revelation 20:1–3; 1 Nephi 22:26; D&C 101:28), the environment will be more controlled" (Monte S. Nyman and Farres H. Nyman, *The Words of the Twelve Prophets: Messages to the Latter-day Saints* [1990], 145).

1 Nephi 22:26. How Will Satan Be Bound?

• Nephi gave a very clear definition in scripture of how Satan is to be bound during the Millennium. Elder Bruce R. McConkie wrote the following explanation concerning this important verse:

"What does it mean to bind Satan? How is he bound? Our revelation says: 'And in that day Satan shall not have power to tempt any man.' (D&C 101:28.) Does this mean that power is withdrawn from Satan so that he can no longer entice men to do evil? Or does it mean that men no longer succumb to his enticements because their hearts are so set on righteousness that they refuse to forsake that which is good to follow him who is evil? Clearly it means the latter. Satan was not bound in heaven, in the very presence of God, in the sense that he was denied the right and power to preach false doctrine and to invite men to walk away from that God whose children they were; nay, in this sense, he could not have been bound in heaven, for even he must have his agency.

"How, then, will Satan be bound during the Millennium? It will be by the righteousness of the people" (*The Millennial Messiah* [1982], 668).

Points to Ponder

• Nephi explained in 1 Nephi 19:18 that he wrote to "persuade" his people to "remember the Lord their Redeemer." How can remembering Nephi's reason for writing help you in your personal study of the scriptures?

• Ponder the meaning of the phrase in 1 Nephi 21:16 that the Savior has "graven thee upon the palms of [His] hands." How can this give you confidence that the Lord will always remember you?

Suggested Assignments

• Nephi cited the prophecies of Zenock, Neum, and Zenos (see 1 Nephi 19:10). These prophets lived in Old Testament times, but their prophecies are not found in the Bible. Using the scripture index or the Guide to the Scriptures as a resource, list several other prophecies that Zenock and Zenos made. What particular importance did their prophecies have to the Nephites? (see 3 Nephi 10:16). Why are they important to you?

• Answer the first question from each paragraph in the commentary for 1 Nephi 19:21–24 (p. 43).

• In the meridian of time, Jesus "was judged to be a thing of naught" (1 Nephi 19:7, 9). Identify ways that the world today still judges Jesus "to be a thing of naught." Write a paragraph outlining ways you can combat these worldly influences and develop your testimony of the Savior.

Introduction

Lehi's final words of advice and counsel to his children are tender and powerful. In a clear and effective way he taught his son Jacob the relationship between the Creation, the Fall, and the Atonement of Jesus Christ. He gave his son Joseph his prophetic declaration of Joseph the son of Israel, including his witness of the Restoration of the gospel through his latter-day namesake, Joseph Smith Jr. As you study the details of the plan of salvation, as well as the fulfillment of the prophecies regarding the Restoration of the gospel in the latter days, your testimony of God's love and care for all His children will grow.

Gary Kapp, © IRI

Commentary

2 Nephi 1:5–11. "A Land of Liberty"

• President Ezra Taft Benson (1899–1994) testified that America is a land of liberty set apart for the Restoration of the gospel: "Our Father in Heaven planned the coming forth of the Founding Fathers and their form of government as the necessary great prologue leading to the restoration of the gospel. Recall what our Savior Jesus Christ said nearly two thousand years ago when He visited this promised land: 'For it is wisdom in the Father that they should be established in this land, and be set up as a free people by the power of the Father, that these things might come forth' (3 Nephi 21:4). America,

the land of liberty, was to be the Lord's latter-day base of operations for His restored church" (in Conference Report, Oct. 1987, 3; or *Ensign,* Nov. 1987, 4).

• Elder Eduardo Ayala of the Seventy explained that the blessings of the gospel are now available wherever faithful members live: "The conditions of peoples and of nations change due to progress in the world; nevertheless, in many such places, be it in the frosty mountain heights, in the warm valleys, at the rivers' edges, or in the desert places, wherever members of our church are found, there will always be those who live these basic principles, and by so doing they bless the rest of the people" (in Conference Report, Apr. 1995, 39; or *Ensign,* May 1995, 30).

---

2 NEPHI 1:10–11

Under what conditions will the Lord allow the children of Lehi "to be scattered and smitten"?

---

2 Nephi 1:13–23. Awake from "the Sleep of Hell"

• Disobedience to the Lord's commandments allows Satan to deceive us, and we forget the light and truth we have previously learned. President Henry B. Eyring of the First Presidency described this dangerous condition: "One of the effects of disobeying God seems to be the creation of just enough spiritual anesthetic to block any sensation as the ties to God are being cut. Not only [does] the testimony of the truth slowly erode, but even the memories of what it was like to be in the light [begin] to seem . . . like a delusion" ("A Life Founded in Light and Truth," *Brigham Young University 2000–2001 Speeches* [2001], 81).

2 Nephi 1:22. Eternal Destruction

• Verse 22 in 2 Nephi 1 does not mean that the spirit and the body of the wicked will be annihilated or become extinct. Our spirits are eternal in nature, and all people born on earth will have a physical resurrection (see Alma 11:43–44). President Joseph Fielding Smith (1876–1972) explained the meaning of the destruction of the soul, as Nephi used it:

"Destruction does not mean annihilation. We know, because we are taught in the revelations of the Lord, that a soul cannot be destroyed.

"Every soul born into this world shall receive the resurrection and immortality and shall endure forever. Destruction does not mean, then, annihilation. When the Lord says they shall be destroyed, he means that they shall be banished from his presence, that they shall be cut off from the presence of light and truth, and shall not have the privilege of gaining this exaltation; and that is destruction" (*Doctrines of Salvation,* comp. Bruce R. McConkie, 3 vols. [1954–56], 2:227–28). Wickedness destroys the opportunity for a resurrection into a higher degree of glory (see D&C 88:30–31).

2 Nephi 2:2. Consecrate Afflictions for Gain

• In 2 Nephi 2:2 Lehi stated that the trials we endure can turn to our benefit (see also D&C 98:3). Elder Dallin H. Oaks of the Quorum of the Twelve Apostles explained how a sense of gratitude enables us to see our hardships in the context of our purpose here on earth: "When we give thanks in all things, we see hardships and adversities in the context of the purpose of life. We are sent here to be tested. There must be opposition in *all* things. We are meant to learn and grow through that opposition, through meeting our challenges, and through teaching others to do the same" (in Conference Report, Apr. 2003, 103; or *Ensign,* May 2003, 97).

• Elder Richard G. Scott of the Quorum of the Twelve Apostles explained that God provides us with challenges that are designed to help us grow spiritually: "Just when all seems to be going right, challenges often come in multiple doses applied simultaneously. When those trials are not consequences of your disobedience, they are evidence that the Lord feels you are prepared to grow more (see Proverbs 3:11–12). He therefore gives you experiences that stimulate growth, understanding, and compassion which polish you for your everlasting benefit. To get you from where you are to where He wants you to be requires a lot of stretching, and that generally entails discomfort and pain" (in Conference Report, Oct. 1995, 18; or *Ensign,* Nov. 1995, 16–17).

2 Nephi 2:4. "Salvation Is Free"

• Salvation means "to be saved from both physical and spiritual death. All people will be saved from physical death by the grace of God, through the death and resurrection of Jesus Christ. Each individual can also be saved from spiritual death as well by the grace of God, through faith in Jesus Christ. This faith is manifested in a life of obedience to the laws and ordinances of the gospel and service to Christ" (Guide to the Scriptures, "Salvation").

• Through the Atonement of Jesus Christ, the plan of salvation is freely available to everyone. This does not mean that all men and women will receive the same reward. As Alma testified, "Whosoever will come may come and partake of the waters of life freely." But he added this warning: "Whosoever will not come the same is not compelled to come; but in the last day it shall be restored unto him according to his deeds" (Alma 42:27). Salvation is free in the sense that it is provided by the grace of God through the Atonement of Christ for all who will receive it. It is not free in the sense that it is given to all regardless of what they believe or how they choose to live their lives.

2 Nephi 2:6–30. Creation, Fall, and Atonement

• Elder Bruce R. McConkie (1915–85) of the Quorum of the Twelve Apostles shared the following insights about the interrelationship between the Creation, the Fall, and the Atonement: "It is not possible to believe in Christ and his atoning sacrifice, in the true and full sense required to gain salvation, without at the same time believing and accepting the true doctrine of the fall. If there had been no fall, there would have been no need for a Redeemer or Savior. And it is not possible to believe in the fall, out of which immortality and eternal life come, without at the same time believing and accepting the true doctrine of the creation: If there had been no creation of all things in a deathless or immortal state, there could have been no fall, and hence no atonement and no salvation. The Father's eternal plan called for the creation, for the fall, and for the atonement, all woven together into one united whole" (*A New Witness for the Articles of Faith* [1985], 82).

• On another occasion Elder Bruce R. McConkie explained:

"The most important events that ever have or will occur in all eternity . . . are the Creation, the Fall, and the Atonement.

"Before we can even begin to understand the temporal creation of all things, we must know how and in what manner these three eternal verities—the Creation, the Fall, and the Atonement—are inseparably woven together to form one plan of salvation. . . . No one of them stands alone; each of them ties into the other two; and without a knowledge of all of them, it is not possible to know the truth about any one of them. . . .

"But, be it remembered, the Atonement came because of the Fall. Christ paid the ransom for Adam's transgression. If there had been no Fall, there would be no Atonement with its consequent immortality and eternal life. Thus, just as surely as salvation comes because of the Atonement, so also salvation comes because of the Fall" ("Christ and the Creation," *Ensign,* June 1982, 9).

2 Nephi 2:5–6. "By the Law No Flesh Is Justified"

• Justification means "to be pardoned from punishment for sin and declared guiltless. A person is justified by the Savior's grace through faith in him. This faith is shown by repentance and obedience to the laws and ordinances of the gospel. Jesus Christ's atonement enables mankind to repent and be justified or pardoned from punishment they otherwise would receive" (Guide to the Scriptures, "Justification, Justify").

Elder Dallin H. Oaks instructed us that the Book of Mormon teaches that "salvation does not come by keeping the commandments alone. 'By the law no flesh is justified' (2 Nephi 2:5). Even those who serve God with their whole souls are unprofitable servants (see Mosiah 2:21). Man cannot earn his own salvation.

"The Book of Mormon teaches, 'Since man had fallen he could not merit anything of himself' (Alma 22:14). 'There can be nothing which is short of an infinite atonement which will suffice for the sins of the world' (Alma 34:12; see also 2 Nephi 9:7; Alma 34:8–16). 'Wherefore, redemption cometh in and through the Holy Messiah; . . . he offereth himself a sacrifice for sin, to answer the ends of the law' (2 Nephi 2:6–7). And so we 'preach of Christ . . . that our children may know to what source they may look for a remission of their sins' (2 Nephi 25:26)" (in Conference Report, Oct. 1988, 78; or *Ensign,* Nov. 1988, 67).

2 Nephi 2:8. "The Merits, and Mercy, and Grace of the Holy Messiah"

• Prior to his call to the Quorum of the Seventy, Elder Bruce C. Hafen explained that the Atonement is not simply God's method for righting wrongs and satisfying the demands of justice. The Atonement is rehabilitative, a miraculous power that can help us change who we are: "I once wondered if those who refuse to repent but who then satisfy the law of justice by paying for their own sins are then worthy to enter the celestial kingdom. The answer is no. The entrance requirements for celestial life are simply higher than merely satisfying the law of justice. For that reason, paying for our sins will not bear the same fruit as repenting of our sins. Justice is a law of balance and order and it must be satisfied, either through our payment or his. But if we decline the Savior's invitation to let him carry our sins, and then satisfy justice by ourselves, we will not yet have experienced the complete rehabilitation that can occur through a combination of divine assistance and genuine repentance. Working together, those forces have the power permanently to change our hearts and our lives, preparing us for celestial life" (*The Broken Heart: Applying the Atonement to Life's Experiences* [1989], 7–8).

• Elder Richard G. Scott shared his feelings about Christ's mercy in paying our debts: "Jesus Christ possessed *merits* that no other child of Heavenly Father could possibly have. He was a God, Jehovah, before His birth in Bethlehem. His Father not only gave Him His spirit body, but Jesus was His Only Begotten Son in the flesh. Our Master lived a perfect, sinless life and therefore was free from the demands of justice. He was and is perfect in every attribute, including love, compassion, patience, obedience, forgiveness, and humility. His *mercy* pays our debt to justice when we repent and obey Him" (in Conference Report, Apr. 1997, 77–78; or *Ensign,* May 1997, 53).

---

2 Nephi 2:11–13
Why is opposition necessary?

---

2 Nephi 2:11–14. "There Is an Opposition in All Things"

• President Boyd K. Packer, President of the Quorum of the Twelve Apostles, explained that opposition helps us grow stronger: "Life will not be free from challenges, some of them bitter and hard to bear. We may wish to be spared all the trials of life, but that would be contrary to the great plan of happiness, 'for it must needs be, that there is an opposition in all things' (2 Nephi 2:11). This testing is the source of our strength" (in Conference Report, Apr. 2004, 81; or *Ensign,* May 2004, 80).

• President Ezra Taft Benson explained that opposition provides choice:

"The Book of Mormon teaches that 'it must needs be, that there is an opposition in all things' (2 Nephi 2:11)—and so there is. Opposition provides choices, and choices bring consequences—good or bad.

"The Book of Mormon explains that men 'are free to choose liberty and eternal life, through the great Mediator of all men, or to choose captivity and death, according to the captivity and power of the devil' (2 Nephi 2:27).

"God loves us; the devil hates us. God wants us to have a fulness of joy as He has. The devil wants us to be miserable as he is. God gives us commandments to bless us. The devil would have us break these commandments to curse us.

"Daily, constantly, we choose by our desires, our thoughts, and our actions whether we want to be blessed or cursed, happy or miserable" (in Conference Report, Apr. 1988, 5; or *Ensign,* May 1988, 6).

• Elder Neal A. Maxwell (1926–2004) of the Quorum of the Twelve Apostles commented on how opposition relates to happiness: "Indeed, without the existence of choices, without our freedom to choose and without opposition, there would be no real existence. This is so much like Lehi's metaphor of how, in the absence of agency and opposites, things would have resulted in a meaningless, undifferentiated 'compound in one' (2 Nephi 2:11). In such a situation the earth would actually have 'no purpose in the end of its creation' (2 Nephi 2:12). It is a fact that we can neither grow spiritually nor thereby be truly happy unless and until we make wise use of our moral agency" (*One More Strain of Praise* [1999], 80).

2 Nephi 2:15. The Tree of Knowledge of Good and Evil and the Tree of Life

• Elder Bruce R. McConkie of the Quorum of the Twelve Apostles explained the meaning of the tree of life and the tree of knowledge of good and evil: "As to the fall, the scriptures set forth that there were in the Garden of Eden two trees. One was the tree of life, which figuratively refers to eternal life; the other was the tree of knowledge of good and evil, which figuratively refers to how and why and in what manner mortality and all that appertains to it came into being" (*A New Witness for the Articles of Faith,* 86).

2 Nephi 2:15. What Was Forbidden?

• President Joseph Fielding Smith showed how the book of Moses helps us understand why the Lord commanded Adam to not partake of the fruit: "Just why the Lord would say to Adam that he forbade him to partake of the fruit of that tree is not made clear in the Bible account, but in the original as it comes to us in the Book of Moses it is made definitely clear. It is that the Lord said to Adam that if he wished to remain as he was in the garden, then he was not to eat the fruit, but if he desired to eat it and partake of death he was at liberty to do so" (*Answers to Gospel Questions,* comp. Joseph Fielding Smith Jr., 5 vols. [1957–66], 4:81).

2 Nephi 2:15–16, 26–27. 📖 Man Should Act for Himself

• President Howard W. Hunter (1907–95) taught that agency is necessary for us to grow:

"Our Father in Heaven wanted our growth to continue in mortality and to be enhanced by our freedom to choose and learn. He also wanted us to exercise our faith and our will, especially with a new physical body to master and control. But we know from both ancient and modern revelation that Satan wished to deny us our independence and agency in that now-forgotten moment long ago, even as he wishes to deny them this very hour. Indeed, Satan violently opposed the freedom of choice offered by the Father, so violently that John in the Revelation described 'war in heaven' (Revelation 12:7) over the matter. Satan would have coerced us, and he would have robbed us of that most precious of gifts if he could: our freedom to choose a divine future and the exaltation we all hope to obtain.

"Through Christ and his valiant defense of our Father's plan, the course of agency and eternal aspirations prevailed. . . .

"So we came to our mortality, like Jeremiah [see Jeremiah 1:5], known by God as his literal spirit children, having the privilege to choose our personal path on matters of belief and religious conviction. With Christ's triumph in heaven in overcoming Lucifer, and later his triumph on earth in overcoming the effects of Adam's fall and the death of all mankind, 'the children of men' continue 'free forever, knowing good from evil; to act for themselves and not be acted upon.' . . .

"To fully understand this gift of agency and its inestimable worth, it is imperative that we understand that God's chief way of acting is by persuasion and patience and long-suffering, not by coercion and stark confrontation. He acts by gentle solicitation and by sweet enticement. He always acts with unfailing respect for the freedom and independence that we possess.

He wants to help us and pleads for the chance to assist us, but he will not do so in violation of our agency. He loves us too much to do that, and doing so would run counter to his divine character" (in Conference Report, Oct. 1989, 21; or *Ensign,* Nov. 1989, 17–18).

2 Nephi 2:17–18. "An Angel of God . . . Became a Devil"

• President James E. Faust (1920–2007) of the First Presidency explained how Lucifer fell from his position of authority: "Because of his rebellion, Lucifer was cast out and became Satan, the devil, 'the father of all lies, to deceive and to blind men, and to lead them captive at his will, even as many as would not hearken unto my voice' (Moses 4:4). And so this personage who was an angel of God and in authority, even in the presence of God, was removed from the presence of God and his Son (see D&C 76:25). This caused great sadness in the heavens, 'for the heavens wept over him—he was Lucifer, a son of the morning' (D&C 76:26)" (in Conference Report, Oct. 1987, 42; or *Ensign,* Nov. 1987, 35).

2 Nephi 2:22. "All Things" Were Affected by the Fall of Adam

• Elder Bruce R. McConkie explained how all things were connected to the Fall of Adam: "Then comes the Fall; Adam falls; mortality and procreation and death commence. Fallen man is mortal; he has mortal flesh; he is 'the first flesh upon the earth.' And the effects of his fall pass upon all created things. They fall in that they too become mortal. Death enters the world; mortality reigns; procreation commences; and the Lord's great and eternal purposes roll onward" ("Christ and the Creation," *Ensign,* June 1982, 14).

"Mortality and procreation and death all had their beginnings with the Fall. . . .

". . . An infinite Creator, in the primeval day, made the earth and man and all forms of life in such a state that they could fall. This fall involved a change of status. All things were so created that they could fall or change. . . .

". . . In the primeval and Edenic day all forms of life lived in a higher state than now prevails. . . . Death and procreation had yet to enter the world" (*Ensign,* June 1982, 9).

2 Nephi 2:22–23. What Is the Difference Between Sin and Transgression?

• Elder Dallin H. Oaks explained the difference between sin and transgression: "[The] contrast between a *sin* and a *transgression* reminds us of the careful wording in the second article of faith: 'We believe that men will be punished for their own *sins,* and not for Adam's *transgression*' (italics added). It also echoes a familiar distinction in the law. Some acts, like murder, are crimes because they are inherently wrong. Other acts, like operating without a license, are crimes only because they are legally prohibited. Under these distinctions, the act that produced the Fall was not a sin—inherently wrong—but a transgression—wrong because it was formally prohibited. These words are not always used to denote something different, but this distinction seems meaningful in the circumstances of the Fall" (in Conference Report, Oct. 1993, 98; or *Ensign,* Nov. 1993, 73).

---

2 NEPHI 2:22–23
Why was the Fall of Adam essential for our salvation?

---

2 Nephi 2:22–25. 📖 "Adam Fell That Men Might Be"

• Elder Russell M. Nelson of the Quorum of the Twelve Apostles explained why the Fall was necessary:

"The Creation culminated with Adam and Eve in the Garden of Eden. They were created in the image of God, with bodies of flesh and bone. Created in the image of God and not yet mortal, they could not grow old and die. 'And they would have had no children' [2 Nephi 2:23] nor experienced the trials of life. . . . The creation of Adam and Eve was a *paradisiacal creation,* one that required a significant change before they could fulfill the commandment to have children and thus provide earthly bodies for premortal spirit sons and daughters of God.

". . . The Fall of Adam (and Eve) constituted the mortal creation and brought about the required changes in their bodies, including the circulation of blood and other modifications as well. They were now able to have children. They and their posterity also became subject to injury, disease, and death" (in Conference Report, Oct. 1996, 44–45; or *Ensign,* Nov. 1996, 33).

• President James E. Faust added to the description of how the Fall affected Adam and Eve as well as all their posterity:

© 1998 Joseph Brickey

"Because of their transgression, Adam and Eve, having chosen to leave their state of innocence (see 2 Nephi 2:23–25), were banished from the presence of God. This is referred to in Christendom as the Fall, or Adam's transgression. It is a spiritual death because Adam and Eve were separated from the presence of God and given agency 'to act for themselves and not to be acted upon' (2 Nephi 2:26). They were also given the great power of procreation, so that they could keep the commandment to 'multiply, and replenish the earth' and have joy in their posterity (Genesis 1:28).

"All of their posterity were likewise banished from the presence of God (see 2 Nephi 2:22–26). However, the posterity of Adam and Eve were innocent of the original sin because they had no part in it. It was therefore unfair for all of humanity to suffer eternally for the transgressions of our first parents, Adam and Eve. It became necessary to settle this injustice; hence the need for the atoning sacrifice of Jesus in His role as the Savior and Redeemer. Because of the transcendent act of the Atonement, it is possible for every soul to obtain forgiveness of sins, to have them washed away and be forgotten (see 2 Nephi 9:6–9; Talmage, *Articles of Faith,* p. 89). This forgiveness comes about, however, on condition of repentance and personal righteousness" (in Conference Report, Oct. 1988, 13–14; or *Ensign,* Nov. 1988, 12).

• President Brigham Young (1801–77) and President Joseph Fielding Smith help us understand that the Fall of Adam was part of our Heavenly Father's plan:

"Did they [Adam and Eve] come out in direct opposition to God and to his government? No. But they transgressed a command of the Lord, and through that transgression sin came into the world. The Lord knew they would do this, and he had designed that they should" (*Discourses of Brigham Young,* sel. John A. Widtsoe [1954], 103).

"Adam did only what he had to do. He partook of that fruit for one good reason, and that was to open the door to bring you and me and everyone else into this world. . . .

". . . If it hadn't been for Adam, I wouldn't be here; you wouldn't be here; we would be waiting in the heavens as spirits" (Joseph Fielding Smith, in Conference Report, Oct. 1967, 121–22).

We learn from Moses 5:10–11 that Adam and Eve also recognized blessings from the results of the Fall. They understood the following concepts:

"My eyes are opened." They knew good from evil (v. 10).

"In the flesh I shall see God." The Resurrection could take place from the coming of the Lord Jesus Christ (v. 10).

"We . . . should have . . . seed." Procreation came into the world (v. 11).

"We . . . have known good and evil." Adam and Eve had the agency to choose between good and evil (v. 11).

"We . . . have known . . . the joy of our redemption, and the eternal life which God giveth unto all the obedient." The Atonement could take place (v. 11).

2 Nephi 3:4–5. "Great Were the Covenants of the Lord"

• In the Joseph Smith Translation of the Bible, we read that "the Lord hath visited" Joseph, the son of Jacob spoken of in the Old Testament, and that Joseph was given great promises concerning his posterity (JST, Genesis 50:24). As Lehi testified, "Joseph truly saw our day" (2 Nephi 3:5), meaning the day of Lehi and his posterity, and knew that in the future God would raise up "a choice seer" (v. 7), namely the great prophet who was his namesake (see v. 15). Joseph knew also that it would be primarily his descendants whom the Lord would call upon first in these last days to carry the gospel to additional lost members of the house of Israel scattered among the nations of the earth, in compliance with the covenant God made with Abraham (see Bible Dictionary, "Joseph," 716–17; Guide to the Scriptures, "Joseph, Son of Jacob"). Obviously, since the Lord kept His covenant with Joseph, He will also keep His covenants with us if we are righteous as well.

Lehi's teaching is a great example of how Heavenly Father honored the covenant He made with Joseph. We can have the confidence that God will always honor His covenants.

2 Nephi 3:6–9. "A Choice Seer"

• A seer is "a person authorized of God to see with spiritual eyes things which God has hidden from the world (Moses 6:35–38). He is a revelator and a prophet (Mosiah 8:13–16). In the Book of Mormon, Ammon taught that only a seer could use special interpreters, or a Urim and Thummim (Mosiah 8:13; 28:16). A seer knows the past, present, and future. Anciently, a prophet was often called a seer (1 Sam. 9:9; 2 Sam. 24:11).

"Joseph Smith is the great seer of the latter days (D&C 21:1; 135:3)" (Guide to the Scriptures, "Seer"). The Prophet Joseph Smith is the "choice seer" described in 2 Nephi 3:6 as a descendant of Joseph, son of Israel.

© 1994 Paul Mann

• President Brigham Young (1801–77) bore witness of the "choice seer" Joseph Smith, who was known not only in the days of Joseph in Egypt, but even before the

creation of the earth: "It was decreed in the counsels of eternity, long before the foundations of the earth were laid, that he, Joseph Smith, should be the man, in the last dispensation of this world, to bring forth the word of God to the people, and receive the fulness of the keys and power of the Priesthood of the Son of God. The Lord had his eyes upon him, and upon his father, and upon his father's father, and upon their progenitors clear back to Abraham, and from Abraham to the flood, from the flood to Enoch, and from Enoch to Adam. He has watched that family and that blood as it has circulated from its fountain to the birth of that man. He [the Prophet Joseph Smith] was fore-ordained in eternity to preside over this last dispensation" (*Discourses of Brigham Young,* 108).

• Elder Neal A. Maxwell suggested several examples of truths that the Seer Joseph Smith could see with spiritual eyes that had previously been hidden from the world:

1. Revelation about the extent and expanse of the universe (see Moses 1:33; D&C 76:24 📖)
2. Revelation about God's central purpose (see Moses 1:39 📖)
3. Revelation about us as God's children (see D&C 93:29)
4. Revelation about man's destiny (see D&C 84:38 📖)
5. Revelation about God's personal involvement with his children (see Alma 18:32)
6. Revelation about the expanse of the Savior's Atonement (see 2 Nephi 9:7; D&C 88:6)

(See Conference Report, Oct. 2003, 105–7; or *Ensign,* Nov. 2003, 100–101.)

2 Nephi 3:6–15. The Prophecies of Joseph

• The following chart helps explain the specific prophecies that Joseph of Egypt made regarding the Prophet Joseph Smith and their subsequent fulfillment:

Prophecy in 2 Nephi 3	Possible Fulfillments
"A seer shall the Lord my God raise up, who shall be a choice seer unto the fruit of my loins" (v. 6).	The Lord said Joseph Smith Jr. was to "be called a seer, a translator, a prophet" (D&C 21:1) and that Joseph was appointed to stand at the head of this dispensation (see D&C 110:16; 112:32).
"He shall be esteemed highly among the fruit of thy loins" (v. 7).	There are millions of descendants of the Book of Mormon people who recognize Joseph Smith as the prophet of the Restoration.
"He shall do a work for the fruit of thy loins . . . , which shall be of great worth unto them" (v. 7).	Many of the children of Lehi have been blessed by the light of the gospel that was restored by the Prophet Joseph Smith.
"He shall do none other work, save the work which I shall command him" (v. 8).	Joseph Smith's life focused upon doing the will of the Lord. For example, in the beginning of his ministry he was commanded to translate the Book of Mormon: "And you have a gift to translate the plates; and this is the first gift that I bestowed upon you; and I have commanded that you should pretend to no other gift until my purpose is fulfilled in this; for I will grant unto you no other gift until it is finished" (D&C 5:4).
"He shall be great like unto Moses" (v. 9).	Moses gathered Israel from Egypt to the promised land. Joseph Smith was given keys by Moses to gather Israel: "Therefore, I will raise up unto my people a man, who shall lead them like as Moses led the children of Israel" (D&C 103:16). This is one of many ways that Joseph was like Moses.
"I give power to bring forth my word unto the seed of thy loins" (v. 11).	Joseph Smith translated and gave the children of Lehi the record of their ancestors (see D&C 3; 5; 10), as well as many other revelations.

Prophecy in 2 Nephi 3	Possible Fulfillments
"The fruit of thy loins . . . shall grow together, unto the confounding of false doctrines" (v. 12)	The Book of Mormon and other modern revelations give plain and authoritative clarification on many principles and doctrines of the gospel in the Bible (see D&C 20:8–15; 42:12).
"Out of weakness he shall be made strong" (v. 13).	A humble farm boy became the prophet of the Restoration.
"They that seek to destroy him shall be confounded" (v. 14).	As promised by the Lord (see 3 Nephi 21:10), the Prophet Joseph Smith was preserved until he had accomplished his mission (see D&C 121:16–22).
"His name shall be called after me; and it shall be after the name of his father" (v. 15).	Joseph Smith Jr., the third son of Joseph Smith Sr., was named after his father (see Joseph Smith—History 1:4).
"For the thing [the gospel and its ordinances], which the Lord shall bring forth by his hand, by the power of the Lord shall bring my people unto salvation" (v. 15).	It is through the Restoration of the Church and the Lord's ordinances that the Prophet Joseph Smith showed us how to obtain eternal life.

2 Nephi 3:12. The Book of Mormon and the Bible "Shall Grow Together"

• President Boyd K. Packer explained how the Book of Mormon and the Bible have grown together: "The Old Testament and the New Testament . . . and . . . the Book of Mormon . . . are now woven together in such a way that as you pore over one you are drawn to the other; as you learn from one you are enlightened by the other. They are indeed one in our hands" (in Conference Report, Oct. 1982, 75; or *Ensign,* Nov. 1982, 53).

Lyle Beddes, © 1977 IRI

2 Nephi 3:18. Who Are the Different People Spoken of?

• Elder Bruce R. McConkie identified the people spoken of in 2 Nephi 3:18 as follows: "Note these words of the Lord: 'And I, behold, I will give unto him

[Mormon] that he shall write the writing of the fruit of thy loins [the Nephites], unto the fruit of thy loins [the Lamanites]; and the spokesman of thy loins [Joseph Smith] shall declare it.' That is, Mormon wrote the Book of Mormon, but what he wrote was taken from the writings of the Nephite prophets; and these writings, compiled into one book, were translated by Joseph Smith and sent forth by him unto the Lamanites" (*A New Witness for the Articles of Faith* [1985], 426).

Points to Ponder

• In what ways do the Creation, the Fall, and the Atonement interrelate?

• What can we learn about the tactics of Satan from the phrase "the sleep of hell"? (2 Nephi 1:13).

• What is the relationship between the trials, adversity, and afflictions we encounter and what our Heavenly Father knows we can become? (see 2 Nephi 2:2).

Suggested Assignments

• Write a paragraph describing the relationship between the Creation, the Fall, and the Atonement.

• Based on what you learn from 2 Nephi 2:5–10, how would you explain to someone not of our faith the need for the Atonement of Jesus Christ?

• List at least six prophecies in 2 Nephi 3 that relate directly to the Prophet Joseph Smith.

Introduction

Near the end of his life, Lehi blessed his children with the promise that if they kept the commandments they would prosper, but if they were disobedient they would be cut off from the presence of the Lord (see 2 Nephi 4:4). The Lord gave this same promise to Nephi early in his ministry, when He promised Nephi that if he kept the commandments of God he would prosper and "be led to a land of promise; . . . which is choice above all other lands" (1 Nephi 2:20). In addition, the Lord said that if Nephi's brothers rebelled against him, they would be "cut off from the presence of the Lord" (1 Nephi 2:21). This promise was fulfilled when Nephi's people departed from the rebellious followers of Laman and Lemuel.

All of us must choose between good and evil. The importance of making good choices is reflected in 2 Nephi 4–8: (1) when Lehi blessed his grandchildren, (2) in Nephi's reflections and expressions in his heartfelt psalm, (3) during the division of the Nephites and Lamanites, and (4) in Jacob's teachings about the scattering and gathering of Israel.

Commentary

2 Nephi 4:3–11. Lehi Blessed His Family

• To the end of his life, Lehi taught his children the gospel. In our day the Lord's servants continue to emphasize parents' responsibility to teach their children. The First Presidency and the Quorum of the Twelve Apostles declared, "We warn that individuals . . . who fail to fulfill family responsibilities will one day stand accountable before God" ("The Family: A Proclamation to the World," *Ensign,* Nov. 1995, 102; see also D&C 68:25–29).

Like Lehi, most Latter-day Saint parents take this responsibility very seriously. Elder M. Russell Ballard of the Quorum of the Twelve Apostles explained how our focus on the importance of families should impact our parenting: "Our family-centered perspective should make Latter-day Saints strive to be the best parents in the world. It should give us enormous respect for our children, who truly are our spiritual siblings, and it should cause us to devote whatever time is necessary

to strengthen our families. Indeed, nothing is more critically connected to happiness—both our own and that of our children—than how well we love and support one another within the family" (in Conference Report, Oct. 2005, 44; or *Ensign,* Nov. 2005, 42).

> **2 NEPHI 4:5**
> *What important principle of parenting is taught here? How can this principle give courage and faith to parents?*

2 Nephi 4:7–10. Laman's and Lemuel's Children

• God has fulfilled and continues to fulfill Lehi's promise of mercy to Laman's and Lemuel's children. There are several cases in the Book of Mormon where Lehi's promise to the children of Laman and Lemuel were fulfilled (see Alma 17–26; Helaman 5–6; 13–15). In the latter days God has continued to fulfill Lehi's promise of mercy to Laman and Lemuel's children. President Henry B. Eyring of the First Presidency explained:

"Our faithful effort to offer to our family the testimony we have of the truth will be multiplied in power and extended in time.

"We have all seen evidence of that in families we have known. I saw it in South America as I looked into the faces of missionaries. Hundreds of them passed by me, shaking my hand and looking deeply into my eyes. I was nearly overwhelmed with the confirmation that these children of Father Lehi and of Sariah were there in the Lord's service because our Heavenly Father honors His promises to families. To nearly his last breath, Lehi taught and testified and tried to bless his children. Terrible tragedy came among his descendants when they rejected his testimony, the testimonies of other prophets, and of the scriptures. But in the eyes and faces of those missionaries I felt confirmation that God has kept His promises to reach out to Lehi's covenant children and that He will reach out to ours" (in Conference Report, Apr. 1996, 88; or *Ensign,* May 1996, 64).

2 Nephi 4:15–16. "My Soul Delighteth in the Scriptures"

• Sister Cheryl C. Lant, Primary general president, discussed how 2 Nephi 4:15 reveals three ways we can effectively read the scriptures: First, delighting in the scriptures; second, pondering the scriptures; and third, writing the scriptures into our lives:

"This scripture teaches us how to read the Book of Mormon. It mentions three important ideas.

"First, 'My soul delighteth.' I love this phrase! I have thought about hungering and thirsting after knowledge as I read the scriptures, but delighting in them is something else. I find that what I take away from the scriptures is determined by what I bring. Each time I read them, I am, in a sense, bringing a new person with new eyes to the experience. Where I am in my life, the experiences I am having, and my attitude all affect how much I will gain. I love the scriptures. I treasure the truths I find as I read them. Joy fills my heart as I receive encouragement, direction, comfort, strength, and answers to my needs. Life looks brighter, and the way opens before me. I am reassured of my Heavenly Father's love and concern for me every time I read. Surely this is a delight to me. As one little boy in a Sunbeam class put it, 'I feel happy about the scriptures!'

"Second, 'My heart pondereth them.' How I love to carry the scriptures with me in my heart! The spirit of what I have read rests there to bring me peace and comfort. The knowledge I have gained gives me

guidance and direction. I have the confidence born out of obedience. . . .

"[Third] I, of course, do not write scriptures as did Nephi, but when I read the scriptures and live the principles I learn, those scriptures become written in my life. They govern my actions and are written there for my children to see and follow. I can build a legacy, a tradition of righteous living, based on the principles I learn in the scriptures" (in Conference Report, Oct. 2005, 78–79; or *Ensign,* Nov. 2005, 76–77).

2 Nephi 4:15–35. The Psalm of Nephi

• A psalm is "an inspired poem or hymn" (Guide to the Scriptures, "Psalm"). Even those who do not have an understanding of ancient Hebrew poetry can recognize and relate with the heartfelt pleadings of Nephi's psalm in 2 Nephi 4. Psalms are to be read aloud. Try reading Nephi's psalm aloud to sense the spirit with which it was written.

2 Nephi 4:17–18. Overcoming Our Sins and Weaknesses

• Throughout the Book of Mormon we note Nephi's righteousness, his faithfulness in tribulation, and his dedication to God, but still he exclaimed, "O wretched man that I am! . . . I am encompassed about, because of the temptations and the sins which do so easily beset me" (2 Nephi 4:17–18). The Prophet Joseph Smith (1805–44) taught that "the nearer man approaches perfection, the clearer are his views, and the greater his enjoyments, till he has overcome the evils of his life and lost every desire for sin" (*History of the Church,* 2:8). Perhaps Nephi felt burdened by what we might consider trivial weaknesses to the point where they caused him sorrow, and he sought to be free from any vestige of sin.

Nephi's heartfelt plea for the Lord to help him overcome his weaknesses helps us understand how to conquer our own weaknesses. Personal experience teaches us of our need to do likewise. Elder Richard G. Scott of the Quorum of the Twelve Apostles reminded us why we are commanded to repent and admonished us to take advantage of the Lord's redeeming power:

"Why have our Father and His Son commanded us to repent? Because they love us. They know all of us will violate eternal laws. Whether they be small or large, justice requires that every broken law be satisfied to retain the promise of joy in this life and the privilege of returning to Father in Heaven. If not satisfied, in the Day of Judgment justice will cause that we be cast out of the presence of God to be under the control of Satan. [See 2 Nephi 9:8–10; 2:5.]

"It is our Master and His redeeming act that make it possible for us to avoid such condemnation. It is done through faith in Jesus Christ, obedience to His commandments, and enduring in righteousness to the end.

"Are you taking full advantage of the redeeming power of repentance in your life so that you can have greater peace and joy? Feelings of turmoil and despondency often signal a need for repentance. Also, the lack of the spiritual direction you seek in your life could result from broken laws. If needed, full repentance will put your life together. It will solve all of the complex spiritual pains that come from transgression. But in this life it cannot remedy some of the physical consequences that can occur from serious sin. Be wise, and consistently live well within the boundaries of righteousness defined by the Lord" (in Conference Report, Oct. 2000, 31–32; or *Ensign,* Nov. 2000, 25).

• Elder Dallin H. Oaks of the Quorum of the Twelve Apostles taught that, regardless of a person's susceptibility or tendency, we have an obligation to exercise our agency to overcome our personal weaknesses:

"Perhaps these persons, as the saying goes, were 'born that way.' But what does that mean? Does it mean that persons with susceptibilities or strong tendencies have no choice, no free agency in these matters? Our doctrine teaches us otherwise. Regardless of a person's susceptibility or tendency, his will is unfettered. His free agency is unqualified. It is his freedom that is impaired. . . . We are all responsible for the exercise of our free agency.

". . . Most of us are born with thorns in the flesh, some more visible, some more serious than others. We all seem to have susceptibilities to one disorder or

another, but whatever our susceptibilities, we have the will and the power to control our thoughts and our actions. This must be so. God has said that he holds us accountable for what we do and what we think, so our thoughts and actions must be controllable by our agency. Once we have reached the age or condition of accountability, the claim 'I was born that way' does not excuse actions or thoughts that fail to conform to the commandments of God. We need to learn how to live so that a weakness that is mortal will not prevent us from achieving the goal that is eternal.

"God has promised that he will consecrate our afflictions for our gain (see 2 Nephi 2:2). The efforts we expend in overcoming any inherited weakness build a spiritual strength that will serve us throughout eternity. Thus, when Paul prayed thrice that his 'thorn in the flesh' would depart from him, the Lord replied, 'My grace is sufficient for thee: for my strength is made perfect in weakness.' [2 Corinthians 12:9]" ("Free Agency and Freedom," in Monte S. Nyman and Charles D. Tate Jr., ed., *The Book of Mormon: Second Nephi, the Doctrinal Structure* [1989], 13–14).

---

2 NEPHI 4:28–35

What did Nephi do to overcome his weaknesses and sins? What in Nephi's example could you use in overcoming personal weaknesses?

---

2 Nephi 5:5–9. Separate Ourselves from Wickedness

• There are times when it is necessary to physically flee from evil, such as with Nephi and his followers. Notice that it was "those who believed in the warnings and the revelations of God" who went with Nephi (2 Nephi 5:6). In like manner, today those who hearken to the warnings and revelations of modern prophets are the ones who are spiritually following them. We may not always be able, however, to physically move ourselves away from wickedness. Elder Richard G. Scott shared how we can protect ourselves:

"God has provided a way to live in this world and not be contaminated by the degrading pressures evil agents spread throughout it. You can live a virtuous, productive, righteous life by following the plan of protection created by your Father in Heaven: His plan of happiness. It is contained in the scriptures and in the inspired declarations of His prophets. . . .

"Avoid worldly wickedness. Know that God is in control. In time, Satan will completely fail and be punished for his perverse evil. God has a specific plan for your life. He will reveal parts of that plan to you as you look for it with faith and consistent obedience. His Son has made you free—not from the consequences of your acts, but free to make choices. God's eternal purpose is for you to be successful in this mortal life. No matter how wicked the world becomes, you can earn that blessing. Seek and be attentive to the personal guidance given to you through the Holy Spirit. Continue to be worthy to receive it. Reach out to others who stumble and are perplexed, not certain of what path to follow" (in Conference Report, Apr. 2004, 103–4, 106; or *Ensign,* May 2004, 100, 102).

2 Nephi 5:11, 13. "We Did Prosper Exceedingly"

• In 2 Nephi 5:11, 13 Nephi told of his people's success in raising their flocks, herds, and crops. Often we associate prosperity with tangible blessings, such as wealth or the material things of the world. President

Heber J. Grant (1856–1945) taught about what true prosperity is: "When I say prosperity I am not thinking of it in terms of dollars and cents alone. . . . What I count as real prosperity . . . is the growth in a knowledge of God, and in a testimony, and in the power to live the gospel and to inspire our families to do the same. That is prosperity of the truest kind" (*Gospel Standards,* comp. G. Homer Durham [1941], 58; also cited by James E. Faust, in Conference Report, Oct. 1998, 74; or *Ensign,* Nov. 1998, 59).

• Speaking about how paying tithing brings true prosperity, President James E. Faust (1920–2007) of the First Presidency quoted from an experience shared by Sister Yaeko Seki:

"My family and I were spending a day at the Japan Alps National Park. . . . I was pregnant with our fourth child and was feeling rather tired, so I lay down under the trees. . . . I began thinking about our financial problems. My heart became overwhelmed, and I burst into tears. 'Lord, we are full-tithe payers. We have sacrificed so much. When will the windows of heaven open unto us and our burdens be lightened?'

"I prayed with all my heart. Then I turned to watch my husband and children playing and laughing together. . . . Suddenly, the Spirit testified to me that my blessings were abundant and that my family was the greatest blessing Heavenly Father could give me" (in Conference Report, Oct. 1998, 74; or *Ensign,* Nov. 1998, 59).

2 Nephi 5:10–18, 26–27. "After the Manner of Happiness"

• The Prophet Joseph Smith explained that there is a path that leads to happiness: "Happiness is the object and design of our existence; and will be the end thereof, if we pursue the path that leads to it; and this path is virtue, uprightness, faithfulness, holiness, and keeping all the commandments of God" (*History of the Church,* 134–35).

• President Gordon B. Hinckley (1910–2008) taught similarly about happiness: "The Lord wants us to be happy. Nephi said a great thing: 'And . . . we lived after the manner of happiness.' (2 Ne. 5:27.) What a wonderful thing. I want my children to be happy. I want them to do well. I want them to live well and live rightly, properly; and, in the same way, except that my Father in Heaven's love reaches beyond any power of love that I have. I think He wants His sons

and daughters to be happy. Happiness comes of righteousness. 'Wickedness never was happiness.' (Alma 41:10.) Sin never was happiness. Selfishness never was happiness. Greed never was happiness. Happiness lies in living the principles of the gospel of

Jesus Christ" ("Fast-Paced Schedule for the Prophet," *Church News,* Apr. 20, 1996, 3).

2 Nephi 5:20–25. The Lamanites Were Cursed

• Verses 20–25 in 2 Nephi 5 answer at least four questions about the curse that came to the Lamanites:

1. What was the curse?
The curse is clearly defined in verse 20 as being "cut off from the presence of the Lord."

2. What caused the curse?
According to verse 21, the cause of the curse came "because of their iniquity" and "hardened . . . hearts." Since the days of Adam's Fall, wickedness has resulted in being cut off from the presence of the Lord (see 1 Nephi 2:21; 2 Nephi 4:4; 9:6; Alma 9:13; Ether 10:11).

3. What was the mark or sign set upon the Lamanites?
It is also explained in verse 21 that so "they might not be enticing unto my people [the Nephites] the Lord did cause a skin of blackness to come upon them [the Lamanites]." It would appear that this was done to limit the spreading of more wickedness. Later Alma suggested this same motive when he explained that "the skins of the Lamanites were dark . . . that thereby the Lord God might preserve his people, that they might not mix and believe in incorrect traditions" (Alma 3:6, 8). Throughout scripture we find warnings of the Lord not to marry unbelievers (see Deuteronomy 7:2–3; 2 Corinthians 6:14); the result of doing so was often that the righteous were turned away from the Lord (see Deuteronomy 7:4; 1 Kings 11:4; D&C 74:5).

Some people have mistakenly thought that the dark skin placed upon the Lamanites was the curse. President Joseph Fielding Smith (1876–1972) explained that the dark skin was not the curse:

"The dark skin was placed upon the Lamanites so that they could be distinguished from the Nephites and to keep the two peoples from mixing. The dark skin was the sign of the curse [not the curse itself]. The curse was the withdrawal of the Spirit of the Lord. . . .

"The dark skin of those who have come into the Church is no longer to be considered a sign of the curse. . . . These converts are delightsome and have the Spirit of the Lord" (*Answers to Gospel Questions,* comp. Joseph Fielding Smith Jr., 5 vols. [1957–66], 3:122–23).

4. What was the result of the curse?
Finally in verse 24 we learn that the result of the curse—being cut off from the presence of the Lord—is that they "become an idle people, full of mischief and subtlety."

One great blessing is that the curse is only valid as long as people are wicked. If they repent, the "curse of God [will] no more follow them" (Alma 23:18). There are many examples of righteous Lamanites who repented and enjoyed the Spirit of the Lord; one of them even became a prophet (see Helaman 13:5).

2 Nephi 6:1–3. Jacob Taught with Authority

• Jacob taught with power and authority from God. He was "called of God, and ordained after the manner of his holy order" (received the holy priesthood) and "consecrated" (or set apart) by his brother Nephi (2 Nephi 6:2; see also 2 Nephi 5:26). In addition, Jacob employed three important elements of effective teaching, as explained by Elder Jeffrey R. Holland of the Quorum of the Twelve Apostles: "'For *I have exhorted you* with all diligence; and *I have taught you the words of my father;* and *I have spoken unto you concerning all things which are written,* from the creation of the world' [2 Nephi 6:3; italics added]. That is the formula by which the gospel has always been taught, a process used to this day—personal testimony, the teachings of the living prophets, and the written record of the scriptures" (*Christ and the New Covenant* [1997], 65).

• President Joseph Fielding Smith explained what "order" of the priesthood the Nephites exercised: "The Nephites were descendants of Joseph. Lehi discovered this when reading the brass plates. . . . Therefore there were no Levites who accompanied Lehi to the Western Hemisphere. Under these conditions the Nephites officiated by virtue of the Melchizedek Priesthood from the days of Lehi to the days of the appearance of our Savior among them" (*Answers to Gospel Questions,* 1:124).

2 Nephi 6:4–18. Jacob Recounted Jewish History

• Jacob quoted from Isaiah to teach "concerning things which are, and which are to come" (2 Nephi 6:4). He applied Isaiah's teachings to his people because they were part of the house of Israel (see v. 5). These are some of the same verses that Nephi applied to the descendants of Lehi in the latter days (compare vv. 6–7; 1 Nephi 21:22–23). These applications of the same prophecy to different situations are examples of "likening the scriptures" under the influence of the Spirit (see 1 Nephi 19:23 📖; 2 Nephi 11:8).

2 Nephi 6:6–11. The Scattering and Gathering of Israel

• For more information on the scattering of Israel, refer to "Brief History of the Scattering of Israel" in the appendix (p. 415). For more information on the gathering of Israel, refer to "The Gathering of Israel" in the appendix (p. 416).

---

2 NEPHI 6:11–12

What are the promises made to both ancient Israel and the latter-day Gentiles? What conditions must be met for them to be fulfilled?

---

2 Nephi 7:10–11. Walking in the Light of Their Own Fire

• Isaiah asked if any who fear and obey the Lord walk in darkness. The answer, of course, is "no." He then stated that those who "walk in the light of [their own] fire and in the sparks which [they] have kindled . . . shall lie down in sorrow" (2 Nephi 7:11). Many people in our day trust themselves or other people above the Lord; they rely on the arm of their own flesh and follow their own light rather than trusting in God (see D&C 1:19–20; 133:70–74).

• The Savior is the Light of the World. It is unwise for us to attempt to replace His light with light that we have created (see 3 Nephi 18:24). President Joseph F. Smith (1838–1918) warned against those who falsely teach, using their own light when preaching "false doctrines disguised as truths of the gospel." He said they are "the proud and self-vaunting ones, who read by the lamps of their own conceit; who interpret by rules of their own contriving; who have become a law unto themselves, and so pose as the sole judges of their own doings" (*Gospel Doctrine,* 5th ed. [1939], 373).

2 Nephi 8. Latter-day Gathering

• Isaiah's prophecies quoted in 2 Nephi 8 speak of the latter-day gathering of Israel. The Lord promised to "comfort Zion" and "make her wilderness like Eden" (v. 3). He admonished them, "Fear ye not the reproach of men" (v. 7). He promised that "the redeemed of the Lord shall return, and come with singing unto Zion" (v. 11). He would cover them "in the shadow of [His] hand" (v. 16). The early Saints found comfort in this as well as other prophecies of Isaiah.

President Ezra Taft Benson (1899–1994) explained that our forefathers were participating in the fulfillment of these prophecies of Isaiah concerning the gathering of Israel:

"Our forefathers . . . were strong and courageous in the Lord, knowing that He was their defense, their refuge, their salvation. Strengthened by this faith, they relied on their cherished independence, their frugality, and honest toil. And history records that even the climate was tempered for their sakes, and their humble untiring efforts made 'the desert to blossom as the rose.'

"Their faith was renewed by two of Isaiah's remarkable prophecies concerning the last days—the days in which they knew they were living. In the first of these Isaiah announces: 'The wilderness and the solitary place shall be glad for them; and the desert shall rejoice, and blossom as the rose.' (Isaiah 35:1.) And again: 'For the Lord shall comfort Zion: he will comfort all her waste places; and he will make her wilderness like Eden, and her desert like the garden of the Lord; joy and gladness shall be found therein, thanksgiving, and the voice of melody.' (Isaiah 51:3.)

"And while their natural eyes saw only their log cabins and immediate surroundings, they envisioned the day when the words of Micah would be fulfilled: 'But in the last days it shall come to pass, that the mountain of the house of the Lord shall be established in the top of the mountains. . . .' (Micah 4:1–2.)

"We have witnessed the fulfillment of these remarkable prophecies" (*This Nation Shall Endure* [1977], 42).

• Concerning the gathering of the Jews to the land of Israel, Elder Bruce R. McConkie (1915–85) of the Quorum of the Twelve Apostles taught that a spiritual gathering precedes the physical gathering: "Judah will gather to old Jerusalem in due course; of this, there is no doubt. But this gathering will consist of accepting Christ, joining the Church, and receiving anew the Abrahamic covenant as it is administered in holy places. The present assembling of people of Jewish ancestry into the Palestinian nation of Israel is not the scriptural gathering of Israel or of Judah. It may be prelude thereto, and some of the people so assembled may in due course be gathered into the true church and kingdom of God on earth, and they may then assist in building the temple that is destined to grace Jerusalem's soil. But a political gathering is not a spiritual gathering, and the Lord's kingdom is not of this world" (*A New Witness for the Articles of Faith* [1985], 519–20; see also pp. 511, 564–65).

Points to Ponder

• In 2 Nephi 5:5–8 the Lord warned Nephi to "flee into the wilderness." Are there aspects of your life that mirror Nephi's situation? Are there influences from friends, entertainment, work, school, or media that merit consideration of moving away from them?

• In 2 Nephi 8:3–16 are listed many blessings that are offered to members of the house of Israel as they "gather." Which of these blessings have you experienced? Which of them could you still seek? What would you need to do to receive them?

Suggested Assignments

• As you read 2 Nephi 4:15–35, look for what Nephi did to overcome his weaknesses. Try to identify specific principles that Nephi applied or believed would help him overcome his weaknesses. Write your thoughts and feelings about the truths that you identify; listen to the feelings of the Spirit. You may want to write concerning any commitments that the Spirit may prompt you to make as you read.

• President Gordon B. Hinckley has counseled: "Keep balance in your lives. Beware of obsession. Beware of narrowness. Let your interests range over many good fields while working with growing strength in the field of your own profession" ("Four Imperatives for Religious Educators" [address to Church Educational System religious educators, Sept. 15, 1978], 3; see LDS.org under gospel library/additional addresses/CES addresses). Read 2 Nephi 5:10–18, 26–27 and identify principles that you could learn about or learn to live that would help you make a greater contribution in the world.

Introduction

We all know someone who has died. Thankfully, knowledge of Heavenly Father's gospel plan offers us peace in the midst of deep sadness. The Book of Mormon prophet Jacob taught of the great blessings of the Atonement by describing what would happen to our body and our spirit had there been no Atonement. Jacob testified of the greatness of God, who prepared a way for our salvation. He described how the Savior tenderly comforts, pleads for, and redeems Israel. By accepting and following the Lord's commandments, we place ourselves in a position to receive His promised blessings. Consider the impact and blessings of the Atonement in your life.

Commentary

2 Nephi 9:1–3. Rejoice Forever in the Atonement

• Elder Jeffrey R. Holland of the Quorum of the Twelve Apostles explained that Christ and His Atonement should be at the heart of our rejoicings:

"Jacob's testimony was that 'the Mighty God' will always deliver 'his covenant people,' and that the Mighty God is, by his own divine declaration, the Lord Jesus Christ, the 'Savior and . . . Redeemer, the Mighty One of Jacob.'

"Jacob reflected on such teachings—especially those contained in the writings of Isaiah—so that his current audience and future readers 'might know concerning the covenants of the Lord that he has covenanted with all the house of Israel,' giving the parents of every generation cause to 'rejoice' and to 'lift up [their] heads forever, because of the blessings which the Lord God shall bestow upon [their] children.'

"At the heart of that covenant and the reason for such rejoicing is the atoning sacrifice of that 'Mighty God' who is the Savior and Redeemer of the world" (*Christ and the New Covenant* [1997], 66–67).

---

2 NEPHI 9:2

What will the Jews be restored to as an important part of their gathering?

---

2 Nephi 9:5–6. Atonement Central to the Merciful Plan

• The First Presidency and the Quorum of the Twelve Apostles declared to the world the central role of the Savior and His influence on all mankind:

"We offer our testimony of the reality of His matchless life and the infinite virtue of His great atoning sacrifice. None other has had so profound an influence upon all who have lived and will yet live upon the earth.

"He was the Great Jehovah of the Old Testament, the Messiah of the New. . . .

"He instituted the sacrament as a reminder of His great atoning sacrifice. He was arrested and condemned on spurious charges, convicted to satisfy a mob, and sentenced to die on Calvary's cross. He gave His life to atone for the sins of all mankind. His was a great vicarious gift in behalf of all who would ever live upon the earth.

Harry Anderson, © IRI

"We solemnly testify that His life, which is central to all human history, neither began in Bethlehem nor concluded on Calvary. He was the Firstborn of the Father, the Only Begotten Son in the flesh, the Redeemer of the world" ("The Living Christ: The Testimony of the Apostles," *Ensign,* Apr. 2000, 2–3).

• President James E. Faust (1920–2007) of the First Presidency declared the importance of our understanding the power of the Atonement:

"Our salvation depends on believing in and accepting the Atonement. Such acceptance requires a continual effort to understand it more fully. The Atonement advances our mortal course of learning by making it possible for our natures to become perfect. . . .

". . . Any increase in our understanding of His atoning sacrifice draws us closer to Him. Literally, the Atonement means to be 'at one' with Him. The nature of the Atonement and its effects is so infinite, so unfathomable, and so profound that it lies beyond the knowledge and comprehension of mortal man. . . .

"We long for the ultimate blessing of the Atonement—to become one with Him, to be in His divine presence, to be called individually by name as He warmly welcomes us home with a radiant smile, beckoning us with open arms to be enfolded in His boundless love. How gloriously sublime this experience will be if we can feel worthy enough to be in His presence! The free gift of His great atoning sacrifice for each of us is the only way we can be exalted enough to stand before Him and see Him face-to-face. The overwhelming message of the Atonement is the perfect love the Savior has for each and all of us. It is a love which is full of mercy, patience, grace, equity, long-suffering, and, above all, forgiving" (in Conference Report, Oct. 2001, 19, 22; or *Ensign,* Nov. 2001, 18, 20).

2 Nephi 9:7. The Infinite Atonement

• Elder Russell M. Nelson of the Quorum of the Twelve Apostles explained several ways in which the Atonement is infinite:

"His Atonement is infinite—without an end. It was also infinite in that all humankind would be saved from never-ending death. It was infinite in terms of His immense suffering. It was infinite in time, putting an end to the preceding prototype of animal sacrifice. It was infinite in scope—it was to be done once for all. And the mercy of the Atonement extends not only to an infinite

number of people, but also to an infinite number of worlds created by Him. It was infinite beyond any human scale of measurement or mortal comprehension.

"Jesus was the only one who could offer such an infinite atonement, since He was born of a mortal mother and an immortal Father. Because of that unique birthright, Jesus was an infinite Being" (in Conference Report, Oct. 1996, 46; or *Ensign,* Nov. 1996, 35).

> ### 2 NEPHI 9:6–9
> *What did Jacob say would happen to your spirit and to your body if there were no Atonement?*

2 Nephi 9:10. "O How Great the Goodness of Our God"

• President Gordon B. Hinckley (1910–2008) expressed gratitude for the Savior's role in fulfilling the Atonement: "Thanks be to God for the wonder and the majesty of His eternal plan. Thank and glorify His Beloved Son, who, with indescribable suffering, gave His life on Calvary's cross to pay the debt of mortal sin. He it was who, through His atoning sacrifice, broke the bonds of death and with godly power rose triumphant from the tomb. He is our Redeemer, the Redeemer of all mankind. He is the Savior of the world. He is the Son of God, the Author of our salvation" (in Conference Report, Apr. 1985, 69; or *Ensign,* May 1985, 51).

2 Nephi 9:15–16. "They Who Are Filthy Shall Be Filthy Still"

• Elder Dallin H. Oaks of the Quorum of the Twelve Apostles spoke about the Final Judgment and the condition of cleanliness we must achieve:

"Many Bible and modern scriptures speak of a final judgment at which all persons will be rewarded according to their deeds or works or the desires of their hearts. But other scriptures enlarge upon this by referring to our being judged by the *condition* we have achieved.

"The prophet Nephi describes the Final Judgment in terms of what we *have become:* 'And if their works have been filthiness they must needs *be* filthy; and if they *be* filthy it must needs be that they cannot dwell in the kingdom of God' (1 Nephi 15:33; italics added). Moroni declares, 'He that *is* filthy shall be filthy still; and he that *is* righteous shall be righteous still' (Mormon 9:14; italics added; see also Revelation 22:11–12; 2 Nephi 9:16; Alma 41:13; D&C 88:35). The same would be true of 'selfish' or 'disobedient' or any other personal attribute inconsistent with the requirements of God. Referring to the 'state' of the wicked in the Final Judgment, Alma explains that if we are condemned by our words, our works, and our thoughts, 'we shall not be found spotless; . . . and in this awful state we shall not dare to look up to our God' (Alma 12:14)" (in Conference Report, Oct. 2000, 41; or *Ensign,* Nov. 2000, 32).

• President Gordon B. Hinckley used the example of pornography to teach this same principle when he

said: "Let any who may be in the grip of this vise get upon their knees in the privacy of their closet and plead with the Lord for help to free them from this evil monster. Otherwise this vicious stain will continue through life and even into eternity. Jacob, the brother of Nephi, taught, 'And it shall come to pass that when all men shall have passed from this first death unto life, insomuch as they have become immortal, . . . they who are righteous shall be righteous still, and they who are filthy shall be filthy still' (2 Nephi 9:15–16)" (in Conference Report, Oct. 2004, 66; or *Ensign,* Nov. 2004, 62).

2 Nephi 9:18. "Endured the Crosses of the World"
• Elder Neal A. Maxwell (1926–2004) of the Quorum of the Twelve Apostles suggested a meaning for the word *crosses:* "What are the 'crosses of the world'? We cannot be sure, but the imagery suggests the bearing of a cross placed upon us by the world, as Jesus did; there may be persecutors and unhelpful onlookers, and the Church member is set apart (if not set upon), yet he does not flinch when accused and scoffed at by those who would make him ashamed, for he has no

real reason to be ashamed" (*Wherefore, Ye Must Press Forward* [1977], 110).

2 Nephi 9:20. God "Knoweth All Things"
• The *Lectures on Faith* teach why the omniscience of God is necessary: "Without the knowledge of all things God would not be able to save any portion of his creatures; for it is by reason of the knowledge which he has of all things, from the beginning to the end, that enables him to give that understanding to his creatures by which they are made partakers of eternal life; and if it were not for the idea existing in the minds of men that God had all knowledge it would be impossible for them to exercise faith in him" ([1985], 51–52).

• Elder Neal A. Maxwell explained that God must know all things in order to accomplish His work of bringing to pass our immortality and eternal life:

"Those who try to qualify God's omniscience fail to understand that He has no need to avoid ennui [tedium] by learning new things. Because God's love is also perfect, there is, in fact, divine delight in that 'one eternal round' which, to us, seems to be all routine and repetition. God derives His great and continuing joy and glory by increasing and advancing His creations, and not from new intellectual experiences.

"There is a vast difference, therefore, between an omniscient God and the false notion that God is on some sort of post-doctoral fellowship, still searching for additional key truths and vital data. Were the latter so, God might, at any moment, discover some new truth not previously known to Him that would restructure, diminish, or undercut certain truths previously known by Him. Prophecy would be mere prediction. Planning assumptions pertaining to our redemption would need to be revised. Fortunately for us, however, His plan of salvation is constantly *underway*—not constantly *under revision. . . .*

"In a very real sense, all we need to know is that God knows all!" (*All These Things Shall Give Thee Experience* [1979], 14–15, 21).

2 Nephi 9:21–24. Everyone Can Be Saved

• President Brigham Young (1801–77) spoke of the extent of the Savior's efforts to save mankind: "This is the plan of salvation. Jesus will never cease his work until all are brought up to the enjoyment of a kingdom in the mansions of his Father, where there are many kingdoms and many glories, to suit the works and faithfulness of all men that have lived on the earth. Some will obey the celestial law and receive of its glory, some will abide the terrestrial and some the telestial" (*Discourses of Brigham Young,* sel. John A. Widtsoe [1954], 56).

2 Nephi 9:25–26. No Law, No Punishment

• Elder James E. Talmage (1862–1933) of the Quorum of the Twelve Apostles explained the role of knowledge in our accountability: "According to the technical definition of sin it consists in the violation of law, and in this strict sense sin may be committed inadvertently or in ignorance. It is plain, however, from the scriptural doctrine of human responsibility and the unerring justice of God, that in his transgressions as in his righteous deeds man will be judged according to his ability to comprehend and obey law. To him who has never been made acquainted with a higher law the requirements of that law do not apply in their fulness. For sins committed without knowledge—that is, for laws violated in ignorance—a propitiation has been provided in the atonement wrought through the sacrifice of the Savior; and sinners of this class do not stand condemned, but shall be given opportunity yet to learn and to accept or reject the principles of the Gospel" (*Articles of Faith,* 12th ed. [1924], 58).

• President Boyd K. Packer, President of the Quorum of the Twelve Apostles, clarified the position of those who do not have knowledge of God's laws:

"Provision is made in the plan for those who live in mortality without knowing of the plan. 'Where there is no law given there is no punishment; and where there is no punishment there is no condemnation . . . because of the atonement; for they are delivered by the power of him' (2 Nephi 9:25).

"Without that sacred work of the redemption of the dead, the plan would be incomplete and would really be unfair" ("The Play and the Plan" [CES fireside for young adults, May 7, 1995], 4, www.ldsces.org).

• Elder Jeffrey R. Holland described some of those who do not have the gospel law: "In the broad reach of the Atonement, generous provision is made for those who die without a knowledge of the gospel or the opportunity to embrace it, including children under the age of accountability, the mentally impaired, those who never came in contact with the gospel, and so forth" (*Christ and the New Covenant,* 215).

2 Nephi 9:28. 📖 "They Think They Are Wise"

• President Gordon B. Hinckley described the weakness of trusting intellect over faith:

"The intellect is not the only source of knowledge. There is a promise, given under the inspiration of the Almighty, set forth in these beautiful words: 'God shall give unto you knowledge by his holy Spirit, yea, by the unspeakable gift of the Holy Ghost' (D&C 121:26).

"The humanists who criticize us, the so-called intellectuals who demean us, speak only from ignorance of this manifestation. They have not heard the voice of the Spirit. They have not heard it because they have not sought after it and prepared themselves to be worthy of it. Then, supposing that knowledge comes only of reasonings and of the workings of the mind, they deny that which comes by the power of the Holy Ghost. . . .

"Do not be trapped by the sophistry of the world, which for the most part is negative and which seldom, if ever, bears good fruit. Do not be ensnared by those clever ones whose self-appointed mission it is to demean that which is sacred, to emphasize human weakness, and undermine faith, rather than inspire strength" ("Be Not Afraid, Only Believe" [CES fireside for young adults, Sept. 9, 2001], 4, www.ldsces.org).

2 Nephi 9:29. "To Be Learned Is Good"

• President Gordon B. Hinckley described the good that comes from learning all we can: "You face great challenges that lie ahead. You are moving into a world of fierce competition. You must get all of the education you can. The Lord has instructed us concerning the importance of education. It will qualify you for greater opportunities. It will equip you to do something worthwhile in the great world of opportunity that lies ahead. If you can go to college and that is your wish, then do it. If you have no desire to attend college, then go to a vocational or business school to sharpen your skills and increase your capacity" (in Conference Report, Apr. 1997, 70; or *Ensign,* May 1997, 49–50).

2 Nephi 9:34. "Wo unto the Liar"

• Second Nephi 9:34 and several other scriptures teach the seriousness of the sin of lying (see Proverbs 6:16–19; D&C 63:17–18; 76:98, 103). President James E. Faust (1920–2007) explained the meaning of telling the truth:

"We believe in being honest [Articles of Faith 1:13]. . . .

"We all need to know what it means to be honest. Honesty is more than not lying. It is truth telling, truth speaking, truth living, and truth loving. . . .

". . . Honesty is a moral compass to guide us in our lives. . . .

"Honesty is a principle, and we have our moral agency to determine how we will apply this principle. We have the agency to make choices, but ultimately we will be accountable for each choice we make. We may deceive others, but there is One we will never deceive. From the Book of Mormon we learn, 'The keeper of the gate is the Holy One of Israel; and he employeth no servant there; and there is none other way save it be by the gate; for he cannot be deceived, for the Lord God is his name' [2 Nephi 9:41].

"There are different shades of truth telling. When we tell little white lies, we become progressively color-blind. It

is better to remain silent than to mislead. The degree to which each of us tells the whole truth and nothing but the truth depends on our conscience. . . .

". . . As President Gordon B. Hinckley has said, 'Let the truth be taught by example and precept—that to steal is evil, that to cheat is wrong, that to lie is a reproach to anyone who indulges in it'" (in Conference Report, Oct. 1996, 57–61; or *Ensign,* Nov. 1996, 41–44).

> ### 2 NEPHI 9:29–38
> *What sins did Jacob warn us of? What makes each of these sins so serious?*

2 Nephi 9:41. Christ Is the "Keeper of the Gate"

• President James E. Faust discussed the value of knowing that one day we will stand before the Savior to account for our lives: "I recall a study some years ago that was made to determine what influences keep young people moving on the straight and narrow track. Of course there were several critical influences. All were important. They included the influence of parents, priesthood advisers, Young Women advisers, Scoutmasters, and peer association. But I was surprised to find that one golden thread of singular importance ran through this study. It was the belief that one day each of us would have to account for our actions to the Lord. Many believed that 'the keeper of the gate is the Holy One of Israel; and he employeth no servant there; and there is none other way save it be by the gate; for he cannot be deceived, for the Lord God is his name' [2 Nephi 9:41]. Those who had an eternal perspective had an extra amount of spiritual strength and resolve. Feeling a personal accountability to the Savior for our actions and stewardships and responding to it provide a profound spiritual protection" ("Who Do You Think You Are?" *New Era,* Mar. 2001, 6–7).

• Elder Neal A. Maxwell described a reassuring aspect to the principle that Jesus Himself and no other will be the final Judge: "Jacob, in 2 Nephi 9:41, in speaking of the straight and narrow, reminds us that 'the keeper of the gate is the Holy One of Israel' and that Jesus 'employeth no servant there.' The emphasis rightly is on the fact that Jesus 'cannot be deceived.' There is another dimension of reassurance, too: not only will the ultimate judgment not be delegated in order to serve the purposes of divine justice, but also divine mercy can best be applied by him who knows these things what only he can know—the quiet moments of courage in the lives of his flock, the un-noticed acts of Christian service, the unspoken thoughts which can be 'credited' in no other way, except through perfect judgment" (*For the Power Is in Them* . . . [1970], 37).

Elder Maxwell further explained: "The self-assigned gatekeeper is Jesus Christ, who awaits us out of a deep divine desire to *welcome* us as much as to *certify* us; hence, 'He employeth no servant there.' (2 Nephi 9:41.) If we acknowledge Him now, He will lovingly acknowledge and gladly admit us then!" (*Notwithstanding My Weakness* [1981], 124).

2 Nephi 9:50–51. "Buy . . . without Money"

• Elder Bruce R. McConkie (1915–85) of the Quorum of the Twelve Apostles explained what it means to "buy . . . without money": "Salvation is available to all men, not just a select few. Eternal life is not reserved for apostles and prophets, for the saints in Enoch's day, or for the martyrs of the Christian Dispensation. 'All mankind may be saved, by obedience to the laws and ordinances of the Gospel.' (Third Article of Faith.) God is no respecter of persons; 'he inviteth them all to come unto him and partake of his goodness; and he denieth none that come unto him, black and white, bond and free, male and female; and he remembereth the heathen; and all are alike unto God, both Jew and Gentile.' (2 Ne. 26:33.) The eternal call of the Eternal God is: 'Ho, every one that thirsteth, come ye to the waters, and he that hath no money; come ye, buy, and eat; yea, come, buy wine and milk without money and without price' (Isa. 55:1), for 'salvation is free!' (2 Ne. 2:4.)" (*Doctrinal New Testament Commentary*, 3 vols. [1971–73], 3:416–17).

2 Nephi 10:3. "Christ . . . Should Be His Name"

• The title *Christ* was revealed to Jacob by an angel. "*Christ* (a Greek word) and *Messiah* (a Hebrew word) mean 'the anointed.' Jesus Christ is the Firstborn of

the Father in the spirit (Heb. 1:6; D&C 93:21). He is the Only Begotten of the Father in the flesh (John 1:14; 3:16). He is Jehovah (D&C 110:3–4) and was foreordained to his great calling before the creation of the world. Under the direction of the Father, Jesus created the earth and everything on it (John 1:3, 14; Moses 1:31–33)" (Guide to the Scriptures, "Jesus Christ"; see also Bible Dictionary, "Christ," 633; Topical Guide, "Jesus Christ—Jehovah," 248).

Hebrew	Greek	English
Messiah	Christ	Anointed One (see Bible Dictionary, "Christ," 633)
Joshua	Jesus	Savior (see Bible Dictionary, "Jesus," 713)

2 Nephi 10:6–8. The Scattering and Gathering Is First Spiritual

• Jacob made it clear that iniquity led to the scattering of the Jews (see 2 Nephi 10:6). Similarly, he emphasized the order of the gathering. The Jews, he declared, will be gathered "*when* the day cometh that they shall believe in [Christ]" (v. 7; italics added).

Elder Bruce R. McConkie clarified the reasons the scattering and gathering of all the tribes of Israel are first *spiritual* and second *physical:*

"Why was Israel scattered? The answer is clear; it is plain; of it there is no doubt. Our Israelite forebears were scattered because they rejected the gospel, defiled the priesthood, forsook the church, and departed from the kingdom. They were scattered because they turned from the Lord, worshipped false gods, and walked in all the ways of the heathen nations. They were scattered because they forsook the Abrahamic covenant, trampled under their feet the holy ordinances, and rejected the Lord Jehovah, who is the Lord Jesus, of whom all their prophets testified. Israel was scattered for apostasy. . . .

"What, then, is involved in the gathering of Israel? The gathering of Israel consists in believing and accepting and living in harmony with all that the Lord once offered his ancient chosen people. It consists of having faith in the Lord Jesus Christ, of repenting, of being baptized and receiving the gift of the Holy Ghost, and of keeping the commandments of God. It consists of believing the gospel, joining the Church, and coming into the kingdom. . . . And it may also consist of assembling to an appointed place or land of worship" (*A New Witness for the Articles of Faith* [1985], 515).

• Elder Russell M. Nelson emphasized the importance of the doctrine of the gathering: "This doctrine of the gathering is one of the important teachings of The Church of Jesus Christ of Latter-day Saints. The Lord has declared, 'I give unto you a sign . . . that I shall gather in, from their long dispersion, my people, O house of Israel, and shall establish again among them my Zion' [3 Nephi 21:1]. The coming forth of the Book of Mormon is a sign to the entire world that the Lord has commenced to gather Israel and fulfill covenants He made to Abraham, Isaac, and Jacob [see Genesis 12:2–3; 26:3–4; 35:11–12]. We not only teach this doctrine, but we participate in it. We do so as we help to gather the elect of the Lord on both sides of the veil" (in Conference Report, Oct. 2006, 84; or *Ensign,* Nov. 2006, 80).

• Elder Bruce R. McConkie explained where the Saints should gather:

"[The] revealed words speak of . . . congregations of . . . covenant people of the Lord in every nation, speaking every tongue, and among every people when the Lord comes again. . . .

"The place of gathering for the Mexican Saints is in Mexico; the place of gathering for the Guatemalan Saints is in Guatemala; the place of gathering for the Brazilian Saints is in Brazil; and so it goes throughout the length and breadth of the whole earth. . . . Every nation is the gathering place for its own people" (in Conference Report, Mexico and Central America Area Conference 1972, 45).

• For more information on the scattering of Israel, refer to "Brief History of the Scattering of Israel" in the appendix (p. 415). For more information on the gathering of Israel, refer to "The Gathering of Israel" in the appendix (p. 416).

> **2 NEPHI 10:11–14**
> *What are some of the characteristics of liberty?*

2 Nephi 10:20–22. Separated from Their Brethren

• Jacob taught that God led various members of the house of Israel to other areas of the world from time to time and referred to them as "brethren" (see 2 Nephi 10:20–21). They were brethren both by lineage and belief. The Lord has a purpose for all of these branches and knows where each group is. The Book of Mormon speaks of at least three such colonies: Lehi's group, the Jaredites (as recorded in the book of Ether), and the Mulekites (see Mosiah 25:2; Helaman 6:10; 8:21). Undoubtedly, there are others we are not aware of, such as the lost tribes from the ancient kingdom of northern Israel and possibly other groups led elsewhere (see Jacob 5:20–25).

Points to Ponder

• In what ways can you help in the gathering of the Lord's people?

• Why is it important to realize that Jesus Christ's atoning sacrifice applies to you as an individual? What can you do to deepen your understanding of the Lord's Atonement?

• How can you know if your life is pleasing to the Lord?

• Why do you think the Atonement needed to be infinite?

Suggested Assignments

• Read and think about 2 Nephi 9:4–7, contemplating how the Atonement frees us from both physical and spiritual death.

• In 2 Nephi 10 is a description of a nation with great promises to be raised up in the latter days. Find descriptions of that nation mentioned in chapter 10.

• Describe what must happen before the ultimate redemption of the house of Israel takes place as described in 2 Nephi 10.

Introduction

President Boyd K. Packer, President of the Quorum of the Twelve Apostles, wrote of the difficulty encountered by many readers of the Book of Mormon:

"Most [readers] readily understand the narrative of the Book of Mormon.

"Then, just as you settle in to move comfortably along, you will meet a barrier. . . . Interspersed in the narrative, are chapters reciting the prophecies of the Old Testament prophet Isaiah. They loom as a barrier, like a roadblock or a checkpoint beyond which the casual reader, one with idle curiosity, generally will not go.

"You, too, may be tempted to stop there, but do not do it! Do not stop reading! Move forward through those difficult-to-understand chapters of Old Testament prophecy, even if you understand very little of it. Move on, if all you do is skim and merely glean an impression here and there. Move on, if all you do is look at the words" (in Conference Report, Apr. 1986, 76; or *Ensign,* May 1986, 61).

Both Nephi and Jacob specifically declared that Isaiah's writings are to be "likened" to ourselves (1 Nephi 19:23 📖; 2 Nephi 6:5). However, even Nephi's people, who lived less than 100 years after Isaiah, found his writings difficult (see 2 Nephi 25:1–4). Remember that when Jesus Christ came personally to the Nephites in America He taught "great are the words of Isaiah" and instructed the Nephites that they "ought to search these things. Yea, a commandment I give unto you that ye search these things diligently" (3 Nephi 23:1; see commentary for 1 Nephi 20–21 on p. 43.)

The following commentary will help you with the context, the dualistic nature, and the symbolism of Isaiah's writings. Because of space limitations in the Book of Mormon footnotes, much of the footnote information concerning Isaiah is only in the Bible footnotes and was not repeated in the Book of Mormon footnotes. Therefore, to study 2 Nephi 12–24 and help in your understanding of Isaiah, use the LDS Bible footnotes for Isaiah 2–14. You should be diligent in trying to understand Isaiah's words and seek the Spirit to guide you. If you have some difficulty, do not be discouraged. Over a period of time through study and prayer, the Lord will bless you and you will come to understand the writings of Isaiah.

Commentary

2 Nephi 11:1–3. Nephi, Jacob, and Isaiah—Three Special Witnesses

• Elder Jeffrey R. Holland of the Quorum of the Twelve Apostles wrote of the significance of the testimonies of these three great prophets:

"The Lord's manner of teaching and affirming, especially when it involves a covenant, has always provided more than one testimony. His admonition has always been that 'in the mouth of two or three witnesses shall every word be established.' Indeed, when the Book of Mormon was to come forth through the inspired hand of the Prophet Joseph Smith, it was prophesied that 'three shall . . . be shown [the plates] by the power of God. . . . And in the mouth of three witnesses shall these things be established. . . .

"Those three witnesses were to be Oliver Cowdery, David Whitmer, and Martin Harris. . . .

"In keeping with this same covenantal principle, it is interesting to note that there were three earlier witnesses—special witnesses—not only of the divine origins of the Book of Mormon but also of Divinity himself. These early witnesses were Nephi, Jacob, and Isaiah, and it is not by coincidence that their testimonies appear so conspicuously at the beginning of this ancient record. . . .

". . . What *is* known is that most of the 'greater views' of the gospel found in the teachings of the small plates of Nephi come from the personal declarations of these three great prophetic witnesses of the premortal Jesus Christ—Nephi, Jacob, and Isaiah. These three doctrinal and visionary voices make clear at the very outset of the Book of Mormon why it is 'another testament of Jesus Christ.' . . .

"One could argue convincingly that the primary purpose for recording, preserving, and then translating the small plates of Nephi was to bring forth to the dispensation of the fulness of times the testimony of these three witnesses. Their writings constitute a full 135 of the [143] pages from the small plates. By the time one has read Nephi, Jacob, and Isaiah in these first pages, a strong foundation has been laid for what Nephi called 'the doctrine of Christ'" (*Christ and the New Covenant* [1997], 33–35).

2 Nephi 11:4. The "Typifying" of Jesus Christ

• At times, Isaiah wrote using symbols or types. Nephi spoke of the importance of understanding that all things typify Jesus Christ. The word *typify* means "to represent by an image, form, model, or resemblance" (*Noah Webster's First Edition of an American Dictionary of the English Language, 1828* [1967]). These things serve as a reminder or an emblem of Christ. The scriptures constantly bear witness of and teach about Jesus Christ. Some examples of types include the sacrifice of a male lamb without blemish, which was a "similitude of the sacrifice of the Only Begotten of the Father" (Moses 5:7; see also Leviticus 1:3–5). The symbols of the sacrament bread and wine represent or typify the atoning sacrifice (see Moroni 4:3; 5:2). These reminders of the Lord and His saving mission for mankind are designed to instruct us and help us draw closer to the Lord our Redeemer.

---

2 NEPHI 11:4–7

Nephi declared that his soul delighted in proving "the truth of the coming of Christ" (v. 4). Identify some of the things Nephi delighted in.

---

2 Nephi 11:5. "Deliverance from Death"

• Elder Dallin H. Oaks of the Quorum of the Twelve Apostles said, concerning the promise of immortality offered through the Atonement of Jesus Christ:

"I wonder if we fully appreciate the enormous significance of our belief in a literal, universal resurrection. The assurance of immortality is fundamental to our faith. The Prophet Joseph Smith declared:

"'The fundamental principles of our religion are the testimony of the Apostles and Prophets, concerning Jesus Christ, that He died, was buried, and rose again the third day, and ascended into heaven; and all other things which pertain to our religion are only

appendages to it' (*Teachings of the Prophet Joseph Smith,* sel. Joseph Fielding Smith [1976], 121).

"Of all things in that glorious ministry, why did the Prophet Joseph Smith use the testimony of the Savior's death, burial, and Resurrection as the fundamental principle of our religion, saying that 'all other things . . . are only appendages to it'? The answer is found in the fact that the Savior's Resurrection is central to what the prophets have called 'the great and eternal plan of deliverance from death' (2 Nephi 11:5)" (in Conference Report, Apr. 2000, 17; or *Ensign,* May 2000, 15).

2 Nephi 12–16. Isaiah in the Book of Mormon

• Second Nephi chapters 12–24 contain quotations from the brass plates' version of the book of Isaiah (compare Isaiah 2–14). Nephi included these chapters to add another witness of the revelations that were given to him about the future of his people and the reality of Jesus Christ. Even though his people were a branch of Israel broken off and transplanted elsewhere, Nephi used the writings of Isaiah to show how the merciful plan of the Lord extends to them as well. Nephi felt that those who read these prophecies would "lift up their hearts and rejoice for all men" (2 Nephi 11:8; see also v. 2).

Repeating what he and his brother Jacob had previously taught, Nephi encouraged us to "liken" the words of Isaiah to ourselves (see 1 Nephi 19:23 ; 2 Nephi 6:5; 11:8). We liken the scriptures to ourselves by recognizing similarities between the events recorded in the scriptures and events that occur in our lives. We also liken the scriptures to ourselves by identifying principles that the scriptures teach. Those principles can guide our decisions.

Isaiah wrote a little over 100 years before Nephi's time (740–700 B.C.). While the writings seem quite distant from our day, for Nephi and Jacob, they were closer than the revelations and prophecies of Joseph Smith are for modern readers. Isaiah's inspired prophecies of Israel's scattering and the Lord's merciful plan to redeem His people influenced Nephi to include major portions to support his own written testimony and prophecies of the Messiah. These Isaiah portions underscore four major themes: (1) the judgments of God and needed repentance, (2) the covenants of God and His promises to the house of Israel, (3) Christ's first and second coming, and (4) major events relating to the latter days.

• The Bible Dictionary observes that quotations from the prophet Isaiah appear in the standard works:

"Isaiah is the most quoted of all the prophets, being more frequently quoted by Jesus, Paul, Peter, and John (in his Revelation) than any other [Old Testament] prophet. Likewise the Book of Mormon and the Doctrine and Covenants quote from Isaiah more than from any other prophet. The Lord told the Nephites that 'great are the words of Isaiah,' and that all things Isaiah spoke of the house of Israel and of the gentiles would be fulfilled (3 Ne. 23:1–3). . . .

"The reader today has no greater written commentary and guide to understanding Isaiah than the Book of Mormon and the Doctrine and Covenants. As one understands these works better he will understand Isaiah better, and as one understands Isaiah better, he more fully comprehends the mission of the Savior, and the meaning of the covenant that was placed upon Abraham and his seed by which all the families of the earth would be blessed" ("Isaiah," 707; see commentary for 1 Nephi 20–21 on p. 43).

2 Nephi 12:1. "Concerning Judah and Jerusalem"

• Isaiah saw and spoke of the future of Judah and Jerusalem and their final destiny. His words quoted in the Book of Mormon, however, also address all the house of Israel (see 2 Nephi 6:5; 3 Nephi 23:1–2).

---

2 NEPHI 12:2

Why is the phrase "top of the mountains" significant? What are some of the high places where the Lord visited and taught His prophets?

---

2 Nephi 12:2. "The Mountain of the Lord's House"

• A significant part of what Isaiah saw will begin to be fulfilled ("shall come to pass") in a time period focusing upon another location in the earth, namely the latter-day Zion of The Church of Jesus Christ of Latter-day Saints with headquarters in Salt Lake City, Utah.

Elder LeGrand Richards (1886–1983) of the Quorum of the Twelve Apostles spoke of the fulfillment of this prophecy:

"Isaiah saw the mountain of the Lord's house established in the top of the mountains in the latter days. . . .

"How literally that has been fulfilled, in my way of thinking, in this very house of the God of Jacob right here on this block! This temple, more than any other building of which we have any record, has brought people from every land to learn of his ways and walk in his paths" (in Conference Report, Apr. 1971, 143; or *Ensign,* June 1971, 98).

Elder Bruce R. McConkie (1915–85) of the Quorum of the Twelve Apostles expanded the meaning of the phrase "top of the mountains" in reference to temples: "All of the holy temples of our God in the latter days shall be built in the mountains of the Lord, for his mountains—whether the land itself is a hill, a valley, or a plain—are the places where he comes, personally and by the power of his Spirit, to commune with his people" (*The Millennial Messiah* [1982], 275).

• America, as a prophesied location of "the mountain of the Lord's house" (2 Nephi 12:2), has been a land of immigration from its earliest discovery and settlement. Isaiah prophesied that "all nations shall flow unto it" (2 Nephi 12:2). The great immigrations from Europe during the 19th century, and continuing from all parts of the world today, peopled and blessed the land, its institutions, and the Church. Many Latter-day Saints trace their ancestry to this movement of people from the old world to the new. In addition, people from around the world, both members and nonmembers of the Lord's Church, continue to visit the area of the Salt Lake Temple and the headquarters of The Church of Jesus Christ of Latter-day Saints. Many members of the Church attend general conference sessions semiannually in Salt Lake City, Utah, while others in various nations around the world view and listen to conference by means of modern communication systems.

2 Nephi 12:3. "Out of Zion Shall Go Forth the Law, and the Word of the Lord from Jerusalem"

• President Joseph Fielding Smith (1876–1972) explained the meaning of the law going out of Zion and the word from Jerusalem:

© Richard Cleave

"Jerusalem of old . . . shall become a holy city where the Lord shall dwell and from whence he shall send forth his word unto all people. Likewise, on this continent [America], the city of Zion, New Jerusalem, shall be built, and from it the law of God shall also go forth. . . .

". . . These two cities, one in the land of Zion and one in Palestine, are to become capitals for the kingdom of God during the millennium" (*Doctrines of Salvation,* comp. Bruce R. McConkie, 3 vols. [1954–56], 3:69–71).

• The phrase "out of Zion shall go forth the law" (2 Nephi 12:3) is an excellent example of how prophecies can have more than one application. President Gordon B. Hinckley (1910–2008) remarked:

"As I contemplate this marvelous structure adjacent to the temple [the Conference Center], there comes to mind the great prophetic utterance of Isaiah:

"'And it shall come to pass in the last days, that the mountain of the Lord's house shall be established in the top of the mountains, and shall be exalted above the hills; and all nations shall flow unto it.' . . .

"I believe that prophecy applies to the historic and wonderful Salt Lake Temple. But I believe also that it is related to this magnificent hall. For it is from this pulpit that the law of God shall go forth, together with the word and testimony of the Lord" (in Conference Report, Oct. 2000, 89; or *Ensign,* Nov. 2000, 69).

2 Nephi 12:4. Time of Peace

• Elder Dallin H. Oaks spoke of the peace that will finally come to the earth after the Lord's Second Coming. He also identified the reason why there will be no peace prior to that time: "Many take comfort from the Old Testament prophecy that nations will 'beat their swords into plowshares, and their spears into pruning hooks' (Micah 4:3). But this prophecy only applies to that time of peace which follows the time when the God of Jacob 'will teach us of his ways, and we will walk in his paths' (4:2). For now, we have wars and conflicts, and everywhere they are rooted in violations of the commandments of God" (in Conference Report, Apr. 1990, 92; or *Ensign,* May 1990, 72).

2 Nephi 12:5–9. "O House of Jacob"

• The "house of Jacob" refers to the descendants of this great patriarch who had gained the covenant name of Israel through personal righteousness. However, both the northern and southern kingdoms of Israel fell, though at different times, because they replaced God with apostate worship. They were "replenished from the east" (2 Nephi 12:6) or, according to Isaiah 2:6 footnote *a,* they were "filled, supplied with teachings, alien beliefs" of false gods, "like the Philistines." In other words, they forsook the gospel of the Lord for teachings and priorities from the world. Their hearts were set on riches and wickedness, and their worship turned to idols.

2 Nephi 12:9. The Mean Man and the Great Man

• The phrase "the mean [ordinary or common] man boweth not down, and the great man humbleth himself not" (2 Nephi 12:9) indicates that from the lowest to the highest in society, none were humble enough to accept God.

2 Nephi 12:11–22. "The Lofty Looks of Man"

• People of all nations who are "proud and lofty" shall be "brought low" (2 Nephi 12:12) and their "lofty looks" (2 Nephi 12:11) shall cease, for at the day of the Lord—the Second Coming—His glory will smite them. Verses 13–22 describe some of the status symbols of the day, including commodities acquired by the most wealthy, the high mountains and hills of false worship and apostate religion, the manmade defenses of towers and walls, and beautiful crafts or pleasure ships. In summary, the haughty and proud will fall, and their worldly treasures shall crumble away in the presence of the Lord's coming (see 3 Nephi 25:1; Malachi 4:1).

• President Henry B. Eyring of the First Presidency suggested that learning to be humble is essential preparation for the great day of the Second Coming of the Lord, when the Savior will be exalted among the nations:

"I began to read in 2 Nephi 12 and thought: 'The Lord is speaking to me. What is it He wants to tell me directly?' Then I came to a verse in the Isaiah passages that jumped out as if it were already underlined: 'And it shall come to pass that the lofty looks of man shall be humbled, and the haughtiness of men shall be bowed down, and the Lord alone shall be exalted in that day' (2 Ne. 12:11).

"This is describing a day when the Savior will come, a day we all look for and want our students to prepare for. This scripture says that in that day, all of us who thought we were special and wonderful will seem smaller, and the Lord will be exalted. We will see better who He is, how much we love Him, and how humble we should be. . . .

". . . I understood why Isaiah told me it would be helpful to foresee the day when the Lord would be exalted and to know how much I depend upon Him. We need Him, and the faith we have in Him makes us see Him as great and exalted and ourselves as small and dependent" ("The Book of Mormon Will Change Your Life," *Ensign,* Feb. 2004, 10–11).

2 Nephi 13:1–15. Punishment of Judah and Jerusalem

• In 2 Nephi 13, Nephi quoted Isaiah's description of the eventual fall of Judah and Jerusalem and the wicked Gentiles in the last days. The foretold destructions did come to the house of Jacob, prefiguring the destructions at the Second Coming.

2 Nephi 13:1. "The Stay and the Staff"

• The necessities of bread and water will dwindle during the siege. "The stay and the staff" described in 2 Nephi 13:1 foreshadows a spiritual famine of those who reject the Lord, who is "the whole staff of bread"—the bread of life—and "the whole stay of water"—the living water.

2 Nephi 13:2–3. "Mighty Man . . . Eloquent Orator"

• All men in Judah and Jerusalem, regardless of their status in society (11 categories are mentioned in 2 Nephi 13:2–3), will be brought into captivity.

2 Nephi 13:4. "Babes Shall Rule over Them"

• The untrained and young who had no status in society will be appointed to rule in captivity over those listed in 2 Nephi 13:2–3.

2 Nephi 13:6. "Thou Hast Clothing"

• The people are so poor and desperate due to devastation and anarchy that even one with clothing would qualify as a leader.

2 Nephi 13:7. "I Will Not Be a Healer; . . . Make Me Not a Ruler"

• Even the one nominated to lead because of his clothing will be powerless to alleviate the hunger and suffering.

2 Nephi 13:8. "Jerusalem Is Ruined"

• About 587 B.C. the city of Jerusalem fell and Judah was taken into captivity by Nebuchadnezzar, king of Babylon (see Bible Dictionary, "Chronology: Kings of Judah and Israel," capture of Jerusalem, 639). The Romans destroyed Jerusalem and scattered the Jews to various parts of the world in A.D. 70 (see Bible

Dictionary, "Chronology: Jewish History," 645), and again in A.D. 132–35. Surely they had, as Isaiah said, "rewarded evil unto themselves" (2 Nephi 13:9).

2 Nephi 13:9. "The Show of Their Countenance"

• Righteousness and wickedness affect both attitude and appearance. President Brigham Young (1801–77) said, "Those who have got the forgiveness of their sins have countenances that look bright, and they will shine with the intelligence of heaven" ("Speech," *Times and Seasons,* July 1, 1845, 956).

President David O. McKay (1873–1970) taught: "No man can disobey the word of God and not suffer for so doing. No sin, however secret, can escape retribution. True, you may lie and not be detected; you may violate virtue without it being known by any who would scandalize you; yet you cannot escape the judgment that follows such transgression. The lie is lodged in the recesses of your mind, an impairment of your character that will reflect sometime, somehow in your countenance or bearing" (in Conference Report, Oct. 1951, 8).

Jeremiah wrote that the people had become so sinful that they lost their ability to blush (see Jeremiah 6:15).

2 Nephi 13:12. "Cause Thee to Err"

• President Ezra Taft Benson (1899–1994) interpreted 2 Nephi 13:12: "And so today, the undermining of the home and family is on the increase, with the devil anxiously working to displace the father as the head of the home and create rebellion among the children. The Book of Mormon describes this condition when it states 'And my people, children are their oppressors, and women rule over them.' And then these words follow—and consider these words seriously when you think of those political leaders who are promoting birth control and abortion: 'O my people, they who lead thee cause thee to err and destroy the way of thy paths.' (2 Ne. 13:12.)" (in Conference Report, Oct. 1970, 21).

2 Nephi 13:16–24. "Daughters of Zion"

• President Joseph Fielding Smith explained who the phrase "daughters of Zion" was referring to and what these verses in 2 Nephi 13 said about them: "The standards expressed by the General Authorities of the Church are that women, as well as men, should dress modestly. They are taught proper deportment and modesty at all times. It is, in my judgment, a sad reflection on the 'daughters of Zion' when they dress immodestly. Moreover, this remark pertains to the men as well as to the women. The Lord gave commandments to ancient Israel that both men and women should cover their bodies and observe the law of chastity at all times" (*Answers to Gospel Questions,* comp. Joseph Fielding Smith Jr., 5 vols. [1957–66], 5:174; see also footnotes for Isaiah 3:16–26).

2 Nephi 14. Zion Shall Be Redeemed

• The millennial day will bring the redemption of Zion and the cleansing of her daughters.

2 Nephi 14:1. "Seven Women . . . One Man"

• A great number of the men will be killed in battle or taken captive, leaving the women with the destitution of being both widows and childless.

2 Nephi 14:2. In That Day

• In Hebrew the term *branch* often symbolized the Messiah (see Jeremiah 23:5–6). It can also refer to righteous groups of the house of Israel who have been cleansed and redeemed (see Isaiah 60:21; 2 Nephi 3:5; 10:1; Jacob 2:25).

"Escaped of Israel" (2 Nephi 14:2) refers to members of the house of Israel who, through personal righteousness, escaped the judgments that came upon the wicked.

2 Nephi 15. A Song of the Lord's Vineyard

• The terrible darkness and apostasy described in 2 Nephi 15:1–25 will abound prior to the destruction of the wicked. During this same time, however, Isaiah also prophesied that the Lord will gather His people and provide hope (see vv. 26–30). Elder Bruce R. McConkie portrayed the circumstances described in 2 Nephi 15 using words modern readers may understand:

"The vision of the future is not all sweetness and light and peace. All that is yet to be shall go forward in the midst of greater evils and perils and desolations than have been known on earth at any time.

"As the Saints prepare to meet their God, so those who are carnal and sensual and devilish prepare to face their doom.

"As the meek among men make their calling and election sure, so those who worship the God of this world sink ever lower and lower into the depths of depravity and despair.

"Amid tears of sorrow—our hearts heavy with forebodings—we see evil and crime and carnality covering the earth. . . .

"We see evil forces everywhere uniting to destroy the family, to ridicule morality and decency, to glorify all that is lewd and base. . . . Satan reigns in the hearts of men; it is the great day of his power.

"But amid it all, the work of the Lord rolls on. . . .

"Amid it all, there are revelations and visions and prophecies. There are gifts and signs and miracles. There is a rich outpouring of the Holy Spirit of God.

"Amid it all believing souls . . . prepare themselves to dwell with God and Christ and holy beings in the eternal kingdom.

"Is it any wonder that we both rejoice and tremble at what lies ahead?

"Truly the world is and will be in commotion, but the Zion of God will be unmoved. The wicked and ungodly shall be swept from the Church, and the little stone will continue to grow until it fills the whole earth" (in Conference Report, Apr. 1980, 99; or *Ensign,* May 1980, 72–73).

2 Nephi 15:18, 20–21. Warnings against Sin

• In 2 Nephi 15:18 the effects of sin are compared to "a cart rope." People guilty of sin are like those who "are tied to their sins like beasts to their burdens [or oxen to their carts]" (Isaiah 5:18c).

President Harold B. Lee (1899–1973) described how sin is like a burden: "If I were to ask you what is the heaviest burden one may have to bear in this life, what would you answer? The heaviest burden that one has to bear in this life is the burden of sin" (in Conference Report, Apr. 1973, 177; or *Ensign,* July 1973, 122).

President James E. Faust (1920–2007) of the First Presidency described the importance of clearly seeing and choosing right from wrong: "The gap between what is popular and what is righteous is widening. As prophesied by Isaiah, many today 'call evil good, and good evil' [Isaiah 5:20]. Revelations from the prophets of God are not like offerings at the cafeteria, some to be selected and others disregarded" (in Conference Report, Oct. 2003, 21; or *Ensign,* Nov. 2003, 22).

2 Nephi 15:26. "Lift Up an Ensign to the Nations"

• In the latter days the Lord will raise an ensign to gather and protect righteous Israel as the desolation of the wicked begins. The gathering of Israel will be a necessary precursor to the Second Coming of Jesus Christ, accompanied by the preaching of the gospel of Jesus Christ among all nations of the earth.

• President Joseph Fielding Smith defined the meaning of the ensign spoken of by Isaiah: "Over 125 years ago, in the little town of Fayette, Seneca County, New York, the Lord set up an ensign to the nations. It was in fulfillment of the prediction made by the Prophet Isaiah, which I have read [Isaiah 11:11–12]. That ensign was the Church of Jesus Christ of Latter-day Saints, which was established for the last time, never again to be  destroyed or given to other people [see Daniel 2:44]. It was the greatest event the world has seen since the day that the Redeemer was lifted upon the cross and worked out the infinite and eternal atonement. It meant more to mankind than anything else that has occurred since that day" (*Doctrines of Salvation,* 3:254–55).

2 Nephi 15:27–29. Horses' Hoofs like Flint, Wheels like a Whirlwind, Roaring like a Lion

• Elder LeGrand Richards (1886–1983) of the Quorum of the Twelve Apostles suggested possible symbolism for the Isaiah verses in 2 Nephi 15:27–29; he directed our attention to the great missionary labor taking place in our time:

"In fixing the time of the great gathering, Isaiah seemed to indicate that it would take place in the day of the railroad train and the airplane. . . .

"Since there were neither trains nor airplanes in that day, Isaiah could hardly have mentioned them by name. However, he seems to have described them in unmistakable words. How better could 'their horses' hoofs be counted like flint, and their wheels like a whirlwind' than in the modern train? How better could 'their roaring . . . be like a lion' than in the roar of the airplane? Trains and airplanes do not stop for night. Therefore, was not Isaiah justified in saying: 'none shall slumber nor sleep; neither shall the girdle of their loins be loosed, nor the latchet of their shoes be broken'? With this manner of transportation the Lord can really 'hiss unto them from the end of the earth,' that 'they shall come with speed swiftly.' Indicating that Isaiah must have foreseen the airplane, he stated: 'Who are these that fly as a cloud, and as the doves to their windows?' (Isaiah 60:8.)" (*Israel! Do You Know?* [1954], 182).

---

2 NEPHI 16:1–13

In what ways does Isaiah's calling mirror the calling of prophets today? Why is the calling of a prophet significant?

---

2 Nephi 16:1. Who Was King Uzziah?

• Uzziah was the tenth king in the southern kingdom of Judah. He began to rule at age 16 when his father, Amaziah, was killed by conspirators in about 767 B.C. Uzziah sought for and followed the counsel of the prophet Zechariah. While he followed the ways of righteousness, the Lord prospered him (see 2 Kings 15:34; 2 Chronicles 26:5). He led the kingdom of Judah in several successful military campaigns against local enemies. He strengthened the walls of Jerusalem. He supported agriculture. He raised the kingdom of Judah to a condition of prosperity that it had not known since the death of Solomon. Toward the end of his life, as an unauthorized servant of the Lord, Uzziah tried to offer

incense on the altar in the temple, at which time he was struck with leprosy (see 2 Chronicles 26:19). His leprosy stayed with him until his death in about 742 B.C. (see Merrill F. Unger, *The New Unger's Bible Dictionary,* ed. R. K. Harrison and others [1988], 1322–23).

2 Nephi 16. Isaiah's Calling to Prophesy

• Isaiah described his call to be a prophet of the Lord to all of Israel in symbolic language, using images and terms that his readers could identify with. His call included a vision of Jehovah (see 2 Nephi 16:1), the ministering of angels (see 2 Nephi 16:2–3, 6–7), recognition of his mortal weakness in contrast with the glory of Jehovah (see 2 Nephi 16:5), and acceptance of the call after a cleansing and strengthening spiritual experience (see 2 Nephi 16:6–8).

2 Nephi 16:2. Seraphim

• "*Seraphs* are angels who reside in the presence of God, giving continual glory, honor, and adoration to him. . . .

"In Hebrew the plural of seraph is *seraphim.* . . . The fact that these holy beings were shown to him as having wings was simply to symbolize their 'power, to move, to act, etc.' as was the case also in visions others had received. (D. & C. 77:4.)" (Bruce R. McConkie, *Mormon Doctrine,* 2nd ed. [1966], 702–3). The basic meaning in Hebrew for *seraph* is "to burn," perhaps to indicate the purified state necessary to be in God's presence.

2 Nephi 16:4. "The House Was Filled with Smoke"

• "The posts of the door moved . . . , and the house was filled with smoke" (2 Nephi 16:4). The shaking and the smoke are symbols of the presence of the Lord (see Revelation 15:8).

2 Nephi 16:9–12. "Hear Ye Indeed, but They Understood Not"

• Isaiah was commissioned to preach the gospel of Jesus Christ even though the people were "hard of hearing" and failed to "see" the truth of the gospel. He was advised that his preaching to a wayward people would generally not be received. Their hearts would "fatten" against the truth and their ears would be "heavy," not willing to accept the gospel as preached in clarity. Isaiah was not commissioned to make the people resistant to the truth; rather, he was advised of the difficulty of his mission. Even so, in answer to Isaiah's query of "how long?" (2 Nephi 16:11), the Lord answered that the people should have the opportunity to accept the gospel until "the land be utterly desolate." The Lord will graciously continue His mission of salvation through His servants "so long as time shall last, or the earth shall stand, or there shall be one man upon the face thereof to be saved" (Moroni 7:36).

2 Nephi 16:13. Holy Seed

• The use of *tenth* in 2 Nephi 16:13 represents a remnant of the house of Israel.

• "Holy seed" refers to the faithful remnant that will regenerate new life out of scattered Israel like new branches growing from the stump of a tree that has been cut down.

Brad Teare, Courtesy of Church History Museum

Points to Ponder

• If the great work of the latter days is setting up an ensign to the nations and bringing the gospel to them (see 2 Nephi 15:26), how can you best fulfill your role as a Latter-day Saint?

Suggested Assignments

• Read 2 Nephi 12:1–4; 15:26–27; and Elder Bruce R. McConkie's teachings in the commentary for 2 Nephi 15 (pp. 77–78) and President Joseph Fielding Smith's statement in the commentary for 2 Nephi 15:26 (p. 78). Write a paragraph about how the Lord's work in restoring the gospel in the latter days has personally blessed you.

• Isaiah was told that he would be preaching to a people who would hear his words but not understand them. Read 2 Nephi 16:9–12. Ponder and pray about how you can improve in regularly "hearing" the words of the prophets. Then write a plan you can follow that will help you understand and apply their words.

CHAPTER 11

2 Nephi 17–24

Introduction

Understanding the writings of Isaiah quoted by Nephi requires diligent study and effort on your part. Use the commentary and your understanding of the gospel to apply the prophecies and visions of Isaiah concerning the last days preceding the Second Coming. Look for how the birth of Jesus Christ, His life and mission, and the destructions and judgments that will befall the wicked in the last days prepare the world for His coming. Pay close attention to those writings that describe the circumstances of the Restoration. In addition, identify the behaviors of the evil world as foreseen by Isaiah. Recognizing and identifying the prophesied iniquity of the last days will help you make righteous choices and avoid the great judgments that will befall the wicked.

Commentary

2 Nephi 17–24. Overview and Background

• Many people have difficulty understanding Isaiah's writings because of the dual nature of his prophecies. On one hand, these prophecies relate directly to Isaiah's calling as a prophet and the circumstances surrounding his time and setting. On the other hand, he used those same events to describe events in the meridian of time as well as in the last days. It is helpful to be aware of the historical, geographical, and political context in which Isaiah prophesied (see 2 Nephi 25:5–6).

When Isaiah prophesied, there were two kingdoms of Israelites—the southern kingdom of Judah and the northern kingdom of Israel (also called Ephraim). A third country, Syria, was sometimes an enemy and sometimes an ally with either or both Israel and Judah (see Bible Dictionary, "Chronology: Kings of Judah and Israel," 637–39). These countries were referred to by the following terms:

Country	Capital city	Territory or Tribe	Leader
Judah	Jerusalem	Judah	Ahaz, of the house of David
Syria	Damascus	Aram	Rezin
Israel	Samaria	Ephraim	Pekah, son of Remaliah

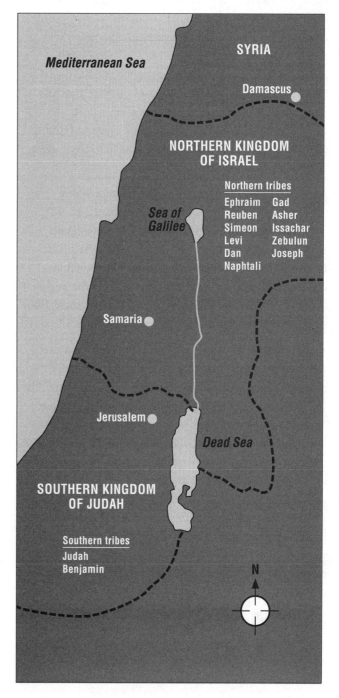

• Isaiah's call to the ministry came during the decline of Judah's and Israel's power and prosperity. The northern kingdom of Israel (Ephraim) had formed an alliance with Syria for mutual strength and protection against the conquering empire of Assyria. When Judah refused to join the alliance, Israel and Syria attacked Judah (see 2 Nephi 17:1).

Isaiah was directed to warn Ahaz, the king of Judah, against seeking political alliances for Judah in order to defend his people, but Ahaz rejected the Lord's warning (see 2 Kings 16:7–20). Ahaz made an agreement with the Assyrian monarch, Tiglath-pileser II (Pul), and Judah became a vassal state, paying tribute to Assyria to escape the threat of Syria and Israel. Assyria gradually devoured the smaller kingdoms, however. First Damascus (Syria) fell in 732 B.C., then Samaria (Israel) in 722 B.C., and even all of Judah, except for Jerusalem, was overrun by Assyria by 701 B.C.

As with many of Isaiah's prophecies, there was a fulfillment during his own time (see 2 Kings 16–18), which is shown in the history of ancient Israel and Judah. A careful reading of 2 Nephi 17–24 (see also Isaiah 7–14) together with the chapter introductions teach that Isaiah's prophecies also relate to the Second Coming of the Lord Jesus Christ and the judgments that precede that wonderful, anticipated event.

• Elder Dallin H. Oaks of the Quorum of the Twelve Apostles noted the "multiple fulfillments" of Isaiah's prophecies in succeeding generations and the role of the Holy Ghost in understanding these important writings: "The book of Isaiah contains numerous prophecies that seem to have multiple fulfillments. One seems to involve the people of Isaiah's day or the circumstances of the next generation. Another meaning, often symbolic, seems to refer to events in the meridian of time. . . . Still another meaning or fulfillment of the same prophecy seems to relate to the events attending the Second Coming of the Savior. The fact that many of these prophecies can have multiple meanings underscores the importance of our seeking revelation from the Holy Ghost to help us interpret them" ("Scripture Reading and Revelation," *Ensign*, Jan. 1995, 8).

2 Nephi 17:2. The House of David

• In 2 Nephi 17:2 the "house of David" refers to King Ahaz, a descendant of King David and heir to the throne of the kingdom of Judah.

• *Confederate* means to make an alliance with. Syria had formed an alliance with Ephraim, the northern kingdom of Israel.

• The phrase "heart was moved" shows that Ahaz and his people were afraid when they learned that Syria and Ephraim were allies.

2 Nephi 17:3. Meet at the Upper Pool

• The name of Isaiah's son *Shearjashub* meant "the remnant shall return" (see 2 Nephi 20:21–22; Isaiah 7:3a).

• The conduit referred to in 2 Nephi 17:3 is an aqueduct. Ahaz may have been checking the city's water supply in case of a siege during war.

• The fuller's field was a place where clothes were washed.

2 Nephi 17:4. "Smoking Firebrands"

• The description of kings Rezin and Pekah in 2 Nephi 17:4 as "smoking firebrands" is the image of a torch burned out, symbolic of having spent their strength. Rezin and Pekah were, in fact, powerless and soon to be crushed by Assyria.

2 Nephi 17:6. "Against Judah"

• To *vex* means to irritate or torment.

• The phrase "make a breach" indicates that Syria and Ephraim were going to try and force their way into Jerusalem.

• The son of Tabeal was a Syrian chosen by Syria and Ephraim to be the puppet ruler in Jerusalem.

2 Nephi 17:8. "Ephraim Be Broken"

• A score equals 20. Consequently, "three score and five years" means 65 years.

• The northern kingdom of Israel was captured by Assyria in 722 B.C., and many of the inhabitants (known today as the lost tribes of Israel) were carried away. Captives from other lands were relocated in the area and eventually intermarried with the remaining Israelites and became known as the Samaritans. "Ephraim be broken" happened as prophesied; within the span of 65 years, Ephraim was no more.

2 Nephi 17:9–14. "The Lord Himself Shall Give You a Sign"

• The Hebrew word for virgin (*'almah*) literally means "young woman," also having the connotation of a virgin.

• *Immanuel,* a name for Jesus Christ, comes from words in Hebrew that mean "God with us." Immanuel is a name-title given as a sign of God's deliverance (see Isaiah 7:14). Isaiah's reference to Immanuel had both a possible historic meaning and a prophetic meaning. In its most immediate meaning, it could indicate a child to be born in Isaiah's time whose coming of age operated as a sign (see 2 Nephi 17:16–19). In its more important prophetic meaning, Immanuel is specifically identified by Matthew as a prophecy of Jesus's birth into mortality (see Matthew 1:18–25). The name also appears in latter-day scripture (see 2 Nephi 17:14; 18:8; D&C 128:22). (For more information, see Guide to the Scriptures, "Immanuel," 117; Bible Dictionary, "Immanuel," 706.)

• "God with us" was meant to reassure King Ahaz that if he turned to the Lord, then God would help him. Elder Jeffrey R. Holland of the Quorum of the Twelve Apostles explained how this also became another type and shadow of the Savior: "There are plural or parallel elements to this prophecy, as with so much of Isaiah's writing. The most immediate meaning was probably focused on Isaiah's wife, a pure and good woman who

© 1987 Greg K. Olsen

brought forth a son about this time, the child becoming a type and shadow of the greater, later fulfillment of the prophecy that would be realized in the birth of Jesus Christ. The symbolism in the dual prophecy acquires additional importance when we realize that Isaiah's wife may have been of royal blood, and therefore her son would have been royalty of the line of David. Here again is a type, a prefiguration of the greater Immanuel, Jesus Christ, the ultimate son of David, the royal King who would be born of a literal virgin. Indeed, his title *Immanuel* would be carried forward to the latter days, being applied to the Savior in section 128 verse 22 of the Doctrine and Covenants" (*Christ and the New Covenant* [1997], 79).

Themes	Isaiah 7:14–17 (2 Nephi 17:14–17)	Isaiah 8:3–7 (2 Nephi 18:3–7)	Matthew 1:21
Mother	Virgin	Prophetess	She (Mary)
Conception	Shall conceive	Conceived	Bring forth
Child is a son	Bear a son	Bare a son	A son
Naming of son	Call his name Immanuel	Call his name Maher-shalal-hash-baz	Call his name Jesus

Donald W. Parry, Jay A. Parry, Tina M. Peterson, *Understanding Isaiah* (1998), 74.

2 Nephi 17:16–22. The Destruction of Ephraim and Syria

• In contrast to the promise that Judah would not totally perish, Isaiah prophesied the fall of the northern kingdom, "the land that thou abhorrest," which opposed Ahaz (2 Nephi 17:16). The two kings in the north at that time were put to death by the Assyrians.

• The two nations of Ephraim and Syria would be destroyed by Assyria. Syria's destruction came in

732 B.C. and Ephraim's followed in 722 B.C. As noted by Elder Holland (see commentary for 2 Nephi 17:14 on p. 83), the historic child of Isaiah's time would be about 12 or 13 years old, the age set by Judaic law for moral responsibility.

2 Nephi 17:20. Shaving Head and Beard

• Shaving the head and beard was customarily done to mourn a death in the family. The forcible shearing of a captive, however, insulted and identified the one in subjection.

2 Nephi 17:22. "Butter and Honey"

• Butter and honey may seem like luxury items, but the land was laid waste by the Assyrians (see 2 Nephi 17:23). Consequently, the survivors had to live off the land like nomadic Bedouins with no crops to eat. Butter and honey likely referred to the curdled yogurt that would come from goats or sheep and any wild honey that could be found.

2 Nephi 18. Assyria, the Lord's Instrument

• Chapter 18 of 2 Nephi is a continuation of the historical events introduced in chapter 17. Again, Isaiah warned Judah against alliances because, as he prophesied, they would be ineffective. The messianic promise of Immanuel ("God with us") would prevail in their behalf. The Assyrian invasion would come, but Judah would still survive. Isaiah concluded his writing with a warning against the false teachings and practices that would pull Judah away from the commandments that had been revealed to them.

2 Nephi 18:1. Maher-shalal-hash-baz

• The name of Isaiah's son, Maher-shalal-hash-baz, means "destruction is imminent" (see 2 Nephi 20:6). The name likely symbolizes Assyria coming to destroy Israel (see Isaiah 8:1d).

2 Nephi 18:3. Prophetess

• The term prophetess refers to Isaiah's wife. She may have had prophetic ability, and her son is probably the initial fulfillment of the prophecy recorded in 2 Nephi 17:14.

2 Nephi 18:4. "Knowledge to Cry"

• The description "the child shall not have knowledge to cry, My father, and my mother" refers to Isaiah's son Maher-shalal-hash-baz at about the age of two. By 732 B.C. Syria and the northern part of Samaria (Israel) were destroyed by Assyria. Israel was not completely conquered until 722 B.C.

2 Nephi 18:6–7. "The Waters of Shiloah That Go Softly"

• One commentary explains a possible meaning of the comparison between "the waters of Shiloah that go softly" (2 Nephi 18:6) and the "strong and many" (v. 7) waters of the river: "Isaiah describes and then contrasts two forms of waters—the soft, rolling waters of Shiloah, located near the temple mount of Jerusalem, and the waters of the Euphrates, a great river that often floods out of control. The waters of Shiloah are controlled and inviting, whereas the Euphrates is dangerous and destructive. The waters of Shiloah bring life to those who drink them; the Euphrates brings death to those who are swept up in its flood. Isaiah's images of the two waters are symbolic: the former represents Jesus, the King of Heaven, who is likened to the waters of life; the latter is the king of Assyria, who leads his great, destructive armies and 'cover the earth [like a flood . . . and] destroy the inhabitants thereof' (Jer. 46:8). Inasmuch as the inhabitants of Judah had rejected Jesus, or the waters of Shiloah, the Lord set upon them the king of Assyria, or the strong and mighty waters of the river that would overflow their banks and cover the entire land with its destruction" (Donald W. Parry, Jay A. Parry, Tina M. Peterson, *Understanding Isaiah* [1998], 83).

2 Nephi 18:8. "Even to the Neck"

• The symbolic expression "even to the neck" indicates that the king of Assyria will conquer Judah's lands, even to Jerusalem. By 701 B.C., Assyria had overrun all of Judah except its capital city.

2 Nephi 18:8, 10. "God Is with Us"

• At the point when Assyria overran Judah, all seemed to be lost, but Immanuel, or "God is with us," prevented the destruction of Jerusalem (2 Nephi 18:10).

Isaiah 37:33–36 describes this miraculous event where not even an arrow flew over the walls.

2 Nephi 18:14. A Sanctuary, "a Stone of Stumbling"

• Elder Bruce R. McConkie (1915–85) of the Quorum of the Twelve Apostles noted the ability of "Immanuel" to both save and condemn: "When the stone of Israel comes, he shall be a sanctuary for the righteous; they shall find peace and safety under the shelter of his gospel; but he shall be a Stone of Stumbling and a Rock of Offense (as also a gin and a snare) to the rebellious and disobedient in Jerusalem and in all Israel. They shall stumble and fall because of him; they shall take offense because of his teachings and be condemned and broken and snared and taken for rejecting them" (*Doctrinal New Testament Commentary,* 3 vols. [1971–73], 3:292–93).

2 Nephi 18:17. "I Will Wait upon the Lord"

• Elder Robert D. Hales of the Quorum of the Twelve Apostles spoke of the spiritual strength that follows when we place our trust in the Lord:

"As we put our faith and trust in the Lord, we must battle our pain day by day and sometimes hour by hour, even moment by moment; but in the end, we understand that marvelous counsel given to the Prophet Joseph Smith as he struggled with his pain of feeling forgotten and isolated in Liberty Jail:

"'My son, peace be unto thy soul; thine adversity and thine afflictions shall be but a small moment;

"'And then, if thou endure it well, God shall exalt thee on high; thou shalt triumph over all thy foes' (D&C 121:7–8).

"My dear brothers and sisters, when pain, tests, and trials come in life, draw near to the Savior. 'Wait upon the Lord, . . . look for him' (Isaiah 8:17; 2 Nephi 18:17). 'They that wait upon the Lord shall renew their strength; they shall mount up with wings as eagles; they shall run, and not be weary; and they shall walk, and not faint' (Isaiah 40:31). Healing comes in the Lord's time and the Lord's way; be patient" (in Conference Report, Oct. 1998, 19; or *Ensign,* Nov. 1998, 17).

2 Nephi 18:19. "Familiar Spirits, and . . . Wizards That Peep"

• In those dark times, the people resorted to consulting the spirits of the dead instead of trusting in the Lord. The peeping and muttering of the wizards refers to the chirping noises and whispered chants of a medium supposedly contacting the dead.

2 Nephi 19. "Unto Us a Child Is Born"

• As the Assyrians swept down against the alliance of Israel (Ephraim) and the Syrians, they destroyed Damascus and captured the northern region of Israel, later called Galilee (see 2 Kings 15:27–31). The text in  2 Nephi 19:1 refers to this occurrence as a "vexation" that brought "dimness." In spite of this invasion and the threat it posed for the rest of Israel and for Judah in the south, Isaiah prophesied of the coming of the Messiah to this region as the coming of "a great light" (2 Nephi 19:2). The lands inherited by the tribes of Zebulun and Naphtali were in northern Israel, or Galilee, where Jesus was raised and spent most of His ministry. Matthew and John saw the fact that the Messiah dwelt in the area of Galilee as the fulfillment of Isaiah's prophecy (see Matthew 4:12–16; John 1:5).

2 Nephi 19:6–7. "The Government Shall Be upon His Shoulder"

• Elder Jeffrey R. Holland wrote of the fulfillment of Isaiah's prophecy in 2 Nephi 19:6–7 being related to both the Atonement and the time of the Millennium: "The fact that the government would eventually be upon his shoulders affirms what all the world will one day acknowledge—that he is Lord of lords and King of kings and will one day rule over the earth and his Church in person, with all the majesty and sacred vestments belonging to a holy sovereign and a high priest. All can take comfort from the fact that because the government—and the burdens thereof—will be upon his shoulders, they will be lifted in great measure from our own. This is yet another reference in Isaiah to the Atonement, the bearing away of our sins (or at very least in this reference, our temporal burdens) on the shoulders of Christ" (*Christ and the New Covenant,* 80).

---

2 NEPHI 19:6–7

How can each of the titles assigned to the Lord Jesus Christ add new meaning to our understanding of the Savior?

• Elder Jeffrey R. Holland also helped us see the importance of the various titles applied to the Lord Jesus Christ:

"As 'Wonderful Counselor,' he will be our mediator, our intercessor, defending our cause in the courts of heaven. 'The Lord standeth up to plead, and standeth to judge the people,' Isaiah (and Nephi) reminded earlier [2 Nephi 13:13]. Note the wonderful compassion of our counselor and spokesman in this passage of latter-day scripture:

"'Listen to him who is the advocate with the Father, who is pleading your cause before him—

"'Saying: Father, behold the sufferings and death of him who did no sin, in whom thou wast well pleased; behold the blood of thy Son which was shed, the blood of him whom thou gavest that thyself might be glorified;

"'Wherefore, Father, spare these my brethren that believe on my name, that they may come unto me and have everlasting life' [D&C 45:3–5].

"Of course, as noted by Isaiah, Christ is not only a mediator but also a judge [see Mosiah 3:10; Moroni 10:34; Moses 6:57]. It is in that role of judge that we may find even greater meaning in Abinadi's repeated expression that 'God himself' will come down to redeem his people [Mosiah 13:28; see also Mosiah 13:34; 15:1; Alma 42:15]. It is as if the judge in that great courtroom in heaven, unwilling to ask anyone but himself to bear the burdens of the guilty people standing in the dock, takes off his judicial robes and comes down to earth to bear their stripes personally.

Christ as merciful judge is as beautiful and wonderful a concept as that of Christ as counselor, mediator, and advocate.

"'Mighty God' conveys something of the power of God, his strength, omnipotence, and unconquerable influence. Isaiah sees him as always able to overcome the effects of sin and transgression in his people and to triumph forever over the would-be oppressors of the children of Israel.

"'Everlasting Father' underscores the fundamental doctrine that Christ is a Father—Creator of worlds without number, the Father of restored physical life through the Resurrection, the Father of eternal life for his spiritually begotten sons and daughters, and the One acting for the Father (Elohim) through divine investiture of authority. All should seek to be born of him and become his sons and his daughters [see Mosiah 5:7].

"Lastly, with the phrase 'Prince of Peace,' we rejoice that when the King shall come, there will be no more war in the human heart or among the nations of the world. This is a peaceful king, the king of Salem, the city that would later become Jeru-Salem. Christ will bring peace to those who accept him in mortality in whatever era they live, and he will bring peace to all those in his millennial and postmillennial realms of glory" (*Christ and the New Covenant,* 80–82).

2 Nephi 19:11–12. "His Hand Is Stretched Out Still"

• The "adversaries of Rezin" were the Assyrians.

• While the phrase "his hand is stretched out still" is most often an expression of righteous anger, it is elsewhere portrayed as a hand of mercy (see 2 Nephi 28:32; Jacob 6:4–5).

2 Nephi 19:18–19. "Fuel of the Fire"

• In 2 Nephi 19:5 the bloody battle gear is fuel for the fire in preparation for the joy and peace of the "great light" (v. 2). In contrast, the fuel for the fire in verses 18–19 is wickedness, including the people who continue in darkness to the point of not sparing even their own brother.

2 Nephi 20. God's Judgment on Assyria

• Although the Assyrians were allowed to prevail against Israel and Judah, they also faced the judgments of God for their unrighteousness. Chapter 20 of 2 Nephi contains a prophecy concerning the destiny of Assyria, the fulfillment of which has been historically confirmed. Isaiah mentioned some of the successful military campaigns of Assyria (see v. 9) and prophesied of the eventual intrusion and success against Judah, even listing the names of many of the cities of Judah that would fall to Assyria (see vv. 28–32). Nevertheless, the Assyrians eventually failed and the destruction of both Israel and Assyria is described as complete (see vv. 15–19). The destruction of Israel and Assyria is also a type of the destruction of the wicked in any age, including the latter days.

2 Nephi 20:5–6. "The Rod of Mine Anger"

• In His mercy the Lord sent prophets repeatedly to call His people to repentance. When the prophets were rejected, the Lord allowed Assyria to become a punishing rod to His people. When that purpose had been fulfilled, the Lord then punished Assyria for its wickedness (see 2 Nephi 20:12) by the hand of another nation, Babylon.

> ### *2 NEPHI 20:12–14*
> *Compare Moses 4:1–4 with these verses. How is the king of Assyria a model by which Isaiah can teach you of the adversary?*

2 Nephi 20:12–15. "Shall the Ax Boast Itself . . . ?"

• The Lord compared Assyria to an ax that boasts against the one holding the handle. The ax (Assyria) has no strength in and of itself, and its reign is about to collapse.

2 Nephi 20:16–19. The Wicked to Be Destroyed in One Day

• Isaiah used the fall of Assyria as a type and shadow of the destruction of the wicked at the Second Coming. Elder Bruce R. McConkie instructed readers of this passage how to arrange and understand the writings in the context of the Second Coming: "It is Isaiah, speaking of the Second Coming, who says: 'And the light of Israel shall be for a fire, and his Holy One for a flame: and it shall burn and devour his thorns and his briers in one day.' So it is said of the day of burning when the vineyard is cleansed. 'And [the fire] shall consume the glory of his forest, and of his fruitful field, both soul and body,' the account continues. 'And the rest of the trees of his forest shall be few, that a child may write them.' The wickedness of men is so widespread, and their evils are so great, that few—comparatively—shall abide the day. 'And it shall come to pass in that day'—the day of burning, the day when every corruptible thing is consumed, the day when few men are left—'that the remnant of Israel, and such as are escaped of the house of Jacob, shall no more again stay upon him that smote them; but shall stay upon the Lord, the Holy One of Israel, in truth. The remnant shall return, even the remnant of Jacob, unto the mighty God.' (Isa. 10:17–21.) They shall be gathered after the coming of the Lord" (*The Millennial Messiah* [1982], 315–16).

2 Nephi 21. The Branch of Jesse

• The Lord taught Isaiah profound truths concerning the latter days by providing comprehensive visions. Like Moroni (see Mormon 8:34–35), Isaiah saw the circumstances of our day and the events by which the Lord would bring to pass the great millennial day. Many of Isaiah's prophecies relate directly to the Restoration of the gospel through the Prophet Joseph Smith.

2 Nephi 21:1–5, 10. The Stem, Branch, and Rod

• When Moroni appeared to Joseph Smith on September 21, 1823, "he quoted the eleventh chapter of Isaiah, saying that it was about to be fulfilled" (Joseph Smith—History 1:40). Who is the stem of Jesse and who is the rod to come forth out of that stem? The Lord answered these questions in Doctrine and Covenants 113:1–4. Still, careful reading and pondering are needed to decide who is meant by each symbolic term.

Elder Bruce R. McConkie identified Christ as the Branch during the Millennium: "'Behold, the days come, saith the Lord, that I will raise unto David a righteous Branch, and a King shall reign and prosper.' . . . (Jer. 23:3–6.) That is to say, the King who shall reign personally upon the earth during the Millennium shall be the Branch who grew out of the house of David. . . . He is the Lord Jehovah, even him whom we call Christ" (*The Promised Messiah: The First Coming of Christ* [1978], 193).

An additional insight regarding the Lord's kingdom in the latter days is interwoven with the messianic prediction in 2 Nephi 21:1: "There shall come forth a rod out of the stem of Jesse." Latter-day revelation identifies this rod as "a servant in the hands of Christ" (D&C 113:4). The idea of a latter-day servant is repeated poetically in 2 Nephi 21:10, this time referred to as "a root of Jesse." This root is identified as an individual who will hold the priesthood "and the keys of the kingdom, for an ensign, and for the gathering of my people in the last days" (D&C 113:6). The Prophet Joseph Smith was such an individual. So also is each succeeding prophet of The Church of Jesus Christ of Latter-day Saints.

Elder Bruce R. McConkie expressed this same feeling: "Are we amiss in saying that the prophet here mentioned is Joseph Smith, to whom the priesthood came, who received the keys of the kingdom, and who raised the ensign for the gathering of the Lord's people in our dispensation? And is he not also the 'servant in the hands of Christ, who is partly a descendant of Jesse as well as of Ephraim, or of the house of Joseph, on whom there is laid much power'? (D&C 113:4–6.) Those whose ears are attuned to the whisperings of the Infinite will know the meaning of these things" (*Millennial Messiah*, 339–40).

2 Nephi 21:9. "The Earth Shall Be Full of the Knowledge of the Lord"

• Elder Dallin H. Oaks taught that the outpouring of knowledge from the heavens includes a knowledge of God's ways, an increase in the presence of the Holy Ghost, and an understanding of the doctrine of the priesthood:

"In our day we are experiencing an explosion of knowledge about the world and its people. But the people of the world are not experiencing a comparable expansion of knowledge about God and his plan for his children. On that subject, what the world needs is not more scholarship and technology but more righteousness and revelation.

"I long for the day prophesied by Isaiah when 'the earth shall be full of the knowledge of the Lord' (Isaiah 11:9; 2 Nephi 21:9). In an inspired utterance, the Prophet Joseph Smith described the Lord's 'pouring down knowledge from heaven upon the heads of the Latter-day Saints' (D&C 121:33). This will not happen for those whose 'hearts are set so much upon the things of this world, and aspire to the honors of men'  (121:35). Those who fail to learn and use 'principles of righteousness' (121:36) will be left to themselves to kick against those in authority, 'to persecute the saints, and to fight against God' (121:38). In contrast, the Lord makes this great promise to the faithful:

"'The doctrine of the priesthood shall distil upon thy soul as the dews from heaven.

"'The Holy Ghost shall be thy constant companion, and thy scepter an unchanging scepter of righteousness and truth; and thy dominion shall be an everlasting dominion, and without compulsory means it shall flow unto thee forever and ever' (D&C 121:45–46)" (in Conference Report, Apr. 1989, 38–39; or *Ensign,* May 1989, 30).

2 Nephi 21:10–16. The Latter-day Gathering
• On September 21–22, 1823, the angel Moroni appeared to the Prophet Joseph Smith five different times. In four of the five visits, among other instructions, Isaiah chapter 11 was quoted with the declaration that it was about to be fulfilled (see Joseph Smith—History 1:40). Within a few years the Prophet Joseph Smith was given the priesthood keys necessary to begin fulfilling this prophecy (see D&C 110:11).

2 Nephi 21:11. The Second Gathering
• The Prophet Joseph Smith (1805–44) taught that the time for the second gathering of the house of Israel is specifically reserved for the last days:

"The time has at last arrived when the God of Abraham, of Isaac, and of Jacob, has set His hand again the second time to recover the remnants of his people, which have been left from Assyria, and from Egypt, and from Pathros, and from Cush, and from Elam, and from Shinar, and from Hamath, and from the islands of the sea, and with them to bring in the fulness of the Gentiles, and establish that covenant with them, which was promised when their sins should be taken away. . . . This covenant has never been established with the house of Israel, nor with the house of Judah. . . .

"Christ, in the day of His flesh, proposed to make a covenant with them, but they rejected Him and His proposals, and in consequence thereof, they were broken off, and no covenant was made with them at that time. . . .

"Thus after this chosen family had rejected Christ and His proposals, the heralds of salvation said to them, 'Lo, we turn unto the Gentiles;' and the Gentiles received the covenant, and were grafted in from whence the chosen family were broken off" (*History of the Church,* 1:313).

2 Nephi 22. Songs of Praise
• Chapter 22 of 2 Nephi contains two hymns of thanksgiving and praise for the millennial day. They present the great promise that the people will accept the Lord, praise Him, and enjoy His blessings. It will be a time when all will share their testimonies, gratitude, and love for each other. Hymn 89, "The Lord Is My Light," in the LDS hymnbook is based on this phrase used by Isaiah in chapter 12, verse 2.

2 Nephi 22:3. "Water out of the Wells of Salvation"
• Elder Joseph B. Wirthlin (1917–2008) of the Quorum of the Twelve Apostles identified the source of living water: "The Lord provides the living water that can quench the burning thirst of those whose lives are parched by a drought of truth. He expects us to supply to them the fulness of the gospel by giving them the scriptures and the words of the prophets and to bear personal testimony as to the truth of the restored gospel to alleviate their thirst. When they drink from the cup of gospel knowledge, their thirst is satisfied as they come to understand our Heavenly Father's great plan of happiness" (in Conference Report, Apr. 1995, 23; or *Ensign,* May 1995, 19).

2 Nephi 23. The Destruction of Babylon
• Isaiah foresaw the graphic destruction of Babylon, the degradation of its nobility, and the universal wickedness of its masses. God issued a call for forces to gather together to overthrow Babylon (see 2 Nephi 13:2–6). The call was answered when an alliance of Medes and Persians under Cyrus the Great dammed the Euphrates River and marched through the riverbed and under the walls of Babylon to capture the city and overthrow the empire in 538 B.C. The significance of the incident is more clearly indicated by considering the imagery of the term *Babylon* in a spiritual sense. In his prophecies Isaiah also used the term *Babylon* to typify the general spiritual condition of the world in the last days. The call is for the "sanctified ones" (2 Nephi 23:3), the Saints of the latter days, to gather together

and join with God in overthrowing wickedness (Babylon) from the world.

Paul Gustave Dore

2 Nephi 23:6. "The Day of the Lord"

• The phrase "the day of the Lord" is used many times to describe the judgments of the Lord that will punish the wicked and preserve the righteous. In preparation for that day the Lord said, "If ye are prepared ye shall not fear" (D&C 38:30).

2 Nephi 24:4–20. The Fall of Lucifer and the Fall of Babylon

• In 2 Nephi 24 the Lord, through Isaiah, condemned the wickedness of the house of Israel. He prophesied that great judgments would come upon it because of the evils within it. Generally, these judgments were to be carried out by other nations. Isaiah's prophetic vision of this destruction highlights the role of the adversary as the principal mover of the distress among the nations. By prophetic authority, we see that ultimately Lucifer will fail.

2 Nephi 24:12. Lucifer

• The only places in the Bible and the Book of Mormon where the name *Lucifer* is used are Isaiah 14:12 and 2 Nephi 24:12. In Doctrine and Covenants 76:25–28 we learn that Lucifer (which means

"lightbearer") was the premortal name of Satan. Because of his rebellion against God, he fell from his position of "authority in the presence of God" (v. 25) and "was called Perdition" (v. 26), which means "destruction."

Isaiah used the story of Lucifer's pride and his fall from heaven (see 2 Nephi 24:12–19) to typify the king of Babylon's ambitions and eventual downfall (see v. 4).

Isaiah's description of Babylon and her rulers are also a type and shadow of when Satan will be bound and will have no power over the nations during the Millennium. While he will be loosed for a little season after the Millennium, he will ultimately lose all power at the end of the earth's mortal history. He and the sons of perdition will be relegated to "outer darkness."

• President Ezra Taft Benson (1899–1994) identified the principal flaw in Satan's character that led to his fall from heaven:

"In the premortal council, it was pride that felled Lucifer, 'a son of the morning' (2 Nephi 24:12–15; see also D&C 76:25–27; Moses 4:3). . . .

"In the pre-earthly council, Lucifer placed his proposal in competition with the Father's plan as advocated by Jesus Christ (see Moses 4:1–3). He wished to be honored above all others (see 2 Nephi 24:13). In short, his prideful desire was to dethrone God (see D&C 29:36; 76:28)" (in Conference Report, Apr. 1989, 3–4; or *Ensign,* May 1989, 4–5).

> ### *2 NEPHI 24:12–20*
> *In what ways has Lucifer made his presence felt among the nations of the earth? What will the consequences be for his behavior?*

Points to Ponder

- As you study 2 Nephi 17–19, look for ways the life of Jesus Christ is central to the purposes of the last days.

- Which of Isaiah's warnings concerning the judgments of the last days are the most significant to you?

- In what ways will the Second Coming be both "great" and "dreadful"?

Suggested Assignments

- Once you have carefully read and studied these chapters of Isaiah and the interpretive commentary on them, write on a separate sheet of paper what you consider to be the most important prophetic insights that have significance and application for you as a Latter-day Saint and our world today.

Identify a major theme from each of the following scripture blocks:

2 Nephi 17–18 _____

_____

2 Nephi 19 _____

_____

2 Nephi 20:12–19 _____

_____

2 Nephi 21:10–14 _____

_____

2 Nephi 22 _____

_____

2 Nephi 23 _____

_____

CHAPTER 12

2 Nephi 24 _____

_____

Introduction

Nephi offered prophetic commentary about the prophecies of Isaiah that he quoted. Pay close attention to Nephi's insights concerning the role of the Savior in bringing to pass the salvation of Heavenly Father's children, the great evils facing those desiring to be righteous in the last days, and the blessings of the promised Restoration. A significant part of the prophesied Restoration was the coming forth of the Book of Mormon. In addition to preparing the world to recognize the great work of the Lord in the last days, Nephi's writings will help you know how to apply the Atonement for your personal forgiveness.

Commentary

2 Nephi 25:1–8. Helps for Understanding Isaiah

• For helps on understanding Isaiah, see commentary for 1 Nephi 20–21 on page 43.

2 Nephi 25:4. "Filled with the Spirit of Prophecy"

• President Joseph Fielding Smith (1876–1972) clarified the phrase "the spirit of prophecy" and how we might attain this gift:

"Revelation may be given to every member of the Church. The Prophet said that every man should be a prophet; that the testimony of Jesus is the spirit of prophecy. It is not only the privilege but the duty of each member of the Church to know the truth which will make him free. This he cannot know unless it is revealed to him. . . .

"The gift of the Holy Ghost is given to the members of the Church so that they may have the spirit of prophecy and revelation. Let it be understood however, that they will not receive revelation for the guidance of the Church" (*Church History and Modern Revelation,* 2 vols. [1953], 2:217–18).

2 Nephi 25:9–30:18. Nephi's Sermon to Jews, Children of Lehi, and Gentiles

• The following overview provides a summary of 2 Nephi, chapters 25–30, which make up a sermon given by Nephi to three different groups of people—the Jews, the children of Lehi, and the Gentiles.

Nephi's Message to the Jews (2 Nephi 25:10–20)

• Destruction of Jerusalem; captivity in Babylon; return to Jerusalem (see vv. 10–11)
• Jewish rejection of Christ; His Crucifixion and Resurrection (see vv. 12–13)
• Jerusalem destroyed again in A.D. 70 and A.D. 135 (see v. 14)
• Subsequent scattering of the Jews (see vv. 17–20)

Nephi's Message to the Children of Lehi (2 Nephi 25:21–26:11)

• Nephi's writings preserved and handed down; Joseph's posterity to be preserved (see 25:21)
• Nephites rejoice in Christ; purpose of the law of Moses (see 25:23–30)
• Signs followed by destruction; Christ visited the Nephites; destruction of the Nephites (see 26:1–11)

Nephi's Message to the Gentiles (2 Nephi 26:12–29:14)

• Jesus is the Christ (see 26:12–13)
• Prophecies of the last days (see 26:14–29:14)
  1. The coming forth of the Book of Mormon (see 2 Nephi 27)
  2. The worth of the Book of Mormon (see 2 Nephi 28)
  3. A warning to those who reject the Book of Mormon (see 2 Nephi 29)

Summary (2 Nephi 30:1–8)

• To the Gentiles (see vv. 1–3)
• To the children of Lehi (see vv. 4–6)
• To the Jews (see vv. 7–8)

2 Nephi 25:13. "With Healing in His Wings"

• Elder Richard G. Scott of the Quorum of the Twelve Apostles spoke of the need for the healing effects of the Atonement—not just for forgiveness of transgressions, but for all of life's hardships:

Harry Anderson, © IRI

"[The Savior] has risen from the dead 'with healing in his wings.'

"Oh, how we all need the healing the Redeemer can provide. Mine is a message of hope for you who yearn for relief from heavy burdens that have come through no conscious act of your own while you have lived a worthy life. It is based on principles embodied in the teachings of the Savior. Your challenge may be a serious physical disability, a struggle with lingering illness, or a daily wrestle with a life-threatening disease. It may have roots in the death of a loved one, the anguish caused by another bound by sin, or abuse in any of its evil forms. Whatever the cause, I testify that lasting relief is available on conditions established by the Lord" (in Conference Report, Apr. 1994, 7; or *Ensign,* May 1994, 7).

2 Nephi 25:15–17. The Return of Judah

• President Wilford Woodruff (1807–98) spoke to the people of the tribe of Judah, highlighting the great blessings to be realized as they fulfill the work prophetically appointed to them—that of gathering to take possession of their homeland and rebuilding the great temple in Jerusalem: "This is the will of your great Elohim, O house of Judah, and whenever you shall be called upon to perform this work, the God of Israel will help you. You have a great future and destiny before you and you cannot avoid fulfilling it; you are the royal chosen seed, and the God of your father's house has kept you distinct as a nation for eighteen hundred years, under all the oppression of the whole Gentile world. . . . When you meet with Shiloh your king, you will know him; your destiny is marked out, you cannot avoid it. It is true that after you return and gather your nation home, and rebuild your City and Temple, that the Gentiles may gather together their armies to go against you to battle . . . ; but when this affliction comes, the living God, that led Moses through the wilderness, will deliver you, and your Shiloh will come and stand in your midst and will fight your battles; and you will know him, and the afflictions of the Jews will be at an end" (quoted in Matthias F. Cowley, *Wilford Woodruff: History of His Life and Labors,* 2nd ed. [1909], 509–10).

---

2 NEPHI 25:17–20

What are the main purposes of the "marvelous work and a wonder" that Nephi prophesied would come forth in the last days?

---

2 Nephi 25:17. "A Marvelous Work and a Wonder"

• The phrase "marvelous work and a wonder" also appears in Isaiah 29:14 and refers to the Restoration of the gospel in the latter days. In 2 Nephi 27 we read of the important role of the Book of Mormon in this Restoration. Isaiah prophesied that as the Book of Mormon would help dispel the darkness of almost 2,000 years of apostasy, the "wisdom" of the supposed "wise and learned" would "perish, and the understanding of their prudent" would come to naught (2 Nephi 27:26).

• President Gordon B. Hinckley (1910–2008) related some of the remarkable events that constitute this marvelous work and wonder:

"That glorious day dawned in the year 1820, when a boy, earnest and with faith, walked into a grove of trees and lifted his voice in prayer, seeking that wisdom which he felt he so much needed.

"There came in response a glorious manifestation. God the Eternal Father and the risen Lord Jesus Christ appeared and spoke with him. The curtains which had been closed for much of two millennia were parted to usher in the dispensation of the fulness of times.

"There followed the restoration of the holy priesthood, first the Aaronic and then the Melchizedek, under the hands of those who had held it anciently. Another testament, speaking as a voice from the dust, came forth as a second witness to the reality and the divinity of the Son of God, the great Redeemer of the world.

"Keys of divine authority were restored, including those keys which were necessary to bind together families for time and eternity in a covenant which death could not destroy.

"The stone was small in the beginning. It was hardly noticeable. But it has grown steadily and is rolling forth to fill the earth" (in Conference Report, Oct. 1999, 94; or *Ensign,* Nov. 1999, 74).

2 Nephi 25:19. "His Name Shall Be Jesus Christ"

• It is significant that the name *Jesus Christ* appears often in the Book of Mormon. The worship of the source of salvation, clearly identified as Jesus Christ, is a common tie between members of The Church of Jesus Christ of Latter-day Saints and the ancient worshippers of Christ in the early Americas. He is also the same individual who established His Church among the New Testament Saints, and it was Jesus Christ in whose name Adam was baptized (see Moses 6:52). Thus the Saints in all ages of the world look to Jesus Christ as the source of strength and salvation, who Nephi testified is "the Son of God" (2 Nephi 25:19).

2 Nephi 25:20–21. Nephi's Records Preserved for Future Generations

• Nephi was commanded by the Lord to keep his record. He knew he had been commanded to write and he knew what to write; he may not have always known why he should write. But he "did know that their records would be preserved and given to future generations to assist in the Restoration" (Robert J. Matthews, *Selected Writings of Robert J. Matthews: Gospel Scholars Series* [1999], 356).

© 1988 Paul Mann

2 Nephi 25:22. Judged by Our Willingness to Receive the Book of Mormon

• President Ezra Taft Benson (1899–1994) discussed the importance of studying the Book of Mormon and how neglecting that study may have unforeseen consequences:

"Do eternal consequences rest upon our response to this book? Yes, either to our blessing or our condemnation.

"Every Latter-day Saint should make the study of this book a lifetime pursuit. Otherwise he is placing his soul in jeopardy and neglecting that which could give spiritual and intellectual unity to his whole life. There is a difference between a convert who is built on the rock of Christ through the Book of Mormon and stays hold

of that iron rod, and one who is not" (*A Witness and a Warning* [1988], 7–8).

2 Nephi 25:23. The Doctrine of Grace

• Grace refers to divine help or strength, given through the bounteous mercy and love of Jesus Christ. "It is through the grace of the Lord Jesus, made possible by his atoning sacrifice, that mankind will be raised in immortality, every person receiving his body from the grave in a condition of everlasting life. It is likewise through the grace of the Lord that individuals, through faith in the atonement of Jesus Christ and repentance of their sins, receive strength and assistance to do good works that they otherwise would not be able to maintain if left to their own means. This grace is an enabling power that allows men and women to lay hold on eternal life and exaltation after they have expended their own best efforts.

"Divine grace is needed by every soul in consequence of the fall of Adam and also because of man's weaknesses and shortcomings. However, grace cannot suffice without total effort on the part of the recipient. Hence the explanation, 'It is by grace that we are saved, after all we can do' (2 Ne. 25:23). It is truly the grace of Jesus Christ that makes salvation possible. This principle is expressed in Jesus' parable of the vine and the branches (John 15:1–11). See also John 1:12–17; Eph. 2:8–9; Philip. 4:13; D&C 93:11–14)" (Bible Dictionary, "Grace," 697).

• Elder Dallin H. Oaks of the Quorum of the Twelve Apostles discussed the effects of grace and how grace is an important doctrine for members of The Church of Jesus Christ of Latter-day Saints:

"Some Christians accuse Latter-day Saints . . . of denying the grace of God through claiming they can earn their own salvation. We answer this accusation with the words of two Book of Mormon prophets. Nephi taught, 'For we labor diligently . . . to persuade our children . . . to believe in Christ, and to be reconciled to God; for we know that it is by grace that we are saved, after all we can do' (2 Nephi 25:23). And what is 'all we can do'? It surely includes repentance (see Alma 24:11) and baptism, keeping the commandments, and enduring to the end. Moroni pleaded, 'Yea, come unto Christ, and be perfected in him, and deny yourselves of all ungodliness; and if ye shall deny yourselves of all ungodliness, and love God with all your might, mind and strength, then is his grace sufficient for you, that by his grace ye may be perfect in Christ' (Moroni 10:32).

"We are not saved *in* our sins, as by being unconditionally saved through confessing Christ and then, inevitably, committing sins in our remaining lives (see Alma 11:36–37). We are saved *from* our sins (see Helaman 5:10) by a weekly renewal of our repentance and cleansing through the grace of God and His blessed plan of salvation (see 3 Nephi 9:20–22)" (in Conference Report, Apr. 1998, 77; or *Ensign,* May 1998, 56).

2 Nephi 25:26. "Rejoice in Christ"

• President Gordon B. Hinckley noted that knowledge gained through the Restoration allows us to truly rejoice in our Savior: "As a Church we have critics, many of them. They say we do not believe in the traditional Christ of Christianity. There is some substance to what they say. Our faith, our knowledge is not based on ancient tradition, the creeds which came of a finite understanding and out of the almost infinite discussions of men trying to arrive at a definition of the risen Christ. Our faith, our knowledge comes of the witness of a prophet in this dispensation who saw before him the great God of the universe and His Beloved Son, the resurrected Lord Jesus Christ. They spoke to him. He spoke with Them. He testified openly, unequivocally, and unabashedly of that great vision. It was a vision of the Almighty and of the Redeemer of the world, glorious beyond our understanding but certain and unequivocating in the knowledge which it brought. It is out of that knowledge, rooted deep in the soil of modern revelation, that we, in the words of Nephi, 'talk of Christ, we rejoice in Christ, we preach of Christ, we prophesy of Christ, and we write according to our prophecies, that [we and] our children may know to what source [we] may look for a remission of [our] sins' (2 Nephi 25:26)" (in Conference Report, Apr. 2002, 107–8; or *Ensign,* May 2002, 90–91).

• Elder Jeffrey R. Holland of the Quorum of the Twelve Apostles connected rejoicing in Jesus Christ with the mandate to obey the laws and ordinances of the gospel:

"My greatest thrill and the most joyful of all realizations is that I have the opportunity, as Nephi phrased it, to 'talk of Christ, . . . rejoice in Christ, . . . preach of Christ, [and] prophesy of Christ' (2 Nephi 25:26) wherever I may be and with whomever I may find myself until the last breath of my life is gone. Surely there could be no higher purpose or greater privilege than that of 'special [witness] of the name of Christ in all the world' (D&C 107:23).

"But my greatest anxiety stems from that very same commission. A line of scripture reminds us with searing understatement that 'they which preach the gospel should live . . . the gospel' (1 Corinthians 9:14). Beyond my words and teachings and spoken witness, my life must be part of that testimony of Jesus. My very being should reflect the divinity of this work. I could not bear it if anything I might ever say or do would in any way diminish your faith in Christ, your love for this church, or the esteem in which you hold the holy apostleship" (in Conference Report, Oct. 1994, 39–40; or *Ensign,* Nov. 1994, 31).

2 Nephi 25:28. Follow Christ and His Leaders

• Elder Charles Didier of the Seventy indicated the importance of listening to the Savior and His leaders on earth to strengthen testimony:

"Once a testimony is in place, just like a fire that needs fuel and oxygen to burn, it needs to be fed and tended or it will burn out and die. A dying testimony corresponds, in fact, to a forthcoming denial of Christ, our Savior and Redeemer. . . .

"Unfortunately, there are those who gain testimonies and then deny them and lose them. How does this happen? If you follow the steps to obtain a testimony, you do exactly the opposite to deny it or lose it. Do not pray; the door to revelation will be closed. Do not be humble but listen to your own superior voice. Do not participate in the ordinances of the gospel but follow the practices of the world. Do not follow Church leaders but be critical of them. Do not listen to prophets and follow their counsel but interpret their declarations according to your own desires. Do not obey the commandments but live according to your own appetites and desires" (in Conference Report, Oct. 1991, 86; or *Ensign,* Nov. 1991, 63).

2 Nephi 26:11. "The Spirit of the Lord Will Not Always Strive with Man"

• Elder Joseph B. Wirthlin (1917–2008) of the Quorum of the Twelve Apostles taught the importance of diligent effort to merit the continued presence of the Holy Ghost: "As with all gifts, [the gift of the Holy Ghost] must be received and accepted to be enjoyed. When priesthood hands were laid upon your head to confirm you a member of the Church, you heard the words, 'Receive the Holy Ghost.' This did not mean that the Holy Ghost unconditionally became your constant companion. Scriptures warn us that the Spirit of the Lord will 'not always strive with man.' When we are confirmed, we are given the *right* to the companionship of the Holy Ghost, but it is a right that we must continue to earn through obedience and worthiness. We cannot take this gift for granted" (in Conference Report, Apr. 2003, 27; or *Ensign,* May 2003, 27).

2 Nephi 26:15–16. Speech Out of the Dust

• Nephi paraphrased Isaiah 29:4 to show that even though his people shall be destroyed, "those who shall be destroyed shall speak unto them out of the ground, and their speech shall be low out of the dust, and their voice shall be as one that hath a familiar spirit" (2 Nephi 26:16). The original meaning of "familiar

spirit" is a noun, meaning a spirit who prompts an individual or the spirit of a dead person. While this meaning may sound odd to us today, in the past it commonly conveyed the sense that departed ones can have influence beyond the grave into this life. In that sense, the voice of Nephi's people "who have slumbered in the dust" (2 Nephi 27:9) for centuries are now whispering "out of the dust" through the pages of the Book of Mormon, which Joseph Smith literally took "out of the ground" (Isaiah 29:4; see Joseph Smith—History 1:51–52).

> ### 2 NEPHI 26:20–30
> *Identify some of the great transgressions and their accompanying behaviors that exist in the last days. What can we do to avoid them?*

2 Nephi 26:22. "He Leadeth Them by the Neck with a Flaxen Cord"

• While serving in the Seventy, Elder Carlos E. Asay (1926–99) explained how a flaxen cord is made and becomes a yoke of unbreakable oppression: "The first wrongdoing is like a single strand of flaxen thread; it is easily broken and thrown aside. But each time the wrong is repeated another strand is intertwined around the first, and on and on it goes until an almost unbreakable cord of multi-strands is woven. 'The chains of habit,' said Samuel Johnson, 'are too small to be felt until they are too strong to be broken'" (*The Road to Somewhere: A Guide for Young Men and Women* [1994], 88).

2 Nephi 26:29. The Sin of Priestcraft

• Nephi explained that priestcraft occurs when men "set themselves up for a light unto the world" (2 Nephi 26:29). In contrast, Jesus taught the Nephites, "I am the light which ye shall hold up" (3 Nephi 18:24).

• Elder M. Russell Ballard of the Quorum of the Twelve Apostles added that priestcraft can occur both in the Church and from enemies to the Church: "Therefore, let us beware of false prophets and false teachers, both men and women, who are self-appointed declarers of the doctrines of the Church and who seek to spread their false gospel and attract followers by sponsoring symposia, books, and journals whose contents challenge fundamental doctrines of the Church. Beware of those who speak and publish in opposition to God's true prophets and who actively proselyte others with reckless disregard for the eternal well-being of those whom they seduce. Like Nehor and Korihor in the Book of Mormon, they rely on sophistry to deceive and entice others to their views. They 'set themselves up for a light unto the world, that they may get gain and praise of the world; but they seek not the welfare of Zion' (2 Nephi 26:29)" (in Conference Report, Oct. 1999, 78; or *Ensign,* Nov. 1999, 63).

2 Nephi 26:33. "He Inviteth Them All to Come unto Him"

• President James E. Faust (1920–2007) of the First Presidency challenged us to set aside prejudice and to labor as brothers and sisters in the kingdom:

"I hope we can all overcome any differences of culture, race, and language. . . .

". . . In my experience, no race or class seems superior to any other in spirituality and faithfulness. . . .

"Spiritual peace is not to be found in race or culture or nationality but rather through our commitment to God and to the covenants and ordinances of the gospel" (in Conference Report, Apr. 1995, 80–81, 83; or *Ensign,* May 1995, 61, 63).

• Elder M. Russell Ballard explained that the gospel blessings are for every one of God's children:

"Our Father in Heaven loves all of His children equally, perfectly, and infinitely. His love is no different for His daughters than for His sons. Our Savior, the Lord Jesus Christ, also loves men and women equally. His Atonement and His gospel are for all of God's children. During His earthly ministry Jesus served men and women alike: He healed both men and women and He taught both men and women.

". . . For example, faith, repentance, baptism, and the gift of the Holy Ghost are requirements for all of God's children, regardless of *gender.* The same is true of temple covenants and blessings. Our Father's work and glory is to bring to pass the immortality and eternal life of His children (see Moses 1:39). . . . His greatest gift, the gift of eternal life, is available to all" ("Equality through Diversity," *Ensign,* Nov. 1993, 89).

2 Nephi 27. The Lord Shall Do "a Marvelous Work and a Wonder"

• The last of Isaiah's writings quoted by Nephi (Isaiah 29) reveals that many important prophecies of the Restoration of the gospel in the latter days are missing from the biblical record. A careful comparison of Isaiah 29 and the same chapter from the brass plates (2 Nephi 27) shows that some of the "plain and most precious" parts that have been "taken away" (1 Nephi 13:26–27) include:

1. Latter-day context of the prophecy (see 2 Nephi 27:1).

2. A "book" that Isaiah prophesied would come forth in the last days (v. 6).

3. The book would be "sealed" (vv. 7–8).

4. Roles of Moroni and Joseph Smith in bringing forth the Book of Mormon (see vv. 9–10).

5. "Three witnesses" who would behold the "book" and testify "to the truth of the . . . things therein" (vv. 12–13).

It is not hard to imagine that by removing these prophecies of the coming Restoration, the adversary schemed to "pervert the right ways of the Lord that

[he] might blind the eyes and harden the hearts of the children of men" (1 Nephi 13:27).

2 Nephi 27:1–2. "Drunken with Iniquity"

• President Boyd K. Packer, President of the Quorum of the Twelve Apostles, shared his concern about the great problems in today's society:

"I know of nothing in the history of the Church or in the history of the world to compare with our present circumstances. Nothing happened in Sodom and Gomorrah which exceeds in wickedness and depravity that which surrounds us now.

"Words of profanity, vulgarity, and blasphemy are heard everywhere. Unspeakable wickedness and perversion were once hidden in dark places; now they are in the open, even accorded legal protection.

"At Sodom and Gomorrah these things were localized. Now they are spread across the world, and they are among us" ("The One Pure Defense" [an evening with President Boyd K. Packer, Feb. 6, 2004], 4, www.ldsces.org).

2 Nephi 27:7–11. "Behold the Book Shall Be Sealed"

• Elder Neal A. Maxwell (1926–2004) of the Quorum of the Twelve Apostles spoke of scriptures yet to be revealed, especially those from the Book of Mormon:

"Many more scriptural writings will yet come to us, including those of Enoch (see D&C 107:57), all of the writings of the Apostle John (see Ether 4:16), the records of the lost tribes of Israel (see 2 Nephi 29:13), and the approximately two-thirds of the Book of Mormon plates that were sealed: 'And the day cometh that the words of the book which were sealed shall be read upon the house tops; and they shall be read by the power of Christ; and all things shall be revealed unto the children of men which ever have been among the children of men, and which ever will be even unto the end of the earth' (2 Nephi 27:11). Today we carry convenient quadruple combinations of the scriptures, but one day, since more scriptures are coming, we may need to pull little red wagons brimful with books" (*A Wonderful Flood of Light* [1990], 18).

2 Nephi 27:12. "Three Witnesses Shall Behold It"

• Elder Dallin H. Oaks gave the following insight into the Three Witnesses' powerful testimonies: "The three men chosen as witnesses of the Book of Mormon were Oliver Cowdery, David Whitmer, and Martin Harris. Their written 'Testimony of Three Witnesses' has been included in all of the almost 100 million copies of the Book of Mormon the Church has published since 1830. These witnesses solemnly testify that they 'have seen the plates which contain this record' and 'the engravings which are upon the plates.' They witness that these writings 'have been translated by the gift and power of God, for his voice hath declared it unto us.' They testify, 'We declare with words of soberness, that an angel of God came down from heaven, and he brought and laid before our eyes, that we beheld and saw the plates, and the engravings thereon; and we know that it is by the grace of God the Father, and our Lord Jesus Christ, that we beheld and bear record that these things are true'" (in Conference Report, Apr. 1999, 45; or *Ensign,* May 1999, 35).

• Refer to the chart "The Witnesses of the Book of Mormon Plates" in the appendix (p. 409). It lists information about each of the Three Witnesses and the Eight Witnesses.

2 Nephi 27:13. A "Few" More Will "Bear Testimony" of the Plates

• In addition to the Three Witnesses to the gold plates, there were eight more who saw the plates and were

called to bear witness of them (see "The Testimony of Eight Witnesses" in the front of the Book of Mormon; see also the chart "The Witnesses of the Book of Mormon Plates," which lists information about each of the witnesses, in the appendix on p. 409).

2 Nephi 27:15–19. "Deliver the Book . . . unto the Learned"

• The Lord directed Joseph Smith to have Martin Harris visit a learned man. Oliver Cowdery reported that during Moroni's initial visit to Joseph Smith on September 21–22, 1823, Moroni quoted the prophecy of Isaiah cited here in 2 Nephi 27 and said that Joseph was to fulfill it: "'Yet,' said he, 'the scripture must be fulfilled before it is translated, which says that the words of a book, which were sealed, were presented to the learned; for thus has God determined to leave men without excuse, and show to the meek that his arm is not shortened that it cannot save'" ("Letter IV. To W. W. Phelps," *Messenger and Advocate,* Feb. 1835, 80). This prophecy was fulfilled in 1828 when Martin Harris visited the "learned" man, Charles Anthon (see Joseph Smith—History 1:63–65).

Elder Neal A. Maxwell of the Quorum of the Twelve Apostles expanded on the singular event with Professor Anthon to include the general reaction of the learned of this world to the Book of Mormon: "This is not solely a reference to Professor Anthon, since the plural pronoun *they* is used [2 Nephi 27:20]. The reference suggests a mind-set of most of the learned of the world, who, by and large, do not take the Book of Mormon seriously. Even when they read it, they do not *really* read it, except with a mind-set which excludes miracles, including the miracle of the book's coming forth by the 'gift and power of God'" ("The Book of Mormon: A Great Answer to 'the Great Question,'" in Monte S. Nyman and Charles D. Tate Jr.,

eds., *The Book of Mormon: First Nephi, The Doctrinal Foundation* [1988], 9).

2 Nephi 27:20. "I Am Able to Do Mine Own Work"

• Elder Neal A. Maxwell spoke of how the Lord will ultimately overcome all objections to His work: "God lives in an eternal now where the past, present, and future are constantly before Him (see D&C 130:7). His divine determinations are guaranteed, since whatever He takes in His heart to do, He will surely do it (see Abraham 3:17). He knows the end from the beginning! (see Abraham 2:8). God is fully 'able to do [His] . . . work' (2 Nephi 27:20) and to bring all His purposes to pass, something untrue of the best-laid plans of man since we so often use our agency amiss!" (in Conference Report, Apr. 2003, 72; or *Ensign,* May 2003, 70).

• In an earlier setting, Elder Maxwell also noted that God fulfills His purposes without nullifying the agency of man: "Because the centerpiece of the Atonement is already in place, we know that everything else in God's plan will likewise finally succeed. God is surely able to do His own work! (See 2 Nephi 27:20–21.) In His plans for the human family, long ago God made ample provision for all mortal mistakes. His purposes will all triumph and without abrogating man's moral agency. Moreover, all His purposes will come to pass in their time (see D&C 64:32)" (in Conference Report, Oct. 1990, 17; or *Ensign,* Nov. 1990, 15).

2 Nephi 27:21. "In Mine Own Due Time"

• Elder Neal A. Maxwell discussed our timing and God's timing: "Faith also includes trust in God's timing, for He has said, 'All things must come to pass in their time' (D&C 64:32). Ironically, some who acknowledge God are tried by His timing, globally and personally!" (in Conference Report, Apr. 1991, 119; or *Ensign,* May 1991, 90).

On another occasion, Elder Maxwell said: "Faith in the timing of God [is] to be able to say Thy *timing* be done, even when we do not fully understand it" ("Glorify Christ" [an evening with Elder Neal A. Maxwell, Feb. 2, 2001], 7, www.ldsces.org).

2 Nephi 27:35. "They That Murmured Shall Learn Doctrine"

• Elder Bruce R. McConkie (1915–85) of the Quorum of the Twelve Apostles indicated how people who murmur against revealed truth shall learn new doctrines: "Such is the purpose of the Book of Mormon. Members of false churches who err in spirit, who think they have the truth, are brought by the Book of Mormon to the fulness of the gospel. Those who have based their beliefs on isolated verses and obscure passages, and who have wondered and murmured at seeming biblical conflicts, come to learn sound doctrine. No longer do they worry about the atonement, salvation by grace alone, infant baptism, the priesthood, the gifts of the Spirit, the passages about an apostasy, a gospel restoration, and the gathering of Israel. All things fall into place because of this new witness for Christ and his gospel" (*The Millennial Messiah* [1982], 174–75).

Points to Ponder

• What does the phrase "after all we can do" mean to you as it relates to being saved by grace? (2 Nephi 25:23).

• How have you seen pride and the love of money contribute to declining spirituality in those around you?

• Nephi discussed the importance of witnesses in 2 Nephi 27. Identify the different witnesses he refers to (see vv. 12–14). How does each member of the Church, including you, play a role as a witness in establishing God's word? (see v. 14).

Suggested Assignments

• To a family member or trusted friend, explain the doctrine of grace as declared by the prophet Nephi.

• Prepare a talk or family home evening lesson concerning the fulfillment of Isaiah's prophecy of the "marvelous work and a wonder" (2 Nephi 27:26) the Lord is performing in the latter days.

Introduction

Some themes and teachings that were first presented in 2 Nephi 26 are built on in 2 Nephi 28. Nephi identified some of the false teachings and beliefs that are rampant in the latter days, and then he taught us what we must do to avoid being led astray. As you read 2 Nephi 29, look for ways the marvelous work of the coming forth of the Book of Mormon and the Restoration will help overcome false doctrines, false churches, and pride in the last days. Throughout your study, identify characteristics of God's covenant people and the blessings that come to them as they repent and serve Him in righteousness.

Commentary

2 Nephi 28:1. "The Spirit Hath Constrained Me"

• Nephi felt "constrained" by the Spirit to record his prophecies of the last days. *Constrained* means being compelled or doing something out of necessity. There are other examples of being constrained by the Spirit (see 1 Nephi 4:10; Alma 14:11; 4 Nephi 1:48; D&C 63:64).

2 Nephi 28:2. This "Book Shall Be of Great Worth"

• The book mentioned in 2 Nephi 28:2 is the Book of Mormon and is the same book Nephi referred to in 2 Nephi 26–27, 29. Nephi said "the book shall be of great worth" to us because of conditions in the last days. President Ezra Taft Benson (1899–1994) taught how we can recognize the great worth of the Book of Mormon:

"Each of the major writers of the Book of Mormon testified that he wrote for future generations. . . .

"If they saw our day and chose those things which would be of greatest worth to us, is not that how we should study the Book of Mormon? We should constantly ask ourselves, 'Why did the Lord inspire Mormon (or Moroni or Alma) to include that in his record? What lesson can I learn from that to help me live in this day and age?' . . .

". . . In the Book of Mormon we find lessons for dealing with persecution and apostasy. We learn much about how to do missionary work. And more than anywhere else, we see in the Book of Mormon the dangers of materialism and setting our hearts on the things of the world. Can anyone doubt that this book was meant for us and that in it we find great power, great comfort, and great protection?" (in Conference Report, Oct. 1986, 5–6; or *Ensign,* Nov. 1986, 6–7).

2 Nephi 28:6–9. 📖 "False and Vain and Foolish Doctrines"

• Nephi exposed some of the "false and vain and foolish doctrines" that Satan professes and will continue to use (2 Nephi 28:9). Each of the phrases found in 2 Nephi 28:6–9 📖 conveys a spiritually dangerous philosophy. Modern prophets have identified these ideas and have spoken against them:

"Eat, drink, and be merry, for tomorrow we die" (v. 7). Elder Neal A. Maxwell (1926–2004) of the Quorum of the Twelve Apostles cautioned against this attitude:

"The philosophy of ritual prodigalism is 'eat, drink, and be merry, . . . [and] God will beat us with a few stripes' (2 Nephi 28:8). This is a cynical and shallow view of God, of self, and of life. God never can justify us 'in committing a little sin' (v. 8). He is the God of the universe, not some night-court judge with whom we can haggle and plea bargain!

"Of course God is forgiving! But He knows the intents of our hearts. He also knows what good we might have done while AWOL [absent without leave]. In any case, what others do is no excuse for the discipline from whom much is required (see Alma 39:4). Besides, on the straight and narrow path, there are simply no corners to be cut (see D&C 82:3)" (in Conference Report, Oct. 1988, 40; or *Ensign,* Nov. 1988, 33).

"God . . . will justify in committing a little sin" (v. 8). The Doctrine and Covenants is clear: "For I the Lord cannot look upon sin with the least degree of allowance; nevertheless, he that repents and does the commandments of the Lord shall be forgiven" (D&C 1:31–32).

Elder Dallin H. Oaks of the Quorum of the Twelve Apostles commented on the foolishness of thinking that we are better off for having sinned for the experience of it: "The idea that one is better off after one has sinned and repented is a devilish lie of the adversary. Does anyone here think that it is better to learn firsthand that a certain blow will break a bone or a certain mixture of chemicals will explode and sear off our skin? Are we better off after we have sustained and then healed such injuries? I believe we all can see that it is better to heed the warnings of wise persons who know the effects on our bodies" ("Sin and Suffering," in *Brigham Young University 1989–90 Devotional and Fireside Speeches* [1990], 151).

"Lie a little" (v. 8). President Gordon B. Hinckley (1910–2008) admonished us to resist the temptation to lie a little: "Nephi so describes the people of his day, as he also describes so many of our day. How easy it is for us to say, 'We believe in being honest, true, chaste, benevolent' (Articles of Faith 1:13). But how difficult for so many to resist the temptation to lie a little, cheat a little, steal a little, bear false witness in speaking gossipy words about others. Rise above it. . . . Be strong in the simple virtue of honesty" (in Conference Report, Oct. 1992, 74; or *Ensign,* Nov. 1992, 52).

"God will beat us with a few stripes, and at last we shall be saved" (v. 8). President James E. Faust (1920–2007) of the First Presidency spoke against this falsehood:

"[One deception] is what some erroneously call 'premeditated repentance.' There is no such doctrine in this Church. This may sound subtly appealing, but it is in fact pernicious and a false concept. Its objective is to persuade us that we can consciously and deliberately transgress with the forethought that quick repentance will permit us to enjoy the full blessings of the gospel, such as temple blessings or a mission. True repentance

can be a long, painful process. This foolish doctrine was foreseen by Nephi:

"'And there shall also be many which shall say: Eat, drink, and be merry; nevertheless, fear God—he will justify in committing a little sin; . . . there is no harm in this; and do all these things, for tomorrow we die; and if it so be that we are guilty, God will beat us with a few stripes, and at last we shall be saved in the kingdom of God' [2 Nephi 28:8].

". . . All of our covenants must not only be received through ordinances but, to be eternal, must also be sealed by the Holy Spirit of Promise. This divine stamp of approval is placed upon our ordinances and covenants only through faithfulness. The false idea of so-called premeditated repentance involves an element of deception, but the Holy Spirit of Promise cannot be deceived" (in Conference Report, Oct. 2000, 61; or *Ensign,* Nov. 2000, 46).

---

2 NEPHI 28:14
What challenge faces the humble followers of Christ? How can we avoid falling prey to this challenge?

---

2 Nephi 28:19–22. Strategies of the Devil

• As Nephi earlier identified false doctrines promoted by Satan, he also identified some of the strategies that promote "the kingdom of the devil" (2 Nephi 28:19). Our modern-day prophets and apostles have continued to identify the tactics used by Satan. Bishop Richard C. Edgley of the Presiding Bishopric warned us of the reality of the attacks of the adversary:

"We have . . . had very specific warnings regarding Satan's power, influence, and determination. Nephi prophesied more than twenty-five hundred years ago of the trials and turbulence that you would face. You all know the scripture. It is found in the 28th chapter of 2 Nephi: [2 Nephi 28:20–21]

"I believe this scripture is true. I believe the time is now. And I believe the target is you. For the most part, Satan has made great strides in establishing and selling his value system, which is based upon the son of man, not the Son of God: 'Eat, drink, and be merry, for tomorrow we die' (2 Nephi 28:7) and 'There is no hell' (2 Nephi 28:22). His is a value system based upon selfishness, self-indulgence, and immediate gratification. Thus we see devastating decisions constantly being made by those of your age. We see cultures infested with drugs, sex, alcohol, pornography, laziness, and many other spiritually devastating practices. But that does not have to be you.

"President Gordon B. Hinckley has warned us and pleaded with us: 'I wish to say in the strongest language of which I am capable, stay away from moral iniquity. You know what is right and wrong. You cannot use ignorance as an excuse for unacceptable behavior. . . .

"'I beg of you, my dear young friends, to avoid such behavior. It will not be easy. It will require self-discipline. . . . You need the strength that comes of prayer' ("To Men of the Priesthood," *Ensign,* Nov. 2002, 58–59)" ("Becoming You" [CES fireside for young adults, Nov. 3, 2002], 4, www.ldsces.org).

"They be stirred up to anger" (2 Nephi 28:19). Elder Marvin J. Ashton (1915–94) of the Quorum of the Twelve Apostles identified the danger that comes from following Satan's temptations to take advantage of each other:

"It should come as no surprise that one of the adversary's tactics in the latter days is stirring up hatred among the children of men. He loves to see us criticize each other, make fun or take advantage of our neighbor's known flaws, and generally pick on each other. The Book of Mormon is clear from where all anger, malice, greed, and hate come from.

". . . By the looks of what we constantly see depicted in the news media, it appears that Satan is doing a pretty good job. In the name of reporting the news, we are besieged with sometimes graphic depictions—too often in living color—of greed, extortion, violent sexual crimes, and insults between business, athletic, or political opponents" (in Conference Report, Apr. 1992, 24–25; or *Ensign,* May 1992, 19).

"Pacify, and lull them away into carnal security" (2 Nephi 28:21). Bishop Richard C. Edgley commented on the carnal desires so prevalent in today's world:

"Nephi describes [Satan's] sales techniques as pacifying, flattering, and lulling as he declares, 'All is well' (2 Nephi 28:21–22). Among other things Satan would have us put in our bags is immorality in all its forms, including pornography, language, dress, and behavior. But such evil deeds bring emotional distress, loss of spirituality, loss of self-respect, lost opportunity for a mission or temple marriage, and sometimes even unwanted pregnancy. Satan would enslave us by having us put drugs, alcohol, tobacco, and other addictive behaviors into our bags" (in Conference Report, Oct. 2000, 57; or *Ensign,* Nov. 2000, 43).

"There is no hell; and . . . I am no devil, for there is none" (2 Nephi 28:22). One of the greatest lies perpetuated is that there is no devil. President Marion G. Romney (1897–1988) of the First Presidency affirmed the reality of Satan with this testimony:

"A corollary to the pernicious falsehood that God is dead is the equally pernicious doctrine that there is no devil. Satan himself is the father of both of these lies. To believe them is to surrender to him. Such surrender has always led, is leading now, and will continue to lead men to destruction.

"Latter-day Saints know that there is a God. With like certainty, they know that Satan lives, that he is a powerful personage of spirit, the archenemy of God, of man, and of righteousness.

"The reality of the existence of both God and the devil is conclusively established by the scriptures and by human experience" (in Conference Report, Apr. 1971, 22; or *Ensign,* June 1971, 35).

2 Nephi 28:28–30. "Wo Be unto Him That Shall Say . . . We Have Enough" Scripture

• Nephi indicated that when the Book of Mormon goes forth to confound the false doctrines and philosophies mentioned in 2 Nephi 28, many people would be "angry because of the truth of God" and will say "we need no more of the word of God, for we have enough!" (vv. 28–29). Making such a claim seals the heavens, discounts the need for living prophets, and denies the power of the Holy Ghost. Nephi warned those who nurture this attitude: "From them shall be taken away even that which they have" (v. 30).

Greg K. Olsen, © 1990 IRI

The Prophet Joseph Smith (1805–44) explained the shortcomings of the Bible: "Much instruction has been given to man since the beginning which we do not possess now. . . . Some of our friends . . . are bold to say that we have everything written in the Bible which God ever spoke to man since the world began. . . . Does it remain for a people who never had faith enough to call down one scrap of revelation from heaven, and for all they have now are indebted to the faith of another people who lived hundreds and thousands of years before them, does it remain for them to say how much God has spoken and how much he has not spoken? . . . It is nowhere said in that volume by the mouth of God, that He would not, after giving, what is there contained, speak again" (*History of the Church,* 2:18).

• To say that the Lord "cannot speak" today as in days past would be to put limitations on God. President James E. Faust explained the need for modern revelation: "Does God love us less than those led by the ancient prophets? Do we need his guidance and instruction less? Reason suggests that this cannot be. Does he not care? Has he lost his voice? Has he gone on a permanent vacation? Does he sleep? The unreasonableness of each of these proposals is

self-evident" (in Conference Report, Apr. 1980, 16; or *Ensign,* May 1980, 13).

2 Nephi 29:2. The Book of Mormon "Shall Hiss Forth"

• President Ezra Taft Benson proclaimed the need for members of the Church to actively declare the truths of the Restoration. By so doing, we become the "hissers" spoken of in 2 Nephi 29:2–3:

"Our main task is to declare the gospel and do it effectively. We are not obligated to answer every objection. Every man eventually is backed up to the wall of faith, and there he must make his stand. . . .

"The Book of Mormon is to be used 'for a standard unto my people, which are of the house of Israel,' the Lord says, and its words 'shall hiss forth unto the ends of the earth.' (2 Ne. 29:2.) We, the members of the Church, and particularly the missionaries, have to be the 'hissers,' or the tellers and testifiers, of the Book of Mormon unto the ends of the earth.

"The Book of Mormon is the great standard we are to use. . . . The Book of Mormon is the great finder of the golden contact. It does not contain things which are 'pleasing unto the world' (1 Ne. 6:5). . . . It is a great sieve" (in Conference Report, Apr. 1975, 95–96; or *Ensign,* May 1975, 65).

• President Gordon B. Hinckley shared the following example of how the Book of Mormon changed a life forever:

"[The Book of Mormon] has touched for good the lives of millions who have prayerfully read it and pondered its language. May I tell you of one such I recently met in Europe.

"He was a businessman, successful in his undertakings. In the course of his travels he met two of our missionaries. They tried to set up an appointment to teach him. He put them off but finally agreed to listen. He somewhat perfunctorily accepted what they had to say. He became convinced in his mind that they spoke the truth, but he was not moved in his heart.

"He decided that he would read the Book of Mormon. He said that he had been a man of the world, never given to crying. But as he read the book, tears coursed his cheeks. It did something to him. He read it again and felt the same emotions. What had been conversion of the mind became conversion of the heart.

"His way of life was altered, his perspective changed. He threw himself into the work of the Lord. Today he fills a high and holy calling in the cause he has come to love" (in Conference Report, Oct. 1990, 70; or *Ensign,* Nov. 1990, 52).

• Refer to the chart "The Stick of Judah and the Stick of Joseph" in the appendix (p. 412).

2 Nephi 29:3. The Coming Forth of Additional Scripture

• Satan seeks to discredit the Book of Mormon by getting people to reject it on the grounds that all truth is contained in the Bible alone. Elder Bruce R. McConkie (1915–85) of the Quorum of the Twelve Apostles commented on those who reject the Book of Mormon: "Strange as it may seem to present day enemies of the truth, their very opposition to the receipt of more of the word of the Lord by way of the Book of Mormon is one of the signs of the times. Their opposition, summarized in the canting chant, 'A Bible! A Bible! We have got a Bible, and there cannot be any more Bible,' brings forth this severe rebuke from the Lord: 'Thou fool, that shall say: A Bible, we have got a Bible, and we need no more Bible. . . . Wherefore murmur ye, because that ye shall receive more of my word?' (2 Ne. 29.)" (*Mormon Doctrine,* 2nd ed. [1966], 719).

2 NEPHI 29:6–9
What do we learn about Father in Heaven and His purposes?

2 Nephi 29:7–14. The Testimony of Two Nations

• President Joseph Fielding Smith (1876–1972) identified the two nations referred to in 2 Nephi 29:7–8:

"This was spoken by prophecy to the gentiles of the present day. It should be remembered also, that the law given to Israel was that 'the testimony of two men is

true,' providing they are honorable witnesses. Here the Lord applies the law to nations. Why should it not be so?

Grant Heaton, © 1986 IRI

"If the word of the Lord is to be established by two chosen witnesses, then we may well look for two chosen nations to stand as witnesses for Jesus Christ. One such nation was Israel in Palestine, the other was Israel in America, Judah speaking from the Old World and Joseph from the New. Today these two testimonies for God and his truth have run together" (*Doctrines of Salvation,* comp. Bruce R. McConkie, 3 vols. [1954–56], 1:278).

2 Nephi 29:12–13. Additional Records Yet to Come Forth

• Elder Neal A. Maxwell testified that other records yet to come forth will testify of Jesus Christ: "Lost books are among the treasures yet to come forth. Over twenty of these are mentioned in the existing scriptures. Perhaps most startling and voluminous will be the records of the lost tribes of Israel (see 2 Nephi 29:13). We would not even know of the impending third witness for Christ except through the precious Book of Mormon, the second witness for Christ! This third set of sacred records will thus complete a triad of truth. Then, just as the Perfect Shepherd has said, 'My word also shall be gathered in one' (v. 14). There will be 'one fold and one shepherd' (1 Nephi 22:25) in a welding together of all the Christian dispensations of human history (see D&C 128:18)" (in Conference Report, Oct. 1986, 70; or *Ensign,* Nov. 1986, 52).

• The coming together of sacred records is a major theme of the Book of Mormon. This concept is taught in 2 Nephi 29:12–13. Later examples in the Book of Mormon include King Limhi and Ammon returning with the Jaredite record (see Mosiah 28:12, 14), King Limhi and Ammon returning with their own records (see Mosiah 7:1–2, 17–33; 8:1, 3–4), and Alma's colony returning with their records (see Mosiah 22:16; 25:1–6).

2 Nephi 30:7–8. "Jews . . . Shall Begin to Believe in Christ"

• Elder Bruce R. McConkie discussed the prophesied conversion of the Jews following the Second Coming of Jesus Christ:

"'And it shall come to pass that the Jews which are scattered also shall *begin* to believe in Christ; and they shall begin to gather in upon the face of the land.' (2 Ne. 30:7.) Much of the old Jewish bitterness against Christ has ceased; many now accept him as a great Rabbi, though not the Son of God. A few have accepted him in the full sense, coming into the true Church along with the gathered remnants of Ephraim and his fellows.

"But the great conversion of the Jews, their return to the truth as a nation, is destined to follow the Second Coming of their Messiah.
Those able to abide that day, in their extremity and mourning, will ask: 'What are these wounds in thine hands and in thy feet? Then shall they know that I am the Lord; for I will say unto them: These wounds are the wounds with which  Robert Barrett, © IRI I was wounded in the house of my friends. I am he who was lifted up. I am Jesus that was crucified. I am

the Son of God.' (D. & C. 45:51–52; Zech. 12:8–14; 13:6.)" (*Mormon Doctrine*, 722–23).

> **2 NEPHI 30:11–18**
> *What are some of the conditions of the Millennium?*

Points to Ponder

• After reading 2 Nephi 28, what false doctrines and teachings of Satan are you now more aware of?

• How has additional scripture increased your knowledge of the doctrines of the restored gospel?

• In what ways does the Book of Mormon testify that the Lord is God over the whole earth?

Suggested Assignments

• List as many false doctrines and beliefs as you can as explained in 2 Nephi 28:2–14. 📖 Counter the false doctrines by listing true doctrines next to them. Identify a scripture reference that affirms each true doctrine.

• Explain in a family home evening setting what is wrong with the claim of accepting the Bible as the word of God while rejecting the Book of Mormon.

Introduction

Nephi's final writings encompass what he defined as "the doctrine of Christ" (2 Nephi 31:2, 21; 32:6). Elder Jeffrey R. Holland of the Quorum of the Twelve Apostles explained:

"In the Book of Mormon, 'the doctrine of Christ' is simple and direct. It focuses on the first principles of the gospel exclusively, including an expression of encouragement to endure, to persist, to press on. Indeed, it is in the clarity and simplicity of 'the doctrine of Christ' that its impact is found. . . .

". . . The doctrine of Christ is not complicated. It is profoundly, beautifully, single-mindedly clear and complete" (*Christ and the New Covenant* [1997], 49–50, 56).

Strive to focus your life upon the simple but profound aspects of the doctrine of Christ that will bring you the companionship and guidance of the Holy Ghost and eternal happiness and joy.

Commentary

2 Nephi 31:2. "The Doctrine of Christ"

• Elder Jeffrey R. Holland explained the meaning of "the doctrine of Christ" as used in 2 Nephi 31: "Although a phrase like 'the doctrine of Christ' could appropriately be used to describe any or all of the Master's teachings, nevertheless those magnificently broad and beautiful expressions spread throughout the Book of Mormon, New Testament, and latter-day scriptures might more properly be called 'the *doctrines* of Christ.' Note that the phrase Nephi used is distinctly singular. In Nephi's concluding testimony, and later in the Savior's own declaration to the Nephites at his appearance to them, the emphasis is on a precise, focused, singular sense of Christ's doctrine, specifically that which the Prophet Joseph Smith declared to be 'the first principles and ordinances of the Gospel'" (*Christ and the New Covenant*, 49).

2 Nephi 31:4–10. "He Having Set the Example Before Them"

• While mankind must be baptized for the remission of sins, the Savior, who was holy and without sin, was baptized as an example of humility and obedience.

Elder Robert D. Hales of the Quorum of the Twelve Apostles explained that by being baptized, Jesus Christ provided an example for all people to follow in His footsteps:

"Entering into the kingdom of God is so important that Jesus was baptized to show us 'the straitness of the path, and the narrowness of the gate, by which [we] should enter' (2 Nephi 31:9). . . .

"Born of a mortal mother, Jesus was baptized to fulfill His Father's commandment that sons and daughters of God should be baptized. He set the example for all of us to humble ourselves before our Heavenly Father. We are all welcome to come into the waters of baptism. He was baptized to witness to His Father that He would be obedient in keeping His commandments. He was baptized to show us that we should receive the gift of the Holy Ghost (see 2 Nephi 31:4–9).

"As we follow the example of Jesus, we, too, demonstrate that we will repent and be obedient in keeping the commandments of our Father in Heaven. We humble ourselves with a broken heart and a contrite spirit as we recognize our sins and seek forgiveness of our trespasses (see 3 Nephi 9:20). We covenant that we are willing to take upon ourselves the name of Jesus Christ and always remember Him" (in Conference Report, Oct. 2000, 5; or *Ensign,* Nov. 2000, 7–8).

> **2 NEPHI 31:6–10**
> *What must we do to fulfill the Savior's commandment to follow Him?*

2 Nephi 31:13. "Full Purpose of Heart, Acting No Hypocrisy"

• "Full purpose of heart" suggests a total commitment to Jesus Christ, with pure and sincere motives, rather than only pretending to follow the Lord. President Marion G. Romney (1897–1988) of the First Presidency observed such hypocrisy: "There are individuals who try to serve the Lord without offending the devil" ("The Price of Peace," *Ensign,* Oct. 1983, 6).

• Elder Joseph B. Wirthlin (1917–2008) of the Quorum of the Twelve Apostles emphasized the importance of sincerely following the Lord:

"Do we, indeed, actually live the gospel, or do we just *manifest* the appearance of righteousness so that those around us *assume* we are faithful when, in reality, our hearts and unseen actions are *not* true to the Lord's teachings?

"Do we take on only the 'form of godliness' while denying the 'power thereof'? [Joseph Smith—History 1:19].

"Are we righteous in fact, or do we feign obedience only when we think others are watching?

"The Lord has made it clear that He will not be fooled by appearances, and He has warned us not to be false to Him or to others. He has cautioned us to be wary of those who project a false front, who put on a bright pretense that hides a darker reality. We know that the Lord 'looketh on the heart' and *not* on the 'outward appearance' [1 Samuel 16:7]" (in Conference Report, Apr. 1997, 17–18; or *Ensign,* May 1997, 15–16).

2 Nephi 31:13–14, 17. "The Baptism of Fire"

• Jesus Christ taught that all people must be baptized of water and also of the Spirit (see John 3:5). Baptism by water must be followed by baptism of the Spirit, which is sometimes referred to as the baptism of fire. President Marion G. Romney taught: "The importance of receiving the gift of the Holy Ghost is beyond expression. It is the baptism of fire referred to by John. (See Luke 3:16.) It is the 'spirit' birth of which Jesus spoke to Nicodemus [John 3:5]" (in Conference Report, Apr. 1974, 134; or *Ensign,* May 1974, 92).

• Elder David A. Bednar of the Quorum of the Twelve Apostles clarified that being confirmed does not mean that person has received the baptism of the Spirit:

"Following our baptism, each of us had hands placed upon our head by those with priesthood authority and was confirmed a member of The Church of Jesus Christ of Latter-day Saints, and the Holy Ghost was conferred upon us (see D&C 49:14). The statement 'receive the Holy Ghost' in our confirmation was a directive to strive for the baptism of the Spirit.

"The Prophet Joseph Smith taught: 'You might as well baptize a bag of sand as a man, if not done in view of the remission of sins and getting of the Holy Ghost. Baptism by water is but half a baptism, and is good for nothing without the other half—that is, the baptism of the Holy Ghost' (*History of the Church,* 5:499). We were baptized by immersion in water for the remission of sins. We must also be baptized by and immersed in the Spirit of the Lord, 'and then cometh a remission of your sins by fire and by the Holy Ghost' (2 Nephi 31:17)" (in Conference Report, Apr. 2006, 29; or *Ensign,* May 2006, 29).

• Elder Lynn A. Mickelsen of the Seventy explained that through the Atonement of the Savior, the baptism of fire brings a cleansing from sin: "Through the Atonement, the Savior, giving Himself as the ransom for our sins, authorizes the Holy Ghost to cleanse us in a baptism of fire. As the Holy Ghost dwells in us, His purifying presence burns out the filthiness of sin. As soon as the commitment is made, the cleansing process begins" (in Conference Report, Oct. 2003, 11; or *Ensign,* Nov. 2003, 12).

2 Nephi 31:15–16. The Voice of the Father

• On one of the rare occasions when the voice of the Father was heard, He testified: "Yea, the words of my Beloved are true and faithful. He that endureth to the end, the same shall be saved" (2 Nephi 31:15). He later said that those who endure to the end "shall have eternal life" (v. 20). These sacred words that Nephi heard from the Father illustrate that one of the most significant promises of the gospel is that those who endure "to the end will [receive] eternal life" (3 Nephi 15:9).

2 Nephi 31:15–16. "Endure to the End"

• The term "endure to the end" is frequently used to suggest the need to patiently suffer hardships throughout our lives. Elder Joseph B. Wirthlin explained that to endure to the end also means to continue in faithfulness to Christ until the end of our lives:

"Enduring to the end is the doctrine of continuing on the path leading to eternal life after one has entered into the path through faith, repentance, baptism, and receiving the Holy Ghost. Enduring to the end requires our whole heart—or, as the Book of Mormon prophet Amaleki taught, we must 'come unto him, and offer [our] whole souls as an offering unto him, and continue in fasting and praying, and endure to the end; and as the Lord liveth [we] will be saved.' [Omni 1:26].

"Enduring to the end means that we have planted our lives firmly on gospel soil, staying in the mainstream of the Church, humbly serving our fellowmen, living Christlike lives, and keeping our covenants. Those who endure are balanced, consistent, humble, constantly improving, and without guile. Their testimonies are not based on worldly reasons—they are based on truth, knowledge, experience, and the Spirit" (in Conference Report, Oct. 2004, 107; or *Ensign,* Nov. 2004, 101).

2 Nephi 31:17–20. Baptism Is the Gate

• President Boyd K. Packer, President of the Quorum of the Twelve Apostles, taught that not only is baptism the entrance to the Church, baptism is also the necessary path to obtain eternal life: "When the Lord was upon the earth He made it very clear that there was one way, and one way only, by which man may be saved. 'I am the way, the truth, and the life: no man cometh unto the Father, but by me.' (John 14:6.) To proceed on that

way, these two things emerge as being very fixed. First, in His name rests the authority to secure the salvation of mankind. 'For there is none other name under heaven given . . . whereby we must be saved.' (Acts 4:12.) And next, there is an essential ordinance—baptism—standing as a gate through which every soul must pass to obtain eternal life" (in Conference Report, Oct. 1975, 145; or *Ensign,* Nov. 1975, 97).

2 Nephi 31:19–20. Press Forward

• Elder David A. Bednar taught that coming unto Christ requires a lifetime of pressing forward in consistent obedience: "Coming unto Christ is not a single event with a fixed point of beginning or ending; rather, it is a process that develops and deepens during a lifetime. As an initial step in the process, we certainly must obtain knowledge and *learn about Jesus* and His life, teachings, and ministry. But truly coming unto Him also requires consistent obedience and striving to *become like Jesus* in our thoughts, motives, communications, and actions. As we 'press forward' (2 Ne. 31:20) on the pathway of discipleship, we can draw near unto the Savior with the expectation that He will draw near unto us; we can seek Him diligently with the hope that we shall find Him; we can ask with confidence that we shall receive; and we can knock anticipating that the door shall be opened unto us (see D&C 88:63)" ("Because We Have Them before Our Eyes," *New Era,* Apr. 2006, 2).

2 Nephi 31:20; 32:3. 📖 "Feast upon the Words of Christ"

• "Feasting upon the word of Christ" (2 Nephi 31:20) compares our willingness to receive the words of Christ with eating a sumptuous meal. Elder Russell M. Nelson of the Quorum of the Twelve Apostles taught that we feast upon Christ's words when we desire and obey them: "To feast means more than to taste. To feast means to savor. We savor the scriptures by studying them in a spirit of delightful discovery and faithful obedience. When we feast upon the words of Christ, they are embedded 'in fleshy tables of the heart' [2 Corinthians 3:3]. They become an integral part of our nature" (in Conference Report, Oct. 2000, 19; or *Ensign,* Nov. 2000, 17).

Where can we find the "word of Christ" to feast upon? President Ezra Taft Benson (1899–1994) clarified: "In Book of Mormon language, we need to 'believe in Christ and deny him not.' (2 Nephi 25:28.) . . . We need to 'come unto Christ, and be perfected in him.' (Moroni 10:32.) . . . We need to come 'feasting upon the word of Christ' (2 Nephi 31:20), as we receive it through His scriptures, His anointed, and His Holy Spirit" (*A Witness and a Warning* [1988], 51).

• Elder Robert D. Hales explained that to feast upon the words of Christ, one must absorb and incorporate His teachings, just as one absorbs and incorporates a meal: "If you and I are to feast upon the words of Christ, we must study the scriptures and absorb His words through pondering them and making them a part of every thought and action" (in Conference Report, Oct. 1998, 16; or *Ensign,* Nov. 1998, 15).

• More recently, Elder Hales spoke of feasting upon the scriptures as the means of hearing the voice of the Lord in our lives:

"If we don't have the word of God or don't cling to and heed the word of God, we will wander off in strange paths and be lost as individuals, as families, and as nations.

"As with voices from the dust, the prophets of the Lord cry out to us on earth today: take hold of the scriptures! Cling to them, walk by them, live by them, rejoice in them, feast on them. Don't nibble. They are 'the power of God unto salvation' [D&C 68:4] that lead us back to our Savior Jesus Christ.

"If the Savior were among us in the flesh today, He would teach us from the scriptures as He taught when He walked upon the earth. . . . His words ring out: 'Search the scriptures; for . . . they are they which testify of me' [John 5:39]—a testimony borne by the Holy Ghost, for 'by the power of the Holy Ghost ye may know the truth of all things' [Moroni 10:5]. . . .

"What a glorious blessing! For when we want to speak to God, we pray. And when we want Him to speak to us, we search the scriptures; for His words are spoken through His prophets. He will then teach us as we listen to the promptings of the Holy Spirit" (in Conference Report, Oct. 2006, 26–27; or *Ensign,* Nov. 2006, 26–27).

2 Nephi 32:2–3. "Speak with the Tongue of Angels"

• After a person has received the Holy Ghost and been baptized by fire, the Holy Ghost inspires them with the ability and the vocabulary to "speak with the tongue of angels" so that they might "shout praises unto the Holy One of Israel" (2 Nephi 31:13). Speaking with the tongue of angels does not necessarily mean that a person would speak in another language.

President Boyd K. Packer explained that we speak with the tongue of angels when we speak by the influence of the Holy Ghost: "Nephi explained that angels speak by the power of the Holy Ghost, and you can speak with the tongue of angels, which simply means that you can speak with the power of the Holy Ghost. It will be quiet. It will be invisible. There will not be a dove. There will not be cloven tongues of fire. But the power will be there" ("The Gift of the Holy Ghost: What Every Member Should Know," *Ensign,* Aug. 2006, 49–50).

2 Nephi 32:5. "All Things What Ye Should Do"

• The Book of Mormon promises that "the words of Christ will tell you all things what ye should do" (2 Nephi 32:5). Elder W. Rolfe Kerr of the Seventy explained that the words of Christ can guide us just as the Liahona guided Lehi's family through the wilderness: "So we see, brethren and sisters, that the words of Christ can be a personal Liahona for each of us, showing us the way. Let us not be slothful because of the easiness of the way. Let us in faith take the words of Christ into our minds and into our hearts as they are recorded in sacred scripture and as they are uttered by living prophets, seers, and revelators. Let us with faith and diligence feast upon the words of Christ, for the words of Christ will be our spiritual Liahona telling us all things what we should do" (in Conference Report, Apr. 2004, 38; or *Ensign,* May 2004, 37).

• President Henry B. Eyring of the First Presidency confirmed the importance and benefits of the presence of the Holy Ghost through regular daily scripture study: "Another simple thing to do, which allows God to give us strength, is to feast on the word of God: read and ponder the standard works of the Church and the words of living prophets. There is a promise of help from God that comes with that daily practice. Faithful study of scriptures brings the Holy Ghost to us" (in Conference Report, Apr. 2004, 16; or *Ensign,* May 2004, 18).

• Elder Spencer J. Condie of the Seventy noted that the scriptures facilitate the companionship of the Holy Ghost when we are faced with important decisions: "You may be facing decisions about a mission, your future career, and, eventually, marriage. As you read the scriptures and pray for direction, you may not actually see the answer in the form of printed words on a page, but as you read you will receive distinct impressions and promptings, and, as promised, the Holy Ghost 'will show unto you all things what ye should do' [2 Nephi 32:5]" (in Conference Report, Apr. 2002, 53; or *Ensign,* May 2002, 45).

2 Nephi 32:8–9. 📖 "Ye Must Pray Always"

• President James E. Faust (1920–2007) of the First Presidency counseled that prayer is a lifeline to God: "When God placed man on the earth, prayer became

the lifeline between mankind and God. Thus, in Adam's generation, men began 'to call upon the name of the Lord' [Genesis 4:26]. Through all generations since that time, prayer has filled a very important human need. Each of us has problems that we cannot solve and weaknesses that we cannot conquer without reaching out through prayer to a higher source of strength. That source is the God of heaven, to whom we pray in the name of Jesus Christ [see 2 Nephi 32:9; 3 Nephi 20:31]. As we pray we should think of our Father in Heaven as possessing all knowledge, understanding, love, and

compassion" (in Conference Report, Apr., 2002, 67; or *Ensign,* May 2002, 59).

2 Nephi 33:1–4. Carried into the Heart

• Elder Dallin H. Oaks of the Quorum of the Twelve Apostles gave an example of carrying the gospel "unto the hearts of the children of men" (2 Nephi 33:1):

"President Hinckley stated an important corollary to the command to teach by the Spirit when he issued this challenge:

"'We must . . . get our teachers to speak out of their hearts rather than out of their books, to communicate their love for the Lord and this precious work, and somehow it will catch fire in the hearts of those they teach' [*Teachings of Gordon B. Hinckley* (1997), 619–20].

"That is our objective—to have love of God and commitment to the gospel of Jesus Christ 'catch fire' in the hearts of those we teach" (in Conference Report, Oct. 1999, 103; or *Ensign,* Nov. 1999, 80).

• Elder David A. Bednar explained that the hearer of the word must also be willing to receive by the Spirit: "Nephi teaches us, 'when a man speaketh by the power of the Holy Ghost the power of the Holy Ghost carrieth [the message] unto the hearts of the children of men' (2 Nephi 33:1). Please notice how the power of the Spirit carries the message *unto* but not necessarily *into* the heart. A teacher can explain, demonstrate, persuade, and testify, and do so with great spiritual power and effectiveness. Ultimately, however, the content of a message and the witness of the Holy Ghost penetrate into the heart only if a receiver allows them to enter" ("Seek Learning by Faith" [an evening with Elder David A. Bednar, Feb. 3, 2006], 1, www.ldsces.org; see also D&C 50:14, 17–20).

> ### *2 NEPHI 33:10–11*
> *Why are the "words of Christ" so important to us? How can you take greater advantage of having His words available to read and ponder?*

2 Nephi 33:11. These Are the Words of Jesus Christ

• President Ezra Taft Benson taught that one of our roles as members of the Church is to declare to others that these are the words of Jesus Christ through His servants: "Our main task is to declare the gospel and do it effectively. We are not obligated to answer every objection. Every man eventually is backed up to the wall of faith, and there he must make his stand. 'And if they are not the words of Christ, judge ye,' said Nephi, 'for Christ will show unto you, with power and great glory, that they are his words, at the last day; and you and I shall stand face to face before his bar; and ye shall know that I have been commanded of him to write these things.' (2 Ne. 33:11.) Every man must judge for himself, knowing God will hold him accountable" (in Conference Report, Apr. 1975, 95–96; or *Ensign,* May 1975, 65).

2 Nephi 33:11. The Judgment Bar

• Nephi said he would meet us at the judgment bar. Interestingly, Jacob and Moroni made very similar comments (see Jacob 6:13; Moroni 10:27).

Points to Ponder

• Why is pressing forward an important part of enduring to the end?

• Nephi counseled that we must "pray always" (2 Nephi 32:9). Given your circumstances in life, how can this best be done?

• What impresses you most with Nephi's final testimony? (see 2 Nephi 33:10–14).

Suggested Assignments

• After reading the commentary in this chapter, evaluate your own habits of personal scripture study and prayer. Do they qualify as feasting upon the words of Christ and as praying always? (see 2 Nephi 32:3, 9). Make the necessary adjustments to your scripture study to bring it more into alignment with Nephi's teachings.

• Prepare a family home evening lesson from 2 Nephi 31–33 on Nephi's exposition of the "doctrine of Christ" (2 Nephi 31:2). Help the members of your family understand what Nephi meant when he said, "This is the way; and there is none other way nor name given under heaven whereby man can be saved in the kingdom of God" (2 Nephi 31:21).

Introduction

Because of pride and exceeding wealth, the Nephites during the time of Jacob succumbed to many sins, particularly the sin of immorality. Feeling the weight of his prophetic calling, Jacob denounced these evil practices and boldly called the people to repentance. When have you witnessed the prophet and other Church leaders speak plainly to share an important message? By understanding the divine mandate of a priesthood leader to give spiritual correction, you will better understand the warning voice of modern-day prophets in an ever-increasingly wicked world.

Note that after teaching the Nephites the consequences of their sins, Jacob turned their attention to the Savior. He taught that we have power to overcome sin and weakness through the grace of Christ. Therefore he asked, "Why not speak of the atonement of Christ . . . ?" By so doing, we gain "knowledge of a resurrection and the world to come" (Jacob 4:12). Then we can develop a greater appreciation for the gift of redemption from sin and death that the Savior provides.

Commentary

Jacob 1:2–8. Jacob's Purpose in Writing

• Notice that Jacob had the same intent that his brother Nephi did as he prepared to continue keeping the record on the small plates. Elder Jeffrey R. Holland of the Quorum of the Twelve Apostles put Jacob's intent into perspective:

"Jacob seems to have been particularly committed to presenting the doctrine of Christ. Given the amount of space he gave to his witness of the Savior's atonement, Jacob clearly considered this basic doctrine the most sacred of teachings and the greatest of revelations.

" 'We . . . had many revelations, and the spirit of much prophecy,' Jacob said, 'wherefore, we knew of Christ and his kingdom, which should come.

" 'Wherefore, we labored diligently among our people, that we might persuade them to come unto Christ. . . .

" 'Wherefore, we would to God . . . that all men would believe in Christ, and view his death, and suffer his cross and bear the shame of the world.' [Jacob 1:6–8].

"No prophet in the Book of Mormon, by temperament or personal testimony, seems to have gone about that work of persuasion any more faithfully than did Jacob. He scorned the praise of the world, he taught straight, solid, even painful doctrine, and he knew the Lord personally. His is a classic Book of Mormon example of a young man's decision to suffer the cross and bear the shame of the world in defense of the name of Christ. Life, including those difficult early years when he saw the wickedness of Laman and Lemuel bring his father and mother down to their graves in grief, was never easy for this firstborn in the wilderness" (*Christ and the New Covenant* [1997], 62–63).

Jacob 1:9–19. Nephi and the Reign of the Nephite Kings

• After Nephi separated from his brethren, who later became known as Lamanites (see 2 Nephi 5), he established a kingdom among his people, and they came to be known as Nephites. Although reluctant, Nephi became the first king (see 2 Nephi 5:18–19). Nephi referred to his time as a king-leader as "my reign" (1 Nephi 10:1). The second king and the other kings who succeeded him were all referred to as Nephi (see Jacob 1:11–15). The record of the kings and the secular history was primarily kept in the large plates of Nephi (see Jarom 1:14; Omni 1:11; Words of Mormon 1:10).

Major Leaders during Nephite History—600 B.C. to A.D. 421

Year-Reign of Judges	Christian Year	King, Chief Judge, or Governor	Historical or Church Leader	Military Leader
	600 B.C.	Nephi (2 Nephi 5:18–19)	Nephi (1 Nephi 1:1–3; 19:1–4)	Nephi (2 Nephi 5:14; Jacob 1:10)
	544 B.C.	Others designated (Jacob 1:9)	Jacob (2 Nephi 5:26; Jacob 1:1–4, 17–18)	
	544–420 B.C.		Enos and many prophets (Enos 1:22, 26)	
	399 B.C.	"Mighty men in the faith of the Lord" (Jarom 1:7)	Jarom and the prophets of the Lord (Jarom 1:1, 10–11)	"Mighty men in the faith of the Lord" (Jarom 1:7)
	361 B.C.		Omni (Omni 1:1–3)	
	317 B.C.		Amaron (Omni 1:4–8) Chemish (Omni 1:9)	
	279–130 B.C.	Mosiah¹ (Omni 1:12–23) Benjamin (Omni 1:23–25; Words of Mormon)	Abinadom (Omni 1:10–11) Amaleki (Omni 1:12) Benjamin with the holy prophets (Words of Mormon 1:16–18; Mosiah 1–6)	Mosiah¹ (Omni 1:12–23) Benjamin (Omni 1:23–25)
	124 B.C.	Mosiah² (Mosiah 1:15)	Mosiah² (Mosiah 6:3)	
	122 B.C.		Alma¹ (Mosiah 25:19; 26:28)	
1	91 B.C.	Alma² (Mosiah 29:44)	Alma² (Mosiah 29:42)	Alma² (Alma 2:16)
9	83 B.C.	Nephihah (Alma 4:17, 20)		
18	74 B.C.			Moroni (Alma 43:17)
19	73 B.C.		Helaman¹ (Alma 37:1; 45:20–23)	
24	68–67 B.C.	Pahoran (Alma 50:39–40)		
32	60 B.C.			Moronihah (Alma 62:43)
36	56 B.C.		Shiblon (Alma 63:1)	
39	53 B.C.		Helaman² (Alma 63:11)	
40	52 B.C.	Pahoran² (Helaman 1:1, 5) and Pacumeni (Helaman 1:13)		
42	50 B.C.	Helaman² (Helaman 2:1–2)		
53	39 B.C.	Nephi¹ (Helaman 3:37)	Nephi¹ (Helaman 3:37)	

Year-Reign of Judges	Christian Year	King, Chief Judge, or Governor	Historical or Church Leader	Military Leader
62	30 B.C.	Cezoram (Helaman 4:18; 5:1)		Last reference to Moronihah (Helaman 4:18)
66	26 B.C.	Cezoram's son (Helaman 6:15)		
?	?	Seezoram (Helaman 6:39; 9:23)		
92	A.D. 1	Lachoneus[1] (3 Nephi 1:1)	Nephi[2] (3 Nephi 1:1–2)	
	A.D. 16			Gidgiddoni (3 Nephi 3:18)
	A.D. 30	Lachoneus[2] (3 Nephi 6:19)		
	?		Nephi[3] (?) (Superscription to 4 Nephi)	
	A.D. 110		Amos[1] (4 Nephi 1:19–20)	
	A.D. 194		Amos[2] (4 Nephi 1:21)	
	A.D. 305		Ammaron (4 Nephi 1:47)	
	c. A.D. 321–335		Mormon (Mormon 1:1–3)	
	A.D. 326			Mormon (Mormon 2:2)
	A.D. 385		Moroni (Mormon 6:6)	

Jacob 1:15. What Is a *Concubine?*

• *Concubines* in the Old Testament "were considered to be *secondary wives,* that is, wives who did not have the same standing in the caste system then prevailing as did those wives who were not called concubines" (Bruce R. McConkie, *Mormon Doctrine,* 2nd ed. [1966], 154). Concubines had full protection as wives and did not violate the law of chastity when the marriages were approved by the Lord (see D&C 132:34–43). During the time period of the Book of Mormon, however, concubines were not approved by the Lord (see Jacob 2:27; Mosiah 11:2).

Jacob 1:18. "Consecrated Priests and Teachers"

• President Joseph Fielding Smith (1876–1972) defined the kind of priests and teachers that were referred to in Jacob 1:18: "The Nephites officiated by virtue of the Melchizedek Priesthood from the days of Lehi to the days of the appearance of our Savior among them.

It is true that Nephi 'consecrated Jacob and Joseph' that they should be priests and teachers over the land of the Nephites, but the fact that plural terms *priests and teachers* were used indicates that this was not a reference to the definite office in the priesthood in either case, but it was a general assignment to teach, direct, and admonish the people" (*Answers to Gospel Questions,* comp. Joseph Fielding Smith Jr., 5 vols. [1957–66], 1:124).

Jacob 1:19. "We Did Magnify Our Office unto the Lord"

• While discussing the duty of priesthood holders to serve others, President Thomas S. Monson explained:

"What does it mean to magnify a calling? It means to build it up in dignity and importance, to make it honorable and commendable in the eyes of all men, to enlarge and strengthen it, to let the light of heaven shine through it to the view of other men.

"And how does one magnify a calling? Simply by performing the service that pertains to it. An elder magnifies the ordained calling of an elder by learning what his duties as an elder are and then by doing them. As with an elder, so with a deacon, a teacher, a priest, a bishop, and each who holds office in the priesthood" (in Conference Report, Apr. 2005, 59; or *Ensign,* May 2005, 54).

Jacob 1:19; 2:2. "Answering the Sins of the People upon Our Own Heads"

• Individuals who have a responsibility to lead in the Church shoulder a sobering responsibility. Jacob taught that when a leader neglects to teach the word of God to those whom he is called to lead, he becomes partly responsible for their sins. President Hugh B. Brown (1883–1975) of the First Presidency elaborated on the responsibility Jacob described:

"President John Taylor said on one occasion, speaking to the brethren of the priesthood, 'If you do not magnify your callings, God will hold you responsible for those you might have saved, had you done your duty.'

"This is a challenging statement. If I by reason of sins of commission or omission lose what I might have had in the hereafter, I myself must suffer and, doubtless, my loved ones with me. But if I fail in my assignment as a bishop, a stake president, a mission president, or one of the General Authorities of the Church—if any of us fail to teach, lead, direct, and help to save those under our direction and within our jurisdiction, then the Lord will hold us responsible if they are lost as the result of our failure" (in Conference Report, Oct. 1962, 84).

Jacob 2:8–10. Admonish "According to the Strict Commands of God"

• Rather than teach "the word which healeth the wounded soul" (Jacob 2:8) or speak "the pleasing word of God" (v. 9), Jacob felt compelled by the Lord to address a subject that, regretfully, would "enlarge the wounds of those who [were] already wounded" (v. 9). Sometimes blunt and challenging words are necessary when a priesthood leader cries repentance to Church members.

Elder Jeffrey R. Holland of the Quorum of the Twelve Apostles described the challenging balance of teaching the truth both sensitively and boldly:

"Jacob spends much of ten full verses apologizing, in effect, for the sins he must address and the language he must use in addressing them. He notes that he does so with 'soberness,' being 'weighed down with much more desire and anxiety for the welfare of [his hearers'] souls' (Jacob 2:2–3). Knowing him as we do, we would be surprised if he had said otherwise.

"Listen to the mournful tone of these passages— literally the grief of them—as he single-mindedly pursues what he has always been single-minded about—steadfast loyalty to God and His commandments.

"'Yea, it grieveth my soul and causeth me to shrink with shame before the presence of my Maker, that I must testify unto you concerning the wickedness of your hearts. . . .

"'Wherefore, it burdeneth my soul that I should be constrained, because of the strict commandment which I have received from God, to admonish you according to your crimes, to enlarge the wounds of those who are already wounded, instead of consoling and healing their wounds; and those who have not been wounded, instead of feasting upon the pleasing word of God have daggers placed to pierce their souls and wound their delicate minds.' (Jacob 2:6–7, 9.)

"We are not even into the discourse per se before we sense that, quite literally, this bold and unyielding manner of preaching is almost as hard on Jacob as it is on the guilty ones in his audience. But perhaps that is as it should be always, and why Christ in his preaching was ofttimes 'a man of sorrows.' The commandments have to be kept, sin has to be rebuked. But even such bold positions must be taken compassionately. Even the sternest of prophets must preach from the depths of a sensitive soul" ("Jacob the Unshakable," in *Heroes from the Book of Mormon* [1995], 39–40).

• Elder Dallin H. Oaks of the Quorum of the Twelve Apostles taught that when priesthood leaders feel "constrained" by the Spirit to give admonitions and warnings, members of the Church have a responsibility to act upon the correction and instruction given to them:

"Last week I was talking with a member of the Quorum of the Twelve about comments we had received on our April conference talks. My friend said someone told him, 'I surely enjoyed your talk.' We agreed that this is not the kind of comment we like to receive. As my friend said, 'I didn't give that talk to be *enjoyed*. What does he think I am, some kind of entertainer?' Another member of our quorum joined the conversation by saying, 'That reminds me of the story of a good minister. When a parishioner said, "I surely enjoyed your sermon today," the minister replied, "In that case, you didn't understand it." '

"You may remember that this April conference I spoke on pornography. No one told me they 'enjoyed' that talk—not one! In fact, there was nothing enjoyable in it even for me.

"I speak of these recent conversations to teach the principle that a message given by a General Authority at a general conference—a message prepared under the influence of the Spirit to further the work of the Lord—is not given to be enjoyed. It is given to inspire, to edify, to challenge, or to correct. It is given to be heard under the influence of the Spirit of the Lord, with the intended result that the listener learns from the talk and from the Spirit what he or she should *do* about it" ("The Dedication of a Lifetime" [CES fireside for young adults, May 1, 2005], 1, www.ldsces.org).

Jacob 2:12–19. "Before Ye Seek for Riches"

• Jacob taught that God does not condemn the wealthy for their riches. Instead, any condemnation comes from their pride or misuse of their abundance (see Jacob 2:13–14). Some of the people of Nephi chose riches rather than God as the center of their lives. Their search for wealth led them to persecute their brethren rather than assist them (see vv. 18–19).

• President David O. McKay (1873–1970) counseled us to be cautious regarding that which we seek. Though we may obtain almost anything we work for, it may come at a high price: "What seek ye first? What do you cherish as the dominant, the uppermost thought in your mind? What this is will largely determine your destiny. . . . You may win in this world almost anything for which you strive. If you work for wealth, you can get it, but before you make it an end in itself, take a look at those men who have sacrificed all to the accomplishment of this purpose, at those who have desired wealth for the sake of wealth itself. Gold does not corrupt man; it is in the motive of acquiring that gold that corruption occurs" (*Treasures of Life* [1962], 174–75).

• President Boyd K. Packer, President of the Quorum of the Twelve Apostles, provided additional instruction concerning the pursuits of life:

"We want our children and their children to know that the choice of life is not between fame and obscurity, nor is the choice between wealth and poverty. The choice is between good and evil, and that is a very different matter indeed.

"When we finally understand this lesson, thereafter our happiness will not be determined by material things. We may be happy without them or successful in spite of them.

"Wealth and prominence do not always come from having earned them. Our worth is not measured by renown or by what we own. . . .

"Our lives are made up of thousands of everyday choices. Over the years these little choices will be bundled together and show clearly what we value.

"The crucial test of life, I repeat, does not center in the choice between fame and obscurity, nor between wealth and poverty. The greatest decision of life is between good and evil" (in Conference Report, Oct. 1980, 28–29; or *Ensign,* Nov. 1980, 21).

Jacob 2:17. "Free with Your Substance"

• In The Church of Jesus Christ of Latter-day Saints, fast offerings assist the poor and needy. Church leaders encourage members to be generous with their offerings. Elder Joseph B. Wirthlin (1917–2008) of the Quorum of the Twelve Apostles provided counsel regarding how much to contribute:

"How much should we pay in fast offerings? My brothers and sisters, the measure of our offering to bless the poor is a measure of our gratitude to our Heavenly Father. Will we, who have been blessed so abundantly, turn our backs on those who need our help? Paying a generous fast offering is a measure of our willingness to consecrate ourselves to relieve the suffering of others.

"Brother Marion G. Romney, who was the bishop of our ward when I was called on a mission and who later served as a member of the First Presidency of the Church, admonished:

"'Be liberal in your giving, that you yourselves may grow. Don't give just for the benefit of the poor, but give for your own welfare. Give enough so that you can give yourself into the kingdom of God through consecrating of your means and your time' (*Ensign,* July 1982, 4)" (in Conference Report, Apr. 2001, 97; or *Ensign,* May 2001, 75).

Jacob 2:20–22. "Proud in Your Hearts"

• Pride is sometimes called the great sin of the spirit; it was Satan's sin in the premortal realm (see Isaiah 14:12–14; Moses 4:1–2). Furthermore, pride leads to failure and destruction as the Lord repeatedly warns us:

"Beware of pride, lest thou shouldst enter into temptation" (D&C 23:1).

"For the hour is nigh and the day soon at hand when the earth is ripe; and all the proud and they that do wickedly shall be as stubble; and I will burn them up,

saith the Lord of Hosts, that wickedness shall not be upon the earth" (D&C 29:9).

"Be not ashamed, neither confounded; but be admonished in all your high-mindedness and pride, for it bringeth a snare upon your souls" (D&C 90:17).

"He that exalteth himself shall be abased, and he that abaseth himself shall be exalted" (D&C 101:42).

> ### *JACOB 2:20–21*
> *What truth does Jacob teach to demonstrate how persecution of others is "abominable unto him who created all flesh"?*

Jacob 2:23–30. Plural Marriage

• Jacob clearly taught that the Lord did not want the Nephites to practice any form of plural marriage. He stated that men were to have only one wife unless the Lord commanded otherwise (see Jacob 2:27–30). In our time President Gordon B. Hinckley (1910–2008) stated the Church's position on plural marriage:

"I wish to state categorically that this Church has nothing whatever to do with those practicing polygamy. They are not members of this Church. Most of them have never been members. They are in violation of the civil law. They know they are in violation of the law. They are subject to its penalties. The Church, of course, has no jurisdiction whatever in this matter.

"If any of our members are found to be practicing plural marriage, they are excommunicated, the most serious penalty the Church can impose. Not only are those so involved in direct violation of the civil law, they are in violation of the law of this Church. An article of our faith is binding upon us. It states, 'We believe in being subject to kings, presidents, rulers, and magistrates, in obeying, honoring, and sustaining the law' (Articles of Faith 1:12). One cannot obey the law and disobey the law at the same time. . . .

"More than a century ago God clearly revealed unto His prophet Wilford Woodruff that the practice of plural marriage should be discontinued, which means that it is now against the law of God. Even in countries where civil or religious law allows polygamy, the Church teaches that marriage must be monogamous and does not accept into its membership those practicing plural marriage" (in Conference Report, Oct. 1998, 92; or *Ensign,* Nov. 1998, 71–72).

Jacob 2:28. Chastity

• Elder Richard G. Scott of the Quorum of the Twelve Apostles clearly defined the law of chastity when he taught: "Any sexual intimacy outside of the bonds of marriage—I mean any intentional contact with the sacred, private parts of another's body, with or without clothing—is a sin and is forbidden by God. It is also a transgression to intentionally stimulate these emotions within your own body" (in Conference Report, Oct. 1994, 51; or *Ensign,* Nov. 1994, 38).

Elder Scott also affirmed the divine sanction of marital intimacy, as well as the divine condemnation of sexual immorality. He warned:

"Those intimate acts are forbidden by the Lord outside the enduring commitment of marriage because they undermine His purposes. Within the sacred covenant of marriage, such relationships are according to His plan. When experienced any other way, they are against His will. They cause serious emotional and spiritual harm. Even though participants do not realize that is happening now, they will later.

"Sexual immorality creates a barrier to the influence of the Holy Spirit with all its uplifting, enlightening, and empowering capabilities. It causes powerful physical and emotional stimulation. In time, that creates an unquenchable appetite that drives the offender to ever more serious sin. It engenders selfishness and can produce aggressive acts such as brutality, abortion,

sexual abuse, and violent crime. Such stimulation can lead to acts of homosexuality, and they are evil and absolutely wrong" (in Conference Report, Oct. 1994, 50–51; or *Ensign,* Nov. 1994, 38).

Jacob 2:31–35. "Many Hearts Died, Pierced with Deep Wounds"

• Many Nephite husbands had broken the hearts of their wives and lost the confidence of their children. Families can be destroyed when the law of chastity is broken. Elder Neal A. Maxwell (1926–2004) of the Quorum of the Twelve Apostles explained how more than just those who participate in the sin are affected by the consequences:

"Unchastity and infidelity bring serious consequences such as the rippling, even haunting effects of illegitimacy and fatherlessness, along with disease and the shredding of families. So many marriages hang by a thread or have already snapped. . . .

"Therefore, the keeping of the seventh commandment is such a vital *shield!* (see Exodus 20:14). By our lowering or losing that shield, the much-needed blessings of heaven are lost. No person or nation can prosper for long without those blessings" (in Conference Report, Oct. 2001, 96; or *Ensign,* Nov. 2001, 78).

JACOB 3:1–2
What blessings did Jacob identify would come to the pure in heart who had been betrayed or afflicted?

Jacob 3:10. Damage Caused by Poor Examples

• Children constantly learn from the examples set by those around them. Unfortunately, an unrighteous example can have a destructive influence on the young. Elder Vaughn J. Featherstone of the Seventy cautioned, "A word to adults and parents: Elder Bruce R. McConkie's father [Oscar Walter McConkie] counseled that when we violate any commandment, however small, our youth may choose to violate a commandment later on in life perhaps 10 times or

100 times worse and justify it on the basis of the small commandment we broke" (in Conference Report, Oct. 1999, 15; or *Ensign,* Nov. 1999, 14).

• Elder Jeffrey R. Holland of the Quorum of the Twelve Apostles admonished parents of the Church to demonstrate personal faith and righteousness to their children:

"I think some parents may not understand that even when they feel secure in their own minds regarding matters of personal testimony, they can nevertheless make that faith too difficult for their children to detect. We can be reasonably active, meeting-going Latter-day Saints, but if we do not live lives of gospel integrity and convey to our children powerful, heartfelt convictions regarding the truthfulness of the Restoration and the divine guidance of the Church from the First Vision to this very hour, then those children may, to our regret but not surprise, turn out *not* to be visibly active, meeting-going Latter-day Saints or sometimes anything close to it.

"Not long ago Sister Holland and I met a fine young man who came in contact with us after he had been roaming around through the occult and sorting through a variety of Eastern religions, all in an attempt to find religious faith. His father, he admitted, believed in nothing whatsoever. But his grandfather, he said, was actually a member of The Church of Jesus Christ of Latter-day Saints. 'But he didn't do much with it,' the young man said. 'He was always pretty cynical about the Church.' From a grandfather who is cynical to a son who is agnostic to a grandson who is now looking desperately for what God had already once given his family! . . .

"To lead a child (or anyone else!), even inadvertently, away from faithfulness, away from loyalty and bedrock belief simply because we want to be clever or independent is license no parent nor any other person has ever been given. . . .

"Live the gospel as conspicuously as you can. Keep the covenants your children know you have made. Give priesthood blessings. And bear your testimony! Don't just assume your children will somehow get the drift of your beliefs on their own" (in Conference Report, Apr. 2003, 91–92; or *Ensign,* May 2003, 86).

Jacob 3:11. "The Second Death"

• The second death is also referred to as spiritual death. The Guide to the Scriptures explains that spiritual death is "separation from God and his influences." The spiritual death or second death Jacob referred to "occurs following the death of the mortal body. Both resurrected beings and the devil and his angels will be judged. Those who have willfully rebelled against the light and truth of the gospel will suffer spiritual death. . . . (Alma 12:16; Hel. 14:16–19; D&C 76:36–38)" (Guide to the Scriptures, "Death, Spiritual").

Jacob 4:5. Worship the Father in the Name of Jesus Christ

• Jacob's writings provide us with an important insight into the law of Moses and the Old Testament. In Jacob 4:5 we learn that the Old Testament prophets prior to Jacob's time knew of both Christ and the Father as distinct individuals and appropriately worshipped the Father in Christ's name. Jacob's words indicate that the law of Moses was far more than simply a law of strict commandments and legal codes, as some  modern scholars claim. The law of Moses testified of Jesus Christ and led the righteous to sanctification through the Atonement of Jesus Christ.

Jacob 4:10. "Seek Not to Counsel the Lord"

• President Marion G. Romney (1897–1988) of the First Presidency explained what it meant to "counsel the Lord": "Now I do not think that many members of the Church consciously urge the persuasions of men or their own counsel instead of heeding the Lord's. However, when we do not keep ourselves advised as to what the counsel of the Lord is, we are prone to substitute our own counsel for His. As a matter of fact, there is nothing else we can do but follow our own counsel when we do not know the Lord's instructions" ("Seek Not to Counsel the Lord," *Ensign,* Aug. 1985, 5).

Jacob 4:14–18. "Looking beyond the Mark"

• While serving in the Seventy, Elder Dean L. Larsen explained that the Israelites in ancient times "got themselves into great difficulty" because they "placed themselves in serious jeopardy in spiritual things because they were unwilling to accept simple, basic principles of truth. They entertained and intrigued themselves with 'things that they could not understand' (Jacob 4:14). They were apparently afflicted with a pseudosophistication and a snobbishness that gave them a false sense of superiority over those who came among them with the Lord's words of plainness. They went beyond the mark of wisdom and prudence, and obviously failed to stay within the circle of fundamental gospel truths, which provide a basis for faith. They must have reveled in speculative and theoretical matters that obscured for them the fundamental spiritual truths. As they became infatuated by these 'things that they could not understand,' their comprehension of and faith in the redeeming role of a true Messiah was lost, and the purpose of life became confused. A study of Israel's history will confirm Jacob's allegations" (in Conference Report, Oct. 1987, 11–12; or *Ensign,* Nov. 1987, 11).

• Elder Neal A. Maxwell explained how "looking beyond the mark" can be avoided today: "This incredible blindness which led to the rejection of those truths spoken by prophets and which prevented the recognition of Jesus for who he was, according to Jacob, came 'by looking beyond the mark.' Those who look beyond plainness, beyond the prophets, beyond Christ, and beyond his simple teachings waited in vain then, as they will wait in vain now. For only the gospel of Jesus Christ teaches us of things as they *really* are and as they *really* will be" ("On Being a Light" [address delivered at the Salt Lake Institute of Religion, Jan. 2, 1974], 1).

JACOB 4:14–15

What did Jacob say happened to the Jews anciently because they "looked beyond the mark"? (see Deuteronomy 32:4; Helaman 5:12).

Points to Ponder

• Jacob mentioned that he received his "errand from the Lord" (Jacob 1:17). What must a person do in order to receive an errand from the Lord?

• Jacob taught that we should treat everyone as a valued child of God (see Jacob 2:21). How can you do this more fully?

• What are some of the consequences, immediate and extended, that come when someone violates the law of chastity? What have you chosen to do so that you will not violate this sacred commandment of God?

• What does it mean to "counsel the Lord" rather than to "take counsel from his hand?" (Jacob 4:10).

Suggested Assignments

• From the following scriptures, make a list of the Lord's counsel concerning financial matters: Jacob 2:12–19; Mosiah 4:16–26. Use the list you have compiled to develop some personal financial guidelines to follow throughout your life.

• After reading Nephi's counsel to Jacob concerning what should be recorded on the small plates in Jacob 1:1–4, make a plan to improve the strength of your personal history.

Introduction

Zenos's allegory of the olive trees reveals God's personal involvement in the history and destiny of the house of Israel (see Jacob 6:4). President Joseph Fielding Smith (1876–1972) encouraged us to ponder the depth of Jacob 5: "The parable of Zenos, recorded by Jacob in chapter five of his book, is one of the greatest parables ever recorded. This parable in and of itself stamps the Book of Mormon with convincing truth. No mortal man, without the inspiration of the Lord, could have written such a parable. It is a pity that too many of those who read the Book of Mormon pass over and slight the truths which it conveys in relation to the history, scattering, and final gathering of Israel" (*Answers to Gospel Questions,* comp. Joseph Fielding Smith Jr., 5 vols. [1957–66], 4:141).

After recording the allegory, Jacob concluded his writings by relating Sherem's attempts to lead the people away from Jesus Christ. Learning how Jacob exposed Sherem's arguments as deceptions from the devil can help you fortify yourself against anti-Christs in our day (see Jacob 7:2–22).

Commentary

Jacob 5. The Allegory of the Olive Trees

• An allegory uses symbolic representations to convey moral or spiritual ideas. These symbols provide additional meaning to the story when studied. The value of the allegory lies in understanding what it represents. Elder Jeffrey R. Holland of the Quorum of the Twelve Apostles presented the principal theme of Zenos's allegory:

"This allegory as recounted by Jacob is from the outset intended to be about Christ. . . .

"Even as the Lord of the vineyard and his workers strive to bolster, prune, purify, and otherwise make productive their trees in what amounts to a one-chapter historical sketch of the scattering and gathering of Israel, the deeper meaning of the Atonement undergirds and overarches their labors. In spite of cuttings and graftings and nourishings that mix and mingle trees in virtually all parts of the vineyard, it is bringing them back to their source that

is the principal theme of this allegory. Returning, repenting, reuniting—at-one-ment—this is the message throughout.

". . . At least fifteen times the Lord of the vineyard expresses a desire to bring the vineyard and its harvest to his 'own self,' and he laments no less than eight times, 'It grieveth me that I should lose this tree.' One student of the allegory says it should take its place beside the parable of the prodigal son, inasmuch as both stories 'make the Lord's mercy so movingly memorable.'

"Clearly this at-one-ment is hard, demanding, and, at times, deeply painful work, as the work of redemption always is. There is digging and dunging. There is watering and nourishing and pruning. And there is always the endless approaches to grafting—all to one saving end, that the trees of the vineyard would 'thrive exceedingly' and become 'one body; . . . the fruits [being] equal,' with the Lord of the vineyard having 'preserved unto himself the . . . fruit.' From all the distant places of sin and alienation in which the children of the Father find themselves, it has always been the work of Christ (and his disciples) in every dispensation to gather them, heal them, and unite them with their Master" (*Christ and the New Covenant* [1997], 165–66).

• For more information on the scattering of Israel, refer to "Brief History of the Scattering of Israel" in the appendix (p. 415). For more information on the gathering of Israel, refer to "The Gathering of Israel" in the appendix (p. 416).

Jacob 5:1. Who Was Zenos?

• Zenos was a Hebrew prophet whose writings appeared on the brass plates but who is not mentioned in the Old Testament. He lived sometime after the prophet Abraham and before the prophet Isaiah (see Helaman 8:19–20). We know he testified concerning the death and redemption of the Son of God (see 1 Nephi 19:10; Alma 8:19). Zenos is most particularly known because of his famous allegory of the olive tree. From this allegory it is clear that he was a prophet and a seer (see Jacob 5).

Jacob 5:3. "I Will Liken Thee, O House of Israel, Like unto a Tame Olive-Tree"

• Cultivating and growing olive trees was common to those who lived in ancient Israel. Elder Jeffrey R. Holland explained why Zenos's use of the olive tree was a powerful symbol of God's love for the house of Israel:

"One writer has said of this extended symbolic portrayal, 'One Jewish legend identifies the tree of life as the olive tree, and with good reason. The olive tree is an evergreen, not a deciduous tree. Its leaves do not seasonally fade nor fall. Through scorching heat and winter cold they are continually rejuvenated. Without cultivation the olive is a wild, unruly, easily corrupted tree. Only after long, patient cultivating, usually eight to ten years, does it begin to yield fruit. Long after that, new shoots often come forth from apparently dead roots. [The appearance of gnarled trunks gives] the impression of travail—of ancient life and renewing life.' [Truman Madsen, "The Olive Press: A Symbol of Christ," in *The Allegory of the Olive Tree,* ed. Stephen D. Ricks and John W. Welch (1994), 2.]

"As Lehi himself taught, no symbol could serve more powerfully and profoundly of God's expansive, constant, redeeming love—including especially the love represented in the gift of his Only Begotten Son—than does the olive tree" (*Christ and the New Covenant,* 163–64).

© Richard Cleave

Jacob 5:3–77. Symbolic Elements in the Allegory of Zenos

• An allegory or a parable should not be stretched too far in an attempt to correlate every item precisely with some symbolic meaning. Certain major elements, however, need to be defined if the parable is to be understood. An overriding principle throughout Zenos's allegory is the Lord's loving care for His people. Additionally, the following items will help you understand the allegory's meaning (see also "Brief History of the Scattering of Israel" in the appendix on p. 415 and "The Gathering of Israel" in the appendix on p. 416).

Symbol	Meaning
The vineyard	The world
Tame olive tree	The house of Israel, the Lord's covenant people
Wild olive tree	Gentiles, or non-Israel (later in the parable, wild branches represent apostate Israel)
Branches	Groups of people
The roots of the tame olive tree	The gospel covenants and promises the Lord makes with His children, a constant source of strength and life to the faithful
Fruit of the tree	The lives or works of men
Digging, pruning, fertilizing	The Lord's work with His children, which seeks to persuade them to be obedient and produce good fruit
Transplanting the branches	Scattering of groups throughout the world, or restoring them to their original position
Grafting	The process of spiritual rebirth through which one is joined to the covenant
Decaying branches	Wickedness and apostasy
Casting the branches into the fire	The judgment of God

The Olive Tree Allegory: Jacob 5

The Scattering of Israel
Before the Time of Christ (vv. 3–14)

Tame olive tree (Israel) is dying (vv. 3–4).

The master prunes and fertilizes; a few new branches grow but the top is still dying (vv. 4–6).

Main branches are removed and wild branches are grafted in; tender branches are hidden (vv. 7–14).

The Time of Christ
(vv. 15–28)

Good fruit (vv. 15–18)

Natural branches are hidden in the nethermost part of the vineyard.

Withered branches are burned (vv. 7, 9).

Wild olive tree (Gentiles; vv. 7, 9).

Poor ground; good fruit (vv. 20–22)

Poorer ground; good fruit (v. 23)

Fruit (this branch is not mentioned again; v. 24)

Good ground; good and bad fruit (v. 25)

God saw the apostasy of ancient Israel. He sent prophets to cry repentance, but few people listened. He allowed the wicked to be destroyed and brought in the Gentiles. A few righteous branches of Israel were scattered around the world.

God saw that Israel (the old root tree) was saved and produced good fruit. The scattered branches of Israel also produced good fruit, except for the Nephites and Lamanites, whose fruit was partly good and partly bad.

The Great Apostasy

(vv. 29–49)

Evil fruit
(vv. 29–37)

Evil fruit
(vv. 39, 46)

Evil fruit
(vv. 39, 46)

Evil fruit only
(vv. 39, 46)

God found that Christianity (the old root tree made up of both Israelites and Gentiles) had become corrupt, but the roots were still good. The natural branches that were scattered were also corrupt.

The Gathering of Israel

The Gospel Goes to All the World
(vv. 50–76)

The Millennium (vv. 76–77)

All trees become as one and bear natural fruit (vv. 74–76).

As the natural branches grow, the wild branches are burned (vv. 57–58, 65–73).

Branches of the scattered trees are grafted back into the original tree (vv. 52–53).

Branches of the original tree are grafted into the scattered trees (vv. 54–56).

When the bad fruit comes again, the good fruit will be gathered out and the vineyard will be burned (v. 77).

God and His servants restore the gospel in its purity. They begin to gather scattered Israel and take the gospel to all the world. As righteousness increases, the wicked are destroyed until no wickedness remains (the Second Coming of Jesus Christ). Righteousness prevails for a long time (the Millennium). When evil again enters the world, God will separate the righteous from the wicked and cleanse the earth by fire.

Jacob 5:8–10. What Does It Mean to Graft Branches?

• In the process of grafting, healthy, living branches are cut from a tree and inserted into the trunk of another tree to grow. The branches in this allegory represent groups of people whom the Lord takes from one place and plants in another. Ultimately, the regrafting in of Israel will include their coming to "the knowledge of the true Messiah" (1 Nephi 10:14).

Jacob 5:23–25. "I Have Planted Another Branch"

• Zenos's allegory helps us understand that the scattering of Israel all over the world was a blessing to Israel and to the rest of Heavenly Father's children. President Joseph Fielding Smith taught: "In that parable the olive tree is the House of Israel. . . . In its native land it began to die. So the Lord took branches like the Nephites, like the lost tribes, and like others that the Lord led off that we do not know anything about, to other parts of the earth. He planted them all over his vineyard, which is the world" (*Answers to Gospel Questions,* 4:204).

President James E. Faust (1920–2007) of the First Presidency explained the purpose of scattering Israel throughout the world: "The scattering of Israel throughout the world sprinkled the blood that believes, so that many nations may now partake of the gospel plan" (in Conference Report, Oct. 1982, 127; or *Ensign,* Nov. 1982, 87).

Jacob 5:41, 47, 49. "What Could I Have Done More for My Vineyard?"

• The Lord asked three times, "What could I have done more for my vineyard?" (Jacob 5:41, 47, 49). Elder Jeffrey R. Holland commented on how this question helps us understand the true nature of God and His unceasing efforts on behalf of His children:

"After digging and dunging, watering and weeding, trimming, pruning, transplanting, and grafting, the great Lord of the vineyard throws down his spade and his pruning shears and weeps, crying out to any who would listen, 'What could I have done more for my vineyard?'

"What an indelible image of God's engagement in our lives! What anguish in a parent when His children do not choose Him nor 'the gospel of God' [Romans 1:1] He sent!" (in Conference Report, Oct. 2003, 74; or *Ensign,* Nov. 2003, 72).

Jacob 5:47–48. Develop Spiritual Roots

• President Spencer W. Kimball (1895–1985) explained why the development of a deep spiritual root system must precede branches and fruit:

"I believe we find a great lesson in this regard in the parable of the vineyard found in the fifth chapter of Jacob in the Book of Mormon. . . .

"'. . . The branches have overcome the roots thereof, *behold they grew faster than the strength of the roots,* taking strength unto themselves. Behold, I say, is not this the cause that the trees of thy vineyard have become corrupted?' (Jacob 5:47–48; italics added).

"It seems that some [Latter-day Saints] among us have this same problem; they want bountiful harvests—both spiritual and temporal—without developing the root system that will yield them. There are far too few who are willing to pay the price, in discipline and work, to cultivate hardy roots. Such cultivation should begin in our youth. Little did I know as a boy that daily chores in the garden, feeding the cattle, carrying the water, chopping the wood, mending fences, and all the labor of a small farm was an important part of sending down roots, before being called on to send out branches. I'm so grateful that my parents understood the relationship between roots and branches. Let us each cultivate deep roots, so that we may secure the desired fruits of our welfare labors" (in Conference Report, Oct. 1978, 113; or *Ensign,* Nov. 1978, 74–75).

Jacob 5:62–75. "Labor with Our Might This Last Time"

• While serving as a member of the Seventy, Elder Dean L. Larsen declared that each of us is part of this final effort to prepare the world for the coming of Jesus Christ:

"[Now] is the period during which the Lord and his servants will make the final great effort to take the message of truth to all the peoples of the earth and to reclaim the descendants of ancient Israel who have lost their true identity.

"The prophet Zenos, whom Jacob quotes in the Book of Mormon, compares this effort to the work of the laborers who prune and nurture a vineyard and gather its fruit for the last time. Zenos likens the Savior to the master of the vineyard, who says to those who are his helpers, 'Wherefore, let us go to and labor with our might this last time, for behold the end draweth nigh, and this is the last time that I shall prune my vineyard' (Jacob 5:62).

"You have come to the earth when the foundation has been laid for this great work. The gospel has been restored for the last time. The Church has been established in almost every part of the world. The stage is set for the final dramatic scenes to be enacted. You will be the principal players. You are among the last laborers in the vineyard. This is the yoke that is set upon your necks. This is the service for which you are chosen" (in Conference Report, Apr. 1983, 47; or *Ensign*, May 1983, 33).

Jacob 6:10. "Lake of Fire and Brimstone"

• The phrase "lake of fire and brimstone" is repeatedly mentioned in the scriptures (Revelation 19:20; 20:10; 2 Nephi 9:16, 19, 26; 28:23; Jacob 3:11; 6:10; Mosiah 3:27; Alma 12:17; 14:14; D&C 76:36). This phrase is generally used to describe either the place that awaits

the unrepentant individual after the Judgment or the mental anguish associated with sin.

In reference to the place that awaits those who are unrepentant, modern revelation states: "[The wicked] shall go away into the lake of fire and brimstone, with the devil and his angels" (D&C 76:36).

In reference to mental anguish, the Prophet Joseph Smith (1805–44) said: "A man is his own tormentor and his own condemner. Hence the saying, They shall go into the lake that burns with fire and brimstone. The torment of disappointment in the mind of man is as exquisite as a lake burning with fire and brimstone" (*History of the Church*, 6:314).

> **JACOB 7:2, 4, 7**
> *What were some of Sherem's arguments and methods? What are modern-day versions of these same arguments and methods?*

Jacob 7:1–23. Sherem, the Anti-Christ

• Jacob 7 introduces the first anti-Christ in the Book of Mormon (see commentary for Alma 30:6 on p. 213). Sherem, like others who followed, used "much power of speech" and flattering words to teach that "there should be no Christ" (Jacob 7:2, 4).

President Ezra Taft Benson (1899–1994) taught that one of the major purposes of the Book of Mormon is to help us discern between truth and error, revealing the motives of individuals like Sherem: "The Book of Mormon exposes the enemies of Christ. It confounds false doctrines and . . . fortifies the humble followers of Christ against the evil designs, strategies, and doctrines of the devil in our day. The type of apostates in the Book of Mormon are similar to the type we have today. God, with his infinite foreknowledge, so molded the Book of Mormon that we might see the error and know how to combat false educational, political, religious, and philosophical concepts of our time" (in Conference Report, Apr. 1975, 94–95; or *Ensign*, May 1975, 64).

Jacob 7:2–4. How to Avoid Being Deceived

• President Ezra Taft Benson shared the following three questions we can ask ourselves to avoid being deceived:

"1. What do the standard works have to say about it? . . .

"The Book of Mormon, Brigham Young said, was written on the tablets of his heart and no doubt helped save him from being deceived. . . .

"2. The second guide is: what do the latter-day Presidents of the Church have to say on the subject—particularly the living President? . . .

"3. The third and final test is the Holy Ghost—the test of the Spirit. . . . This test can only be fully effective if one's channels of communication with God are clean and virtuous and uncluttered with sin. Said Brigham Young:

"'You may know whether you are led right or wrong . . . for every principle God has revealed carries its own convictions of its truth to the human mind. . . .

"'What a pity it would be if we were led by one man to utter destruction!'" (in Conference Report, Oct. 1963, 16–17).

Jacob 7:13. "Show Me a Sign"

• The Lord has said that "an evil and adulterous generation seeketh after a sign" (Matthew 12:39). Those who desire a sign without first exercising faith reveal their spiritual condition.

The Prophet Joseph Smith gave a modern example of this principle: "When I was preaching in Philadelphia, a Quaker called out for a sign. I told him to be still. After the sermon, he again asked for a sign. I told the congregation the man was an adulterer; that a wicked and adulterous generation seeketh after a sign; and that the Lord had said to

me in a revelation, that any man who wanted a sign was an adulterous person. 'It is true,' cried one, 'for I caught him in the very act,' which the man afterwards confessed, when he was baptized" (*History of the Church,* 5:268).

President Joseph F. Smith (1838–1918) explained the weakness of requiring a sign to uphold faith: "Show me Latter-day Saints who have to feed upon miracles, signs and visions in order to keep them steadfast in the Church, and I will show you members of the Church who are not in good standing before God, and who are walking in slippery paths.

It is not by marvelous manifestations unto us that we shall be established in the truth, but it is by humility and faithful obedience to the commandments and laws of God" (in Conference Report, Apr. 1900, 40).

Jacob 7:13–20. Signs Follow Those Who Believe

• The Lord declared, "Faith cometh not by signs, but signs follow those that believe" (D&C 63:9; see also vv. 10–12). Elder Bruce R. McConkie (1915–85) explained that the righteous will have signs in their lives as a result of their faith:

"*Signs flow from faith.* They may incidentally have the effect of strengthening the faith of those who are already spiritually inclined, but *their chief purpose is not to convert people to the truth, but to reward and bless those already converted.* . . .

"Signs are sacred grants of divine favor reserved for the faithful and concerning which the recipients are commanded not to boast" (*Mormon Doctrine,* 2nd ed. [1966], 713–14).

Jacob 7:27. Adieu

• Some have questioned the use of the French word *adieu* in Jacob 7:27. One author explained:

"The choice of words came through the manner of the language of Joseph Smith, so that we might have understanding. This is why words not known in Book of Mormon times are found in the translated text.

"The word *adieu* is defined in a dictionary of Joseph Smith's day as 'a farewell; an expression of kind wishes at the parting of friends' [meaning that I commend you to God]. (Noah Webster, *An American Dictionary of the English Language,* 1828). While the word is of French origin, it had found common usage in early nineteenth century New England" (Edward J. Brandt, "I Have a Question," *Ensign,* Oct. 1985, 17).

Points to Ponder

- What does Zenos's allegory teach concerning God's efforts on behalf of His children?

- President Joseph Fielding Smith said, "Today Latter-day Saints are going to all parts of the world as servants in the vineyard to gather this fruit and lay it in store for the time of the coming of the Master" (*Answers to Gospel Questions,* 4:142). In addition to missionary work, how can you assist the Lord in gathering fruit?

- Why are the tactics Sherem used so successful in today's world? How can you fortify yourself against them?

Suggested Assignments

- Record in your journal gospel principles you have identified in Zenos's allegory (see Jacob 5). Compare them to the gospel principles Jacob emphasized in Jacob 6:3–13.

- Read Alma 30:12–18 and the accompanying commentary for those verses (see p. 214). Compare Korihor's arguments to Sherem's arguments in Jacob 7:2–13. Teach a friend or family member how we can protect ourselves from the deceptions of anti-Christs.

- Review the story under Jacob 7:13 regarding the preacher who demanded a sign from the Prophet Joseph Smith. Read Jacob 7:13–20 and Alma 30:49–59 and compare what Sherem and Korihor experienced for demanding a sign. Read Doctrine and Covenants 63:7–12 and outline why faith does not result from signs.

Introduction

As you study the books of Enos, Jarom, Omni, and Words of Mormon, look for ways you can receive guidance from the Lord as Enos did. The story of Enos demonstrates God's willingness to bless and direct us in response to personal prayer. The account of the Nephites who fled the land of Lehi-Nephi illustrates that God also directs His people through prophetic warnings and counsel. Through personal prayer and by following the prophet, we gain a testimony of the Lord's infinite love and care for us.

© 1999 Scott Snow

Commentary

Enos 1:1. "Nurture and Admonition of the Lord"

• President Ezra Taft Benson (1899–1994) counseled fathers to follow the pattern of teaching modeled by righteous fathers in the Book of Mormon:

"What did the righteous fathers of the Book of Mormon teach their sons? They taught them many things, but the overarching message was 'the great plan of the Eternal God'—the Fall, rebirth, Atonement, Resurrection, Judgment, eternal life. (See Alma 34:9.) Enos said he knew his father was a just man, 'for he taught me in his language, and also in the nurture and admonition of the Lord—and blessed be the name of my God for it' (Enos 1:1).

"Those in the Book of Mormon who were taught nothing concerning the Lord but only concerning worldly knowledge became a cunning and wicked people. (See Mosiah 24:5, 7.)

"All truths are not of the same value. The saving truths of salvation are of greatest worth. These truths the fathers taught plainly, frequently, and fervently. Are we fathers doing likewise?" (in Conference Report, Oct. 1985, 47; or *Ensign,* Nov. 1985, 36).

Enos 1:2. A Wrestle before God

• Enos did not wrestle *with* God. The record states that Enos wrestled *before* God in prayer. Such wrestling is the struggle to find and express one's real desires under the inspiration of the Holy Ghost. Praying in this manner requires that a person eliminate vain, trite, or insincere repetitions and to pour the deepest desires of his or her heart into words. Each phrase becomes an expression of yearning and desire to do

Robert Barrett, © IRI

God's will. Such prayers are assisted and guided by the Holy Spirit, "for we know not what we should pray for as we ought: but the Spirit itself maketh intercession for us with groanings which cannot be uttered" (Romans 8:26).

> **ENOS 1:3–4**
> *What words or phrases demonstrate Enos's sincerity and faith as he called upon God?*

Enos 1:3–15. Preparing to Receive an Answer to Prayer

• Elder Robert D. Hales of the Quorum of the Twelve Apostles spoke of the process Enos went through that increased his faith and prepared him to receive the answer to his prayer:

"First, Enos heard the gospel truths from his father, just as you are hearing them in your families and in this conference.

"Second, he let his father's teachings about 'eternal life, and the joy of the saints' [Enos 1:3] sink deep into his heart.

"Third, he was filled with a desire to know for himself whether these teachings were true and where he himself stood before his Maker. To use Enos's words, 'My soul hungered' [Enos 1:4]. By this intense spiritual appetite, Enos qualified himself to receive the Savior's promise: 'Blessed are all they who do hunger and thirst after righteousness, for they shall be filled with the Holy Ghost' [2 Nephi 12:6].

"Fourth, Enos obeyed the commandments of God, which enabled him to be receptive to the Spirit of the Holy Ghost.

"Fifth, Enos records, 'I kneeled down before my Maker, and I cried unto him in mighty prayer and supplication for mine own soul; and all the day long did I cry unto him; yea, and when the night came I did still raise my voice high that it reached the heavens' [Enos 1:4]. It wasn't easy. Faith did not come quickly. In fact, Enos characterized his experience in prayer as a 'wrestle which [he] had before God' [Enos 1:2]. But faith did come. By the power of the Holy Ghost, he did receive a witness for himself.

"We cannot find Enos-like faith without our own wrestle before God in prayer. I testify that the reward is worth the effort. . . . I promise that if you do these things sincerely and unceasingly, the words Christ spoke to His disciples will be fulfilled in your life: 'Ask, and it shall be given you; seek, and ye shall find; knock, and it shall be opened unto you.' [Matthew 7:7]" (in Conference Report, Oct. 2004, 73–74; or *Ensign,* Nov. 2004, 72).

• Elder Neal A. Maxwell (1926–2004) of the Quorum of the Twelve Apostles compared receiving answers to prayers to the opening of a combination lock. It is a step-by-step process: "Petitioning in prayer has taught me, again and again, that the vault of heaven with all its blessings is to be opened only by a combination lock. One tumbler falls when there is faith, a second when there is personal righteousness; the third and final tumbler falls only when what is sought is, in God's judgment—not ours—right for us. Sometimes we pound on the vault door for something we want very much and wonder why the door does not open. We would be very spoiled children if that vault door opened any more easily than it does. I can tell, looking back, that God truly loves me by inventorying the petitions He has refused to grant me. Our rejected petitions tell us much about ourselves but also much about our flawless Father" ("Insights," *New Era,* Apr. 1978, 6).

Enos 1:5–8. "Enos, Thy Sins Are Forgiven Thee"

• Elder Richard G. Scott of the Quorum of the Twelve Apostles taught how full repentance can cleanse an individual through the Atonement of Jesus Christ: "The Redeemer can settle your individual account with justice

Del Parson, © 2000 IRI

and grant forgiveness through the merciful path of repentance [see Alma 42:15]. Full repentance is absolutely essential for the Atonement to work its complete miracle in your life. By understanding the Atonement, you will see that God is not a jealous being who delights in persecuting those who misstep. He is an absolutely perfect, compassionate, understanding, patient, and forgiving Father" (in Conference Report, Apr. 1995, 101; or *Ensign,* May 1995, 75).

Enos 1:9–14. A Desire for the Welfare of Others

• After feeling the blessings of the Atonement for himself, Enos prayed for the welfare of his own people, the Nephites, and then for the spiritual welfare of his enemies, the Lamanites. Elder Robert D. Hales spoke about the concern those who have been converted feel for others: "The scriptures confirm that the truly converted do more than just forsake the enticements of the world. They love God and their fellowmen. Their minds and hearts are centered on the Savior's atoning sacrifice. From the moment of their respective conversions, Enos, Alma the Younger, Paul, and others turned wholeheartedly to the task of bringing themselves and their fellowmen to God" (in Conference Report, Oct. 2000, 6; or *Ensign,* Nov. 2000, 8). (See also commentary for Mosiah 28:3 on p. 168.)

Enos 1:13–16

What did Enos desire of the Lord in case the Nephites were destroyed? How does this demonstrate his love for his fellowman?

Enos 1:10. "The Voice of the Lord Came into My Mind"

• Revelation or inspiration comes in several ways, including thoughts, impressions, and feelings (see D&C 6:15; 8:2–3). President Boyd K. Packer, President of the Quorum of the Twelve Apostles, discussed how we can recognize the voice of the Lord:

"Answers to prayers come in a quiet way. The scriptures describe that voice of inspiration as a still, small voice. . . .

"I have come to know that inspiration comes more as a feeling than as a sound. . . .

"Put difficult questions in the back of your minds and go about your lives. Ponder and pray quietly and persistently about them.

"The answer may not come as a lightning bolt. It may come as a little inspiration here and a little there, 'line upon line, precept upon precept' (D&C 98:12).

"Some answers will come from reading the scriptures, some from hearing speakers. And, occasionally, when it is important, some will come by very direct and powerful inspiration. The promptings will be clear and unmistakable" (in Conference Report, Oct. 1979, 28, 30; or *Ensign,* Nov. 1979, 19–21).

• The Prophet Joseph Smith (1805–44) shared this explanation of how the Lord communicates with us: "A person may profit by noticing the first intimation of the spirit of revelation; for instance, when you feel pure intelligence flowing into you, it may give you sudden strokes of ideas, so that by noticing it, you may find it fulfilled the same day or soon; (i.e.) those things that were presented unto your minds by the Spirit of God, will come to pass; and thus by learning the Spirit of God and understanding it, you may grow into the

principle of revelation, until you become perfect in Christ Jesus" (*History of the Church,* 3:381).

Enos 1:23; Words of Mormon 1:17. Speaking with Sharpness

• Church leaders must speak out at times with directness and sharpness in warning members of the Church of anything that may jeopardize their salvation. President Spencer W. Kimball (1895–1985) referred to this obligation as he spoke to young adults: "I am sure that Peter and James and Paul found it unpleasant business to constantly be calling people to repentance and warning them of dangers, but they continued unflinchingly. So we, your leaders, must be everlastingly at it; if young people do not understand, then the fault may be partly ours. But, if we make the true way clear to you, then we are blameless" (*Love versus Lust,* Brigham Young University Speeches of the Year [Jan. 5, 1965], 6).

Enos 1:27. "The Place of My Rest"

• Concerning eternal rest, the Prophet Joseph Smith taught: "God has in reserve a time, or period appointed . . . when He will bring all His subjects, who have obeyed His voice and kept His commandments, into His celestial rest. This rest is of such perfection and glory, that man has need of a preparation before he can, according to the laws of that kingdom, enter it and enjoy its blessings. . . . God has given certain laws to the human family, which, if observed, are sufficient to prepare them to inherit this rest" (*History of the Church,* 2:12).

Jarom 1:5. "They Profaned Not; Neither Did They Blaspheme"

• President Gordon B. Hinckley (1910–2008) affirmed the need to keep our words pure:

"I say this to the boys. I say it also to any of you older men who have a similar problem. I do so with love. I know that the Lord is pleased when we use clean and virtuous language, for He has set an example for us. His revelations are couched in words that are affirmative, that are uplifting, that encourage us to do what is right and to go forward in truth and goodness.

"Don't swear. Don't profane. Avoid so-called dirty jokes. Stay away from conversation that is sprinkled with foul and filthy words. You will be happier if you do so, and your example will give strength to others" (in Conference Report, Oct. 1987, 59; or *Ensign,* Nov. 1987, 48).

Jarom 1:11. "Believe in Him to Come as Though He Already Was"

• True prophets, such as Jarom, who lived before Jesus Christ's birth, wrote about His Coming and His Atonement as though it had already happened. King Benjamin said, "The Lord God hath sent his holy prophets among all the children of men, to declare these things to every kindred, nation, and tongue, that thereby whosoever should believe that Christ should come, the same might receive remission of their sins, and rejoice with exceedingly

great joy, *even as though he had already come among them*" (Mosiah 3:13; italics added). Abinadi said, "If Christ had not come into the world, *speaking of things to come as though they had already come,* there could have been no redemption" (Mosiah 16:6; italics added).

Omni 1:12–17. Three Separate Civilizations in the Record

• In this short account, we learn of three groups of people whom the Lord brought to the land of promise in the Western Hemisphere. The first group mentioned was Lehi's colony. The majority of the Book of Mormon relates their story and that of their descendants.

The Book of Mormon also identifies a second group, referred to as the people of Zarahemla, who were descendants of Mulek and who joined the Nephites (see Mosiah 25:2). Mulek, a son of King Zedekiah, left Jerusalem and traveled to the Americas after Babylon destroyed Jerusalem around 587 B.C. (see Omni 1:15). Without a scriptural record, the people of Zarahemla were a living witness of what the Spirit said to Nephi that a whole nation would dwindle

in unbelief (see 1 Nephi 4:13). The Mulekites then joined with the Nephites under the rule of King Mosiah (see Omni 1:19).

The third group was the Jaredites, who came to the land of promise following the time of the "great tower" mentioned in Genesis 11. The original Jaredite colony grew into a great race. Eventually, however, they annihilated themselves in a great civil war sometime between 600 and 300 B.C., leaving only Coriantumr, their last king, and Ether, a prophet of the Lord (see Ether 15:29–34). Ether finished the record, and Coriantumr apparently wandered until he found the people of Zarahemla, where he lived "for the space of nine moons" (Omni 1:21) before dying. Little is known of the Jaredites other than what is recorded by Moroni in the book of Ether.

Omni 1:23–25. King Benjamin Received the Small Plates

• From 1 Nephi through Omni the prophets kept the small plates and the king kept the large plates (see Jarom 1:14). A major shift happened at this point. Amaleki gave the small plates to King Benjamin; the small plates were full at this point (see Omni 1:30). From King Benjamin's time forward, the religious and the historical information were kept on the large plates. The small plates were not added until after 130 B.C. Mosiah through 4 Nephi is Mormon's abridgement of the large plates.

OMNI 1:26

What did Amaleki counsel us to do to be saved?

Omni 1:26. "Offer Your Whole Souls as an Offering unto Him"

• Elder Neal A. Maxwell taught the meaning of offering ourselves to the Lord: "Real, personal sacrifice never was placing an animal on the altar. Instead, it is a willingness to put the animal in us upon the altar and letting it be consumed!" (in Conference Report, Apr. 1995, 91; or *Ensign,* May 1995, 68).

On the same topic, Elder Maxwell later taught: "As you submit your wills to God, you are giving Him the *only* thing you *can* actually give Him that is really yours to give" (in Conference Report, Apr. 2004, 48; or *Ensign,* May 2004, 46).

Words of Mormon. A Bridge between the Small and Large Plates of Nephi

• Among the records the Nephites kept were the small and large plates of Nephi (see 1 Nephi 9:2). The large plates primarily contained the secular history of the people, while the small plates included the sacred history (see 1 Nephi 9:2–4). The books of 1 Nephi through Omni were recorded on the small plates of Nephi. The books of Mosiah through 4 Nephi are Mormon's abridgement taken from the large plates (see commentary for 1 Nephi 9:1–5 on p. 23).

Words of Mormon 1:7. "The Lord Knoweth All Things Which Are to Come"

• Nephi did not make the small plates until 30 years after Lehi's colony left Jerusalem (see 2 Nephi 5:28–31). He did not understand why he was commanded to make a second set of records, but he had faith that it was "for a wise purpose" in the Lord (1 Nephi 9:5). Nearly 1,000 years later the prophet Mormon echoed similar words to Nephi's when he testified that in addition to his abridgment of the large plates of Nephi he was including the small plates of Nephi "for a wise purpose" (Words of Mormon 1:7).

Joseph Smith started the translation of the Book of Mormon with Mormon's abridgment of the large plates of Nephi. He had completed 116 manuscript pages when Martin Harris pleaded with Joseph to let him take the manuscript and show it to family members. Joseph asked God three different times if Martin could take the manuscript, and permission was finally given. The manuscript fell into the hands of wicked men (see

D&C 10:8) and became known as the lost manuscript, or the lost 116 pages.

The loss of the manuscript clearly demonstrates why the Lord commanded Nephi to write the small plates and why Mormon was inspired to include them. Joseph Smith was told not to retranslate the portion he had already completed, but to replace it by translating the small plates of Nephi (see D&C 10:30, 38–45). The translation of the 116 pages covered 600–130 B.C.—from the time of Lehi to the time of King Benjamin. The small plates also covered 600–130 B.C.— from Lehi to King Benjamin. The Lord in His omniscience had the second record, the small plates, cover the exact time period that was covered in the stolen 116 pages. This also allowed the Lord to keep His covenant with Enos that "he would preserve the records" (Enos 1:16).

• Elder Jeffrey R. Holland of the Quorum of the Twelve Apostles affirmed that the portion of the Book of Mormon that comes from the small plates provides more information than was lost on the 116 pages:

"At least six times in the Book of Mormon the phrase 'for a wise purpose' is used in reference to the making, writing, and preserving of the small plates of Nephi (see 1 Nephi 9:5; Words of Mormon 1:7; Alma 37:2, 12, 14, 18). You and I know *the* wise purpose—the most obvious one—was to compensate for the loss of the earlier mentioned 116 pages of manuscript.

"But it strikes me that there is a wiser purpose than that. . . . The key to such a suggestion of a wiser purpose is in verse 45 of Doctrine and Covenants section 10. As the Lord instructs Joseph . . . he says, 'Behold, there are many things engraven upon the [small] plates of Nephi which do throw *greater views* upon my gospel' (emphasis added).

"So, clearly, this was not . . . tit for tat, this for that—you give me 116 pages of manuscript and I'll give you 142 pages of printed text. Not so. We got back more than we lost. And it was known from the beginning that it would be so. It *was* for a wiser purpose. We do not know exactly what we missed in the 116 pages, but we do know that what we received on the small plates was the personal declarations of three great witnesses [Nephi, Jacob, and Isaiah], three of the great doctrinal voices of the Book of Mormon, testifying that Jesus is the Christ. . . .

"In fact, I think you could make a pretty obvious case that the *sole* purpose of the small plates was to give a platform for these three witnesses" ("A Standard unto My People" [Church Educational System symposium on the Book of Mormon, Aug. 9, 1994], 9–10; see LDS.org under gospel library/additional addresses/CES addresses).

• Elder Neal A. Maxwell testified of the foreknowledge of God and how it builds our faith in Him:

"Few doctrines, save those pertaining to the reality of the existence of God, are more basic than the truth that God is omniscient. . . .

". . . God is perfect in the attributes of divinity, and one of these is knowledge: '. . . seeing that without the knowledge of all things, God would not be able to save any portion of his creatures; for it is by reason of the knowledge which he has of all things, from the beginning to the end, that enables him to give that understanding to his creatures by which they are made partakers of eternal life; and if it were not for the idea existing in the minds of men that God had all knowledge it would be impossible for them to exercise faith in him.' (Lecture 4, paragraph 11.) . . .

"God, who knows the beginning from the end, knows, therefore, all that is in between" (*All These Things Shall Give Thee Experience* [1979], 6–7).

Words of Mormon 1:10–11. Amaleki Delivered the Plates to King Benjamin

• The plates that Amaleki gave to King Benjamin were the small plates. The large plates were continually added to and handed down from record keeper to record keeper until A.D. 385, when Mormon received the large plates and abridged them. His abridgement was written on the gold plates or the plates of Mormon.

• To help you gain perspective of the number of pages of the Book of Mormon that are devoted to various time periods, see the chart "Nephite Record Keepers" in the appendix (p. 408).

Points to Ponder

• How is prayer necessary for you to enjoy the blessings of the Atonement?

• The language of the people of Zarahemla had become corrupted because they had no records. How do records and language help us grow spiritually?

• What examples have you seen of the foreknowledge of God demonstrated in the events of your life? (see commentary for Words of Mormon 1:7 on p. 134).

Suggested Assignments

• Briefly write about some of the "wrestling" you have had before God that led to spiritual growth (see commentary for Enos 1:2 on p. 130). Refer to these recorded spiritual events from time to time to refresh your memory of how the Lord has guided you.

• Study and discuss with a friend what "sharp" counsel we have received from modern prophets to warn us of spiritual danger (see commentary for Enos 1:23; Words of Mormon 1:17 on p. 132).

• Using the story of the 116 lost pages as an example, prepare a short lesson that teaches about the omniscience of God and His ability to bring about His purposes.

Introduction

With the assistance of the holy prophets who were among his people, King Benjamin labored "with all the might of his body and the faculty of his whole soul" to "establish peace in the land" (Words of Mormon 1:18). Near the end of his life, Benjamin called the people together at the temple. During this assembly, he reported on his reign as king, appointed his son Mosiah to succeed him, taught concerning Christ's gospel and Atonement, and exhorted the Nephites to take upon themselves the name of Jesus Christ. The portion of Benjamin's address discussed in this chapter of the manual demonstrates the ideals he espoused—willingness to serve others, gratitude for divine providence, and dependence upon the Savior. We can grow in humility and strengthen our covenant relationship with God by living according to the principles King Benjamin taught.

Commentary

• It may be instructive to compare the length of books in the Book of Mormon and the time periods they covered. Refer to the chart "Book of Mormon Pages and Time Periods" in the appendix (p. 411).

Mosiah 1:1–2. Shift from First Person Accounts to Third Person in the Book of Mosiah

• There is a shift from the first person accounts of the early books in the Book of Mormon to the third person account in the book of Mosiah. The books of 1 Nephi through Omni were translated from the small plates of Nephi and are the works of the original writers; consequently, they were written in the first person. The books of Mosiah through 4 Nephi, however, all come from Mormon's abridgement of the large plates of Nephi. These books are Mormon's abridgement of the original authors' records.

Mosiah 1:3–10. Mysteries of God

• The term "mysteries of God" as used in the Book of Mormon (Mosiah 1:3) includes the saving principles of the gospel of Jesus Christ. They are termed mysteries not because they are mysterious or difficult to understand, but because they are revealed from God based upon our faith and obedience. They are intended to lead God's children to eternal life. "A mystery is a truth that cannot be known except through divine revelation—a sacred secret. . . . In our day such great truths as those pertaining to the restoration of the Priesthood, the work for the dead, and the re-establishment of the Church are 'mysteries,' because they could not have been discovered except by revelation" (Hyrum M. Smith and Janne M. Sjodahl, *The Doctrine and Covenants Commentary*, rev. ed. [1972], 141).

MOSIAH 1:4–7
According to King Benjamin, what would have happened to the Nephites if they were without a scriptural record?

Mosiah 1:4–6. "The Language of the Egyptians"

• Benjamin, Nephi (see 1 Nephi 1:2), and Moroni (see Mormon 9:32) all referred to the Egyptian language. In Mosiah 1:4–6, King Benjamin makes it clear there was a reason his sons needed to learn "the language of the Egyptians." It was necessary in order to study the commandments contained on the brass plates and the plates of Nephi (see Mosiah 1:6). From the time of Nephi down to Moroni, the Nephites had a form of the Egyptian language (see commentary for 1 Nephi 1:2 on p. 12 and for Mormon 9:32–34 on p. 359).

Mosiah 1:10. Mosiah to Be the New King

• A close examination of the Book of Mormon reveals numerous traditions and customs that have their origins in ancient Israel. There is a striking similarity between Mosiah's ascendancy to the Nephite throne in the first chapters of Mosiah and how kings were crowned in the Old Testament (see Stephen D. Ricks, "King, Coronation, and Covenant in Mosiah 1–6," in John L. Sorenson and Melvin J. Thorne, ed., *Rediscovering the Book of Mormon* [1991], 209).

Some notable similarities between Book of Mormon and Old Testament coronation ceremonies include: (1) a belief that kings were chosen by heaven (see

Mosiah 1:9–10; 6:3, 5; 1 Kings 2:15; 2 Kings 15:5); (2) the sanctuary as the place of the coronation (see Mosiah 1:18; 1 Kings 1:39–45); (3) bestowal of sacred relics, artifacts, or other objects at the time of coronation (see Mosiah 1:15–16; 2 Kings 11:12); (4) anointing (see Mosiah 6:3; 1 Kings 1:33–34) (see Ricks, in *Rediscovering the Book of Mormon,* 210, 213–14).

"In addition, the ideal was that the new king take office before the death of the old one, and this transfer of power was connected with the ceremony where the people make or renew their covenant with God" (Ricks, in *Rediscovering the Book of Mormon,* 216). This took place a little later with King Benjamin's people when they proclaimed, "we are willing to enter into a covenant with our God to do his will, and to be obedient to his commandments" (Mosiah 5:5).

Mosiah 1:11–12. The Name King Benjamin Wanted to Give His People

• The major purpose for King Benjamin to gather his people together was to give them a name. He wanted to lift them spiritually. He and many other holy prophets had spent years preaching to the people and preparing them to be spiritually ready to take upon them the name of Christ (see Words of Mormon 1:5–18). Throughout his address, King Benjamin spoke of how to worthily accept the name he desired to give them. Then, in Mosiah 5:8–11, he clearly identified the name as being that of Jesus Christ.

MOSIAH 2:9

How could you use King Benjamin's teachings to improve your personal worship?

Mosiah 2:17. 📖 Service

• President Howard W. Hunter (1907–95) taught that righteousness should be at the heart of all service we give: "Continue to seek opportunities for service. Don't be overly concerned with status. . . . It is important to be appreciated. But our focus should be on

righteousness, not recognition; on service, not status. The faithful visiting teacher, who quietly goes about her work month after month, is just as important to the work of the Lord as those who occupy what some see as more prominent positions in the Church. Visibility does not equate to value" ("To the Women of the Church," *Ensign,* Nov. 1992, 96–97).

• Elder Robert J. Whetten of the Seventy explained how the service we render to others can be used to measure the depth of our personal conversion:

"Conversion means consecrating your life to caring for and serving others who need your help and sharing your gifts and blessings. . . .

"Every unselfish act of kindness and service increases your spirituality. God would use you to bless others. Your continued spiritual growth and eternal progress are very much wrapped up in your relationships—in how you treat others. Do you indeed love others and become a blessing in their lives? *Isn't the measure of the level of your conversion how you treat others?* The person who does only those things in the Church that concern himself alone will never reach the goal of perfection. Service to others is what the gospel and exalted life are all about" (in Conference Report, Apr. 2005, 96; or *Ensign,* May 2005, 91).

• Elder Dallin H. Oaks of the Quorum of the Twelve Apostles helped us understand that in addition to what service we do, it is very important why we do it:

"The last motive . . . is, in my opinion, the highest reason of all. In its relationship to service, it is what the scriptures call 'a more excellent way' (1 Corinthians 12:31). . . .

"If our service is to be most efficacious, it must be accomplished for the love of God and the love of his children" (in Conference Report, Oct. 1984, 16; or *Ensign,* Nov. 1984, 14).

Mosiah 2:21–24, 34. "Indebted unto Him"

• Elder Joseph B. Wirthlin (1917–2008) of the Quorum of the Twelve Apostles taught that we should spend all our days in pursuit of eternal life as a means of showing gratitude for the debt Jesus Christ paid on our behalf:

"How can we ever repay the debt we owe to the Savior? He paid a debt He did not owe to free us from a debt we can never pay. Because of Him we will live forever. Because of His infinite Atonement, our sins can be swept away, allowing us to experience the greatest of all the gifts of God: eternal life [see D&C 14:7].

"Can such a gift have a price? Can we ever make compensation for such a gift? The Book of Mormon prophet King Benjamin taught 'that if you should render all the thanks and praise which your whole soul has power to possess . . . [and] serve him with all your whole souls yet ye would be unprofitable servants' [Mosiah 2:20–21]" (in Conference Report, Apr. 2004, 44; or *Ensign,* May 2004, 43).

• One of the best ways for each of us to demonstrate gratitude for what Heavenly Father and Jesus Christ give us is to keep the commandments. President Joseph Fielding Smith (1876–1972) taught:

"We are extremely ungrateful to our Father and to his Beloved Son when in all humility with 'broken hearts and contrite spirits' we are unwilling to keep the commandments. The violation of any divine commandment is a most ungrateful act, considering all that has been accomplished for us through the atonement of our Savior.

"We will never be able to pay the debt. The gratitude of our hearts should be filled to overflowing in love and obedience for his great and tender mercy. For what he has done, we should never fail him. He bought us with a price, the price of his great suffering and the spilling of his blood in sacrifice on the cross.

"Now, he has asked us to keep his commandments. He says they are not grievous, and there are so many of us who are not willing to do it. I am speaking now generally of the people of the earth. We are not willing to do it. That certainly is ingratitude. We are ungrateful.

"Every member of this Church who violates the Sabbath day, who is not honest in the paying of his tithing, who will not keep the Word of Wisdom, who willfully violates any of the other commandments the Lord has given us, is ungrateful to the Son of God, and when ungrateful to the Son of God is ungrateful to the Father who sent him" (*Doctrines of Salvation,* comp. Bruce R. McConkie, 3 vols. [1954–56], 1:131–32).

Mosiah 2:25. Your Body "Belongeth to Him Who Created You"

• Mosiah 2:25 is the Lord's response to those who claim that "It's my body and I can do what I want with it." King Benjamin's point that our bodies belong to God is consistent with the teachings of Paul when he wrote, "For ye are bought with a price: therefore glorify God in your body, and in your spirit, which are God's" (1 Corinthians 6:20).

Mosiah 2:34–41. Willfully Rebelling against God

• When a person knows what is right and does not do it, he or she not only violates the actual law, but puts himself or herself in a state of opposition to God—a serious offense in and of itself. President Gordon B. Hinckley (1910–2008) shared the following simple illustration of such rebellion: "I recall a bishop's telling me of a woman who came to get a recommend. When asked if she observed the Word of Wisdom, she said that she occasionally drank a cup of coffee. She said, 'Now, bishop, you're not going to let that keep me from going to the temple, are you?' To which he replied, 'Sister, surely *you* will not let a cup of coffee stand between you and the house of the Lord'" (in Conference Report, Apr. 1990, 67; or *Ensign,* May 1990, 51).

Mosiah 3:5, 17–18. What Does the Term *Lord Omnipotent* Mean?

• Of all the prophets recorded in the Book of Mormon, King Benjamin is the only one to use the term *omnipotent,* which Elder Bruce R. McConkie (1915–85) of the Quorum of the Twelve Apostles defined this way: "Christ is the *Lord Omnipotent* (Mosiah 3:5, 17–18, 21; 5:2, 15; Rev. 19:6), meaning that as Lord of all he has all power" (*Mormon Doctrine,* 2nd ed. [1966], 452).

Mosiah 3:7. So Great Was His Anguish

• Elder Neal A. Maxwell (1926–2004) of the Quorum of the Twelve Apostles referred to the suffering experienced by Jesus Christ as "the awful arithmetic of the Atonement":

"Imagine, Jehovah, the Creator of this and other worlds, 'astonished'! Jesus knew cognitively what He must do, but not experientially. He had never personally known the exquisite and exacting process of an atonement before. Thus, when the agony came in its fulness, it was so much, much worse than even He with his unique intellect had ever imagined! No wonder an angel appeared to strengthen him! (See Luke 22:43.)

Del Parson, © 1987 RI

"The cumulative weight of all mortal sins—past, present, and future—pressed upon that perfect, sinless, and sensitive Soul! All our infirmities and sicknesses were somehow, too, a part of the awful arithmetic of the Atonement. (See Alma 7:11–12; Isaiah 53:3–5; Matthew 8:17.) The anguished Jesus not only pled with the Father that the hour and cup might pass from Him, but with this relevant citation. 'And he said, Abba, Father, all things are possible unto thee; take away this cup from me' (Mark 14:35–36).

"Had not Jesus, as Jehovah, said to Abraham, 'Is any thing too hard for the Lord?' (Genesis 18:14). Had not His angel told a perplexed Mary, 'For with God nothing shall be impossible'? (Luke 1:37; see also Matthew 19:28; Mark 10:27; Luke 18:27).

"Jesus' request was not theater!

"In this extremity, did He, perchance, hope for a rescuing ram in the thicket? I do not know. His suffering—as it were, *enormity* multiplied by *infinity*—evoked His later soul-cry on the cross, and it was a cry of forsakenness. (See Matthew 27:46.)

"Even so, Jesus maintained this sublime submissiveness, as He had in Gethsemane: 'Nevertheless not as I will, but as thou wilt' (Matthew 26:39)" (in Conference Report, Apr. 1985, 92; or *Ensign,* May 1985, 72–73).

• One commentator wrote that the Savior's suffering was the total weight of the consequence of the Fall: "Jesus knew that the awful hour of His deepest humiliation had arrived—that from this moment till the utterance of that great cry with which He expired, nothing remained for Him on earth but the torture of physical pain and the poignancy of mental anguish. All that the human frame can tolerate of suffering was to be heaped upon His shrinking body; every misery that cruel and crushing insult can inflict was to weigh heavy upon His soul; and in this torment of body and agony of soul even the high and radiant serenity of His divine spirit was to suffer a short but terrible eclipse. Pain in its acutest sting, shame in its most overwhelming brutality, all the burden of the sin and mystery of man's existence in its apostasy and fall—this was what He must now face in all its most inexplicable accumulation" (F. W. Farrar, *The Life of Christ* [London: Cassell and Co., 1874], pp. 622–23; quoted in Bruce R. McConkie, *The Mortal Messiah, Book 4* [1981], 126).

Mosiah 3:17. "No Other Name Given"

• The First Presidency and the Quorum of the Twelve Apostles affirmed that salvation comes through Jesus Christ: "We bear testimony, as His duly ordained Apostles—that Jesus is the Living Christ, the immortal Son of God. He is the great King Immanuel, who stands today on the right hand of His Father. He is the light, the life, and the hope of the world. His way is the path that leads to happiness in this life and eternal life in the world to come" ("The Living Christ: The Testimony of the Apostles," *Ensign,* Apr. 2000, 3).

Mosiah 3:19. 📖 The Natural Man

• The terms *natural* or *by nature,* as commonly used, indicate an inherent part of our identity, something with which we are born. In the scriptures, however, *natural* means fallen or sinful. Though born innocent (see D&C 93:38), all men, through the Fall of Adam, come into a fallen world and into a state of spiritual death (see Alma 42:9), separated from the presence of God. Knowing good and evil (see Moses 4:11; 5:11) and living in this imperfect state, all men sin (see Romans 3:23; 1 John 1:8, 10) and experience a resultant "fall" of their own (see Moses 6:49, 55). In other words, it is through transgression of God's law that one becomes a "natural man" (see Alma 42:10, 12; D&C 20:20). Hence, a natural man is an enemy to God (see Mosiah 3:19 📖) until he qualifies for the cleansing influence of the Atonement through living the commandments of God (see Mosiah 3:11–12, 19 📖).

• King Benjamin taught that to put off the natural man we must yield to the enticings of the Holy Spirit (see Mosiah 3:19 📖). In a conference address, Elder Neal A. Maxwell discussed how we might accomplish this task: "*Personal* righteousness, worship, prayer, and scripture study are so crucial in order to '[put] off the natural man' (Mosiah 3:19)" (in Conference Report, Oct. 2000, 46; or *Ensign,* Nov. 2000, 36).

In an earlier address, Elder Maxwell suggested another tool, along with a caution, for putting off the natural man: "Hope is particularly needed in the hand-to-hand combat required to put off the natural man (see Mosiah 3:19). Giving up on God and on oneself constitutes simultaneous surrender to the natural man" (in Conference Report, Oct. 1994, 46; or *Ensign,* Nov. 1994, 36).

Mosiah 3:19. 📖 Becoming a Saint

• While discussing what it means to be a Saint, Elder Quentin L. Cook of the Quorum of the Twelve Apostles cited this definition and then provided examples of things we must separate ourselves from:

"The word *saint* in Greek denotes 'set apart, separate, [and] holy' [in Daniel H. Ludlow, ed., *Encyclopedia of Mormonism,* 5 vols. (1992), 3:1249]. If we are to be Saints in our day, we need to separate ourselves from evil conduct and destructive pursuits that are prevalent in the world.

"We are bombarded with visual images of violence and immorality. Inappropriate music and pornography are increasingly tolerated. The use of drugs and alcohol is rampant. There is less emphasis on honesty and character. Individual rights are demanded, but duties, responsibilities, and obligations are neglected. There has been a coarsening of dialogue and increased exposure to that which is base and vulgar. The adversary has been relentless in his efforts to undermine the plan of happiness. If we separate ourselves from this worldly conduct, we will have

the Spirit in our lives and experience the joy of being worthy Latter-day Saints" (in Conference Report, Oct. 2003, 100–101; or *Ensign,* Nov. 2003, 95).

Mosiah 3:19. 📖 "As a Child"

• President Henry B. Eyring of the First Presidency taught how becoming "as a child" (Mosiah 3:19) leads to spiritual safety:

"King Benjamin makes it clear how we can . . . have our natures changed through the Atonement of Jesus Christ. That is the only way we can build on the sure foundation and so stand firm in righteousness during the storms of temptation.

"King Benjamin describes that change with a beautiful comparison, used by prophets for millennia and by the Lord Himself. It is this: that we can, and we must, become as a child—a little child.

"For some that will not be easy to understand or to accept. Most of us want to be strong. We may well see being like a child as being weak. . . .

"But King Benjamin, who understood as well as any mortal what it meant to be a man of strength and courage, makes it clear that to be like a child is not to be childish. It is to be like the Savior, who prayed to His Father for strength to be able to do His will and then did it. Our natures must be changed to become as a child to gain the strength we must have to be safe in the times of moral peril. . . .

"We are safe on the rock which is the Savior when we have yielded in faith in Him, have responded to the Holy Spirit's direction to keep the commandments long enough and faithfully enough that the power of the Atonement has changed our hearts. When we have, by that experience, become as a child in our capacity to love and obey, we are on the sure foundation.

"From King Benjamin we learn what we can do to take us to that safe place. But remember: the things we do are the means, not the end we seek. What we do allows the Atonement of Jesus Christ to change us into what we must be. Our faith in Jesus Christ brings us to repentance and to keeping His commandments. We obey and we resist temptation by following the promptings of the Holy Ghost. In time our natures will change. We will become as a little child, obedient to God and more loving. That change, if we do all we must to keep it, will qualify us to enjoy the gifts which come through the Holy Ghost. Then we will be safe on the only sure rock" (in Conference Report, Apr. 2006, 14–15; or *Ensign,* May 2006, 15–16).

MOSIAH 3:19 📖
What attributes of little children must we have? How do we obtain those qualities?

Points to Ponder

- In what ways has serving others helped you draw nearer to God?

- How does the Atonement allow you to overcome the natural man? Why is it only through the Atonement of Christ that you can become a Saint? (see Mosiah 3:19 📖).

- Mosiah 1:5–6 explains that having the scriptures "before [their] eyes" kept the Nephites from dwindling in unbelief. Why is it important for you to have a personal daily habit of scripture study?

Suggested Assignments

- King Benjamin explained that when we are taught the word of God we are "found no more blameless" in His sight (Mosiah 3:22). Write a response to the following argument: If hearing the word of God makes us more accountable, why would it be an advantage to study the gospel and learn more? (see D&C 130:18–19; 131:6). Find and list at least three scriptures that describe the blessings of gospel study.

- From Mosiah 3, create an outline that demonstrates and explains the mission of the Savior through mortality and in the postmortal life.

Introduction

The Nephites listening to King Benjamin recognized their need for the redeeming power of the Atonement. As a result, they prayed for forgiveness, received peace of conscience, and took upon themselves the name of Jesus Christ. Like those Nephites, we can also experience a change of heart and live in such a way that we will "always rejoice, and be filled with the love of God, and always retain a remission of [our] sins." King Benjamin's sermon instructs us how to "grow in the knowledge of the glory of him that created [us]" (Mosiah 4:12) through faith, repentance, and making and keeping covenants.

Commentary

Mosiah 4:1–2, 5, 11. "Less Than the Dust of the Earth"

• King Benjamin's people viewed themselves "even less than the dust of the earth." This expression described the fact that while the dust of the earth is obedient to the commands of God (see Helaman 12:7–8), they as God's children had not always been obedient to His commands. They recognized their utter dependence upon God—that man must rely upon God for everything: life and breath, food and the ability to produce it, health and strength, salvation and eternal life. Without God and the Atonement, man is, in a very real sense, nothing. Humility comes from realizing our dependence upon the Lord. The key to our greatness is to remember our nothingness without Christ and His Atonement. As Jacob taught, if there were no Atonement we would never live again and we would become angels to the devil (see 2 Nephi 9:7–9).

Mosiah 4:2–3. Applying the "Atoning Blood of Christ"

• King Benjamin's people recognized their need for power beyond their own to overcome their sinful condition. They prayed for mercy and asked that Heavenly Father "apply the atoning blood of Christ" (Mosiah 4:2) so they could be forgiven of their sins. President Boyd K. Packer, President of the Quorum of the Twelve Apostles, taught how the Atonement can heal us of our errors:

"We all make mistakes. Sometimes we harm ourselves and seriously injure others in ways that we alone cannot repair. We break things that we alone cannot fix. It is then in our nature to feel guilt and humiliation and suffering, which we alone cannot cure. That is when the healing power of the Atonement will help. . . .

"If Christ had not made His Atonement, the penalties for mistakes would be added one on the other. Life would be hopeless. But He willingly sacrificed in order that we may be redeemed. . . .

"We can even 'retain a remission of [our] sins' [Mosiah 4:12]. Baptism by immersion is for the remission of our sins. That covenant can be renewed by partaking of the sacrament each week [see D&C 27:2].

"The Atonement has practical, personal, everyday value; apply it in your life. It can be activated with so simple a beginning as prayer. You will not thereafter be free from trouble and mistakes but can erase the guilt through repentance and be at peace" (in Conference Report, Apr. 2001, 28–29; or *Ensign,* May 2001, 23–24).

Mosiah 4:3. "Peace of Conscience"

• Elder Richard G. Scott of the Quorum of the Twelve Apostles testified that peace of conscience comes from sincere repentance and righteous living:

"God wants each of His children to enjoy the transcendent blessing of peace of conscience [see Mosiah 4:2–3]. A tranquil conscience invites freedom from anguish, sorrow, guilt, shame, and self-condemnation. It provides a foundation for happiness. . . .

". . . You can regain peace of conscience by repenting of personal transgressions that cause you internal turmoil. . . .

"Broken law from sin or transgression causes anguish of mind and heart from an offended conscience. Knowing that all of His spirit children save His Only Begotten, Jesus Christ, would unintentionally or intentionally violate His laws, our Eternal Father provided a means to correct the consequences of such acts. Whether the violation be great or small, the solution is the same: full repentance through faith in

Jesus Christ and His Atonement with obedience to His commandments" (in Conference Report, Oct. 2004, 14–15; or *Ensign,* Nov. 2004, 15–16).

• President Boyd K. Packer admonished those who seek peace of conscience through repentance to persevere until they obtain forgiveness:

"The gospel teaches us that relief from torment and guilt can be earned through repentance. Save for those few who defect to perdition after having known a fulness, there is no habit, no addiction, no rebellion, no transgression, no offense exempted from the promise of complete forgiveness. . . .

"That great morning of forgiveness may not come at once. Do not give up if at first you fail. Often the most difficult part of repentance is to forgive yourself. Discouragement is part of that test. Do not give up. That brilliant morning will come.

"Then 'the peace of God, which passeth . . . understanding' comes into your life once again. [Philippians 4:7]. Then you, like Him, will remember your sins no more. How will you know? You will know! [see Mosiah 4:1–3]" (in Conference Report, Oct. 1995, 22, 24; or *Ensign,* Nov. 1995, 19–20).

Mosiah 4:4–8. Come to a Knowledge of the Atonement

• President James E. Faust (1920–2007) of the First Presidency testified of the need for every Latter-day Saint to study and accept the Atonement:

"My beloved brothers and sisters and friends, I come humbly to this pulpit this morning because I wish to speak about the greatest event in all history. That singular event was the incomparable Atonement of our Lord and Savior, Jesus the Christ. This was the most transcendent act that has ever taken place, yet it is the most difficult to understand.

"My reason for wanting to learn all I can about the Atonement is partly selfish: Our salvation depends on believing in and accepting the Atonement [see Mosiah 4:6–7]. Such acceptance requires a continual effort to understand it more fully. The Atonement advances our mortal course of learning by making it possible for our natures to become perfect [see Moroni 10:32]. All of us

have sinned and need to repent to fully pay *our* part of the debt. When we sincerely repent, the Savior's magnificent Atonement pays the *rest* of that debt [see 2 Nephi 25:23]" (in Conference Report, Oct. 2001, 19; or *Ensign,* Nov. 2001, 18).

Mosiah 4:12. "Retain a Remission of Your Sins"

• Elder Neal A. Maxwell (1926–2004) of the Quorum of the Twelve Apostles counseled us to frequently and regularly repent to retain a remission of sins: "Much emphasis was given by King Benjamin to retaining a remission of our sins (see Mosiah 4:26). We do not ponder that concept very much in the church. We ought to think of it a lot more. Retention clearly depends on the regularity of our repentance. In the church we worry, and should, over the retention of new members, but the retention of our remissions is cause for even deeper concern" ("King Benjamin's Sermon: A Manual for Discipleship," in John W. Welch and Stephen D. Ricks, eds., *King Benjamin's Speech: "That Ye May Learn Wisdom"* [1998], 16).

Mosiah 4:14–15. Raising Righteous Children

• King Benjamin taught the importance of the family and the need for righteous parents. Modern prophets also testify that the Lord commands His faithful disciples to bring up their children in righteousness and teach them gospel principles:  "Parents have a sacred duty to rear their children in love and righteousness, to provide for their physical and spiritual needs, and to teach them to love and serve one another, [and] to observe the commandments of God" ("The Family: A Proclamation to the World," *Ensign,* Nov. 1995, 102).

• As a modern witness of parents' responsibility to teach their children, Elder Russell M. Nelson of the Quorum of the Twelve Apostles identified several scriptures that help parents understand their role: "Scriptures direct parents to teach faith in Jesus Christ, repentance, baptism, and the gift of the Holy Ghost [see Moroni 8:10]. Parents are to teach the plan of salvation [see Moses 6:58–62] and the importance of living in complete accord with the commandments of God [see Leviticus 10:11; Deuteronomy 6:7; Mosiah 4:14]. Otherwise, their children will surely suffer in ignorance of God's redeeming and liberating law [see 2 Nephi 2:26]. Parents should also teach by example how to consecrate their lives—using their time, talents, tithing, and substance [see Mosiah 4:21–26; 18:27; Alma 1:27] to establish the Church and kingdom of God upon the earth [see JST, Matthew 6:38]. Living in that manner will literally bless their posterity" (in Conference Report, Oct. 2001, 85; or *Ensign,* Nov. 2001, 71).

Mosiah 4:16–25. Imparting to the Poor

• King Benjamin reminded us that we are all beggars before God and that we should show mercy to others if we expect mercy in return. Similarly, President Gordon B. Hinckley (1910–2008) counseled us to look upon others with compassion:

"Let us be more merciful. Let us get the arrogance out of our lives, the conceit, the egotism. Let us be more compassionate, gentler, filled with forbearance and patience and a greater measure of respect one for another. In so doing, our very example will cause others to be more merciful, and we shall have greater claim upon the mercy of God who in His love will be generous toward us.

"'For behold, are we not all beggars? . . .' [Mosiah 4:19].

"So spoke King Benjamin. To which I add that the power of the Master is certain and His word is sure. He will keep His promise toward those who are compassionate. 'Blessed are the merciful: for they shall obtain mercy' (Matthew 5:7).

"I am confident that a time will come for each of us when, whether because of sickness or infirmity, of poverty or distress, of oppressive measures against us by man or nature, we shall wish for mercy. And if,

through our lives, we have granted mercy to others, we shall obtain it for ourselves" (in Conference Report, Apr. 1990, 89; or *Ensign,* May 1990, 70).

Mosiah 4:27. "Not Requisite That a Man Should Run Faster than He Has Strength"

• Elder Neal A. Maxwell pointed out that we have limited time and energy, so we must focus on that which is most important:

"When we run faster than we are able, we get both inefficient and tired. . . .

"I have on my office wall a wise and useful reminder by Anne Morrow Lindbergh concerning one of the realities of life. She wrote, 'My life cannot implement in action the demands of all the people to whom my heart responds.' That's good counsel for us all, not as an excuse to forego duty, but as a sage point about pace and the need for quality in relationships" (*Deposition of a Disciple* [1976], 58).

> **MOSIAH 4:30**
>
> *What must we watch and do to avoid perishing?*

Mosiah 5:2. "A Mighty Change in Us"

• Elder Robert D. Hales of the Quorum of the Twelve Apostles explained the process by which we experience the change of heart: "Once we receive a witness of the Spirit, our testimony is strengthened through study, prayer, and living the gospel. Our growing testimony brings us increased faith in Jesus Christ and His plan of happiness. We are motivated to repent and obey the commandments, which, with a mighty change of heart, leads to our conversion. And our conversion brings divine forgiveness, healing, joy, and the desire to bear our witness to others" (in Conference Report, Oct. 2003, 31–32; or *Ensign,* Nov. 2003, 30).

Mosiah 5:7–8. Becoming Children of Christ

• President Joseph Fielding Smith (1876–1972) explained how we may consider Jesus Christ as our Father:

"If we speak of Jesus Christ as being our Father, we are not making any mistake because, spiritually, he begot us. No question about it—he united spirit and body, providing a resurrection for every living thing. We do not make any mistake in speaking of the Savior as our God, as our Father, and also as the Son of God because he received all authority. Jesus declared the Father conferred all authority upon him, and so he becomes to us a Father. Moreover, he begot us spiritually in the Resurrection. . . .

". . . We are his sons and daughters. He is a Father to us because he begot us and saved us from death, uniting spirit and body. What is a father but one who gives life?" ("The Fatherhood of Christ" [unpublished address to seminary and institute of religion personnel, Brigham Young University, July 17, 1962], 5–6).

See commentary for Mosiah 15:1–7 (p. 153).

Mosiah 5:8–10. Taking upon Us His Name

• Elder Dallin H. Oaks of the Quorum of the Twelve Apostles deepened our understanding of taking the name of Jesus Christ upon us:

"We see that we take upon us the name of Christ when we are baptized in his name, when we belong to his Church and profess our belief in him, and when we do the work of his kingdom.

"There are other meanings as well, deeper meanings that the more mature members of the Church should understand and ponder as he or she partakes of the sacrament.

"It is significant that when we partake of the sacrament we do not witness that we *take upon us* the name of Jesus Christ. We witness that we are *willing* to do so. (See D&C 20:77.) The fact that we only witness to our willingness suggests that something else must happen before we actually take that sacred name upon us in the most important sense. . . .

"Willingness to take upon us the name of Jesus Christ can therefore be understood as willingness to take upon us the authority of Jesus Christ. According to this meaning, by partaking of the sacrament we witness our willingness to participate in the sacred ordinances of the temple and to receive the highest blessings

available through the name and by the authority of the Savior when he chooses to confer them upon us.

". . . Our willingness to take upon us the name of Jesus Christ affirms our commitment to do all that we can to be counted among those whom he will choose to stand at his right hand and be called by his name at the last day. In this sacred sense, our witness that we are willing to take upon us the name of Jesus Christ constitutes our declaration of candidacy for exaltation in the celestial kingdom. Exaltation is eternal life, 'the greatest of all the gifts of God' (D&C 14:7)" (in Conference Report, Apr. 1985, 102–3, 105; or *Ensign,* May 1985, 80–81, 83).

Mosiah 5:12. "Know the Voice"

• Learning to recognize and follow the Lord's voice is vital for spiritual progression. Elder M. Russell Ballard of the Quorum of the Twelve Apostles taught that God expects us to hear and know His voice in this life: "When my ministry is all over, it will not be any talk that I gave that will be very important in the sight of the Lord; but what will be important to him will be my hearing his voice and responding to his promptings" ("Respond to the Prompting of the Spirit" [an evening with Elder M. Russell Ballard, Jan. 8, 1988], 4, www.ldsces.org).

> **MOSIAH 5:7–12**
> *What must we do to be found on the right hand of God?*

Mosiah 6:4–7. King Mosiah

• King Benjamin named his son after his father. We might, therefore, refer to King Benjamin's father as Mosiah[1] and to King Benjamin's son as Mosiah[2]. It was Mosiah[1] who was commanded by the Lord to take those who would follow him and depart out of the land of Nephi into the wilderness because of the wickedness of the Nephites (see Omni 1:12). The book of Mosiah, however, is named after Mosiah[2]; he is the one who kept the record.

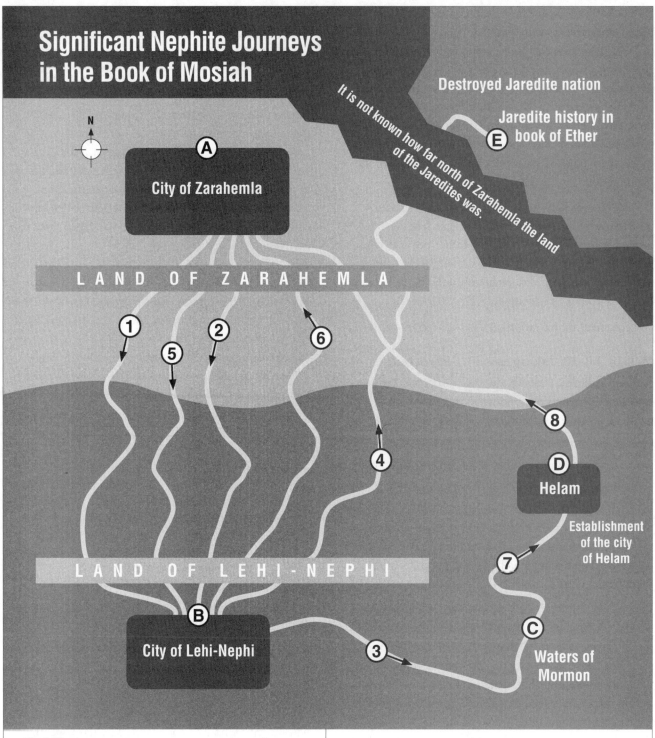

Significant Nephite Journeys in the Book of Mosiah

Destroyed Jaredite nation

Jaredite history in book of Ether

It is not known how far north of Zarahemla the land of the Jaredites was.

City of Zarahemla

LAND OF ZARAHEMLA

LAND OF LEHI-NEPHI

City of Lehi-Nephi

Helam

Establishment of the city of Helam

Waters of Mormon

Key to Map

1. The ill-fated expedition. Read Omni 1:27–28; Mosiah 9:1–2.

2. Zeniff's expedition. Read Omni 1:29; Mosiah 7:9; 9:3–7.

3. Alma's escape to the Waters of Mormon. Read Mosiah 18:1–7, 30–33.

4. The expedition of 43 men to find Zarahemla. Read Mosiah 8:8–9; 21:25–27.

5. Ammon's expedition to find Zeniff's colony. Read Mosiah 7:2–3.

6. Limhi's escape to Zarahemla. Read Mosiah 22:3–13.

7. Alma's people flee to Helam. Read Mosiah 23:1–5, 19.

8. Alma's escape to Zarahemla. Read Mosiah 24.

Mosiah 7:1–14; 8:7–21. Nephite Journeys

• To understand the historical setting of Mosiah 7–8, you may need to review the events contained in Omni 1:27–30 and the chapter summaries from Mosiah 7–8. These references discuss the leaders of the people in the land of Zarahemla (Mosiah¹, King Benjamin, and Mosiah²) as well as the kings in the land of Lehi-Nephi (Zeniff, Noah, and Limhi). They also refer to the journeys of various groups of people between the city of Zarahemla and Zeniff's colony in the land of Lehi-Nephi. To better understand these travels, study the accompanying map.

Mosiah 8:13. Interpreters

• President Joseph Fielding Smith provided this historical overview of the "interpreters" referred to in the Book of Mormon:

"King Mosiah possessed '. . . two stones which were fastened into the two rims of a bow' [Mosiah 28:13] called by the Nephites 'Interpreters,' with which he translated the Jaredite record [Mosiah 28:11–14], and these were handed down from generation to generation for the purpose of interpreting languages. How Mosiah came into possession of these 'two stones' or Urim and Thummim, the record does not tell us, more than to say that it was a 'gift from God' [Mosiah 21:28]. Mosiah had this 'gift' or Urim and Thummim before the people of Limhi discovered the record of Ether. They may have been received when the 'large stone' was brought to Mosiah with engravings upon it, which he interpreted by the 'gift and power of God' [Omni 1:20–21]. They may have been given to him, or to some other prophet before his day, just as the brother of Jared received them—from the Lord.

"That the Urim and Thummim, or two stones, given to the brother of Jared were those in the possession of Mosiah appears evident from the following statements in the Book of Mormon:

"The brother of Jared was commanded to seal up his writings of the vision he had when Christ appeared to him, so that they could not be read by his people. This vision was in a language which was confounded, for it was not to go forth until after the resurrection of Christ. The Urim and Thummim were also sealed up so that they could not be used for the purpose of interpreting those sacred writings of this vision, until such time as the Lord should grant to man to interpret them. When they were to be revealed, they were to be interpreted by the aid of the same Urim and Thummim [Ether 3:21–28]. . . .

"Joseph Smith received with the 'breastplate' and the plates of the Book of Mormon, the Urim and Thummim, which were hid up by Moroni to come forth in the last days as a means by which the ancient record might be translated, which Urim and Thummim were given to the brother of Jared [D&C 17:1]" (*Answers to Gospel Questions,* comp. Joseph Fielding Smith Jr., 5 vols. [1957–66], 1:160–62).

Mosiah 8:15. "A Seer Is Greater than a Prophet"

• President Howard W. Hunter (1907–95) explained the unique role of a seer and how a seer views things

Alvin Gittins, © 1959 IRI

differently than others: "A seer is one who sees. This does not mean that he sees through his natural eyes but rather through spiritual eyes. The seeric gift is a supernatural endowment" (*The Teachings of Howard W. Hunter,* ed. Clyde J. Williams [1997], 224).

• Elder John A. Widtsoe (1872–1952) of the Quorum of the Twelve Apostles further described a seer as one who "perceives the meaning of that which seems obscure to others; therefore he is an interpreter and clarifier of eternal truth. He foresees the future from the past and the present. This he does by the power of the Lord operating through him directly, or indirectly with the aid of divine instruments such as the Urim and Thummim. In short, he is one who sees, who walks in the Lord's light with open eyes" (*Evidences and Reconciliations,* arr. G. Homer Durham [1960], 258).

MOSIAH 8:13–18
What are the characteristics of a seer?

Points to Ponder

- What do you need to do to "retain a remission of your sins"? (Mosiah 4:12; see also vv. 9–30 📖).

- What must you do to become a son or daughter of Jesus Christ? (Mosiah 5:7; see also Mosiah 27:24–27; Ether 3:14).

Suggested Assignments

- Examine Mosiah 4:5–13 and discover some of the attributes of God identified by King Benjamin in his discourse.

- Mosiah 4:12–16 reviews several aspects of gospel living. Select two of them that are most meaningful to you and create a plan to apply them in your life more fully.

Introduction

Mosiah 9–24 recounts the history of a colony led by Zeniff from the land of Zarahemla to the land of Lehi-Nephi. The record covers a period of almost 80 years, from about 200 B.C. until their return to the land of Zarahemla in about 121 B.C. This was about the same time period that Kings Mosiah¹, Benjamin, and Mosiah² were reigning in the land of Zarahemla; Zeniff, Noah, and Limhi reigned in the land of Lehi-Nephi.

During the reign of King Noah, the prophet Abinadi warned the people to repent. He also prophesied of pending destruction for turning from God. Abinadi's teachings also demonstrated the Savior's divinity, His unity with the Father, and the great sacrifice the Savior would make in the Atonement process. By studying the words of Abinadi, you can renew feelings of gratitude for the Savior's sacrifice and gain deeper appreciation of the Atonement.

Abinadi's martyrdom exhibits his great courage. Abinadi's testimony led to the conversion of Alma but cost Abinadi his life. As you ponder the events of Abinadi's ministry, consider the influence that one righteous man had on future generations. Through his one known convert—Alma—came the next several generations of prophets who prepared the people for the coming of Jesus Christ. Like Abinadi, you too can profoundly affect your family and others you know by testifying of truth and by living righteously.

Commentary

Insert before Mosiah 9

• The inserted heading prior to the chapter summary of Mosiah 9 is part of the original record given to the Prophet Joseph Smith (see commentary for The First Book of Nephi: His Reign and Ministry on p. 12). The phrase "Comprising chapters 9 to 22 inclusive" was added when the Book of Mormon was published in chapter format in the 1879 edition.

Mosiah 9. The Record of Zeniff

• Mosiah 9:1–4 and Omni 1:27–29 both relate the story of Zeniff's first expedition to recolonize the land of Nephi-Lehi; however, Mosiah 9:1–2 reveals why the first expedition fought a civil war and was forced

to return to the land of Zarahemla. Zeniff did not delight in war but desired to live in peace among the Lamanites. Mosiah 9–10 was written by Zeniff without abridgement or comment by Mormon. Note that the date for Mosiah 8 is 121 B.C. The date for Mosiah 9 is 200 B.C. The record reverted back in time 80 years to tell what happened in the land of Lehi-Nephi during the time period of Benjamin and Mosiah's reign in Zarahemla.

Mosiah 9:16–18; 10:10–11, 19. "In the Strength of the Lord"

• Zeniff recorded that they fought "in the strength of the Lord" when battling the Lamanites (see Mosiah 9:16–18; 10:10–11, 19). Although Zeniff's people were greatly outnumbered, they overcame their Lamanite aggressors with comparatively few casualties. Their success was due to their faithfulness to God. The Lord heard their cries and blessed them with strength. Throughout the Book of Mormon we see that giving strength to His people is one of God's tender mercies. Benjamin's people in Zarahemla were victorious over the Lamanites because they fought "in the strength of the Lord" (Words of Mormon 1:14).

In the book of Alma, the success of the Nephite armies can be attributed to their ability to trust in God to assist them in their battles and not in the size of the army (see Alma 2:27–31; 43:49–51; 56:56). Although our battles may not be physical warfare, the phrase "in the strength of the Lord" teaches us that we too can ask for assistance from God to grant us strength to triumph over our foes.

Mosiah 9–22. The History of Zeniff and His People

• The book of Mosiah is often confusing because of the different storylines and historical flashbacks that are part of the book (refer to the chart "Flashbacks from Omni through Mosiah" in the appendix, p. 413). The history contained in Mosiah chapters 9–22 flashes back approximately 80 years to the time when Zeniff and a small band of followers left the land of Zarahemla to return to the land of Nephi. The record contains the history of Kings Zeniff, Noah, and Limhi. The flashback narrative takes the reader back to the Book of Mormon history as Zeniff's group is reunited with the people of Zarahemla in Mosiah 25.

Mosiah 10:11–17. False Traditions

• The Lamanites came to accept as truth a distorted version of events concerning their original journey from Jerusalem. These false traditions were handed down from generation to generation, creating deep prejudices or an "eternal hatred" among the Lamanites against the Nephites (Mosiah 10:17). In latter-day revelation the Lord warned that Satan uses false traditions to take "away truth and light" (D&C 93:39; see also D&C 123:7–8). Because of these traditions the Lamanites felt justified in murdering, robbing, and attempting to destroy or enslave the Nephites (see Mosiah 10:17).

• Elder Richard G. Scott of the Quorum of the Twelve Apostles taught what we should do when a family or cultural tradition conflicts with God's plan or standards. He counseled us to carefully examine our lives to determine what traditions may differ from the teachings of the Lord:

"Your Heavenly Father assigned you to be born into a specific lineage from which you received your inheritance of race, culture, and traditions. That lineage can provide a rich heritage and great reasons to rejoice. Yet you have the responsibility to determine if there is any part of that heritage that must be discarded because it works against the Lord's plan of happiness.

"You may ask how can one determine when a tradition is in conflict with the teachings of the Lord and should be abandoned? That is not easily done. I have found how difficult it is as I work to overcome some of my own incorrect traditions. . . . Customs and traditions become an inherent part of us. They are not easy to evaluate objectively. Carefully study the scriptures and counsel of the prophets to understand how the Lord wants you to live. Then evaluate each part of your life and make any adjustments needed. Seek help from another you respect who has been able to set aside some deeply held convictions or traditions that are not in harmony with the Lord's plan. . . .

"Is yours a culture where the husband exerts a domineering, authoritarian role, making all of the

important decisions for the family? That pattern needs to be tempered so that both husband and wife act as equal partners, making decisions in unity for themselves and their family. . . .

"These are other traditions that should be set aside—any aspect of heritage:

"That would violate the Word of Wisdom.

"That is based on forcing others to comply by the power of station often determined by heredity.

"That encourages the establishment of caste systems.

"That breeds conflict with other cultures" (in Conference Report, Apr. 1998, 112–13; or *Ensign,* May 1998, 86).

Mosiah 11:2–19, 27. Noah Walked "after the Desires of His Own Heart"

• For discussion on concubines, see commentary for Jacob 1:15 on page 115.

• Mormon vividly described the wickedness of King Noah (see Mosiah 11:2–19, 27). Later, Mosiah used the example of King Noah as the primary reason to eliminate government by kings: "How much iniquity doth one wicked king cause to be committed, yea, and what great destruction! Yea, remember king Noah" (Mosiah 29:17–18). King Noah's complete selfishness in seeking the desires of the flesh stands as a warning to modern readers of the fate of such individuals.

Mosiah 11:20. The Prophet Abinadi

• Elder M. Russell Ballard of the Quorum of the Twelve Apostles highlighted Abinadi's courage and willingness to obey the Lord: "Abinadi infuriated wicked King Noah with his courageous testimony of the Lord Jesus Christ. Eventually this great missionary offered the ultimate sacrifice for his witness and faith but not before his pure testimony touched one believing heart. Alma, one of King Noah's priests, 'repented of his sins . . . , [accepted Jesus as the Christ,] and went about privately among the people, and began to teach the words of Abinadi' (Mosiah 18:1). Many were converted to the gospel of Jesus Christ as a direct result of Abinadi's powerfully borne testimony of the

Savior, believed by one soul—Alma" (in Conference Report, Oct. 2004, 43; or *Ensign,* Nov. 2004, 41).

• While serving in the Seventy, Elder Cree-L Kofford discussed Abinadi's influence and example: "What is there that is so special about Abinadi? Perhaps it was his total obedience as he went, presumably alone, among those whom he must have known would take his life, to deliver the word of the Lord and to cry repentance to the people. Perhaps it is the very fact that we know so little about him, or perhaps it was simply the way with which he faced the adversities which came into his life in such a straightforward, 'square-to-the-world' way. Whatever the reason, Abinadi was and is special. His life, lived so long ago, still has the power to excite the mind and cause the pulse to pound" ("Abinadi," in *Heroes from the Book of Mormon* [1995], 69–70). We know that Abinadi was a man who came from among the people, not from outside their society. He was obviously a righteous man called to warn his own people that if they did not repent, bondage and destruction would follow.

Mosiah 11:21; 12:1–2, 8. Abinadi's Warnings

• The failure of the people of Noah to hearken to Abinadi's first warning (see Mosiah 11:21) led to a more serious warning when he returned two years later. The consequence became that they would be in bondage, and if they did not repent they would be destroyed (see Mosiah 12:1–2, 8). This is often the case in life—when we put off obedience or delay following the prophet, we bring more serious consequences upon ourselves.

Mosiah 12:15–24. "Him That Bringeth Good Tidings"

• One of King Noah's wicked priests challenged Abinadi: "What meaneth the words . . . : How beautiful upon the mountains are the feet of him that bringeth good tidings; that publisheth peace; that bringeth good tidings of good"? (Mosiah 12:20–21). As you read Mosiah 12–15, note how thoroughly Abinadi responded to this question.

MOSIAH 12:25, 27
Why were the priests unable to understand the scriptures? How can we keep from falling into the same error?

Mosiah 12:34–36; 13:11–26. The Ten Commandments

• President Gordon B. Hinckley (1910–2008) declared that the Ten Commandments (see Exodus 20:3–17 📖) are an essential part of the gospel of Jesus Christ in every generation: "[The] Ten Commandments [were] written by the finger of Jehovah on tablets of stone for the salvation and safety, for the security and happiness of the children of Israel and for all of the generations which were to come after them" (in Conference Report, Oct. 1991, 71; or *Ensign,* Nov. 1991, 51).

Mosiah 13:28. "Salvation Doth Not Come by the Law Alone"

• Elder Dallin H. Oaks of the Quorum of the Twelve Apostles testified of the absolute need for Jesus Christ, even when we live righteously: "Men and women unquestionably have impressive powers and can bring to pass great things. But after all our obedience and good works, we cannot be saved from death or the effects of our individual sins without the grace extended by the atonement of Jesus Christ. The Book of Mormon makes this clear. It teaches that 'salvation doth not come by the law alone' (Mosiah 13:28). In other words, salvation does not come simply by keeping the commandments. 'By the law no flesh is justified' (2 Ne. 2:5). Even those who try to obey and serve God with all their heart, might, mind, and strength are 'unprofitable servants' (Mosiah 2:21). Man cannot earn his own salvation" ("Another Testament of Jesus Christ," *Ensign,* Mar. 1994, 67).

Mosiah 13:34. "God Himself Should Come Down"

• The term *God* generally refers to our Heavenly Father, and it is Him whom we ultimately worship. It is also true that Jesus Christ is God. Saints of the Old Testament era knew Him as Jehovah, the God of Abraham, Isaac, and Jacob. Elder James E. Talmage (1862–1933) of the Quorum of the Twelve Apostles taught that the scriptures help us understand the divinity of Jesus Christ and His role as a God: "We claim scriptural authority for the assertion that Jesus Christ was and is God the Creator, the God who revealed Himself to Adam, Enoch, and all the antediluvial patriarchs and prophets down to Noah; the God of Abraham, Isaac and Jacob; the God of Israel as a united people, and the God of Ephraim and Judah after the disruption of the Hebrew nation; the God who made Himself known to the prophets from Moses to Malachi; the God of the Old Testament record; and the God of the Nephites. We affirm that Jesus Christ was and is Jehovah, the Eternal One" (*Jesus the Christ,* 3rd ed. [1916], 32).

Mosiah 13:27–35. The Law of Moses and Jesus Christ

• Elder Jeffrey R. Holland of the Quorum of the Twelve Apostles taught how the law of Moses relates to the gospel of Jesus Christ:

"The modern reader should not see the Mosaic code—anciently or in modern times—as simply a tedious set of religious rituals slavishly (and sometimes militantly) followed by a stiffnecked people who did not accept the Christ and his gospel. This historic covenant, given by the hand of God himself . . . was . . . a guide to spirituality, a gateway to Christ. . . .

". . . It is crucial to understand that the law of Moses was overlaid upon, and thereby included, many basic parts of the gospel of Jesus Christ, which had existed before it. It was never intended to be something apart or separated from, and certainly not something antagonistic to, the gospel of Jesus Christ. . . . Its purpose was never to have been different from the higher law. Both were to bring people to Christ" (*Christ and the New Covenant* [1997], 136–37, 147).

> **MOSIAH 14:2–5**
> *What do we learn of the Savior?*

Mosiah 14:1–12. Isaiah's Messianic Prophecy

• To powerfully teach the importance of the Atonement, Abinadi quoted from the writings of Isaiah. Elder Jeffrey R. Holland explained the significance of Isaiah 53 (Mosiah 14) as a witness of the Savior's role: "Surely the most sublime, the lengthiest and most lyrical declaration of the life, death, and atoning sacrifice of the Lord Jesus Christ is that found in the 53rd chapter of Isaiah, quoted in its entirety in the Book of Mormon by Abinadi as he stood in chains before King Noah" (*Christ and the New Covenant,* 89).

Mosiah 14:5. "With His Stripes We Are Healed"

• In reference to the suffering of Jesus Christ during the Atonement and its healing power, Elder M. Russell Ballard shared the following:

"What peace, what comfort this great gift is which comes through the loving grace of Jesus Christ, the Savior and Redeemer of all mankind. . . .

". . . Even though His life was pure and free of sin, He paid the ultimate penalty for sin—yours, mine, and everyone's who has ever lived. His mental, emotional, and spiritual anguish were so great they caused Him to bleed from every pore (see Luke 22:44; D&C 19:18). And yet Jesus suffered willingly so we might all have the opportunity to be washed clean—through having faith in Him. . . . Without the Atonement of the Lord, none of these blessings would be available to us, and we could not become worthy and prepared to return to dwell in the presence of God" (in Conference Report, Apr. 2004, 86–87; or *Ensign,* May 2004, 84–85).

Mosiah 15:1–7. How Christ Is Both the Father and the Son

• Sometimes the scriptures refer to Jesus Christ by using the title "Father." Elder M. Russell Ballard explained why Jesus Christ is sometimes referred to as both the Father and the Son:

"How can Jesus Christ be both the Father and the Son? It really isn't as complicated as it sounds. Though He is the Son of God, He is the head of the Church, which is the family of believers. When we are spiritually born again, we are adopted into His family. He becomes our Father or leader. . . .

"In no way does this doctrine denigrate the role of God the Father. Rather, we believe it enhances our understanding of the role of God the Son, our Savior, Jesus Christ. God our Heavenly Father is the Father of our spirits; we speak of God the Son as the Father of the righteous. He is regarded as the 'Father' because of the relationship between Him and those who accept His gospel, thereby becoming heirs of eternal life. And the third member of the Godhead, God the Holy Ghost, has the specific mission to teach and to testify of truth as it pertains to the divinity of both God the Father and God the Son" ("Building Bridges of Understanding," *Ensign,* June 1998, 66–67).

• On June 30, 1916, under the leadership of President Joseph F. Smith, the Brethren set forth a detailed statement on the Father and the Son entitled "The Father and the Son: A Doctrinal Exposition by the First Presidency and the Quorum of the Twelve Apostles." A portion of this exposition explains how Jesus Christ is identified in the scriptures as both the "Son" and at times as the "Father":

"'Father' as Creator. . . . Scriptures that refer to God in any way as the Father of the heavens and the earth are to be understood as signifying that God is the Maker, the Organizer, the Creator of the heavens and the earth.

"With this meaning, as the context shows in every case, Jehovah, who is Jesus Christ the Son of Elohim, is called 'the Father,' and even 'the very Eternal Father of heaven and of earth' [see Ether 4:7; Alma 11:38–39; Mosiah 15:4; 16:15]. . . .

"**Jesus Christ the 'Father' of Those Who Abide in His Gospel.** [Another] sense in which Jesus Christ is regarded as the 'Father' has reference to the relationship between Him and those who accept His gospel and thereby become heirs of eternal life. . . .

"To His faithful servants in the present dispensation the Lord has said, 'Fear not, little children, for you are mine, and I have overcome the world, and you are of them that my Father hath given me' (D&C 50:41). . . .

"**Jesus Christ the 'Father' by Divine Investiture of Authority.** . . . Jesus the Son has represented and yet represents Elohim His Father in power and authority. . . . Thus the Father placed His name upon the Son; and Jesus Christ spoke and ministered in and through the Father's name; and so far as power, authority, and godship are concerned His words and acts were and are those of the Father" ("The Father and The Son," *Ensign,* Apr. 2002, 14–15, 17).

Mosiah 15:10–13. The Seed of Christ

• Elder Dallin H. Oaks explained how one becomes a son or daughter of Jesus Christ: "In these great scriptures from the Book of Mormon, we learn that those who are qualified by faith and repentance and compliance with the laws and ordinances of the gospel will have their sins borne by the Lord Jesus Christ. In spiritual and figurative terms they will become the sons and daughters of Christ, heirs to his kingdom. These are they who will be called by his name in the last day" (in Conference Report, Apr. 1985, 104; or *Ensign,* May 1985, 82).

• While serving as Presiding Bishop, Elder Merrill J. Bateman described how Jesus would see His seed: "The Savior, as a member of the Godhead, knows each of us personally. Isaiah and the prophet Abinadi said that when Christ would 'make his soul an offering for sin, he shall see his seed' (Isaiah 53:10; compare Mosiah 15:10). Abinadi explains that 'his seed' are the righteous, those who follow the prophets (see Mosiah 15:11). In the garden and on the cross, Jesus saw each of us and not only bore our sins but also experienced our deepest feelings so he would know how to comfort and strengthen us" (in Conference Report, Apr. 1995, 15–16; or *Ensign,* May 1995, 14).

Mosiah 15:13–20. How Beautiful Are the Feet

• Paraphrasing Isaiah, Abinadi extolled the great blessings that have come and will come to all the holy prophets who publish peace (see Mosiah 15:15–17) and to the Savior, who "is the founder of peace" (see Mosiah 15:18). That peaceful message is that the Redeemer would come and indeed has come to redeem his people from sin and has brought to pass the resurrection of the dead (see Mosiah 15:18, 20).

• While serving in the Seventy, Elder Carlos E. Asay (1926–99) shared an insight into the imagery of this statement from Isaiah:

"No one is more beautiful or more blessed than those who serve God by preaching and exemplifying the truth. It is the most sanctifying and beautifying labor of all! . . .

"The feet, the voices, the faces, and the whole being of those preachers who share saving truths will always be precious and beautiful to new converts, especially to those who have suffered in their sins. In the eyes of those who have learned of Christ and of his power to save, there are few if any blemishes in the missionaries who walked long distances to bring the gospel message" (*The Seven M's of Missionary Service* [1996], 135–36).

Mosiah 15:20–31. The First Resurrection

• Jesus Christ was the first person on this earth to be resurrected. Consequently, the period of time referred to in the scriptures as the First Resurrection commenced with His triumph over the grave and continues through the Millennium. Abinadi taught that those who would come forth in the First Resurrection would include "the prophets, and all those that have believed in their words" (Mosiah 15:22), those who have died in ignorance without having "salvation declared unto them" (Mosiah 15:24; see also D&C 45:54), and little children who die before they are accountable (see Mosiah 15:25; Moroni 8:1–24).

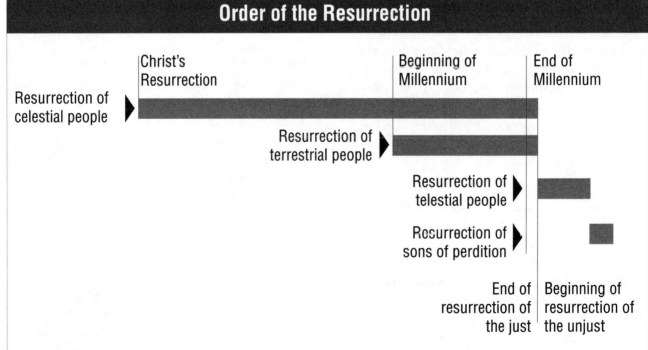

Brian D. Garner, *Search These Things Diligently* (2003), 151.

Mosiah 15:25. Little Children Have Eternal Life

• Concerning the salvation of little children, the Prophet Joseph Smith (1805–44) taught, "Children will be enthroned in the presence of God and the Lamb . . . ; they will there enjoy the fullness of that light, glory and intelligence, which is prepared in the celestial kingdom" (*History of the Church,* 4:555–56).

Mosiah 17:6–20. The Example of Abinadi

• Elder Robert D. Hales of the Quorum of the Twelve Apostles emphasized the need to follow the example of Abinadi's courage in keeping the commandments:

"What a powerful example Abinadi should be to all of us! He courageously obeyed the Lord's commandments—even though it cost him his life!

"Prophets of all dispensations have willingly put their lives on the line and, with courage, have done the will and proclaimed the word of God.

"The Prophet Joseph Smith went 'like a lamb to the slaughter' (D&C 135:4), never wavering as he fulfilled the Lord's commandments.

"And think of our Savior's example. . . . He endured to the end, fulfilling His divine mission and completing the atoning sacrifice for all mankind.

". . . Let us follow the example of our Lord Jesus Christ and His prophets, past and present. It may not be required of us to give our lives as martyrs, as did many of the prophets. What is required is our obedience to the Lord's commandments and our faithfulness to the covenants we have made with Him" (in Conference Report, Apr. 1996, 49; or *Ensign,* May 1996, 35).

Points to Ponder

• What do you think it means to have the Lord's commandments "written in your hearts"? (Mosiah 13:11).

• Why is it important to know that the Savior was and is a God? How should this knowledge affect our faith in His ability to save us?

• How can you live a righteous life regardless of the wickedness that is all around?

Suggested Assignments

• As you read through Mosiah 12:34–13:24, find and mark each of the Ten Commandments. Choose one of these commandments to obey more fully. Record in your journal how you will accomplish this.

• Read Mosiah 14 and compare it with Mosiah 3:7–8. Write a one-page summary of Mosiah 14 in your own words, or write a one-page testimony of what the Savior means to you.

Introduction

The people who followed Alma into the wilderness humbled themselves by believing the word of God, repenting, and accepting the covenant of baptism. Even so, they fell captive to the Lamanites for a length of time. In the same period of history, the people of Limhi continued to live under Lamanite domination. They eventually humbled themselves after failing to free themselves by their own strength and were delivered by God. Alma's people and Limhi's people both experienced bondage and oppression, and both groups experienced the blessing of being set free by the hand of the Lord. Look for ways the Lord provides redemption from the difficulties of mortality by strengthening us and assisting us in our troubles. By comparing and contrasting the circumstances of the two societies, we can learn principles to help us deal with our challenges.

Commentary

Mosiah 18:8. Becoming the Lord's People through Baptism

• Elder Jeffrey R. Holland of the Quorum of the Twelve Apostles summarized the expectations that come to those who accept baptism:

"Alma began baptizing all who wished to make a covenant with Christ. He asked that they 'serve [God] and keep his commandments, that he may pour out his Spirit more abundantly' upon them. These new disciples would also demonstrate their faith by:

"Coming into the fold of God.

"Being called his people.

"Bearing one another's burdens.

"Mourning with those that mourn.

"Comforting those who stand in need of comfort.

"Standing as witnesses of God at all times and in all things and in all places.

"Entering into a covenant to serve God and keep his commandments.

"This declaration by Alma at the Waters of Mormon still stands as the most complete scriptural statement on

record as to what the newly baptized commit to do and be" (*Christ and the New Covenant* [1997], 106).

Elder Joseph B. Wirthlin (1917–2008) of the Quorum of the Twelve Apostles described the blessings of accepting the covenants of baptism: "I have noted throughout my life that when people come to fully understand the blessings and the power of their baptismal covenant, whether as new converts or as lifelong members of the Church, great joy comes into their lives and they approach their duties in the kingdom with contagious enthusiasm" ("Alma the Elder: A Role Model for Today," in *Heroes from the Book of Mormon* [1995], 84).

Mosiah 18:9. "Stand as Witnesses of God at All Times"

• Elder M. Russell Ballard of the Quorum of the Twelve Apostles declared that our baptismal covenants require righteousness no matter how difficult the circumstances: "When we covenant in the waters of baptism to 'stand as witnesses of God at all times and in all things, and in all places,' we're not talking solely about fast and testimony meetings. It may not always be easy, convenient, or politically correct to stand for truth and right, but it is always the right thing to do—always" (in Conference Report, Oct. 1997, 51; or *Ensign,* Nov. 1997, 37).

Mosiah 18:10. "Ye Have Entered into a Covenant with Him"

• Sister Bonnie D. Parkin, as Relief Society general president, explained how Heavenly Father tutors us as we make and keep covenants: "Covenants—or binding promises between us and Heavenly Father—are essential for our eternal progression. Step-by-step, He tutors us to become like Him by enlisting us in His work. At baptism we covenant to love Him with all our hearts and love our sisters and brothers as ourselves.

In the temple we further covenant to be obedient, selfless, faithful, honorable, charitable. We covenant to make sacrifices and consecrate all that we have. Forged through priesthood authority, our kept covenants bring blessings to fill our cups to overflowing. How often do you reflect that your covenants reach beyond mortality and connect you to the Divine? Making covenants is the expression of a willing heart; keeping covenants, the expression of a faithful heart" ("With Holiness of Heart," *Ensign,* Nov. 2002, 103).

Mosiah 18:10. Having His Spirit

• Elder Robert D. Hales of the Quorum of the Twelve Apostles observed that having the Holy Ghost influences our conduct and solidifies our testimonies:

"The Holy Ghost gives us the strength and courage to conduct our lives in the ways of the kingdom of God and is the source of our testimony of the Father and the Son. . . .

"By choosing to be in His kingdom, we separate—not isolate—ourselves from the world. Our dress will be modest, our thoughts pure, our language clean. The movies and television we watch, the music we listen to, the books, magazines, and newspapers we read will be uplifting. We will choose friends who encourage our eternal goals, and we will treat others with kindness. We will shun the vices of immorality, gambling, tobacco, liquor, and illicit drugs. Our Sunday activities will reflect the commandment of God to remember the Sabbath day and keep it holy. We will follow the example of Jesus Christ in the way we treat others. We will live to be worthy to enter the house of the Lord" (in Conference Report, Oct. 2000, 6–7; or *Ensign,* Nov. 2000, 8).

Mosiah 18:12–18. Alma Held the Priesthood

• President Joseph Fielding Smith (1876–1972) explained that Alma had authority to baptize:

"We may conclude that Alma held the priesthood before he, with others, became disturbed with King Noah. Whether this is so or not makes no difference because in the Book of Mosiah it is stated definitely that he had authority [see Mosiah 18:13].

"If he had authority to baptize that is evidence that he had been baptized. Therefore, when Alma baptized himself with Helam that was not a case of Alma baptizing himself, but merely as a token to the Lord of his humility and full repentance" (*Answers to Gospel Questions,* comp. Joseph Fielding Smith Jr., 5 vols. [1957–66], 3:203).

> **MOSIAH 18:21–29**
> *What did Alma teach his people to do to "walk uprightly before God"? (v. 29).*

Mosiah 18:21. "Hearts Knit Together in Unity and in Love"

• Through modern revelation the Lord counseled, "Be one; and if ye are not one ye are not mine" (D&C 38:27). President Henry B. Eyring of the First Presidency commented on the division prevalent in our fallen world and how keeping the commandments brings unity:

"With the Fall it became clear that living in unity would not be easy. . . .

". . . We need hope that we can experience unity in this life and qualify to have it forever in the world to come. . . .

"If we are to have unity, there are commandments we must keep concerning how we feel. We must forgive and bear no malice toward those who offend us" (in

Conference Report, Apr. 1998, 85–86, 88; or *Ensign,* May 1998, 66, 68).

• Unity and love came as the people of Alma recommitted themselves to living the commandments of God. While serving in the Seventy, Elder C. Max Caldwell described this increase in love as a condition that needs to be developed:

"Jesus' love was inseparably connected to and resulted from his life of serving, sacrificing, and giving in behalf of others. We cannot develop Christlike love except by practicing the process prescribed by the Master. . . .

"Charity is not just a precept or a principle, nor is it just a word to describe actions or attitudes. Rather, it is an internal condition that must be developed and experienced in order to be understood. We are possessors of charity when it is a part of our nature. People who have charity have a love for the Savior, have received of his love, and love others as he does" (in Conference Report, Oct. 1992, 40; or *Ensign,* Nov. 1992, 30).

Mosiah 18:23. "Observe the Sabbath Day, and Keep It Holy"

• "Because the Sabbath is a holy day, it should be reserved for worthy and holy activities. . . . If we merely lounge about doing nothing on the Sabbath, we fail to keep the day holy" (*True to the Faith: A Gospel Reference* [2004], 146).

Elder L. Tom Perry of the Quorum of the Twelve Apostles spoke about how the Sabbath is a special time for families to be together and reviewed 10 other activities of the many that are worthy of the Sabbath day: "This is the time we are to attend our regular meetings together, study the life and teachings of the Savior and of the prophets. 'Other appropriate Sunday activities include (1) writing personal and family journals, (2) holding family councils, (3) establishing and maintaining family organizations for the immediate and extended family, (4) personal interviews between parents and children, (5) writing to relatives and missionaries, (6) genealogy, (7) visiting relatives and those who are ill or lonely, (8) missionary work, (9) reading stories to children, and (10) singing Church hymns.' ["Suggestions for Individual and Family

Sabbath-Day Activities," *Ensign,* Mar. 1980, 76]" (in Conference Report, Apr. 2003, 44; or *Ensign,* May 2003, 42).

• Elder Mark E. Petersen (1900–1984) of the Quorum of the Twelve Apostles taught that our observance of the Sabbath day reflects our appreciation of the Atonement of Jesus Christ:

"We can readily see that observance of the Sabbath is an indication of the depth of our conversion.

"Our observance or nonobservance of the Sabbath is an unerring measure of our attitude toward the Lord personally and toward his suffering in Gethsemane, his death on the cross, and his resurrection from the dead. It is a sign of whether we are Christians in very deed, or whether our conversion is so shallow that commemoration of his atoning sacrifice means little or nothing to us" (in Conference Report, Apr. 1975, 72; or *Ensign,* May 1975, 49).

Mosiah 18:28. "They Should Impart of Their Substance of Their Own Free Will"

• President Marion G. Romney (1897–1988) of the First Presidency counseled us to develop charity by giving ourselves fully to the work of the Lord: "Some may ask, 'How do I obtain these righteous feelings in giving? How do I overcome giving grudgingly? How do I obtain the "pure love of Christ?"' To those I would say: Faithfully live all the commandments, give of yourselves, care for your families, serve in church callings, perform missionary work, pay tithes and offerings, study the scriptures—and the list could go on. As you lose yourself in this service, the Lord will touch and soften your heart" (in Conference Report, Oct. 1981, 131–32; or *Ensign,* Nov. 1981, 93).

Mosiah 19–24. People of Limhi Compared to People of Alma

• When the prophet Abinadi first went to the wicked people of King Noah, he told them that if they did not repent they would come under bondage (see Mosiah 11:21). When the Lord commanded Abinadi to return to them two years later, they still had not repented (see Mosiah 12:1). Therefore, according to the word of the Lord, all of them would inevitably come under bondage. Furthermore, the second time Abinadi preached to them, the Lord's warning to the people of King Noah was even stronger. In addition to being brought into bondage, many would be slain. Others would experience famine and pestilence, and if they still refused to repent, they would be destroyed (see Mosiah 12:2–8).

After Abinadi's second visit, there was a division among the people. Alma believed Abinadi, and a group of people listened to Alma, repented, and became righteous. However, the majority of the people—under the leadership of King Noah and then his son Limhi—did not repent until much later. Although both groups eventually came under bondage because they refused to repent after the first warning of the Lord, consider the following differences between what happened to Alma's group, who voluntarily repented, and Limhi's group, who were compelled to repent.

Time Period	People of Limhi	People of Alma
Abinadi's second visit	Noah's people rejected and killed Abinadi (Mosiah 17). They continued in their wickedness.	Alma believed Abinadi (Mosiah 17:2–4). Alma was forced to flee.
Aftermath of Abinadi's second visit	Noah-Limhi's people continued in wickedness (Mosiah 19:2–20). They were divided (v. 2). They were contentious (v. 3). They were attacked by the Lamanites (vv. 6–7). King Noah was killed by his own people (v. 20). The people were brought into Lamanite bondage and had to pay a 50 percent tribute to the Lamanites (v. 15).	A small group believed Alma (Mosiah 18:3–21). They traveled to hear Alma preach (v. 4). They were taught to repent and have faith (v. 7). They covenanted with God (vv. 8–11). They escaped the efforts of King Noah to destroy them (vv. 33–34).
Two years from the time of Abinadi's death (Mosiah 19:29)	Limhi's people endured bondage (Mosiah 19:22–20:22). They endured bondage and 50 percent tribute (19:22). The Lamanites attacked (20:7). They fought back (20:8–11). They accepted bondage (20:22).	Alma's people prospered (Mosiah 23:2–5). The Lord strengthened them (v. 2). They built a city (v. 5).
A period of time following the first two years (Mosiah 19:29)	Conditions of bondage intensified (Mosiah 21:3–6). The Lamanites smote them on the cheeks and exercised authority over them (v. 3). The Lamanites gave Limhi's people heavy burdens and drove them like animals (v. 3). The people murmured because of their trials (v. 6). Limhi's people went to war three times to deliver themselves and were defeated each time. Many were killed and there was much sorrow (vv. 7–12).	Alma's people continued in peace and prosperity (Mosiah 23:19–20). They lived in righteousness (vv. 14–15). They prospered exceedingly (vv. 19–20).

Time Period	People of Limhi	People of Alma
Continued after the first two years	Limhi's people repented and turned to the Lord (Mosiah 21:7–14, 25–26). They were compelled to be humble (vv. 13–14). They accepted their bondage and abuse (v. 13). They cried mightily to the Lord (v. 14). They sent men to find help in Zarahemla (vv. 25–26).	Alma's people continued in peace and prosperity.
Continued after the first two years	The Lord eventually delivered them from Lamanite bondage (Mosiah 21:15–22:16). The Lord was slow to hear them, but He softened the hearts of their enemies, who eased their burdens (21:15). They were not delivered at first (21:15). They prospered by degrees (21:16). They helped others (21:17). They covenanted to serve God (21:31). They gave wine to the Lamanite guards, who then fell asleep (22:7, 10). They escaped (22:11).	Alma's people continued in peace and prosperity.
c. 120–121 B.C. (Mosiah 22; 24:25 footnotes)	Limhi's people arrived in the land of Zarahemla (Mosiah 22:13). A Lamanite army pursued Limhi's people (vv. 15–16).	Alma's people experienced bondage and delivery from the Lord (Mosiah 23–24). The Lamanite army sent after Limhi's people discovered Alma's people in the land of Helam (Mosiah 23:25). Alma's people were taken into bondage (Mosiah 24:8–10). They remained faithful and endured patiently (vv. 10–16). The Lord eased their burdens and strengthened them (vv. 14–15). The Lord delivered them out of bondage and into the land of Zarahemla (v. 20).

• Limhi's people were forced to remember the Lord during their Lamanite bondage. Alma's people willingly repented after Abinadi's second warning. Consequently, the suffering of Limhi's group was greater and more prolonged. Some years later, Alma the Younger explained a principle that helps us understand the different results experienced by these two groups: Some "are compelled to be humble . . . for a man sometimes, if he is compelled to be humble, seeketh repentance" (Alma 32:13), and "blessed are they who humble themselves without being compelled to be humble" (v. 16).

Mosiah 21:13–14. Humility Fortifies Our Dependence upon the Lord

• After failing the third time to fight their way out of bondage, Limhi's colony finally turned to God in humility and prayer and sought deliverance by His hand. Their experiences compelled them to seek the Lord and not to put their trust in the arm of the flesh (see Alma 32:13–16; see also 2 Nephi 4:34).

President Ezra Taft Benson (1899–1994) taught that humility strengthens our dependence upon the Lord: "Humility, of course, is not a sign of weakness. Humility does not mean timidity. A person can be humble, powerful, and courageous. The Prophet Joseph is a good example. Humility is an acknowledged recognition of our dependence on a higher power" (*The Teachings of Ezra Taft Benson* [1988], 369).

> ### MOSIAH 21:15–22
> *In what ways did the people of Limhi begin to "prosper by degrees in the land"? (v. 16). How can we receive similar help?*

Mosiah 21:15. "The Lord Did Hear Their Cries"

• Even though many people in Limhi's colony brought their distress upon themselves, the Lord was merciful and answered their prayers. The Prophet Joseph Smith (1805–44) described the Lord's mercy in response to the sorrow the Prophet felt as a result of his mistakes: "I have called to mind all the past moments of my life, and am left to mourn and shed tears of sorrow for my folly in suffering the adversary of my soul to have so much power over me as he has had in times past. But God is merciful and has forgiven my sins, and I rejoice that he sendeth forth the Comforter unto as many as believe and humbleth themselves before him" (*The Personal Writings of Joseph Smith,* comp. Dean C. Jessee [1984], 238; punctuation, spelling, and capitalization standardized).

Mosiah 23:21. "He Trieth Their Patience and Their Faith"

• Even though the people who followed Alma had repented and been faithful, the Lord allowed them to be temporarily oppressed by the Lamanites in fulfillment of Abinadi's prophecy (see Mosiah 12:1–5) and as a trial of their patience and faith. Elder Orson F. Whitney (1855–1931) of the Quorum of the Twelve Apostles taught that everything we experience teaches us valuable lessons: "No pain that we suffer, no trial that we experience is wasted. It ministers to our education, to the development of such qualities as patience, faith, fortitude and humility. All that we suffer and all that we endure, especially when we endure it patiently, builds up our characters, purifies our hearts,

expands our souls, and makes us more tender and charitable, more worthy to be called the children of God . . . and it is through sorrow and suffering, toil and tribulation, that we gain the education that we come here to acquire and which will make us more like our Father and Mother in heaven" (cited in Spencer W. Kimball, *Faith Precedes the Miracle* [1972], 98).

Mosiah 23–24. The History of Alma's People

• Mosiah chapters 23–24 is a flashback within a flashback (see commentary for Mosiah 9–22 on p. 149). The history of Alma, from the time they were driven into the wilderness by the people of King Noah until they arrived in Zarahemla, was added to the record. This small flashback occupies approximately 20 years. When the reader finishes chapters 23–24, both Zeniff's people and Alma's people have returned to Zarahemla and King Mosiah (see the chart "Flashbacks from Omni through Mosiah" in the appendix, p. 413).

Mosiah 24:13–15. "They Did Submit Cheerfully and with Patience to All the Will of the Lord"

• If we are entirely dependent upon God, then He can take our limitations and our weaknesses and magnify them into strengths useful for His divine purposes. Elder Richard G. Scott of the Quorum of the Twelve Apostles encouraged us to cheerfully rely on the Lord when we face the challenges of mortality:

"Problems or trials in our lives need to be viewed in the perspective of scriptural doctrine. Otherwise they can easily overtake our vision, absorb our energy, and deprive us of the joy and beauty the Lord intends us to receive here on earth. Some people are like rocks thrown into a sea of problems. They are drowned by them. Be a cork. When submerged in a problem, fight to be free to bob up to serve again with happiness. . . .

"The Lord is intent on your personal growth and development. That progress is accelerated when you willingly allow Him to lead you through every growth experience you encounter, whether initially it be to your individual liking or not. When you trust in the Lord, when you are willing to let your heart and your mind be centered in His will, when you ask to be led by the Spirit to do His will, you are assured of the greatest happiness along the way and the most fulfilling attainment from this mortal experience. If you question everything you are asked to do, or dig in your heels at every unpleasant challenge, you make it harder for the Lord to bless you [see 1 Nephi 3:7]" (in Conference Report, Apr. 1996, 32–33; or *Ensign,* May 1996, 24–25).

Points to Ponder

- Reflect upon the baptismal covenants recorded in Mosiah 18:8–10. What can you do this week to live your covenants more fully?
- In what ways has your faith been strengthened by trials?
- How can the example of Alma and his followers help you trust in the Savior's Atonement and power?

Suggested Assignments

- Find a scripture for each aspect of our redemption through the Savior's Atonement described in Mosiah 18:2, including His power, suffering, death, resurrection, and ascension into heaven. You may want to write your references in the margin of your scriptures next to Mosiah 18:2.
- Study and outline the baptismal covenant as described by Alma in Mosiah 18:8–10.
- Call, visit, or write a letter to a Church priesthood leader, teacher, or adviser who has nourished you "with things pertaining to righteousness" (Mosiah 23:18) and express your appreciation and testimony to him or her.

CHAPTER 22

Mosiah 25–29

Introduction

Many of the "rising generation" rejected the testimony of their fathers and led some Church members to "commit many sins" (see Mosiah 26:1, 6). As a result, Alma sought the Lord's guidance on how to deal with members of the Church who broke the laws of God. He also prayed that his own son might "be brought to the knowledge of the truth" (see Mosiah 27:14). The answers to both petitions provide valuable teachings for us today. We learn the manner in which priesthood leaders must admonish those who commit serious sin and help them through the repentance process. We also see the need for all mankind to be "born of God" in the story of Alma the Younger and the four sons of Mosiah. Through your study, contemplate how accepting the Atonement of Jesus Christ leads to repentance, full conversion, and the desire to labor for the salvation of others.

Commentary

Mosiah 25–29. Mosiah²

• The book of Mosiah is often confusing because of the different storylines and historical flashbacks that are part of the book. Refer to the chart "Flashbacks from Omni through Mosiah" in the appendix (p. 413).

Mosiah 25:5–11. The Power of the Scriptures

• In Mosiah 25:5–11, Mosiah "caused" the scriptures to be read to the people. The following list shows the effects that the scriptures had on the people:

1. They were "struck with wonder and amazement" (v. 7).

2. They "were filled with exceedingly great joy" (v. 8).

3. They felt "sorrow" for the deaths of so many (v. 9).

4. They recognized the "goodness of God" (v. 10).

5. They felt the need to "give thanks to God" (v. 10).

6. The sins of others "filled [them] with pain and anguish" (v. 11).

Jerry Thompson, © IRI

Mosiah 26:1–4. The Rising Generation

• President Henry B. Eyring of the First Presidency emphasized the need to teach the youth of the Church to believe in God: "No charge in the kingdom is more important than to build faith in youth. Each child in each generation chooses faith or disbelief. Faith is not an inheritance; it is a choice. Those who believed King Benjamin learned that. Many of their children chose later not to believe. The scriptures give as a reason, 'for they would not call upon the Lord their God' (Mosiah 26:4)" ("Inquire of the Lord" [remarks at an evening with Elder Neal A. Maxwell, Feb. 2, 2001], 1, www.ldsces.org).

• Speaking to the youth of the Church, Elder Jeffrey R. Holland of the Quorum of the Twelve Apostles explained why older Church members mentor those younger than them: "So much that we do in this church is directed toward you, those whom the Book of Mormon calls 'the rising generation' (Mosiah 26:1; Alma 5:49). We who have already walked that portion of life's path that you are now on try to call back to you something of what we have learned. We shout encouragement. We try to warn of pitfalls or perils along the way. Where possible we try to walk with you and keep you close to our side" (in Conference Report, Apr. 1995, 52; or *Ensign,* May 1995, 38).

> ### *MOSIAH 26:1–6*
> *What were the challenges Alma faced with the rising generation?*

Mosiah 26:8–12. Why Did King Mosiah Decline to Judge Church Members?

• After King Mosiah (as king and prophet) gave Alma authority to establish churches throughout the land, it seemed natural for Alma to bring the disobedient Church members to Mosiah to be judged. The king, however, having delegated priesthood authority to Alma, indicated that Alma was responsible for dealing with those who transgressed the laws of the Church. Mosiah retained the judgment of those who broke the laws of the land.

Mosiah 26:20. "Thou Shalt Have Eternal Life"

• The Lord declared that Alma should "have eternal life" (Mosiah 26:20). The Prophet Joseph Smith (1805–44) outlined the process by which one obtains this promise: "After a person has faith in Christ, repents of his sins, and is baptized for the remission of his sins and receives the Holy Ghost, (by the laying on of hands), . . . then let him continue to humble himself before God, hungering and thirsting after righteousness, and living by every word of God, and the Lord will soon say unto him, Son, thou shalt be exalted. When the Lord has thoroughly proved him, and finds that the man is determined to serve Him at all hazards, then the man will find his calling and his election made sure, then it will be his privilege to receive the other Comforter, which the Lord hath promised the Saints, as is recorded in the testimony of St. John" (*History of the Church*, 3:380).

Mosiah 26:24–28. Knowing the Lord

• Elder Joseph B. Wirthlin (1917–2008) of the Quorum of the Twelve Apostles explained how we can know the Lord: "We can choose to know the Lord by reading the scriptures every day; by communicating with him in fervent prayer at least morning and night, and in times of trial, every hour or more, if needed; and by keeping his commandments. Remember, 'Hereby we do know that we know him, if we keep his commandments. He that saith, I know him, and keepeth not his commandments, is a liar, and the truth is not in him. But whoso keepeth his word, in him verily is the love of God perfected: hereby know we that we are in him.' (1 John 2:3–5.)" (*Finding Peace in Our Lives* [1995], 74).

Mosiah 26:29–30. Confession of Sins

• Confession of sins is required as part of the repentance process. The Lord declared, "By this ye may know if a man repenteth of his sins—behold, he will confess them and forsake them" (D&C 58:43 📖). In *True to the Faith: A Gospel Reference* (2004), we read the following description:

"*Confession.* 'He that covereth his sins shall not prosper: but whoso confesseth and forsaketh them shall have mercy' (Proverbs 28:13). Essential to forgiveness is a willingness to disclose fully to your

Heavenly Father all that you have done. Kneel before Him in humble prayer, acknowledging your sins. Confess your shame and guilt, and then plead for help.

"Serious transgressions, such as violations of the law of chastity, may jeopardize your membership in the Church. Therefore, you need to confess these sins to both the Lord and His representatives in the Church. This is done under the care of your bishop or branch president and possibly your stake or mission president, who serve as watchmen and judges in the Church. While only the Lord can forgive sins, these  priesthood leaders play a critical role in the process of repentance. They will keep your confession confidential and help you throughout the process of repentance. Be completely honest with them. If you partially confess, mentioning only lesser mistakes, you will not be able to resolve a more serious, undisclosed transgression. The sooner you begin this process, the sooner you will find the peace and joy that come with the miracle of forgiveness" ([2004], 134).

> ### MOSIAH 26:31
> *What is the result of refusing to forgive others who trespass against us?*

Mosiah 26:32–36. "Their Names Were Blotted Out"

• "Blotted out" in Mosiah 26:36 refers to excommunication. When a Church member commits serious sin, the Lord's servants must take steps to assist the sinner through repentance. Sometimes this involves formal or informal Church discipline. Elder Dallin H. Oaks of the Quorum of the Twelve Apostles explained:

"Church discipline encourages members to keep the commandments of God. Its mere existence . . . stresses the seriousness and clarifies the meaning of the commandments of God. This is extremely important in an otherwise permissive society. . . .

"The shepherd has a responsibility to protect the flock. . . . That responsibility may require him to deny [the sinner] the fellowship of the Saints or even to sever his membership in the flock. As Jesus taught: 'If he repent not he shall not be numbered among my people, that he may not destroy my people, for behold I know my sheep, and they are numbered.' (3 Ne. 18:31; see also Mosiah 26:34–36.)" (*The Lord's Way* [1991], 216, 227).

• President James E. Faust (1920–2007) of the First Presidency identified offenses that warrant Church discipline:

"Church discipline is not limited to sexual sins but includes other acts such as murder, abortions, burglary, theft, fraud and other dishonesty, deliberate disobedience to the rules and regulations of the Church, advocating or practicing polygamy, apostasy, or any other unchristian conduct, including defiance or ridicule of the Lord's anointed, contrary to the law of the Lord and the order of the Church. . . .

"Among the activities considered apostate to the Church include when members '(1) repeatedly act in clear, open, and deliberate public opposition to the Church or its leaders; (2) persist in teaching as Church doctrine information that is not Church doctrine after being corrected by their bishops or higher authority; or (3) continue to follow the teachings of apostate cults (such as those that advocate plural marriage) after being corrected by their bishops or higher authority' (*General Handbook of Instructions* [1989], p. 10-3)" (in Conference Report, Oct. 1993, 52–53; or *Ensign*, Nov. 1993, 37–38).

• In 1985 the First Presidency issued an invitation for everyone to come back, which reminded us of our duty toward those who have had their names "blotted out":

"We are aware of some who are inactive, of others who have become critical and are prone to find fault, and of those who have been disfellowshipped or excommunicated because of serious transgressions.

"To all such we reach out in love. We are anxious to forgive in the spirit of Him who said: 'I, the Lord, will forgive whom I will forgive, but of you it is required to forgive all men.' (D&C 64:10)

"We encourage Church members to forgive those who may have wronged them. To those who have ceased activity and to those who have become critical, we say, 'Come back. Come back and feast at the table of the Lord, and taste again the sweet and satisfying fruits of fellowship with the saints.'

"We are confident that many have longed to return, but have felt awkward about doing so. We assure you that you will find open arms to receive you and willing hands to assist you" (Ezra Taft Benson, Gordon B. Hinckley, and Thomas S. Monson, "An Invitation to Come Back," *Church News*, Dec. 22, 1985, 3).

Mosiah 27:14. An Angel Sent from God

• One of the roles an angel fulfills is to call the wicked to repentance (see Moroni 7:29, 31). Note that the angel did not come to Alma and the four sons of Mosiah because of their righteousness but "that the prayers of his servants might be answered according to their faith" (Mosiah 27:14).

• The ministering of angels must be in harmony with the will of God and does not always occur according to the timetable of the petitioner. Speaking of a man who had prayed for the visitation of angels, President Wilford Woodruff (1807–98) said:

"I said to him that if he were to pray a thousand years to the God of Israel for that gift, it would not be granted, unless the Lord had a motive in sending an angel to him. I told him that the Lord never did nor never will send an angel to anybody merely to gratify the desire of the individual to see an angel. If the Lord sends an angel to anyone, He sends him to perform a work that cannot be performed only by the  administration of an angel. I said to him that those were my views. The Lord had sent angels to men from the creation of the world, at different times, but always with a message or with something to perform that could not be performed without. I rehearsed to him different times when angels appeared to men. Of course, I referred to the angel visiting Joseph Smith. The Revelator John said that in the last days an angel would fly in the midst of heaven, having the everlasting Gospel to preach to them that dwelt on the earth. The reason it required an angel to do this work was, the Gospel was not on the earth. The Gospel and the Priesthood had been taken from among men. Hence God had to restore it again.

"Now, I have always said, and I want to say it to you, that the Holy Ghost is what every Saint of God needs. It is far more important that a man should have that gift than he should have the ministration of an angel, unless it is necessary for an angel to teach him something that he has not been taught" ("The Administration of Angels," in Brian H. Stuy, comp. *Collected Discourses,* 5 vols. [1987–92], 5:233).

MOSIAH 27:14
How can righteous parents influence wayward children?

Mosiah 27:22–23. Ministering to Those Who Have Strayed

• One of the chief duties God requires of those He calls to serve is to help those who have strayed come back to the fold. While serving in the Seventy, Elder Theodore M. Burton (1907–89) shared his feelings about this sacred work: "I have been asked the question, 'Isn't it depressing to have to review the sins and transgressions of people involved in such difficulties?' It would be if I were looking for sins and transgressions. But I am working with people who are repenting. These are sons and daughters of God who have made mistakes—some of them very serious. But they are *not* sinners. They *were*

sinners in the past but have learned through bitter experience the heartbreak that results from disobedience to God's laws. *Now* they are no longer sinners. They are God's repentant children who want to come back to Him and are striving to do so. They have made their mistakes and have paid for them. Now they seek understanding, love, and acceptance" (in Conference Report, Oct. 1985, 80–81; or *Ensign,* Nov. 1985, 64).

Mosiah 27:25. Being Born Again

• President Ezra Taft Benson (1899–1994) gave us an important reminder as we seek to be born again and become like our Savior Jesus Christ:

"We must be careful, as we seek to become more and more godlike, that we do not become discouraged and lose hope. Becoming Christlike is a lifetime pursuit and very often involves growth and change that is slow, almost imperceptible. The scriptures record remarkable accounts of men whose lives changed dramatically, in an instant, as it were: Alma the Younger, Paul on the road to Damascus, Enos praying far into the night, King Lamoni. Such astonishing examples of the power to change even those steeped in sin give confidence that the Atonement can reach even those deepest in despair.

"But we must be cautious as we discuss these remarkable examples. Though they are real and powerful, they are the exception more than the rule. For every Paul, for every Enos, and for every King Lamoni, there are hundreds and thousands of people who find the process of repentance much more subtle, much more imperceptible. Day by day they move closer to the Lord, little realizing they are building a godlike life. They live quiet lives of goodness, service, and commitment. They are like the Lamanites, who the Lord said 'were baptized with fire and with the Holy Ghost, *and they knew it not.*' (3 Ne. 9:20; italics added.)" ("A Mighty Change of Heart," *Ensign,* Oct. 1989, 5).

• For additional information on the subject of being born again and experiencing a mighty change of heart, refer to the commentary for Mosiah 5:2 (see p. 144), Alma 5:12–14 (see p. 178), and Alma 36:17–21 (see p. 234).

• Elder Dallin H. Oaks discussed the meaning of being born again:

"The question of whether a person has been saved is sometimes phrased in terms of whether that person has been 'born again.' Being 'born again' is a familiar reference in the Bible and the Book of Mormon. As noted earlier, Jesus taught that except a man was 'born again' (John 3:3) of water and of the Spirit, he could not enter into the kingdom of God (see John 3:5). The Book of Mormon has many teachings about the necessity of being 'born again' or 'born of God' (Mosiah 27:25; see verses 24–26; Alma 36:24, 26; Moses 6:59). As we understand these scriptures, our answer to whether we have been born again is clearly 'yes.' We were born again when we entered into a covenant relationship with our Savior by being born of water and of the Spirit and by taking upon us the name of Jesus Christ. We can renew that rebirth each Sabbath when we partake of the sacrament.

"Latter-day Saints affirm that those who have been born again in this way are spiritually begotten sons and daughters of Jesus Christ (see Mosiah 5:7; 15:9–13; 27:25). Nevertheless, in order to realize the intended blessings of this born-again status, we must still keep our covenants and endure to the end. In the meantime, through the grace of God, we have been born again as new creatures with new spiritual parentage and the prospects of a glorious inheritance" (in Conference Report, Apr. 1998, 77; or *Ensign,* May 1998, 56).

Mosiah 27:28. After Much Tribulation Comes the Blessing

• Though Alma the Younger had to wade through much tribulation, the end result of his repentance was exquisite and exceeding joy (see Alma 36:21). The following chart helps illustrate the effect of Alma's repentance:

Before	After
"Carnal and fallen," to be "cast off" (Mosiah 27:25–27; Alma 36:11)	Redeemed of God, "born of the Spirit" (Mosiah 27:24–25; Alma 36:23)
"Wading through much tribulation" (Mosiah 27:28)	Snatched "out of an everlasting burning" (Mosiah 27:28)

Before	After
In "the gall of bitterness and bonds of iniquity" (Mosiah 27:29)	"Redeemed from the gall of bitterness and bonds of iniquity" (Mosiah 27:29)
"In the darkest abyss" (Mosiah 27:29)	Beheld "the marvelous light of God" (Mosiah 27:29)
"Racked with eternal torment" (Mosiah 27:29)	Soul "pained no more" (Mosiah 27:29)
"Harrowed up by the memory" of his many sins (Alma 36:17)	No longer "harrowed up by the memory" of his sins (Alma 36:19)
Felt exquisite and exceeding pain (Alma 36:20–21)	Felt exquisite and exceeding joy (Alma 36:20–21)
Soul racked with horror at the thought of being in the presence of God (Alma 36:14–15)	Soul longed to be in the presence of God (Alma 36:22)

• Elder Jeffrey R. Holland explained we must realize that the price of sin is high and that though repentance can be difficult, the end result is always worth much more than the cost:

"We learn that repentance is a very painful process. By his own admission Alma said he wandered 'through much tribulation,' repenting nigh unto death,' that he was consumed with an 'everlasting burning. . . . I was in the darkest abyss,' he said. 'My soul was racked with eternal torment' (Mosiah 27:28–29). . . .

"For three seemingly endless days and nights he was torn 'with the pains of a damned soul' (Alma 36:16), pain so real that he was physically incapacitated and spiritually terrorized by what appeared to be his ultimate fate. No one should think that the gift of forgiveness is fully realized without significant effort on the part of the forgiven. No one should be foolish enough to sin willingly or wantonly, thinking forgiveness is easily available.

"Repentance of necessity involves suffering and sorrow. Anyone who thinks otherwise has not read the life of the young Alma, nor tried personally to repent. In the process of repentance we are granted just a taste of the suffering we would endure if we failed to turn away from evil. That pain, though only momentary for the repentant, is the most bitter of cups. No man or woman should be foolish enough to think it can be sipped, even briefly, without consequence. . . .

"We learn that when repentance is complete, we are born again and leave behind forever the self we once were. To me, none of the many approaches to teaching repentance falls more short than the well-intentioned suggestion that 'although a nail may be removed from a wooden post, there will forever be a hole in that post.' We know that repentance (the removal of that nail, if you will) can be a very long and painful and difficult task. Unfortunately, some will never have the incentive to undertake it. We even know that there are a very few sins for which no repentance is possible. But where repentance is possible, and its requirements are faithfully pursued and completed, there is no 'hole left in the post' for the bold reason that it is no longer the same post. It is a new post. We can start again, utterly clean, with a new will and a new way of life" (*However Long and Hard the Road* [1985], 83–84).

MOSIAH 28:3–4
How did the conversion of the sons of Mosiah influence their desire to be missionaries?

Mosiah 28:3. "Salvation Should Be Declared to Every Creature"

• President Howard W. Hunter (1907–95) described how desire to share the gospel is a natural result of personal conversion:

"There is the example of the four sons of Mosiah—Ammon, Aaron, Omner, and Himni—who received a forgiveness of sins through the Atonement and then labored for years among the Lamanites to bring them to Christ. The record states that they could not bear the thought that any soul should perish (see Mosiah 28:3). . . .

"A great indicator of one's personal conversion is the desire to share the gospel with others. For this reason the Lord gave an obligation to every member of the Church to be missionaries" (*The Teachings of Howard W. Hunter,* ed. Clyde J. Williams [1997], 249).

• Elder M. Russell Ballard of the Quorum of the Twelve Apostles suggested one effective way Church members could share the gospel today: "The key to successful member missionary work is the exercise of faith. One way to show your faith in the Lord and His promises is to prayerfully set a date to have someone prepared to meet with the missionaries. I have received hundreds of letters from members who have exercised their faith in this simple way. Even though families had no one in mind with whom they could share the gospel, they set a date, prayed, and then talked to many more people. The Lord is the Good Shepherd, and He knows His sheep who have been prepared to hear His voice. He will guide us as we seek His divine help in sharing His gospel" (in Conference Report, Apr. 2006, 89; or *Ensign,* May 2006, 86).

Mosiah 28:11–20. The Jaredite Record and Seer Stones

• President Joseph Fielding Smith (1876–1972) discussed Mosiah's use of the interpreters in translating the Jaredite record:

"The people of Limhi brought to Mosiah a record, '. . . engraven on plates of ore,' [Mosiah 21:27] which record Mosiah translated by the aid of 'two stones which were fastened into the two rims of a bow.' . . .

"Joseph Smith received with the 'breastplate' and the plates of the Book of Mormon, the Urim and Thummim, which were hid up by Moroni to come forth in the last days as a means by which the ancient record might be translated, which Urim and Thummim were given to the brother of Jared [see D&C 17:1]" (*Answers to Gospel Questions,* comp. Joseph Fielding Smith Jr., 5 vols. [1957–66], 1:161–62).

Mosiah 29:26–27. The Danger of the Majority Choosing "That Which Is Not Right"

• Elder Neal A. Maxwell (1926–2004) of the Quorum of the Twelve Apostles warned that we must not be indifferent to wickedness in society, because destruction awaits nations that choose unrighteousness:

"Speaking behaviorally, when what was once the lesser voice of the people becomes more dominant, then the judgments of God and the consequences of foolish selfishness follow (see Mosiah 29:26–27).

"Cultural decline is accelerated when single-interest segments of society become indifferent to general values once widely shared. This drift is facilitated by the indifferent or the indulgent as society is led carefully down to hell (see 2 Nephi 28:21). Some may not join in this drift, but instead they step aside, whereas once they might have constrained, as is their representative right. . . .

"We actually have an obligation to notice genuine, telltale societal signs. . . .

"For what happens in cultural decline both leaders and followers are really accountable. Historically, of course, it is easy to criticize bad leaders, but we should not give followers a free pass. Otherwise, in their rationalization of their degeneration they may say they were just following orders, while the leader was just ordering followers! However, much more is required of followers in a democratic society, wherein individual character matters so much in both leaders and followers" (in Conference Report, Apr. 1999, 28–30; or *Ensign,* May 1999, 23–24).

• President Boyd K. Packer also spoke of the recent trends of distorting tolerance:

"The virtue of tolerance has been distorted and elevated to a position of such prominence as to be thought equal to and even valued more than morality. It is one thing to be tolerant, even forgiving of individual conduct. It is quite another to collectively legislate and legalize to protect immoral conduct that can weaken, even destroy the family.

"There is a dangerous trap when tolerance is exaggerated to protect the rights of those whose conduct endangers the family and injures the rights of the more part of the people. We are getting dangerously close to the condition described by the prophet Mosiah [in Mosiah 29:26–27]" ("Children of God," *BYU Women's Conference,* May 5, 2006, 6).

Mosiah 29:41–44. The Reign of the Judges

• The change in the government instituted through King Mosiah was so significant that from then until the birth of Christ (see 3 Nephi 2:8) the Nephites recorded their time in relation to the beginning of the reign of the judges. Previously the Nephites kept track of time from the year Lehi left Jerusalem.

Points to Ponder

• What do you think motivates those who have been fully converted to share the gospel with others?

• Why do you feel it is important to keep records in our families and in the Church?

Suggested Assignments

• Volunteer to teach a family home evening lesson about the conversion of Alma the Younger and the sons of Mosiah in Mosiah 27–28. Challenge those you teach to apply the principles demonstrated by Alma and the sons of Mosiah found in Mosiah 27:32–36; 28:3.

• Create a special entry in your personal journal that describes a "change of heart" you experienced in the development of your testimony.

Introduction

Alma the Younger faced severe challenges while serving simultaneously as the high priest over the Church and the first elected chief judge over the Nephites (see Alma 4:18). Both the Church and the government were threatened by men seeking to use religion and politics for their own gain. Nehor undermined the Church by using priestcraft to establish a religious movement and profession that attracted many (see Alma 1). Amlici, a man after the order of Nehor, made war against the newly elected government of judges after failing to obtain his desire to be king (see Alma 2–3). Notice how Alma prayed, exercised faith in God, and then took action to overcome each of the problems he faced. Consider how you can follow Alma's model as you deal with your own personal challenges.

Commentary

Book of Alma

• As compiler of the Book of Mormon, Mormon faced difficult challenges in determining what to include in the abridged record. At least two directives guided his selections. First, the Lord told Mormon to "write the things which have been commanded" (3 Nephi 26:12). Second, Mormon saw our day and the conditions that would exist (see Mormon 8:34–35). We understand, then, that when Mormon made editorial decisions, these two factors were his governing concerns.

It is instructive to compare the length of books in the Book of Mormon and the time periods they covered. The inordinate amount of writing for a rather small period of history alerts the reader that the time of Book of Mormon history covered by the book of Alma is especially parallel and relevant for our time. For more comparison, see the chart "Book of Mormon Pages and Time Periods" in the appendix (p. 411).

Alma 1:3–4. Nehor Taught That a "Teacher Ought to Become Popular"

• Nehor used flattery and false doctrine to attract followers and attack the church of God. His teachings were popular because they excused sin in the name of religion. He encouraged wickedness, rationalizing that

"in the end, all men should have eternal life" regardless of their personal behavior (Alma 1:4).

Elder L. Tom Perry of the Quorum of the Twelve Apostles urged us to have the courage to reject modern-day Nehors and their popular messages: "Nehor's words appealed to the people, but his doctrine, while popular to many, was incorrect. As we face the many decisions in life, the easy and popular messages of the world will not usually be the right ones to choose, and it will take much courage to choose the right" (in Conference Report, Oct. 1993, 88–89; or *Ensign*, Nov. 1993, 67).

• In Alma 1:4 Nehor taught that "all men should have eternal life." Verse 16 states that priestcraft was "preaching false doctrines . . . for the sake of riches and honor." One of the false doctrines often promoted by those guilty of priestcraft is that "all mankind should be saved at the last day, and that they need not fear nor tremble" (v. 4). A major problem with priestcraft is that there is no teaching of repentance, "For they were of the profession of Nehor, and did not believe in the repentance of their sins" (Alma 15:15).

• Elder Dallin H. Oaks of the Quorum of the Twelve Apostles instructed gospel teachers to look to the Savior and to help their students do the same. "A gospel teacher will never obscure [students'] view of the Master by standing in the way or by shadowing the lesson with self-promotion or self-interest. This means that a gospel teacher must never indulge in priestcrafts, which are 'that men preach and set themselves up for a light unto the world, that they may get gain and praise of the world' (2 Nephi 26:29). A gospel teacher does not preach 'to become popular' (Alma 1:3) or 'for the sake of riches and honor' (Alma 1:16). He or she follows the marvelous Book of Mormon example in which 'the preacher was no better than the hearer, neither was the teacher any better than the learner' (Alma 1:26). Both will always look to the Master" (in Conference Report, Oct. 1999, 102; or *Ensign,* Nov. 1999, 79).

Alma 1:5–6, 16. Priestcrafts

• Nehor encouraged priestcrafts and self-promotion to gain riches and honor. Nehor's example shows that we should be suspicious of those who seek personal fame or wealth from their preaching. Nephi previously defined priestcraft: "Priestcrafts are that men preach and set themselves up for a light unto the world, that they may get gain and praise of the world; but they seek not the welfare of Zion. Behold, the Lord hath forbidden this thing" (2 Nephi 26:29–30).

• Elder David A. Bednar of the Quorum of the Twelve Apostles also defined priestcraft for teachers in the Church: "Anything you or I do as an instructor that knowingly and intentionally draws attention to self—in the messages we present, in the methods we use, or in our personal demeanor—is a form of priestcraft that inhibits the teaching effectiveness of the Holy Ghost. 'Doth he preach it by the Spirit of truth or some other way? And if it be by some other way it is not of God' (D&C 50:17–18)" ("Seek Learning by Faith" [an evening with Elder David A. Bednar, Feb. 3, 2006, 4, www.ldsces.org).

ALMA 1:7–9

How did Gideon first respond to Nehor's false teachings? What can we learn from Gideon's experience?

Alma 1:7–9. Gideon "Was an Instrument in the Hands of God"

• The record states that Gideon "was an instrument in the hands of God" (Alma 1:8). As a member of the colony that lived in the land of Nephi, he resisted the wicked leadership of King Noah (see Mosiah 19:4). Later, Gideon became "the king's captain" during the reign of Limhi and played a significant part in preserving the colony and helping them escape to Zarahemla (see Mosiah 20:17; 22:3–9). Once in Zarahemla, he met the high standards set forth to become a teacher in the Church (see Mosiah 23:14). When confronted by Nehor's false teachings, Gideon admonished Nehor "with the words of God" (Alma 1:7). As a result, Gideon was slain for defending the faith. This captain, teacher, and martyr was so respected by the people that they named both a valley and a city in his honor (see Alma 2:20; 6:7).

Alma 1:13–15. What Is an *Ignominious* Death?

• Nehor was put to death for murdering Gideon. The scriptures say "he suffered an ignominious death" (Alma 1:15), which means "very shameful; reproachful; dishonorable" (*Noah Webster's First Edition of an American Dictionary of the English Language, 1828* [1967]).

Alma 1:17–18. Capital Punishment

• The law of God is "Whoso sheddeth man's blood, by man shall his blood be shed" (Genesis 9:6). In 1889 the First Presidency and the Quorum of the Twelve Apostles prepared a declaration regarding the Church's position on capital punishment:

"We solemnly make the following declarations, viz.:

"That this Church views the shedding of human blood with the utmost abhorrence. That we regard the killing of human beings, except in conformity with the civil law, as a capital crime which should be punished by shedding the blood of the criminal, after a public trial before a legally constituted court of the land. . . .

"The revelations of God to this Church make death the penalty for capital crime, and require that offenders against life and property shall be delivered up to and tried by the laws of the land" ("Official Declaration," *Millennial Star,* Jan. 20, 1890, 33–34).

Alma 1:19–20, 25. Enduring Persecution

• Those who follow the teachings of Jesus Christ have always faced persecution. President Harold B. Lee

(1899–1973) admonished those who are persecuted neither to allow their trials to stop their spiritual progression nor to deter their righteous zeal:

"To be persecuted for righteousness sake in a great cause where truth and virtue and honor are at stake is god-like. . . . The great harm that may come from persecution is not from the persecution itself but from the possible effect it may have upon the persecuted who may thereby be deterred in their zeal for the righteousness of their cause. Much of that persecution comes from lack of understanding, for men are prone to oppose that which they do not comprehend. Some of it comes from men intent upon evil. But from whatever cause, persecution seems to be so universal against those engaged in a righteous cause. . . .

". . . If you stand firmly for the right despite the jeers of the crowd or even physical violence, you shall be crowned with the blessedness of eternal joy. Who knows but that again in our day some of the saints or even apostles, as in former days, may be required to give their lives in defense of the truth? If that time should come, God grant they would not fail!" (*Decisions for Successful Living* [1973], 61–62).

ALMA 1:26
How did the priests regard those they taught? Why is this attitude important when we are teaching others?

Alma 1:26. "The Priests Left Their Labor to Impart the Word of God"

• In Alma 1, note Mormon's comparison between the pride of Nehor and the humble priests from the church of God. Nehor wore "very costly apparel," preached "for the sake of riches," and was lifted up in the pride of his heart, believing he was superior to others (see

Alma 1:5–6, 16). On the other hand, the true priests did not wear costly apparel, taught out of a desire to see others improve without monetary compensation, labored with their hands for their own support, and did not esteem themselves above their hearers (see Alma 1:26–27; see also Mosiah 18:24; 27:5). Throughout the Book of Mormon various apostate groups adopted the teachings or order of Nehor (see Alma 1:16; 16:1–12). This order exalted their so-called spiritual leaders to the point of creating an elite priestly class and social ranks among the people. These self-appointed elites often exploited the lay population and persecuted the poor (see Mosiah 11:3–6; 23:39; 24:8–9; Alma 31:23–32:5). In contrast, Alma 1:26 teaches that the Lord's way is to call a lay ministry of priesthood leaders.

Alma 1:26–31. The Affairs of the Church Established

• President James E. Faust (1920–2007) of the First Presidency explained that establishing the Lord's Church requires more than performing baptisms:

"We recognize that the process of establishing the Lord's church encompasses much more than baptizing people. In the first chapter of Alma in the Book of Mormon we find an instructive sequence of events outlining the way by which the Lord's church is established. . . .

"Let us take note of this process:

"First, the doctrines are taught [see Alma 1:26].

"Second, members esteem each other as themselves (see v. 26).

"Third, they all labor; they work and earn that which they receive (see v. 26).

"Fourth, they impart of their substance to the less fortunate; they serve one another (see v. 27).

"Fifth, they discipline their own appetites while at the same time caring appropriately for their own needs (see v. 27). . . .

"This mighty change happened, not because the people were given things, but rather because they were taught and began to help themselves and to care for those who were less fortunate. It was when they gave of themselves in the Lord's way that their circumstances began to improve.

"This process of establishing the Church can apply anywhere" (in Conference Report, Oct. 1979, 133–34; or *Ensign,* Nov. 1979, 91).

Alma 1:27. Dress and Appearance

• The Book of Mormon repeatedly warns against the sins of pride and class distinction that are manifest when people begin to wear "very costly apparel" (Alma 1:6). Members of the Lord's Church have been counseled to avoid extremes in clothing and appearance. They also should avoid becoming preoccupied with expensive fashions (see D&C 42:40). Nevertheless, disciples of Christ are to be "neat and comely" (Alma 1:27).

The *For the Strength of Youth* pamphlet states: "When you are well groomed and modestly dressed, you invite the companionship of the Spirit. . . . Always be neat and clean and avoid being sloppy or inappropriately casual in dress, grooming, and manners. Ask yourself, 'Would I feel comfortable with my appearance if I were in the Lord's presence?'" ([2001], 15–16).

ALMA 2:4

Why did Amlici want to be king? What did he do when the majority of the people voted against him? (see Alma 2:7–10).

Alma 2:4–6. The Voice of the People

• Amlici's attempt to deprive the people of their religious rights and privileges was defeated by the voice of the people. Consider the result if righteous Nephites in Amlici's day had abstained from voting. In democratic nations of our day, every Latter-day Saint has a sacred obligation to vote and to influence his or her society for good by upholding honest, wise, good, and honorable leaders and laws (see D&C 98:10).

• Elder M. Russell Ballard of the Quorum of the Twelve Apostles encouraged us to raise our voices against the wicked trends in our day: "We need to remember Edmund Burke's statement: 'The only thing necessary for the triumph of evil is for good men to do nothing.' We need to raise our voices with other concerned citizens throughout the world in opposition to current trends. We need to tell the sponsors of offensive media that we have had enough. We need to support programs and products that are positive and uplifting. Joining together with neighbors and friends who share our concerns, we can send a clear message to those responsible. The Internet Web sites and their local affiliates will have their addresses. Letters and e-mails have more effect than most people realize" (in Conference Report, Oct. 2003, 17; or *Ensign,* Nov. 2003, 18).

Alma 2:28–31. Alma and the Nephites Were Strengthened by God

• Previously the Lord had promised the Nephites that He would sustain them against the Lamanites if they were righteous (see 2 Nephi 5:25). Consequently, in the time of their greatest need, the Nephites called upon God and were "strengthened by the hand of the Lord" (Alma 2:28). During the same battle, God "strengthened" Alma with the ability to defeat his enemies, in response to his faith (see Alma 2:30–31).

Alma 3:4. The Amlicites Marked Their Bodies

• The Amlicites "marked themselves with red in their foreheads" to distinguish themselves from the Nephites (Alma 3:4, 18). In our time, President Gordon B. Hinckley (1910–2008) admonished young men and women to keep their bodies sacred by not marking themselves with tattoos:

"Now comes the craze of tattooing one's body. I cannot understand why any young man—or young woman, for that matter—would wish to undergo the painful process of disfiguring the skin with various multicolored representations of people, animals, and various symbols. With tattoos, the process is permanent unless there is another painful and costly undertaking to remove it. Fathers, caution your sons against having their bodies tattooed. They may resist your talk now, but the time will come when they will thank you. A tattoo is graffiti on the temple of the body.

"Likewise the piercing of the body for multiple rings in the ears, in the nose, even in the tongue. Can they possibly think that is beautiful? . . . The First Presidency and the Quorum of the Twelve have declared that we discourage tattoos and also 'the piercing of the body for other than medical purposes.' We do not, however, take any position 'on the minimal piercing of the ears by women for one pair of earrings'—one pair" (in Conference Report, Oct. 2000, 70–71; or *Ensign,* Nov. 2000, 52).

Alma 3:5. The Amlicites Changed Their Appearance to Follow the Lamanites

• The Amlicites changed their appearance to look like the Lamanites. Many Latter-day Saints today feel pressured to follow the dress trends of the world. Extremes in clothing and appearance serve to distinguish the disobedient from the disciples of Jesus Christ. Those who follow these worldly trends "disobey the prophet and, instead, follow the fads of the world" (see "Questions and Answers," *New Era,* Mar. 2006, 14; *For the Strength of Youth,* 14–16).

• Elder M. Russell Ballard taught young men who hold the priesthood that worldly trends in dress and appearance will chase away the Spirit of the Lord:

"There is an entire subculture that celebrates contemporary gangs and their criminal conduct with music, clothing styles, language, attitudes, and behaviors. Many of you have watched as trendy friends have embraced the style as something that was 'fashionable' and 'cool,' only to be dragged into the subculture. . . .

". . . I do not believe that you can stand for truth and right while wearing anything that is unbecoming one who holds the priesthood of God" (in Conference Report, Oct. 1997, 51–53; or *Ensign,* Nov. 1997, 38–39).

Alma 3:6–15. The Mark and the Curse

• There is a difference between the mark and the curse. The mark placed upon the Lamanites was a dark skin (see Alma 3:6). The curse was not the dark skin but being "cut off from the presence of the Lord" (2 Nephi 5:20). Notice that in both Alma 3:7 and Alma 3:14 the conjunction *and* is used between the curse *and* the mark. This implies that they are not the same thing. The people brought the curse upon themselves: "And even so doth every man that is cursed bring upon himself his own condemnation" (Alma 3:19). Through righteousness the curse may be removed, but the mark may remain as it has with the Lamanites (see commentary for 2 Nephi 5:20–25 on p. 62).

> ### ALMA 3:14–19
> What prophecy did Nephi give that was fulfilled by the Amlicites marking themselves?

Alma 3:26–27. "Every Man Receiveth Wages of Him Whom He Listeth to Obey"

• The phrase "every man receiveth wages of him whom he listeth to obey" figuratively invites the reader to consider himself as an employee whose choices determine whether his ultimate employer is God or Satan (see Alma 3:27). In this context, the word *list* refers to leaning or tilting to one side or another. Therefore, those who tilt or lean toward Satan soon find themselves employed by him and receive "eternal misery" (Alma 3:26).

Eventually, the choices of a lifetime will reveal whom one has chosen as an eternal employer. President Boyd K. Packer, President of the Quorum of the Twelve Apostles, taught this truth when he declared: "Our lives are made up of thousands of everyday choices. Over the years these little choices will be bundled together and show clearly what we value" (in Conference Report, Oct. 1980, 29; or *Ensign,* Nov. 1980, 21).

Alma 4:9–12. "A Great Stumbling-Block"

• As Church members became proud, their negative examples became a stumbling-block to those who did not belong to the Church (see Alma 4:9–12; 39:11). President Gordon B. Hinckley related the story of a young man who faced terrible odds to learn about the gospel because of the way Church members treated him:

"He was not a member of the Church. He and his parents were active in another faith.

"He recalls that when he was growing up, some of his LDS associates belittled him, made him feel out of place, and poked fun at him.

"He came to literally hate this Church and its people. He saw no good in any of them.

"Then his father lost his employment and had to move. In the new location, at the age of 17, he was able to enroll in college. There, for the first time in his life, he felt the warmth of friends, one of whom, named Richard, asked him to join a club of which he was president. He writes:

"'For the first time in my life someone wanted me around. I didn't know how to react, but thankfully I joined. . . . It was a feeling that I loved, the feeling of having a friend. I had prayed for one my whole life. And now after 17 years of waiting, God answered that prayer.'

"At the age of 19 he found himself as a tent partner with Richard during their summer employment. He noticed Richard reading a book every night. He asked what he was reading. He was told that he was reading the Book of Mormon. He adds:

"'I quickly changed the subject and went to bed. After all, that is the book that ruined my childhood. I tried forgetting about it, but a week went by and I couldn't sleep. Why was he reading it every night? I soon couldn't stand the unanswered questions in my head. So one night I asked him what was so important in that book. What was in it? . . . He started to read where he had stopped. He read about Jesus and about an

appearance in the Americas. I was shocked. I didn't think that the Mormons believed in Jesus.' . . .

"On a subsequent occasion this young man and his friend were traveling. Richard handed him a Book of Mormon and asked that he read it aloud. He did so, and suddenly the inspiration of the Holy Spirit touched him.

"Time passed and his faith increased. He agreed to be baptized. . . .

"That is the end of the story, but there are great statements in that story. One is the sorry manner in which his young Mormon associates treated him.

"Next is the manner in which his newfound friend, Richard, treated him. It was totally opposite from his previous experience. It led to his conversion and baptism in the face of terrible odds" (in Conference Report, Apr. 2006, 62–63; or *Ensign,* May 2006, 59–60).

Alma 4:14. Retaining a Remission of Sins

• The Book of Mormon not only teaches that through the Atonement of Jesus Christ you can receive a remission of your sins, but it also teaches that you must

retain a remission of your sins (see Alma 4:14; also Mosiah 4:11). President Marion G. Romney (1897–1988) of the First Presidency taught that being true to our covenants and caring for others allows us to retain a remission of our sins: "Is there any doubt that retaining a remission of sins depends on our caring for one another? If we believe these teachings, if we profess to follow the Savior and his prophets, if we want to be true to our covenants and have the Spirit of the Lord in our lives, then we must do the things that the Savior said and did" (in Conference Report, Oct. 1980, 136; or *Ensign,* Nov. 1980, 92).

> **ALMA 4:15–19**
> *Why did Alma give up the judgment-seat?*
> *What can you learn from his example?*

Alma 4:19. Bearing Pure Testimony

• In order to reclaim the people, Alma knew that "the preaching of the word had a great tendency to lead the people to do that which was just—yea, it had had more powerful effect upon the minds of the people than the sword, or anything else" (Alma 31:5). President Gordon B. Hinckley emphasized the world's need to hear pure testimonies:

"You will recall that Alma gave up the judgment seat so that he might have time and strength for a greater work: [Alma 4:19]

"For this same reason, the world today needs the power of pure testimony. It needs the gospel of Jesus Christ, and if the world is to hear that gospel, there must be messengers to teach it" ("There Must Be Messengers," *Ensign,* Oct. 1987, 2).

• Elder M. Russell Ballard counseled Latter-day Saints to bear pure testimony:

"Simply stated, testimony—real testimony, born of the Spirit and confirmed by the Holy Ghost—changes lives. It changes how you think and what you do. It changes what you say. It affects every priority you set and every choice you make. . . .

"My experience throughout the Church leads me to worry that too many of our members' testimonies linger on 'I am thankful' and 'I love,' and too few are able to say with humble but sincere clarity, 'I know.' As a result, our meetings sometimes lack the testimony-rich, spiritual underpinnings that stir the soul and have meaningful, positive impact on the lives of all those who hear them.

"Our testimony meetings need to be more centered on the Savior, the doctrines of the gospel, the blessings of the Restoration, and the teachings of the scriptures. We need to replace stories, travelogues, and lectures with pure testimonies. . . .

". . . To bear testimony is 'to bear witness by the power of the Holy Ghost; to make a solemn declaration of truth based on personal knowledge or belief' (Guide to the Scriptures, "Testify"). Clear declaration of truth makes a difference in people's lives. That is what changes hearts. That is what the Holy Ghost can confirm in the hearts of God's children.

"Although we can have testimonies of many things as members of the Church, there are basic truths we need to constantly teach one another and share with those not of our faith. Testify that God is our Father and Jesus is the Christ. The plan of salvation is centered on the Savior's Atonement. Joseph Smith restored the fulness of the everlasting gospel of Jesus Christ, and the Book of Mormon is evidence that  our testimony is true" (in Conference Report, Oct. 2004, 42–43; or *Ensign,* Nov. 2004, 40–41).

• President Howard W. Hunter (1907–1995) offered a caution with regard to emotions in testimonies:

"Let me offer a word of caution on this subject. . . . I get concerned when it appears that strong emotion or free-flowing tears are equated with the presence of the Spirit. Certainly the Spirit of the Lord can bring strong emotional feelings, including tears, but that outward manifestation ought not to be confused with the presence of the Spirit itself.

"I have watched a great many of my brethren over the years and we have shared some rare and unspeakable spiritual experiences together. Those experiences have all been different, each special in its own way, and such sacred moments may or may not be accompanied by tears. Very often they are, but sometimes they are accompanied by total silence" ("Eternal Investments" [an evening with President Howard W. Hunter, Feb. 10, 1989], 3, www.ldsces.org).

Points to Ponder

- Why do you think the Book of Mormon repeatedly warns against wearing "costly apparel" (Alma 1:6, 27, 32) and focusing on material possessions? What are some current styles, fashions, or trends that Latter-day Saints should avoid?

- How can you use your voice to defend the standards, rights, and privileges of the Church today?

Suggested Assignments

- Read Alma 1–4, marking all the verses that refer to riches, costly clothing, and the vain things of the world. Note the effect that their display of wealth had on the righteousness of members of the Church. Write a three- to five-minute talk on principles that Church members can follow to keep themselves from experiencing negative spiritual effects from materialism.

- Compare Alma 1:3–6, 16–20 to Alma 31:12–29 and make a list of the similarities. Why did Nehor's teachings and the apostate Zoramite's religion appeal to so many?

- In the heat of battle, Alma cried to God for assistance (see Alma 2:30). In response to Alma's faith, God "strengthened" him with the ability to defeat his enemies (Alma 2:31). Find at least two other experiences in the Book of Mormon where God strengthened others. Think of a time when you have been strengthened by the Lord, and record the experience in your journal, if you have not already written about it.

CHAPTER 24

Alma 5–7

Introduction

Alma yielded up the judgment seat so that he might go forth "among the people of Nephi . . . to stir them up in remembrance of their duty, . . . bearing down in pure testimony against them" (Alma 4:19). The record of his labors among the people of Zarahemla and the people of Gideon allows us to reflect upon our own spiritual standing before the Lord. As you study these chapters, consider how Alma's questions, counsel, and testimony can help you remember your duty toward God and your fellowman. Look for what brings about spiritual rebirth and for what will help you emulate the attributes of the Savior.

Commentary

Alma 5:7. "The Chains of Hell"

• Alma defined the "chains of hell" as being brought into subjection to the adversary and placing ourselves at risk for everlasting destruction (see Alma 12:6, 11).

Alma 5:12–14. A "Mighty Change in Your Hearts"

• President Marion G. Romney (1897–1988) of the First Presidency described conversion—experiencing a mighty change of heart—as a transformation process involving and affecting every aspect of one's life: "The verb *convert* means 'to turn from one belief or course to another,' [and] *conversion* is 'a spiritual and moral *change* attending a *change* of belief with conviction.' As used in the scriptures, *converted* generally implies not merely mental acceptance of Jesus and his teachings, but also a motivating faith in him and in his gospel, a faith which works a transformation, an actual *change* in one's understanding of life's meaning and in one's allegiance to God—in interest, in thought, and in conduct. While *conversion* may be accomplished in stages, one is not really converted in the full sense of the term unless and until he is at heart a new person" (in Conference Report, Oct. 1975, 107–8; or *Ensign,* Nov. 1975, 71).

• President Ezra Taft Benson (1899–1994) shared some characteristics of those who have experienced a mighty change of heart:

"When you choose to follow Christ, you choose to be changed. . . .

"The Lord works from the inside out. The world works from the outside in. The world would take people out of the slums. Christ takes the slums out of people, and then they take themselves out of the slums. The world would mold men by changing their environment. Christ changes men, who then change their environment. The world would shape human behavior, but Christ can change human nature. . . .

"Yes, Christ changes men, and changed men can change the world.

"Men changed for Christ will be captained by Christ. Like Paul they will be asking, 'Lord, what wilt thou have me to do?' (Acts 9:6). Peter stated, they will 'follow his steps' (1 Peter 2:21). John said they will 'walk, even as he walked' (1 John 2:6).

"Finally, men captained by Christ will be consumed in Christ. To paraphrase President Harold B. Lee, they set fire in others because they are on fire. (See *Stand Ye in Holy Places* [Salt Lake City: Deseret Book Co., 1974], p. 192.)

"Their will is swallowed up in His will. (See John 5:30.)

"They do always those things that please the Lord. (See John 8:29.)

"Not only would they die for the Lord, but more important they want to live for Him.

"Enter their homes, and the pictures on their walls, the books on their shelves, the music in the air, their words and acts reveal them as Christians.

"They stand as witnesses of God at all times, and in all things, and in all places. (See Mosiah 18:9.)

"They have Christ on their minds, as they look unto Him in every thought. (See D&C 6:36.)

"They have Christ in their hearts as their affections are placed on Him forever. (See Alma 37:36.)

"Almost every week they partake of the sacrament and witness anew to their Eternal Father that they are willing to take upon them the name of His Son, always remember Him, and keep His commandments.

(See Moroni 4:3.)" (in Conference Report, Oct. 1985, 4–6; or *Ensign,* Nov. 1985, 5–7).

Alma 5:14. "Born of God"

• Elder Russell M. Nelson of the Quorum of the Twelve Apostles described how conversion leads to being born again:

"Conversion means 'to turn with.' Conversion is a turning *from* the ways of the world *to,* and staying *with,* the ways of the Lord. Conversion includes repentance and obedience. Conversion brings a mighty change of heart [see Mosiah 5:2; Alma 5:12–14]. Thus, a true convert is 'born again,' [see John 3:3–7; Mosiah 27:24–26] walking with a newness of life [see Romans 6:3–4].

"As true converts, we are motivated to do what the Lord wants us to do [see Mosiah 5:2–5] and to be who He wants us to be [see 3 Nephi 27:21, 27]" (in Conference Report, Oct. 2005, 90; or *Ensign,* Nov. 2005, 86).

• The Prophet Joseph Smith (1805–44) stated that "being born again, comes by the Spirit of God through ordinances" (*History of the Church,* 3:392).

Elder Bruce R. McConkie (1915–85) of the Quorum of the Twelve Apostles described what a true miracle it is to be born again: "Perhaps the greatest miracle . . . is the healing of sin-sick souls so that those who are spiritually blind and deaf and diseased become again pure and clean and heirs of salvation. Perhaps the greatest miracle of all is that which happens in the life of each person who is born again; who receives the sanctifying power of the Holy Spirit of God in his life; who has sin and evil burned out of his soul as though by fire; who lives again spiritually" (*The Mortal Messiah, Book 4* [1981], 3:269).

• For additional insights on being born of God, see the commentary for Mosiah 5:2 (p. 144) and for Mosiah 27:25 (p. 166).

Alma 5:14, 19. "The Image of God Engraven upon Your Countenances"

• While serving as an Assistant to the Quorum of the Twelve Apostles, Elder Theodore M. Burton (1907–89) observed that those who follow Heavenly Father appear more like Him: "If we truly accept God in our lives and

live in accordance with his commandments, God will work a mighty change in our appearance and we will begin to appear more like our Heavenly Father, in whose image we have been created. Could it be this appearance we recognize when we meet men and women who are trying to live close to the Lord?" (in Conference Report, Oct. 1973, 151; or *Ensign,* Jan. 1974, 114).

• President James E. Faust (1920–2007) of the First Presidency recounted an experience in which an associate of the Church remarked concerning light in the countenance of Latter-day Saint students:

"I recently recalled a historic meeting in Jerusalem about 17 years ago. It was regarding the lease for the land on which the Brigham Young University's Jerusalem Center for Near Eastern Studies was later built. Before this lease could be signed, President Ezra Taft Benson and Elder Jeffrey R. Holland, then president of Brigham Young University, agreed with the Israeli government on behalf of the Church and the university not to proselyte in Israel.

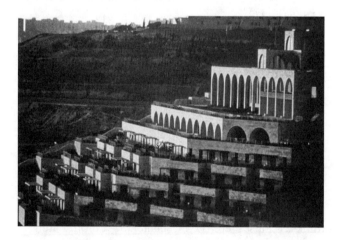

"You might wonder why we agreed not to proselyte. We were required to do so in order to get the building permit to build that magnificent building which stands in the historic city of Jerusalem. To our knowledge, the Church and BYU have scrupulously and honorably kept that nonproselyting commitment. After the lease had been signed, one of our friends insightfully remarked, 'Oh, we know that you are not going to proselyte, but what are you going to do about the light that is in their eyes?' He was referring to our students who were studying in Israel" (in Conference Report, Oct. 2005, 19; or *Ensign,* Nov. 2005, 20).

Alma 5:21–22. "Garments . . . Cleansed from All Stain"

• The reference to "garments" in Alma 5:22 represents our spiritual standing before the Lord. Elder Lynn A. Mickelsen of the Seventy identified the similarity between the cleansing we receive through the Atonement and the washing of soiled laundry: "There is a parallel between our garments being washed clean through the blood of the Lamb and how we wash our own dirty linen. It is through His atoning sacrifice that our garments will be cleansed. The scriptural reference to garments encompasses our whole being. The need for cleansing comes as we become soiled through sin. The judgment and forgiving are the Savior's prerogative, for only He can forgive and wash away our sins [see Alma 5:21–27; D&C 64:10]" (in Conference Report, Oct. 2003, 9; or *Ensign,* Nov. 2003, 11).

Alma 5:28. Being "Stripped of Pride"

• For insights on the topic of pride, see the commentary for Helaman 3:33–34, 36; 4:12 (p. 264) and for Helaman 12:5–6 (p. 278).

Alma 5:29. Being "Stripped of Envy"

• Elder Jeffrey R. Holland of the Quorum of the Twelve Apostles taught that envy, born of worldly influences, stands in opposition to God's perfect love:

"It has been said that envy is the one sin to which no one readily confesses, but just how widespread that tendency can be is suggested in the old Danish proverb, 'If envy were a fever, all the world would be ill.' . . . As others seem to grow larger in our sight, we think we must therefore be smaller. So, unfortunately, we occasionally act that way.

"How does this happen, especially when we wish so much that it would not? I think one of the reasons is that every day we see allurements of one kind or another that tell us what we have is not enough. Someone or something is forever telling us we need to be more handsome or more wealthy, more applauded or more admired than we see ourselves as being. We are told we haven't collected enough possessions or gone to enough fun places. We are bombarded with the message that on the *world's* scale of things we

have been weighed in the balance and found wanting [see Daniel 5:27]. . . .

"But God does not work this way. . . .

". . . I testify that no one of us is less treasured or cherished of God than another. I testify that He loves each of us—insecurities, anxieties, self-image, and all. He doesn't measure our talents or our looks; He doesn't measure our professions or our possessions. He cheers on *every* runner, calling out that the race is against sin, *not* against each other. I know that if we will be faithful, there is a perfectly tailored robe of righteousness ready and waiting for *everyone* [see Isaiah 61:10; 2 Nephi 4:33; 9:14], 'robes . . . made . . . white in the blood of the Lamb' [Revelation 7:14]. May we encourage each other in our effort to win that prize" (in Conference Report, Apr. 2002, 72, 74; or *Ensign,* May 2002, 63–64).

Alma 5:46–47. "The Spirit of Revelation"

• Alma had seen an angel, but he testified in Alma 5:46–47 that it was fasting and prayer that had allowed him to come to know, not seeing an angel. President Heber J. Grant (1856–1945) explained: "Many men say: 'If I could only see an angel, if I could only hear an angel proclaim something, that would cause me to be faithful all the days of my life!' It had no effect upon these men [Laman and Lemuel] that were not serving the Lord, and it would have no effect today" (in Conference Report, Apr. 1924, 159).

President Joseph Fielding Smith (1876–1972) explained why the Holy Ghost can be more powerful than a visitation of an angel: "Christ . . . declared that the manifestations we might have . . . from a visitation of an angel, a tangible resurrected being, would not leave the impression . . . which we receive through a manifestation of the Holy Ghost. Personal visitations might become dim as time goes on, but this guidance of the Holy Ghost is renewed and continued, day after day, year after year, if we live to be worthy of it" (*Doctrines of Salvation,* comp. Bruce R. McConkie, 3 vols. [1954–56], 1:44).

• The spirit of revelation is communication from God to man by the power of the Holy Ghost to the mind and heart (see D&C 8:2). Elder Richard G. Scott of the

Quorum of the Twelve Apostles described how to recognize communication from the Holy Ghost:

"An impression to the *mind* is very specific.

"Detailed words can be heard or felt and written as though the instruction were being dictated.

"A communication to the *heart* is a more general impression. The Lord often begins by giving impressions. Where there is a recognition of their importance and they are obeyed, one gains more capacity to receive more detailed instruction to the *mind*. An impression to the heart, if followed, is fortified by a more specific instruction to the mind" ("Helping Others to Be Spiritually Led" [Church Educational System symposium on the Doctrine and Covenants, Aug. 11, 1998], 3–4; see LDS.org under gospel library/additional addresses/CES addresses).

Alma 5:53–54. "Vain Things of the World"

• *Vain* is defined as "empty; worthless; having no substance, value or importance. . . . Elated with a high opinion of one's own accomplishments" (*Noah Webster's First Edition of an American Dictionary of the English Language, 1828* [1967]).

• Elder Dallin H. Oaks of the Quorum of the Twelve Apostles counseled Latter-day Saints to avoid becoming preoccupied with the vain things of the world: "Jesus taught that 'a man's life consisteth not in the abundance of the things which he possesseth' (Luke 12:15). Consequently, we should not lay up for ourselves 'treasures upon earth, where moth and rust doth corrupt, and where thieves break through and steal' (Matthew 6:19). In other words, the treasures of our hearts—our priorities—should not be what the scriptures call 'riches [and] the vain things of this world' (Alma 39:14). The 'vain things of [the] world' include every combination of that worldly quartet of property, pride, prominence, and power. As to all of these, the scriptures remind us that 'you cannot carry

them with you' (Alma 39:14). We should be seeking the kind of treasures the scriptures promise the faithful: 'great treasures of knowledge, even hidden treasures' (D&C 89:19)" (in Conference Report, Apr. 2001, 109; or *Ensign,* May 2001, 84).

• Elder Jeffrey R. Holland also noted that vanity of physical appearance is spiritually dangerous: "In terms of preoccupation with self and a fixation on the physical, this is more than social insanity; it is spiritually destructive and it accounts for much of the unhappiness . . . in the modern world. And if adults are preoccupied with appearance—tucking and nipping and implanting and remodeling everything that can be remodeled—those pressures and anxieties will certainly seep through to children. At some point the problem becomes what the Book of Mormon called 'vain imaginations' [1 Nephi 12:18]. And in secular society both vanity *and* imagination run wild. One would truly need a great and spacious makeup kit to compete with beauty as portrayed in media all around us" (in Conference Report, Oct. 2005, 30–31; or *Ensign,* Nov. 2005, 30).

Alma 5:57. "Come Ye Out from the Wicked . . . and Be Ye Separate"

• Elder David R. Stone of the Seventy discussed how techniques used in the construction of the Manhattan New York Temple provide an example of how to remove oneself from the influence of the world:

"Too many of the people of the world have come to resemble the Babylon of old by walking in their own ways and following a god 'whose image is in the likeness of the world' [D&C 1:16].

"One of the greatest challenges we will face is to be able to live in that world but somehow not be of that world. We have to create Zion in the midst of Babylon. . . .

"My involvement with the building of the Manhattan Temple gave me the opportunity to be in the temple quite often prior to the dedication. It was wonderful to sit in the celestial room and be there in perfect silence, without a single sound to be heard coming from the busy New York streets outside. How was it possible that the temple could be so reverently silent when the hustle and bustle of the metropolis was just a few yards away?

"The answer was in the construction of the temple. The temple was built within the walls of an existing building, and the inner walls of the temple were connected to the outer walls at only a very few junction points. That is how the temple (Zion) limited the effects of Babylon, or the world outside.

"There may be a lesson here for us. We can create the real Zion among us by limiting the extent to which Babylon will influence our lives. . . .

"Wherever we are, whatever city we may live in, we can build our own Zion by the principles of the celestial kingdom and ever seek to become the pure in heart. . . .

"We do not need to become as puppets in the hands of the culture of the place and time. We can be courageous and can walk in the Lord's paths and follow His footsteps" (in Conference Report, Apr. 2006, 94–97; or *Ensign*, May 2006, 90–93).

Alma 5:57–58; 6:3. "Names Were Blotted Out"

• For a discussion of names being blotted out, refer to the commentary for Mosiah 26:32–36 (p. 164) and for Moroni 6:7 (p. 387).

ALMA 6:8

Which principles guided Alma as he declared the word of God to the city of Gideon?

Alma 7:10. Jesus Born at Jerusalem

• President Joseph Fielding Smith explained the location of the Savior's birth as declared by Alma:

"There is no conflict or contradiction in the Book of Mormon with any truth recorded in the Bible. A careful reading of what Alma said will show that he had no intention of declaring that Jesus would be born *in* Jerusalem. Alma knew better. So did Joseph Smith and those who were associated with him in the bringing forth of the Book of Mormon. Had Alma said, 'born *in*

Jerusalem, the *city* of our fathers,' it would have made all the difference in the world. Then we would have said he made an error. Alma made no mistake, and what he said is true.

"Dr. Hugh Nibley, in his course of study for the priesthood for 1957, *An Approach to the Book of Mormon,* in Lesson 8, page 85, has this to say on this point:

"'. . . One of the favorite points of attack on the Book of Mormon has been the statement in Alma 7:10 that the Savior would be born "at Jerusalem which is the *land* of our forefathers." Here Jerusalem is not the city "*in* the land of our forefathers," it *is* the land. Christ was born in a village some six miles from the city of Jerusalem; it was not in the city, but it was in what we now know the ancients themselves designated as "the land of Jerusalem"'" (*Answers to Gospel Questions,* comp. Joseph Fielding Smith Jr., 5 vols. [1957–66], 1:174).

• Both Jerusalem and Bethlehem have been called the city of David, which has caused some confusion. Luke 2:11 refers to Bethlehem as the city of David. Yet 2 Samuel 5:6–8; 2 Kings 14:20; 1 Chronicles 11:4–8 all refer to Jerusalem as the city of David.

ALMA 7:6, 19–20

What did Alma discern about the spiritual state of the people of Gideon?

Alma 7:11–12. Our Pains, Afflictions, Temptations, Sicknesses, and Infirmities

• Elder Neal A. Maxwell (1926–2004) of the Quorum of the Twelve Apostles wrote of the Savior's familiarity with the afflictions of mortality and with our individual transgressions: "He knows by actual, personal experience, because not only did He suffer pains, afflictions, and temptations of every kind during His second estate, but He took upon Himself our sins as well as our pains, sicknesses, and infirmities. (See Alma 7:11–12.) Thus He knew, not in abstraction but in actuality, 'according to the flesh,' the whole of human suffering. He bore our infirmities before we bore them. He knows perfectly well how to succor us. We can tell Him nothing of pain, temptation, or affliction; He learned 'according to the flesh,' and His triumph was complete!" (*We Will Prove Them Herewith* [1982], 46).

Alma 7:12. "Succor His People"

• Teaching about the word *succor,* Elder Jeffrey R. Holland stated: "[Succor] is used often in the scriptures to describe Christ's care for and attention to us. It means literally 'to run to.' What a magnificent way to describe the Savior's urgent effort in our behalf. Even as he calls us to come to him and follow him, he is unfailingly running to help us" ("Come unto Me" [CES fireside for young adults, Mar. 2, 1997], 7, www.ldsces.org).

ALMA 7:15–16

What was Alma's counsel and promise to the people of Gideon?

Alma 7:22–24. Responsibilities of the Melchizedek Priesthood

• Alma 7:22–24 includes instruction to priesthood holders and a list of qualities they should possess to appropriately officiate in the priesthood. This instruction is similar to instruction given to priesthood holders in Doctrine and Covenants 121:41–42. These verses in Alma 7 and Doctrine and Covenants 121 help those who hold the priesthood know how to act to increase their power in the priesthood.

President Boyd K. Packer, President of the Quorum of the Twelve Apostles, explained the importance of living righteously as a priesthood holder:

"The priesthood is very, very precious to the Lord. He is very careful about how it is conferred, and by whom. It is never done in secret.

"I have told you how the *authority* is given to you. The *power* you receive will depend on what you do with this sacred, unseen gift.

"Your authority comes through your ordination; your power comes through obedience and worthiness" (in Conference Report, Oct. 1981, 47; or *Ensign,* Nov. 1981, 32).

Alma 7:23. "Temperate in All Things"

• Elder Russell M. Nelson remarked on the safety temperance brings:

"Temperance suggests sobriety and self-restraint in action. It reminds one of covenants made. . . .

"Repeatedly, scriptures teach that we be 'temperate in all things' (1 Corinthians 9:25; Alma 7:23; 38:10; D&C 12:8). Temperance can protect each of us from the aftermath of excess" (in Conference Report, Oct. 1991, 81; or *Ensign,* Nov. 1991, 60).

Points to Ponder

• Even after seeing an angel, Alma still had to repent, exercise faith in Jesus Christ, and put forth great effort to obtain his testimony. How does Alma 5:45–48 describe the process by which Alma obtained knowledge of "the Son, the Only Begotten of the Father"?

• What similarities and differences do you see in Alma's ministering among the people of Zarahemla and the people of Gideon?

• How has your understanding and appreciation of the Atonement deepened as you studied Alma 7:11–13?

Suggested Assignments

• Alma asked over 40 questions in chapter 5. Read the questions Alma asked, and choose one of them to answer by writing a paragraph that includes your understanding, feelings, or insights about the subject of the question.

• Research and discover the meaning of any attribute listed in Alma 7:23 that you may not be familiar with.

Introduction

Alma's ministry to the city of Ammonihah illustrates how God supports His servants who faithfully obey Him, even in times of great difficulty or personal sacrifice (see 1 Nephi 1:20). After an initial attempt to preach in a wicked city, Alma was blessed with a visit from an angel, who assured him of his standing before God and instructed him to return to Ammonihah. There, a man named Amulek had received instruction from an angel who told him to receive Alma. Later, both men were inspired to know how to contend with skilled lawyers who were intent upon creating discord for personal profit. Alma's and Amulek's experiences serve as a model for us today. Although you still have challenges to face, Heavenly Father will bless you with reassurance, inspiration, and assistance as you seek to obey Him.

In addition, these chapters illustrate the power of "bearing down in pure testimony" (Alma 4:19) against those opposed to the work of the Lord. Notice the impact the doctrines of the Resurrection and the Final Judgment had upon Zeezrom. Consider how these doctrines can affect your heart and testimony, as well as those around you.

Commentary

Alma 8:10. "Mighty Prayer"

• The phrase "mighty prayer" indicates powerful, faith-filled communication with God. Elder Joseph B. Wirthlin (1917–2008) of the Quorum of the Twelve Apostles suggested ways we can evaluate and seek to improve the strength of our prayers:

"May I ask you today to consider the effectiveness of your prayers? How close do you feel to your Heavenly Father? Do you feel that your prayers are answered? Do you feel that the time you spend in prayer enriches and uplifts your soul? Is there room for improvement?

"There are many reasons our prayers lack power. Sometimes they become routine. Our prayers become hollow when we say similar words in similar ways over and over so often that the words become more of a recitation than a communication. This is what the Savior described as 'vain repetitions' (Matthew 6:7). Such prayers, He said, will not be heard. . . .

"Do your prayers at times sound and feel the same? Have you ever said a prayer mechanically, the words pouring forth as though cut from a machine? Do you sometimes bore yourself as you pray?

"Prayers that do not demand much of your thought will hardly merit much attention from our Heavenly Father. When you find yourself getting into a routine with your prayers, step back and think. Meditate for a while on the things for which you really are grateful" ("Improving Our Prayers," in *Brigham Young University 2002–2003 Speeches* [2003], 160).

Alma 8:10–16. The Lord Will Help Us When We Are Faithful

• After having noteworthy success preaching the gospel in other cities, Alma was reviled, spit upon, and cast out of Ammonihah. Then came reassurance from the angel that Alma's efforts were acceptable to the Lord and that Alma should return and preach again to the people (see Alma 8:15–16). Commenting to those who sometimes feel that their best efforts are not enough or that they have failed, President Thomas S. Monson stated:

" 'Do your duty; that is best. Leave unto the Lord the rest' ['The Legend Beautiful' by Henry Wadsworth Longfellow]

"Should there be anyone who feels he is too weak to change the onward and downward course of his life, or should there be those who fail to resolve to do better because of that greatest of fears—the fear of failure—there is no more comforting assurance to be had than these words of the Lord: 'My grace is sufficient for all men that humble themselves before me; for if they humble themselves before me, and have faith in me, then will I make weak things become strong unto them' [Ether 12:27].

"Miracles are everywhere to be found when priesthood callings are magnified. When faith replaces doubt, when selfless service eliminates selfish striving, the power of God brings to pass His purposes" (in Conference Report, Oct. 1999, 64–65; or *Ensign,* Nov. 1999, 50).

Alma 8:18. Alma "Returned Speedily"

• After hearing the angel's message, Alma "returned speedily" to Ammonihah. President Henry B. Eyring of the First Presidency taught that prompt obedience to the Lord is necessary to our spiritual well-being:

"However much faith to obey God we now have, we will need to strengthen it continually and keep it refreshed constantly. We can do that by deciding now to be more quick to obey and more determined to endure. Learning to start early and to be steady are the keys to spiritual preparation. . . .

"A loving Heavenly Father and His Beloved Son have given us all the help They can to pass the test of life set before us. But we must decide to obey and then do it. We build the faith to pass the tests of obedience over time and through our daily choices. We can decide now to do quickly whatever God asks of us" (in Conference Report, Oct. 2005, 39, 41; or *Ensign,* Nov. 2005, 38, 40).

Alma 8:26. Fasting

• Alma fasted to prepare his mind and soul to preach to the inhabitants of Ammonihah. Fasting often indicates to the Lord the seriousness of our request. President James E. Faust (1920–2007) of the First Presidency taught: "At times fasting is appropriate as a strong evidence of our sincerity. . . . When we fast we humble our souls, which brings us more in tune with God and His holy purposes" (in Conference Report, Apr. 2002, 68; or *Ensign,* May 2002, 60).

• Elder Joseph B. Wirthlin enumerated some of the blessings that flow into our lives when we add prayer to an appropriate fast:

"Fasting, coupled with mighty prayer, is powerful. It can fill our minds with the revelations of the Spirit. It can strengthen us against times of temptation.

"Fasting and prayer can help develop within us courage and confidence. They can strengthen our character and build self-restraint and discipline. Often when we fast, our righteous prayers and petitions have greater power. Testimonies grow. We mature spiritually and emotionally and sanctify our souls. Each time we fast, we gain a little more control over our worldly appetites and passions. . . .

"Fasting in the proper spirit and in the Lord's way will energize us spiritually. It will strengthen our self-discipline, fill our homes with peace, lighten our hearts with joy, fortify us against temptation, prepare us for times of adversity, and open the windows of heaven" (in Conference Report, Apr. 2001, 95, 97–98; or *Ensign,* May 2001, 73, 75).

Alma 9:14–23. Great Blessings Bring Great Responsibilities

• Alma warned that although the Lamanites were a wicked people at that time, the Lord would look more favorably upon them than upon the people of Ammonihah on the day of judgment (see Alma 9:14). The Lamanites were following incorrect traditions that had been handed down to them, while the Nephites in general and the people of Ammonihah in particular had been "a highly favored people of the Lord; . . . above every other nation, kindred, tongue, or people" (Alma 9:20). With great blessings come great responsibilities.

Sister Sheri L. Dew, then a counselor in the Relief Society general presidency, taught: "'Unto whom much is given much is required' (D&C 82:3), and at times the demands of discipleship are heavy. But shouldn't we expect the journey towards eternal glory to stretch us? We sometimes rationalize our preoccupation with this world and our casual attempts to grow spiritually by trying to console each other with the notion that living the gospel really shouldn't require all that much of us. The Lord's standard of behavior will always be more demanding than the world's, but then the Lord's rewards are infinitely more glorious—including true joy, peace, and salvation" ("We Are Women of God," *Ensign,* Nov. 1999, 98).

Alma 10:2–3. Lehi—"a Descendent of Manasseh"

• Lehi's lineage as a descendant of Manasseh is partial fulfillment of a promise to Joseph of old. Shortly before his death, Joseph of Egypt related assurances that the Lord made unto him concerning his posterity:

"I have obtained a promise of the Lord, that . . . the Lord God will raise up a righteous branch out of my loins. . . .

"And it shall come to pass that they shall be scattered again; and a branch shall be broken off, and shall be carried into a far country; nevertheless they shall be remembered in the covenants of the Lord, when the Messiah cometh. . . .

"Thus saith the Lord God of my fathers unto me. . . .

"Wherefore the fruit of thy loins shall write, and the fruit of the loins of Judah shall write; and that which shall be written by the fruit of thy loins, and also

that which shall be written by the fruit of the loins of Judah, shall grow together unto the confounding of false doctrines, and laying down of contentions, and establishing peace among the fruit of thy loins, and bringing them to a knowledge of their fathers in the latter days; and also to the knowledge of my covenants, saith the Lord" (JST, Genesis 50:24–25, 27, 31; see also 2 Nephi 3:5, 12).

• Prior to their flight into the wilderness, Lehi and Ishmael, both descendants of Joseph, lived with their families in Jerusalem, which was part of the kingdom of Judah. One writer suggested an explanation for why Lehi's ancestry, though descended from Joseph, lived in Jerusalem, which for the most part was made up of

descendants of Judah: "Some students of the Book of Mormon have wondered how descendants of Joseph were still living in Jerusalem in 600 B.C. when most members of the tribes of Ephraim and Manasseh were taken into captivity by the Assyrians about 721 B.C. A scripture in 2 Chronicles may provide a clue to this problem. This account mentions that in about 941 B.C. Asa, the king of the land, gathered together at Jerusalem all of Judah and Benjamin 'and the strangers with them out of Ephraim and Manasseh.' (2 Chronicles 15:9.) These 'strangers . . . out of Ephraim and Manasseh' who were gathered to Jerusalem in approximately 941 B.C. may have included the forefathers of Lehi and Ishmael" (Daniel H. Ludlow, *A Companion to Your Study of the Book of Mormon* [1976], 199).

Alma 10:22–23. "Prayers of the Righteous"

• Note the effect that the prayers of the righteous had upon a nation. The prayers of the righteous also kept the Nephites from being destroyed later during the days of Captain Moroni and Samuel the Lamanite (see Alma 62:40; Helaman 13:12–14).

President Spencer W. Kimball (1895–1985) said the following about prayers offered in our day: "There are many many upright and faithful who live all the commandments and whose lives and prayers keep the world from destruction" (in Conference Report, Apr. 1971, 7; or *Ensign,* June 1971, 16). Once the righteous were destroyed or removed from Ammonihah, the prayers of the righteous ceased to protect the city and "every living soul of the Ammonihahites was destroyed" (Alma 16:9).

Alma 11:22. "Six Onties of Silver"

• An *onti* was the greatest monetary value in Nephite society. One possible purpose for the inclusion of the Nephite coinage in Alma 11 is to demonstrate the extent of the bribe Zeezrom offered if Amulek would "deny the existence of a Supreme Being" (Alma 11:22). It appears that six onties of silver was the equivalent of 42 days wages for a judge in the society of the people of Ammonihah (see Alma 11:3, 11–13).

ALMA 11:34–37

What is the difference between the Savior's declaration in 3 Nephi 9:21 and Amulek's response to Zeezrom in Alma 11:34–37?

Alma 11:40. Whom Does the Atonement Cover?

• There is often a misunderstanding in Alma 11:40—some people have thought that Amulek was teaching that Christ suffered only for those who believe and repent. This is not correct. The scriptures tell us that the Savior "suffereth the pains of all men, yea, the pains of every living creature, both men, women, and children" (2 Nephi 9:21; see also Mosiah 4:7). If mankind will not repent, however, the Savior indicates that "my blood shall not cleanse them" (D&C 29:17). Clearly, what Amulek was intending to convey is the fact that the Atonement in part may go unused when the wicked choose not to repent—not that the Savior only suffered for those who would repent.

Alma 11:41–45. Resurrection

• The Bible Dictionary defines the Resurrection as "the uniting of a spirit body with a body of flesh and bones, never again to be divided" ("Resurrection," 761; see also Guide to the Scriptures, "Resurrection"). Knowledge of the Resurrection adds greater meaning to mortal life.

Elder Dallin H. Oaks of the Quorum of the Twelve Apostles described the "lively hope" that comes to individuals who possess faith and trust in this sacred truth and the impact it can have on day to day living:

"The 'lively hope' we are given by the resurrection is our conviction that death is not the conclusion of our identity but merely a necessary step in the destined transition from mortality to immortality. This hope changes the whole perspective of mortal life. . . .

"The assurance of resurrection gives us the strength and perspective to endure the mortal challenges faced by each of us and by those we love, such things as the physical, mental, or emotional deficiencies we bring with us at birth or acquire during mortal life. Because of the resurrection, we know that these mortal deficiencies are only temporary!

"The assurance of resurrection also gives us a powerful incentive to keep the commandments of God during our mortal lives. . . .

". . . Moreover, unless our mortal sins have been cleansed and blotted out by repentance and forgiveness (see Alma 5:21; 2 Nephi 9:45–46; D&C 58:42), we will be resurrected with a 'bright recollection' (Alma 11:43) and a 'perfect knowledge of all our guilt, and our uncleanness' (2 Nephi 9:14; see also Alma 5:18). The seriousness of that reality is emphasized by the many scriptures suggesting that the resurrection is followed immediately by the Final Judgment (see 2 Nephi 9:15, 22; Mosiah 26:25; Alma 11:43–44; 42:23; Mormon 7:6; 9:13–14). Truly, 'this life is the time for men to prepare to meet God' (Alma 34:32📖). . . .

"Our sure knowledge of a resurrection to immortality also gives us the courage to face our own death—even a death that we might call premature. . . .

"The assurance of immortality also helps us bear the mortal separations involved in the death of our loved ones. . . . We should all praise God for the assured resurrection that makes our mortal separations temporary and gives us the hope and strength to carry on" (in Conference Report, Apr. 2000, 17–18; or *Ensign,* May 2000, 15–16).

• While serving as a member of the Seventy, Elder Sterling W. Sill (1903–94) described some of the blessings of the Resurrection when he taught that a resurrected body "is beautiful beyond all comprehension, with quickened senses, amplified powers of perception, and vastly increased capacity for love, understanding, and happiness" (in Conference Report, Oct. 1976, 67; or *Ensign,* Nov. 1976, 48).

• President Joseph Fielding Smith (1876–1972) also explained what the Resurrection would do to our physical bodies: "There is no reason for any person to be concerned as to the appearance of individuals in the resurrection. Death is a purifying process as far as the body is concerned. We have reason to believe that the appearance of old age will disappear and the body will be restored with the full vigor of manhood and womanhood. Children will arise as children, for there is no growth in the grave. Children will continue to grow until they reach the full stature of their spirits" (*Answers to Gospel Questions,* comp. Joseph Fielding Smith Jr., 5 vols. [1957–66], 4:185).

ALMA 12:9

What does this verse teach us about acquiring more knowledge from God?

Alma 12:9. What Are the "Mysteries of God"?

• President Joseph Fielding Smith explained that the mysteries of God are simply those divine principles of the gospel necessary for our salvation that are not understood by the world: "The Lord has promised to reveal his mysteries to those who serve him in faithfulness. . . . The Gospel is very simple, so that even children at the age of accountability may understand it. Without question, there are principles which in this life we cannot understand, but when the fulness comes we will see that all is plain and reasonable and within our comprehension. The

'simple' principles of the Gospel, such as baptism, the atonement, are mysteries to those who do not have the guidance of the Spirit of the Lord" (*Church History and Modern Revelation,* 2 vols. [1953], 1:43).

The mysteries of God should not be confused with the unworthy pursuit of "mysteries," or things that God has not revealed. Speaking of this latter use of the word *mysteries,* Elder Bruce R. McConkie (1915–85) of the Quorum of the Twelve Apostles explained: "There is also a restricted and limited usage of the expression

mysteries; it is more of a colloquial than a scriptural usage, and it has reference to that body of teachings in the speculative field, those things which the Lord has not revealed in plainness in this day. It is to these things that reference is made when the elders are counseled to leave the mysteries alone" (*Mormon Doctrine,* 2nd ed. [1966], 524).

Alma 12:10–12. We Receive "the Lesser Portion of the Word" When We Harden Our Heart

• Elder Dallin H. Oaks explained that if we reject revelation through the Holy Ghost, we limit how much we can learn: "We teach and learn the mysteries of God by revelation from his Holy Spirit. If we harden our hearts to revelation and limit our understanding to what we can obtain by study and reason, we are limited to what Alma called 'the lesser portion of the word'" (*The Lord's Way* [1991], 42).

Alma 12:12–14. Judged According to our Words, Works, and Thoughts

• Elder Dallin H. Oaks taught that the Judgment is not merely a review of actions taken in mortality, but is instead an assessment of who and what we have become as a result of our actions:

"The prophet Nephi describes the Final Judgment in terms of what we *have become:* 'And if their works have been filthiness they must needs *be* filthy; and if they *be* filthy it must needs be that they cannot dwell in the kingdom of God' (1 Nephi 15:33; italics added). Moroni declares, 'He that *is* filthy shall be filthy still; and he that *is* righteous shall be righteous still' (Mormon 9:14; italics added; see also Revelation 22:11–12; 2 Nephi 9:16; D&C 88:35). The same would be true of 'selfish' or 'disobedient' or any other personal attribute inconsistent with the requirements of God. Referring to the 'state' of the wicked in the Final Judgment, Alma explains that if we are condemned by our words, our works, and our thoughts, 'we shall not be found spotless; . . . and in this awful state we shall not dare to look up to our God' (Alma 12:14).

"From such teachings we conclude that the Final Judgment is not just an evaluation of a sum total of good and evil acts—what we have *done.* It is an acknowledgment of the final effect of our acts and thoughts—what we have *become*. It is not enough for anyone just to go through the motions. The commandments, ordinances, and covenants of the gospel are not a list of deposits required to be made in some heavenly account. The gospel of Jesus Christ is a plan that shows us how to become what our Heavenly Father desires us to become" (in Conference Report, Oct. 2000, 41; or *Ensign,* Nov. 2000, 32).

Alma 12:15–18. "Second Death, Which Is a Spiritual Death"

• For information on the second death, see commentary for Jacob 3:11 (p. 120), Alma 40:26 (p. 244), and Helaman 14:15–19 (p. 284).

Alma 12:21. Cherubim

• Cherubim are "figures representing heavenly creatures, the exact form being unknown. They are found in the Holy of Holies, on the Mercy Seat of the Ark (Ex. 25:18, 22; 1 Kings 6:23–28; Heb. 9:5), and in the visions of Ezekiel (Ezek. 10; 11:22). In the account of the Fall, cherubim are represented as keeping 'the way of the tree of life' (Gen. 3:24)" (Bible Dictionary, "Cherubim," 632).

Alma 12:24. "Probationary State"

• The term *probationary state* or *probationary time* is a phrase used only by Alma in the Book of Mormon (see Alma 42:4, 10, 13). Elder L. Tom Perry of the Quorum of the Twelve Apostles described this probationary time: "The main purpose of earth life is to allow our spirits, which existed before the world was, to be united with our bodies for a time of great opportunity in mortality. The association

of the two together has given us the privilege of growing, developing, and maturing as only we can with spirit and body united. With our bodies, we pass through a certain amount of trial in what is termed a probationary state of our existence. This is a time of learning and testing to prove ourselves worthy of eternal opportunities. It is all part of a divine plan our Father has for His children" (in Conference Report, Apr. 1989, 16; or *Ensign,* May 1989, 14).

> ### ALMA 12:25–33
> *Why is the title "plan of redemption" an appropriate name for God's preparations for His children?*

Alma 12:32. Commandments *after* Knowing the Plan

• President Boyd K. Packer, President of the Quorum of the Twelve Apostles, taught that knowledge of God's plan provides answers to difficult questions. Speaking to teachers of youth, he said:

"Young people wonder 'why?'—Why are we commanded *to do* some things, and why we are commanded *not* to do other things? A knowledge of the plan of happiness, even in outline form, can give your minds a 'why.' . . .

"Most of the difficult questions we face in the Church right now, and we could list them—abortion and all the rest of them, all of the challenges of who holds the priesthood and who does not—cannot be answered without some knowledge of the plan as a background.

"Alma said this, and this is, I think of late, my favorite scripture, although I change now and again: 'God gave unto them *commandments, after* having made known unto them the *plan of redemption*' (Alma 12:32; emphasis added). . . .

". . . If you are trying to give [students] a 'why,' follow that pattern: 'God gave unto them commandments, *after* having made known unto them the plan of redemption'" ("The Great Plan of Happiness" [Church Educational System symposium on the Doctrine and

Covenants, Aug. 10, 1993], 3; see LDS.org under gospel library/additional addresses/CES addresses).

Points to Ponder

- Alma 8:18 records that Alma "returned speedily" to Ammonihah. In Genesis 22:3 we read that Abraham "rose up early in the morning" to take Isaac upon the mount. How might you apply these verses to yourself when you receive a prompting from God?

- Read Alma 10:6. What do you suppose Amulek meant when he said he was "called many times" but "would not hear"?

Suggested Assignments

- Alma 9:8–14 highlights the importance of remembering. Make a short list of significant spiritual experiences you have been privileged to have. You might also talk to your parents and grandparents and make a similar list of significant spiritual experiences from their lives as well. What blessings might come from regularly reviewing these lists and continually adding to them?

- Alma 11–12 records much detail about the Resurrection. Write a short paper from these chapters about key doctrines of the Resurrection and the impact your knowledge of the Resurrection and Judgment has had on your life.

CHAPTER 26

Alma 13–16

Introduction

You used your agency in the pre-earth life to make righteous choices and to prepare for mortality (see Alma 13:3–5). As a result of your premortal righteousness, further blessings and opportunities have been prepared for you in mortality—upon condition of your continued faithfulness. Note that Alma emphasized our need to be sanctified in mortality and to prepare for the ultimate goal of entering "into the rest of the Lord" (Alma 13:12).

Remember that God's mercy and justice are greater than the wickedness of this world. In Ammonihah those who repented and accepted the teachings of Alma received the Lord's blessings even though many of them were cast out or destroyed (see commentary for Alma 14:7–11 on p. 195). Amulek pleaded with Alma to petition the Lord to save the righteous from the actions of the wicked. Alma's explanation to Amulek, however, confirms the principle of agency and the blessings awaiting those who suffer for the gospel's sake. The wicked will receive God's justice either in this life or in the life to come.

Commentary

Alma 13:1–2. Priests Ordained "After the Order of His Son"

• Alma referred to priests who were ordained "after the order of his Son" (Alma 13:1). The phrase *after the order of his Son* is a reference to the Melchizedek Priesthood. In modern revelation, the Lord stated that before the days of Melchizedek, the priesthood was called "the Holy Priesthood, after the Order of the Son of God. But out of respect or reverence to the name" of God, the name was changed to the Melchizedek Priesthood (D&C 107:3–4).

Elder Bruce R. McConkie (1915–85) of the Quorum of the Twelve Apostles explained why Alma 13, like many other passages in the Book of Mormon, does not distinguish between *priests* of the Aaronic Priesthood and *high priests* of the Melchizedek Priesthood: "Book of Mormon prophets gave the title *priest* to officers known in this dispensation as *high priests*. That is, they were priests of the Melchizedek Priesthood, or as Alma expressed it, *'the Lord God ordained priests, after his holy order, which was after the order of his Son.'* (Alma 13:1–20.)" (*Mormon Doctrine,* 2nd ed. [1966], 599).

Alma 13:3–5. "Called and Prepared" before the Foundation of the World

• The Prophet Joseph Smith (1805–44) taught that those who are ordained to a calling in mortality were foreordained to that calling in the pre-earth life: "Every man who has a calling to minister to the inhabitants of the world was ordained to that very purpose in the Grand Council of heaven before this world was. I suppose that I was ordained to this very office in that Grand Council" (*History of the Church,* 6:364).

• Those who were "called and prepared from the foundation of the world" were chosen by God in the pre-earth life because of their "exceeding faith and good works" (Alma 13:3; see also D&C 138:55–56; Abraham 3:22–23).

President Wilford Woodruff (1807–98) taught that all of the elders of Israel who hold the Melchizedek Priesthood were foreordained, in addition to the prophets: "Joseph Smith was appointed by the Lord before he was born as much as Jeremiah was. . . . So I say with regard to Joseph Smith, he received his appointment from before the foundation of the world, and he came forth in the due time of the Lord to establish this work on the earth. And so it is the case with tens of thousands of the elders of Israel. The Lord Almighty has conferred upon you the Holy Priesthood and made you the instrument in His hands to build up this kingdom. Do we contemplate these things as fully as we ought?" (*Discourses of Wilford Woodruff,* ed. G. Homer Durham [1990], 281–82; see also *Teachings of Presidents of the Church: Wilford Woodruff* [2004], 15).

• President Spencer W. Kimball (1895–1985) taught that both men and women were given assignments in the pre-earth life: "In the world before we came here, faithful women were given certain assignments while

191

faithful men were foreordained to certain priesthood tasks. While we do not now remember the particulars, this does not alter the glorious reality of what we once agreed to. You are accountable for those things which long ago were expected of you just as are those we sustain as prophets and apostles!" ("The Role of Righteous Women," *Ensign*, Nov. 1979, 102).

• Elder Neal A. Maxwell (1926–2004) of the Quorum of the Twelve Apostles described the responsibilities God's children have in mortality regardless of their chosen state in the premortal life: "Premortality is not a relaxing doctrine. For each of us, there are choices to be made, incessant and difficult chores to be done, ironies and adversities to be experienced, time to be well spent, talents and gifts to be well employed. Just because we were chosen 'there and then,' surely does not mean we can be indifferent 'here and now.' Whether foreordination for men, or foredesignation for women, those called and prepared must also prove 'chosen, and faithful.' (See Revelation 17:14; D&C 121:34–36.)" (in Conference Report, Oct. 1985, 21; or *Ensign*, Nov. 1985, 17).

• President Harold B. Lee (1899–1973) described the source of some of the blessings we receive in this life: "All these rewards were seemingly promised, or foreordained, before the world was. Surely these matters must have been determined by the kind of lives we had lived in that premortal spirit world. Some may question these assumptions, but at the same time they will accept without any question the belief that each one of us will be judged when we leave this earth according to his or her deeds during our lives here in mortality. Isn't it just as reasonable to believe that what we have received here in this earth [life] was given to each of us according to the merits of our conduct before we came here?" (in Conference Report, Oct. 1973, 7–8; or *Ensign*, Jan. 1974, 5).

Alma 13:4. Agency Existed in the Premortal World

• How were those in the premortal world able to "reject the Spirit of God"? (Alma 13:4). President Joseph Fielding Smith (1876–1972) confirmed the eternal principle of agency as he answered this question:

"God gave his children their free agency even in the [premortal] spirit world, by which the individual spirits had the privilege, just as men have here, of choosing the good and rejecting the evil, or partaking of the evil to suffer the consequences of their sins. Because of this, some even there were more faithful than others in keeping the commandments of the Lord. . . .

"The spirits of men had their free agency. . . . The spirits of men were not equal. They may have had an equal start, and we know they were all innocent in the beginning; but the right of free agency which was given to them enabled some to outstrip others, and thus, through the eons of immortal existence, to become more intelligent, more faithful, for they were free to act for themselves, to think for themselves, to receive the truth or rebel against it" (*Doctrines of Salvation*, comp. Bruce R. McConkie, 3 vols. [1954–56], 1:58–59).

• As spirits in the pre-earth life, we developed worthy characteristics that showed our abilities. God observed our progress and gave us responsibilities according to our faithfulness. President Joseph Fielding Smith taught: "During the ages in which we dwelt in the pre-mortal state we not only developed our various characteristics and showed our worthiness and ability, or the lack of it, but we were also where such progress could be observed. It is reasonable to believe that there was a Church organization there. The heavenly beings were living in a perfectly arranged society. Every person knew his place. Priesthood, without any question, had been conferred and the leaders were chosen to officiate. Ordinances pertaining to that pre-existence were required and the love of God prevailed. Under such conditions it was natural for our Father to discern and choose those who were most worthy and evaluate the talents of each individual. He knew not only what each of us *could* do, but also what each of us *would* do when put to the test and when responsibility was given us. Then, when the time came for our habitation on mortal earth, all things were prepared and the servants of the Lord chosen and ordained to their respective missions" (*The Way to Perfection* [1970], 50–51).

ALMA 13:6, 18

What responsibility does one have after being ordained to the high priesthood?

Alma 13:9. "They Become High Priests Forever"

• Because the Melchizedek Priesthood is "without beginning of days or end of years" (Alma 13:9; D&C 84:17; see also Hebrews 7:3), those who obtain the priesthood on earth continue to exercise it even after death. Thus, holders of the Melchizedek Priesthood who die righteous "become high priests forever" (Alma 13:9).

President Harold B. Lee recounted an experience, explaining that every priesthood office a person holds in this life will have an effect in the next world:

"I had reorganized the presidency of the Ensign Stake. We had named the bishop of one of the wards as stake president. . . .

"Six weeks after they were sustained, the stake president suddenly passed away.

"Then I began to receive a barrage of letters. Where in the world was the inspiration for you to call a man whom the Lord was going to let die in six weeks? They invited me to talk at his services, and some seemed to be expecting me to try to explain why I had appointed a man that the Lord was going to take home in six weeks.

"President Joseph Fielding Smith sat on the stand and heard my attempt to satisfy these people, and he said to me, 'Don't you let that bother you. If you have called a man to a position in this church and he dies the next day, that position would have a bearing on what he will be called to do when he leaves this earth.'

"I believe that. I believe that every President of this church, every apostle of this church, every bishop, every stake president, every presiding position will have a bearing on what one is called to do when he leaves this earth" (in Conference Report, Oct. 1972, 129–30; or *Ensign*, Jan. 1973, 107).

Alma 13:10–13. Many Were Called and Foreordained

• Alma taught that there were many who were called in the pre-earth life because of their "exceeding faith" (Alma 13:10). He pled with his brethren to exercise faith again and to "bring forth fruit" to obtain their blessings (Alma 13:13).

President Harold B. Lee explained that although many were called and foreordained in the premortal life because of their valiance, they must exercise faith and good works during mortality to realize the full blessings of their calling (see D&C 121:34):

"God may have called and chosen men in the spirit world or in their first estate to do a certain work, but whether they will accept that calling here and magnify it by faithful service and good works while in mortality is a matter in which it is their right and privilege to exercise their free agency to choose good or evil.

". . . I fear there are many among us who because of their faithfulness in the spirit world were 'called' to do a great work here, but like reckless spendthrifts they are exercising their free agency in riotous living and are losing their birthright and the blessings that were theirs had they proved faithful to their calling. Hence as the Lord has said, 'there are many called but few are chosen'" (*Decisions for Successful Living* [1973], 169).

Alma 13:11–12. Sanctification

• Alma taught that many became clean through the "blood of the Lamb" and were "sanctified by the Holy Ghost" (Alma 13:11–12; see also Moroni 10:32–33). Once sanctified, they "could not look upon sin save it were with abhorrence" (Alma 13:12; see also 2 Nephi 4:31). However, even after a person has been sanctified and has felt cleansed by the Holy Ghost, he or she will continue to be tempted throughout mortality. Modern revelation warns, "Therefore let the church take heed and pray always, lest they fall into temptation; yea, and even let those who are sanctified take heed also" (D&C 20:33–34).

President Brigham Young (1801–77) defined sanctification as follows:

"I will put my own definition to the term sanctification, and say it consists in overcoming every sin and bringing all into subjection to the law of Christ. God has placed in us a pure spirit; when this [the spirit] reigns predominant, without let or hindrance, and triumphs over the flesh and rules and governs and controls . . . , this I call the blessing of sanctification. Will sin be perfectly destroyed? No, it will not, for it is not so designed in the economy of heaven.

"Do not suppose that we shall ever in the flesh be free from temptations to sin. Some suppose that they can in the flesh be sanctified body and spirit and become so pure that they will never again feel the effects of the power of the adversary of truth. Were it possible for a person to attain to this degree of perfection in the flesh, he could not die, neither remain in a world where sin predominates. Sin has entered into the world, and death by sin. [Rom. 5:12.] I think we shall more or less feel the effects of sin so long as we live, and finally have to pass the ordeals of death" (in Daniel H. Ludlow, *A Companion to Your Study of the Book of Mormon* [1976], 2:248–49).

Alma 13:13–19. Melchizedek, the Great High Priest

• The high priest Melchizedek holds a place of great respect among Latter-day Saints. Alma noted the importance of Melchizedek when he said "none were greater" (Alma 13:19). Who was this great prophet? Melchizedek lived about 2000 B.C. and was the high priest and king of Salem (Jerusalem; see Genesis 14:18). He was the presiding priesthood authority in his day and was the one Abraham paid tithing to (see Genesis 14:20). When Melchizedek was a child, "he feared God, and stopped the mouths of lions, and quenched the violence of fire" (JST, Genesis 14:26). Although he is mentioned only briefly in the Bible, modern revelation confirms he was a man of great faith. Because of Melchizedek's righteousness, his ministry foreshadowed the ministry of Jesus Christ and thus became the namesake of the higher priesthood (see Hebrews 7:15; D&C 107:2–4).

Alma 13:16. "The Rest of the Lord"

• Alma 13:6, 12–13, 16, 29 mention the "rest of the Lord" (see also D&C 84:24). President Joseph F. Smith (1838–1918) commented on the meaning of this phrase when he said: "What does it mean to enter into the rest of the Lord? Speaking for myself, it means that through the love of God I have been won over to Him, so that I can feel at rest in Christ, that I may no more be disturbed by every wind of doctrine, by the cunning and craftiness of men, whereby they lie in wait to deceive; and that I am established in the knowledge and testimony of Jesus Christ, so that no power can turn me aside from the straight and narrow path that leads back into the presence of God, to enjoy exaltation in His glorious kingdom; that from this time henceforth I shall enjoy that rest until I shall *rest* with Him in the heavens" (*Teachings of Presidents of the Church: Joseph F. Smith* [1998], 426).

Alma 13:20. What Does It Mean to "Wrest" the Scriptures?

• The dictionary defines *wrest* as, "To twist. . . . To distort; to turn from truth or twist from its natural meaning . . . ; to pervert" (*Noah Webster's First Edition of an American Dictionary of the English Language, 1828* [1967]). Thus, those who *wrest* the scriptures change or distort the actual meaning to match their own personal opinion or interpretation. Those who manipulate the scriptures to stir up contention are inspired by Satan (see Alma 12:1–6; 14:6–7). The fate of those who *wrest* the scriptures is their own destruction (see Alma 13:20).

Alma 13:22–26. The Reality of Angels

• The Book of Mormon testifies of the authenticity and purpose of angels (see Alma 13:22–26; 32:23; 3 Nephi 17:24; Moroni 7:29–31; D&C 20:10). In reference to the reality of angels, Elder Jeffrey R. Holland of the Quorum of the Twelve Apostles said:

"I am convinced that one of the profound themes of the Book of Mormon is the role and prevalence and central participation of angels in the gospel story. . . .

"One of the things that will become more important in our lives the longer we live is the reality of angels, their work and their ministry. I refer here not alone to the angel Moroni but also to those more personal ministering angels who are with us and around us, empowered to help us and who do exactly that (see 3 Ne. 7:18; Moro. 7:29–32, 37; D&C 107:20). . . .

Harry Anderson, © IRI

"I believe we need to speak of and believe in and bear testimony of the ministry of angels more than we sometimes do. They constitute one of God's great methods of witnessing through the veil, and no document in all this world teaches that principle so clearly and so powerfully as does the Book of Mormon" ("For a Wise Purpose," *Ensign,* Jan. 1996, 16–17).

ALMA 13:27
What do you learn from this verse about Alma's love for the people of Ammonihah?

Alma 13:28. You Will Not Be Tempted "Above That Which Ye Can Bear"

• President Brigham Young taught of the constant battle we wage against Satan and sin: "The men and women, who desire to obtain seats in the celestial kingdom, will find that they must battle [with the enemy of all righteousness] every day" (*Discourses of Brigham Young,* sel. John A. Widtsoe [1954], 392). Each of us must actively choose to avoid and to resist temptation.

Alma taught that we must "watch and pray continually" to avoid being tempted "above that which ye can bear" (Alma 13:28). The Apostle Paul also declared that "God is faithful, who will not suffer you to be tempted above that ye are able; but will with the temptation also make a way to escape, that ye may be able to bear it" (1 Corinthians 10:13). By following Alma's counsel in Alma 13:28, we will always be able to resist temptation.

Alma 14:7–11. The Martyrdom of the Righteous

• Through the power of the priesthood he held and his faith, Alma had the ability to deliver the faithful women and children of Ammonihah from their terrible deaths. The Lord did not permit him to do so, however (see Alma 14:11). Alma explained to Amulek that the Lord would receive the righteous martyrs unto Himself as a testimony against the evil acts of their persecutors (see Alma 14:11; 60:13).

While serving in the Seventy, Elder Ronald E. Poelman affirmed that, at times, the Lord permits the righteous to suffer when others exercise agency in unrighteousness: "Adversity in the lives of the obedient and faithful may be the consequence of disease, accidental injury, ignorance, or the influence of the adversary. To preserve free agency, the Lord also at times permits the righteous to suffer the consequences of evil acts by others (see 1 Nephi 18:16)" (in Conference Report, Apr. 1989, 29; or *Ensign,* May 1989, 23).

• Certainly we grieve to consider the deaths of the righteous who suffered at the hands of the wicked. But we rejoice in knowing of their rewards in the spirit world (see Alma 40:12) as well as their final state in the celestial kingdom (see D&C 76:50–70). Doctrine and Covenants 42:46 reminds us: "Those that die in me shall not taste of death, for it shall be sweet unto them." This does not mean that there is no pain involved in the death of the righteous, but that the eternal rewards for them are so great that in comparison their pains are nothing.

President Joseph F. Smith explained: "It is true I am weak enough to weep at the death of my friends and kindred. I may shed tears when I see the grief of others. I have sympathy in my soul for the children of men. I can weep with them when they weep; I can rejoice with them when they rejoice; but I have no cause to mourn, nor to be sad because death comes into the world. . . . All fear of this death has been removed from the Latter-day Saints. They have no dread of the temporal death, because they know that as death came upon them by the transgression of Adam, so by the righteousness of Jesus Christ shall life come unto them, and though they die they shall live again. Possessing this knowledge, they have joy even in death, for they know that they shall rise again and shall meet again beyond the grave" (in Conference Report, Oct. 1899, 70).

• When the righteous and innocent suffer, some become critical or lose faith. President Spencer W. Kimball offered the following counsel for when we witness suffering:

"If we looked at mortality as the whole of existence, then pain, sorrow, failure, and short life would be calamity. But if we look upon life as an eternal thing stretching far into the premortal past and on into the eternal post-death future, then all happenings may be put in proper perspective.

"Is there not wisdom in his giving us trials that we might rise above them, responsibilities that we might achieve, work to harden our muscles, sorrows to try our souls? Are we not exposed to temptations to test our strength, sickness that we might learn patience, death that we might be immortalized and glorified?

"If all the sick for whom we pray were healed, if all the righteous were protected and the wicked destroyed, the whole program of the Father would be annulled and the basic principle of the gospel, free agency, would be ended. No man would have to live by faith.

"If joy and peace and rewards were instantaneously given the doer of good, there could be no evil—all would do good but not because of the rightness of doing good. There would be no test of strength, no development of character, no growth of powers, no free agency, only satanic controls.

"Should all prayers be immediately answered according to our selfish desires and our limited understanding, then there would be little or no suffering, sorrow, disappointment, or even death, and if these were not, there would also be no joy, success, resurrection, nor eternal life and godhood" (*Faith Precedes the Miracle* [1973], 97).

Alma 14:25–28. The Deliverance of Alma and Amulek

• Elder Richard G. Scott of the Quorum of the Twelve Apostles used the story of Alma and Amulek to illustrate that the Lord will deliver us from our afflictions, but only after we have proven our faith by submitting to His will:

"Help from the Lord always follows eternal law. The better you understand that law, the easier it is to receive His help. . . .

". . . The example of Alma and Amulek is enlightening. While striving to do good among the people of Ammonihah, they were taken captive. Amulek trusted his more seasoned companion, Alma, who led him to greater confidence in the Lord. Forced to observe women and children consumed by fire, Amulek said, 'Perhaps they will burn us also.' Alma answered, *'Be it according to the will of the Lord'*—a vital principle. 'But . . . our work is not finished; therefore they burn us not' [Alma 14:12–13; italics added].

"The chief judge and others over many days smote, spit upon, starved, questioned, and harassed them with mocking words and threats. Though commanded to speak, they withstood, bound and naked, in silence waiting patiently for the Lord to inspire them to act. Then 'the power of God was upon Alma and Amulek, and they rose.' Alma cried, 'Give us strength *according to our faith which is in Christ, even unto deliverance.* And they broke the cords with which they were bound' [Alma 14:26; italics added; see vv. 15–26]. The earth shook; the prison walls were rent. All who smote Alma and Amulek were slain, and they were freed. . . .

". . . The Lord will give relief with divine power when you seek deliverance in humility and *faith in Jesus Christ*" (in Conference Report, Apr. 1994, 7–8; or *Ensign,* May 1994, 7–8).

Alma 15:2–3. Zeezrom

• The change in Zeezrom demonstrates the love God has for each of His children and shows His willingness to forgive those who covenant to follow His Son. Zeezrom was a deceitful lawyer in the city of Ammonihah who used his position to accuse Alma and Amulek and destroy that which was good (see Alma 10:13, 31; 11:21). Zeezrom's deception was revealed, however, and he began to "tremble under a consciousness of his guilt" (Alma 12:1, 7). He changed from an antagonist to a sincere investigator (see Alma 12:8). When Alma and Amulek arrived in the city of Sidom, they found Zeezrom suffering "great tribulations of his mind on account of his wickedness" (Alma 15:3). But as a repentant believer, Zeezrom was healed according to his faith in Christ, was baptized, and became a powerful preacher from that time forth (see Alma 15:6–12). Years later Zeezrom served a mission with Alma and Amulek among the Zoramites (see Alma 31:6).

Alma 15:3–5. Sins Harrowed Up the Mind of Zeezrom

• While repenting and seeking forgiveness, Zeezrom's spirit and mind had been harrowed up and "become exceedingly sore" (Alma 15:3). President Boyd K. Packer, President of the Quorum of the Twelve Apostles, spoke of the reality of spiritual disorders that can cause powerful suffering:

"There is another part of us, not so tangible, but quite as real as our physical body. This intangible part of us is described as mind, emotion, intellect, temperament, and many other things. Very seldom is it described as spiritual.

"But there is a *spirit* in man; to ignore it is to ignore reality. There are spiritual disorders, too, and spiritual diseases that can cause intense suffering.

"The body and the spirit of man are bound together. Often, very often, when there are disorders, it is very difficult to tell which is which" (in Conference Report, Oct. 1977, 89; or *Ensign,* Nov. 1977, 59).

ALMA 15:16

What did Amulek give up by choosing to live the gospel and serve as a missionary? What did he gain? (see also Alma 34:8; Ether 12:12–13).

Alma 16:2–3, 9–10. The Words of Alma Were All Fulfilled

• Alma pleaded with "great anxiety" from the "inmost part" of his heart for the people of Ammonihah to repent (Alma 13:27). As their prophet, Alma warned them to repent or be utterly destroyed "from off the face of the earth" (Alma 9:12). The Lord has promised to fulfill all the words of his prophets (see D&C 1:37–38). Alma 16:2–3, 9–10 documents the fulfillment of the words of Alma by recording the destruction of those who rejected the prophets and executed the innocent.

Points to Ponder

• How did men demonstrate in premortal life that they were worthy to be foreordained to receive the Melchizedek Priesthood? (see Alma 13:3–5).

• Why does the Lord sometimes allow the innocent to suffer at the hands of the wicked? (see Alma 14:9–11).

• What can Zeezrom's change from deceitful lawyer to powerful preacher help you learn?

Suggested Assignments

• Why did Alma say the following regarding Melchizedek: "Now, there were many before him, and also there were many afterwards, but none were greater; therefore, of him they have more particularly made mention"? (Alma 13:19). Answer this question by researching the following verses to determine why Alma praised the importance of Melchizedek's mission: Alma 13:14–19; Genesis 14:18–20; JST, Genesis 14:25–40; JST, Hebrews 7:3; Doctrine and Covenants 107:2–4.

• Using scriptures from Alma 14 and materials from the commentary for Alma 14:7–11 (p. 195), write a brief essay that answers the following questions: Why does tragedy happen to righteous people? How do God's mercy and justice impact the tragedies of mortality?

Introduction

Because of their demonstration of love and their understanding of the worth of a soul, Ammon and his companions are models for servants of the Lord everywhere. Through their experience you will see the importance of personal preparation, the power of setting a righteous example, and the need to build meaningful relationships with those you serve. Furthermore, Ammon and his brethren understood that those they served held strong beliefs. Look for ways they found to share gospel truths concerning the Spirit, love, and testimony. By emulating their example, you can be a powerful servant in the Lord's hands to help bring others to Christ.

Commentary

Alma 17:2. Those Who Serve Together Develop a Bond of Friendship

• Those who labor in the Lord's vineyard share a bond of love that comes from laboring in the "harvest" together. This bond is deepened by common experiences of faith and testimony. Elder L. Tom Perry of the Quorum of the Twelve Apostles shared a personal example of meeting his first missionary companion after several years had passed:

"I had an experience a few years ago of receiving a call from my son, Lee. He told me that my first missionary companion was in his neighborhood, and he wanted to spend a few minutes with me. . . . We had a special experience of being together after many years of not seeing one another.

"As missionaries we were given the opportunity of opening up a new town in Ohio to missionary work. Because of this assignment, we were allowed to labor together for 10 months. He was my trainer, my first companion. . . . It was difficult for me to keep up with him, but as we served together we drew close together as companions.

"Our companionship did not end with the 10-month assignment. World War II was raging, and when I returned home I had only a short time to adjust before

I was drafted into military service. On my first Sunday in boot camp, I attended an LDS service. I saw the back of a head that was very familiar to me. It was my first missionary companion. We spent most of the next two and a half years together.

"Although circumstances were very different for us in military service, we tried to continue the practices of missionary service. As often as we could, we prayed together. When circumstances allowed, we had scripture study together. . . .

"We were both set apart as group leaders, and we again had the opportunity to serve and teach together the glorious gospel of our Lord and Savior. We were more successful in the military than we had been as full-time missionaries. Why? Because we were experienced returned missionaries.

"My visit with my first missionary companion was the last opportunity I had to be with him. He was suffering from an incurable disease and died only a few months later. It was a wonderful experience to relive our missions together and then tell about our lives following our missionary service. We recounted our service in bishoprics, high councils, and stake presidencies, and, of course, we bragged about our children and our grandchildren. As we sat and thrilled at the opportunity of being together again, I couldn't help but think of the account in the 17th chapter of the book of Alma" (in Conference Report, Oct. 2001, 94–95; or *Ensign,* Nov. 2001, 77).

ALMA 17:2–3

What did Ammon and his brethren do to prepare to share the gospel with power and authority? What can you do to implement these principles?

Alma 17:2. They "Searched the Scriptures Diligently"

• The sons of Mosiah searched the scriptures as an essential part of their missionary preparation. Likewise, Hyrum Smith received counsel from the Lord to prepare for missionary service by first seeking to obtain His word (see D&C 11:21–22). The missionary handbook *Preach My Gospel* emphasizes the importance of seeking the Holy Ghost, having a strong desire to learn, and putting what we learn into action as key components of effective gospel study:

"Your gospel study is most effective when you are taught by the Holy Ghost. Always begin your gospel study by praying for the Holy Ghost to help you learn. He will bring knowledge and conviction that will bless your life and allow you to bless the lives of others. Your faith in Jesus Christ will increase. Your desire to repent and improve will grow.

"This kind of study prepares you for service, offers solace, resolves problems, and gives you the strength to endure to the end. Successful gospel study requires desire and action. 'For he that diligently seeketh shall find; and the mysteries of God shall be unfolded unto them, by the power of the Holy Ghost, as well as in these times as in times of old' (1 Nephi 10:19). Like Enos, as you hunger to know the words of eternal life and as you allow these words to '[sink] deep into [your] heart' (Enos 1:3), the Holy Ghost will open your mind and heart to greater light and understanding.

"Learning the gospel is also a process of receiving revelation (see Jacob 4:8)" ([2004], 18).

• In addition, *Preach My Gospel* recommends the use of a scripture journal as one way to increase the power of your scripture study. By recording your thoughts and impressions while studying your scriptures, you open new avenues of receiving personal revelation:

"A study journal [can] help you understand, clarify, and remember what you are learning. Elder Richard G. Scott taught, 'Knowledge carefully recorded is knowledge available in time of need. Spiritually sensitive information should be kept in a sacred place that communicates to the Lord how you treasure it. This practice enhances the likelihood of your receiving further light' ('Acquiring Spiritual Knowledge,' *Ensign*, Nov. 1993, 86). Review your study journal to recall spiritual experiences, see new insights, and recognize your growth.

"Your study journal may be a bound journal, a notebook, or a binder. Record and organize your

thoughts and impressions in a way that fits how you learn. Develop your own system to easily access key information in the future. Use it often to review, access, and apply what you have learned. Use your study journal to take notes and record impressions" (p. x).

Alma 17:3. The Benefits of Prayer and Fasting

• Elder M. Russell Ballard of the Quorum of the Twelve Apostles illustrated the power of fasting and prayer in the Lord's service with the following story: "Some years ago a faithful convert, Brother George McLaughlin, was called to preside over a small branch of 20 members in Farmingdale, Maine. He was a humble man who drove a milk delivery truck for a living. Through his fasting and earnest prayer, the Spirit taught him what he and the members of his branch needed to do to help the Church grow in their area. Through his great faith, constant prayer, and powerful example, he taught his members how to share the gospel. It's a marvelous story—one of the great missionary stories of this dispensation. In just one year there were 450 convert baptisms in the branch. The next year there were an additional 200 converts" (in Conference Report, Apr. 2003, 39; or *Ensign*, May 2003, 38–39).

Alma 17:9. Pray and Fast for Those without the Truth

• President Gordon B. Hinckley (1910–2008) counseled every member to work and pray for missionary opportunities:  "Let there be cultivated an awareness in every member's heart of his own potential for bringing others to a knowledge of the truth. Let him work at it. Let him pray with great earnestness about it" ("Find the Lambs, Feed the Sheep," *Ensign*, May 1999, 106).

• Elder M. Russell Ballard admonished us to pray for guidance in doing the Lord's work: "In gospel-sharing homes we pray for guidance for ourselves, and we pray for the physical and spiritual well-being of others. We pray for the people the missionaries are teaching, for our acquaintances, and for those not of our faith. In the gospel-sharing homes of Alma's time, the people would 'join in fasting and mighty prayer in behalf of the welfare of the souls of those who knew not God' (Alma 6:6)" (in Conference Report, Apr. 2006, 88; or *Ensign,* May 2006, 85).

ALMA 17:11, 21–29
What was the commission and the promise the Lord gave the sons of Mosiah?

Alma 17:11. "Show Forth Good Examples"

• Ammon and his brethren learned to live in peace with the Lamanites before they were able to share the gospel with them. Elder M. Russell Ballard suggested three important things we can do to be better neighbors to those not of our faith:

"First, get to know your neighbors. Learn about their families, their work, their views. Get together with them, if they are willing, and do so without being pushy and without any ulterior motives. Friendship should never be offered as a means to an end; it can and should be an end unto itself. . . .

". . . Let us cultivate meaningful relationships of mutual trust and understanding with people from different backgrounds and beliefs.

"Second, I believe it would be good if we eliminated a couple of phrases from our vocabulary: *nonmember* and *non-Mormon.* Such phrases can be demeaning and even belittling. Personally, I don't consider myself to be a 'non-Catholic' or a 'non-Jew.' I am a Christian. I am a member of The Church of Jesus Christ of Latter-day Saints. That is how I prefer to be identified—for who and what I am, as opposed to being identified for what I am not. Let us extend that same courtesy to those who live among us. If a collective description is needed, then 'neighbors' seems to work well in most cases.

"And third, if neighbors become testy or frustrated because of some disagreement with The Church of Jesus Christ of Latter-day Saints or with some law we support for moral reasons, please don't suggest to them—even in a humorous way—that they consider

moving someplace else. I cannot comprehend how any member of our Church can even think such a thing! Our pioneer ancestors were driven from place to place by uninformed and intolerant neighbors. They experienced extraordinary hardship and persecution because they thought, acted, and believed differently from others. If our history teaches us nothing else, it should teach us to respect the rights of all people to peacefully coexist with one another" (in Conference Report, Oct. 2001, 45; or *Ensign,* Nov. 2001, 37–38).

• Elder L. Tom Perry illustrated how our example can lead others to draw nearer to the Lord:

"A nineteen-year-old missionary . . . would never forget his first day in the mission field, for it taught him a great lesson about using his talents to teach the gospel.

"He and his senior companion were assigned to open a new city some distance from the mission headquarters. As they arrived in this new city and walked down the street, they passed a church with a minister standing at the front door. As they walked by the church, the minister went in and called to his whole congregation to follow him out into the street. There they followed the missionaries and started calling them names; then they became more violent and started to throw rocks at them.

"The young elder was excited about this experience—his first day in the mission field and already he was being stoned, he thought. Then, a big rock suddenly hit him squarely in the middle of the back, and his feeling changed to anger. Before entering the mission field he had been quite a baseball pitcher; and in the flush of anger he wheeled around, grabbed the first rock he could find on the ground, reared back in his famous pitching pose, and was just ready to let the rock fly at the crowd when suddenly he realized why he was there. He had not been sent all the way to Brazil to throw rocks at people; he was there to teach them the gospel. But what was he to do with the rock in his hand? If he dropped it to the ground, they would think it a sign of weakness and probably continue to throw rocks at them. Yet he could not throw it at the crowd. Then he saw a telephone post some distance away. That was the way to save face! He reared back and let the rock fly directly at the telephone post, hitting it squarely in the middle.

"The people in the crowd took a couple of steps back. They suddenly realized that that rock probably could have hit any one of them right between the eyes. Their mood changed; instead of throwing rocks at the missionaries, they began to throw them at the telephone post. After this incident, every time the elder went down that street he was challenged to a rock-throwing contest. The rock-throwing contests led to discussions of the gospel, which led to conversions, which led to the establishment of a branch of the Church in that community" ("Prophecies, Visions, and Dreams," in *1979 Devotional Speeches of the Year* [1980], 3).

Alma 18:3–9. Service Softens Hearts

• President Henry B. Eyring of the First Presidency explained how temporal service can soften a heart and lead to a miracle:

"When the other servants brought the evidence of what Ammon had done, King Lamoni said, 'Where is he?' They said, 'Oh, he is in the stables. He is doing every little thing to serve you' (see Alma 18:8–9).

"Isn't that odd? He was called to teach the doctrines of salvation, but he was in the stables. Don't you think he should have been praying and fasting and polishing his teaching plan? No, he was in the stables.

"King Lamoni had been brought up with a belief that there was a God but that whatever the king did was right. He had been specifically taught false doctrine that might have made him impervious to feelings of guilt. Do you remember that when he heard where Ammon was, a feeling of guilt, of fear that he had done wrong in the killing of the servants, came over him (see Alma 18:5)? . . .

"I have always focused before on how mixed up Lamoni was in his doctrine, without seeing the miracle. The miracle was that a spiritual need was created in a man, that he might be taught the gospel of Jesus Christ. His heart was broken. He felt guilt. And it came from the temporal things that Ammon had done. . . .

". . . Never, never underestimate the spiritual value of doing temporal things well for those whom you serve.

". . . Be their servants, and you will love them. And they will feel your love. And more important, they will feel God's love" ("The Book of Mormon Will Change Your Life," *Ensign,* Feb. 2004, 13–14).

> **ALMA 18:10**
> What can you do to respond more like Ammon in this regard? How do Alma 17:25 and 18:3 relate to 18:10?

Alma 18:24. Ammon Began to Speak with Boldness

• Many members of the Church feel concern about how to begin gospel conversations. Ammon's approach was to ask Lamoni questions about his belief in God. Others have found it natural to simply talk about their "Church life" with their friends. Elder M. Russell Ballard gave valuable counsel about starting gospel conversations with our friends:

Jerry Thompson, © IRI

"Creating a gospel-sharing home does not mean that we are going to have to dedicate large amounts of time to meeting and cultivating friends with whom to share the gospel. These friends will come naturally into our lives, and if we are open about our membership in the Church from the very beginning, we can easily bring gospel discussions into the relationship with very little risk of being misunderstood. Friends and acquaintances will accept that this is part of who we are, and they will feel free to ask questions. . . .

"A sister in France was asked about the secret of her success. She said, 'I simply share my joy. I treat everyone as if they were already a member of the Church. If I'm standing by someone in line and strike up a conversation, I share with them how much I enjoyed my Church meetings on Sunday. When co-workers ask, "What did you do this weekend?" I do not skip from Saturday night to Monday morning. I share with them that I went to church, what was said, and my experiences with the Saints. I talk about how I live, think, and feel'" (in Conference Report, Apr. 2006, 89; or *Ensign,* May 2006, 86).

Alma 18:24–28. Building on Common Beliefs

• While serving as a member of the Seventy, Elder Loren C. Dunn (1930–2001) spoke on the importance of showing respect for others' beliefs and building on common ground: "Today we live in times of conflict, dissent, differences of opinion, charges, countercharges, disagreements. There is a need for us, perhaps more than ever before, to reach within ourselves and allow the quality of mutual respect, mingled with charity and forgiveness, to influence our actions with one another; to be able to disagree without becoming disagreeable; to lower our voices and build on common ground with the realization that once the storm has passed, we will still have to live with one another" (in Conference Report, Apr. 1991, 109; or *Ensign,* May 1991, 82).

• The first question Ammon asked when he began to teach King Lamoni was, "Believest thou that there is a God?" (Alma 18:24). When Ammon learned that Lamoni believed in a Great Spirit, he testified, "This is God" (Alma 18:28). Technically, God is not a "great spirit." But Ammon looked beyond that and focused instead on their common belief in a Supreme Being and taught from that point. Ammon took Lamoni's fundamental belief in a Creator and added eternal truths that would "light up his mind" (Alma 19:6).

President Gordon B. Hinckley explained how we also should build on the good that others already possess: "We say in a spirit of love, bring with you all that you have of good and truth which you have received from whatever source, and come and let us see if we may add to it. This invitation I extend to men and women

everywhere" (in Conference Report, Oct. 2002, 87; or *Ensign,* Nov. 2002, 81).

Alma 18:36–39; 22:7–14. Teaching the Plan of Salvation

• When Ammon taught Lamoni, "he began at the creation of the world," then he taught "concerning the fall of man" (Alma 18:36); finally, he "expounded unto them [the king and his servants] the plan of redemption," particularly "concerning the coming of Christ" (Alma 18:39). Likewise, Aaron taught these important basic principles of the plan of salvation to Lamoni's father (see Alma 22:12–14). By learning the reality of the Creation, the Fall, and the Atonement, one can understand his place in mortality and his potential in eternity.

Elder Bruce R. McConkie (1915–85) of the Quorum of the Twelve Apostles called these foundation doctrines—the Creation, the Fall, and the Atonement—the "three pillars of eternity" and the "greatest events that have ever occurred in all eternity." He explained:

"If we can gain an understanding of them, then the whole eternal scheme of things will fall into place, and we will be in a position to work out our salvation. . . .

". . . These three are the foundations upon which all things rest. Without any one of them all things would lose their purpose and meaning and the plans and designs of Deity would come to naught" ("The Three Pillars of Eternity," in *Brigham Young University 1981 Firesides and Devotional Speeches* [1981], 27).

• Elder Russell M. Nelson of the Quorum of the Twelve Apostles explained how each component of the plan is essential: "The plan required the Creation, and that in turn required both the Fall and the Atonement. These are the three fundamental components of the plan. The creation of a paradisiacal planet came from God. Mortality and death came into the world through the Fall of Adam. Immortality and the possibility of eternal life were provided by the Atonement of Jesus Christ. The Creation, the Fall, and the Atonement were planned long before the actual work of the Creation began" (in Conference Report, Apr. 2000, 105; or *Ensign,* May 2000, 84).

Alma 18:41–43; 22:15–18. Our Dependence on Christ

• Ammon and Aaron helped Lamoni and his father understand how much they needed the redemption of Christ in their lives. Understanding our dependence on Christ leads to conversion. Both Lamoni and his father became aware of their fallen nature and of their need for help. They came to know that their only hope for redemption was through the Atonement that Christ had wrought.

Walter Rane, Courtesy of Museum of Church History and Art

Alma 18:42. Dramatic Conversions Are the Exception

• See the statement by President Ezra Taft Benson under the commentary for Mosiah 27:25 (see p. 166).

Alma 20:30. "A More Hardened and a More Stiff-Necked People"

• The record states that Aaron and his companions served among those who were "a more hardened and a more stiff-necked people" (Alma 20:30). Their experience parallels the experience of many who try to teach those who either have no interest in, or who are antagonistic toward the gospel. President Henry B. Eyring explained why we must still try to reach every soul:

"Why should I speak to anyone about the gospel who seems content? What danger is there to them or to me if I do or say nothing?

"Well, the danger may be hard to see, but it is real, both for them and for us. For instance, at some moment in the world to come, everyone you will ever meet will know what you know now. They will know that the only way to live forever in association with our families and in the presence of our Heavenly Father and His Son, Jesus Christ, was to choose to enter into the gate by baptism at the hands of those with authority from God. They will know that the only way families can be together forever is to accept and keep sacred covenants offered in the temples of God on this earth. And they will know that you knew. And they will remember whether you offered them what someone had offered you" (in Conference Report, Oct. 1998, 41; or *Ensign,* Nov. 1998, 33).

> ### ALMA 22:15–18
> *What was Lamoni's father willing to give up to know God? How might such willingness help us draw nearer to God? (see also Omni 1:26).*

Alma 22:18. "I Will Give Away All My Sins to Know Thee"

• Like Lamoni's father, we must be willing to sacrifice all things to be born of God. In the *Lectures on Faith* we learn the importance of sacrifice in our eternal progression: "Let us here observe, that a religion that does not require the sacrifice of all things never has power sufficient to produce the faith necessary unto life and salvation; for, from the first existence of man, the faith necessary unto the enjoyment of life and salvation never could be obtained without the sacrifice of all earthly things. It was through this sacrifice, and this only, that God has ordained that men should enjoy eternal life; and it is through the medium of the sacrifice of all earthly things that men do actually know that they are doing the things that are well pleasing in the sight of God. When a man has offered in sacrifice all that he has for the truth's sake, not even withholding his life, and believing before God that he has been called to make this sacrifice because he seeks to do his will, he does know, most assuredly, that God does and will accept his sacrifice and offering, and that he has not, nor will not seek his face in vain. Under these circumstances, then, he can obtain the faith necessary for him to lay hold on eternal life" ([1985], 69).

• While serving in the Seventy, Elder Alexander B. Morrison taught concerning the sacrifices we must make to come unto Christ:

"To take His name upon us means a willingness to do whatever He requires of us.

"Someone has said that the price of a Christian life is the same today as always: it is simply to give all that we have, holding back nothing, to 'give away all [our] sins to know [Him]' (Alma 22:18). When we fall short of that standard by reason of sloth, indifference, or wickedness; when we are evil or envious, selfish, sensual, or shallow; we, in a sense at least, crucify Him afresh. And when we try consistently to be our very best, when we care for and serve others, when we overcome selfishness with love, when we place the welfare of others above our own, when we bear each other's burdens and 'mourn with those that mourn,' when we 'comfort those that stand in need of comfort, and . . . stand as witnesses of God at all times and in all things, and in all places' (Mosiah 18:8–9), then we honor Him and draw from His power and become more and more like Him, growing 'brighter and brighter,' if we persist, 'until the perfect day' (D&C 50:24)" (in Conference Report, Oct. 1999, 33; or *Ensign,* Nov. 1999, 27).

Points to Ponder

• How did Ammon prepare Lamoni's heart to receive the gospel? What could you do to prepare someone's heart to receive the truths of the gospel?

• What do we learn from the example of Aaron and his brethren when they experienced rejection "and all kinds of afflictions"? (Alma 20:29).

Suggested Assignments

• As Ammon and his brethren approached the land of Nephi, the Lord charged them (1) to establish His word, (2) to be patient in afflictions, and (3) to be good examples, promising them that He would bless them with success (see Alma 17:11). Write these three headings on a piece of paper. Then, as you study Alma 17–22, list examples under each heading that demonstrate their obedience to the Lord's instruction. Also write how each example you list helped bring the Lamanites to a knowledge of the truth.

• Make a list of principles related to missionary work (see Alma 17–22). Prayerfully identify specific ways you could apply these principles in your life.

Introduction

The Anti-Nephi-Lehies clearly demonstrated the powerful change that comes upon individuals who accept the gospel and make covenants to follow Jesus Christ. They provided an example of profound, full conversion that comes from a sincere effort to emulate the Savior in every aspect of life. Along with the converted Lamanites, the sons of Mosiah and Alma also showed the spiritual power that comes from the continuous desire to repent, to keep covenants, and to serve the Lord through missionary work and righteous living. As you study Alma 23–29, look for specific actions and attitudes that will help you deepen the strength of your personal conversion. Also look at the numerous descriptions of joy and rejoicing that come as a result of being engaged in sharing the gospel with others.

Commentary

Alma 23:1–5. "The Word of God Might Have No Obstruction"

• The king of the Lamanites removed restrictions that had kept the gospel from being taught among his people, and the missionaries went forth preaching throughout the land. President Thomas S. Monson related a similar event as he described the circumstances surrounding the decision made by the government of the German Democratic Republic to allow missionaries to preach in that land after years of restricted Church activity:

"Our ultimate goal was to seek permission for the doorway of missionary work to open. Elder Russell M. Nelson, Elder Hans B. Ringger, and I, along with our local German Democratic Republic church leaders, headed by President Henry Burkhardt, President Frank Apel, and President Manfred Schutze, initially met with State Secretary for Religious Affairs Kurt Löffler as he hosted a lovely luncheon in our honor. He addressed our group by saying, 'We want to be helpful to you. We've observed you and your people for twenty years. We know you are what you profess to be: honest men and women.'

"Government leaders and their wives attended the dedication of a stake center at Dresden and a chapel at Zwickau. As the Saints sang 'God be with you till we meet again'—'Auf Wiedersehen, Auf Wiedersehen'—we remembered Him, the Prince of Peace, who died on the cross at Calvary. I contemplated our Lord and Savior, when He walked the path of pain, the trail of tears, even the road of righteousness. His penetrating declaration came to mind: 'Peace I leave with you, my peace I give unto you: not as the world giveth, give I unto you. Let not your heart be troubled, neither let it be afraid' (John 14:27).

"Then it was back to Berlin for the crucial meetings with the head of the nation, even Chairman Erich Honecker.

". . . We were driven to the chambers of the chief representatives of the government.

"Beyond the exquisite entry to the building, we were greeted by Chairman Honecker. We presented to him the statuette *First Step,* depicting a mother helping her child take its first step toward its father. He was highly pleased with the gift. He then escorted us into his private council room. There, around a large round table, we were seated. Others at the table included Chairman Honecker and his deputies of government.

"Chairman Honecker began, 'We know members of your Church believe in work; you've proven that. We know you believe in the family; you've demonstrated that. We know you are good citizens in whatever country you claim as home; we have observed that. The floor is yours. Make your desires known.'

"I began, 'Chairman Honecker, at the dedication and open house for the temple in Freiberg, 89,890 of your countrymen stood in line, at times up to four hours, frequently in the rain, that they might see a house of God. In the city of Leipzig, at the dedication of the stake center, 12,000 people attended the open house. In the city of Dresden there were 29,000 visitors; in the city of Zwickau, 5,300. And every week of the year 1,500 to 1,800 people visit the temple grounds in the city of Freiberg. They want to know what we believe. We would like to tell them that we believe in honoring and obeying and sustaining the law of the land. We would like to explain our desire to achieve strong family units. These are but two of our beliefs. We cannot answer questions, and we cannot convey our feelings, because we have no missionary representatives here as we do in other countries. The young men and young women whom we would like to have come to your country as missionary representatives would love your nation and your people. More particularly, they would leave an influence with your people which would be ennobling. Then we would like to see young men and young women from your nation who are members of our Church serve as missionary representatives in many nations, such as in America, in Canada, and in a host of others. They will return better prepared to assume positions of responsibility in your land.'

"Chairman Honecker then spoke for perhaps thirty minutes, describing his objectives and viewpoints and detailing the progress made by his nation. At length, he smiled and addressed me and the group, saying, 'We know you. We trust you. We have had experience with you. Your missionary request is approved.'

"My spirit literally soared out of the room. The meeting was concluded. As we left the beautiful government chambers, Elder Russell Nelson turned to me and said, 'Notice how the sunshine is penetrating this hall. It's almost as though our Heavenly Father is saying, "I am pleased."'

"The black darkness of night had ended. The bright light of day had dawned. The gospel of Jesus Christ would now be carried to the millions of people in that nation. Their questions concerning the Church will be answered, and the Kingdom of God will go forth.

"As I reflect on these events, my thoughts turn to the Master's words, 'In nothing doth man offend God, or against none is his wrath kindled, save those who confess not his hand in all things' (D&C 59:21). I confess the hand of God in the miraculous events pertaining to the Church in the German Democratic

Republic" (in Conference Report, Apr. 1989, 68–69; or *Ensign,* May 1989, 52–53).

Alma 23:6. Converted unto the Lord and Never Did Fall Away

• It is remarkable that not one of the Anti-Nephi-Lehies ever left the Church or became less active (see Alma 27:27). President Gordon B. Hinckley (1910–2008) has repeatedly stressed the importance of retaining recent converts. He has said there is no point in doing missionary work unless those converted stay active:

Del Parson, © 1982 IRI

"With the increase of missionary work throughout the world, there must be a comparable increase in the effort to make every convert feel at home in his or her ward or branch. Enough people will come into the Church this year to constitute more than 100 new average-size stakes. Unfortunately, with this acceleration in conversions, we are neglecting some of these new members. I am hopeful that a great effort will go forward throughout the Church, throughout the world, to retain every convert who comes into the Church.

"This is serious business. There is no point in doing missionary work unless we hold on to the fruits of that effort. The two must be inseparable" (in Conference Report, Oct. 1997, 69–70; or *Ensign,* Nov. 1997, 50).

Alma 23:17. What Does the Name *Anti-Nephi-Lehi* Mean?

• The name *Anti-Nephi-Lehi* could indicate the joining together of the descendants of Nephi and those who followed him with the other posterity of Lehi: "The name 'Anti' of 'Anti-Nephi-Lehi' may be a reflex of the Egyptian *nty* 'he of, the one of.' Thus, rather than having the sense 'against,' it has the meaning 'the one of Nephi and Lehi'" (Stephen D. Ricks, "Anti-Nephi-Lehi," in Dennis L. Largey, ed., *Book of Mormon Reference Companion* [2003], 67).

Alma 24:10. Guilt Taken Away through the Atonement

• President Boyd K. Packer, President of the Quorum of the Twelve Apostles, testified that we can apply the Atonement of Jesus Christ to remove our guilt:

"For some reason we think the Atonement of Christ applies *only* at the end of mortal life to redemption from the Fall, from spiritual death. It is much more than that. It is an ever-present power to call upon in everyday life. When we are racked or harrowed up or tormented by guilt or burdened with grief, He can heal us. While we do not fully understand how the Atonement of Christ was made, we can experience 'the peace of God, which passeth all understanding' [Philippians 4:7]. . . .

"We all make mistakes. Sometimes we harm ourselves and seriously injure others in ways that we alone cannot repair. We break things that we alone cannot fix. It is then in our nature to feel guilt and humiliation and suffering, which we alone cannot cure. That is when the healing power of the Atonement will help.

"The Lord said, 'Behold, I, God, have suffered these things for all, that they might not suffer if they would repent' [D&C 19:16]. . . .

"The Atonement has practical, personal, everyday value; apply it in your life. It can be activated with so simple a beginning as prayer. You will not thereafter be free from trouble and mistakes but can erase the guilt through repentance and be at peace" (in Conference Report, Apr. 2001, 28–29; or *Ensign,* May 2001, 23–24).

Alma 24:11. "All That We Could Do" to Repent

• The Anti-Nephi-Lehies did "all that [they] could do . . . to repent" (Alma 24:11). In 2 Nephi 25:23 Nephi explained: "It is by grace that we are saved, after all we can do." From the king of the Anti-Nephi-Lehies we learn that part of all we can do is "to repent of all our sins."

Alma 24:17–19. Burying Our Weapons Deep

• By burying their weapons deep in the earth, the Anti-Nephi-Lehies promised the Lord that they would never use them again. Scripture records, "They were firm, and would suffer even unto death rather than commit sin" (Alma 24:19). Their actions demonstrate the complete abandonment of sin following sincere repentance.

President Spencer W. Kimball (1895–1985) taught that abandonment of sins often requires a change in our lifestyle: "In abandoning sin one cannot merely wish for better conditions. He must make them. He may need to come to hate the spotted garments and loathe the sin. He must be certain not only that he has abandoned the sin but that  he has changed the situations surrounding the sin. He should avoid the places and conditions and circumstances where the sin occurred, for these could most readily breed it again. He must abandon the people with whom the sin was committed. He may not hate the persons involved but he must avoid them and everything associated with the sin. . . . He must eliminate anything which would stir the old memories" (*The Miracle of Forgiveness* [1969], 171–72).

Alma 24:22–27. The Examples of the Righteous Resulted in the Conversion of Many

• Elder L. Tom Perry of the Quorum of the Twelve Apostles remarked that our resolve to keep our covenants may lead to the conversion of others:

"The king of the Anti-Nephi-Lehies instructed his people to bury their weapons deep in the ground that they might not be tempted to use them when their Lamanite brethren came to do battle against them. The people followed their king's instructions, viewing their actions as 'a testimony to God, and also to men, that they never would use weapons again for the shedding of man's blood' (Alma 24:18). When the Lamanites attacked, the Anti-Nephi-Lehies 'went out to meet them, and prostrated themselves' on the ground before their attackers (Alma 24:21). The Lamanites killed a thousand and five of the Anti-Nephi-Lehies before the slaughter stopped. Why did the slaughter stop, and what were its consequences? From the account in Alma we learn the answers to these questions: . . .

"'Now when the Lamanites saw this they did forbear from slaying them; and there were many whose hearts had swollen . . . , for they repented of the things which they had done. . . .

"'. . . The people of God were joined that day by more than the number who had been slain; and those who had been slain were righteous people, therefore we have no reason to doubt but what they were saved.' (Alma 24:24–26) . . .

"While the message of the story is not to insist on universal pacifism, we do learn that by not returning aggressions from others we can have a profound effect on them. Literally, we can change their hearts when we follow Christ's example and turn the other cheek. Our examples as peaceable followers of Christ inspire others to follow him" (*Living with Enthusiasm* [1996], 127–28).

Alma 24:30. Leaving Neutral Ground

• A person who falls away from the Church after having been a member is typically "worse than [if]

they had never known these things" (Alma 24:30). The Prophet Joseph Smith explained this position in a conversation with another member. A brother Isaac Behunin once told the Prophet Joseph Smith, "'If I should leave this Church I would not do as those men have done: I would go to some remote place where Mormonism had never been heard of, settle down, and no one would ever learn that I knew anything about it.'

"The great Seer immediately replied: 'Brother Behunin, you don't know what you would do. No doubt these men once thought as you do. Before you joined this Church you stood on neutral ground. When the gospel was preached, good and evil were set before you. You could choose either or neither. There were two opposite masters inviting you to serve them. When you joined this Church you enlisted to serve God. When you did that you left the neutral ground, and you never can get back on to it. Should you forsake the Master you enlisted to serve, it will be by the instigation of the evil one, and you will follow his dictation and be his servant'" (*Teachings of Presidents of the Church: Joseph Smith* [2007], 324).

Alma 25:1–12. Prophecy Fulfilled

• Alma 25:1–12 records the fulfillment of Abinadi's prophecy regarding the wicked priests of King Noah (see Mosiah 17:15–20). Note how Mormon documented for the reader the fulfillment of the prophecies of Abinadi. Consider the results of those who reject the prophets, like Abinadi, and claim that the prophet has sinned. Modern revelation also contains a warning to those who "lift up the heel against mine anointed" (see D&C 121:16–22).

Alma 25:17. The Lord "Verified His Word unto Them in Every Particular"

• One of the great lessons that emerges from this section of the book of Alma is that God always keeps His promises. The Lord had told King Mosiah that many would believe his sons' teachings and that He would deliver them "out of the hands of the Lamanites" (Mosiah 28:7). For the fulfillment of these promises, see Alma 17:4, 35–39; 19:22–23; 26:1–4. This is just one of numerous scriptural illustrations that reinforce the doctrinal truth that God is bound when we do what He says (see D&C 82:10 📖).

Alma 26:5–7. What Are Sheaves?

• The word *sheaves* means quantities of stalks and heads of grain bound together. Ammon's mention of sheaves in Alma 26:5 refers to the converts brought into the Church by faithful missionaries who thrust in their sickles.

ALMA 26:11–14

What evidences do you find that Ammon's rejoicing was in the Savior's power and mercy, rather than boasting of himself?

Alma 26:15–16. "Who Can Glory Too Much in the Lord?"

• Just as Ammon felt to glory in the Lord and to sing His praises, so should we. Sister Sheri L. Dew, while serving as a counselor in the Relief Society general presidency, taught us concerning the role Jesus Christ plays in our daily lives:

"*Is* it possible to be happy when life is hard? To feel peace amid uncertainty and hope in the midst of cynicism? Is it possible to change, to shake off old habits and become new again? Is it possible to live with integrity and purity in a world that no longer values the virtues that distinguish the followers of Christ?

"Yes. The answer is yes because of Jesus Christ, whose Atonement ensures that we need not bear the burdens of mortality alone. . . .

"Through the years I, like you, have experienced pressures and disappointments that would have crushed me had I not been able to draw upon a source of wisdom and strength far greater than my own. He has never forgotten or forsaken me, and I have come to know for myself that Jesus is the Christ and that this is His Church. With Ammon I say, '[For] who can glory too much in the Lord? Yea, who can say too much of his great power, and of his mercy . . . ? Behold, . . . I cannot say the smallest part which I feel' (Alma 26:16).

I testify that in this, the twilight of the dispensation of the fulness of times, when Lucifer is working overtime to jeopardize our journey home and to separate us from the Savior's atoning power, the only answer for *any* of us is Jesus Christ" (in Conference Report, Apr. 1999, 85–86; or *Ensign,* May 1999, 67).

Alma 26:27. Perseverance Leads to Success

• The success the sons of Mosiah experienced among the Lamanites exceeded their expectations (see Alma 26:30–31). As they began their missions, the Lord promised, "I will make an instrument of thee in my hands unto the salvation of many souls" (Alma 17:11). With this promise they "took courage to go forth unto the Lamanites to declare unto them the word of God" (Alma 17:12). Success in their endeavors did not come automatically, even though the Lord had promised it. During the course of their 14-year mission, they experienced "all manner of afflictions" (Alma 26:30). The record further indicates their hearts became "depressed, and [they] were about to turn back" (Alma 26:27). Yet, trusting in the promises of the Lord, they continued their efforts. Then, as He always does, the Lord honored His promises and rewarded their perseverance.

Jerry Thompson, © IRI

Alma 26:27–30. The Realities of Missionary Service

• Elder F. Burton Howard of the Seventy shared how his reading Alma 26 as a young missionary impacted his testimony of the truthfulness of the Book of Mormon:

"I was reading again the twenty-sixth chapter of Alma and the story of Ammon's mission. I read out loud, as

I sometimes do, trying to put myself in the position of the characters in the book, imagining that I was saying or hearing the words, that I was there. Once more I went over the report, and, with a clarity which cannot be described and which would be difficult to comprehend by one who has not experienced it, the Spirit spoke to my soul, saying, *Did you notice? Everything that happened to Ammon happened to you?*

"It was a totally unexpected sentiment. It was startling in its scope; it was a thought that had never occurred to me before. I quickly reread the story. Yes, there were times when my heart had been depressed and I had thought about going home. I too had gone to a foreign land to teach the gospel to the Lamanites. I had gone forth among them, had suffered hardships, had slept on the floor, endured the cold, gone without eating. I too had traveled from house to house, knocking on doors for months at a time without being invited in, relying on the mercies of God.

"There had been other times when we had entered houses and talked to people. We had taught them on their streets and on their hills. We had even preached in other churches. I remembered the time I had been spit upon. I remembered the time when I, as a young district leader assigned by the mission president to open up a new town, had entered, with three other elders, the main square of a city that had never had missionaries before. We went into the park, sang a hymn, and a crowd gathered.

"Then the lot fell on me, as district leader, to preach. I stood upon a stone bench and spoke to the people. I told the story of the restoration of the gospel, of the boy Joseph going in to the grove and the appearance of the Father and the Son to him. I remembered well a group of teenage boys, in the evening shadows, throwing rocks at us. I remembered the concern about being hit or injured by those who did not want to hear the message.

"I remembered spending time in jail while my legal right to be a missionary in a certain country was decided by the police authorities. I didn't spend enough time in prison to compare myself to Ammon, but I still remember the feeling I had when the door was closed and I was far away from home, alone, with only the mercies of the

Lord to rely on for deliverance. I remembered enduring these things with the hope that 'we might be the means of saving some soul' (Alma 26:30).

"And then on that day as I read, the Spirit testified to me again, and the words remain with me even today: *No one but a missionary could have written this story. Joseph Smith could never have known what it was like to be a missionary to the Lamanites, for no one he knew had ever done such a thing before*" ("Ammon: Reflections on Faith and Testimony," in *Heroes from the Book of Mormon* [1995], 124–25).

Alma 27:21–24. Forgiving Our Enemies

• Alma had previously called upon the inhabitants of Zarahemla to change their hearts (see Alma 5:6, 12–14, 26). He also declared that the Lord "sendeth an invitation unto all men" (Alma 5:33). This matches a similar invitation by the Lord through Nephi, that God "denieth none that come unto him, black and white, bond and free, male and female; . . . all are alike unto God" (2 Nephi 26:33). The inhabitants of Zarahemla embraced Alma's message, and when it became necessary to forgive their enemies, they offered land and protection to the people of Ammon.

President Howard W. Hunter (1907–95) admonished each of us to similarly forgive our enemies:

"Consider, for example, this instruction from Christ to his disciples. He said, 'Love your enemies, bless them that curse you, do good to them that hate you, and pray for them which despitefully use you, and persecute you' (Matthew 5:44).

"Think what this admonition alone would do in your neighborhood and mine, in the communities in which you and your children live, in the nations which make up our great global family. I realize this doctrine poses a significant challenge, but surely it is a more agreeable challenge than the terrible tasks posed for us by the war and poverty and pain the world continues to face. . . .

"We all have significant opportunity to practice Christianity, and we should try it at every opportunity. For example, we can all be a little more forgiving" (in Conference Report, Oct. 1992, 22–23; or *Ensign,* Nov. 1992, 18).

Alma 28:1–12. Hope Follows the Death of the Righteous

• Elder Robert D. Hales of the Quorum of the Twelve Apostles shared the following experience he had with a righteous priesthood leader dying of a terminal disease:

"My friend came to accept the phrase 'Thy will be done' as he faced his own poignant trials and tribulations. As a faithful member of the Church, he was now confronted with some sobering concerns. Particularly touching were his questions, 'Have I done all that I need to do to faithfully endure to the end?' 'What will death be like?' 'Will my family be prepared to stand in faith and be self-reliant when I am gone?'

"We had the opportunity to discuss all three questions. They are clearly answered in the doctrine taught to us by our Savior. We discussed how he had spent his life striving to be faithful, to do what God asked of him, to be honest in his dealings with his fellowmen and all others, to care for and love his family. Isn't that what is meant by enduring to the end? We talked about what happens immediately after death, about what God has taught us about the world of spirits. It is a place of paradise and happiness for those who have lived righteous lives. It is not something to fear.

"After our conversation, he called together his wife and the extended family—children and grandchildren—to teach them again the doctrine of the Atonement that all will be resurrected. Everyone came to understand that just as the Lord has said, while there will be mourning at the temporary separation, there is no sorrow for those who die in the Lord (see Revelation 14:13; D&C 42:46). His blessing promised him comfort and reassurance that all would be well, that he would not have pain, that he would have additional time to prepare his family for his departure, and even that he would know the time of his departure. The family related to me that on the night before he passed away,

he said he would go on the morrow. He passed away the next afternoon at peace, with all his family at his side. This is the solace and comfort that comes to us when we understand the gospel plan and know that families are forever.

"Contrast these events with an incident which happened to me when I was a young man in my early twenties. While serving in the Air Force, one of the pilots in my squadron crashed on a training mission and was killed. I was assigned to accompany my fallen comrade on his final journey home to be buried in Brooklyn. I had the honor of standing by his family during the viewing and funeral services and of representing our government in presenting the flag to his grieving widow at the graveside. The funeral service was dark and dismal. No mention was made of his goodness or his accomplishments. His name was never mentioned. At the conclusion of the services, his widow turned to me and asked, 'Bob, what is really going to happen to Don?'

"I was then able to give her the sweet doctrine of the Resurrection and the reality that, if baptized and sealed in the temple for time and all eternity, they could be together eternally. The clergyman standing next to her said, 'That is the most beautiful doctrine I have ever heard'" (in Conference Report, Oct. 1996, 88–89; or *Ensign,* Nov. 1996, 66).

Alma 29:4–5. God Grants unto Men According to Their Desires

• Elder Neal A. Maxwell (1926–2004) of the Quorum of the Twelve Apostles taught that our desires affect our personal development and eventually determine our eternal blessings:

"Desires . . . become real determinants, even when, with pitiful naïveté, we do not really want the consequences of our desires. . . .

"Therefore, what we insistently desire, over time, is what we will eventually become and what we will receive in eternity. . . .

"Righteous desires need to be relentless, therefore, because, said President Brigham Young, 'the men and women, who desire to obtain seats in the celestial kingdom, will find that they must battle every day' (in

Journal of Discourses, 11:14). Therefore, true Christian soldiers are more than weekend warriors. . . .

". . . Remember, brothers and sisters, it is our own desires which determine the sizing and the attractiveness of various temptations. We set our thermostats as to temptations.

"Thus, educating and training our desires clearly requires understanding the truths of the gospel, yet even more is involved. President Brigham Young confirmed, saying, 'It is evident that many who understand the truth do not govern themselves by it; consequently, no matter how true and beautiful truth is, you have to take the passions of the people and mould them to the law of God' (in *Journal of Discourses,* 7:55). . . .

". . . Therefore, declared President Joseph F. Smith, 'the education then of our desires is one of far-reaching importance to our happiness in life' (*Gospel Doctrine,* 5th ed. [1939], 297). Such education can lead to sanctification until, said President Brigham Young, 'holy desires produce corresponding outward works' (in *Journal of Discourses,* 6:170). Only by educating

and training our desires can they become our allies instead of our enemies!" (in Conference Report, Oct. 1996, 26–28; or *Ensign,* Nov. 1996, 21–22).

Points to Ponder

- How can the example of the Anti-Nephi-Lehies help you deepen the strength of your own conversion?

- Just as the Anti-Nephi-Lehies buried their weapons in a covenant with God (see Alma 24:17–18), what are you doing on a regular basis to demonstrate to the Lord that you also have been fully converted?

- How might Alma's missionary efforts among the Nephites (see Alma 4–15) have prepared him to receive the converted Lamanites who had been taught by the sons of Mosiah?

Suggested Assignments

- Just as the Lamanites buried their weapons of war so that they would never again use them, we have to rid ourselves of sins or weaknesses that keep us from coming unto God. Identify a sin or weakness in your life that you would like to eliminate. Outline a plan to help you overcome it, and put your plan into action.

- Read Alma 26 and 28, looking for the reasons Ammon and Alma gave for their joy. List these reasons and choose one or more to more fully make part of your life.

Introduction

Chapters 30–31 of Alma identify people and ideas that oppose Jesus Christ. President Ezra Taft Benson (1899–1994) said:

"The Book of Mormon brings men to Christ through two basic means. First, it tells in a plain manner of Christ and his gospel. . . .

"Second, the Book of Mormon exposes the enemies of Christ. It confounds false doctrines and lays down contention. (See 2 Ne. 3:12.) It fortifies the humble followers of Christ against the evil designs, strategies, and doctrines of the devil in our day. The type of apostates in the Book of Mormon are similar to the type we have today. God, with his infinite foreknowledge, so molded the Book of Mormon that we might see the error and know how to combat false educational, political, religious, and philosophical concepts of our time" (in Conference Report, Apr. 1975, 94–95; or *Ensign,* May 1975, 64).

By studying how Korihor sought to destroy the faith of the Nephites, you will better recognize those same destructive arguments in our day. By studying Alma's response to Korihor, you will be better prepared to defend yourself and others from those who would destroy your faith.

Commentary

Alma 30. Modern-day Korihors

• Elder Gerald N. Lund, formerly of the Seventy, explained that Korihor has many modern-day equivalents:

"Today, the world is permeated with philosophies similar to those taught by Korihor. We read them in books, see them championed in the movies and on television, and hear them taught in classrooms and sometimes in the churches of our time. . . .

". . . We see clear evidence of Mormon's inspiration to give us a full account of Korihor and his teachings. Korihor's teachings are old doctrine, and yet they are ideas as modern as today's high-speed printing presses and satellite dishes" ("Countering Korihor's Philosophy," *Ensign,* July 1992, 20).

Alma 30:6. Anti-Christs

• The Bible Dictionary states that an anti-Christ is "anyone or anything that counterfeits the true gospel or plan of salvation and that openly or secretly is set up in opposition to Christ. The great antichrist is Lucifer, but he has many assistants both as spirit beings and as mortals" ("Antichrist," 609).

Elder Bruce R. McConkie (1915–85) of the Quorum of the Twelve Apostles further taught: "An *antichrist* is an opponent of Christ; he is one who is in opposition to the true gospel, the true Church, and the true plan of salvation. (1 John 2:19; 4:4–6.) He is one who offers salvation to men on some other terms than those laid down by Christ. Sherem (Jac. 7:1–23), Nehor (Alma 1:2–16), and Korihor (Alma 30:6–60) were antichrists who spread their delusions among the Nephites" (*Mormon Doctrine,* 2nd ed. [1966], 39–40).

Alma 30:7, 11. "No Law against a Man's Belief"

• If there was "no law against a man's belief," some people might ask why Korihor was arrested. King Mosiah had issued a proclamation declaring that it was against Nephite law for any "unbeliever [to] persecute any of those who belonged to the church of God" (Mosiah 27:2).

Clearly, Korihor was entitled to his beliefs, but when he sought to destroy the Church, he broke King Mosiah's proclamation. It is interesting to note that whereas many in Zarahemla embraced Korihor and his teachings, the people of Ammon, who had lived most of their lives following Korihor-like beliefs, "caused that he should be carried out of the land" (Alma 30:21; see also vv. 18–20). They understood the danger of Korihor's teachings.

ALMA 30:12–18

How do Korihor's teachings fit the arguments used to attack our faith in these days?

Chapter 29

Alma 30:12–18. Strategies of Korihor

• One gospel scholar explained how closely Korihor's philosophy aligns with many modern philosophies: "Korihor insisted on a strictly rational and scientific approach to all problems, anything else being but 'the effect of a frenzied mind' (Alma 30:13–16); he crusaded against the tyranny of ancient traditions and primitive superstitions, which led people to believe things which just 'are not so' (Alma 30:16), calling for an emancipation from 'the silly traditions of their fathers' (Alma 30:31). He called for a new morality with the shedding of old inhibitions (Alma 30:17–18, 25). He called for economic liberation from priestly exploitation (Alma 30:27),

Scott Snow, © 1982 IRI

demanding that all be free to 'make use of that which is their own' (Alma 30:28). He preached a strict no-nonsense naturalism: 'When a man was dead, that was the end thereof' (Alma 30:18), and its corollary, which was a strict materialism: 'Every man fared in this life according to the management of the creature' (Alma 30:17). From this followed a clear-cut philosophy of laissez-faire: 'Therefore every man prospereth according to his genius, and . . . every man conquered according to his strength,' with right and wrong measured only by nature's iron rule of success and failure: 'And whatsoever a man did was no crime' (Alma 30:17). It was survival of the fittest applied to human behavior, and the removal of old moral and sentimental restraints was good news to many people, 'causing them to lift up their heads in their wickedness, yea, leading many away . . . to commit whoredoms' (Alma 30:18). Along with his attitude of emancipation Korihor cultivated a crusading zeal and intolerance of any opposition, which has been thoroughly characteristic of his school of thought in modern times, calling all opposition 'foolish' (Alma 30:13–14), 'silly' (Alma 30:31), and the evidence of frenzied and deranged minds (Alma 30:16). And while for Alma a free society was one in which anybody could think and say whatever he chose (Alma 30:7–12), for Korihor the

only free society was one in which everyone thought exactly as *he* thought (Alma 30:24)" (Hugh W. Nibley, *Since Cumorah,* 2nd ed. [1988], 379–80).

Alma 30:15–16. Korihor's False Teaching

• Korihor's teaching that "ye cannot know of things which ye do not see" is the philosophy that all ideas and knowledge are derived from and can be tested by experience and that we can only know those things we experience through our senses: sight, smell, touch, hearing, or taste. Since spiritual experiences involving revelation from God rarely pass through the senses of sight, smell, touch, hearing, or taste, those who hold to Korihor's philosophy count them as meaningless.

President Boyd K. Packer, President of the Quorum of the Twelve Apostles, described an experience he had that illustrated the fact that spiritual matters do not typically include the common five senses:

"I will tell you of an experience I had before I was a General Authority which affected me profoundly. I sat on a plane next to a professed atheist who pressed his disbelief in God so urgently that I bore my testimony to him. 'You are wrong,' I said, 'there is a God. I *know* He lives!'

"He protested, 'You don't *know.* Nobody *knows* that! You can't *know* it!' When I would not yield, the atheist, who was an attorney, asked perhaps the ultimate question on the subject of testimony. 'All right,' he said in a sneering, condescending way, 'you say you know. Tell me *how* you know.'

"When I attempted to answer, even though I held advanced academic degrees, I was helpless to communicate.

"Sometimes in your youth, you young missionaries are embarrassed when the cynic, the skeptic, treat you with contempt because you do not have ready answers for everything. Before such ridicule, some turn away in shame. (Remember the iron rod, the spacious building, and the mocking? See 1 Ne. 8:28.)

"When I used the words *Spirit* and *witness,* the atheist responded, 'I don't know what you are talking about.' The words *prayer, discernment,* and *faith,* were equally meaningless to him. 'You see,' he said, 'you

214

don't really know. If you did, you would be able to tell me *how you know.*'

"I felt, perhaps, that I had borne my testimony to him unwisely and was at a loss as to what to do. Then came the experience! Something came into my mind. And I mention here a statement of the Prophet Joseph Smith: 'A person may profit by noticing the first intimation of the spirit of revelation; for instance, when you feel pure intelligence flowing into you, it may give you sudden strokes of ideas . . . and thus by learning the Spirit of God and understanding it, you may grow into the principle of revelation, until you become perfect in Christ Jesus.' (*Teachings of the Prophet Joseph Smith*, comp. Joseph Fielding Smith, Salt Lake City: Deseret Book Co., 1977, p. 151.)

"Such an idea came into my mind and I said to the atheist, 'Let me ask if you know what salt tastes like.'

"'Of course I do,' was his reply.

"'When did you taste salt last?'

"'I just had dinner on the plane.'

"'You just think you know what salt tastes like,' I said.

"He insisted, 'I know what salt tastes like as well as I know anything.'

"'If I gave you a cup of salt and a cup of sugar and let you taste them both, could you tell the salt from the sugar?'

"'Now you are getting juvenile,' was his reply. 'Of course I could tell the difference. I know what salt tastes like. It is an everyday experience—I know it as well as I know anything.'

"'Then,' I said, 'assuming that I have never tasted salt, explain to me just what it tastes like.'

"After some thought, he ventured, 'Well-I-uh, it is not sweet and it is not sour.'

"'You've told me what it isn't, not what it is.'

"After several attempts, of course, he could not do it. He could not convey, in words alone, so ordinary an experience as tasting salt. I bore testimony to him once again and said, 'I know there is a God. You ridiculed that testimony and said that if I *did* know, I would be able to tell you exactly *how* I know. My friend,

spiritually speaking, I have tasted salt. I am no more able to convey to you in words how this knowledge has come than you are to tell me what salt tastes like. But I say to you again, there is a God! He does live! And just because you don't know, don't try to tell me that I don't know, for I do!'

"As we parted, I heard him mutter, 'I don't need your religion for a crutch! I don't need it.'

"From that experience forward, I have never been embarrassed or ashamed that I could not explain in words alone everything I know spiritually" ("The Candle of the Lord," *Ensign,* Jan. 1983, 51–52).

Alma 30:17. Korihor Taught That "Whatsoever a Man Did" Was Not Sin

• Despite what some people in the world believe, the gospel teaches that there is no such thing as a relative value system. Some cultures seem to allow or even encourage this value-free approach to life, encouraging subtle forms of dishonesty in government, business, and personal relations. The Book of Mormon teaches us, however, that there is a right and wrong and gives us the key by which to judge (see Moroni 7:16–17 📖).

• Korihor's philosophy that a person prospers "according to his genius, and that every man conquered according to his strength" precludes the necessity of God in our life. His philosophy that "whatsoever a man did was no crime" would create a self-centered and relative value system in man.

• Elder Neal A. Maxwell (1926–2004) of the Quorum of the Twelve Apostles exposed the selfishness in Korihor's teachings:

"Some of the selfish wrongly believe that there is no divine law anyway, so there is no sin (see 2 Nephi 2:13). Situational ethics are thus made to order for the selfish. So in the management of self, one can conquer by his genius and strength, because there really is no crime whatsoever (see Alma 30:17).

"Unsurprisingly, therefore, selfishness leads to terrible perceptual and behavioral blunders. For instance, Cain, corrupted by his seeking of power, said after slaying Abel, 'I am free' (Moses 5:33; see also Moses 6:15).

"One of the worst consequences of severe selfishness, therefore, is this profound loss of proportionality, like straining at gnats while swallowing camels (see Matthew 23:24; see also Joseph Smith Translation, Matthew 23:21, footnote 24a). Today there are, for example, those who strain over various gnats but swallow the practice of partial-birth abortions. Small wonder, therefore, that selfishness magnifies a mess of pottage into a banquet and makes 30 pieces of silver look like a treasure trove" (in Conference Report, Apr. 1999, 29; or Ensign, May 1999, 24).

Alma 30:20–23. The Teachings of Ecclesiastical Leaders

• The high priest Giddonah confronted Korihor and asked him why he spoke against the prophets and against the reality of Jesus Christ. Korihor evaded the question and mounted a verbal attack against the believers and their leaders. He sought to make it appear foolish for anyone to follow their ecclesiastic leaders. President Henry B. Eyring of the First Presidency taught to the contrary:

"Korihor was arguing, as men and women have falsely argued from the beginning of time, that to take counsel from the servants of God is to surrender God-given rights of independence. But the argument is false because it misrepresents reality. When we reject the counsel which comes from God, we do not choose to be independent of outside influence. We choose another influence. We reject the protection of a perfectly loving, all-powerful, all-knowing Father in Heaven, whose whole purpose, as that of His Beloved Son, is to give us eternal life, to give us all that He has, and to bring us home again in families to the arms of His love. In rejecting His counsel, we choose the influence of another power, whose purpose is to make us miserable and whose motive is hatred. We have moral agency as a gift of God. Rather than the right to choose to be free of influence, it is the inalienable right to submit ourselves to whichever of those powers we choose.

"Another fallacy is to believe that the choice to accept or not accept the counsel of prophets is no more than deciding whether to accept good advice and gain its benefits or to stay where we are. But the choice not to take prophetic counsel changes the very ground upon which we stand. It becomes more dangerous. The failure to take prophetic counsel lessens our power to take inspired counsel in the future. The best time to have decided to help Noah build the ark was the first time he asked. Each time he asked after that, each failure to respond would have lessened sensitivity to the Spirit. And so each time his request would have seemed more foolish, until the rain came. And then it was too late" (in Conference Report, Apr. 1997, 33; or Ensign, May 1997, 25).

© 2000 Steve Bunderson

Alma 30:25. Anti-Christs Often Use Half Truths

• A common tactic used by those who are trying to destroy faith is called a "straw man" argument. This is done by setting up a false image—a straw man—of the truth and then attacking the false image in order to convince others the true image is false. A simple example of this is a child accusing parents who won't let him play until he gets his work done of not wanting him to have any fun. This is faulty reasoning, but it is often used to deceive others.

Sometimes others claim that Latter-day Saints believe something that we don't believe. They claim that the false belief is false and then show that it is false. It has nothing to do with what we really believe but is an attempt to make us seem to be in error. Korihor did this to Giddonah: "This argument is called a straw man. That is, he attributed to Giddonah something that Giddonah does not believe—the idea that children inherit guilt through Adam's transgression. Korihor knows that he cannot fight truth fairly and come off victorious, so he attributes bad doctrine to Giddonah, a straw man to which he can give a good verbal licking" (Joseph Fielding McConkie and Robert L. Millet, *Sustaining and Defending the Faith* [1985], 90).

Alma 30:29. Avoid Arguments and Contention

• The Prophet Joseph Smith (1805–44) taught that we should avoid contention: "Let the Elders be exceedingly careful about unnecessarily disturbing and harrowing up the feelings of the people. Remember that your business is to preach the Gospel in all humility and meekness, and warn sinners to repent and come to Christ. Avoid contentions and vain disputes with men of corrupt minds, who do not desire to know the truth. Remember that 'it is a day of warning, and not a day of many words.' If they receive not your testimony in one place, flee to another, remembering to cast no reflections, nor throw out any bitter sayings. If you do your duty, it will be just as well with you, as though all men embraced the Gospel" (*History of the Church,* 1:468).

ALMA 30:37–44

List at least three approaches Alma used to refute Korihor's attack on the true Church. How can we similarly be ready to defend the truth?

Alma 30:39. The Power of Personal Testimony

• Elder Jeffrey R. Holland of the Quorum of the Twelve Apostles explained one way to respond to an anti-Christ:

"Korihor ridiculed the 'foolish . . . [and] silly traditions' of believing in a Christ who should come.

"Korihor's arguments sound very contemporary to the modern reader, but Alma used a timeless and ultimately undeniable weapon in response—the power of personal testimony. Angry that Korihor and his like were essentially against happiness, Alma asked, 'Why do you teach this people that there shall be no Christ, to interrupt their rejoicings?' [Alma 30:22] 'I know there is a God'" (*Christ and the New Covenant* [1997], 121).

Alma 30:40. "What Evidence Have Ye That There Is No God"

• Elder Gerald N. Lund explained the impossibility of proving that there is no God:

"When questioned, Korihor categorically denies that he believes there is a God. Alma then asks, 'What evidence have ye that there is no God, or that Christ cometh not? I say unto you that ye have none, save it be your word only.' (Alma 30:40.)

"It is an inspired insight on Alma's part. Korihor is not consistent in his own thinking. If we truly can know only those things for which we have empirical evidence, then we cannot teach there is no God unless we have evidence for that belief. And Korihor has no evidence.

"Korihor will consider only evidence that can be gathered through the senses. In such a system, it is much easier to prove there *is* a God than to prove there is not a God. To prove there is a God, all it takes is for one person to see, hear, or otherwise have an experience with God, and thereafter the existence of God cannot be disproved. But here is what it would take to *prove* there is no God: Since God is not confined to this earth, we would have to search throughout the universe for him. We assume God is able to move about, so it would not be enough to start at point A in the universe and search through to point Z. What if after we leave point A, God moves there and stays there for the rest of the search?

"In other words, for Korihor to say that there is no God, based on the very criteria he himself has established, he would have to perceive every cubic meter of the universe simultaneously. This creates a paradox: In order for Korihor to prove there is no God, *he would have to be a god* himself! Therefore, in declaring there is no God, he is acting on 'faith,' the very thing for which he so sharply derides the religious leaders!" ("Countering Korihor's Philosophy," *Ensign,* July 1992, 21).

Alma 30:41. "I Have All Things as a Testimony That These Things Are True"

• President Gordon B. Hinckley (1910–2008) spoke of the power of God's creations to strengthen testimony when he said:

"Can any man who has walked beneath the stars at night, can anyone who has seen the touch of spring upon the land doubt the hand of divinity in creation? So observing the beauties of the earth, one is wont to speak as did the Psalmist: 'The heavens declare the glory of God; and the firmament sheweth his handywork. Day unto day uttereth speech, and night unto night sheweth knowledge.' (Ps. 19:1–2.)

"All of beauty in the earth bears the fingerprint of the Master Creator" (in Conference Report, Apr. 1978, 90; or *Ensign,* May 1978, 59).

Alma 30:48. Sign Seekers

• The Prophet Joseph Smith taught, "Whenever you see a man seeking after a sign, you may set it down that he is an adulterous man" (*History of the Church,* 3:385).

Later, the Prophet noted: "When I was preaching in Philadelphia, a Quaker called out for a sign. I told him to be still. After the sermon, he again asked for a sign. I told the congregation the man was an adulterer; that a wicked and adulterous generation seeketh after a sign; and that the Lord had said to me in a revelation, that any man who wanted a sign was an adulterous person. 'It is true,' cried one, 'for I caught him in the very act,' which the man afterwards confessed, when he was baptized" (*History of the Church,* 5:268).

• President Joseph F. Smith (1838–1918) further explained the dangers of depending on miracles for our faith: "Show me Latter-day Saints who have to feed upon miracles, signs and visions in order to keep them steadfast in the Church, and I will show you members of the Church who are not in good standing before God, and who are walking in slippery paths" (*Gospel Doctrine,* 5th ed. [1939], 7).

Alma 30:52. Lies and Lying

• To better understand the evils of lying, Robert J. Matthews, a former dean of religion at BYU, explained

that "the seriousness of lying is not measured only in injury or pain inflicted on the one deceived. Lying has a devastating effect also on the perpetrator. It robs the liar of self-respect, and deadens his ability to recognize the difference between truth and error. When a lie is told often enough, even the one who knowingly spread it may begin to believe it. This was the case with the antichrist Korihor in the Book of Mormon (see Alma 30:52–53)" ("Thou Shalt Not Bear False Witness," *Ensign,* Oct. 1994, 56).

• The Prophet Joseph Smith spoke of the tragedy of individuals like Korihor: "Nothing is a greater injury to the children of men than to be under the influence of a false spirit when they think they have the Spirit of God" (*History of the Church,* 4:573).

Alma 30:53. The Devil's Deception and the Carnal Mind

• To be carnally minded is to focus on physical pleasures or material things rather than on the things of the Spirit. It is hard for carnally-minded people to experience the things of the Spirit. Elder Neal A. Maxwell noted that they are "'past feeling,' having been sedated by pleasing the carnal mind" (in Conference Report, Apr. 1999, 29; or *Ensign,* May 1999, 24).

Alma 31:3, 8–29. The Zoramites' False Theology

• Even though the Zoramites killed Korihor, they seem to have adopted a similar belief system. Note the following phrases from Alma 31 that describe the Zoramite beliefs:

Jerry Thompson, © IRI

"They had fallen into great errors" (v. 9).

They had rejected traditions that they felt were "handed down . . . by the childishness of their fathers" (v. 16).

They did not want to "be led away after the foolish traditions of [their] brethren, which doth bind them down to a belief of Christ" (v. 17).

They refused "to believe in things to come, which they knew nothing about" (v. 22).

• Elder Jeffrey R. Holland commented about Korihor's influence on the Zoramites' false teachings:

"[Korihor's] brand of teaching inevitably had its influence among some of the less faithful who, like the neighboring Zoramites, were already given to 'perverting the ways of the Lord.'

"Zoram and his followers are one of the most memorable apostate groups mentioned in the Book of Mormon primarily because they considered themselves so unusually righteous. . . . Once a week they stood atop a prayer tower called a Rameumptom and, using always 'the selfsame prayer,' thanked God that they were better than everyone else, 'a chosen and a holy' people 'elected' by God to be saved while all around them were equally 'elected' to be cast down to hell. In the reassuring safety of all this, they were also spared any belief in such 'foolish traditions' (evidence of Korihor's legacy emerging here) as a belief in a Savior, for it had been 'made known' to them there should be no Christ. . . .

"Alma lost little time in countering such unholy prayer and its equally unholy theology with his own prayer for divine assistance against this form of self-serving iniquity that made him literally sick at heart" (*Christ and the New Covenant*, 121–22).

ALMA 31:5

According to Alma, why is the preaching of the word so powerful? How does this help explain why daily scripture study is so important?

Alma 31:5. The Power of the Word

• The virtue or power of the word of God is in part explained by the fact that it is attended by the witness of the Spirit. The Lord said that when His words are conveyed by His Spirit they are His voice (see D&C 18:34–36). Alma considered resorting to preaching the word to the apostate Zoramites even though they had already heard and rejected it (see Alma 31:8–9).

President Boyd K. Packer explained one reason why we must learn the doctrines of the kingdom:

"True doctrine, understood, changes attitudes and behavior.

"The study of the doctrines of the gospel will improve behavior quicker than a study of behavior will improve behavior. . . . That is why we stress so forcefully the study of the doctrines of the gospel" (in Conference Report, Oct. 1986, 20; or *Ensign,* Nov. 1986, 17).

• President Spencer W. Kimball (1895–1985) spoke of the power of scriptures to help us draw nearer to God:

"I find that when I get casual in my relationships with divinity and when it seems that no divine ear is listening and no divine voice is speaking, that I am far, far away. If I immerse myself in the scriptures, the distance narrows and the spirituality returns. I find myself loving more intensely those whom I must love with all my heart and mind and strength, and loving them more. I find it easier to abide their counsel" ("What I Hope You Will Teach My Grandchildren and All Others of the Youth of Zion" [address to Church Educational System religious educators, July 11, 1966], 4).

• President Ezra Taft Benson explained how the scriptures can be a powerful way to bless us and answer the difficult questions of life: "Often we spend great effort in trying to increase the activity levels in our stakes. We work diligently to raise the percentages of those attending sacrament meetings. We labor to get a higher percentage of our young men on missions. We strive to improve the numbers of those marrying in the temple. All of these are commendable efforts and important to the growth of the kingdom. But when individual members and families immerse themselves in the scriptures regularly and consistently, these other areas of activity will automatically come. Testimonies will increase. Commitment will be strengthened. Families will be fortified. Personal revelation will flow" ("The Power of the Word," *Ensign,* May 1986, 81).

Alma 31:9–11. Avoiding the Causes of Apostasy

• In Antionum, the missionary force of Alma and his companions came across a group of Nephite dissenters known as the Zoramites. Mormon not only recorded that the Zoramites had previously had the word of God preached unto them, but he further identified the cause of their apostasy: they would not keep the commandments, they no longer petitioned the Lord daily in prayer, they perverted the ways of the Lord, and what prayers they did offer to the Lord were vain and meaningless. They ignored the basics, such as having a daily habit of meaningful prayer and scripture study.

Elder Donald L. Staheli of the Seventy emphasized the importance of daily consistency in the basics of the gospel:

"Daily fervent prayers seeking forgiveness and special help and direction are essential to our lives and the nourishment of our testimonies. When we become hurried, repetitive, casual, or forgetful in our prayers, we tend to lose the closeness of the Spirit, which is so essential in the continual direction we need to successfully manage the challenges of our everyday lives. Family prayer every morning and night adds additional blessings and power to our individual prayers and to our testimonies.

"Personal, sincere involvement in the scriptures produces faith, hope, and solutions to our daily challenges. Frequently reading, pondering, and applying the lessons of the scriptures, combined with prayer, become an irreplaceable part of gaining and sustaining a strong, vibrant testimony" (in Conference Report, Oct. 2004, 40; or *Ensign,* Nov. 2004, 39).

Alma 31:6–38. Apostate Zoramites

• Alma 30:59 indicates that the Zoramites had dissented from the Nephites under the leadership of a man named Zoram. The following is a summary of what we know about their apostate beliefs and practices:

They did not observe the law of Moses (see Alma 31:9).

They had forsaken daily prayer (see v. 10).

They perverted the ways of the Lord (see v. 11).

They built synagogues for the purpose of worshipping one day a week (see v. 12).

Today there are those who have also fallen into similar false practices. Unless we are careful to guard against it, we too could fall into some of the same traps of routine prayers, worshipping only weekly during the three-hour block and not thinking of God again during the week, only praying in a set place, or becoming materialistic and prideful.

ALMA 31:26–35

Read Alma's prayer on behalf of the Zoramites. What do we learn about how a disciple of Christ should feel toward his or her fellowmen?

Alma 31:26–35. Alma's Prayer in Behalf of the Zoramites

• Alma recognized that the souls of the apostate Zoramites were precious to God. Thus, Alma prayed for the power and wisdom to bring them back to the Lord. Alma's prayer exemplifies the attitude all members and missionaries must develop. All people are of great worth, and through the power of God they can be brought back to Him.

While serving as a member of the Seventy, Elder Carlos E. Asay (1926–99) taught that all people are precious to God and should be to us:

"The souls of our brothers and sisters who may seem to be more feeble and less honorable are precious. The Church has need of them. We should make every attempt to know them and to help them claim the full blessings and joys of the gospel of Jesus Christ. Our prayers should be as Alma's: 'Give unto us, O Lord, power and wisdom that we may bring these, our brethren, again unto thee.' (See Alma 31:35.)

"We must remember that our salvation is intertwined with the salvation of others. We must *care more* for those who seem to *care less* for their faith" ("Nurturing the Less Active," *Ensign,* Oct. 1986, 15).

Alma 31:31–33. Comfort in Afflictions

• President Lorenzo Snow (1814–1901) spoke of the blessings that come through tribulation:

"I suppose I am talking to some who have had worry and trouble and heart burnings and persecution, and have at times been caused to think that they never expected to endure quite so much. But for everything you have suffered, for everything that has occurred to you which you thought an evil at that time, you will receive fourfold, and that suffering will have had a tendency to make you better and stronger and to feel that you have been blessed. When you look back over your experiences you will then see that you have advanced far ahead and have gone up several rounds of the ladder toward exaltation and glory. . . .

"Take it individually or take it collectively, we have suffered and we shall have to suffer again; and why? Because the Lord requires it at our hands for our sanctification" (*The Teachings of Lorenzo Snow,* comp. Clyde J. Williams [1984], 117–18).

Points to Ponder

• Why would Korihor's teachings seem attractive to certain individuals? What are some examples of such teachings today?

• Alma seemed to be motivated to reclaim the Zoramites out of love of God and love of the Zoramites. How can we develop this same kind of love?

• How was Alma's prayer different from the Zoramites' prayer? In what ways might our prayers be similar to the Zoramites' prayers? (see Alma 31:15–18). How might they be similar to Alma's prayers? (see Alma 31:30–35).

Suggested Assignments

• What were some of the false teachings of Korihor? Explain to a friend why such arguments ultimately fail (see Alma 30:13–18).

• When Korihor asked for a sign of God's existence, what signs did Alma put forth as evidence that God lives? (see Alma 30:44). How have these evidences helped strengthen your faith? Write a paragraph that briefly explains how the design and order in the universe is evidence of God's existence.

Introduction

Alma and his brethren preached the word of God to the Zoramites, who were in a state of apostasy. Because of their trials, a group of Zoramites were prepared to receive the word. Alma and Amulek's teachings concerning individual and institutional worship touch upon some of the most significant aspects of the gospel of Jesus Christ: the power of the Atonement, repentance, faith, the word of God, and the importance of prayer. In addition to their own testimonies, Alma and Amulek drew upon the testimonies and messages of three ancient prophets. The doctrine and principles contained herein constitute a powerful witness of Jesus Christ.

Commentary

Alma 32. Having Faith in the Word of God

• A central point of Alma 32 is that of having faith in the word of God. Alma observed that when the word of God is planted in the fertile soil of the heart, it will begin to swell and grow. Through experimenting upon the word, or nurturing it through obedience, the word of God will bring forth fruit that is most precious, sweet above all that is sweet, white above all that is white, and pure above all that is pure. Neglecting the word of God will result in no such fruit.

How do we nurture our faith in the word so that we may feast upon this fruit? President Joseph Fielding Smith (1876–1972) taught, "If we want to have a living, abiding faith, we must be active in the performance of every duty as members of this Church" (*Doctrines of Salvation*, comp. Bruce R. McConkie, 3 vols. [1954–56], 2:311).

Elder Joseph B. Wirthlin (1917–2008) of the Quorum of the Twelve Apostles similarly taught: "Faith exists when absolute confidence in that which we cannot see combines with action that is in absolute conformity to the will of our Heavenly Father. Without all three—first, absolute confidence; second, action; and third, absolute conformity—without these three, all we have is a counterfeit, a weak and watered-down faith" (in Conference Report, Oct. 2002, 89; or *Ensign,* Nov. 2002, 83).

Alma 32–34. Tree of Life

• Elder Jeffrey R. Holland of the Quorum of the Twelve Apostles emphasized the importance of studying Alma 32–34 as a coherent whole:

"In [the] brilliant discourse [of Alma 32], Alma moves the reader from a general commentary on faith in the seedlike word of God to a focused discourse on faith in Christ as the Word of God, grown to a fruit-bearing tree, a tree whose fruit is exactly that of Lehi's earlier perception of Christ's love. . . . Christ is the bread of life, the living water, the true vine. Christ is the seed, the tree, and the fruit of eternal life.

"But the profound and central Tree of Life imagery in this discourse is lost, or at least greatly diminished, if the reader does not follow it on into the next two chapters of the Book of Mormon" (*Christ and the New Covenant* [1997], 169).

Jerry Thompson, © IRI

Alma 32:8–16. "Blessed Are They Who Humble Themselves"

• Alma perceived the readiness of the poor Zoramites to be taught the gospel. Their rejection by the wealthy Zoramites contributed to their state of humility.

Bishop Richard C. Edgley of the Presiding Bishopric taught that humility and submissiveness are virtues allowing one to access gospel blessings: "Many of us live or work in an environment where humility is often misunderstood and considered a weakness. Not many corporations or institutions include humility as a value statement or a desired characteristic of their management. Yet as we learn about the workings of God, the power of a humble and submissive spirit becomes apparent. In the kingdom of God, greatness begins with humility and submissiveness. These companion virtues are the first critical steps to opening the doors to the blessings of God and the power of the priesthood. It matters not who we are or how lofty our credentials appear. Humility and submissiveness to the Lord, coupled with a grateful heart, are our strength and our hope" (in Conference Report, Oct. 2003, 104; or *Ensign,* Nov. 2003, 98).

• Humility is important enough in the eyes of the Lord that He sometimes helps us be humble. Alma 32:8–16 speaks of two ways to become humble. Verse 13 describes those who are "compelled to be humble"; verses 14 and 16 speak of others who humble themselves voluntarily "because of the word."

• Elder Carlos E. Asay (1926–99) of the Seventy also described these two groups: "Most of us seem to have the 'Nephite cycle' as part of our character. There is a point when we are teachable; our humility enables us to grow and to ride the crest of spirituality. Then there are other times when we begin to feel self-sufficient and puffed up with pride. . . . How much better it would be if we kept in remembrance our God and our religion and broke the cycle by consistent worship and righteous living. How much better it would be if we were humbled by the word of the Lord and strong enough in spirit to remember our God in whatsoever circumstances we find ourselves" (*Family Pecan Trees: Planting a Legacy of Faith at Home* [1992], 193–94).

For more information and a diagram depicting the pride cycle, refer to "The Cycle of Righteousness and Wickedness" in the appendix (p. 414).

• President Ezra Taft Benson (1899–1994) described ways that we could humble ourselves and avoid the trials that sometimes accompany being compelled to be humble:

"We can choose to humble ourselves by conquering enmity toward our brothers and sisters, esteeming them as ourselves, and lifting them as high or higher than we are (see D&C 38:24; 81:5; 84:106).

"We can choose to humble ourselves by receiving counsel and chastisement (see Jacob 4:10; Helman

15:3; D&C 63:55; 101:4–5; 108:1; 124:61, 84; 136:31; Proverbs 9:8).

"We can choose to humble ourselves by forgiving those who have offended us (see 3 Nephi 13:11, 14; D&C 64:10).

"We can choose to humble ourselves by rendering selfless service (see Mosiah 2:16–17).

"We can choose to humble ourselves by going on missions and preaching the word that can humble others (see Alma 4:19; 31:5; 48:20).

"We can choose to humble ourselves by getting to the temple more frequently.

"We can choose to humble ourselves by confessing and forsaking our sins and being born of God (see D&C 58:43; Mosiah 27:25–26; Alma 5:7–14, 49).

"We can choose to humble ourselves by loving God, submitting our will to His, and putting Him first in our lives (see 3 Nephi 11:11; 13:33; Moroni 10:32)" (in Conference Report, Apr. 1989, 6; or *Ensign,* May 1989, 6–7).

Alma 32:17–18. Faith Is Not Built upon Signs

• Elder Dallin H. Oaks of the Quorum of the Twelve Apostles spoke of the dangers accompanying the seeking of signs for faith:

"The showing of a sign can work to the condemnation of those who are brought to knowledge by that means. They miss the opportunity to develop faith, and they subject themselves to a more severe punishment for backsliding than those whose spiritual development is proceeding along the normal pathway of developing faith.

"There are other 'condemnations' to those who seek signs without first developing the faith God has required as a prerequisite.

"One condemnation is to be misled. God warned ancient Israel against following prophets who gave signs and wonders and then sought to lead them away to the worship of strange gods. (Deut. 13:1–3.) The Savior taught his apostles that in the last days 'there shall also arise false Christs, and false prophets, and shall show great signs and wonders, insomuch that, if possible, they shall deceive the very elect, who are the elect according to the covenant.' (JST Matt. 24:23; also see Matt. 24:24; Mark 13:22.) . . .

". . . In our day, God does not use miracles or signs as a way of teaching or convincing the unbeliever. As a result, we should not ask for signs for this purpose, and we should be deeply suspicious of the so-called spiritual evidences of those who do" (*The Lord's Way* [1991], 85–86).

Alma 32:21. Faith and Hope

• President Boyd K. Packer, President of the Quorum of the Twelve Apostles, helps us better understand the meaning of faith:

"Faith, to be faith, must center around something that is not known. Faith, to be faith, must go beyond that for which there is confirming evidence. Faith, to be faith, must go into the unknown. Faith, to be faith, must walk to the edge of the light, and then a few steps into the darkness. If everything has to be known, if everything has to be explained, if everything has to be certified, then there is no need for faith. Indeed, there is no room for it. . . .

"There are two kinds of faith. One of them functions ordinarily in the life of every soul. It is the kind of faith born by experience; it gives us certainty that a new day will dawn, that spring will come, that growth will take place. It is the kind of faith that relates us with confidence to that which is scheduled to happen. . . .

"There is another kind of faith, rare indeed. This is the kind of faith that *causes* things to happen. It is the kind of faith that is worthy and prepared and unyielding, and it calls forth things that otherwise would not be. It is the kind of faith that moves people. It is the kind of faith that sometimes moves things. . . . It comes by gradual growth. It is a marvelous, even a transcendent, power, a power as real and as invisible as electricity. Directed and channeled, it has great effect. . . .

"In a world filled with skepticism and doubt, the expression 'seeing is believing' promotes the attitude, 'You show me, and I will believe.' We want all of the proof and all of the evidence first. It seems hard to take things on faith.

"When will we learn that in spiritual things it works the other way about—that believing is seeing? Spiritual belief precedes spiritual knowledge. When we believe in things that are not seen but are nevertheless true, then we have faith" ("What Is Faith?" in *Faith* [1983], 42–43).

• Elder Neal A. Maxwell (1926–2004) of the Quorum of the Twelve Apostles described the relationship between hope, faith, and knowledge and explained how they exist in a profound and dynamic relationship: "Faith and hope are constantly interactive and may not always be precisely distinguished or sequenced. Though not perfect knowledge either, hope's enlivened expectations are 'with surety' true (Ether 12:4; see also Romans 8:24; Hebrews 11:1; Alma 32:21)" (in Conference Report, Oct. 1994, 45; or *Ensign,* Nov. 1994, 35).

ALMA 32:21–37 📖

How did Alma differentiate between faith and knowledge?

Alma 32:23. Little Children Receive Inspiration

• The faith of little children often leads to divine insights. Elder Neal A. Maxwell described how their example can serve to instruct those who are older:

"Children often have the 'thoughts and [the] intents of [their] hearts' focused on the Master. Though not full of years, such children are full of faith! Too young for formal Church callings, they have been 'called to serve' as exemplifiers, doing especially well when blessed with 'goodly parents' (1 Ne. 1:1).

"Just as the scriptures assure, 'little children do have words given unto them many times' (Alma 32:23). For example, the resurrected Jesus revealed things to the Nephite children, who then taught adults and their parents 'even greater' things than Jesus had taught (3 Ne. 26:14).

"It has been a privilege to seal several adopted children to Nan and Dan Barker, now of Arizona. Some time ago Nate, then just over three, said: 'Mommy, there is another little girl who is supposed to come to our family. She has dark hair and dark eyes and lives a long way from here.'

"The wise mother asked, 'How do you know this?'

"'Jesus told me, upstairs.'

"The mother noted, 'We don't have an upstairs,' but quickly sensed the significance of what had been communicated. After much travail and many prayers, the Barker family were in a sealing room in the Salt Lake Temple in the fall of 1995, where a little girl with dark hair and dark eyes, from Kazakhstan, was sealed to them for time and eternity. Inspired children still tell parents 'great and marvelous things' (3 Nephi 26:14)" (in Conference Report, Apr. 1996, 95–96; or *Ensign,* May 1996, 69–70).

Alma 32:27–37. Experimenting on the Word of God Brings Conversion

• Elder M. Russell Ballard of the Quorum of the Twelve Apostles taught that a willingness to perform Alma's experiment leads to conversion:

"We know that both members and nonmembers are more likely to be thoroughly converted to the gospel of Jesus Christ when they are willing to experiment upon the word (see Alma 32:27). This is an attitude of both mind and heart that includes a desire to know the truth and a willingness to act on that desire. For those investigating the Church, the experiment can be as  simple as agreeing to read the Book of Mormon, to pray about it, and to earnestly seek to know if Joseph Smith was the Lord's prophet.

"True conversion comes through the power of the Spirit. When the Spirit touches the heart, hearts are changed. When individuals, both members and investigators, feel the Spirit working with them, or when they see the evidence of the Lord's love and mercy in their lives, they are edified and strengthened spiritually, and their faith in Him increases. These experiences with the Spirit follow naturally when a person is willing to experiment upon the word. This is how we come to *feel* the gospel is true" (in Conference Report, Oct. 2000, 97; or *Ensign,* Nov. 2000, 75).

• At times the swelling motions, the enlarging of souls, the enlightening of understanding, and the beginning of delicious feelings from the Spirit spoken of in Alma 32:28 are difficult to verbally express. However, being hard to express does not discount the truthfulness of the feeling.

President Boyd K. Packer, President of the Quorum of the Twelve Apostles, shared an experience that describes the difficulty of verbal expression. He bore his testimony to an atheist that there is a God. The man said he could not *know* such a thing. President Packer compared his testimony and knowledge with knowing what salt tastes like (see commentary for Alma 30:15–16 on p. 214; see also "The Candle of the Lord," *Ensign,* Jan. 1983, 51–52).

Alma 32:28–30. "Give Place, That a Seed May Be Planted" and Begin to Grow

• Increased faith in God's word is one of the fruits that come from seeds of faith planted in the fertile ground of a soft heart. President James E. Faust (1920–2007) of the First Presidency described the necessary prerequisites for faith and knowledge to grow and mature: "We . . . need to prepare our own seedbeds of faith. To do this we need to plow the soil through daily humble prayer, asking for strength and forgiveness. We need to harrow the soil by overcoming our feelings of pride. We need to prepare the seedbed by keeping the commandments to the best of our ability. We need to be honest with the Lord in the payment of our tithing and our other offerings. We need to be worthy and able to call forth the great powers of the priesthood to bless ourselves, our families, and others for whom we have responsibility. There is no better place for the spiritual seeds of our faith to be nurtured than within the hallowed sanctuaries of our temples and in our homes" (in Conference Report, Oct. 1999, 61; or *Ensign,* Nov. 1999, 48).

• The planted seed of faith does not grow suddenly. President Boyd K. Packer explained the importance of patience while waiting for the seed to grow:

"My experience has been that a testimony does not burst upon us suddenly. Rather, it grows, as Alma said, from a seed of faith. . . .

"Do not be disappointed if you have read and reread and yet have not received a powerful witness. You may be somewhat like the disciples spoken of in the Book of Mormon who were filled with the power of God in great glory 'and they knew it not' (3 Nephi 9:20).

"Do the best you can. Think of this verse: 'See that all these things are done in wisdom and order; for it is not requisite that a man should run faster than he has strength. And again, it is expedient that he should be diligent, that thereby he might win the prize; therefore, all things must be done in order' (Mosiah 4:27)" (in Conference Report, Apr. 2005, 7; or *Ensign,* May 2005, 8).

Alma 32:28–35. "It Beginneth to Be Delicious to Me"

• Alma used the concept of taste to describe the growth of testimony. The Prophet Joseph Smith (1805–44) also used taste to teach about discernment of true doctrine: "This is *good* doctrine. It *tastes* good. I can *taste* the principles of eternal life, and *so can you.* . . . I know that when I tell you these words of eternal life as they are given to me, you *taste* them, and I know that you believe them. You say honey is sweet, and so do I. I can also *taste* the spirit of eternal life. I know that it is good; and when I tell you of these things which were given me by inspiration of the Holy Spirit, you are

bound to receive them as *sweet,* and rejoice more and more" (*History of the Church,* 6:312; italics added).

• Sister Janette Hales Beckham, former general Young Women president, spoke of the feelings associated with scripture reading: "Learning to discern the teachings of the Spirit is an important part of helping faith become a reality. My daughter Karen shared her experience. She said: 'When I was just a little girl, I started reading the Book of Mormon for the first time. After many days of reading, I came one night to 1 Nephi 3:7. . . . I didn't know this was a famous verse, but as I read that verse, I felt strongly impressed. I was impressed that Heavenly Father would help us keep His commandments, but the deep impression was really more of a feeling. I had seen my parents mark verses in their scriptures with red pencils. So I got up and searched through the house until I found a red pencil, and with a great sense of solemnity and importance, I marked that verse in my own Book of Mormon.' Karen continued: 'Over the years as I read the scriptures, that experience was repeated time and time again—reading a verse and feeling deeply impressed. In time I came to recognize that feeling as the Holy Ghost' " (in Conference Report, Oct. 1997, 104; or *Ensign,* Nov. 1997, 75).

Alma 32:35. "O Then, Is Not This Real?"

• As Alma spoke to the poor Zoramites, he asked them to discern the truth of his message for themselves. One person cannot learn a gospel principle for another. Elder Neal A. Maxwell explained that each of us can know the certainty of divine truths:

"Alma describes the growth of faith and how faith can actually become knowledge with the accompanying intellectual and emotional experiences of the believer. After the understanding of the believer has been enlarged and his mind has been expanded, Alma asks, 'O then, is not this real?' It is real, he says, because it is 'discernible, therefore ye must know that it is good.' (Alma 32:35.)

"The truth of each divine doctrine is actually discernible by us in a system of certification and confirmation that justifies our saying, 'I know!' " (*Things As They Really Are* [1978], 10).

ALMA 32:33–43

In what ways do the teachings of Alma in this passage of scripture help you better understand Lehi's vision of the tree of life in 1 Nephi 8?

Alma 32:33–43. Nourish the Word

• Elder Bruce C. Hafen of the Seventy, using Alma's metaphor of cultivation, identified two aspects of nourishment that bring the blessings of the gospel into our lives: "We grow in two ways—removing negative weeds and cultivating positive flowers. The Savior's grace blesses both parts—if we do our part. First and repeatedly we must uproot the weeds of sin and bad choices. It isn't enough just to *mow* the weeds. Yank them out by the roots, repenting fully to satisfy the conditions of mercy. But being forgiven is only part of our growth. We are not just paying a debt. Our purpose is to become celestial beings. So once we've cleared our heartland, we must continually plant, weed, and nourish the seeds of divine qualities. And then as our sweat and discipline stretch us to meet His gifts, 'the flow'rs of grace appear' ["There Is Sunshine in My Soul Today," *Hymns,* no. 227], like hope and meekness. Even a tree of life can take root in this heart-garden, bearing fruit so sweet that it lightens all our burdens 'through the joy of his Son' [Alma 33:23]. And when the flower of charity blooms here, we will love others with the power of Christ's own love [see Moroni 7:48]" (in Conference Report, Apr. 2004, 100–101; or *Ensign,* May 2004, 97).

Alma 32:37–38, 42–43. Being a Disciple of Christ

• President Dieter F. Uchtdorf of the First Presidency taught members of the Church how to become a disciple of Christ:

"This is the peaceable way of the follower of Jesus Christ.

"Nevertheless, it is not a quick fix or an overnight cure.

"A friend of mine recently wrote to me, confiding that he was having a difficult time keeping his testimony strong and vibrant. He asked for counsel.

"I wrote back to him and lovingly suggested a few specific things he could do that would align his life more closely with the teachings of the restored gospel. To my surprise, I heard back from him only a week later. The essence of his letter was this: 'I tried what you suggested. It didn't work. What else have you got?'

"Brothers and sisters, we have to stay with it. We don't acquire eternal life in a sprint—this is a race of endurance. We have to apply and reapply the divine gospel principles. Day after day we need to make them part of our normal life.

"Too often we approach the gospel like a farmer who places a seed in the ground in the morning and expects corn on the cob by the afternoon. When Alma compared the word of God to a seed, he explained that the seed grows into a fruit-bearing tree gradually, as a result of our 'faith, and [our] diligence, and patience, and long-suffering' [Alma 32:43]. It's true that some blessings come right away: soon after we plant the seed in our hearts, it begins to swell and sprout and grow, and by this we know that the seed is good. From the very moment we set foot upon the pathway of discipleship, seen and unseen blessings from God begin to attend us.

"But we cannot receive the fulness of those blessings if we 'neglect the tree, and take no thought for its nourishment' [v. 38].

"Knowing that the seed is good is not enough. We must 'nourish it with great care, that it may get root' [v. 37]. Only then can we partake of the fruit that is 'sweet above all that is sweet, and . . . pure above all that is pure' and 'feast upon this fruit even until [we] are filled, that [we] hunger not, neither shall [we] thirst' [v. 42].

"Discipleship is a journey. We need the refining lessons of the journey to craft our character and purify our hearts. By patiently walking in the path of discipleship, we demonstrate to ourselves the measure of our faith and our willingness to accept God's will rather than ours.

"It is not enough merely to speak of Jesus Christ or proclaim that we are His disciples. It is not enough to surround ourselves with symbols of our religion. Discipleship is not a spectator sport. We cannot expect to experience the blessings of faith by standing inactive on the sidelines any more than we can experience the benefits of health by sitting on a sofa watching sporting events on television and giving advice to the athletes. And yet for some, 'spectator discipleship' is a preferred if not a primary way of worshipping.

"Ours is not a secondhand religion. We cannot receive the blessings of the gospel merely by observing the good that others do. We need to get off the sidelines and practice what we preach. . . .

". . . Now is the time to embrace the gospel of Jesus Christ, become His disciples, and walk in His way" ("The Way of the Disciple, *Ensign,* May 2009, 76–77).

Alma 33:2–19. False Doctrines of the Zoramites

• Alma used the scriptures repeatedly to address the false doctrines taught by the Zoramites. He first dealt with the false notion that you can only pray on the Rameumptom. Using the scriptures he explained that they could pray and worship God anywhere; in their "wilderness," in their "field," in their "house," and even in their "closet" (see Alma 33:2–11). Alma then addressed the fact that all the prophets have testified of the coming of a Christ (see Alma 33:14–22; see also Jacob 7:11).

Alma 33:3–11; 34:17–27, 39. Hearts Drawn Out in Prayer Continually

• President Henry B. Eyring of the First Presidency explained what it means to be in a continuous attitude of prayer:

"When God has commanded us to pray, He has used words like 'pray unceasingly' and 'pray always' and 'mighty prayer.'

"Those commands do not require using many words. In fact, the Savior has told us that we need not multiply words when we pray. The diligence in prayer which God requires does not take flowery speech nor long hours of solitude. . . .

"Our hearts can be drawn out to God only when they are filled with love for Him and trust in His goodness" (in Conference Report, Oct. 2001, 17; or *Ensign,* Nov. 2001, 16).

Alma 33:19–23. A Type of Christ Was Raised in the Wilderness

• Because of the ancient Israelites' murmuring in the wilderness, the Lord sent venomous serpents to humble the spiritually poisoned. Many people died, and the repentant people turned to their prophet and pled with him to ask the Lord to remove the serpents. God told Moses to make a serpent of brass and elevate it on a pole. The Lord promised that everyone who looked upon the raised serpent would be healed (see Numbers 21:4–9).

The brass serpent was a *type.* Elder Dallin H. Oaks explained that a *type* is "a likeness or reminder of something else" (in Conference Report, Oct. 1992, 51; or *Ensign,* Nov. 1992, 37).

Jesus Christ taught that the type raised up in the wilderness testified of Him: "As Moses lifted up the serpent in the wilderness, even so must the Son of man be lifted up: that whosoever believeth in him should not perish, but have eternal life" (John 3:14–15).

Because of their hard hearts and disbelief, many of the Israelites refused to take advantage of the simple manner of healing (see 1 Nephi 17:41). Alma invited everyone to "begin to believe in the Son of God, that he will come to redeem his people, and . . . atone for their sins" (Alma 33:22; see also Helaman 8:14–15). Alma promised that nourishing this testimony will lighten one's burdens and lead to everlasting life (see Alma 33:23).

Alma 34:9–12. The Atonement of Jesus Christ Is Infinite and Eternal

• Elder Bruce R. McConkie (1915–85) of the Quorum of the Twelve Apostles defined the scope of the infinite and eternal sacrifice of the Lord: "When the prophets speak of an *infinite* atonement, they mean just that. Its effects cover all men, the earth itself and all forms of life thereon, and reach out into the endless expanses of eternity" (*Mormon Doctrine,* 2nd ed. [1966], 64; see also Moses 7:30).

• Elder Russell M. Nelson of the Quorum of the Twelve Apostles enumerated some of the ways the Atonement of Jesus Christ is infinite:

"His Atonement is infinite—without an end [see 2 Nephi 9:7; 25:16; Alma 34:10, 12, 14]. It was also infinite in that all humankind would be saved from never-ending death. It was infinite in terms of His immense suffering. It was infinite in time, putting an end to the preceding prototype of animal sacrifice. It was infinite in scope— it was to be done once for all [see Hebrews 10:10]. And the mercy of the Atonement extends not only to an infinite number of people, but also to an infinite number of worlds created by Him [see D&C 76:24; Moses 1:33]. It was infinite beyond any human scale of measurement or mortal comprehension.

"Jesus was the only one who could offer such an infinite atonement, since He was born of a mortal mother and an immortal Father. Because of that unique birthright, Jesus was an infinite Being" (in Conference Report, Oct. 1996, 46; or *Ensign,* Nov. 1996, 35).

Alma 34:14. "Every Whit Pointing to That Great and Last Sacrifice"

• Amulek declared that the whole meaning of the law of Moses was to point the people to the eventual "great and last sacrifice" of Jesus Christ in Gethsemane and Golgotha. The animal sacrifices, the feasts and festivals, and other daily rituals were full of numerous types and shadows, pointing the children of Israel to Christ. The sacrament similarly reminds us today of the atoning mission of Jesus Christ. Likewise, anciently Passover was a yearly reminder that the Lord brought Israel out of physical bondage in Egypt. Today Easter is a yearly reminder that through the Atonement and Resurrection of the Lord we can be redeemed out of spiritual bondage.

© 1995 Del Parson

Alma 34:14–17. "Faith unto Repentance"

• While serving as a member of the Seventy, Elder Robert E. Wells spoke of the faith required to bring changes in our lives sufficient to participate in the Atonement of Jesus Christ:

" 'Just how much faith do I need for the atonement of Christ to work for me?' In other words, how much faith do I need to receive salvation? In the book of Alma . . . we find the answer. The prophet Amulek taught this simple but grand principle: 'The Son of God, . . . bringeth about means unto men that they may have *faith unto repentance*' (Alma 34:14–15; emphasis added).

"Please note those three words: *faith unto repentance.* That is the clue. Four times in three verses he uses that expression [see Alma 34:15–17]. . . .

"So the combination of faith in Christ plus *faith unto repentance* is vitally important. That concept is one of the greatest insights we have into the importance of simple, clear faith—faith sufficient to repent.

Apparently faith great enough to move mountains is not required; faith enough to speak in tongues or to heal the sick is not needed; all that we need is just enough faith to recognize that we have sinned and to repent of our sins, to feel remorse for them, and to desire to sin no more but to please Christ the Lord. Then the greatest miracle of all, the Atonement, whereby Christ rescues us from our deserved punishment, is in effect in our behalf" ("The Liahona Triad," in Bruce A. Van Orden and Brent L. Top, eds., *Doctrines of the Book of Mormon: The 1991 Sperry Symposium* [1992], 6–7).

Alma 34:15–16. "Mercy Can Satisfy the Demands of Justice"

• There are two aspects of justice:

1. Obedience to law results in blessings that bring joy (see D&C 130:20–21).

2. Disobedience to law results in punishments that bring sorrow (see Alma 42:22).

• There are two ways to satisfy justice:

1. Never violate the law.

2. If you do violate the law, pay the penalty.

Problem: No flesh is justified by the law (see 2 Nephi 2:5); everyone has sinned (see Romans 3:23). Thus, a penalty must be paid.

• There are two effects of sin:

1. By temporal law we are cut off—justice is violated (see Alma 42:14).

2. By spiritual law we perish—"there cannot any unclean thing enter into the kingdom of God" (1 Nephi 15:34).

Jesus "offereth himself a sacrifice for sin, to answer the ends of the law" (2 Nephi 2:7).

• Christ initiated the law of mercy, but how?

1. He kept the law perfectly and was without sin. He was justified by the law.

2. In the Garden of Gethsemane and on the cross, He suffered and paid the price for the penalty as though He was guilty of every sin ever committed.

3. He is our Advocate with the Father (see Alma 33:11; D&C 45:3–5).

Alma 34:32–34. "Do Not Procrastinate the Day of Your Repentance"

• Procrastination and indecision can impact our efforts to return to our Heavenly Father. President Joseph Fielding Smith taught, "Procrastination, as it may be applied to Gospel principles, is the thief of eternal life—which is life in the presence of the Father and the Son" (*The Way to Perfection* [1970], 202).

> ### ALMA 34:32–34
> *What circumstances did Amulek warn about that make repentance after this life difficult?*

Alma 34:34–35. That Same Spirit Will Possess Us

• Amulek made it clear that we are, by our daily choices, ultimately giving ourselves over to the control or influence of either the Spirit of the Lord or the spirit of the devil. President Harold B. Lee (1899–1973) gave the following explanation of Alma 34:35: "To those who die in their wicked state, not having repented, the scriptures say the devil shall seal them as his own (see Alma 34:35), which means that until they have paid the uttermost farthing for what they have done, they shall not be redeemed from his grasp. When they shall have been subjected to the buffetings of Satan sufficient to have satisfied justice, then they shall be brought forth out of the grasp of Satan and shall be assigned to that place in our Father's celestial, terrestrial, or telestial world merited by their life here upon this earth" (*The Teachings of Harold B. Lee,* ed. Clyde J. Williams [1996], 59).

• Elder Melvin J. Ballard (1873–1939) of the Quorum of the Twelve Apostles emphasized the importance of repenting during mortality:

"This life is the time in which men are to repent. Do not let any of us imagine that we can go down to the grave not having overcome the corruptions of the flesh and then lose in the grave all our sins and evil tendencies. They will be with us. They will be with the spirit when separated from the body.

"... [Mortality] is the time when men are more pliable and susceptible" (*The Three Degrees of Glory: A Discourse* [Sept. 22, 1922], 11–12).

Alma 35. The Nephite-Lamanite Wars Recorded in Alma 43–62

• Chronologically, Alma 43 follows Alma 35. "Alma, being grieved for the iniquity of his people, yea for the wars, and the bloodsheds," gathered his sons "separately" to address "things pertaining unto righteousness" (Alma 35:15–16). Mormon specifically noted his interjection of Alma's words to his sons Helaman, Shiblon, and Corianton—before returning to the "account of the wars between the Nephites and the Lamanites" (Alma 43:3; compare the dates at the bottom of the pages of Alma 35 and Alma 43).

Alma 35 explains the buildup that led to the Lamanite-Nephite war, comprising chapters 43–62. The conflict and eventual war may be summarized from Alma 35:

1. The "popular part of the Zoramites ... were angry because of the word, for it did destroy their craft [priestcraft]" (v. 3).

2. The converted Zoramites, being "cast out of the land; and they were many" (v. 6), went and dwelt among the people of Jershon (people of Ammon). Here they were nourished, clothed, given lands for their inheritance, and had all of their wants satisfied (see v. 9). In their previous land they were looked upon as poor, filthy, and coarse (see Alma 32:2–3).

3. The kindness of the people of Jershon receiving the new converts infuriated the Zoramites (see Alma 35:8). The chief ruler of the Zoramites "breathed out many threatenings against them" (v. 9). "The people of Ammon did not fear" (v. 9), further angering the Zoramites and their ruler.

4. The unconverted Zoramites "began to mix with the Lamanites and to stir them up also to anger" against the people of Ammon, who were Lamanite converts (v. 10; see also Alma 43:6–7).

The events recorded in Alma 35 reveal how the lengthy Nephite-Lamanite wars recorded in Alma 43–62 began. Satan stirred the hearts of the Zoramites to anger (see 2 Nephi 28:20). In turn, they influenced the Lamanites and other Nephite dissenters to anger and to take up weapons of war against those who were good.

Points to Ponder

• In what ways might a person's heart be "full, drawn out in prayer" continually to the Lord? (Alma 34:27).

• Why was Jesus Christ the only one who could make an infinite atonement?

• Why do people sometimes procrastinate repentance? What danger results from this delay?

Suggested Assignments

• Create a detailed outline of Alma's teachings on the development of faith from Alma 32. Show how faith is nourished from hope to perfect knowledge and what role the word of God plays in this process.

• Using the instructions on prayer in Alma 33–34, identify specific ways that your prayers could become more productive.

CHAPTER 31

Alma 36–39

Introduction

Alma 36–39 contains Alma's final counsel to his three sons: Helaman, Shiblon, and Corianton. The counsel given to faithful Helaman and Shiblon differed greatly from the counsel given to wayward Corianton. To a certain extent we determine what kind of counsel we might receive in our lives by how faithful we are to the counsel we have already been given (see Alma 12:9–11).

Alma's conversion story provides one of the clearest examples of how we can know when we have been forgiven of our sins. Through Alma's counsel to Shiblon, we learn the power and value of steadfastness in our lives. Finally, the poignant counsel given to Corianton teaches how serious and destructive sexual transgression is.

Commentary

Alma 36. Chiasmus

• *Chiasmus,* sometimes called an inverted parallelism, is a Hebrew literary form where words or ideas are arranged in a certain order and then repeated in reverse order. This repetition emphasizes important ideas and words. In addition, the writer's main idea is often located at the center of the chiasmus.

Alma used chiasmus to tell the story of his conversion to his son Helaman. The presence of Semitic literary forms such as chiasmus in the Book of Mormon is an external witness that the book is what the Prophet Joseph Smith taught that it is: a translation of an ancient text written in a Middle Eastern language.

The following chart will help you recognize the chiasmus in Alma 36. For convenience, positions are designated in the chart from left to right, starting with the letter *A* and ending with the letter *P.* Thus, the thought expressed in the beginning verse of the chiasmus, Alma 36:1 (labeled position *A*), is repeated in the last verse of the chiasmus, Alma 36:30 (also in position *A*). The thought in Alma 36:2 (labeled position *D*) is repeated in verse 29 (also in position *D*), and so forth.

A. Give ear to my words (v. 1)
 B. Keep the commandments of God, and ye shall prosper in the land (v. 1)
  C. Do as I have done (v. 2)
   D. Remember the captivity of our fathers, for they were in bondage (v. 2)
    E. He surely did deliver them (v. 2)
     F. Trust in God (v. 3)
      G. Supported in their trials, and their troubles, and their afflictions (v. 3)
       H. Lifted up at the last day (v. 3)
        I. I would not that ye think that I know of myself— but of God (v. 4)
         J. Born of God (v. 5)
          K. I went about seeking to destroy the church of God (v. 6)
           L. Neither had I the use of my limbs (v. 10)
            M. I thought that I might not be brought to the presence of my God (v. 15)
             N. The pains of a damned soul (v. 16)
              O. Harrowed up by the memory of my many sins (v. 17)
               P. I remembered one Jesus Christ, a Son of God (v. 17)
               P. I cried within my heart: O Jesus, thou Son of God (v. 18)
              O. Harrowed up by the memory of my sins no more (v. 19)
             N. Joy as exceeding as was my pain (v. 20)
            M. My soul did long to be there (in the presence of God) (v. 22)
           L. My limbs received strength again (v. 23)
          K. I labored to bring souls to repentance (v. 24)
         J. Born of God (v. 26)
        I. My knowledge is of God (v. 26)
       H. Supported under trials, troubles, and afflictions (v. 27)
      G. Trust in him (v. 27)
     F. He will deliver me and raise me up (vv. 27–28)
    E. He has delivered them out of bondage and captivity (v. 28)
   D. Retain a remembrance of their captivity (v. 29)
  C. Know as I do know (v. 30)
 B. Keep the commandments of God, and ye shall prosper (v. 30)
A. This according to his word (v. 30)

Notice that the central message of the chiasmus focuses on the time in Alma's life when he experienced great pain and sorrow and turned to Jesus Christ for relief (see Alma 36:17–18).

Alma 36:2–3. Remembering the Mercies of God

• Alma 36:2–3 continues a theme emphasized throughout the Book of Mormon. Nephi began his account by saying he would show us that "the tender mercies of the Lord are over all those whom he hath chosen, because of their faith, to make them mighty even unto the power of deliverance" (1 Nephi 1:20). In Alma 36, Alma taught his sons to remember the captivity of their fathers and how God delivered those who trusted in Him (see Alma 36:2–3, 29).

Later, Moroni exhorted us to "remember how merciful the Lord hath been unto the children of men, from the creation of Adam" (Moroni 10:3). It might have been stated most emphatically by Alma the Younger: "And now behold, I say unto you, my brethren, you that belong to this church, have you sufficiently retained in remembrance the captivity of your fathers? Yea, and have you sufficiently retained in remembrance his mercy and long-suffering towards them? And moreover, have ye sufficiently retained in remembrance that he has delivered their souls from hell?" (Alma 5:6).

Alma 36:6–10. Alma "Fell to the Earth"—Two Days or Three?

• "Some readers of the Book of Mormon have claimed there is a discrepancy in the accounts of the conversion of Alma as recorded in Mosiah 27:23 and Alma 36:10. It is true that one account mentions 'two days and two nights' and the other says 'three days and three nights,' but there is no apparent discrepancy because they are not referring to exactly the same thing. In the

account in the book of Mosiah the time element clearly refers to the period of fasting by the priests; no exact length of time is indicated for Alma's unconscious state.

Note the major details of the account: After Alma was confronted by an angel and realized the enormity of his sins, he fell to the earth almost as if dead. Then he was carried to his father in this helpless condition. The father of Alma then called in the priests of the church and *'after they had fasted and prayed for the space of two days and two nights,* the limbs of Alma received their strength, and he stood up.' (Mosiah 27:22–23. Italics added.) In the account in the book of Alma, however, the term 'three days and three nights' clearly refers to the *total time* Alma could not open his mouth nor use his limbs. (Alma 36:10.)" (Daniel H. Ludlow, *A Companion to Your Study of the Book of Mormon* [1976], 217–18).

Alma 36:11–16. Godly Sorrow

• President Ezra Taft Benson (1899–1994) taught about the difference between worldly sorrow and the deeper godly sorrow necessary for repentance:

"It is not uncommon to find men and women in the world who feel remorse for the things they do wrong. Sometimes this is because their actions cause them or loved ones great sorrow and misery. Sometimes their sorrow is caused because they are caught and punished for their actions. Such worldly feelings do not constitute 'godly sorrow.' . . .

"Godly sorrow is a gift of the Spirit. It is a deep realization that our actions have offended our Father and our God. It is the sharp and keen awareness that our behavior caused the Savior, He who knew no sin, even the greatest of all, to endure agony and suffering. Our sins caused Him to bleed at every pore. This very real mental and spiritual anguish is what the scriptures refer to as having 'a broken heart and a contrite spirit.' (See 3 Ne. 9:20; Moro. 6:2; D&C 20:37; 59:8; Ps. 34:18; 51:17; Isa. 57:15.) Such a spirit is the absolute prerequisite for true repentance" ("A Mighty Change of Heart," *Ensign,* Oct. 1989, 4).

• Elder Richard G. Scott of the Quorum of the Twelve Apostles further explained one of the reasons for godly sorrow: "The painful consequences of sin were purposely put in His plan of happiness by a compassionate Father in Heaven so that you need not follow that tragic path in life. A sinner will not only suffer in this life, but sins that have not been forgiven through true repentance will cause anguish beyond the veil [see D&C 19:4, 15–24]" (in Conference Report, Oct. 2002, 94; or *Ensign,* Nov. 2002, 87).

ALMA 36:17–21
How did Alma obtain relief from his personal agony? How did he describe being forgiven?

Alma 36:17–21. "I Could Remember My Pains No More"

• President Spencer W. Kimball (1895–1985) pointed out the need to completely rely on Jesus Christ in the repentance process:

"In Alma's account the sensitive reader can in a measure identify with him, feel his pains, experience his great sense of horror at the recognition of the depth of his sin. The reader can then share also in the great relief which Alma was to find. How did he gain this relief? In the same way every transgressor does—by partaking of the miracle of forgiveness through genuine repentance and by casting himself wholly on the mercies of Jesus Christ. . . .

"Now anguish was turned to joy, pain to calm, darkness to light. Only now could Alma have peace. He emphasized to his son Shiblon the sole source of that peace.

" '. . . And never, until I did cry out unto the Lord Jesus Christ for mercy, did I receive a remission of my sins. But behold, I did cry unto him and I did find peace to my soul' (Al. 38:8.)" (*Miracle of Forgiveness* [1969], 365–66).

• President Ezra Taft Benson explained that sincere repentance requires a change of heart:

"Repentance means more than simply a reformation of behavior. Many men and women in the world demonstrate great willpower and self-discipline in overcoming bad habits and the weaknesses of the flesh. Yet at the same time they give no thought to the Master, sometimes even openly rejecting Him. Such

changes of behavior, even if in a positive direction, do not constitute true repentance. . . .

". . . Repentance involves not just a change of actions, but a change of heart" ("A Mighty Change of Heart," *Ensign,* Oct. 1989, 2).

Alma 36:23–24. Evidence That a Person Has Been Born Again

• President Ezra Taft Benson described the change that is a part of the new birth: "When we have undergone this mighty change, which is brought about only through faith in Jesus Christ and through the operation of the Spirit upon us, it is as though we have become a new person. Thus, the change is likened to a new birth. Thousands of you have experienced this change. You have forsaken lives of sin, sometimes deep and offensive sin, and through applying the blood of Christ in your lives, have become clean. You have no more disposition to return to your old ways. You are in reality a new person. This is what is meant by a change of heart" ("A Mighty Change of Heart," *Ensign,* Oct. 1989, 4).

Alma 36:30. "Prosper in the Land"

• Alma referred to a recurring theme in the Book of Mormon of prospering in the land. Alma 36:30 gives contextual meaning to that phrase. It is not necessarily intended that all inhabitants will become materially rich in this life. Rather, there is a spiritual meaning to the word *prosper.* This verse teaches us that if we do not "keep the commandments of God," then we shall not prosper but be "cut off from his presence." Therefore, those who prosper in the land are those who are successful in obtaining the spiritual blessings of being close to the Lord. They are on a track that will lead to entering the Lord's presence.

Alma 37. The Importance and Value of Scripture

• To help prepare his son Helaman to be the spiritual leader and the new record keeper for the people, Alma stressed the importance of the scriptures. Some of the major points he made are that the Lord would preserve the brass plates and the Nephite record in a marvelous but simple way (see Alma 37:1–5). He commanded his son to keep a record of his people and taught him that the scriptures are designed to enlarge our memory, convince us of the error of our ways, and bring us to a knowledge of God and His plan of salvation (see vv. 8–9). Then he reminded his son that only one who keeps the commandments is worthy to record scripture (vv. 14–16). Alma further promised his son, and us, that following the words of Christ will "carry us beyond this vale of sorrow into a far better land of promise" (v. 45).

Elder David A. Bednar of the Quorum of the Twelve Apostles described ways we could get more from our personal scripture study: "The scriptures contain the words of Christ and are a reservoir of living water to which we have ready access and from which we can drink deeply and long. You and I must look to and come unto Christ, who is 'the fountain of living waters' (1 Nephi 11:25; compare Ether 8:26; 12:28), by reading (see Mosiah 1:5), studying (see D&C 26:1), searching (see John 5:39; Alma 17:2), and feasting (see 2 Nephi 32:3) upon the words of Christ as contained in the holy scriptures. By so doing, we can receive both spiritual direction and protection during our mortal journey" ("A Reservoir of Living Water" [CES fireside for young adults, Feb. 4, 2007], 1).

Alma 37:1–8 📖

What topic was Alma addressing when he spoke of the power of small and simple things? In what ways does scripture study fit this principle?

Alma 37:6–7. 📖 "Small and Simple Things"

• Elder M. Russell Ballard of the Quorum of the Twelve Apostles taught the importance of giving heed to small and simple things:

"We observe vast, sweeping world events; however, we must remember that the purposes of the Lord in our personal lives generally are fulfilled through the small and simple things and not the momentous and spectacular. . . .

"Great and marvelous events seem to motivate us, but small things often do not hold our attention. Noting that the Liahona worked by faith, Alma stated, 'Nevertheless, because those miracles were worked by small means . . . [the people of Lehi] were slothful, and forgot to exercise their faith and diligence and then those marvelous works ceased, and they did not progress in their journey' (Alma 37:41).

"Is our journey sometimes impeded when we forget the importance of small things? (see Alma 37:46). Do we realize that small events and choices determine the direction of our lives just as small helms determine the direction of great ships? (see James 3:4; D&C 123:16). . . .

". . . We need to have family and personal prayers; study the scriptures, particularly the Book of Mormon; hold family home evenings; follow the admonition of the Savior to love one another; and be thoughtful, kind, and gentle within the family. Through these and other similar small and simple things, we have the promise that our lives will be filled with peace and joy" (in Conference Report, Apr. 1990, 4, 8; or *Ensign,* May 1990, 6, 8).

Alma 37:19. The Power of the Book of Mormon

• Elder Bruce R. McConkie (1915–85) of the Quorum of the Twelve Apostles listed some ways in which the power of the Book of Mormon is and will be demonstrated: "What then is the power of the Book of Mormon? It will proclaim the everlasting gospel; it will gather Israel; it will build the New Jerusalem; it will prepare a people for the Second Coming; it will usher in the Millennium—at least it will play such an important part in all of these that its value and power can scarcely be overstated" (*The Millennial Messiah* [1982], 171).

Alma 37:21, 27–29, 32. Not Reveal Secret Works of Darkness

• President Boyd K. Packer, President of the Quorum of the Twelve Apostles, explained that teaching about sin in too much detail may stir one's curiosity to experiment with sin:

"I am convinced that two of the major mistakes are to teach too much about the subject and to teach it at the wrong time. . . .

"I know of more than one instance in which a young person has been led to experiment in gross and perverted immorality because of a suggestion that originated with his bishop in an interview.

"Those who teach, and I refer to leaders, to teachers, and to parents, should keep in mind this message. Picture a father and mother leaving home for a period of time. Just as they go out the door they say to their little children who are to be left untended during their absence, 'Now children, be good. Whatever you do while we are gone, do not take the footstool into the pantry, and do not climb to the fourth shelf and move the cracker box and reach back and get the sack of beans and take a bean and put it up your nose, will you?'

"Some of us are just that foolish. The humor of the illustration is wry humor when you think of the first thing that happens after the parents are gone. Surely we can be wiser than that. Young people should know from the very beginning that chastity is a sacred subject" (*Teach Ye Diligently* [1975], 256–57).

Alma 37:35. What Blessings Come from Learning in Our "Youth to Keep the Commandments of God"?

• President Ezra Taft Benson described the power that comes from learning to keep the commandments early in life while still young: "Give me a young man who has kept himself morally clean and has faithfully attended his Church meetings. Give me a young man who has magnified his priesthood and has earned the Duty to God Award and is an Eagle Scout. Give me a young man who is a seminary graduate and has a burning testimony of the Book of Mormon. Give me such a young man and I will give you a young man who can perform miracles for the Lord in the mission field and throughout his life" (in Conference Report, Apr. 1986, 59; or *Ensign*, May 1986, 45).

• The scriptures give several examples of the Lord calling those who are still in their youth to be His leaders: Joseph Smith was 14 years old (see Joseph Smith—History 1:7); Mormon was 15 years old (see Mormon 1:15); the Old Testament Samuel was still a "child" when called by the Lord (1 Samuel 3:1–10).

President Joseph F. Smith testified of the relationship between keeping the commandments early in life and being called to serve the Lord later: "You may look around today, and who are the leaders among the people but those who early and zealously devoted themselves to the faith? And you may foretell who are to be the leaders by observing the boys who show self-respect and purity and who are earnest in all good works. The Lord will not choose men from any other class of his people. . . . The opposite course, waiting to serve the Lord until the wild oats of youth are sown, is reprehensible. There is always something lacking in the man who spends his youth in wickedness and sin, and then turns to righteousness in later years. . . . There are regrets and heartburnings in repenting late in life from the follies and sins of youth, but there are consolation and rich reward in serving the Lord in the vigorous days of early manhood" (*Gospel Doctrine*, 5th ed. [1939], 335).

> ***ALMA 37:38–47***
> *What specific parallels do you see between the Liahona and the scriptures or between the Liahona and the Holy Spirit in our day?*

Alma 37:38–47. The Liahona

• Over the years several General Authorities have described different means in which the Lord continues to guide us in our journey of life, like a Liahona.

Elder W. Rolfe Kerr of the Seventy compared the words of Christ to the Liahona: "So we see, brethren and sisters, that the words of Christ can be a personal Liahona for each of us, showing us the way. Let us not be slothful because of the easiness of the way. Let us in faith take the words of Christ into our minds and into our hearts as they are recorded in sacred scripture and as they are uttered by living prophets, seers, and revelators. Let us with faith and diligence feast upon the words of Christ, for the words of Christ will be our spiritual Liahona telling us all things what we should do" (in Conference Report, Apr. 2004, 38; or *Ensign*, May 2004, 37).

• President Thomas S. Monson compared the Liahona to an individual's patriarchal blessing: "The same Lord who provided a Liahona for Lehi provides for you and for me today a rare and valuable gift to give direction to our lives. . . . The gift to which I refer is known as a patriarchal blessing" (*Live the Good Life* [1988], 36).

President Spencer W. Kimball compared the Liahona to the light of Christ, or our conscience:

"Wouldn't you like to have that kind of a ball . . . ?

". . . The Lord gave to . . . every person, a conscience which tells him everytime he starts to go on the wrong path. . . .

". . . Every child is given it" (in Conference Report, Oct. 1976, 117; or *Ensign,* Nov. 1976, 79).

• Elder David A. Bednar compared the Liahona to the gift of the Holy Ghost:

"As we each press forward along the pathway of life, we receive direction from the Holy Ghost just as Lehi was directed through the Liahona. . . .

"The Holy Ghost operates in our lives precisely as the Liahona did for Lehi and his family, according to our faith and diligence and heed. . . .

"And the Holy Ghost provides for us today the means whereby we can receive, 'by small and simple things' (Alma 37:6), increased understanding about the ways of the Lord. . . .

"The Spirit of the Lord can be our guide and will bless us with direction, instruction, and spiritual protection during our mortal journey" (in Conference Report, Apr. 2006, 31; or *Ensign,* May 2006, 30–31).

Alma 38:12. "Bridle All Your Passions"

• A bridle is the headgear used on a horse. It includes reins and a bit, which give the rider control.

Elder Bruce C. Hafen of the Seventy and his wife Marie explained that a bridle was meant to direct, not destroy, desires and

passions: "Is self-denial wise because something is wrong with our passions, or because something is right with our passions? Alma taught his son: 'See that ye bridle all your passions, *that ye may be filled with love.*' (Alma 38:12; emphasis added.) He did not say eliminate or even suppress your passions, but *bridle* them—harness, channel, and focus them. Why? Because discipline makes possible a richer, deeper love" (*The Belonging Heart* [1994], 302).

Alma 39. The Law of Chastity

• "Do not have any sexual relations before marriage, and be completely faithful to your spouse after marriage. Satan may tempt you to rationalize that sexual intimacy before marriage is acceptable when two people are in love. That is not true. In God's sight, sexual sins are extremely serious because they defile the power God has given us to create life. . . .

"Before marriage, do not do anything to arouse the powerful emotions that must be expressed only in marriage. Do not participate in passionate kissing, lie on top of another person, or touch the private, sacred parts of another person's body, with or without clothing. Do not allow anyone to do that with you. Do not arouse those emotions in your own body.

"In cultures where dating or courting is acceptable, always treat your date with respect, never as an object to be used for your lustful desires. Stay in areas of safety where you can easily control your physical feelings. Do not participate in talk or activities that arouse sexual feelings.

"Homosexual activity is a serious sin. If you find yourself struggling with same-gender attraction, seek counsel from your parents and bishop. They will help you.

"Victims of rape, incest, or other sexual abuse are not guilty of sin. If you have been a victim of any of these crimes, know that you are innocent and that God loves you. Seek your bishop's counsel immediately so he can help guide you through the process of emotional healing" (*For the Strength of Youth: Fulfilling Our Duty to God* [2001], 27–28).

Alma 39:3. The Seriousness of Sexual Sin

• Elder Jeffrey R. Holland spoke of the devastating impact of sexual sin and the importance of preserving your virtue until you are married: "*In matters of human intimacy, you must wait!* You must wait until you can give everything, and you cannot give everything until you are legally and lawfully married. To give illicitly that which is not yours to give (remember, 'you are not your own' [1 Corinthians 6:19]) and to give only part of that which cannot be followed with the gift of your whole self is emotional Russian roulette. If you persist in pursuing physical satisfaction without the sanction of heaven, you run the terrible risk of such spiritual, psychic damage that you may undermine *both* your longing for physical intimacy *and* your ability to give wholehearted devotion to a later, truer love. You may come to that truer moment of ordained love, of real union, only to discover to your horror that what you should have saved you have spent, and that only God's grace can recover the piecemeal dissipation of the virtue you so casually gave away. On your wedding day the very best gift you can give your eternal companion is your very best self—clean and pure and worthy of such purity in return" (in Conference Report, Oct. 1998, 100; or *Ensign,* Nov. 1998, 76–77).

• President Boyd K. Packer described the relationship between the power of creation and the plan of salvation:

"The power of creation—or may we say procreation—is not just an incidental part of the plan: it is essential to it. Without it the plan could not proceed. The misuse of it may disrupt the plan.

"Much of the happiness that may come to you in this life will depend on how you use this sacred power of creation" (in Conference Report, Apr. 1972, 136–37; or *Ensign,* July 1972, 111).

> **ALMA 39:4**
> *What did Alma say Corianton should have been doing that would have kept him safe from temptation? How can you apply that in your life?*

Alma 39:5. Next to Murder in Seriousness

• Elder Jeffrey R. Holland explained the connection between the worth of a soul and the Atonement, helping us understand why sexual transgression is so serious:

"In exploiting the body of another—which means exploiting his or her soul—one desecrates the Atonement of Christ, which saved that soul and which makes possible the gift of eternal life. And when one mocks the Son of Righteousness, one steps into a realm of heat hotter and holier than the noonday sun. You cannot do so and not be burned.

"Please, never say: 'Who does it hurt? Why not a little freedom? I can transgress now and repent later.' Please don't be so foolish and so cruel. You cannot with impunity 'crucify Christ afresh' [see Hebrews 6:6]. 'Flee fornication' [1 Corinthians 6:18], Paul cries, and flee *'anything like unto it'* [D&C 59:6; italics added], the Doctrine and Covenants adds. Why? Well, for one reason, because of the incalculable suffering in both body and spirit endured by the Savior of the world so that we *could* flee. We owe Him something for that. Indeed, we owe Him everything for that. 'Ye are not your own,' Paul says. 'Ye [have been] bought with a price: therefore *glorify God in your body, and in your spirit, which are God's*' [1 Corinthians 6:19–20; italics added]. In sexual transgression the soul is at stake—the body and the spirit" (in Conference Report, Oct. 1998, 99–100; or *Ensign,* Nov. 1998, 76).

Alma 39:6. What Is the Unpardonable Sin?

• The Prophet Joseph Smith (1805–44) gave further knowledge about the unpardonable sin: "All sins shall be forgiven, except the sin against the Holy Ghost; for Jesus will save all except the sons of perdition. What must a man do to commit the unpardonable sin? He must receive the Holy Ghost, have the heavens opened unto him, and know God, and then sin against him. After a man has sinned against the Holy Ghost, there is no

Alvin Gittins, © 1959 IRI

repentance for him. He has got to say that the sun does not shine while he sees it; he has got to deny Jesus Christ when the heavens have been opened unto him, and to deny the plan of salvation with his eyes open to the truth of it; and from that time he begins to be an enemy. This is the case with many apostates of the Church of Jesus Christ of Latter-day Saints" (*History of the Church,* 6:314).

Alma 39:9. "Go No More after the Lusts of Your Eyes"

• How does going "no more after the lusts of your eyes" apply to us? In today's world with advanced technology, there are many ways Satan offers such temptations. Many prophets in recent years have warned us about the dangers of pornography in its many forms.

Elder Dallin H. Oaks of the Quorum of the Twelve Apostles explained the dangers of allowing evil into our minds: "Our Savior emphasized the importance of sexual purity when he taught that it was sinful for a man to even look upon a woman to lust after her [see Matthew 5:28]. . . . We are surrounded by the promotional literature of illicit sexual relations, on the printed page and on the screen. For your own good, avoid it. Pornographic or erotic stories and pictures are worse than filthy or polluted food. The body has defenses to rid itself of unwholesome food. With a few fatal exceptions bad food will only make you sick but do no permanent harm. In contrast, a person who feasts upon filthy stories or pornographic or erotic pictures and literature records them in this marvelous retrieval system we call a brain. The brain won't vomit back filth. Once recorded, it will always remain subject to recall, flashing its perverted images across your mind and drawing you away from the wholesome things in life" ("Things They're Saying," *New Era,* Feb. 1974, 18).

• President Ezra Taft Benson described several ways Satan tries to get pornography into our minds:

"Consider carefully the words of the prophet Alma to his errant son, Corianton, 'Forsake your sins, and go no more after the lusts of your eyes' (Alma 39:9).

"'The lusts of your eyes.' In our day, what does that expression mean?

"Movies, television programs, and video recordings that are both suggestive and lewd.

"Magazines and books that are obscene and pornographic.

"We counsel you, young men, not to pollute your minds with such degrading matter, for the mind through which this filth passes is never the same afterwards. Don't see R-rated movies or vulgar videos or participate in any entertainment that is immoral, suggestive, or pornographic. Don't listen to music that is degrading" (in Conference Report, Apr. 1986, 58; or *Ensign,* May 1986, 45).

• President Gordon B. Hinckley (1910–2008) added his testimony to the evils of pornography:

"Pornography is printed and pictorial material designed to excite us and attract us into areas that will only bring regret. It is enticing in its appeal. It plays on the instincts that lie within all of us, God-given instincts placed within us for his great purposes. Pornography is a tool of the devil to twist those instincts to forbidden ends. It most often involves beautiful young women and handsome young men. The purpose of its creation is to put dollars in the pockets of its creators. The result of its use is to warp the minds and excite the passions of those who fall into its trap. It brings billions to its creators. It leads to heartache and pain and regret for those who indulge in it.

"It is found in magazines that can be bought at most newsstands, in theaters showing R- and X-rated movies, and on our television screens in our homes" (*Teachings of Gordon B. Hinckley* [1997], 460).

• The phrase "cross yourself," as used in Alma 39:9, is not familiar to us today. However, in Webster's 1828 dictionary, we find the following helpful definitions that relate to Alma's counsel to his son: "To erase, to cancel, to counteract, to stop, to preclude" (*Noah Webster's First Edition of an American Dictionary of the English Language, 1828* [1967]). All of these actions apply well to what one must do to avoid moral transgression, the topic Alma was teaching his son Corianton. Refer also to the footnote for Alma 39:9*b,* which refers to self-mastery in the Topical Guide (p. 461)).

Alma 39:11–12. Leading Others from the Truth

• In Alma 39:11–12, Alma explained to Corianton, his wayward son, the fact that our negative examples can lead others away from the gospel.

President Joseph Fielding Smith (1876–1972) warned of the seriousness of leading people away from the truth:

"I think the greatest crime in all this world is to lead men and women, the children of God, away from the true principles. We see in the world today philosophies of various kinds, tending to destroy faith, faith in God, faith in the principles of the gospel. What a dreadful thing that is.

"The Lord says if we labor all our days and save but one soul, how great will be our joy with him; on the other hand how great will be our sorrow and our condemnation if through our acts we have led one soul away from this truth.

"He who blinds one soul, he who spreads error, he who destroys, through his teachings, divine truth, truth that would lead a man to the kingdom of God and to its fulness, how great shall be his condemnation and his punishment in eternity. For the destruction of a soul is the destruction of the greatest thing that has ever been created" (*Doctrines of Salvation,* comp. Bruce R. McConkie, 3 vols. [1954–56], 1:314).

Alma 39:12–13, 15. "Turn to the Lord" and Acknowledge Your Faults

• "If you have committed sexual transgressions, begin the process of repentance now so you can find inner peace and have the full companionship of the Spirit. Seek the Lord's forgiveness. Talk with your bishop. He will help you obtain the forgiveness available to those who truly repent" (*For the Strength of Youth,* 28).

• Elder Richard G. Scott explained what you must do in order to "turn to the Lord" and be forgiven of serious sins, such as immorality: "For a moment I speak to anyone who has succumbed to serious temptation. Please stop now. You can do it with the help from an understanding parent, bishop, or stake president. Serious transgression such as immorality requires the help of one who holds keys of authority, such as a bishop or stake president, to quietly work out the repentance process to make sure that it is complete and appropriately done. Do not make the mistake to believe that because you have confessed a serious transgression, you have repented of it. That is an essential step, but it is not all that is required. Nor assume that because someone did not ask you all the important details of a transgression, you need not mention them. You personally must make sure that the bishop or stake president understands those details so that he can help you properly through the process of repentance for full forgiveness" (in Conference Report, Oct. 1998, 89; or *Ensign,* Nov. 1998, 69–70).

• Elder Jeffrey R. Holland taught that the Lord will be with and strengthen you as you properly repent: "To you is extended the peace and renewal of repentance available through the atoning sacrifice of the Lord Jesus Christ. In such serious matters the path of repentance is not easily begun or painlessly traveled. But the Savior of the world will walk that essential journey with you. He will strengthen you when you waver. He will be your light when it seems most dark. He will take your hand and be your hope when hope seems all you have left. His compassion and mercy, with all their cleansing and healing power, are freely given to all who truly wish complete forgiveness and will take the steps that lead to it" (in Conference Report, Oct. 1998, 101–2; or *Ensign,* Nov. 1998, 78).

Alma 39:17–19. The Plan of Salvation Was Known Before the World Was Created

• Some religions recognize a life of some kind after mortality; however, very few proclaim belief in a life before mortality. The Prophet Joseph Smith explained what the Lord knew even before the Creation: "The great Jehovah contemplated the whole of the events connected with the earth, pertaining to the plan of salvation, before it rolled into existence . . . ; the past, the present, and the future were and are, with Him, one eternal 'now;' He knew of the fall of Adam, the iniquities of the antediluvians, of the depth of iniquity that would be connected with the human family . . . ;

He comprehended the fall of man, and his redemption; He knew the plan of salvation and pointed it out; He was acquainted with the situation of all nations and with their destiny; . . . He knows the situation of both the living and the dead, and has made ample provision for their redemption" (*History of the Church,* 4:597).

Points to Ponder

• When Alma was convinced of the reality of God and the gospel, he immediately began to suffer great sorrow for his past sins. Why do you think that happened? How does that apply to us today?

• Alma emphasized the importance of the scriptures to his son Helaman. Modern prophets continue to do the same with us. Do you or someone you know enjoy the blessings of daily scripture study? In what ways do the scriptures bless the lives of those who regularly feast on them? How can you establish or strengthen your personal scripture study habit?

• What can we learn from Shiblon's example that will help us remain strong through both good and bad times?

Suggested Assignments

• The principles of Alma's repentance and forgiveness experience are the same for us today even though the circumstances are different than ours. Write a one-page paper summarizing some of the principles involved and how they apply to us now.

• Alma told Corianton that sexual transgressions are next to murder in seriousness. Write out a specific plan of steps you can take now to safeguard your purity.

Introduction

What happens to people after they die? Alma 40–42 focuses on Alma's counsel to his wayward son Corianton, who had a similar question. In his response, Alma taught about the spirit world, the Judgment, the Resurrection, the law of restoration, and the punishment of sinners. As Alma concluded his teachings to Corianton, he answered questions about what life would be like without repentance, sin, law, and punishment. Alma's answers to his son also help us understand the plan of happiness and the justice and mercy of God and how they affect our eternal progression.

Commentary

Alma 40:4–10. "All Is as One Day with God"

• After testifying to Corianton of the reality of the Resurrection, Alma expressed uncertainty of the timing of the Resurrection as it relates to all of mankind. Such concerns did not matter to Alma, for he said "all is as one day with God" (Alma 40:8). The Prophet Joseph Smith (1805–44) revealed that for God all things "are manifest, past, present, and future, and are continually before the Lord" (D&C 130:7).

Elder Neal A. Maxwell (1926–2004) of the Quorum of the Twelve Apostles explained how things are done in God's way:

"God was redemptively at work long before mortal time began on this earth—and He will still be at work even after mortal time is no more (see D&C 88:110; Alma 40:8). . . .

"Mercifully, things then will 'be done in [God's] own way,' not ours (D&C 104:16). Then God's purposes, His patience, His power, and His profound love, which were at work long before time was, will also be at work even after time will be no more (see D&C 84:100; Alma 40:8).

"These and other truths are among what Paul called 'the deep things of God' (1 Corinthians 2:10)" (*A Wonderful Flood of Light* [1990], 50, 58–59).

The Prophet Joseph Smith also said that "the great Jehovah contemplated the whole of the events connected with the earth, pertaining to the plan of salvation, before it rolled into existence, or ever 'the morning stars sang together' for joy; the past, the present, and the future were and are, with Him, one eternal 'now'" (*History of the Church,* 4:597).

Alma 40:11. The Spirits of All Men "Are Taken Home to That God Who Gave Them Life"

• If at death we enter the spirit world, not God's actual presence, how are we to understand Alma's words?

President Joseph Fielding Smith (1876–1972) explained that Alma did not necessarily mean that we are brought back into God's presence: "These words of Alma [40:11] as I understand them, do not intend to convey the thought that all spirits go back into the presence of God for an assignment to a place of peace or a place of punishment and before him receive their individual sentence. 'Taken home to God' [compare Ecclesiastes 12:7] simply means that their mortal existence has come to an end, and they have returned to the world of spirits, where they are assigned to a place according to their works with the just or with the unjust, there to await the resurrection. 'Back to God' is a phrase which finds an equivalent in many other well known conditions. For instance: a man spends a stated time in some foreign mission field. When he is released and returns to the United States, he may say, 'It is wonderful to be back home'; yet his home may be somewhere in Utah or Idaho or some other part of the West" (*Answers to Gospel Questions,* comp. Joseph Fielding Smith Jr., 5 vols. [1957–66], 2:85).

President George Q. Cannon (1827–1901) of the First Presidency explained that Alma "does not intend to convey the idea that they are immediately ushered into the personal presence of God. He evidently uses that phrase in a qualified sense" (*Gospel Truth: Discourses and Writings of President George Q. Cannon,* sel. Jerreld L. Newquist [1987], 58).

Alma 40:11–15. The State of the Soul between Death and the Resurrection

• The following clarification helps us understand the condition of spirit beings after death and prior to their resurrection: "When the physical body dies, the spirit continues to live. In the spirit world, the spirits of the righteous 'are received into a state of happiness, which is called paradise, a state of rest, a state of peace, where they shall rest from all their troubles and from all care, and sorrow' (Alma 40:12). A place called spirit prison is reserved for 'those who [have] died in their sins, without a knowledge of the truth, or in transgression, having rejected the prophets' (D&C 138:32). The spirits in prison are 'taught faith in God, repentance from sin, vicarious baptism for the remission of sins, the gift of the Holy Ghost by the laying on of hands, and all other principles of the gospel that [are] necessary for them to know' (D&C 138:33–34). If they accept the principles of the gospel, repent of their sins, and accept ordinances performed in their behalf in temples, they will be welcomed into paradise" (*True to the Faith: A Gospel Reference* [2004], 46–47).

© 1985 Robert Barrett

• President Brigham Young (1801–77) helped us better understand the difference between the location of the spirit world and God's abode: "When you lay down this tabernacle, where are you going? Into the spiritual world. Are you going into Abraham's bosom? No, not anywhere nigh there but into the spirit world. Where is the spirit world? It is right here. Do the good and evil spirits go together? Yes, they do. Do they both inhabit one kingdom? Yes, they do. Do they go to the sun? No. Do they go beyond the boundaries of the organized earth? No, they do not. They are brought forth upon this earth" (*Discourses of Brigham Young*, sel. John A. Widtsoe [1954], 376).

Alma 40:16–22. The First Resurrection

• Alma was speaking of the First Resurrection in relation to earthly time. Jesus Christ would be resurrected first, followed shortly thereafter by the righteous who had lived and died from the beginning of time for our mortal earth down to the time of Christ's Resurrection (see Alma 40:16, 20; D&C 133:54–55). This resurrection is what Alma called the First Resurrection.

• President Joseph Fielding Smith explained that the First Resurrection includes different time periods and events:

"While there was a general resurrection of the righteous at the time Christ arose from the dead, it is customary for us to speak of the resurrection of the righteous at the Second Coming of Christ as the first resurrection. It is the first to us, for we have little thought or concern over that which is past. The Lord has promised that at the time of his Second Advent the graves will be opened, and the just shall come forth to reign with him on the earth for a thousand years. . . .

"At the time of the [second] coming of Christ, 'They who have slept in their graves shall come forth, for their graves shall be opened; and they also shall be caught up to meet him in the midst of the pillar of heaven—They are Christ's, the first fruits, they who shall descend with him first, and they who are on the earth and in their graves, who are first caught up to meet him; and all this by the voice of the sounding of the trump of the angel of God' [D&C 88:97–98]. These are the just, 'whose names are written in heaven, where God and Christ are the judge of all. These are they who are just men made perfect through Jesus the mediator of the new covenant, who wrought out this perfect atonement through the shedding of his own blood' [D&C 76:68–69].

"Following this great event, and after the Lord and the righteous who are caught up to meet him have descended upon the earth, there will come to pass another resurrection. This may be considered as a part of the first, although it comes later. In this resurrection will come forth those of the terrestrial order, who were not worthy to be caught up to meet him, but who are worthy to come forth to enjoy the millennial reign" (*Doctrines of Salvation,* comp. Bruce R. McConkie, 3 vols. [1954–56], 2:295–97).

• Elder Bruce R. McConkie (1915–85) of the Quorum of the Twelve Apostles gave the following explanation regarding the First Resurrection, which is also referred to as the Resurrection of the Just and as the Resurrection of Life: "Those coming forth in the morning of this resurrection do so with celestial bodies and shall inherit a celestial glory; these are they who are Christ's the firstfruits. Those coming forth in the afternoon of this resurrection do so with terrestrial bodies and consequently shall inherit that kingdom; they are described as being Christ's at this coming. All who have been resurrected so far have received celestial bodies; the coming forth of terrestrial beings does not commence until after the Second Coming. (D.&C. 76:50–80; 88:95–99.)" (*Doctrinal New Testament Commentary,* 3 vols. [1971–73], 1:196).

Alma 40:23. "Proper and Perfect Frame"

• Elder Dallin H. Oaks of the Quorum of the Twelve Apostles referred to the comfort brought by knowing that defects will be corrected in the Resurrection:

"What a comfort to know that all who have been disadvantaged in life from birth defects, from mortal injuries, from disease, or from the natural deterioration of old age will be resurrected in 'proper and perfect frame.' . . .

© 2000 Del Parson

"The assurance of resurrection gives us the strength and perspective to endure the mortal challenges faced by each of us and by those we love, such things as the physical, mental, or emotional deficiencies we bring with us at birth or acquire during mortal life. Because of the resurrection, we know that these mortal deficiencies are only temporary!" (in Conference Report, Apr. 2000, 16–17; or *Ensign,* May 2000, 14).

• President Joseph F. Smith (1838–1918) had the following to say in relation to deformities in the Resurrection: "Deformity will be removed; defects will be eliminated, and men and women shall attain to the perfection of their spirits, to the perfection that God designed in the beginning. It is his purpose that men and women, his children, born to become heirs of God, and joint heirs with Jesus Christ, shall be made perfect, physically as well as spiritually, through obedience to the law by which he has provided the means that perfection shall come to all his children" (*Gospel Doctrine,* 5th ed. [1939], 23).

Alma 40:26. "An Awful Death Cometh upon the Wicked"

• The following statement helps us understand what this "awful death" refers to: "The scriptures sometimes speak of salvation from the second death. The second death is the final spiritual death—being cut off from righteousness and denied a place in any kingdom of glory (see Alma 12:32; D&C 88:24). This second death will not come until the Final Judgment, and it will come to very few (see D&C 76:31–37). Almost every person who has ever lived on the earth is assured salvation from the second death (see D&C 76:40–45)" (*True to the Faith,* 153).

Alma 41. The Law of Restoration

• Like some people today, Corianton may have wondered why it was important to live righteously if everyone receives the blessings of resurrection. Alma 41 addresses these concerns.

For Heavenly Father's children, the outcome of the law of restoration is dependent upon their faithfulness in keeping His commandments. Thus Alma explained to Corianton that one cannot "be restored from sin to happiness" (Alma 41:10 📖). This is akin to the law of the harvest: as we sow, so shall we reap (see Galatians 6:7; D&C 130:20–21 📖). Alma encouraged his son to "do good continually" in order to "have good rewarded unto you again. For that which ye do send out shall return unto you again, and be restored" (Alma 41:14–15).

Alma also taught his son that the law of restoration provides for a perfect restitution of the body in the

Resurrection: "The soul shall be restored to the body . . . ; yea, even a hair of the head shall not be lost" (Alma 40:23). However, the degree of glory of the resurrected body is dependent upon the degree of faithfulness of each individual (see D&C 88:28–32).

Alma 41:10. "Wickedness Never Was Happiness"

• The following counsel reinforces the importance of seeking happiness by living gospel standards:

"Many people try to find happiness and fulfillment in activities that are contrary to the Lord's commandments. Ignoring God's plan for them, they reject the only source of real happiness. They give in to the devil, who 'seeketh that all men might be miserable like unto himself' (2 Nephi 2:27). Eventually they learn the truth of Alma's warning to his son Corianton: 'Wickedness never was happiness' (Alma 41:10). . . .

"As you seek to be happy, remember that the only way to real happiness is to live the gospel. You will find peaceful, eternal happiness as you strive to keep the commandments, pray for strength, repent of your sins, participate in wholesome activities, and give meaningful service. You will learn to have fun within the limits set by a loving Father in Heaven" (*True to the Faith,* 79–80).

ALMA 41:11–14

What do we receive if we "deal justly, judge righteously, and do good continually"?

Alma 42:1–10. "A Probationary Time"

• Elder L. Tom Perry of the Quorum of the Twelve Apostles explained the purpose of the probationary time called mortality: "The main purpose of earth life is to allow our spirits, which existed before the world was, to be united with our bodies for a time of great opportunity in mortality. The association of the two together has given us the privilege of growing, developing, and maturing as only we can with spirit and body united. With our bodies, we pass through a certain amount of trial in what is termed

a probationary state of our existence. This is a time of learning and testing to prove ourselves worthy of eternal opportunities. It is all part of a divine plan our Father has for His children" (in Conference Report, Apr. 1989, 16; or *Ensign,* May 1989, 13–14).

• While serving as a member of the Seventy, Elder Ronald E. Poelman added that mortality is a time to learn of opposites and to choose between them: "The plan of salvation presented to and accepted by us in our premortal state includes a probationary period on earth, during which we experience opposites, make choices, learn the consequences thereof, and prepare to return to the presence of God. Experiencing adversity is an essential part of the process. Knowing this, we elected to come into mortality. (See 2 Nephi 2:11–16.)" (in Conference Report, Apr. 1989, 29; or *Ensign,* May 1989, 23).

• Elder William R. Bradford of the Seventy concluded that the purpose of mortality is to become like our Father in Heaven: "This life is a probationary period. It is a marvelous gift of time during which we can learn to be like our Heavenly Father by following the teachings of His Son, Jesus Christ. The path He leads us on is not a cluttered path. It is simple and straight and lighted by the Spirit" (in Conference Report, Apr. 1992, 40; or *Ensign,* May 1992, 29).

Alma 42:11–31. The Laws of Justice and Mercy

• President Boyd K. Packer, President of the Quorum of the Twelve Apostles, explained that the Savior's sacrifice allows mercy to be extended to us without violating the law of justice:

"Each of us lives on a kind of spiritual credit. One day the account will be closed, a settlement demanded. However casually we may view it now, when that day comes and the foreclosure is imminent, we will look around in restless agony for someone, anyone, to help us.

"And, by eternal law, mercy cannot be extended save there be one who is both willing and able to assume our debt and pay the price and arrange the terms for our redemption.

"Unless there is a mediator, unless we have a friend, the full weight of justice untempered, unsympathetic, must, positively must fall on us. The full recompense for every transgression, however minor or however deep, will be exacted from us to the uttermost farthing.

"But know this: Truth, glorious truth, proclaims there is such a Mediator.

"'For there is one God, and one mediator between God and men, the man Christ Jesus.' (1 Tim. 2:5.)

Justice

"Through Him mercy can be fully extended to each of us without offending the eternal law of justice.

"This truth is the very root of Christian doctrine. . . .

"The extension of mercy will not be automatic. It will be through covenant with Him. It will be on His terms, His generous terms, which include, as an absolute essential, baptism by immersion for the remission of sins.

Justice   Mercy

"All mankind can be protected by the law of justice, and at once each of us individually may be extended the redeeming and healing blessing of mercy" (in Conference Report, Apr. 1977, 80; or *Ensign,* May 1977, 55–56).

• Elder Neal A. Maxwell shared this insight: "The justice and mercy of God will have been so demonstrably perfect that at the Final Judgment there will be no complaints, including from those who once questioned what God had allotted in the mortal framework (see 2 Nephi 9:14–15; Alma 5:15–19; 12:3–14; 42:23–26, 30)" (in Conference Report, Apr. 2000, 92; or *Ensign,* May 2000, 74).

Alma 42:18–30. Remorse of Conscience

• President Boyd K. Packer explained the value remorse of conscience can have:

"It is my purpose to ease the pain of those who suffer from the very unpleasant feeling of guilt. I feel like the doctor who begins his treatment by saying, 'Now, this may hurt a little. . . .'

"Every one of us has at least tasted the pain of conscience which follows our mistakes.

"John said, 'If we say that we have no sin, we deceive ourselves, and the truth is not in us' [1 John 1:8]. Then he said it more strongly: 'If we say that we have not sinned, we make [the Lord] a liar, and his word is not in us' [1 John 1:10].

"All of us sometime, and some of us much of the time, suffer remorse of conscience from things we did wrong or things left undone. That feeling of guilt is to the spirit what pain is to the physical body. . . .

"We all make mistakes. Sometimes we harm ourselves and seriously injure others in ways that we alone cannot repair. We break things that we alone cannot fix. It is then in our nature to feel guilt and humiliation and suffering, which we alone cannot cure. That is when the healing power of the Atonement will help.

"The Lord said, 'Behold, I, God, have suffered these things for all, that they might not suffer if they would repent [D&C 19:16]" (in Conference Report, Apr. 2001, 27–28; or *Ensign,* May 2001, 22–23).

• President Spencer W. Kimball (1895–1985) spoke of the value of a sensitive conscience: "How wonderful that God should endow us with this sensitive yet strong guide we call a conscience! Someone has aptly remarked that 'conscience is a celestial spark which God has put into every man for the purpose of saving his soul.' Certainly it is the instrument which awakens the soul to consciousness of sin, spurs a person to make up his mind to adjust, to convict himself of the transgression without soft-pedaling or minimizing the error, to be willing to face facts, meet the issue and pay necessary penalties—and until the person is in this frame of mind he has not begun to repent. To be sorry is an approach, to abandon the act of error is a beginning, but until one's conscience has been sufficiently stirred to cause him to move in the matter, so long as there are excuses and rationalizations, one has hardly begun his approach to forgiveness. This is what Alma meant in telling his son Corianton that 'none but the truly penitent are saved.' (Al. 42:24.)" (*The Miracle of Forgiveness* [1969], 152).

Alma 42:23. "The Atonement Bringeth to Pass the Resurrection"

• President Gordon B. Hinckley (1910–2008) bore the following witness of the magnificence of the atoning sacrifice which made the Resurrection possible:

Paul Gustave Doré

"The magnificent expression of His love came in His death, when He gave His life as a sacrifice for all men. That Atonement, wrought in unspeakable pain, became the greatest event of history, an act of grace for which men gave nothing but which brought the assurance of the Resurrection to all who have or would walk the earth.

"No other act in all of human history compares with it. Nothing that has ever happened can match it. Totally unselfish and with unbounded love for all mankind, it became an unparalleled act of mercy for the whole human race.

"Then with the Resurrection that first Easter morn came the triumphal declaration of immortality. Well was Paul able to declare, 'For as in Adam all die, even so in Christ shall all be made alive' (1 Corinthians

15:22). He not only granted the blessing of the Resurrection to all, but opened the way to eternal life to those who observe His teachings and commandments" (in Conference Report, Oct. 1999, 92; or *Ensign,* Nov. 1999, 73).

ALMA 42:27–30
What relationship between agency and accountability is suggested in these verses?

Points to Ponder

• Why can wickedness never lead to happiness? Why does it sometimes seem that wicked people are happy?

• What must we do to have the Savior's Atonement applied in our behalf?

• How does the law of justice work in your favor?

• How does the law of mercy work in your favor?

Suggested Assignments

• Prepare and if possible deliver a short talk on the spirit world using two or more references from Alma 40–42.

• What did Alma teach his son Corianton about resurrection?

• Write a brief definition or explanation for each of the following: the law of restoration, the law of justice, the law of mercy.

Introduction

Contention, dissension, and war placed the survival of the Nephite nation in jeopardy. The Lamanites, however, were not the only source of conflict. Dissenting Nephites eager for power led to many serious problems. The Nephites overcame their enemies by exercising faith in Jesus Christ and following His prophets as well as other righteous military leaders.

Contrast the motives and intentions of Captain Moroni with those of Amalickiah. The prophet Mormon wrote of Captain Moroni, "If all men had been, and were, and ever would be, like unto Moroni, behold, the very powers of hell would have been shaken forever; yea, the devil would never have power over the hearts of the children of men" (Alma 48:17). Like Moroni, you too can remain "firm in the faith of Christ" (Alma 48:13) even in difficult and trying circumstances.

Commentary

Alma 43:2–3. "The Wars between the Nephites and the Lamanites"

• At this point in the book of Alma, chapters 43–62, Mormon alerted the reader that he would "return to an account of the wars" (Alma 43:3). Some people wonder why the Book of Mormon contains so much about war. President Ezra Taft Benson (1899–1994) stated that "from the Book of Mormon we learn how disciples of Christ live in times of war" (in Conference Report, Oct. 1986, 5; or *Ensign,* Nov. 1986, 7).

Since Mormon saw our day and knew we would live in a time of "wars and rumors of wars" (D&C 45:26; see also Revelation 9), he included how to live righteously during these times. Many Latter-day Saints have been and will be involved in military conflicts. Look for the gospel principles Mormon included in these war chapters. Mormon revealed the tremendous suffering caused by conflict and also explained why war may be necessary in the defense of life and liberty. Both Mormon and modern prophets have described circumstances when war is justified (see commentary for Alma 43:45–47 on p. 250 and for Alma 51:13 on p. 255).

President Gordon B. Hinckley (1910–2008) related the heavenly sorrow that accompanies such events, even when wars are justified: "I think our Father in Heaven must have wept as He has looked down upon His children through the centuries as they have squandered their divine birthright in ruthlessly destroying one another" (in Conference Report, Apr. 2003, 82; or *Ensign,* May 2003, 79). The Nephites and Captain Moroni showed the proper attitude toward war and bloodshed (see commentary for Alma 43:54; 44:1–2; 48:11, 22–23 on p. 251).

• At the time of World War II, the First Presidency issued the following statement, clarifying the Church's position on war:

"Members must give allegiance to their sovereign and render it loyal service when called thereto. [This includes military service.] But the Church, itself, as such, has no responsibility for these policies, as to which it has no means of doing more than urging its members fully to render that loyalty to their country and to free institutions which the loftiest patriotism calls for.

". . . There is an obligation running from every citizen or subject to the state. This obligation is voiced in that Article of Faith which declares:

"'We believe in being subject to kings, presidents, rulers, and magistrates, in obeying, honoring, and sustaining the law.' . . .

"Obedient to these principles, the members of the Church have always felt under obligation to come to the defense of their country when a call to arms was made. . . .

"Thus the Church is and must be against war. . . . It cannot regard war as a righteous means of settling international disputes; these should and could be settled—the nations agreeing—by peaceful negotiation and adjustment.

"But the Church membership are citizens or subjects of sovereignties over which the Church has no control. . . .

". . . When, therefore, constitutional law, obedient to these principles, calls the manhood of the Church into the armed service of any country to which they owe allegiance, their highest civic duty requires that they meet that call. If, harkening to that call, and obeying those in command over them, they shall take the lives of those who fight against them, that will not make of them murderers" (Heber J. Grant, J. Reuben Clark Jr., and David O. McKay, in Conference Report, Apr. 1942, 92–94; also cited in Boyd K. Packer, Conference Report, Apr. 1968, 34–35).

Alma 43:4–8. Nephite Dissenters Appointed Chief Captains over Lamanite Armies

• The Zoramites once belonged to the Nephite nation. Due to pride, however, "the Zoramites became Lamanites" (Alma 43:4). Before their defection, Nephite leaders rightly feared that the Zoramites might enter into an alliance with the Lamanites, thus placing the Nephite nation at risk (see Alma 31:4). In order to prevent this mass defection, Alma led a mission to reclaim the Zoramites, many of whom had already abandoned the true faith. Even though some of the Zoramites were restored to the faith, the majority were angry and "began to mix with the Lamanites and to stir them up" in preparation for war (Alma 35:10–11). Lamanite war leaders appointed the more bloodthirsty Zoramites and Amalekites as chief captains in an effort to gain an advantage over the Nephites.

"The Zoramites . . . invited the Lamanite hordes to move in and occupy their country as the first major move against the Nephites (Alma 43:5). At their head came the Lamanite commander-in-chief, the Amalekite Zerahemnah. The Amalekites were Nephite dissenters of an earlier day, and like most dissenters were more bitter against the Nephites and 'of a more wicked and murderous disposition than the Lamanites were' (Alma 43:6). Zerahemnah had seen to it that all the key commands in the army had gone to Amalekites like himself or to equally ferocious Zoramites (Alma 43:6)" (Hugh Nibley, *Since Cumorah,* 2nd ed. [1988], 296).

Alma 43:13–14. Outnumbered and Compelled to Stand against Their Enemy

• The number of Nephite dissenters who became Lamanites was almost as large as the number of Nephites who remained true (see Alma 43:14). This large number, combined with the Lamanite armies, placed the Nephites at a serious numerical disadvantage (see Alma 43:51; see also Mosiah 25:3; Alma 2:27, 35). Relying on their faith, however, the Nephites trusted that God would strengthen them during their battles against overwhelming odds, just as He had done for Gideon's army (see Judges 7–9), Elisha (see 2 Kings 6:15–23), King Benjamin (see Words of Mormon 1:14), and Alma (see Alma 2:27–35).

Alma 43:15–54. Captain Moroni Used Faith and Strategy to Defend the Nephites

• During his service as chief captain, Moroni relied on his strengths and the Lord's power to defend the Nephites. Alma 43 is an example of how Captain Moroni blended his good judgment with his obedience to God's counsel. He prepared each soldier with improved military armor (see vv. 19–21), and he sought the prophet's advice before entering battle (see vv. 23–24).

"The Lamanite campaign was directed by Amalekite and Zoramite officers, whose knowledge of Nephite military secrets and methods would have given them an enormous advantage over any commander but Moroni. Right at the outset his foresight had robbed them of their first and logical objective—the buffer land of Jershon (Alma 43:22). He had taken up his main defensive position there, but when the messengers returned from consulting the prophet he learned that the Lamanites were planning a surprise by directing their push against the more inaccessible but weaker land of Manti, where they would not be expected (Alma 43:24). Immediately Moroni moved his main army into Manti and put the people there in a state of preparedness (Alma 43:25–26).

"Informed of every Lamanite move by his spies and scouts, Moroni was able to lay a trap for the enemy, catching them off-guard as they were fording the river Sidon (Alma 43:28–35)" (Hugh Nibley, *Since Cumorah,* 297–98).

Captain Moroni expected the blessings of the Lord because he had given his best efforts. He was perhaps the brightest military mind of his day, and yet he showed humility by following the prophet's counsel. This made Captain Moroni a mighty instrument in the hand of God.

Alma 43:18–22, 37–38. What Protective Armor Do We Have Today?

• Captain Moroni provided his army with protective armor, which made a significant difference in the battles against their enemies (see Alma 43:37–38). President Harold B. Lee (1899–1973) explained one way that we could apply these verses to our lives today:

"We have the four parts of the body that the Apostle Paul said or saw to be the most vulnerable to the powers of darkness. The loins, typifying virtue, chastity. The heart typifying our conduct. Our feet, our goals or objectives in life and finally our head, our thoughts.

". . . We should have our loins girt about with truth. What is truth? Truth, the Lord said, was knowledge of things as they are, things as they were and things as they are to come [D&C 93:24]. . . . 'Our loins shall be girt about with truth,' the prophet said.

"And the heart, what kind of a breastplate shall protect our conduct in life? We shall have over our hearts a breastplate of righteousness. Well, having learned truth we have a measure by which we can judge between right and wrong and so our conduct will always be gauged by that thing which we know to be true. Our breastplate to cover our conduct shall be the breastplate of righteousness.

"[By] what shall we protect our feet, or by what shall we gauge our objectives or our goals in life? . . . 'Your feet should be shod with the preparation of the gospel of peace.' (Ephesians 6:15). . . .

"And then finally the helmet of salvation. . . . What is salvation? Salvation is to be saved. Saved from what? Saved from death and saved from sin. . . .

"Well, now the Apostle Paul . . . had his armoured man holding in his hand a shield and in his other hand a sword, which were the weapons of those days. That shield was the shield of faith and the sword was

the sword of the spirit which is the Word of God. I can't think of any more powerful weapons than faith and a knowledge of the scriptures in the which are contained the Word of God. One so armoured and one so prepared with those weapons is prepared to go out against the enemy" (*Feet Shod with the Preparation of the Gospel of Peace,* Brigham Young University Speeches of the Year [Nov. 9, 1954], 2–3, 6–7; see also Ephesians 6:13–17; D&C 27:15–18).

ALMA 43:23–25
Why did Captain Moroni seek counsel from the prophet? In what ways can we seek counsel from the prophet?

Alma 43:23–25. Obeying the Prophet Brings Blessings

• Captain Moroni's desire to seek and follow the prophet's counsel led to many victories. Life's battles today will also be won by following the prophet.

President Spencer W. Kimball (1895–1985) emphasized why we need to follow the prophets: "Let us harken to those we sustain as prophets and seers, as well as the other brethren as if our eternal life depended upon it, because it does!" (in Conference Report, Apr. 1978, 117; or *Ensign,* May 1978, 77).

Alma 43:45–47. "Even unto Bloodshed"

• Human life is sacred. Taking an innocent life is "an abomination in the sight of the Lord" (Alma 39:5). One may justifiably take another's life, however, when defending oneself, family, freedom, religion, or country. President Gordon B. Hinckley helped explain the concept of war and bloodshed:

"When war raged between the Nephites and the Lamanites, the record states that 'the Nephites were inspired by a better cause, for they were not fighting for . . . power but they were fighting for their homes and their liberties, their wives and their children, and their all, yea, for their rites of worship and their church.

"'And they were doing that which they felt was the duty which they owed to their God' (Alma 43:45–46).

"The Lord counseled them, 'Defend your families even unto bloodshed' (Alma 43:47). . . .

"It is clear from these and other writings that there are times and circumstances when nations are justified, in fact have an obligation, to fight for family, for liberty, and against tyranny, threat, and oppression. . . .

". . . We are a freedom-loving people, committed to the defense of liberty wherever it is in jeopardy. I believe that God will not hold men and women in uniform responsible as agents of their government in carrying forward that which they are legally obligated to do. It may even be that He will hold us responsible if we try to impede or hedge up the way of those who are involved in a contest with forces of evil and repression" (in Conference Report, Apr. 2003, 83–84; or *Ensign*, May 2003, 80).

Alma 43:54; 44:1–2; 48:11, 22–23. Moroni "Did Not Delight in Bloodshed"

• Captain Moroni "did not delight in bloodshed" (Alma 48:11) even though he was justified in taking another person's life while defending his country. He reluctantly fought the Lamanites for many years (see Alma 48:22). When he did fight, he maintained charity for all, including those on the opposing side. The record states that Captain Moroni stopped the battle on more than one occasion in order to spare as many lives as possible (see Alma 43:54–44:1–2; 55:19). Lives were taken reluctantly and with sorrow that "their

brethren [were sent] out of this world . . . unprepared to meet their God" (Alma 48:23). Captain Moroni firmly believed that those who kept their covenants with God and met with death would be "redeemed by the Lord Jesus Christ" and leave this "world rejoicing" (Alma 46:39).

Some readers may wonder how a man concerned with keeping the covenants of the Lord could be so involved in military affairs. This concern may be why Mormon wrote that Moroni "did not delight in bloodshed" and was taught "never to raise the sword except it were against an enemy, except it were to preserve their lives" (Alma 48:11, 14).

Alma 45 Insert. "Account of the People of Nephi"

• The italic insert before the summary of Alma 45 is part of the original record (for a more detailed explanation, see commentary for The First Book of Nephi: His Reign and Ministry on p. 12). The phrase "comprising chapters 45 to 62 inclusive" was added when the Book of Mormon was published in chapter format in the 1879 edition.

Alma 45:17–19. Alma Departed and "Was Never Heard of More"

• Elder Bruce R. McConkie (1915–85) of the Quorum of the Twelve Apostles explained that the phrase "taken up by the Spirit, or buried by the hand of the Lord" (Alma 45:19) suggests that Alma was translated: "Moses, Elijah, and Alma the younger, were translated. The Old Testament account that Moses died and was buried by the hand of the Lord in an unknown grave is an error. (Deut. 34:5–7.) It is true that he may have been 'buried by the hand of the Lord,' if that expression is a figure of speech which means that he was translated. But the Book of Mormon account, in recording that Alma 'was taken up by the Spirit,' says, 'the scriptures saith the Lord took Moses unto himself; and we suppose that he has also received Alma in the spirit, unto himself.' (Alma 45:18–19.) It should be remembered that the Nephites had the Brass Plates, and that they were the 'scriptures' which gave the account of Moses being taken by way of translation. As to Elijah, the account of his being taken in 'a chariot of fire . . . by a whirlwind into heaven,' is majestically set out in the Old Testament. (2 Kings 2.)" (*Mormon Doctrine,* 2nd ed. [1966], 805).

Alma 46–50. The Contrast between Wicked and Righteous Leadership

• Mormon plainly exposed the striking differences between Amalickiah and Captain Moroni (see Alma 48:7; 49:25–28). Amalickiah wanted to "destroy the foundation of liberty which God had granted" to the Nephites, and Captain Moroni wanted to preserve it (Alma 46:10).

Wicked men like Amalickiah who thrust themselves into power may prosper for a season by the world's standards, but they ultimately bring ruin upon themselves and their followers. By contrast, leaders like Captain Moroni inspire people with noble desires that will ultimately overpower evil designs. The following chart contrasts Moroni and Amalickiah:

Captain Moroni	Amalickiah
Was appointed by "the voice of the people" and the judges as chief captain of the armies (Alma 46:34; see also 43:16).	Obtained power by fraud and deceit (see Alma 47:1–35; 48:7).
Rallied the people to righteousness and taught them to be faithful to God and their covenants (see Alma 46:12–21; 48:7).	Incited the people through hatred and propaganda (see Alma 48:1–3).
Rejoiced in the liberty and freedom of his country and the people (see Alma 48:11).	Sought to destroy the liberty of the people (see Alma 46:10).
Loved his brethren and labored "exceedingly for the welfare and safety of his people" (Alma 48:12).	"Did care not for the blood of his people" and worked to promote his own selfishness (Alma 49:10).
A man governed by righteous principles who taught the Nephites to never raise the sword, except to defend one's family, life, or freedoms (see Alma 48:10, 14).	A man governed by passion who taught the people to aggressively conquer and make oaths to destroy (see Alma 49:13, 26–27).

Captain Moroni	Amalickiah
Humbly sought God's help in preserving life (see Alma 48:16).	Cursed God and swore to kill (see Alma 49:27).
Worked to put an end to contention and dissension (see Alma 51:16).	Worked to create contention and dissension (see Alma 46:6, 10).

ALMA 46:12–13

Why is it a solemn duty to defend our homes, freedoms, and religious rights? How can we defend our homes against the forces of evil?

Alma 46:12–15, 36. The Title of Liberty

• Rallying others for a righteous cause takes courage. President Ezra Taft Benson often taught concerning the importance of Captain Moroni's actions in raising the title of liberty. He frequently emphasized the need to be an active citizen and promote liberty and freedom: "Improve your community by active participation and service. Remember in your civic responsibility that 'the only thing necessary for the triumph of evil is for good men to do nothing' (Edmund Burke). . . . Do something meaningful in defense of your God-given freedom and liberty" (in Conference Report, Apr. 1988, 58; or *Ensign,* May 1988, 51).

© Clark Kelley Price

President Benson further taught:

"In that sacred volume of scripture, the Book of Mormon, we note the great and prolonged struggle for liberty. We also note the complacency of the people and their frequent willingness to give up their liberty for the promises of a would-be provider. . . .

". . . Moroni, like the prophets whose words are recorded in the Book of Mormon, spoke of the

Americas as a chosen land—the land of liberty. He led the people in battle who were willing to fight to 'maintain their liberty.'

"And the record states: '. . . that he caused the title of liberty to be hoisted upon every tower which was in all the land, . . . and thus Moroni planted the standard of liberty among the Nephites.' [Alma 46:36.]

"This is our need today—to plant the standard of liberty among our people throughout the Americas.

"While this incident occurred some seventy years B.C., the struggle went on through one thousand years covered by this sacred Book of Mormon record. In fact, the struggle for liberty is a continuing one—it is with us in a very real sense today" (in Conference Report, Oct. 1962, 14–15).

Alma 46:23–27. The Prophecy of Joseph's Coat

• The torn coat of Moroni—the title of liberty—was a reminder of the preserved remnant of the coat of Joseph of Egypt. Moroni declared that the Nephites

were a remnant of the seed of Joseph and would only continue to be preserved as long as they served God (see Alma 46:22–24). President Joseph Fielding Smith (1876–1972) commented on the symbolism and prophecy regarding the preserved part of Joseph's coat being fulfilled in our day:

© 1994 Robert Barrett

"We are told that there was a prophecy in the destruction of the coat of many colors worn by Joseph. Part of it was preserved, and Jacob, before his death, prophesied that as a remnant of the coat was preserved so should a remnant of Joseph's posterity be preserved [see Alma 46:24].

"That remnant now found among the Lamanites shall eventually partake of the blessings of the Gospel. They shall unite with the remnant which is being gathered from among the nations and they shall be blessed of the Lord forever" (*The Way to Perfection* [1970], 121).

Alma 47:36. Dissension and Contention

• The Book of Mormon repeatedly warns that those who belong to the Church and then "dissent" become hard in their hearts and are apt to "entirely [forget] the Lord their God" (Alma 47:36).

Elder Neal A. Maxwell (1926–2004) of the Quorum of the Twelve Apostles warned that the same problems exist today when dissenters become critical of the Church due to their own pride: "There are the dissenters who leave the Church, either formally or informally, but who cannot leave it alone. Usually anxious to please worldly galleries, they are critical or at least condescending towards the Brethren. They not only seek to steady the ark but also on occasion give it a hard shove! Often having been taught the same true doctrines as the faithful, they have nevertheless moved in the direction of dissent (see Alma 47:36). They have minds hardened by pride (see Daniel 5:20)" (*Men and Women of Christ* [1991], 4).

• Elder Russell M. Nelson of the Quorum of the Twelve Apostles described the consequences of contention and dissension:

"'He that hath the spirit of contention is not of me [saith the Lord]' . . . (3 Nephi 11:29–30). . . .

"Throughout the world, Saints of the Lord . . . have learned that the path of dissent leads to real dangers. The Book of Mormon carries this warning:

"'. . . not long after their dissensions they became more hardened and impenitent, and more wild, wicked and ferocious . . . ; giving way to indolence, and all manner of lasciviousness; yea, entirely forgetting the Lord their God' (Alma 47:36).

"How divisive is the force of dissension! Small acts can lead to such great consequences. Regardless of position or situation, no one can safely assume immunity to contention's terrible toll. . . .

"Contention fosters disunity" (in Conference Report, Apr. 1989, 86–88; or *Ensign*, May 1989, 68, 70).

Alma 48:1–10. Make a Stand for Christian Principles

• Sometimes true followers of Christ must stand as Moroni's people stood in defense of "their liberty, their lands, their wives, and their children, and their peace" (Alma 48:10). Moroni was intent on helping his people "maintain that which was called by their enemies the cause of Christians" (Alma 48:10).

With the tide of wickedness in the world today, President Gordon B. Hinckley has advocated that "there are times when we must stand up for right and decency, for freedom and civilization, just as Moroni rallied his people in his day to the defense of their wives, their children, and the cause of liberty (see Alma 48:10)" (in Conference Report, Oct. 2001, 88; or *Ensign,* Nov. 2001, 72).

> **ALMA 48:10–18**
> *What qualities made Captain Moroni a successful leader?*

Alma 48:19. "No Less Serviceable"

• What does it mean that Helaman was "no less serviceable"? President Howard W. Hunter (1907–95) taught that all righteous service is equally acceptable to God even though not everyone will serve in prominent callings:

"Even though Helaman was not as noticeable or conspicuous as Moroni, he was as serviceable; that is, he was as helpful or useful as Moroni. . . .

"Not all of us are going to be like Moroni, catching the acclaim of our colleagues all day every day. Most of us will be quiet, relatively unknown folks who come and go and do our work without fanfare. To those of you who may find that lonely or frightening or just unspectacular, I say, you are 'no less serviceable' than the most spectacular of your associates. You, too, are part of God's army.

"Consider, for example, the profound service a mother or father gives in the quiet anonymity of a worthy Latter-day Saint home. Think of the Gospel Doctrine teachers and Primary choristers and Scoutmasters and Relief Society visiting teachers who serve and bless millions but whose names will never be publicly applauded or featured in the nation's media.

"Tens of thousands of unseen people make possible our opportunities and happiness every day. As the scriptures state, they are 'no less serviceable' than those whose lives are on the front pages of newspapers.

"The limelight of history and contemporary attention so often focuses on the *one* rather than on the *many*" ("No Less Serviceable," *Ensign,* Apr. 1992, 64).

Alma 49–50. Fortification of Nephite Cities

• Moroni's inspiration and foresight in fortifying the cities proved to be a turning point in the war. Thousands of Nephites were preserved because the cities were prepared. We can apply this lesson by fortifying our own lives with righteous thoughts and deeds in order to withstand evil attacks or "fiery darts of the adversary" (1 Nephi 15:24; see also Helaman 5:12 📖). The Lord has promised that if we humbly seek Him, then He will show us our weakness and will "make weak things become strong" (Ether 12:27 📖). The following chart lists some examples of how the fortifications of the Nephites could apply to us:

How the Nephites Were Fortified	How We Can Fortify
The weaker fortifications were strengthened (see Alma 48:9).	We must strengthen the weak spots in our lives.
The Nephites prepared for the enemy in a manner never before known (see Alma 49:8).	We must prepare as never before to stand against the wiles of the devil.
The Nephites made their weaker cities into strongholds (see Alma 49:14).	If we come unto Christ, He can make weak things become strong to us (see Ether 12:27).
The Nephites were given power over their enemies (see Alma 49:23).	If we are faithful and trust the Lord, He will give us power over our enemies.

How the Nephites Were Fortified	How We Can Fortify
After some Nephite victories, they did not stop in their preparations (Alma 50:1).	When we have successfully overcome a temptation or trial, we must not let our guard down, but continue to endure and watch and pray always to not be overcome (see Alma 13:28).
The Nephites built security towers so they could see the enemy afar off (see Alma 50:4).	As we rely on prophets who are modern watchmen on the tower and see afar off, we will be better prepared for the future.

Alma 51:13. Take Up Arms to Defend One's Country

• As citizens we are subject to the governing laws of our country. Elder Russell M. Nelson offered the following counsel when faced with the duty of taking up arms to defend one's country:

"Men really are brothers because God really is our Father. Nevertheless, scriptures are studded with stories of contention and combat. They strongly condemn wars of aggression but sustain obligations of citizens to defend their families and their freedoms [see Alma 43:45–47; 46:11–12, 19–20; 48:11–16]. . . . Members of this Church will be called into military service of many nations. 'We believe that governments were instituted of God for the benefit of man; and that he

holds men accountable for their acts in relation to them, both in making laws and administering them, for the good and safety of society' [D&C 134:1].

"During the Second World War, when members of the Church were forced to fight on opposing sides, the First Presidency affirmed that 'the state is responsible for the civil control of its citizens or subjects, for their political welfare, and for the carrying forward of political policies, domestic and foreign. . . . But the Church itself, as such, has no responsibility for these policies, [other] than urging its members fully to render . . . loyalty to their country' [in James R. Clark, comp., *Messages of the First Presidency of The Church of Jesus Christ of Latter-day Saints,* 6 vols. (1965–75), 6:155–56]" (in Conference Report, Oct. 2002, 42; or *Ensign,* Nov. 2002, 40).

Points to Ponder

• What would you include in a list of the most important spiritual fortifications you need to be safe from the enemy who seeks your destruction?

• In what ways can Latter-day Saint soldiers serve like Captain Moroni during times of war?

• What impact can a valiant leader have on a country, state, community, or family?

Suggested Assignments

• Since not all of us will be preeminent like Moroni, describe the valuable service given by mothers and fathers. In addition, describe the importance of a Sunday School teacher, Primary chorister, Scoutmaster, a Relief Society visiting teacher, or a Church calling of your choice.

• Write down some of the weak areas in your life and your plans to "fortify" them against wickedness.

Introduction

President Ezra Taft Benson (1899–1994) observed, "From the Book of Mormon we learn how disciples of Christ live in times of war" (in Conference Report, Oct. 1986, 5; or *Ensign,* Nov. 1986, 7). Mormon included several accounts of war in the Book of Mormon for a purpose. These accounts teach about the need to preserve freedom in order to maintain religious rights, the damage traitors inflict, the value of even a few righteous youth, the moral justification for war, and strategies to combat evil while relying upon God's power to intervene.

Commentary

Alma 52–53. War and Bloodshed

• Alma 52–53 are a verification of the Savior's statement that "all they that take the sword shall perish with the sword" (Matthew 26:52). Led by wicked and apostate Nephites (Ammoron and others), the Lamanites sought to violently capture and maintain Nephite cities. Each city was taken at a high price, however: "They had not taken any cities save they had lost much blood" (Alma 52:4). Captain Moroni was always reluctant to take up the sword and far more eager to lay it down for peace (see Alma 52:37). He knew that even when the Nephites were victorious, it cost thousands of lives on both sides.

War would never occur if all people were living the gospel of Jesus Christ. He is the Prince of Peace, and those who follow Him are emissaries of peace.

ALMA 53:9

What caused the Nephites to be placed in dangerous circumstances? What could they have done to avoid such circumstances?

Alma 53:9. Iniquity—The Real Cause of Conflict

• One commentator explained how external trials such as the Nephites endured can sometimes point to internal needs: "So it was a blessing to the Nephites after all to have the Lamanites on their doorstep to 'stir them up to remembrance'—'Happy is the man whom

God correcteth' (Job 5:17). No matter how wicked and ferocious and depraved the Lamanites might be (and they were that!), no matter by how much they outnumbered the Nephites, darkly closing in on all sides, no matter how insidiously they spied and intrigued and infiltrated and hatched their diabolical plots and breathed their bloody threats and pushed their formidable preparations for all-out war, *they were not the Nephite problem.* They were merely kept there to remind the Nephites of their real problem, which was to walk uprightly before the Lord" (Hugh Nibley, *Since Cumorah,* 2nd ed. [1988], 339–40).

Alma 53:10–18. The Importance of Covenants

• Elder M. Russell Ballard of the Quorum of the Twelve Apostles shared how we gain power through keeping our covenants: "Sometimes we are tempted to let our lives be governed more by convenience than by covenant. It is not always convenient to live gospel standards and stand up for truth and testify of the Restoration. . . . But there is no spiritual power in living by convenience. The power comes as we keep our covenants" (in Conference Report, Apr. 1999, 113; or *Ensign,* May 1999, 86).

• President Boyd K. Packer, President of the Quorum of the Twelve Apostles, explained that keeping covenants keeps us safe:

"Keep your covenants and you will be safe. Break them and you will not. . . .

". . . We are not free to break our covenants and escape the consequences" (in Conference Report, Oct. 1990, 107–8; or *Ensign,* Nov. 1990, 84).

Alma 53:16–21. The Example of the Stripling Warriors

• The stripling warriors, who went to battle in place of their fathers, were young men of righteousness. They were committed to defending their country (see Alma 56:5). They were fearless in the face of death and courageous in battle (see Alma 56:45–49, 56). God rewarded their faith with amazing strength and protection. Not one of them died in battle (see Alma 57:25–26). This is not always the case with righteous young men in military service. Sometimes even the righteous "die in the Lord" (D&C 63:49). But in the case of these young men, divine protection was given that preserved their mortal lives in battle. They exemplified the type of manhood that all of God's sons should emulate and stood as a witness to the Nephite nation that God would deliver them if they were faithful.

© Clark Kelley Price

Alma 53:20–21. Being Good Examples in Military Service

• In modern times, the First Presidency has given the following counsel to Church members in military service: "To our young men who go into service, no matter whom they serve or where, we say live clean, keep the commandments of the Lord, pray to Him constantly to preserve you in truth and righteousness, live as you pray, and then whatever betides you the Lord will be with you and nothing will happen to you that will not be to the honor and glory of God and to your salvation and exaltation. There will come into your hearts from the living of the pure life you pray for, a joy that will pass your powers of expression or understanding. The Lord will be always near you; He will comfort you; you will feel His presence in the hour of your greatest tribulation; He will guard and protect you to the full extent that accords with His all-wise purpose. Then, when the conflict is over and you return to your homes, having lived the righteous life, how great will be your happiness—whether you be of the victors or of the vanquished—that you have lived as the Lord commanded. You will return so disciplined in righteousness that thereafter all Satan's wiles and stratagems will leave you untouched. Your faith and testimony will be strong beyond breaking. You will be looked up to and revered as having passed through the fiery furnace of trial and temptation and come forth unharmed. Your brethren will look to you for counsel,

support, and guidance. You will be the anchors to which thereafter the youth of Zion will moor their faith in man" (Heber J. Grant, J. Reuben Clark Jr., and David O. McKay, in Conference Report, Apr. 1942, 96).

Alma 53:20–21. "True at All Times"

• Elder Dallin H. Oaks of the Quorum of the Twelve Apostles discussed what it means to be true at all times:

"That word *true* implies commitment, integrity, endurance, and courage. It reminds us of the Book of Mormon's description of the 2,000 young warriors:

"[Alma 53:20–21.]

"In the spirit of that description I say to our returned missionaries—men and women who have made covenants to serve the Lord and who have already served Him in the great work of proclaiming the gospel and perfecting the Saints—are you being true to the faith? Do you have the faith and continuing commitment to demonstrate the principles of the gospel in your own lives, consistently? You have served well, but do you, like the pioneers, have the courage and the consistency to be true to the faith and to endure to the end?" (in Conference Report, Oct. 1997, 101–2; or *Ensign,* Nov. 1997, 73; italics added).

Alma 56:45–48. "We Do Not Doubt Our Mothers Knew It"

• Elder Neal A. Maxwell (1926–2004) of the Quorum of the Twelve Apostles explained that parents can only give what they themselves already have:

"When a parent's teaching and helping job is done well and when there are receptive children to receive the message, then we encounter those marvelous situations such as the one involving young men in the Book of Mormon who had been  taught so well by their mothers [Alma 56:47–48]. . . .

"The reliance, of course, by these young men on their mothers is touching and profound, but the mothers first had to know 'it' in such a way that the young men, observing them closely and hearing them (as is always the case with children observing parents), did 'not doubt' that their mothers knew that 'it' was true" (*That My Family Should Partake* [1974], 58–59).

• Speaking of the need for women to have more vigilance, Sister Julie B. Beck, Relief Society general president, described covenant women who know who they are:

"In the Book of Mormon we read about 2,000 exemplary young men who were exceedingly valiant, courageous, and strong. 'Yea, they were men of truth and soberness, for they had been taught to keep the commandments of God and to walk uprightly before him' (Alma 53:21). These faithful young men paid tribute to their mothers. They said, 'Our mothers knew it' (Alma 56:48). . . .

"The responsibility mothers have today has never required more vigilance. More than at any time in the history of the world, we need mothers who know. . . . When mothers know who they are and who God is and have made covenants with Him, they will have great power and influence for good on their children" (in Conference Report, Oct. 2007, 80; or *Ensign,* Nov. 2007, 76).

Alma 57:19–21. "Firm and Undaunted"

• President Gordon B. Hinckley (1910–2008) discussed the importance of staying firm and undaunted:

" 'You reflect this Church in all you think, in all you say, and in all you do,' President Hinckley told the youth. 'Be loyal to the Church and kingdom of God.' . . .

"President Hinckley told the youth that they are 'out there as the sons of Helaman in a world that is full of destructive influences. . . . But if you put your trust in the Almighty and follow the teachings of this Church and cling to it notwithstanding your wounds, you will be preserved and blessed and magnified and made happy.'

"Speaking of the world in which they live, President Hinckley told the youth, 'You're in the midst of Babylon. The adversary comes with great destruction. Stand above it, you of the noble birthright. Stand above it' " ("Prophet Grateful for Gospel, Testimony," *Church News,* Sept. 21, 1996, 4).

Alma 58. The Right to Fight for Liberty

• For an insight on fighting for liberty even among bloodshed, see the commentary for Alma 43:45–47 on page 250.

Alma 58:10–11. The Lord Spoke "Peace to Our Souls"

• While serving as a member of the Seventy, Elder Dennis E. Simmons explained that God's peace is not dependent on outward circumstances:

"If all the world is crumbling around us, the promised Comforter will provide His peace as a result of true discipleship. . . . We can have His peace with us irrespective of the troubles of the world. *His* peace is that peace, that serenity, that comfort spoken to our hearts and minds by the Comforter, the Holy Ghost, as we strive to follow *Him* and keep *His* commandments. . . .

"Just as Helaman discovered in the midst of battle that 'he did speak peace to our souls' (Alma 58:11) . . . , all sincere seekers can have that same peace spoken to them. That peace comes from the assurances spoken by a still, small voice" (in Conference Report, Apr. 1997, 41–42; or *Ensign,* May 1997, 31).

> **ALMA 58:10–11**
> *What was the result of the Nephites' prayer of faith? How can these answers apply in our struggle for deliverance?*

Alma 58:34–37. "We Do Not Desire to Murmur"

• Elder Neal A. Maxwell helped us better understand a cause of murmuring: "In a happy day ahead, 'They that murmured shall learn doctrine' (Isaiah 29:24; 2 Nephi 27:35). This suggests that doctrinal illiteracy is a significant cause of murmuring among Church members" ("A Choice Seer," in *Brigham Young University 1985–86 Devotional and Fireside Speeches* [1986], 115).

Alma 59:9. Easier to Keep a City from Falling

• Mormon records that it is far easier to keep a city from falling than to retake it (Alma 59:9). As with cities, so it is with people. It is much more difficult and dangerous to reclaim one who has fallen than to help keep them from falling. In the words of President Ezra Taft Benson (1899–1994), "It is better to prepare and prevent, than to repair and repent" (*The Teachings of Ezra Taft Benson* [1988], 285).

Minerva K. Teichert, Courtesy of BYU Museum of Art

Alma 59:11–12. Cities Lost Because of Wickedness

• The loss of the city of Nephihah illustrates the strong correlation between the wickedness of the Nephites and their inability to defeat their enemies in the "strength of the Lord" (see Mosiah 9:16; 10:10–11; Alma 60:16). The leaders of the Nephite armies were often men who "had the spirit of revelation and also prophecy" (3 Nephi 3:19). These righteous military leaders attributed Nephite defeats not to the Lamanites but to Nephite wickedness. By contrast, faithful Nephites were usually able to defend themselves and recover lost cities, often with relatively minimal loss of life (see Alma 52:19; 56:53–56; 57:7–12; 58:25–28; 62:22–26). The Lord has repeatedly taught that while we may face difficulties and serious problems, if we are righteous and rely on Him, we can always have confidence that He will be with us and His work will ultimately prevail (see D&C 6:34; 10:69; 33:13).

Alma 60:10–14. The Slaying of the Righteous

• Moroni wrote that the Lord permits the righteous to be slain so that "his justice and judgment may come upon the wicked; therefore ye need not suppose that the righteous are lost because they are slain; but behold, they do enter into the rest of the Lord their God" (Alma 60:13).

Soon after the beginning of World War II, the First Presidency of the Church stated: "In this terrible war now waging, thousands of our righteous young men in all parts of the world and in many countries are subject to a call into the military service of their own countries. Some of these, so serving, have already been called back to their heavenly home; others will almost surely be called to follow. But 'behold,' as Moroni said, the righteous of them who serve and are slain 'do enter into the rest of the Lord their God' [Alma 60:13], and of them the Lord has said 'those that die in me shall not taste of death, for it shall be sweet unto them' (D.&C. 42:46). Their salvation and exaltation in the world to come will be secure. That in their work of destruction they will be striking at their brethren will not be held against them. That sin, as Moroni of old said, is to the condemnation of those who 'sit in their places of power in a state of thoughtless stupor,' those rulers in the world who in a frenzy of hate and lust for unrighteous power and dominion over their fellow men, have put into motion eternal forces they do not comprehend and cannot control. God, in His own due time, will pass sentence upon them" (Heber J. Grant, J. Reuben Clark Jr., and David O. McKay, in Conference Report, Apr. 1942, 95–96).

Alma 60:19–36. Moroni's Letter to Pahoran

• Pahoran could have chosen to be offended by the letters sent by Moroni, but he did not. Elder David A. Bednar of the Quorum of the Twelve Apostles described the fact that we, like Pahoran, can choose to not be offended:

"When we believe or say that we have been offended, we usually mean we feel insulted, mistreated, snubbed, or disrespected. And certainly clumsy, embarrassing, unprincipled, and mean-spirited things do occur in our interactions with other people that would allow us to take offense. However, it ultimately is impossible for another person to offend you or to offend me. Indeed, believing that another person offended us is fundamentally false. To be offended is a *choice* we make; it is not a *condition* inflicted or imposed upon us by someone or something else. . . .

"Through the strengthening power of the Atonement of Jesus Christ, you and I can be blessed to avoid and triumph over offense. 'Great peace have they which love thy law: and nothing shall offend them' (Psalm 119:165). . . .

". . . As described by Elder Neal A. Maxwell, the Church is not 'a well-provisioned rest home for the already perfected' (in Conference Report, Apr. 1982, 57; or *Ensign*, May 1982, 38). Rather, the Church is a learning laboratory and a workshop in which we gain experience as we practice on each other in the ongoing process of 'perfecting the Saints.'

"Elder Maxwell also insightfully explained that in this latter-day learning laboratory known as the restored Church, the members constitute the 'clinical material' (see 'Jesus, the Perfect Mentor,' *Ensign*, Feb. 2001, 13) that is essential for growth and development. . . .

"You and I cannot control the intentions or behavior of other people. However, we do determine how we will act. Please remember that you and I are agents endowed with moral agency, and we can choose not to be offended" (in Conference Report, Oct. 2006, 95–97; or *Ensign*, Nov. 2006, 90–91).

Alma 60:23. Cleansing the Inner Vessel

• President Ezra Taft Benson left little room for doubt that these warnings apply to us. He declared: "All is not well in Zion. As Moroni counseled, we must cleanse the inner vessel (see Alma 60:23), beginning first with ourselves, then with our families, and finally with the Church" (in Conference Report, Apr. 1986, 3, or *Ensign*, May 1986, 4).

ALMA 60:23

You may want to mark this verse. Then ask yourself what things you must do to cleanse your inner vessel.

Alma 61. Response to Unjustified Scolding

• Elder Neal A. Maxwell explained how differences can occur even between faithful members: "In a perfect church filled with imperfect people, there are bound to be some miscommunications at times. A noteworthy example occurred in ancient American

Israel. Moroni wrote two times to Pahoran complaining of neglect because much-needed reinforcements did not arrive. Moroni used harsh language, accusing the governor of the land, Pahoran, of sitting on his throne in a state of 'thoughtless stupor.' (Alma 60:7.) Pahoran soon made a very patriotic reply, explaining why he could not do what Moroni wanted. Though censured, Pahoran was not angry; he even praised Moroni for 'the greatness of your heart.' (Alma 61:9.) Given the intense, mutual devotion of disciples, discussions as to how best to move the Lord's work along are bound to produce tactical differences on occasion. Just as in this episode, sometimes scolding occurs that is later shown to be unjustified" (*All These Things Shall Give Thee Experience* [1979], 119).

Alma 62:41. The Effects of Adversity

• Elder Dallin H. Oaks explained that we choose how we will be affected by adversity:

"Surely these great adversities are not without some eternal purpose or effect. They can turn our hearts to God. . . . Even as adversities inflict mortal hardships, they can also be the means of leading men and women to eternal blessings.

"Such large-scale adversities as natural disasters and wars seem to be inherent in the mortal experience. We cannot entirely prevent them, but we can determine how we will react to them. For example, the adversities of war and military service, which have been the spiritual destruction of some, have been the spiritual awakening of others. The Book of Mormon describes the contrast:

"'But behold, because of the exceedingly great length of the war between the Nephites and the Lamanites many had become hardened, because of the exceedingly great length of the war; and many were softened because of their afflictions, insomuch that they did humble themselves before God, even in the depth of humility' (Alma 62:41).

"I read of a similar contrast after the devastating hurricane that destroyed thousands of homes in Florida some years ago. A news account quoted two different persons who had suffered the same tragedy and received the same blessing: each of their homes had been totally destroyed, but each of their family members had been spared death or injury. One said that this tragedy had destroyed his faith; how, he asked, could God allow this to happen? The other said that the experience had strengthened his faith. God had been good to him, he said. Though the family's home and possessions were lost, their lives were spared and they could rebuild the home. For one, the glass was half empty. For the other, the glass was half full. The gift of moral agency empowers each of us to choose how we will act when we suffer adversity" ("Adversity," *Ensign,* July 1998, 7–8).

Alma 63:4–10. Journey to the Land Northward

• "To [a] group of Saints in the South Seas, President [Spencer W.] Kimball observed: 'President Joseph F. Smith, the president of the Church, reported, "You brothers and sisters from New Zealand, I want you to know that you are from the people of Hagoth." For New Zealand Saints, that was that. A prophet of the Lord had spoken. . . . It is reasonable to conclude that Hagoth and his associates were about nineteen centuries on the islands, from about 55 B.C. to 1854 before the gospel began to reach them. They had lost all the plain and precious things which the Savior brought to the earth, for they were likely on the islands when the Christ was born in Jerusalem.' (Temple View Area Conference Report, February 1976, p. 3.)" (Joseph Fielding McConkie and Robert L. Millet, *Doctrinal Commentary on the Book of Mormon,* 4 vols. [1987–91] 3:329).

Minerva K. Teichert, Courtesy of BYU Museum of Art

President David O. McKay (1873–1970) substantiated what happened to some of Hagoth's people when he gave the following proclamation in the dedicatory prayer of the New Zealand Temple: "We express gratitude that to these fertile Islands Thou didst guide descendants of Father Lehi, and hast enabled them to prosper" ("Dedicatory Prayer Delivered by Pres. David O. McKay at New Zealand Temple," *Church News,* May 10, 1958, 2).

Points to Ponder

• What can you do to honor, sustain, and defend your country?

• What lessons can we learn from both Moroni's and Pahoran's letters that could help us in our lives? (see Alma 60–61).

• What is the correlation between righteousness and freedom?

• After reading Alma 52–63, what are some of the greatest principles regarding war that you could teach another person?

Suggested Assignments

• Record in your journal how you can apply Moroni's defense tactics in your own personal battles for righteousness.

• You may wish to record the insights discovered about how to defend yourself against the enemies of your faith.

• Write a family home evening lesson outline from one or more of the subjects listed below:

1. Making use of the means the Lord has provided (see Alma 60:21)

2. Cleansing the inner vessel (see Alma 60:23)

3. Seeking God's glory over the honor of the world (see Alma 60:36)

4. Not taking offense (see Alma 61:9)

Chapter 35

Helaman 1–4

Introduction

Helaman 1–4 presents a stark contrast between the fruits of good and evil. We see the results of evil upon society as well as the individual. The personal growth and blessings obtained by Saints who remain faithful in challenging circumstances can provide us with courage to remain true to righteous principles during difficult times. We can contrast the discord brought by wickedness with the great peace and joy obtained by righteousness. Noting these contrasts provides motivation to chart a course based upon principles that will bring happiness and avoid the misery that comes from disobedience.

Commentary

Helaman 1:1–21. Contention Is Destructive

• The book of Helaman recounts a period of great wickedness among the Nephites. The Gadianton robbers thrived and the masses endured several cycles of wickedness and destructions followed by repentance only to return to wickedness. Many of these troubles could be attributed to "contention" that began in the first chapter of Helaman. While some people might consider "contention" to be a rather innocuous sin, the following General Authorities have commented on the dangers of contention.

President James E. Faust (1920–2007) of the First Presidency stated in forthright terms that the Spirit of the Lord cannot abide contention: "When there is contention, the Spirit of the Lord will depart, regardless of who is at fault" (in Conference Report, Apr. 1996, 57; or *Ensign,* May 1996, 41).

• Elder Joseph B. Wirthlin (1917–2008) of the Quorum of the Twelve Apostles explained that contention is purposely fostered by Satan to serve his own evil purposes: "The sins of corruption, dishonesty, strife, contention, and other evils in this world are not here by chance. They are evidences of the relentless campaign of Satan and those who follow him. He uses every tool and device available to him to deceive, confuse, and mislead" (in Conference Report, Oct. 1994, 100; or *Ensign,* Nov. 1994, 76).

• In contrast to the destructive impact of contention, President Henry B. Eyring of the First Presidency

emphasized the unity of the spirit of peace: "Where people have that Spirit with them, we may expect harmony. The Spirit puts the testimony of truth in our hearts, which unifies those who share that testimony. The Spirit of God never generates contention (see 3 Nephi 11:29). It never generates the feelings of distinctions between people which lead to strife (see Joseph F. Smith, *Gospel Doctrine,* 5th ed. [1939], 131). It leads to personal peace and a feeling of union with others. It unifies souls. A unified family, a unified Church, and a world at peace depend on unified souls" (in Conference Report, Apr. 1998, 86; or *Ensign,* May 1998, 67).

HELAMAN 1:27, 33

What contrast do you note between these verses in the way enemies were treated by opposing armies? What accounts for the difference?

Helaman 1–2. Evil Secret Works Can Destroy Societies

• Elder M. Russell Ballard of the Quorum of the Twelve Apostles explained that the threat of secret combinations still exists in our day:

"The Book of Mormon teaches that secret combinations engaged in crime present a serious challenge, not just to individuals and families but to entire civilizations. Among today's secret combinations are gangs, drug cartels, and organized crime families. The secret combinations of our day function much like the Gadianton robbers of the Book of Mormon times. They have secret signs and code words. They participate in secret rites and initiation ceremonies. Among their purposes are to 'murder, and plunder, and steal, and commit whoredoms and all manner of wickedness, contrary to the laws of their country and also the laws of their God' [Helaman 6:23].

"If we are not careful, today's secret combinations can obtain power and influence just as quickly and just as completely as they did in Book of Mormon times. Do you remember the pattern? The secret combinations began among the 'more wicked part' of society, but eventually 'seduced the more part of the righteous' until the whole society was polluted [Helaman 6:38]. . . .

"The Book of Mormon teaches that the devil is the 'author of all sin' and the founder of these secret combinations [Helaman 6:30; see 2 Nephi 26:22]. He uses secret combinations, including gangs, 'from generation to generation according as he can get hold upon the hearts of the children of men' [Helaman 6:30]. His purpose is to destroy individuals, families, communities, and nations [see 2 Nephi 9:9]. To a degree, he was successful during Book of Mormon times. And he is having far too much success today. That's why it is so important for us as priesthood holders to take a firm stand for truth and right by doing what we can to help keep our communities safe" (in Conference Report, Oct. 1997, 51–52; or *Ensign,* Nov. 1997, 38).

Helaman 1–2. Good People Can Help Thwart the Goals of Evil Organizations

• During the general conference following the terrorist attacks on the World Trade Center and the Pentagon, President Gordon B. Hinckley (1910–2008) referred to terrorist organizations determined to foster murder, tyranny, fear, and wicked control:

"Terrorist organizations . . . must be ferreted out and brought down.

"We of this Church know something of such groups. The Book of Mormon speaks of the Gadianton robbers, a vicious, oath-bound, and secret organization bent on evil and destruction. In their day they did all in their power, by whatever means available, to bring down the Church, to woo the people with sophistry, and to take control of the society. We see the same thing in the present situation.

"We are people of peace. We are followers of the Christ, who was and is the Prince of Peace. But there are times when we must stand up for right and decency, for

freedom and civilization, just as Moroni rallied his people in his day to the defense of their wives, their children, and the cause of liberty (see Alma 48:10)" (in Conference Report, Oct. 2001, 88; or *Ensign,* Nov. 2001, 72).

Helaman 3:20. "That Which Was Right in the Sight of God Continually"

• Although times were difficult and society was threatened by evil forces, Helaman's example of steadfastness in doing the Lord's will is a model for us to follow in the challenging latter days. Like Helaman, we can continually strive to "do what is right; let the consequence follow" ("Do What Is Right," *Hymns,* no. 237). The key word is *continually.*

Elder Spencer J. Condie of the Seventy emphasized the importance of keeping our covenants as a way of developing consistency in doing good:

"Perhaps of all the evidence of true conversion and a remission of sins, this is the most significant: *the disposition to do evil no more, but to do good continually.* . . .

"We can strengthen our disposition to do good each time we make and keep covenants. Each time we participate in priesthood ordinances, the powers from on high reach downward and draw us nearer to the heavens. Those who partake of the sacrament and temple ordinances with pure hearts and who faithfully keep their covenants require no lengthy instructions regarding modest dress, the payment of generous fast offerings and tithing, observance of the Word of Wisdom, or keeping the Sabbath day holy. They need no stern reminders to share the gospel with others, to attend the temple frequently, to conduct family history research, or to do their home teaching or visiting teaching. Nor do they need nudges to visit the sick and to serve those in need.

"These are the faithful Saints of the Most High who keep the sacred covenants they have made in the house of the Lord, 'having a determination to serve him to the end, and truly manifest by their works that they have received the Spirit of Christ unto the remission of their sins' (D&C 20:37). Covenant keepers . . . live the law of consecration. Their time, talents, and financial resources all belong to the Lord.

"Keeping their covenants has caused them to develop a disposition to do good continually" ("A Disposition to Do Good Continually," *Ensign,* Aug. 2001, 14, 19).

Helaman 3:24–25. Prosperity in Our Lives and in the Church

• While serving as a member of the Seventy, Elder Dean L. Larsen observed a relationship between faithfulness to the Lord and prosperity:

"When the lives of the people are in harmony with the Lord's will, all of the essential factors that produce the blessings God deigns to give to his children seem to come into line. Love and harmony prevail. Even the weather, the climate, and the elements seem to respond. Peace and tranquility endure. Industry and progress mark the lives of the people. . . .

". . . We have the Lord's assurance that he will bless and prosper his people if they will keep his commandments and remember to look to him as the source of their blessings" (in Conference Report, Oct. 1992, 58–59; or *Ensign,* Nov. 1992, 41–42).

HELAMAN 3:24–26

What insights do we get from these verses about the meaning of "prosperity"? How does this differ from the prosperity the world has to offer?

Helaman 3:29–30. "Lay Hold upon the Word"

• President Ezra Taft Benson (1899–1994) taught that certain blessings come only through diligent scripture study: "Success in righteousness, the power to avoid deception and resist temptation, guidance in our daily lives, healing of the soul—these are but a few of the promises the Lord has given to those who will come to His word. Does the Lord promise and not fulfill? Surely if He tells us that these things will come to us if we lay hold upon His word,

then the blessings can be ours. And if we do not, then the blessings may be lost. However diligent we may be in other areas, certain blessings are to be found only in the scriptures, only in coming to the word of the Lord and holding fast to it as we make our way through the mists of darkness to the tree of life" ("The Power of the Word," *Ensign,* May 1986, 82).

Helaman 3:30. "Sit Down with Abraham, and Isaac, and with Jacob"

• The phrase "to sit down with Abraham, and Isaac, and with Jacob" means that the faithful will merit the association of these three great patriarchs and the reception of celestial-like rewards. According to Doctrine and Covenants 132:37, "Abraham . . . as Isaac also and Jacob . . . have entered into their exaltation, according to the promises, and sit upon thrones, and are not angels but are gods."

Elder Russell M. Nelson of the Quorum of the Twelve Apostles explained that Church members may become heirs to the blessings of Abraham, Isaac, and Jacob:

"The covenant that the Lord first made with Abraham and reaffirmed with Isaac and Jacob is of transcendent significance. . . .

"We are also children of the covenant. We have received, as did they of old, the holy priesthood and the everlasting gospel. Abraham, Isaac, and Jacob are our ancestors. We are of Israel. We have the right to receive the gospel, blessings of the priesthood, and eternal life. Nations of the earth will be blessed by our efforts and by the labors of our posterity. The literal seed of Abraham and those who are gathered into his family by adoption receive these promised blessings—predicated upon acceptance of the Lord and obedience to his commandments" (in Conference Report, Apr. 1995, 42–43; or *Ensign,* May 1995, 33).

Helaman 3:33–34, 36; 4:12. The Effect of Pride on the Church

• Mormon was careful to point out that pride was not part of the Lord's Church, but because of great riches, it began to enter into the hearts of some of the members of the Church (see Helaman 3:36), which had a detrimental effect on the Church in general.

President Ezra Taft Benson expressed thoughts in a similar vein:

"Think of what pride has cost us in the past and what it is now costing us in our own lives, our families, and the Church.

© Busath.com

"Think of the repentance that could take place with lives changed, marriages preserved, and homes strengthened, if pride did not keep us from confessing our sins and forsaking them (see D&C 58:43).

"Think of the many who are less-active members of the Church because they were offended and their pride will not allow them to forgive or fully sup at the Lord's table.

"Think of the tens of thousands of young men and couples who could be on missions except for the pride that keeps them from yielding their hearts unto God (see Alma 10:6; Helaman 3:34–35).

"Think how temple work would increase if the time spent in this godly service were more important than the many prideful pursuits that compete for our time" (in Conference Report, Apr. 1989, 6; or *Ensign,* May 1989, 6).

• For more information and a diagram depicting the pride cycle, refer to "The Cycle of Righteousness and Wickedness" in the appendix (p. 414).

• Elder D. Todd Christofferson of the Quorum of the Twelve Apostles taught that a paramount step in becoming completely faithful in the gospel is the avoidance or removal of pride:

"How can you make the gospel of Jesus Christ not just an influence in your life but the controlling influence and, indeed, the very core of what you are? . . .

"As a first step, you must lay aside any feeling of pride that is so common in the world today. By this I mean the attitude that rejects the authority of God to rule in our lives. . . . You hear it expressed today in phrases such as 'Do your own thing' or 'Right and wrong depend on what I feel is right for me.' That attitude is a rebellion against God" (in Conference Report, Apr. 2004, 9; or *Ensign,* May 2004, 11).

Helaman 3:35. Sanctification of the Heart

• *Sanctification* has been defined as "the process of becoming free from sin, pure, clean, and holy through the atonement of Jesus Christ (Moses 6:59–60)" (Guide to the Scriptures).

• Faithful Church members in Helaman's day continued their spiritual growth, which resulted in "the sanctification of their hearts" (Helaman 3:35).

President James E. Faust taught that such growth comes with the aid of the Holy Spirit fostering our inmost desires to conduct our lives as the Savior would have us live. During this process, we are sanctified: "Christlike conduct flows from the deepest wellsprings of the human heart and soul. It is guided by the Holy Spirit of the Lord, which is promised in gospel ordinances. Our greatest hope should be to enjoy the sanctification which comes from this divine guidance; our greatest fear should be to forfeit these blessings" (in Conference Report, Apr. 1998, 23; or *Ensign,* May 1998, 20).

• The Saints of Helaman's day continued in good works and became stronger in spiritual qualities, which in turn resulted in sanctification. Elder D. Todd Christofferson explained that sanctification is a step in the path of striving toward perfection: "Personal persistence in the path of obedience is something different than achieving perfection in mortality. Perfection is not, as some suppose, a prerequisite for justification and sanctification. It is just the opposite: justification (being pardoned) and sanctification (being purified) are the prerequisites for perfection. We only become perfect 'in Christ' (see Moro. 10:32), not independently of Him. Thus, what is required of us in order to obtain mercy in the day of judgment is simple diligence" ("Justification and Sanctification," *Ensign,* June 2001, 24–25).

Helaman 3:35. They Did Wax Strong in Their Humility

• The development of humility is a strengthening factor that leads to greater faith and joy in the lives of faithful Church members then and now.

"To be humble is to recognize gratefully your dependence on the Lord—to understand that you have constant need for His support. Humility is an acknowledgment that your talents and abilities are gifts from God. It is not a sign of weakness, timidity, or fear; it is an indication that you know where your true strength lies. You can be both humble and fearless. You can be both humble and courageous. . . .

"The Lord will strengthen you as you humble yourself before Him" (*True to the Faith: A Gospel Reference* [2004], 86).

Helaman 3:35. Firm in the Faith

• The strength of the Church lies in the firm convictions of individual members. Helaman 3:35 describes the lives of Church members who were firm in their faith and works.

Elder Russell M. Nelson pointed out that such firmness in behavior and attitude is obtained individually: "Only as an individual can you develop a firm faith in God and a passion for personal prayer. Only as an individual can you keep the commandments of God. Only as an individual can you repent. Only as an individual can you qualify for the ordinances of salvation and exaltation" (in Conference Report, Oct. 2003, 47; or *Ensign,* Nov. 2003, 44).

Helaman 3:35. Yielding Our Hearts to God

• The phrase "yield our hearts" means to surrender or give our hearts to God. When one yields his or her heart to God, he is surrendering his personal desires in exchange for the Lord's desires. Elder Neal A. Maxwell (1926–2004) of the Quorum of the Twelve Apostles taught that yielding our hearts and souls to God is the highest form of consecration to the Lord:

"Ultimate consecration is the yielding up of oneself to God. *Heart, soul,* and *mind* were the encompassing words of Christ in describing the first commandment, which is constantly, not periodically, operative (see Matthew 22:37). If it is kept, then our performances will in turn be fully consecrated for the lasting welfare of our souls (see 2 Nephi 32:9).

"Such totality involves the submissive converging of feelings, thoughts, words, and deeds" (in Conference Report, Apr. 2002, 41; or *Ensign,* May 2002, 36).

> ### HELAMAN 4:11–13
> *List at least six of the serious sins the Church members in Nephi's day committed that drew them away from the Lord's protection.*

Helaman 4:22–26. Sin Weakens People

• Elder M. Russell Ballard gave this warning: "You must be honest with yourself and remain true to the covenants you have made with God. Do not fall into the trap of thinking you can sin a little and it will not matter. Remember, 'the Lord cannot look upon sin with the least degree of allowance' (D&C 1:31). . . . Some youth foolishly rationalize that it is 'no big deal' to sin now because they can always repent later when they want to go to the temple or on a mission. Anyone who does that is breaking promises made to God both in the premortal life and in the waters of baptism. The idea of sinning a little is self-deception. Sin is sin! Sin weakens you spiritually, and it always places the sinner at eternal risk. Choosing to sin, even with the intent to repent, is simply turning away from God and violating covenants" (in Conference Report, Apr. 1993, 6; or *Ensign,* May 1993, 7).

Points to Ponder

- Mormon referred to "the man of Christ" (Helaman 3:29). What do you think characterizes a man of Christ? What are two or three goals you can set that would lead you toward becoming a man or woman of Christ? What do you need to do to achieve these goals?

- Helaman 3:35 lists benefits that come from being firm in the faith. Which of these blessings have you recently felt? What qualified you for these blessings?

Suggested Assignments

- Analyze yourself to determine where pride might be a problem in your life. Write down goals to overcome that pride.

- Under the title of "prosperity," list as many blessings as you can think of that you have recently received from the Lord.

CHAPTER 36

Helaman 5–9

Introduction

At this crucial point in Nephite history, the wicked outnumbered the righteous. Their laws became so corrupted that they had little effect for good. Like his great-grandfather Alma, Nephi gave up his position as chief judge and devoted himself full-time to the Lord's work (see Alma 4:15–20). During this period of spiritual darkness, the people were "ripening for destruction" (Helaman 5:2). Nephi and his brother Lehi worked diligently to stem the tide of iniquity and turned many back to the Lord.

Commentary

Helaman 5:2. "The Voice of the People"

• When the people desired a king 62 years previously, Mosiah counseled that government should be by "the voice of the people" (Mosiah 29:26), stating it was not common for the majority of the people to desire unrighteousness. Government by the voice of the people was preferred to a monarchy in which an unrighteous king might lead them to destruction. At this time prior to the Savior's coming, however, the Nephites "who chose evil were more numerous than they who chose good" (Helaman 5:2). This corruption proved the truth of Mosiah's caution that should this ever occur, "then is the time that the judgments of God will come upon you; yea, then is the time he will visit you with great destruction" (Mosiah 29:27). This warning was fulfilled with the destruction preceding the Savior's appearance (see 3 Nephi 8–11).

The Lord declared this principle true in our day as well: "When the wicked rule the people mourn" (D&C 98:9).

Helaman 5:5–7. "Remember Your Names"

• Helaman had a special way of transferring his heritage to his sons—he named them after their noble ancestors to help his sons remember their righteous works. The following insight by Elder Carlos E. Asay (1926–99) of the Presidency of the Seventy helps us appreciate what this meant to Nephi and Lehi:

"Though all of Adam's children may not have received names of significance, many have, and it has made a difference. It made a difference in the lives of Helaman's sons, Nephi and Lehi. . . . [See Helaman 5:5–7.]

"The record attests that Nephi and Lehi did pattern their lives after their forebears or namesakes and did bring honor to the names given them" (*Family Pecan Trees: Planting a Legacy of Faith at Home* [1992], 66–67).

• President George Albert Smith (1870–1951) provided a modern illustration of the profound influence that a good name may have upon a person:

"One day . . . I lost consciousness of my surroundings and thought I had passed to the Other Side. I found myself standing with my back to a large and beautiful lake, facing a great forest of trees. . . .

"I began to explore, and soon I found a trail through the woods which seemed to have been used very little, and which was almost obscured by grass. I followed this trail, and after I had walked for some time and had traveled a considerable distance through the forest, I saw a man coming towards me. I became aware that he was a very large man, and I hurried my steps to reach him, because I recognized him as my grandfather. In mortality he weighed over three hundred pounds, so you may know he was a large man. I remember how happy I was to see him coming. I had been given his name and had always been proud of it.

"When Grandfather came within a few feet of me, he stopped. His stopping was an invitation for me to stop. Then—and this I would like the boys and girls and young people never to forget—he looked at me very earnestly and said:

"'I would like to know what you have done with my name.'

"Everything I had ever done passed before me as though it were a flying picture on a screen—everything I had done. Quickly this vivid retrospect came down to the very time I was standing there. My whole life had passed before me. I smiled and looked at my grandfather and said:

"'I have never done anything with your name of which you need be ashamed.'

"He stepped forward and took me in his arms, and as he did so, I became conscious again of my earthly surroundings. My pillow was as wet as though water had been poured on it—wet with tears of gratitude that I could answer unashamed.

"I have thought of this many times, and I want to tell you that I have been trying, more than ever since that time, to take care of that name. So I want to say to the boys and girls, to the young men and women, to the youth of the Church and of all the world: Honor your fathers and your mothers. Honor the names that you bear, because some day you will have the privilege and the obligation of reporting to them (and to your Father in heaven) what you have done with their name" ("Your Good Name," *Improvement Era,* Mar. 1947, 139).

Helaman 5:9. "No Other Way Nor Means Whereby Man Can Be Saved"

• Elder Richard G. Scott of the Quorum of the Twelve Apostles used Helaman 5:9 to teach that only the miraculous Atonement makes salvation possible:

"Full repentance is absolutely essential for the Atonement to work its complete miracle in your life. By understanding the Atonement, you will see that God is not a jealous being who delights in persecuting those who misstep. He is an absolutely perfect, compassionate, understanding, patient, and forgiving Father. He is  willing to entreat, counsel, strengthen, lift, and fortify. He so loves each of us that He was willing to have His perfect, sinless, absolutely obedient, totally righteous Son experience indescribable agony and pain and give Himself in sacrifice for all [see Helaman 5:9]. Through that atonement we can live in a world

where absolute justice reigns in its sphere so the world will have order. But that justice is tempered through mercy attainable by obedience to the teachings of Jesus Christ.

"Which of us is not in need of the miracle of repentance? Whether your life is lightly blemished or heavily disfigured from mistakes, the principles of recovery are the same. The length and severity of the treatments are conditioned to fit the circumstances. Our goal surely must be forgiveness. The only possible path to that goal is repentance, for it is written:

"'There is no other way nor means whereby man can be saved, only through the atoning blood of Jesus Christ'" (in Conference Report, Apr. 1995, 101; or *Ensign,* May 1995, 75).

> **HELAMAN 5:9–11**
> Compare Elder Richard G. Scott's statement regarding the saving power of the Atonement to Helaman's teachings to his sons.

Helaman 5:9–14. 📖 Remember

• President Spencer W. Kimball (1895–1985) taught of the great importance that memory plays in our spirituality: "When you look in the dictionary for the most important word, do you know what it is? It could be *remember.* Because all of you have made covenants—you know what to do and you know how to do it—our greatest need is to remember. That is why everyone goes to sacrament meeting every Sabbath day—to take the sacrament and listen to the priests pray that they 'may always remember him and keep his commandments which he has given them.' Nobody should ever forget to go to sacrament meeting. *Remember* is the word. *Remember* is the program" ("Circles of Exaltation" [address to Church Educational System religious educators, June 28, 1968], 5).

Helaman 5:12. 📖 A Strong Foundation

• Elder Bruce C. Hafen of the Seventy vividly illustrated the necessity of strong foundations for long-term safety and survival:

"Someone once said you can't visually tell the difference between a strand of cobweb and a strand of powerful cable—until stress is put on the strand. Our testimonies are that way, and for most of us, the days of stress for our testimonies have already begun. It may not be the death of a loved one. We might not yet have been asked to give up something that is really precious to us, though the time for such a test may well come to us by and by. Our current stress is more likely to come in the form of overpowering temptations, which show us that a shallow acceptance of the gospel does not have the power to cope with the full fury of the powers of darkness. Perhaps there is a mission call to a place of illness and disappointment, when we had planned on a mission to a place of unbounded opportunity. Or perhaps there are too many questions to which our limited knowledge simply has no answer, and those who claim to know more than we do taunt us with what appears to be a persuasive certainty.

"When those times come, our testimonies must be more than the cobweb strands of a fair-weather faith. They need to be like strands of cable, powerful enough to resist the shafts of him who would destroy us. In our days of stress and trouble, we must be built 'upon the rock of our Redeemer, who is Christ, the Son of God, . . . that when the devil shall send forth his mighty winds, yea, his shafts in the whirlwind, . . . and his mighty storm shall beat upon you, it shall have no power over you, . . . because of the rock upon which ye are built.' (Helaman 5:12.)" (*The Believing Heart,* 2nd ed. [1990], 21–22).

Helaman 5:12. 📖 The Mighty Storm of Satan "Shall Beat upon You"

• President Spencer W. Kimball described the modern storms Satan sends upon Heavenly Father's children today:

"We, too, are faced with powerful destructive forces unleashed by the adversary. Waves of sin, wickedness, immorality, degradation, tyranny, deceitfulness, conspiracy, and dishonesty threaten all of us. They come with great power and speed and will destroy us if we are not watchful.

"But a warning is sounded for us. It behooves us to be alert and to listen and flee from the evil for our eternal lives. Without help we cannot stand against it. We must flee to high ground or cling fast to that which can keep us from being swept away. That to which we must cling for safety is the gospel of Jesus Christ. It is our protection from whatever force the evil one can muster. An inspired Book of Mormon prophet counseled his people: 'Remember that it is upon the rock of our Redeemer, who is Christ, the Son of God, that ye must build your foundation; that when the devil shall send forth his mighty winds, yea, his shafts in the whirlwind, yea, when all his hail and his mighty storm shall beat upon you, it shall have no power over you to drag you down to the gulf of misery and endless wo' (Hel. 5:12)" (in Conference Report, Oct. 1978, 6; or *Ensign,* Nov. 1978, 6).

> ### HELAMAN 5:22–25
> Compare Helaman 5:22–25 with 2 Nephi 1:15 and Alma 34:15–16. How is Christ's love manifest in these experiences?

Helaman 5:35–41. Aminadab and a "Cloud of Darkness"

• We are told in the record that Aminadab "was a Nephite by birth, who had once belonged to the church of God but had dissented from them" (Helaman 5:35). His reactions, as recorded in Helaman 5:35, show that he still had some knowledge of what one must do to repent and turn to the Lord. Elder F. Burton Howard of the Seventy gave the following explanation:

"To find the way back, as Aminadab [remembered], one must repent and pray until doubt and darkness disappear and important things can be seen again. . . .

". . . It is possible to return. It is possible for those who have ceased to pray, to pray again. It is possible for those who are lost to find their way through the dark and come home.

"And when they do, they will know, as I know, that the Lord is more concerned with what a man is than with what he was, and with where he is than with where he has been" (in Conference Report, Oct. 1986, 99–100; or *Ensign,* Nov. 1986, 77–78).

Helaman 5:50–52; 6:1–8. A Dramatic Transformation

• The power and impact of Nephi and Lehi's mission among the Lamanites were dramatic. Following their successful mission, notice the following first-time experiences that occurred in the history of the majority of the Lamanites:

1. The majority of the Lamanites were converted to the gospel (see Helaman 5:50).

2. The Lamanites laid down their weapons and their hatred and false traditions (see Helaman 5:51).

3. They freely yielded up the land that belonged to the Nephites (see Helaman 5:52).

4. The majority of the Lamanites became more righteous than the Nephites (see Helaman 6:1).

5. The Lamanites began to preach the gospel to the Nephites (see Helaman 6:4).

6. There was peace in all the land (see Helaman 6:7).

7. The Lamanites and Nephites had open travel and free trade with one another (see Helaman 6:8).

Helaman 6:17. Setting Hearts upon Riches

• President Henry B. Eyring of the First Presidency taught that worldliness is an obstacle to inspiration

and spirituality: "God is forgotten out of vanity. A little prosperity and peace, or even a turn slightly for the better, can bring us feelings of self-sufficiency. We can feel quickly that we are in control of our lives, that the change for the better is our own doing, not that of a God who communicates to us through the still, small voice of the Spirit. Pride creates a noise within us which makes the quiet voice of the Spirit hard to hear. And soon, in our vanity, we no longer even listen for it. We can come quickly to think we don't need it" (in Conference Report, Oct. 2001, 16; or *Ensign,* Nov. 2001, 16).

> ### HELAMAN 6:21, 26–31
> *What is the motive of Lucifer and his followers? How can that motivate us to stay near our Father in Heaven?*

Helaman 6:18–40. The Evils of Secret Combinations

• Helaman chapter 6 provides several insights into secret combinations, including how they work, what motivates them, and how they come to power:

1. Their two objectives are to get gain and power; then they glory in it (see Helaman 6:17; Ether 8:22; Moses 5:31).

2. Secret combinations require general wickedness to survive (see Helaman 6:21, 31, 38).

3. Secret combinations thrive on secrecy, violation of which is a capital offense (see Helaman 5:22; 6:22; Moses 5:29, 50).

4. Secret combinations involve formal covenant making (see Helaman 6:22; Moses 5:30–31).

5. They use murder, violence, threat of violence, plunder, vice, whoredoms, and flattery to get gain and power (see Helaman 2:4–5; 6:17, 23).

6. Secret combinations operate on laws contrary to the laws of the country (see Helaman 6:23).

7. Satan is the grand conspirator and author (see Helaman 6:26–30).

8. Participants have court trials for their own people—not according to the laws of the land but according to their own set of laws (see Helaman 6:23–24).

9. They seek to take governmental power as rapidly as possible (see Helaman 2:5; 6:39).

10. Participants seek to overthrow freedom for others but seek to maintain freedom for themselves (see Ether 8:25; Moses 5:28–33).

11. Secret combinations cause the destruction of nations (see Alma 37:21, 26, 29; Helaman 2:13; Ether 8:21–22).

12. Secret combinations are abominable in God's sight (see 3 Nephi 9:9; Ether 8:18).

Helaman 8:14–15. "The Brazen Serpent"

• As a witness against wickedness and as a testimony of Christ, Nephi referred to an incident in the Old Testament when the children of Israel were being

plagued by "fiery flying serpents" (1 Nephi 17:41; Numbers 21:6–9). The prelude to the Israelites' trouble was speaking evil of God and His prophet (see Numbers 21:5), just as the corrupt judges of Nephi's day were doing. The lifting up of a brass serpent by Moses was a type (a symbolic representation) of the

crucifixion of Christ. When the people looked upon the brass serpent, they were healed.

Nephi's use of this story emphasizes that we "should look upon the Son of God with faith" and live (Helaman 8:15; see also John 3:14–15). Through the atoning sacrifice of Christ, the poisonous venom of Satan was overcome for all who would repent. He then reminded the people that all of the prophets had testified of Christ (see Helaman 8:16–23).

• Elder Neal A. Maxwell (1926–2004) of the Quorum of the Twelve Apostles further clarified the symbolism of the brazen serpent retold in the Book of Mormon:

"Divinely deliberate and serious symbolism is involved. Without this needed elaboration, the Old Testament episode of the fiery serpents does not give us a fulness of spiritual insight that can clearly be 'for our profit and learning.' (1 Nephi 19:23.) The symbolic emphasis in this episode is upon both the necessity and the simpleness of the way of the Lord Jesus. Ironically, in Moses' time many perished anyway. The promise for the future is as follows: 'And as many as should look upon that serpent should live, even so as many as should look upon the Son of God with faith, having a contrite spirit, might live, even unto that life which is eternal.' (Helaman 8:15. See also 1 Nephi 17:41; Alma 37:46.)

"Thus, now we have the verified and amplified analogy, thanks to the precious and plain things given to us in 'these last records.'

"The whole episode points toward the need to look upon Jesus Christ as our Lord, likewise a simple but unwaivable requirement. How plain and precious in any age!" (*Plain and Precious Things* [1983], 22).

HELAMAN 8:16–25
From Helaman 8 and Doctrine and Covenants 6:9; 11:9; 15:6; 16:6, what is every prophet's message? How do you respond to the message?

Helaman 9:36–41. The Omniscience of God

• Upon seeing Nephi's knowledge of secret and hidden things, there were those who wanted to proclaim him to be God. This is understandable given the universal acknowledgment of certain characteristics of God. Elder Neal A. Maxwell taught that omniscience is one of the characteristics of God:

"The Lord in a revelation for John Whitmer spoke of that which was in the latter's heart, which only the Lord and John Whitmer knew, witnessing that God was omniscient concerning the needs of that individual. (D&C 15:3.)

"Paul said to the saints at Corinth, 'And again, The Lord knoweth the thoughts of the wise, that they are vain.' (1 Corinthians 3:20.) In the period just before the flood God saw not only the wickedness of man in the earth, but he saw also 'every imagination of the thoughts' of men's hearts. (Genesis 6:5.) He knows 'the things that come into your mind.' (Ezekiel 11:5.) Jesus himself said before we pray, 'Your father knoweth what things ye have need of.' (Matthew 6:8.) Indeed, as Nephi said, 'God . . . knoweth all things, and there is not anything save he knows.' (2 Nephi 9:20.)

"Hence omniscience is one of the characteristics of the living God. As we read in Helaman 9:41, 'Except he was a God he could not know of all things.' 'And now, behold, you have received a witness; for if I have told you things which no man knoweth have you not received a witness?' (D&C 6:24.)" (*Things As They Really Are* [1978], 22).

Points to Ponder

• Helaman used the examples of their first fathers, Lehi and Nephi, to strengthen his sons Nephi and Lehi. Who in your family has influenced you for good? What was it about them that made an impact on you?

• What impressions have you given others about your family name by the life you have lived so far?

• What are some of the foundations you are building your life upon? Do you need to make any adjustments? What foundation is the most important to you?

• What are some of the obstacles to spirituality that existed in Nephi's time that are similar to obstacles you face today?

Suggested Assignments

• Research your family history and discover who the first-generation converts in your family were. Talk to members of your family and collect the stories of their faith and conversion for your own personal history.

• Have a discussion with a friend or family member about how you might better keep the commandments, live the principles of the gospel, and stay close to your Father in Heaven in a world that is increasingly filled with wickedness.

Introduction

Being completely trusted by God is a great honor. The *Lectures on Faith* teach that awareness of God's approval is necessary for one's faith: "An actual knowledge to any person, that the course of life which he pursues is according to the will of God, is essentially necessary to enable him to have that confidence in God without which no person can obtain eternal life" ([1985], 7).

Trust and approval come by obedience to all of God's commandments. Helaman chapters 10–12 highlight how important it is to heed the promptings of the Spirit. Only by doing so can we be sure we are living according to God's will. These chapters also highlight how important it is to want what God wants. The Lord knew Nephi would "not ask that which is contrary to [God's] will" (Helaman 10:5). As we prove faithful in the small things, the Lord will trust us with the greater things.

Commentary

Helaman 10:1–3. Pondering

• To ponder is to "meditate and think deeply, often upon the scriptures or other things of God. When combined with prayer, pondering . . . may bring revelation and understanding" (Guide to the Scriptures, "Ponder"). Nephi and other prophets received revelation while pondering. Elder M. Russell Ballard of the Quorum of the Twelve Apostles taught: "All of us would benefit from time to ponder and meditate. In the quiet moments of personal introspection, the Spirit can teach us much" (in Conference Report, Oct. 1995, 4; or *Ensign,* Nov. 1995, 6).

• Elder Richard G. Scott of the Quorum of the Twelve Apostles suggested that a quiet place is conducive to pondering: "Find a retreat of peace and quiet where periodically you can ponder and let the Lord establish the direction of your life" (in Conference Report, Apr. 2001, 8; or *Ensign,* May 2001, 9).

• Elder Russell M. Nelson of the Quorum of the Twelve Apostles shared with us the benefits of pondering: "As you ponder and pray about doctrinal principles, the Holy Ghost will speak to your mind and your heart [see D&C 8:2]. From events portrayed in the scriptures, new insights will come and principles relevant to your situation will distill upon your heart" (in Conference Report, Oct. 2000, 19; or *Ensign,* Nov. 2000, 18).

Helaman 10:4–5. "Thou Shalt Not Ask That Which Is Contrary to My Will"

• Like Nephi, if we learn to ask "in the Spirit" (Helaman 10:17) and according to God's will, then "it is done even as" we ask (see D&C 46:30; 50:29–30). President Marion G. Romney (1897–1988) of the First Presidency shared some necessary aspects of proper petitions:

"When we pray unto the Father in the name of Jesus for specific personal things, we should feel in the very depths of our souls that we are willing to subject our petitions to the will of our Father in heaven. . . .

"The time will come when we shall know the will of God before we ask. Then everything for which we pray will be 'expedient.' Everything for which we ask will be 'right.' That will be when as a result of righteous living, we shall so enjoy the companionship of the spirit that he will dictate what we ask" (in Conference Report, Oct. 1944, 55–56).

President Romney had an experience in which the Lord gave him a promise similar to Nephi's. Elder Jeffrey R. Holland of the Quorum of the Twelve Apostles spoke about it:

"In 1967 Sister Ida Romney suffered a serious stroke. The doctors told then-Elder Romney that the damage from the hemorrhage was severe. They offered to keep her alive by artificial means but did not recommend it. The family braced for the worst. Brother Romney confided to those closest to him that in spite of his anguished, personal yearning for Ida's restored health and continued companionship, above all he wanted 'the Lord's will to be done and to take what he needed to take without whimpering.'

"As the days wore on, Sister Romney became less responsive. She had, of course, been administered to, but Elder Romney was 'reluctant to counsel the Lord about the matter.' Because of his earlier unsuccessful experience of praying that he and Ida might have children, he knew that he could never ask in prayer for something that was not in harmony with the will of the Lord. He fasted that he might know how to show the Lord he had faith and would accept God's will in their lives. He wanted to make sure he had done all he could do. But she continued to fail.

"One evening in a particularly depressed state, with Ida unable to speak or recognize him, Brother Romney went home and turned, as he always had, to the scriptures in an effort to commune with the Lord. He picked up the Book of Mormon and continued where he had left off the night before. He had been reading in Helaman about the prophet Nephi, who had been falsely accused and unfairly charged with sedition. Following a miraculous deliverance from his accusers, Nephi returned home pondering the things he had experienced. As he did so he heard a voice.

"Although Marion Romney had read that story many times before, it now struck him this night as a personal revelation. The words of the scripture so touched his heart that for the first time in weeks he felt he had tangible peace. It seemed as if the Lord were speaking directly to him. The scripture read: 'Blessed art thou, . . . for those things which thou hast done; . . . thou hast not . . . sought thine own life, but hast sought my will, and to keep my commandments. And now, because thou hast done this with such unwearyingness, behold, I will bless thee forever; and I will make thee mighty in word and in deed, in faith and in works; yea, even that all things shall be done unto thee according to thy word, for thou shalt not ask that which is contrary to my will.' (Helaman 10:4–5.)

"There was the answer. He had sought only to know and obey the will of the Lord, and the Lord had spoken. He fell to his knees and poured out his heart, and as he concluded his prayer with the phrase 'Thy will be done,' he either felt or actually heard a voice that said, 'It is not contrary to my will that Ida be healed.'

"Brother Romney rose to his feet quickly. It was past two o'clock in the morning, but he knew what he must do. Quickly he put on his tie and coat, then went out into the night to visit Ida in the hospital. He arrived

shortly before three o'clock. His wife's condition was unchanged. She did not stir as he placed his hands upon her pale forehead. With undeviating faith, he invoked the power of the priesthood in her behalf. He pronounced a simple blessing and then uttered the incredible promise that she would recover her health and her mental powers and would yet perform 'a great mission' upon the earth.

"Even though he did not doubt, Elder Romney was astonished to see Ida's eyes open as he concluded the blessing. Somewhat stunned by all that had happened, he sat down on the edge of the bed only to hear his wife's frail voice for the first time in months. She said, 'For goodness' sake, Marion, what are you doing here?' He didn't know whether to laugh or to cry. He said, 'Ida, how are you?' With that flash of humor so characteristic of both of them, she replied, 'Compared to what, Marion? Compared to what?'

"Ida Romney began her recovery from that very moment, soon left her hospital bed, and lived to see her husband sustained as a member of the First Presidency of the Church, 'a great mission upon the earth' indeed. (F. Burton Howard, *Marion G. Romney: His Life and Faith* [Salt Lake City: Bookcraft, 1988], pp. 137–42.)" (Jeffrey R. Holland and Patricia T. Holland, *On Earth As It Is in Heaven* [1989], 133–35).

HELAMAN 10:4–5
What characteristics do you find in these two verses that enabled Nephi to receive such blessings?

Helaman 10:7. The Sealing Power

• Nephi served with such diligence that the Lord bestowed upon him great power. He was given power over the people and the elements of the earth. He was also granted a sacred bestowal of the sealing power, the same power held by Elijah the prophet: "The power of Elijah is the sealing power of the priesthood by which things that are bound or loosed on earth are bound or loosed in heaven (D&C 128:8–18)" (Guide to the Scriptures, "Elijah").

© 1985 Robert Barrett

• President Joseph Fielding Smith (1876–1972) taught about the sealing power given to various prophets:

"The Lord conferred authority on some of his chosen servants and gave them exceptional powers. . . . In this manner Elijah obtained the keys of power in the priesthood to raise the dead, heal the sick, close the heavens that it did not rain only by his word, and for more than three years there was no rain, and moreover he had the power to call down fire from heaven to destroy the enemies of the Church. . . .

"The Lord gave similar authority to Nephi, son of Helaman, who likewise had authority to close the heavens and perform other mighty works, simply by his faith and the commandment from the Lord [see Helaman 10:7]. This wonderful power has been bestowed on but a few of the servants of the Lord" (*Answers to Gospel Questions,* comp. Joseph Fielding Smith Jr., 5 vols. [1957–66], 4:95).

Helaman 10:13–15. "Notwithstanding That Great Miracle"

• The Prophet Joseph Smith taught that "miracles are the fruits of faith" (*History of the Church,* 5:355). Some people seek faith through miracles; however, that is contrary to the order of heaven. Faith precedes the miracle—it does not follow it. Nephi's miraculous identification of Seantum as the murderer of the chief judge came as a result of the prophet's faith. Sadly, the majority of the people who witnessed this miracle were living without faith. The miracle failed to convert them because "faith cometh not by signs [or miracles], but signs follow those that believe" (D&C 63:9). The necessary change in their lives had to begin with "faith unto repentance" (Alma 34:15–17). Unfortunately, these people who had witnessed a great miracle continued to harden their hearts, and instead of repenting, they persecuted Nephi.

Helaman 11:1–16. Prophets Pray for the People

• Nephi's prayer on behalf of his people illustrates the concern of a prophet for the people. As well as representing God to the people, at times prophets also seek to intervene on behalf of their people. When plagued by poisonous serpents, the children of Israel went to Moses and pled, "pray unto the Lord, that he take away the serpents from us. And Moses prayed for the people" (Numbers 21:7).

In the Americas, Nephi, the son of Lehi, wrote: "I pray continually for [my people] by day, and mine eyes water my pillow by night, because of them; and I cry unto my God in faith" (2 Nephi 33:3).

• Our current prophets continue to pray for us. In the general conference following the tragic terrorist events on September 11, 2001, President Gordon B. Hinckley (1910–2008) prayed:

"O God, our Eternal Father, . . . whose children we are, we look to Thee in faith in this dark and solemn time. Please, dear Father, bless us with faith. Bless us with love. Bless us with charity in our hearts. Bless us with a spirit of perseverance to root out the terrible evils that are in this world. Give protection and guidance to those who are engaged actively in carrying forth the things of battle. Bless them; preserve their lives; save them from harm and evil. Hear the prayers of their loved ones for their safety. . . .

"O Father, look with mercy upon this, our own nation, and its friends in this time of need. Spare us and help us to walk with faith ever in Thee and ever in Thy Beloved Son, on whose mercy we count and to whom we look as our Savior and our Lord. Bless the cause of peace and bring it quickly to us again, we humbly plead with Thee, asking that Thou wilt forgive our arrogance, pass by our sins, be kind and gracious to us, and cause our hearts to turn with love toward Thee. We humbly pray in the name of Him who loves us all, even the Lord Jesus Christ, our Redeemer and our Savior, amen" (in Conference Report, Oct. 2001, 112; or *Ensign,* Nov. 2001, 90).

Helaman 11:4–5. The Lord Sometimes Uses Nature to Correct His Children

• President Spencer W. Kimball (1895–1985) explained that "the Lord uses the weather sometimes to discipline his people for the violation of his laws" (in Conference Report, Apr. 1977, 4; or *Ensign,* May 1977, 4; see also D&C 43:21–25).

Helaman 11:18–12:6. Cycles of Righteousness and Wickedness

• Several times in Book of Mormon history the people passed through a cycle of righteousness, prosperity, riches, pride, wickedness, destruction, humility, and righteousness again. For more information and a diagram depicting the pride cycle, refer to "The Cycle of Righteousness and Wickedness" in the appendix (p. 414).

Elder L. Tom Perry of the Quorum of the Twelve Apostles lamented mankind's failure to break out of negative cycles: "I guess one of the greatest mysteries of mortality is why mankind fails to learn from history" (in Conference Report, Oct. 1992, 19; or *Ensign,* Nov. 1992, 16). Surely the Lord has placed these obvious patterns of behavior in scripture for our benefit, to help us avoid the same problems in our own lives (see D&C 52:14–19).

Helaman 11:22–23. "Points of Doctrine"

• Elder Bruce R. McConkie (1915–85) of the Quorum of the Twelve Apostles indicated what comprised the true doctrine of Christ: "The true doctrine of Christ is that all men must come unto him, gain faith, repent, be baptized, receive the Holy Ghost, and endure in faith to the end in order to gain salvation. (2 Ne. 31:17–21; 3 Ne. 11:29–41; D.&C. 10:67; 68:25.)" (*Mormon Doctrine,* 2nd ed. [1966], 204).

• President Boyd K. Packer, President of the Quorum of the Twelve Apostles, made this statement regarding the power of true doctrine:

"True doctrine, understood, changes attitudes and behavior.

"The study of the doctrines of the gospel will improve behavior quicker than a study of behavior will improve behavior. . . . That is why we stress so forcefully the study of the doctrines of the gospel" (in Conference Report, Oct. 1986, 20; or *Ensign,* Nov. 1986, 17).

Helaman 11:21–38. Wickedness Returned

• The Prophet Joseph Smith taught that "the devil always sets up his kingdom at the very same time in opposition to God" (*History of the Church,* 6:364). Whenever the Savior's Church is established or strengthened, the adversary seeks to create resistance in one form or another to battle the progress made by the Saints of God. We see an example of Satan's opposition emerge in Helaman 11. The Gadianton robbers had been swept off the land. The righteous Nephite and Lamanite members of the Church had great peace (see Helaman 11:21). Only a few years passed, however, before Satan's influence on the people led them to return to iniquity and allowed the Gadianton robbers to regain their power and influence.

Helaman 12:1–3. The Unsteadiness of Men

• Elder Neal A. Maxwell (1926–2004) of the Quorum of the Twelve Apostles explored some possible reasons for spiritual unsteadiness:

"Is it simply unintended forgetfulness? Or is it a failure of intellectual integrity by our refusing to review and to acknowledge past blessings? Or is it a lack of meekness which requires the repetition of such stern lessons, because we neglect the milder and gentler signs beckoning us to 'remember Him'? . . .

". . . We need the Spirit daily to help us remember daily. Otherwise memory lapses will occur when we are most vulnerable. It is not natural to the natural man to remember yesterday's blessings gratefully, especially when today's needs of the flesh press steadily upon him" (*Lord, Increase Our Faith* [1994], 101–2).

• President Henry B. Eyring of the First Presidency added this insight about why we might be unsteady: "Dependence upon God can fade quickly when prayers are answered. And when the trouble lessens, so do the prayers. The Book of Mormon repeats that sad story over and over again" (in Conference Report, Oct. 2001, 15; or *Ensign,* Nov. 2001, 15).

HELAMAN 12:1–9

From these verses, what role does remembering or not remembering play in helping us avoid the pride cycle?

Helaman 12:2. When God Prospers His People, They Forget Him

• President Ezra Taft Benson (1899–1994) described the difficulty that can come with prosperity: "Ours then seems to be the toughest test of all for the evils are more subtle, more clever. It all seems less menacing and it is harder to detect. While every test of righteousness represents a struggle, this particular test seems like no test at all, no struggle and so could be the most deceiving of all tests. Do you know what peace and prosperity can do to a people—it can put them to sleep" (Larry E. Dahl, "Fit for the Kingdom," in

Studies in Scripture, Volume Five: The Gospels, edited by Kent P. Jackson and Robert L. Millet [1986], 5:369).

• President Harold B. Lee (1899–1973) compared the test of "luxury" with other tests of life: "We're tested and we're tried. Perhaps we don't realize the severity of the tests we're going through. In the early days of the Church, there were murders committed, there were mobbings. The Saints were driven out into the desert. They were starving, they were unclad, and they were cold. We're the inheritors of what they gave to us. But what are we doing with it? Today we're basking in the lap of luxury, the like of which we've never seen before in the history of the world. It would seem that probably this is the most severe test of any we've ever had in the history of this Church" (Dahl, "Fit for the Kingdom," in *Studies in Scripture,* 5:369).

Helaman 12:4. "Set Their Hearts upon the Vain Things of the World!"

• Mormon emphasized the foolishness of those who set their hearts upon the vain or worthless, empty, and valueless things of the world. Elder Dallin H. Oaks of the Quorum of the Twelve Apostles remarked: "The 'vain things of [the] world' include every combination of that worldly quartet of property, pride, prominence, and power. As to all of these, the scriptures remind us that 'you cannot carry them with you' (Alma 39:14). We should be seeking the kind of treasures the scriptures promise the faithful: 'great treasures of knowledge, even hidden treasures' (D&C 89:19)" (in Conference Report, Apr. 2001, 109; or *Ensign,* May 2001, 84).

Helaman 12:5–6. "Quick to Be Lifted Up in Pride"

• In his classic discourse on pride, President Ezra Taft Benson characterized the many facets of pride:

"Pride is essentially competitive in nature. We pit our will against God's. When we direct our pride toward God, it is in the spirit of 'my will and not thine be done.' . . .

"The proud cannot accept the authority of God giving direction to their lives (see Helaman 12:6). They pit their perceptions of truth against God's great knowledge, their abilities versus God's priesthood power, their accomplishments against His mighty works.

". . . The proud wish God would agree with them. They aren't interested in changing their opinions to agree with God's. . . .

"Pride results in secret combinations which are built up to get power, gain, and glory of the world (see Helaman 7:5; Ether 8:9, 16, 22–23; Moses 5:31). This fruit of the sin of pride, namely secret combinations, brought down both the Jaredite and the Nephite civilizations and has been and will yet be the cause of the fall of many nations (see Ether 8:18–25)" (in Conference Report, Apr. 1989, 4–5; or *Ensign,* May 1989, 4, 6).

• Elder Joe J. Christensen of the Seventy taught that pride leads to unrighteous comparisons and also may lead to our downfall:

"Pride causes us to become overly concerned, as we compare ourselves with others, about how intelligent we think we are, the brand of our jeans or other clothing—the 'costly apparel' we wear, to what organizations we belong, on which side of town we live, how much money we have, what our race or nationality is, what kind of car we drive, even to what church we belong, how much education we have been privileged to acquire, and on and on and on.

"In the scriptures there are many indications that pride has risen to destroy individuals, nations, and in some cases even the Church itself. . . ."It has been calculated that no fewer than thirty times throughout the Book of Mormon the cycles of prosperity and peace were destroyed, principally by the effects of human pride" (*One Step at a Time: Building a Better Marriage, Family, and You* [1996], 138–39). (See diagram "The Cycle of Righteousness and Wickedness" in the appendix, p. 414.)

Helaman 12:7–19. The Nothingness of Man

• President Joseph Fielding Smith helped us understand that the phrase "the nothingness of the children of men" (Helaman 12:7) is not a reflection of man's worth: "Now this prophet did not mean to say that the Lord has greater concern for and loves the dust of the earth more than he does his children. . . . The point he is making is that the dust of the earth is obedient. It moveth hither and thither at the command

of the Lord. All things are in harmony with his laws. Everything in the universe obeys the law given unto it, so far as I know, except man. Everywhere you look you find law and order, the elements obeying the law given to them, true to their calling. But man rebels, and in this thing man is less than the dust of the earth because he rejects the counsels of the Lord" (in Conference Report, Apr. 1929, 55).

Helaman 12:15. Knowledge of Astronomy

• Helaman 12:14–15 shows that Mormon had a basic understanding of the physical laws of the universe: "Reference is here made to the biblical account that shows Joshua commanding the sun and the moon to stand still so that his army might complete their rout of the Amorites (Joshua 10:12–14). Here a corrective note is added to that account, which supposed the sun to rotate around a stationery earth. (See also Isaiah 38:7–8; 2 Kings 20:8–11.) These verses provide a subtle but certain assurance that the prophet-editor Mormon, like many of the ancient spiritual leaders, was anything but primitive in his understanding concerning God, man, and the universe" (Joseph Fielding McConkie and Robert L. Millet, *Doctrinal Commentary on the Book of Mormon,* 4 vols. [1987–91], 3:397).

Helaman 12:23–24. Repentance Leads Us to Christ's Grace

• Elder David A. Bednar of the Quorum of the Twelve Apostles expounded on the power of God's grace:

"In the Bible Dictionary we learn that the word *grace* frequently is used in the scriptures to connote a strengthening or enabling power:

"'The main idea of the word is divine means of help or strength, given through the bounteous mercy and love of Jesus Christ.

"'. . . It is likewise through the grace of the Lord that individuals, through faith in the atonement of Jesus Christ and repentance of their sins, receive strength and assistance to do good works that they otherwise would not be able to maintain if left to their own means. This grace is an enabling power that allows men and women to lay hold on eternal life and exaltation after they have expended their own best efforts' (p. 697).

"Thus, the enabling and strengthening aspect of the Atonement helps us to see and to do and to become good in ways that we could never recognize or accomplish with our limited mortal capacity. I testify and witness that the enabling power of the Savior's Atonement is real" (in Conference Report, Oct. 2004, 79; or *Ensign,* Nov. 2004, 76–77; see also D&C 93:20, 27–28).

• Elder Gene R. Cook of the Seventy discussed the personal nature of the Savior's grace:

"The grace of the Lord through the Atonement can both cleanse us of sin and assist us in perfecting ourselves through our trials, sicknesses, and even character defects. . . . Christ can repair our flaws and failings that otherwise are not repairable (see Genesis 18:14; Mark 9:23–24).

"That great truth ought to fill us all with hope, as long as we are quick to remember that the effect of grace in our lives is conditioned upon repenting of our sins. . . .

"A repentant heart and good works are the very conditions required to have grace restored to us. When someone pleads fervently in prayer for an answer, the answer may be more conditioned on repentance of personal sins than on any other factor (see D&C 101:7–8; Mosiah 11:23–24).

"To obtain grace, one does not have to be perfect, but he does have to be trying to keep the commandments the best that he can. Then the Lord will allow him to receive that power" (in Conference Report, Apr. 1993, 99–100; or *Ensign,* May 1993, 80–81).

Points to Ponder

• What steps are you taking to avoid the pride cycle in your life?

• Where have you seen the power of the priesthood operate in your life?

• What can you do to reach a point in your prayers where you do not ask anything that is contrary to the Lord's will?

Suggested Assignments

• Share in a family home evening what you have learned from Helaman 12–14 about how and why the Lord chastens His children.

• Write in your journal how you deal with the pride cycle in your life.

CHAPTER 38

Helaman 13–16

Introduction

The gospel of Jesus Christ offers all people the opportunity to change. Throughout much of the Book of Mormon, the Lamanites' "deeds [had] been evil"; however, "the preaching of the Nephites" (Helaman 15:4) led "the more part of them" to receive the gospel (Helaman 6:1) and experience a mighty change of heart. Here in the book of Helaman is an obvious reversal of roles—a people who had once been taught became the teachers. Many

Nephites, on the other hand, had become prideful and ignored their own prophets, so the Lord sent a Lamanite prophet to warn them to repent and prepare for the coming of the Lord. Look for the Nephites' collective and individual response to the Lord's Lamanite messenger. Samuel's words were important enough to the Savior that He endorsed them during His personal ministry in the Americas and testified they had all been fulfilled (see 3 Nephi 23:9–13).

Commentary

Helaman 13:3. "Whatsoever Things Should Come into His Heart"

• Samuel, who was a prophet, did not take it upon himself to decide what to preach to the Nephites. We read in Helaman 13:3 that he taught "whatsoever things should come into his heart." Concerning this revelatory process, President Boyd K. Packer, President of the Quorum of the Twelve Apostles, described how the voice of the Lord often comes:

"Revelation comes as words we *feel* more than *hear.* Nephi told his wayward brothers, who were visited by an angel, 'Ye were past *feeling,* that ye could not *feel* his words' [1 Nephi 17:45; italics added].

"The scriptures are full of such expressions as 'The veil was taken from our minds, and the eyes of our understanding were opened' [D&C 110:1], or 'I will tell you in your mind and in your heart' [D&C 8:2],

or 'I did enlighten thy mind' [D&C 6:5], or 'Speak the thoughts that I shall put into your hearts' [D&C 100:5]. There are hundreds of verses which teach of revelation" (in Conference Report, Oct. 1994, 77; or *Ensign,* Nov. 1994, 60).

Helaman 13:11–16. Spared Because of a Few Righteous People

• There have been times when the wicked were spared from terrible destructions because there were righteous people living among them. The wicked people of Zarahemla had the righteous people to thank for their preservation from destruction, though, of course, they did not know it. In a few years Zarahemla lost this silent and unappreciated protection, and Samuel's words were fulfilled (see 3 Nephi 9:3). Even Sodom and Gomorrah would have been spared if only 10 righteous people had lived there (see Genesis 18:23–33).

How we live really does make a difference. The personal righteousness of a few can become a great blessing to others, especially to those in our own family and local community.

Helaman 13:19–22. Riches and Spirituality

• Elder Dallin H. Oaks of the Quorum of the Twelve Apostles described the relationship between materialism and spirituality:

"Materialism, which gives priority to material needs and objects, is obviously the opposite of spirituality. The Savior taught that we should not lay up 'treasures upon earth, where moth and rust doth corrupt, and where thieves break through and steal' (Matthew 6:19). We should lay up treasures in heaven: 'For where your treasure is, there will your heart be also' (Matthew 6:21). . . .

"There is nothing inherently evil about money. The Good Samaritan used the same coinage to serve his fellowman that Judas used to betray the Master. It is 'the *love of money* [which] is the root of all evil' (1 Timothy 6:10; italics added). The critical difference is the degree of spirituality we exercise in viewing, evaluating, and managing the things of this world and our experiences in it.

"If allowed to become an object of worship or priority, money can make us selfish and prideful, 'puffed up in the vain things of the world' (Alma 5:37). In contrast, if used for fulfilling our legal obligations and for paying our tithes and offerings, money can demonstrate integrity and develop unselfishness. The spiritually enlightened use of property can help prepare us for the higher law of a celestial glory" (in Conference Report, Oct. 1985, 78; or *Ensign,* Nov. 1985, 62–63).

> ### HELAMAN 13:21–22
> To what did Samuel attribute the Nephites' curse? What did they remember and what did they forget? Why is this important in your life?

Helaman 13:23–29. Following the Living Prophet

• Elder M. Russell Ballard of the Quorum of the Twelve Apostles taught the importance of following living prophets and apostles: "Now, my dear brothers and sisters, please pay attention to those things that the leaders of the Church have taught. . . . Apply the teachings that will help you and your family. Let all of us, regardless of our family circumstances, bring into our homes the teachings of the prophets and the apostles to strengthen our relationships with each other, with our Father in Heaven, and with the Lord Jesus Christ. I promise you in the name of the Lord

that if you will listen not just with your ears but also with your heart, the Holy Ghost will manifest the truth unto you of the messages delivered by [the President of the Church], his counselors, the Apostles, and other leaders of the Church. The Spirit will prompt you to know what you should do as individuals and as families in order to follow our counsel, that your testimonies might be strengthened and that you might have peace and joy" (in Conference Report, Apr. 2001, 86; or *Ensign,* May 2001, 67).

Helaman 13:38. Iniquity Is Contrary to the Nature of Happiness

• Samuel warned the Nephites that they had been seeking happiness in doing iniquity, which is contrary to the nature of happiness. Speaking of this problem and how true happiness comes, Elder Richard G. Scott of the Quorum of the Twelve Apostles pointed out that happiness only comes with righteousness:

"Have you noticed how Satan works to capture the mind and emotions with flashing images, blaring music, and the stimulation of every physical sense to excess? He diligently strives to fill life with action, entertainment, and stimulation so that one cannot ponder the consequences of his tempting invitations. Think of it. Some are tempted to violate the most basic commandments of God because of seductive actions portrayed as acceptable. They are made to seem attractive, even desirable. There seems to be no serious consequence, but rather apparent lasting joy and happiness. But recognize that those performances are controlled by scripts and actors. The outcome of decisions made is likewise manipulated to be whatever the producer wants.

"Life is not that way. Yes, moral agency allows you to choose what you will, but you cannot control the outcome of those choices. Unlike the false creations of man, our Father in Heaven determines the consequences of your choices. Obedience will yield happiness, while violation of His commandments will not" (in Conference Report, Apr. 2004, 105; or *Ensign,* May 2004, 102).

> ### HELAMAN 13:38
> In what ways does Alma 41:10–11 📖 relate to Helaman 13:38? Why is it impossible to find happiness in sin?

Helaman 14. Samuel's Prophecy of the Savior's Coming

• One of the most specific prophecies in scripture is the one by Samuel concerning the birth and death of Jesus Christ. The following charts outline Samuel's teachings, including the birth and death of Christ with their recorded fulfillment and Samuel's teachings to direct the people:

Prophecy of the Savior's Birth		Fulfillment
Helaman 14:2	Birth in five years	3 Nephi 1:13
Helaman 14:3–4	No darkness the night before the birth	3 Nephi 1:15
Helaman 14:5	New star	3 Nephi 1:21
Helaman 14:6	Many signs and wonders in heaven	Helaman 16:13; 3 Nephi 2:1
Helaman 14:7	All people amazed and fall to the earth	3 Nephi 1:16–17

Samuel Taught Them to Prepare for the Savior (Helaman 14:8–13)	Teaching
Helaman 14:8	Believe in God
Helaman 14:9, 13	Repent and be forgiven through Christ
Helaman 14:30	You are free to act for yourself

Prophecy of the Savior's Death		Fulfillment
Helaman 14:20, 27	Sun darkened for three days	3 Nephi 8:19–23
Helaman 14:21	Thunder, lightning, earthquakes	3 Nephi 8:6–7
Helaman 14:22	Earth broken up	3 Nephi 8:12, 17–18

Prophecy of the Savior's Death		Fulfillment
Helaman 14:23	Great tempests; mountains laid low and valleys become mountains	3 Nephi 8:5–6
Helaman 14:24	Highways and cities destroyed	3 Nephi 8:8–11, 13–14
Helaman 14:25	Graves open and resurrected Saints minister to people	3 Nephi 23:9–13

Helaman 14:11. "That Ye Might Know the Conditions of Repentance"

• Elder Richard G. Scott taught about the conditions of repentance:

"In *The Miracle of Forgiveness,* Spencer W. Kimball gives a superb guide to forgiveness through repentance. It has helped many find their way back. He identifies five essential elements of repentance:

"*Sorrow for sin.* Study and ponder to determine how serious the Lord defines your transgression to be. That will bring healing sorrow and remorse. It will also bring a sincere desire for change and a willingness to submit to every requirement for forgiveness. . . .

"*Abandonment of sin.* This is an unyielding, permanent resolve to not repeat the transgression. By keeping this commitment, the bitter aftertaste of that sin need not be experienced again. . . .

"*Confession of sin.* You always need to confess your sins to the Lord. If they are serious transgressions, such as immorality, they need to be confessed to a bishop or stake president. Please understand that confession is not repentance. It is an essential step but is not of itself adequate. Partial confession by mentioning lesser mistakes will not help you resolve a more serious, undisclosed transgression. . . .

"*Restitution for sin.* You must restore as far as possible all that which is stolen, damaged, or defiled. Willing restitution is concrete evidence to the Lord that you are committed to do all you can to repent.

"*Obedience to all the commandments.* Full obedience brings the complete power of the gospel into your life with strength to focus on the abandonment of specific sins. It includes things you might not initially consider part of repentance, such as attending meetings, paying tithing, giving service, and forgiving others. . . .

Paul Gustave Dore

"I would add a sixth step: *Recognition of the Savior.* Of all the necessary steps to repentance, I testify that the most critically important is for you to have a conviction that forgiveness comes because of the Redeemer. It is essential to know that only on His terms can you be forgiven" (in Conference Report, Apr. 1995, 102; or *Ensign,* May 1995, 76).

• In addition to the important elements taught above by President Kimball and Elder Scott, repentance must also include change. Elder Jeffrey R. Holland of the Quorum of the Twelve Apostles explained: "We must change anything we can change that may be part of the problem. . . . We thank our Father in Heaven we are *allowed* to change, we thank Jesus we *can* change, and ultimately we do so only with Their divine assistance. Certainly not everything we struggle with is a result of our actions. Often it is the result of the actions of others or just the mortal events of life. But anything *we* can change we *should* change, and we must forgive the rest. In this way our access to the Savior's Atonement becomes as unimpeded as we, with our imperfections, can make it. He will take it from there" (in Conference Report, Apr. 2006, 70–71; or *Ensign,* May 2006, 70).

Helaman 14:11–12. Samuel's Purpose in Teaching

• In Helaman 14:11–12 the prophet Samuel listed four truths he wanted the people to know from his teachings:

Know the judgments of God

Know the conditions of repentance

Know of the coming of Jesus Christ

Know of the signs of His coming

Helaman 14:15–19. The Atonement Overcomes Death

• Samuel the Lamanite described the difference between physical death, the first spiritual death, and the second spiritual death—as well as how the Savior's Atonement helps us overcome these deaths.

Physical death. Elder Earl C. Tingey of the Presidency of the Seventy defined physical death and who will experience it: "Physical death is the separation of the spirit from the physical body. Because of the Fall of Adam, all mankind will suffer physical death" (in Conference Report, Apr. 2006, 74; or *Ensign,* May 2006, 73).

The first spiritual death. Spiritual death when someone is "cut off from the presence of the Lord" (Alma 42:9).

President Spencer W. Kimball (1895–1985) explained that both of these deaths are the result of the Fall of Adam and Eve: "Our first parents, Adam and Eve, disobeyed God. By eating the forbidden fruit, they became mortal. Consequently, they and all of their descendants became subject to both mortal and spiritual death (mortal death, the separation of body and spirit; and spiritual death, the separation of the spirit from the presence of God and death as pertaining to the things of the spirit)" (in Conference Report, Apr. 1978, 7; or *Ensign,* May 1978, 6).

For us, this spiritual death occurred when we left God's presence and were born into mortality. Samuel the Lamanite called being cut off from His presence "the first death" (Helaman 14:16).

Samuel the Lamanite taught that all of Heavenly Father's children who lived in mortality will overcome physical and spiritual death through the powers of the Atonement of Jesus Christ (see Helaman 14:17). Many other scriptures also attest to this fact (see 2 Nephi 2:9–10; 9:15, 22, 38; Alma 11:43–44; 12:12–15, 24; 42:23; 3 Nephi 26:4).

The second spiritual death. The second death is an ultimate or final spiritual death that comes not because of leaving God's presence to be born into mortality, but comes because of unrepented personal sin.

The Savior has also provided help to overcome this second spiritual death. By suffering for our sins, He offers us the opportunity to repent. But to those who do not repent, there "cometh upon them again a spiritual death, yea, a second death, for they are cut off again as to things pertaining to righteousness" (Helaman 14:18). This means that a person with unresolved sin cannot remain in God's presence after he or she is brought back to Him for judgment.

Elder Russell M. Nelson of the Quorum of the Twelve Apostles described this condition:

"If physical death should strike before moral wrongs have been made right, opportunity for repentance will have been forfeited. Thus, 'the [real] sting of death is sin' (1 Corinthians 15:56).

"Even the Savior cannot save us in our sins. He will redeem us from our sins, but only upon condition of our repentance. We are responsible for our own spiritual survival or death (see Romans 8:13–14; Helaman 14:18; D&C 29:41–45)" (in Conference Report, Apr. 1992, 102; or *Ensign,* May 1992, 73).

Helaman 15:3–4. God's Divine Love

• The Lord loves all people but cannot tolerate sin. Although Helaman 15:4 states that the Lord hated the Lamanites "because their deeds have been evil continually," Samuel is an example of the many Lamanites who were taught the gospel message and gained God's favor once they were converted.

Elder Russell M. Nelson addressed the subject of God's love for those who sin: "Does this mean the Lord does not love the sinner? Of course not. Divine love is infinite and universal. The Savior loves both saints and sinners. The Apostle John affirmed, 'We love him, because he first loved us' [1 John 4:19]. And Nephi, upon seeing in vision the Lord's mortal ministry, declared: '. . . Yea, they spit upon him, and he suffereth it, because of his *loving kindness* and his long-suffering towards the children of men' [1 Nephi 19:9; italics added]. We know the expansiveness of the Redeemer's love because He died that *all* who die might live again" ("Divine Love," *Ensign,* Feb. 2003, 24).

Helaman 15:7–8. A Lasting Change of Heart

• President Ezra Taft Benson (1899–1994) understood the power of the scriptures, especially the Book of Mormon, to change our lives. He emphasized the importance of having the doctrines taught in our latter-day scripture deep in our hearts if we are to stay "firm and steadfast in the faith" (Helaman 15:8).

President Benson taught, "Social, ethical, cultural, or educational converts will not survive under the heat of the day unless their taproots go down to the fulness of the gospel which the Book of Mormon contains" (in Conference Report, Apr. 1975, 96; or *Ensign,* May 1975, 65).

Helaman 16:2–3, 6–8. Divine Protection

• The protection Samuel received while he delivered his message of repentance is not unusual. The scriptures include several examples of prophets who were threatened but whose lives were miraculously guarded so they could complete their missions. Consider the following examples and recall how they were able to present the Lord's words while under the threat of injury or death: Noah (see Moses 8:18), Abraham (see Abraham 1:5, 12, 15–19), Lehi (see 1 Nephi 1:19–20; 2:1–4), Nephi (see 1 Nephi 17:48–55), and Abinadi (see Mosiah 13:1–5). Sometimes the Lord's servants eventually lose their life, but not until, as Abinadi declared, they have "delivered the message which the Lord sent [them] to deliver" (Mosiah 13:3).

Elder Robert D. Hales of the Quorum of the Twelve Apostles reminded us:

"Prophets of all dispensations have willingly put their lives on the line and, with courage, have done the will and proclaimed the word of God. . . .

". . . Let us follow the example of our Lord Jesus Christ and His prophets, past and present. It may not be required of us to give our lives as martyrs, as did many of the prophets. What is required is our obedience to the Lord's commandments and our faithfulness to the covenants we have made with Him" (in Conference Report, Apr. 1996, 49; or *Ensign,* May 1996, 35).

Helaman 16:2–20. Reactions to the Prophet

• Helaman 16 records the ways the wicked reacted to the prophet Samuel and his message. President Ezra Taft Benson spoke of how the wicked react to prophets of our day:

"The prophet will not necessarily be popular with the world or the worldly.

"As a prophet reveals the truth it divides the people. The honest in heart heed his words, but the unrighteous either ignore the prophet or fight him. When the prophet points out the sins of the world, the worldly either want to close the mouth of the prophet or else act as if the prophet didn't exist, rather than repent of their sins. Popularity is never a test of truth. Many a prophet has been killed or cast out. As we come closer to the Lord's second coming, you can expect that as the people of the world become more wicked, the prophet will be less popular with them" ("Fourteen Fundamentals in Following the Prophet," in *1980 Devotional Speeches of the Year* [1981], 29; see also *The Teachings of Ezra Taft Benson* [1988], 133).

The following list includes some reasons why the people in Helaman 16:2–21 refused to heed the words of the prophet:

1. Subsequent scattering of the Jews (see vv. 17–20)

2. Personal anger (see v. 2)

3. Prophets just guess right occasionally with their prophecies (see v. 6)

4. People trust more in their own strength and abilities (see v. 15)

5. Teachings are often not reasonable (see v. 18)

6. Teachings of the prophets are confused traditions and cannot be proved (see v. 20)

7. Prophets trick and deceive us rather than doing real miracles (see v. 21)

Helaman 16:15, 18, 20. Depending on One's Own Strength and Wisdom

• Elder Dallin H. Oaks cautioned us against relying solely upon personal study and reason to determine spiritual truths:

"The Book of Mormon describes [an] attitude among a people who depended solely 'upon their own strength and upon their own wisdom' and upon what they could 'witness with [their] own eyes.' (Hel. 16:15, 20.) Upon the basis of reason, these persons rejected the prophecies, saying, 'It is not reasonable that such a being as a Christ shall come.' (Vs. 18.) Applying that same attitude, a prominent professor dismissed the Book of Mormon with the assertion, 'You don't get books from angels. It is just that simple.'

"Those who seek gospel knowledge only by study and reason are particularly susceptible to the self-sufficiency and self-importance that sometimes characterize academic pursuits. As the apostle Paul observed in his day, 'Knowledge puffeth up.' He cautioned the learned: 'Take heed lest by any means this liberty [knowledge] of yours become a stumblingblock to them that are weak. . . . And through thy knowledge shall the weak brother perish, for whom Christ died?' (1 Cor. 8:1, 9, 11.)" (*The Lord's Way* [1991], 46–47).

> ### *HELAMAN 16:22*
> *What is Satan's goal for spreading contention?*

Helaman 16:22. Satan Spreads Contention

• Why is it important to avoid contention with others? Elder Russell M. Nelson explained that the answer reaches back into premortal life:

"To understand why the Lord has commanded us not to 'contend one with another,' we must know the true source of contention. A Book of Mormon prophet revealed this important knowledge even before the birth of Christ. . . . [See Helaman 16:22.] . . .

"Contention existed before the earth was formed. When God's plan for creation and mortal life on the earth was first announced, sons and daughters of God shouted for joy. The plan was dependent on man's agency, his subsequent fall from the presence of God, and the merciful provision of a Savior to redeem mankind. Scriptures reveal that Lucifer sought vigorously to *amend* the plan by destroying the agency of man. . . .

"Satan's selfish efforts to alter the plan of God resulted in great contention in heaven. . . .

"This war in heaven was not a war of bloodshed. It was a war of conflicting ideas—the beginning of contention.

"Scriptures repeatedly warn that the father of contention opposes the plan of our Heavenly Father. Satan's method relies on the infectious canker of contention. Satan's motive: to gain personal acclaim even over God Himself" (in Conference Report, Apr. 1989, 85–86; or *Ensign,* May 1989, 68–69).

Points to Ponder

• Consider if you had lived in the days of Samuel, whether you would have accepted these prophets and perhaps even stood against the masses in their defense. In what ways do you feel you are following the living prophet in your life?

• Helaman 15:7 describes what led the Lamanites to their mighty change. Have you known anyone who has had a life-changing experience after being led to the scriptures?

• Read Helaman 16:22. What have you found to be the most helpful tool to keep peace and harmony with your family and those you associate with?

Suggested Assignments

• Write a letter to a missionary. Include in your letter a description of a principle you learned from Samuel's teachings. Explain how you think it applies in your life.

• Teach a lesson in family home evening on the difference between having a hard heart and a broken heart. Consider using scriptures from Helaman 16:13–23 and 3 Nephi 9:20.

Introduction

President Ezra Taft Benson (1899–1994) observed that "the record of the Nephite history just prior to the Savior's visit reveals many parallels to our own day as we anticipate the Savior's second coming" (in Conference Report, Apr. 1987, 3; or *Ensign,* May 1987, 4). Only those with firm testimonies and full conversions were able to remain steadfast prior to the Savior's appearance in America. The same is true in our day. Only those with firm testimonies and full conversions will be able to remain steadfast prior to the Lord's Second Coming. A careful study of 3 Nephi 1–7 will help you understand how your testimony of Jesus Christ and conversion to His gospel will give you the sustaining strength you need to stay true to the Savior during the challenging days in which you live.

Commentary

It may be instructive to compare the length of books in the Book of Mormon and the time periods they covered. Refer to the chart "Book of Mormon Pages and Time Periods" in the appendix (p. 411).

3 Nephi 1. The Fulfillment of Prophecy

• Nephi prayed mightily to the Lord when enemies threatened to kill those who believed the signs foretold by Samuel the Lamanite. In answer to his prayer, the Lord told Nephi not to fear, for the signs of Christ's birth would be fulfilled that very night. The record carefully documents the fulfillment of all of Samuel's prophecies (see chart in commentary for Helaman 14 on p. 283).

3 Nephi 1:1. The Nephite Calendar Systems

• Throughout the course of the Book of Mormon, the Nephites used three different points of reference for measuring time with their calendars:

Reference Point	When Used	Scripture Block
From the time when Lehi left Jerusalem	600–92 B.C.	1 Nephi 1–Mosiah 29
From the time when the government changed from kings to judges	92 B.C.–A.D. 1	Mosiah 29–3 Nephi 1
From the time of the sign of the birth of Jesus Christ	A.D. 1–421	3 Nephi 1–Moroni 10

Note: The sign was given at Jesus's birth. However, they did not start using it as a point of reference until A.D. 9.

3 Nephi 1:29. We Must Protect Ourselves from Being Led Astray

• Verse 29 of 3 Nephi 1 illustrates that it only takes one generation for apostasy to occur. We read the sad tale of the children of faithful parents who were led away by "lyings and . . . flattering words, to join those Gadianton robbers."

President Henry B. Eyring of the First Presidency taught: "The young people of the Church . . . hold the future in their hands. The Church has always been one generation away from extinction. If a whole generation were lost, which will not happen, we would lose the Church. But even a single individual lost to the gospel of Jesus Christ closes doors for generations of descendants, unless the Lord reaches out to bring some of them back" ("We Must Raise Our Sights" [Church Educational System conference on the Book of Mormon, Aug. 14, 2001], 1; see LDS.org under gospel library/additional addresses/CES addresses).

• President Gordon B. Hinckley (1910–2008) counseled the youth of our day on how to avoid being led away from the truth:

"To our young people, the glorious youth of this generation, I say, be true. Hold to the faith. Stand firmly for what you know to be right.

"You face tremendous temptation. It comes at you in the halls of popular entertainment, on the Internet, in the movies, on television, in cheap literature, and in other ways—subtle, titillating, and difficult to resist. Peer pressure may be almost overpowering. But, my dear young friends, you must not give in. You must be strong. You must take the long look ahead rather than succumbing to the present seductive temptation. . . .

". . . You are the best generation we have ever had. You know the gospel better. You are more faithful in your duties. You are stronger to face the temptations which come your way. Live by your standards. Pray for the guidance and protection of the Lord. He will never leave you alone. He will comfort you. He will sustain you. He will bless and magnify you and make your reward sweet and beautiful. And you will discover that your example will attract others who will take courage from your strength" (in Conference Report, Oct. 2003, 86–88; or *Ensign,* Nov. 2003, 83–84).

3 Nephi 2:1–2. They Began to Disbelieve the Signs That Had Been Given

• Immediately after the sign of Christ's birth was given, Satan sent forth lies to harden the hearts of the people (see 3 Nephi 1:22). Though the impact was not immediate, it was not long before many people became "hard in their hearts, and blind in their minds, and began to disbelieve all which they had heard and seen" (3 Nephi 2:1).

Elder Neal A. Maxwell (1926–2004) of the Quorum of the Twelve Apostles taught that we too can become vulnerable to Satan's attack on our beliefs: "How quickly [Satan] moves in even where people have had special spiritual experiences, seeking to get people who have seen signs *'to disbelieve all which they had heard and seen.'* (3 Nephi 2:1–2.) The adversary has a better chance to persuade us that what we believe is foolish if we worry about looking foolish in front of our fellowmen" (*Things As They Really Are* [1978], 41).

Jerry Thompson, © IRI

What is the lesson believers should learn concerning signs and salvation? (see D&C 63:8–12). Signs flow from faith and are a product of it. They strengthen the faithful and produce faith in the spiritually receptive. The chief purpose of signs, however, is not to produce faith but to reward it (see D&C 68:9–11). Signs do not force faith upon anyone. Sadly, it is common to see both in scripture and in today's world most marvelous signs and evidences of God's power ignored or rationalized away by those without faith.

---

3 NEPHI 2:1–3
How did these people explain away the signs of Christ's birth? What did their disbelief lead to? How does belief affect action?

---

3 Nephi 2:1–4. Why Do the Wicked Sometimes See Signs?

• Scripturally we can see some reasons why the Lord will occasionally show signs to the wicked:

To vindicate prophets. The sign that Nephi, son of Helaman, gave to the people concerning the death of the chief judge showed that Nephi was right (see Mosiah 20:21).

Leave the wicked without excuse. The wicked are completely responsible for their actions thereafter. The

Lord has stated, "He that seeketh signs shall see signs, but not unto salvation" (D&C 63:7).

Show correctness of prophets' words. Since the wicked seek to prove the prophet wrong, the Lord will occasionally show indisputable signs (see Helaman 9:2–4).

Condemn the wicked. When the wicked see signs, it is through the Lord's anger and to their condemnation (see D&C 63:11). The Savior stated, "An evil and adulterous generation seeketh after a sign" (Matthew 12:39).

3 Nephi 3–4. Physical and Spiritual Preparation

• It is easy to see Satan's imprint in Giddianhi's words (3 Nephi 3:1–10) as he used flattery (v. 2), feigned concern (v. 5), and made false promises (vv. 7–8) to accomplish his evil designs. How like the devil's promises were Giddianhi's promises of freedom when all he had to offer was bondage and a promise to share possessions that were not even his to share (see v. 7).

Lachoneus straightway turned his attention to his people. He knew they needed to be physically and spiritually prepared for the imminent attack of Giddianhi's robbers. He had his people build strong fortifications (v. 14) and gather their animals and families (v. 13) into one place—the land of Zarahemla (vv. 22–23). He had them make weapons and armor (v. 26) and gather a seven-year supply of provisions (3 Nephi 4:4). Lachoneus instructed his people to leave the deserted land "desolate" so the robbers would not be able to forage for food (vv. 3–4).

Most importantly, Lachoneus had his people prepare spiritually. He reminded them of the safety of repentance (3 Nephi 3:15). His people repented and prayed mightily unto the Lord (v. 25; 4:8). Thus they wisely prepared themselves both physically and spiritually for the imminent attack of their enemies.

• We have been asked to prepare physically and spiritually in our day for imminent calamities. Elder Dallin H. Oaks of the Quorum of the Twelve Apostles taught what we should do to prepare for the events that precede the Savior's coming:

"What if the day of His coming were tomorrow? If we knew that we would meet the Lord tomorrow—through our premature death or His unexpected coming—what would we do today? What confessions would we make? What practices would we discontinue? What accounts would we settle? What forgivenesses would we extend? What testimonies would we bear?

"If we would do those things then, why not now? Why not seek peace while peace can be obtained? If our lamps of preparation are drawn down, let us start immediately to replenish them.

"We need to make both temporal and spiritual preparation for the events prophesied at the time of the Second Coming. And the preparation most likely to be neglected is the one less visible and more difficult—the spiritual. . . .

"Are we following the Lord's command, 'Stand ye in holy places, and be not moved, until the day of the Lord come; for behold, it cometh quickly'? (D&C 87:8). What are those 'holy places'? Surely they include the temple and its covenants faithfully kept. Surely they include a home where children are treasured and parents are respected. Surely the holy places include our posts of duty assigned by priesthood authority, including missions and callings faithfully fulfilled in branches, wards, and stakes" (in Conference Report, Apr. 2004, 7–8; or *Ensign,* May 2004, 9–10).

3 Nephi 4:10. Faith in God Overcomes Fear

• The Nephites prepared themselves physically and spiritually to meet Giddianhi's robbers. As a final act of submission to the Lord, which was misinterpreted by their foes, they fell to the earth and cried unto the Lord. They then stood on their feet and met their enemy with faith in God. (See 3 Nephi 4:8–10.) We too can stand up to our enemies and replace our fears with faith in God.

Elder M. Russell Ballard of the Quorum of the Twelve Apostles wrote concerning the faith that is needed to face the challenges of our day: "Preparing ourselves and our families for the challenges of the coming years will require us to replace fear with faith. We must be able to overcome the fear of enemies who oppose and threaten us. The Lord has said, 'Fear not, little flock; do good; let earth and hell combine against you, for if ye are built upon my rock, they cannot prevail' (D&C 6:34)" (in Conference Report, Oct. 1989, 43; or *Ensign,* Nov. 1989, 34).

3 Nephi 5:1–3. Faith Leads to Repentance and All Good Works

• While serving as a member of the Seventy, Elder John H. Groberg explained the relationship between faith and repentance:

"If we think deeply, we realize that the first principle—faith in the Lord Jesus Christ—underlies all else; that is, it takes faith in Christ to repent or be baptized or perform any other ordinances of the gospel. Jesus made saving repentance possible and He made baptism meaningful. If we have faith in Him, we will repent and be baptized.

"If we do not repent, or refuse to be baptized, or are unwilling to keep His commandments, it is because we do not have sufficient faith in Him. Thus, repentance, baptism, and all other principles and ordinances are not entirely separate but are actually extensions of our faith in Christ. Without faith in Him, we do little of eternal value. With faith in Him, our lives become focused on doing things of eternal value" (in Conference Report, Oct. 1993, 35; or *Ensign,* Nov. 1993, 26).

---

3 NEPHI 5:1–3; 6:4–5

What did the people know with certainty? What did Mormon say was the only thing that would stop them from prospering?

---

3 Nephi 5:13. "A Disciple of Jesus Christ"

• Mormon described himself as a disciple of Christ. President Joseph Fielding Smith (1876–1972) explained the nature of Mormon's calling: "While in every instance the Nephite twelve are spoken of as disciples, the fact remains that they had been endowed with divine authority to be special witnesses for Christ among their own people. Therefore, they were virtually apostles to the

Nephite race, although their jurisdiction was, as revealed to Nephi, eventually to be subject to the authority and jurisdiction of Peter and the twelve chosen in Palestine" (*Answers to Gospel Questions,* comp. Joseph Fielding Smith Jr., 5 vols. [1957–66], 1:122).

While Mormon's personal call was that of an Apostle, the term *disciple* can also have a more general definition. A disciple is also "a follower of Jesus Christ who lives according to Christ's teachings (D&C 41:5)" (Guide to the Scriptures, "Disciple").

Elder L. Tom Perry of the Quorum of the Twelve Apostles further explained:

"The following has been written about discipleship:

"'The word *disciple* comes from the Latin [meaning] a learner. A disciple of Christ is one who is learning to be like Christ—learning to think, to feel, and to act as he does. To be a true disciple, to fulfill that learning task, is the most demanding regimen known to man. No other discipline compares . . . in either requirements or rewards. It involves the total transformation of a person from the state of the natural man to that of [a] saint, one who loves the Lord and serves with all of his heart, might, mind, and strength' (Chauncey C. Riddle, 'Becoming a Disciple,' *Ensign,* Sept. 1974, 81)" (in Conference Report, Oct. 2000, 77; or *Ensign,* Nov. 2000, 61).

In addition to speaking about discipleship, Mormon here may be making a statement about his authority not just as a disciple but as an Apostle of the Lord Jesus Christ.

3 Nephi 5:22–26. The Meaning of the Gathering in the Latter Days

• Elder Dallin H. Oaks explained the meaning and purpose of the gathering:

"Another sign of the times is the gathering of the faithful (see D&C 133:4). In the early years of this last dispensation, a gathering to Zion involved various locations in the United States: to Kirtland, to Missouri, to Nauvoo, and to the tops of the mountains. Always these were gatherings to prospective temples.

Courtesy of LDS Church Archives

"With the creation of stakes and the construction of temples in most nations with sizable populations of the faithful, the current commandment is not to gather to one place but to gather in stakes in our own homelands. There the faithful can enjoy the full blessings of eternity in a house of the Lord. There, in their own homelands, they can obey the Lord's command to enlarge the borders of His people and strengthen her stakes (see D&C 101:21; 133:9, 14). In this way the stakes of Zion are 'for a defense, and for a refuge from the storm, and from wrath when it shall be poured out without mixture upon the whole earth' (D&C 115:6)" (in Conference Report, Apr. 2004, 6; or *Ensign,* May 2004, 8).

---

3 NEPHI 6:10–16, 18, 29

What led to the apostasy of many Nephites? How can this serve as a warning for us in the latter days?

---

3 Nephi 6:12. Prosperity and Peace Can Lead to Pride

• During the years immediately prior to the Savior's personal ministry among the Nephites, the people enjoyed a period of brief prosperity. Unfortunately, this temporal success led to "pride and boastings because of their exceedingly great riches" (3 Nephi 6:10).

President Henry B. Eyring warned about such challenges in our day: "A little prosperity and peace, or even a turn slightly for the better, can bring us feelings of self-sufficiency. We can feel quickly that we are in

control of our lives, that the change for the better is our own doing, not that of a God who communicates to us through the still, small voice of the Spirit. Pride creates a noise within us which makes the quiet voice of the Spirit hard to hear. And soon, in our vanity, we no longer even listen for it. We can come quickly to think we don't need it" (in Conference Report, Oct. 2001, 16; or *Ensign,* Nov. 2001, 16).

• Several times in Book of Mormon history the people passed through a cycle of righteousness, prosperity, riches, pride, wickedness, destruction, humility, and righteousness again. For more information and a diagram depicting the pride cycle, refer to "The Cycle of Righteousness and Wickedness" in the appendix (p. 414).

3 Nephi 6:12–13. We Determine Our Response to Circumstance

• The record states that "some were lifted up in pride, and others were exceedingly humble" (3 Nephi 6:13). Each of us must determine which way we are going to turn. Elder Marvin J. Ashton (1915–94) of the Quorum of the Twelve Apostles taught of this principle: "Certainly one of our God-given privileges is the right to choose what our attitude will be in any given set of circumstances. We can let the events that surround us determine our actions—or we can personally take charge and rule our lives, using as guidelines the principles of pure religion. Pure religion is learning the gospel of Jesus Christ and then putting it into action. Nothing will ever be of real benefit to us until it is incorporated into our own lives" (in Conference Report, Oct. 1982, 91; or *Ensign,* Nov. 1982, 63).

3 Nephi 6:15–18. Satan Tempted Them to Willfully Sin against God

• Satan, who rebelled against God in our premortal existence (see Moses 4:3; D&C 29:36; 76:25), seeks to stir up rebellion among the Saints of God. The danger of willful participation in sin has to do with the voice we choose to follow. King Benjamin warned:

"And now, I say unto you, my brethren, that after ye have known and have been taught all these things, if ye should transgress and go contrary to that which has been spoken. . . .

"I say unto you, that the man that doeth this, the same cometh out in open rebellion against God; therefore he listeth to obey the evil spirit, and becometh an enemy to all righteousness; therefore, the Lord has no place in him, for he dwelleth not in unholy temples" (Mosiah 2:36–37).

• In connection with this, Elder Neal A. Maxwell observed: "Surely it should give us more pause than it does to think of how casually we sometimes give to [Satan] who could not control his own ego in the premortal world such awful control over our egos here. We often let the adversary do *indirectly* now what we refused to let him do *directly* then" (*We Will Prove Them Herewith* [1982], 45).

• Elder M. Russell Ballard further explained the danger of heeding Satan's temptations:

"In the premortal world before we left the presence of Heavenly Father, He warned and cautioned us about new experiences we would have in mortality. We knew that we each would have a physical body of flesh and bone. Never having been mortal before, we had no experience dealing with the temptations of mortality. But Heavenly Father knew and understood. He charged us to control our mortal bodies and to make them subject to our spirits. Our spirits would have to master the physical temptations that our bodies would encounter in a temporal world. Spiritual power over the influence of Satan comes to us by keeping the commandments of our Lord, Jesus Christ. . . .

"Satan will seek to tempt us at times and in ways that exploit our greatest weaknesses or destroy our strengths. But his promises of pleasure are short-lived deceptions. His evil design is to tempt us into sinning, knowing that when we sin we separate ourselves from our Heavenly Father and the Savior, Jesus Christ. We begin to move away from Heavenly Father's promised blessings toward the misery and anguish in which Satan and his followers languish. By sinning we put ourselves in Satan's power.

"Now, my dear young friends, I understand the struggles you face every day in keeping the commandments of the Lord. The battle for your souls is increasingly fierce. The adversary is strong and cunning. However, you have within your physical body the powerful spirit of a son or daughter of God. Because He loves you and wants you

to come home to Him, our Father in Heaven has given you a conscience that tells your spirit when you are keeping the Lord's commandments and when you are not. If you will pay more attention to your spiritual self, which is eternal, than to your mortal self, which is temporary, you can always resist the temptations of Satan and conquer his efforts to take you into his power" (in Conference Report, Apr. 1993, 5–6; or *Ensign,* May 1993, 6–7).

3 Nephi 7:15–26. The Faithfulness of Nephi and His Followers

• One bright spot in the otherwise sad account of the Nephites' turn from their righteousness is the steadfast faithfulness of Nephi and his people. Their example provides a pattern to help us maintain our righteousness during times of wickedness. We read of Nephi's firm testimony, born of personal experience (see 3 Nephi 7:15), that he boldly taught "repentance and remission of sins through faith on the Lord Jesus Christ" (v. 16). He ministered with power and authority because "great was his faith on the Lord Jesus Christ" (v. 18), and those who responded to his testimony were themselves visited "by the power and Spirit of God" (v. 21). Those who believed were healed (see v. 22), repented, were baptized, and "received a remission of their sins" (see vv. 24–25).

> **3 NEPHI 7:21–25**
>
> *What did those who were converted do? What is your experience with these important principles?*

3 Nephi 7:21–26. Full Conversion

• Elder Richard G. Scott of the Quorum of the Twelve Apostles spoke of the difference between those who are fully converted and those who are still lacking. He further taught the continual need for a cycle of conversion, which builds steadiness in true followers of Christ:

"Each of us has observed how some individuals go through life consistently doing the right things. . . . When difficult choices are to be made, they seem to invariably make the right ones, even though there were enticing alternatives available to them. We know that they are subject to temptation, but they seem oblivious to it. Likewise, we have observed how others are not so valiant in the decisions they make. In a powerfully spiritual environment, they resolve to do better. . . . Yet they are soon back doing the same things they resolved to abandon. . . .

"Sometimes the word *converted* is used to describe when a sincere individual decides to be baptized. However . . . *conversion* means far more than that. . . . President Marion G. Romney explained conversion:

"'Converted means to turn from one belief or course of action to another. Conversion is a spiritual and moral change. *Converted* implies not merely mental acceptance of Jesus and his teachings but also a motivating faith in him and his gospel. A faith which works a transformation, an actual change in one's understanding of life's meaning and in his allegiance to God in interest, in thought, and in conduct. In one who is really wholly converted, desire for things contrary to the gospel of Jesus Christ has actually died. And substituted therefore is a love of God, with a fixed and controlling determination to keep his commandments' [in Conference Report, Guatemala Area Conference 1977, 8]. . . .

"Stated simply, true conversion is the fruit of *faith, repentance,* and *consistent obedience. Faith* comes by hearing the word of God [see Romans 10:17] and responding to it. You will receive from the Holy Ghost a confirming witness of things you accept on *faith* by willingly doing them [see Ether 12:6]. You will be led to *repent* of errors resulting from wrong things done or right things not done. As a consequence, your capacity to *consistently obey* will be strengthened. This cycle of *faith, repentance,* and *consistent obedience* will lead you to greater conversion with its attendant blessings" (in Conference Report, Apr. 2002, 26–28; or *Ensign,* May 2002, 24–25).

Points to Ponder

- What does it mean to be a disciple of Christ? (see 3 Nephi 5:13). What would help you be a more devoted disciple of Jesus Christ?

- The inequality among the Nephites is examined in 3 Nephi 6:14. What did this inequality do to the Church? What did Mormon say was the real cause of this iniquity? (see v. 15). What generally happens when people begin to believe that they are better than others? How does this part of Book of Mormon history substantiate Proverbs 16:18?

- We have been taught the importance of actions accompanying beliefs and the importance of enduring in faith. These chapters contain both positive and negative examples of these concepts. What examples did you see? What can we learn from these examples? Which of them have direct relevance as you strive to remain faithful?

Suggested Assignments

- We learn the importance of individual testimony and conversion in 3 Nephi 1–7. Divide a piece of paper into two columns and put the following two headings at the top of each column:

  1. Attitudes, beliefs, and actions that lead to individual testimony and conversion

  2. Attitudes, beliefs, and actions that destroy individual testimony and conversion

  Then review 3 Nephi 1–7 and list in the appropriate column the teachings, events, principles, and doctrines you discover. Write a short explanation of what you have learned from this exercise and teach it in a family home evening lesson.

- President Ezra Taft Benson taught that many of the events just prior to the Savior's first coming to the Book of Mormon people parallel those of His Second Coming. Make a list of events, teachings, doctrines, and principles from Helaman 14 through 3 Nephi 7 that you believe have parallels to the "last days."

- Memorize 3 Nephi 5:13. As you recite these words, think of ways you could declare the Savior's words to others. You may want to start your declarations of faith with the phrase, "I believe that . . ."

CHAPTER 40

3 Nephi 8–11

Introduction

Ponder the spoken witness from Heavenly Father: "Behold my Beloved Son, in whom I am well pleased, in whom I have glorified my name—hear ye him" (3 Nephi 11:7). Envision how you would have responded if you had been there for this announcement and the appearance of Jesus Christ—the crowning event of the Book of Mormon. Imagine how you would have felt when you heard the Son declare, "Behold, I am Jesus Christ, whom the prophets testified shall come into the world" (3 Nephi 11:10). Consider the impact on the lives of those who received a spiritual and physical witness of the reality of Jesus Christ.

The voice of God was heard several times by this people. As you read 3 Nephi 8–11 look for what He taught. Consider your ability to recognize God's voice and follow His message for you.

Commentary

3 Nephi 8:1. Performing Miracles in the Name of Jesus

• Nephi noted that "there was not any man who could do a miracle in the name of Jesus save he were cleansed every whit from his iniquity" (3 Nephi 8:1; see also D&C 121:36 📖).

The following story told by Elder Vaughn J. Featherstone while serving in the Presiding Bishopric illustrates the need for priesthood holders to be pure at all times:

"People cannot hide sin. You cannot mock God and hold the Lord's holy priesthood and pretend to propose that you are his servant.

"I know of a great man who held his dead son in his arms, and said, 'In the name of Jesus Christ and by the power and authority of the Holy Melchizedek Priesthood, I command you to live.' And the dead boy opened up his eyes.

"This great brother could not have possibly done that had he been looking at a pornographic piece of material a few nights before or if he had been involved in any other transgression of that kind. The priesthood has to have a pure conduit to operate" (in Conference Report, Apr. 1975, 100; or *Ensign,* May 1975, 66).

• Elder Jeffrey R. Holland of the Quorum of the Twelve Apostles explained that although not every priesthood administration will result in a miraculous event, only those who are worthy can perform miracles in the name of Christ. Priesthood holders must keep themselves pure and clean: "Now, my young friends of both the Aaronic and Melchizedek Priesthood, not every prayer is answered so immediately, and not every priesthood declaration can command the renewal or the sustaining of life. Sometimes the will of God is otherwise. But young men, you will learn, if you have not already, that in frightening, even perilous moments, your faith and your priesthood will demand the very best of you and the best you can call down from heaven. You Aaronic Priesthood boys will not use your priesthood in exactly the same way an ordained elder uses the Melchizedek [Priesthood], but all priesthood bearers must be instruments in the hand of God, and to be so, you must, as Joshua said, 'sanctify yourselves' [Joshua 3:5]. You must be ready and worthy to act" (in Conference Report, Oct. 2000, 51; or *Ensign,* Nov. 2000, 39).

3 Nephi 8:6–19. Physical Upheavals Testify of Christ

• "A great and terrible tempest . . . such as never had been known in all the land" unleashed untold natural destruction (3 Nephi 8:6–7). These physical upheavals were signs in America witnessing the crucifixion of Jesus Christ in Jerusalem (see 1 Nephi 19:10–12; Helaman 14:20–21). Some physical upheavals in our day signal the approaching of the Second Coming.

Jerry Thompson, © IRI

Elder Dallin H. Oaks of the Quorum of the Twelve Apostles cited the increase of major earthquakes as one of the signs of the Second Coming: "Signs of the Second Coming are all around us and seem to be increasing in frequency and intensity. For example, the list of major earthquakes in *The World Almanac and Book of Facts, 2004* shows twice as many earthquakes in the decades of the 1980s and 1990s as in the two preceding decades (see pages 189–90). It also shows further sharp increases in the first several years of this century. The list of notable floods and tidal waves and the list of hurricanes, typhoons, and blizzards worldwide show similar increases in recent years (see pages 188–89). Increases by comparison with 50 years ago can be dismissed as changes in reporting criteria, but the accelerating pattern of natural disasters in the last few decades is ominous" (in Conference Report, Apr. 2004, 5–6; or *Ensign,* May 2004, 7–8).

3 Nephi 8:23. Three Days of Darkness

• The three days of darkness symbolized the death of Jesus Christ, who is "the light and the life of the world" (3 Nephi 11:11). Mormon emphasized that the three days of darkness was "a sign" given of the Savior's death (see 1 Nephi 19:10; Helaman 14:27; 3 Nephi 8:23). After describing the damage caused by the "great storm" (3 Nephi 8:5) that lasted for three hours, Mormon documented the complete darkness as one of the signs that was now fulfilled (see 3 Nephi 10:14). The darkness was so intense that "there could not be any light at all" (3 Nephi 8:21). During this time of darkness, the body of Jesus Christ, the Light of the World, lay in the tomb. On the day of His Resurrection, after Christ had overcome death, light came again to the people in America, signifying Christ's victory over death and darkness (see 3 Nephi 10:9–11).

> ### 3 NEPHI 8:24–25
> *What were the reasons the survivors gave for the terrible destruction? How might this apply in our day?*

3 Nephi 8:24–25. Rejecting the Prophets Brings Suffering

• Just as in ancient times, rejection of the prophets today leads to suffering. President N. Eldon Tanner (1898–1982) of the First Presidency compared the suffering of the Saints in America during the destruction following the Savior's death with the destruction in our day of those who choose not to follow modern prophets:

"Today the world is rejecting the messages of the prophets of God. Is it not true that there is weeping and wailing over the face of the land because men are at war one with another? Do we not have among us many who lament the waywardness of their youth and the tragedies that befall them as they turn away from righteousness and suffer the consequences of tampering with alcohol, tobacco, and drugs, and other forbidden things? How many mourners do we have as a result of the lawlessness that is extant in our communities? We need to heed the lessons from the history of the past lest *we* be consumed as were some of those earlier civilizations.

"This was the message Christ brought to those early Nephite people" (in Conference Report, Apr. 1975, 53; or *Ensign,* May 1975, 35–36).

3 Nephi 9:14. "Come unto Me"

• Jesus Christ promised: "Blessed are those who come unto me" (3 Nephi 9:14).

Elder Jeffrey R. Holland explained the meaning of this invitation and how it applies in our lives: "'Come,' [Christ] says lovingly. 'Come, follow me.' Wherever you are going, first come and see what I do, see where and how I spend my time. Learn of me, walk with me, talk with me, believe. Listen to me pray. In turn you will find answers to your own prayers. God will bring rest to your souls. Come, follow me" (in Conference Report, Oct. 1997, 88; or *Ensign,* Nov. 1997, 65).

3 Nephi 9:19–20. A Change in the Commandment to Sacrifice

• The command to offer animal sacrifice was first given to Adam. The purpose of animal sacrifice was to point one's mind to the Savior's ultimate sacrifice.

The faithful were taught that animal sacrifice would cease after the Son of God had offered His blood as the "great and last sacrifice" (Alma 34:10). Amulek explained that following the Atonement of Jesus Christ, animal sacrifice would no longer be required: "There should be, a stop to the shedding of blood; then shall the law of Moses be fulfilled; . . . and that great and last sacrifice will be the Son of God, yea, infinite and eternal" (Alma 34:13–14). Once the offering of Jesus Christ was complete, the voice of God proclaimed to the Book of Mormon people, "I will accept none of your sacrifices and burnt offerings" (3 Nephi 9:19).

• Even though animal sacrifice and burnt offerings were to be "done away" (3 Nephi 9:19), the Lord did not end the law of sacrifice. Using 3 Nephi 9:20, Elder D. Todd Christofferson of the Quorum of the Twelve Apostles explained that today the Lord requires sacrifices of a different nature:

"The Savior said He would no longer accept burnt offerings of animals. The gift or sacrifice He will accept now is 'a broken heart and a contrite spirit' [3 Nephi 9:20]. . . . You can offer the Lord the gift of your broken, or repentant, heart and your contrite, or obedient, spirit. In reality, it is the gift of yourself—what you are and what you are becoming.

"Is there something in you or in your life that is impure or unworthy? When you get rid of it, that is a gift to the Savior. Is there a good habit or quality that is lacking in your life? When you adopt it and make it part of your character, you are giving a gift to the Lord" (in Conference Report, Apr. 2004, 10; or *Ensign,* May 2004, 12).

3 Nephi 9:20. "They Knew It Not"

• President Ezra Taft Benson (1899–1994) explained that there are many who are developing spiritually but are unable to perceive their own subtle growth: "Day by day [Latter-day Saints] move closer to the Lord, little realizing they are building a godlike life. They live quiet lives of goodness, service, and commitment. They are like the Lamanites, who the Lord said 'were baptized with fire and with the Holy Ghost, *and they knew it not.'* (3 Ne. 9:20; italics added)" ("A Mighty Change of Heart," *Ensign,* Oct. 1989, 5).

• President Boyd K. Packer, President of the Quorum of the Twelve Apostles, used this same scripture to express concern that the gift of the Holy Ghost is not recognized as it should be. He encouraged Latter-day Saints to cultivate the gift of the Holy Ghost and gave counsel on how to recognize the Spirit:

"Too many of us are like those whom the Lord said '[came] with a broken heart and a contrite spirit, . . . [and] at the time of their conversion, were baptized with fire and with the Holy Ghost, *and they knew it not"* [3 Nephi 9:20; italics added].

"Imagine that: 'And they knew it not.' It is not unusual for one to have received the gift and not really know it.

". . . There are so many places to go, so many things to do in this noisy world. We can be too busy to pay attention to the promptings of the Spirit" (in Conference Report, Apr. 2000, 8; or *Ensign,* May 2000, 8).

3 Nephi 10:5–6. "As a Hen Gathereth Her Chickens"

• The comparison between a hen gathering her chicks and the Lord gathering His people offers some interesting insights. A hen cares for her chicks and would sacrifice her life to protect them. When danger threatens, she gathers the chicks under her wings for protection. In a similar way, the Lord loves His people, the house of Israel. He gave His life for His people and has sought to  gather them together so he could protect and nourish them. On many occasions, however, Israel has chosen to forsake the Lord.

Commenting on 3 Nephi 10:5–6, President Henry B. Eyring of the First Presidency testified that the Savior will help those who are trying to come to Him:

"More than once He has said that He would gather us to Him as a hen would gather her chickens under her wings. He says that we must choose to come to Him in meekness and with enough faith in Him to repent 'with full purpose of heart' [3 Nephi 10:6].

"One way to do that is to gather with the Saints in His Church. Go to your meetings, even when it seems hard. If you are determined, He will help you find the strength to do it" (in Conference Report, Apr. 2004, 16–17; or *Ensign,* May 2004, 18).

3 Nephi 10:12. "They Who Received the Prophets"

• Safety often comes when we follow the prophets. The Nephites who "received the prophets" were spared from the great destructions (3 Nephi 10:12). Elder M. Russell Ballard of the Quorum of the Twelve Apostles taught that we, like the Nephites, must follow our prophet if we hope to find safety, peace, prosperity, and happiness: "It is no small thing, my brothers and sisters, to have a prophet of God in our midst. Great and wonderful are the blessings that come into our lives as we listen to the word of the Lord given to us through him. . . . When we hear the counsel of the Lord expressed through the words of the President of the Church, our response should be positive and prompt. History shows that there is safety, peace, prosperity, and happiness in responding to prophetic counsel" (in Conference Report, Apr. 2001, 84; *Ensign,* May 2001, 65).

• President Boyd K. Packer testified that blessings come to those who follow the prophets and warned of the consequences for rejecting them:

"On one occasion, Karl G. Maeser was leading a party of young missionaries across the Alps. As they reached the summit, he looked back and saw a row of sticks thrust in the snow to mark the one safe path across the otherwise treacherous glacier.

"Halting the company of missionaries, he gestured toward the sticks and said, 'Brethren, there stands the priesthood [of God]. They are just common sticks like the rest of us, . . . but the position they hold makes them what they are to us. If we step aside from the path they mark, we are lost' (in Alma P. Burton, *Karl G. Maeser, Mormon Educator* [Salt Lake City: Deseret Book Co., 1953], p. 22).

"Although no one of us is perfect, the Church moves forward, led by ordinary people.

"The Lord promised:

"'If my people will hearken unto my voice, and unto the voice of my servants whom I have appointed to lead my people, behold, verily I say unto you, they shall not be moved out of their place.

"'But if they will not hearken to my voice, nor unto the voice of these men whom I have appointed, they shall not be blest' (D&C 124:45–46).

"I bear witness, brethren and sisters, that the leaders of the Church were called of God by proper authority, and it is known to the Church that they have that authority and have been properly ordained by the regularly ordained heads of the Church. If we follow them we will be saved. If we stray from them we will surely be lost" (in Conference Report, Apr. 1985, 45; or *Ensign,* May 1985, 35).

3 Nephi 11:3. "They Heard a Voice"

• Elder Dallin H. Oaks taught that the "small voice" that caused "their hearts to *burn*" (3 Nephi 11:3; italics added) was more of a *feeling* than a sound: "The word 'burning' in this scripture signifies a feeling of comfort and serenity" ("Teaching and Learning by the Spirit," *Ensign,* Mar. 1997, 13). *Serenity* means warmth, gentleness, and calmness.

• Just as the Nephites had to "open their ears" (3 Nephi 11:5) to hear the voice of God, President Boyd K. Packer explained our need to pay attention so we might feel the gentle promptings of the Spirit:

"The voice of the Spirit is described in the scripture as being neither 'loud' nor 'harsh.' It is 'not a voice of thunder, neither . . . voice of a great tumultuous noise.' But rather, 'a still voice of perfect mildness, as if it had been a whisper,' and it can 'pierce even to the very soul' and 'cause [the heart] to burn.' (3 Ne. 11:3; Hel. 5:30; D&C 85:6–7.) Remember, Elijah found the voice of the Lord was not in the wind, nor in the earthquake, nor in the fire, but was a 'still small voice.' (1 Kgs. 19:12.)

"The Spirit does not get our attention by shouting or shaking us with a heavy hand. Rather it whispers. It caresses so gently that if we are preoccupied we may not feel it at all. (No wonder that the Word of Wisdom was revealed to us, for how could the drunkard or the addict feel such a voice?)

"Occasionally it will press just firmly enough for us to pay heed. But most of the time, if we do not heed the gentle feeling, the Spirit will withdraw" ("The Candle of the Lord," *Ensign,* Jan. 1983, 53).

3 Nephi 11:5–7. "Behold My Beloved Son"
• President Ezra Taft Benson spoke of the rare experience of hearing the voice of Heavenly Father:

"How few people in all the history of the world have heard the actual voice of God the Father speaking to them. As the people looked heavenward, 'they saw a Man descending out of heaven; and he was clothed in a white robe; and he came down and stood in the midst of them' [3 Nephi 11:8].

"A glorious, resurrected being, a member of the Godhead, the Creator of innumerable worlds, the God of Abraham, Isaac, and Jacob, stood before their very eyes!" (in Conference Report, Apr. 1987, 4; or *Ensign,* May 1987, 5).

3 Nephi 11:11. The Bitter Cup
• President James E. Faust (1920–2007) of the First Presidency taught that following the Savior's example during hardships helps us endure our personal "bitter cups": "Many members, in drinking of the bitter cup that has come to them, wrongfully think that this cup passes by others. In His first words to the people of the Western continent, Jesus of Nazareth poignantly spoke of the bitter cup the Father had given Him (see 3 Ne. 11:11). Every soul has some bitterness to swallow. Parents having a child who loses his way come to know a sorrow that defies description. A woman whose husband is cruel or insensitive can have her heart broken every day. Members who do not marry may suffer sorrow and disappointment. Having drunk the bitter cup, however, there comes a time when one must accept the situation as it is and reach upward and outward. President Harold B. Lee said, 'Do not let self-pity or despair beckon you from the course you know is right.' The Savior set the compass: we must be born again in spirit and heart" ("A Second Birth," *Ensign,* June 1998, 2).

3 Nephi 11:14–17. The Wounds in His Hands and Feet and Side
• When the resurrected Lord appeared to the Nephites, He invited them to feel the wounds in His hands and feet and side so that they could witness His Resurrection (see 3 Nephi 11:14). Elder Jeffrey R. Holland taught that Jesus Christ's mortal wounds are tokens of His sacrifice:

"However dim our days may seem, they have been a lot darker for the Savior of the world. As a reminder of those days, Jesus has chosen, even in a resurrected, otherwise perfected body, to retain for the benefit of His disciples the wounds in His hands and in His feet and in His side—signs, if you will, that painful things happen even to the pure and the perfect; signs, if you will, that pain in this world is *not* evidence that God doesn't love you; signs, if you will, that problems pass and happiness can be ours. Remind others that it is the wounded Christ who is the Captain of our souls, He who yet bears the scars of our forgiveness, the lesions of His love and humility, the torn flesh of obedience and sacrifice.

"These wounds are the principal way we are to recognize Him when He comes. He may invite us forward, as He has invited others, to see and to feel those marks. If not before, then surely at that time, we will remember with Isaiah that it was for us that a God was 'despised and rejected . . . ; a man of sorrows, and acquainted with grief,' that 'he was wounded for our transgressions, he was bruised for our iniquities: the chastisement of our peace was upon him; and with his stripes we are healed' (Isa. 53:3, 5)" ("Teaching, Preaching, Healing," *Ensign,* Jan 2003, 42).

3 Nephi 11:16–21. Hosanna

• "The word *Hosanna* is a transliteration of a Hebrew word of supplication which means in essence 'Oh, grant salvation.' Evidently the people were asking the Savior to teach them the way to salvation; thus it is not surprising that he immediately teaches them the basic principles and ordinances of the gospel" (Daniel H. Ludlow, *A Companion to Your Study of the Book of Mormon* [1976], 261–62).

3 Nephi 11:21–27. The Importance of Baptism

• There appears to have been some contention among the Nephites concerning the manner of baptism. The Lord clarified how the ordinance should be performed. President Boyd K. Packer explained the significance of baptism and cautioned that we should not alter this sacred ordinance:

"Baptism by immersion for the remission of sins is the first ordinance. Baptism must be by immersion, for it is symbolic of both the coming forth from temporal death, from the grave, and the cleansing required for redemption from spiritual death.

". . . Under the plan, baptism is not just for entrance into the Church of Jesus Christ. It begins a spiritual rebirth that may eventually lead back into the presence of God.

"If we really understood what baptism signifies, we could never consider it trivial nor alter the form of this sacred ordinance. . . . Through the sacrament we renew the covenant" (*Our Father's Plan* [1984], 39–40).

---

3 NEPHI 11:29 📖
Why does the Savior counsel us to avoid contention?

---

3 Nephi 11:28–30. 📖 Avoid Contention

• President Henry B. Eyring helps us understand that the Spirit of God will not lead people into contention: "Where people have that Spirit with them, we may expect harmony. The Spirit puts the testimony of truth in our hearts, which unifies those who share

that testimony. The Spirit of God never generates contention (see 3 Nephi 11:29). It never generates the feelings of distinctions between people which lead to strife (see Joseph F. Smith, *Gospel Doctrine,* 5th ed. [1939], 131). It leads to personal peace and a feeling of union with others. It unifies souls. A unified family, a unified Church, and a world at peace depend on unified souls" (in Conference Report, Apr. 1998, 86; or *Ensign,* May 1998, 67).

• President Thomas S. Monson shared a story illustrating the blessings that come from avoiding contention. After reading 3 Nephi 11:28–30 📖, he said:

"Let me conclude with an account of two men who are heroes to me. Their acts of courage were not performed on a national scale, but rather in a peaceful valley known as Midway, Utah.

"Long years ago, Roy Kohler and Grant Remund served together in Church capacities. They were the best of friends. They were tillers of the soil and dairymen. Then a misunderstanding arose which became somewhat of a rift between them.

"Later, when Roy Kohler became grievously ill with cancer and had but a limited time to live, my wife, Frances, and I visited Roy and his wife, and I gave him a blessing. As we talked afterward, Brother Kohler said, 'Let me tell you about one of the sweetest experiences I have had during my life.' He then recounted to me his misunderstanding with Grant Remund and the ensuing estrangement. His comment was, 'We were sort of on the outs with each other.'

"'Then,' continued Roy, 'I had just put up our hay for the winter to come, when one night, as a result of spontaneous combustion, the hay caught fire, burning the hay, the barn, and everything in it right to the ground. I was devastated,' said Roy. 'I didn't know what in the world I would do. The night was dark, except for the dying embers of the fire. Then I saw coming toward me from the road, in the direction of Grant Remund's place, the lights of tractors and heavy equipment. As the "rescue party" turned in our drive and met me amidst my tears, Grant said, "Roy, you've got quite a mess to clean up. My boys and I are here. Let's get to it."' Together they plunged to the task at hand. Gone forever was the hidden wedge which had separated them for a short time. They worked throughout the night and into the next day, with many others in the community joining in.

"Roy Kohler has passed away, and Grant Remund is getting older. Their sons have served together in the same ward bishopric. I truly treasure the friendship of these two wonderful families" (in Conference Report, Apr. 2002, 22; or *Ensign,* May 2002, 20–21).

3 Nephi 11:28–40. Jesus Spoke of His Doctrine

• The phrase "my doctrine" can be found eight times in verses 28–40 of 3 Nephi 11. The Lord described His doctrine as repentance and baptism. In similar language in 2 Nephi 31, Nephi spent considerable time describing what he called "the doctrine of Christ." Nephi included faith, repentance, baptism, the Holy Ghost, scripture study, and enduring to the end in his list of the doctrines of Christ. Later in His visit to the Book of Mormon people, the Lord repeated these same principles (see 3 Nephi 27) and labeled them "my gospel." These principles remind us of Articles of Faith 1:4: "We believe that the first principles and ordinances of the Gospel are: first, Faith in the Lord Jesus Christ; second, Repentance; third, Baptism by immersion for the remission of sins; fourth, Laying on of hands for the gift of the Holy Ghost."

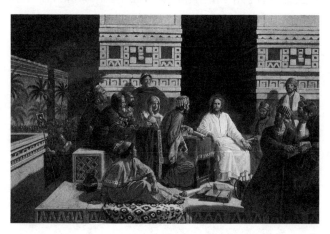

Points to Ponder

• Why is complete darkness an appropriate sign and symbol of the death of the Savior?

• How has the Lord tried to gather you into His fold?

• How does a person gain "a broken heart" and "a contrite spirit"? (3 Nephi 9:20).

• What is the difference between the "spirit of contention" (3 Nephi 11:29) and a discussion to resolve a disagreement? How can people disagree without becoming contentious?

Suggested Assignments

• Only those who had received the prophets were spared the destructions of the Lord's coming. Make a list of instructions spoken in recent general conference sessions by the prophet and members of the Quorum of the Twelve Apostles. Plan how you will implement them in your life.

• Both Nephi and Samuel the Lamanite prophesied specifically about the devastation that would take place in America shortly after Jesus Christ died in Jerusalem. Compare the prophecies in 2 Nephi 26:3–9 and Helaman 14:20–27 with their fulfillment in 3 Nephi 8:5–23.

• Very few people in the history of the world have ever heard the actual voice of God the Father speak to them. Make a chart to compare the words of Heavenly Father when He spoke at the baptism of Jesus Christ (see Matthew 3:17; Mark 1:11; Luke 3:22); on the Mount of Transfiguration (see Matthew 17:5; Mark 9:7; Luke 9:35); to the Nephites (3 Nephi 11:7); and to the Prophet Joseph Smith (Joseph Smith—History 1:17). Describe the significance of each of these statements.

CHAPTER 41

3 Nephi 12–14

Introduction

In His mortal ministry Jesus delivered the Sermon on the Mount to encourage His disciples to strive toward perfection with full purpose of heart. Following His Resurrection, Jesus appeared to the Book of Mormon people in the Western Hemisphere and again delivered this sermon.

The gospel standards contained in this sermon have been reaffirmed in our time through modern revelation. President James E. Faust (1920–2007) of the First Presidency observed: "The Savior's transcendent message in the Sermon on the Mount is of burning-bush importance to all of us: 'But seek ye first to build up the kingdom of God, and to establish his righteousness' [Joseph Smith Translation, Matthew 6:38; see also Matthew 6:33]. This message needs to penetrate into our hearts and souls. As we accept this message, we are taking our personal stand in this life" (in Conference Report, Apr. 2004, 68; or *Ensign,* May 2004, 67).

Through your study of these sacred principles in the Book of Mormon, you will gain insights that will help you stay faithful and remain on the road to perfection.

Commentary

3 Nephi 12–14. A Blueprint for Our Lives

• The Sermon on the Mount as contained in both the Bible and the Book of Mormon is the Lord's blueprint for perfection. Of this sermon, President Harold B. Lee (1899–1973) said: "Christ came not only into the world to make an atonement for the sins of mankind but to set an example before the world of the standard of perfection of God's law and of obedience to the Father. In his Sermon on the Mount the Master has given us somewhat of a revelation of his own character, which was perfect, or what might be said to be 'an autobiography, every syllable of which he had written down in deeds,' and in so doing has given us a blueprint for our own lives" (*Decisions for Successful Living* [1973], 55–56).

3 Nephi 12:1–2. Give Heed to the Apostles

• The Savior began His sermon to the Nephites by calling attention to the importance of following the twelve Nephite disciples, whom He had called and given power and authority. Modern revelation has also emphasized the safety and blessings that come by following the Lord's chosen servants (see D&C 1:38 ; 21:6). Elder Jeffrey R. Holland of the Quorum of the Twelve Apostles explained why it is of critical importance for us to follow the First Presidency and the Quorum of the Twelve Apostles today:

Jerry Thompson, © IRI

"The apostolic and prophetic foundation of the Church was to bless in all times, but *especially* in times of adversity or danger, times when we might feel like children, confused or disoriented, perhaps a little fearful, times in which the devious hand of men or the maliciousness of the devil would attempt to unsettle or mislead. Against such times as come in our modern day, the First Presidency and Quorum of the Twelve are commissioned by God and sustained by you as prophets, seers, and revelators. . . .

". . . Such a foundation in Christ was and is always to be a protection. . . . In such days as we are now in—and will more or less always be in—the storms of life 'shall have no power over you . . .' [Helaman 5:12]" (in Conference Report, Oct. 2004, 5; or *Ensign,* Nov. 2004, 7).

---

3 NEPHI 12:1–2

Compare these verses with Matthew 5:1–2. What does the Book of Mormon account add?

---

3 Nephi 12:3. "Blessed Are the Poor in Spirit Who Come unto Me"

• President Harold B. Lee defined what it means to be poor in spirit:

"The Master said, 'Blessed are the poor in spirit: for theirs is the kingdom of heaven.' (Matthew 5:3.) The poor in spirit, of course, means those who are spiritually needy, who feel so impoverished spiritually that they reach out with great yearning for help. . . .

"Every one of us, if we would reach perfection, must one time ask ourselves this question, 'What lack I yet?' if we would commence our climb upward on the highway to perfection" (*Stand Ye in Holy Places* [1974], 210).

• The phrase "who come unto me" (3 Nephi 12:3) is not found in the New Testament version of the Sermon on the Mount, but it clarifies the Savior's teaching. It is blessed to be poor in spirit *if* we come unto Christ. The Savior described in 3 Nephi 12:2 how we begin to come unto Him. The statement "who come unto me" can in principle also be applied to other Beatitudes. In order to be comforted (v. 4), inherit the earth (v. 5), be filled with the Holy Ghost (v. 6), obtain mercy (v. 7), or see God (v. 8), we must come unto Christ.

As the Savior led into His sermon about coming unto Him, He mentioned baptism 19 times between 3 Nephi 11:21 and 12:2. To completely "come unto Christ" includes accepting the ordinances of salvation.

President Ezra Taft Benson (1899–1994) described additional ways we can come unto Christ: "Come unto Christ through proclaiming the gospel, perfecting our lives, and redeeming our dead. As we come unto Christ, we bless our own lives, those of our families, and our Father in Heaven's children, both living and dead" (in Conference Report, Apr. 1988, 98; or *Ensign,* May 1988, 85).

3 Nephi 12:3–12. The Beatitudes

• The Savior's sermon begins with declarations referred to as the Beatitudes. These start with a series of statements that declare "blessed are . . ." (see 3 Nephi 12:1–11). *Beatitude* means "'to be fortunate,' 'to be happy,' or 'to be blessed'" (Matthew 5:3*a*). Webster's dictionary defines the word as "a state of utmost bliss" (*Merriam-Webster's Collegiate Dictionary,* 11th ed.

[2004], 107). Such words describe the results when Saints apply the teachings of this sermon.

The LDS Bible Dictionary explains that the Beatitudes "describe certain elements that go to form the refined and spiritual character, and all of which will be present whenever that character exists in its perfection. Rather than being isolated statements, the Beatitudes are interrelated and progressive in their arrangement" ("Beatitudes," 620). The Guide to the Scriptures adds, "The Beatitudes are arranged in such a way that each statement builds upon the one that precedes it" ("Beatitudes").

President Harold B. Lee taught that the Beatitudes embody the "constitution for a perfect life": "Four of them have to do with our individual selves," and four "have to do with man's social relations with others" (*Decisions for Successful Living* [1973], 57, 60). The following chart illustrates that relationship:

With Self	With Others
Blessed are the poor in spirit.	Blessed are the meek.
Blessed are all they that mourn.	Blessed are the merciful.
Blessed are all they who do hunger and thirst after righteousness.	Blessed are all the peacemakers.
Blessed are all the pure in heart.	Blessed are all they who are persecuted for my name's sake.

3 Nephi 12:4. "Blessed Are All They That Mourn"

• Elder Spencer J. Condie of the Seventy explained how the Beatitudes could be seen as progressive in nature: "The Beatitudes may be viewed as a recipe for righteousness with incremental steps, beginning with 'the poor in spirit who come unto [Christ]' (3 Nephi

12:3). The next step in the celestial direction is to *mourn,* especially for our sins, for 'godly sorrow worketh repentance to salvation' (2 Corinthians 7:10)" (*Your Agency, Handle with Care* [1996], 8).

3 Nephi 12:5. "Blessed Are the Meek"

• President Spencer W. Kimball (1895–1985), explained that meekness is not weakness:

"If the Lord was meek and lowly and humble, then to become humble one must do what he did in boldly denouncing evil, bravely advancing righteous works, courageously meeting every problem, becoming the master of himself and the situations about him and being near oblivious to personal credit.

"Humility is not pretentious, presumptuous, nor proud. It is not weak, vacillating, nor servile. . . .

"*Humble* and *meek* properly suggest virtues, not weaknesses. They suggest a consistent mildness of temper and an absence of wrath and passion. . . . It is not servile submissiveness. It is not cowed nor frightened. . . .

"How does one get humble? To me, one must constantly be reminded of his dependence. On whom dependent? On the Lord. How remind one's self? By real, constant, worshipful, grateful prayer" (*The Teachings of Spencer W. Kimball,* ed. Edward L. Kimball [1982], 232–33).

3 Nephi 12:6. "Hunger and Thirst after Righteousness"

• While serving in the general Relief Society presidency, Sister Sheri L. Dew explained the connection between *desire* (hungering and thirsting) and *action,* or the ability to work to achieve the desired results: "Our ability to hear spiritually is linked to our willingness to work at it. President Hinckley has often said that the only way he knows to get anything done is to get on his knees and plead for help and then get on his feet and go to work. That combination of faith and hard work is the consummate curriculum for learning the language of the Spirit. The Savior taught, 'Blessed are all they who do *hunger* and *thirst* after righteousness, for they shall be filled with the Holy Ghost' (3 Ne. 12:6; emphasis added). Hungering and

thirsting translate to sheer spiritual labor. Worshiping in the temple, repenting to become increasingly pure, forgiving and seeking forgiveness, and earnest fasting and prayer all increase our receptivity to the Spirit. Spiritual work *works* and is the key to learning to hear the voice of the Lord" ("We Are Not Alone," *Ensign,* Nov. 1998, 96).

3 Nephi 12:8. "Pure in Heart"

• Elder Joseph B. Wirthlin (1917–2008) of the Quorum of the Twelve Apostles explained what it means to be pure in heart:

"To be without guile is to be pure in heart, an essential virtue of those who would be counted among true followers of Christ. . . .

"If we are without guile, we are honest, true, and righteous. These are all attributes of Deity and are required of the Saints. Those who are honest are fair and truthful in their speech, straightforward in their dealings, free of deceit, and above stealing, misrepresentation, or any other fraudulent action. Honesty is of God; dishonesty of the devil, who was a liar from the beginning. Righteousness means living a life that is in harmony with the laws, principles, and ordinances of the gospel" (*Finding Peace in Our Lives* [1995], 181–82).

3 Nephi 12:9. Peacemakers

• Elder Russell M. Nelson of the Quorum of the Twelve Apostles testified of the ultimate source for becoming a peacemaker: "Coming unto Jesus Christ as the 'Prince of Peace' [Isaiah 9:6] is the pathway to peace on earth and goodwill among men [see Luke 2:14]" (in Conference Report, Oct. 2002, 41; or *Ensign,* Nov. 2002, 39).

• Elder Bruce R. McConkie (1915–85) of the Quorum of the Twelve Apostles described how to become a peacemaker: "Peacemakers: In the full sense, only those who believe and spread the fulness of the gospel are peacemakers within the perfect meaning of this Beatitude. The gospel is the message of peace to all mankind. Children of God: Those who have been adopted into the family of God as a result of their devotion to the truth. By such a course they become heirs of God and joint-heirs with Christ. (Rom. 8:14–18;

Gal. 3:26–29; 4:1–7.)" (*Doctrinal New Testament Commentary*, 3 vols. [1971–73], 1:216).

3 Nephi 12:13. "Salt of the Earth"

• The Book of Mormon account indicates that "to be the salt of the earth" is a goal members of the Church should strive for (3 Nephi 12:13). In the Mosaic sacrificial ritual, salt was a reminder that we should remember and preserve our covenants with God (see Numbers 18:19; 2 Chronicles 13:5). In a similar sense, Saints should help restore and preserve the covenants in these latter days. Doctrine and Covenants 101:39–40 indicates what one must do to be accounted as "the salt of the earth."

To be considered "the salt of the earth" carries an important meaning. While serving as a member of the Presidency of the Seventy, Elder Carlos E. Asay (1926–99) explained to priesthood holders:

"'When men are called into mine everlasting gospel, and covenant with an everlasting covenant, they are accounted as the salt of the earth and the savor of men;

"'*They are called to be the savor of men*' (D&C 101:39–40; italics added).

"The word *savor (s-a-v-o-r)* denotes taste, pleasing flavor, interesting quality, and high repute. . . .

"A world-renowned chemist told me that salt will not lose its savor with age. Savor is lost through mixture and contamination. Similarly, priesthood power does not dissipate with age; it, too, is lost through mixture and contamination. . . .

"Flavor and quality flee a man when he contaminates his mind with unclean thoughts, desecrates his mouth by speaking less than the truth, and misapplies his strength in performing evil acts. . . .

"I would offer these simple guidelines, especially to the young men, as the means to preserve one's savor: If it is not *clean*, do not think it; if it is not *true*, do not speak it; if it is not *good*, do not do it (see Marcus Aurelius, 'The Meditations of Marcus Aurelius,' in *The Harvard Classics,* Charles W. Eliot, ed., New York: P. F. Collier and Son, 1909, p. 211)" (in Conference Report, Apr. 1980, 60–61; or *Ensign,* May 1980, 42–43).

3 Nephi 12:14–16. "Let Your Light So Shine"

• Elder Robert D. Hales of the Quorum of the Twelve Apostles referred to personal experience in emphasizing the importance of being a light for others:

"Growing up on Long Island, in New York, I understood how vital light was to those traveling in the darkness on the open sea. How dangerous is a fallen lighthouse! How devastating is a lighthouse whose light has failed!

"We who have the gift of the Holy Ghost must be true to its promptings so we can be a light to others.

"'Let your light so shine before men,' said the Lord, 'that they may see your good works, and glorify your Father which is in heaven' [Matthew 5:15–16].

"We never know who may be depending on us. And, as the Savior said, we 'know not but what they will return and repent, and come unto me with full purpose of heart, and I shall heal them; and ye shall be the means of bringing salvation unto them' [3 Nephi 18:32]" (in Conference Report, Apr. 2002, 82; or *Ensign,* May 2002, 71).

3 Nephi 12:17–20, 46–47. The Law of Moses Was Fulfilled by Jesus Christ

• By the time of the Savior's mortal ministry, the law of Moses had been at the foundation of Israelite religious and social life for over a thousand years. The Nephites possessed written records of the law on the brass plates, and Nephite prophets taught and observed the law. When the Savior visited the Nephites, He taught them that the law had been completely fulfilled in Him. However, they were not to think of the law of Moses as "destroyed" or having "passed away" (3 Nephi 12:17–18). How is it that the Savior "fulfilled" but did not "destroy" the law of Moses? The law of Moses included both *moral* and *ritual* aspects.

The *moral* aspects included such commandments as "Thou shalt not kill" and "Thou shalt not commit adultery." Jesus Christ taught the Nephites that not only were they to avoid murder and adultery, but also anger and lust—conditions of the heart that lead to murder and adultery (see 3 Nephi 12:21–30). Thus the gospel of Jesus Christ fulfilled the law in the sense that it expanded the moral aspects of the law of Moses by being a higher law; it included the moral imperatives of the law of Moses and placed them in the context of broader gospel principles that require a change of heart.

The *ritual* aspects of the law of Moses included commandments about animal sacrifice and burnt offerings—what Abinadi called "performances" and "ordinances" (Mosiah 13:30). The Nephite prophets understood that these parts of the law of Moses were meant to help people look forward to the atoning sacrifice of Jesus Christ (see 2 Nephi 25:24; Jacob 4:5; Mosiah 16:14–15). Therefore, when the Savior's mortal mission was completed, these forward-looking ordinances could no longer look ahead to a future event—the event had happened, and the ordinances were fulfilled in the sense that it concluded. Thus the Savior taught the Nephites that animal sacrifices and burnt offerings were to be "done away," and that His followers were to offer instead the "sacrifice" of "a broken heart and a contrite spirit" (3 Nephi 9:19–20). In place of ordinances that looked forward to the Atonement, the Savior instituted the sacrament, an ordinance of remembrance, to look back to the Savior's atoning sacrifice (see 3 Nephi 18:1–11).

• Elder Bruce R. McConkie stated: "Jesus came to restore that gospel fulness which men had enjoyed before the day of Moses, before the time of the lesser order. Obviously he did not come to destroy what he himself had revealed to Moses anymore than a college professor destroys arithmetic by revealing the principles of integral calculus to his students. Jesus came to build on the foundation Moses laid. By restoring the fulness of the gospel he fulfilled the need for adherence to the terms and conditions of the preparatory gospel. No one any longer needed to walk by the light of the moon, for the sun had risen in all its splendor" (*Doctrinal New Testament Commentary,* 1:219–20; see also Stephen E. Robinson, "The Law after Christ," *Ensign,* Sept. 1983, 68–73).

3 Nephi 12:19. "A Broken Heart and a Contrite Spirit"

• Elder Richard G. Scott of the Quorum of the Twelve Apostles testified of the value of having a broken heart and a contrite spirit: "I witness that 'redemption cometh in and through the Holy Messiah; . . . unto all those who have *a broken heart and a contrite spirit;* and unto none else can the ends of the law be answered' [2 Nephi 2:6–7; italics added]. This absolute requisite of 'a broken heart and a contrite spirit' prescribes the need to be submissive, compliant, humble (that is, teachable), and willingly obedient" (in Conference Report, Apr. 1997, 77; or *Ensign,* May 1997, 53).

3 Nephi 12:22. "Whosoever Is Angry with His Brother"

• The New Testament account of the Savior's teachings is, "Whosoever is angry with his brother without a cause shall be in danger of the judgment" (Matthew 5:22). The Savior's teachings on this subject in the Book of Mormon are the same except that the phrase "without a cause" is deleted. This indicates that it is best to avoid anger altogether. It should be noted that the earliest known manuscript for Matthew 5:22 does not contain the phrase "without a cause" (see Daniel K. Judd and Allen W. Stoddard, "Adding and Taking Away 'Without a Cause' in Matthew 5:22," in *How the New Testament Came to Be,* ed. Kent P. Jackson and Frank F. Judd Jr. [Sidney B. Sperry symposium, 2006], 161).

3 Nephi 12:27–29. Avoid Lust

• Elder Richard G. Scott contrasted both the results and motivation for love versus those of lust: "Love, as defined by the Lord, elevates, protects, respects, and enriches another. It motivates one to make sacrifices for another. Satan promotes counterfeit love, which is lust. It is driven by a hunger to appease personal appetite. One who practices this deception cares little for the pain and destruction caused another. While often camouflaged by flattering words, its motivation is self-gratification" (in Conference Report, Apr. 1991, 43–44; or *Ensign,* May 1991, 35).

3 Nephi 12:30. "Take Up Your Cross"

• Elder Neal A. Maxwell (1926–2004) of the Quorum of the Twelve Apostles explained the phrase "take up your cross":

"The *daily* taking up of the cross means *daily* denying ourselves the appetites of the flesh.

"By emulating the Master, who endured temptations but 'gave no heed unto them,' we, too, can live in a world filled with temptations 'such as [are] common to man' (1 Corinthians 10:13). Of course Jesus noticed the tremendous temptations that came to Him, but He did not process and reprocess them. Instead, He rejected them promptly. If we entertain temptations, soon they begin entertaining us! Turning these unwanted lodgers away at the doorstep of the mind is one way of giving 'no heed.' Besides, these would-be lodgers are actually barbarians who, if admitted, can be evicted only with great trauma" (in Conference Report, Apr. 1987, 88; or *Ensign,* May 1987, 71).

3 Nephi 12:31–32. "Whoso Shall Marry Her Who Is Divorced Committeth Adultery"

• Elder Bruce R. McConkie described who the Savior here was speaking to and how it applies to us today:

"This strict law governing divorce was not given to the Pharisees, nor to the world in general, but to the disciples only, 'in the house,' at a later time as Mark explains. Further, Jesus expressly limited its application. All men could not live such a high standard; it applied only to those 'to whom it is given.'

". . . It may have been in force at various times and among various people, but the Church is not bound by it today. At this time divorces are permitted in the Church for a number of reasons other than sex immorality, and divorced persons are permitted to marry again and enjoy all of the blessings of the gospel" (*Doctrinal New Testament Commentary,* 1:548–49).

• It would appear that one of the purposes of the Savior's words was not to condemn those who marry divorced people, but to teach the people not to turn to divorce as the solution to all the minor irritations that come up in marriage. In speaking about divorce, President Gordon B. Hinckley (1910–2008) has taught:

"Of course, all in marriage is not bliss. Years ago I clipped these words from a column written by Jenkins Lloyd Jones:

"'There seems to be a superstition among many thousands of our young who hold hands and smooch in the drive-ins that marriage is a cottage surrounded by perpetual hollyhocks to which a perpetually young and handsome husband comes home to a perpetually young and ravishing wife. When the hollyhocks wither and boredom and bills appear the divorce courts are jammed. . . .

"'Anyone who imagines that bliss is normal is going to waste a lot of time running around shouting that he has been robbed' ("Big Rock Candy Mountains," *Deseret News,* 12 June 1973, p. A4). . . .

". . . Among the greatest of tragedies, and I think the most common, is divorce. It has become as a great scourge. The most recent issue of the *World Almanac* says that in the United States during the twelve months ending with March 1990, an estimated 2,423,000 couples married. During this same period, an estimated 1,177,000 couples divorced. (See *The World Almanac and Book of Facts 1991* [New York: World Almanac, 1990], p. 834.)

"This means that in the United States almost one divorce occurred for every two marriages. . . .

"Selfishness so often is the basis of . . . problems. . . .

"Too many who come to marriage have been coddled and spoiled and somehow led to feel that everything must be precisely right at all times, that life is a series of entertainments, that appetites are to be satisfied without regard to principle. How tragic  the consequences of such hollow and unreasonable thinking! . . .

". . . The remedy for most marriage stress is not in divorce. It is in repentance. It is not in separation. It is in simple integrity that leads a man to square up his shoulders and meet his obligations. It is found in the Golden Rule. . . .

"There must be a willingness to overlook small faults, to forgive, and then to forget.

"There must be a holding of one's tongue. Temper is a vicious and corrosive thing that destroys affection and casts out love.

"There must be self-discipline that constrains against abuse. . . .

"There may be now and again a legitimate cause for divorce. I am not one to say that it is never justified. But I say without hesitation that this plague among us, which seems to be growing everywhere, is not of God, but rather is the work of the adversary of righteousness and peace and truth" (in Conference Report, Apr. 1991, 94–98; or *Ensign,* May 1991, 72–74).

3 Nephi 12:48. "I Would That Ye Should Be Perfect"

• It is not possible to be perfect in this life. However, President James E. Faust explained that we must seek for perfection now so as to be able to attain it in the next life: "Perfection is an eternal goal. While we cannot be perfect in mortality, striving for it is a commandment which ultimately, through the Atonement, we can keep" (in Conference Report, Apr. 1999, 22; or *Ensign,* May 1999, 19).

• President Spencer W. Kimball also explained the need to strive for perfection: "'Be ye therefore perfect, even as your Father which is in heaven is perfect.' (Matthew 5:48.) Now, that is an attainable goal. We will not be exalted, we shall not reach our destination, unless we are perfect, and now is the best time in the world to start toward perfection. I have little patience with persons who say, 'Oh, nobody is perfect,' the implication being; 'so why try?' Of course no one is wholly perfect, but we find some who are a long way up the ladder" (*Teachings of Spencer W. Kimball,* 165).

3 Nephi 13:1–8, 16–18. Do Not Your Righteous Acts Openly

• These verses in 3 Nephi teach about avoiding the giving of money to the poor openly or praying and fasting openly to be seen of others. The Lord

encourages us to practice righteousness in private. President Thomas S. Monson explained the value of anonymous service:

"I approached the reception desk of a large hospital to learn the room number of a patient I had come to visit. This hospital, like almost every other in the land, was undergoing a massive expansion. Behind the desk where the receptionist sat was a magnificent plaque which bore an inscription of thanks to donors who had made possible the expansion. The name of each donor who had contributed $100,000 appeared in a flowing script, etched on an individual brass placard suspended from the main plaque by a glittering chain.

"The names of the benefactors were well known. Captains of commerce, giants of industry, professors of learning—all were there. I felt gratitude for their charitable benevolence. Then my eyes rested on a brass placard which was different—it contained no name. One word, and one word only, was inscribed: 'Anonymous.' I smiled and wondered who the unnamed contributor could have been. Surely he or she experienced a quiet joy unknown to any other. . . .

"A year ago last winter [1981], a modern jetliner faltered after takeoff and plunged into the icy Potomac River. Acts of bravery and feats of heroism were in evidence that day, the most dramatic of which was one witnessed by the pilot of a rescue helicopter. The rescue rope was lowered to a struggling survivor. Rather than grasping the lifeline to safety, the man tied the line to another, who was then lifted to safety. The rope was lowered again, and yet another was saved. Five were rescued from the icy waters. Among them was not found the anonymous hero. Unknown by name, 'he left the vivid air signed with his honor' (Stephen Spender, 'I think continually of those—' in *Masterpieces of Religious Verse,* ed. James Dalton Morrison [New York: Harper and Brothers Publishers], p. 291.) . . .

"May this truth [service] guide our lives. May we look upward as we press forward in the service of our God and our fellowmen. And may we incline an ear toward Galilee, that we might hear perhaps an echo of the Savior's teachings: 'Do not your alms before men, to be seen of them' (Matthew 6:1). 'Let not thy left hand know what thy right hand doeth' (Matthew 6:3). And of our good deeds: 'See thou tell no man' (Matthew 8:4). Our hearts will then be lighter, our lives brighter, and our souls richer.

"Loving service anonymously given may be unknown to man—but the gift and the giver are known to God" (in Conference Report, Apr. 1983, 73–74, 76; or *Ensign,* May 1983, 55–57).

3 Nephi 13:7. "Use Not Vain Repetitions"

• *Vain* means "empty; worthless; having no substance, value or importance" (*Noah Webster's First Edition of an American Dictionary of the English Language, 1828* [1967]). Our prayers are vain when we offer them out of habit, with little thought or feeling.

"The prophet Mormon warned that if anyone 'shall pray and not with real intent of heart . . . it profiteth him nothing, for God receiveth none such' (Moroni 7:9). To make your prayers meaningful, you must pray with sincerity and 'with all the energy of heart' (Moroni 7:48). . . . Give serious thought to your attitude and to the words you use" (*True to the Faith: A Gospel Reference* [2004], 119).

• Elder Joseph B. Wirthlin cautioned regarding repetition in prayer: "Our prayers become hollow when we say similar words in similar ways over and over so often that the words become more of a recitation than a communication. This is what the Savior described as 'vain repetitions' (see Matt. 6:7)" ("Improving Our Prayers," *Ensign,* Mar. 2004, 24; see also Alma 34:27–28).

---

3 NEPHI 13:9–13

What principles for effective prayer does the Savior teach in these verses?

---

3 Nephi 13:9–13. The Lord's Prayer

• We can use the principles in the Lord's Prayer as a model for our service in the kingdom. President Henry B. Eyring of the First Presidency taught:

"The prayer begins with reverence for our Heavenly Father. Then the Lord speaks of the kingdom and its coming. The servant with a testimony that this is the true Church of Jesus Christ feels joy in its progress and a desire to give his or her all to build it up.

Paul Mann, © 1999 IRI

"The Savior Himself exemplified the standard set by these next words of the prayer: 'Thy will be done, as in heaven, so in earth' (Luke 11:2). That was His prayer in the extremity of offering the Atonement for all mankind and all the world (see Matthew 26:42). The faithful servant prays that even the apparently smallest task will be done as God would have it done. It makes all the difference to work and to pray for His success more than for our own.

"Then the Savior set for us this standard of personal purity: 'And forgive us our sins; for we also forgive every one that is indebted to us. And lead us not into temptation; but deliver us from evil' (Luke 11:4). The strengthening we are to give those we watch over comes from the Savior. We and they must forgive to be forgiven by Him (see Matthew 6:14). We and they can hope to remain clean only with His protection and with the change in our hearts that His Atonement makes possible. We need that change to have the constant companionship of the Holy Ghost. . . .

"You may have confidence in the Lord's service. The Savior will help you do what He has called you to do, be it for a time as a worker in the Church or forever as a parent. You may pray for help enough to do the work and know that it will come" (in Conference Report, Apr. 2000, 83; or *Ensign,* May 2000, 67–68).

3 Nephi 13:19–24. "Lay Not Up for Yourselves Treasures on Earth"

• President Ezra Taft Benson referred to the temporary nature of earthly treasures:

"Our affections are often too highly placed upon the paltry perishable objects. Material treasures of earth are merely to provide us, as it were, room and board while we are here at school. It is for us to place gold, silver, houses, stocks, lands, cattle, and other earthly possessions in their proper place.

"Yes, this is but a place of temporary duration. We are here to learn the first lesson toward exaltation—obedience to the Lord's gospel plan" (in Conference Report, Apr. 1971, 17; or *Ensign*, June 1971, 33).

• Elder Dallin H. Oaks of the Quorum of the Twelve Apostles gave insight regarding the treasures we may lay up for ourselves: "The Savior taught that we should not lay up treasures on earth but should lay up treasures in heaven (see Matthew 6:19–21). In light of the ultimate purpose of the great plan of happiness, I believe that the ultimate treasures on earth and in heaven are our children and our posterity" (in Conference Report, Oct. 1993, 100; or *Ensign*, Nov. 1993, 75).

3 Nephi 13:34. "No Thought for the Morrow"

• The Book of Mormon clarifies the meaning of Matthew 6:25–32 by indicating that Jesus was speaking to the twelve Nephite disciples for this portion of the sermon (see 3 Nephi 13:25–34). After Jesus delivered this charge to them, he then turned and began to speak to the multitude again (see 3 Nephi 14:1). It is helpful to note that Jesus repeatedly turned back and forth between these two audiences throughout His sermon.

3 Nephi 14:1–2. Judging

• Elder Dallin H. Oaks clarified the meaning of verses 1–2 in 3 Nephi 14 by explaining the difference between righteous and unrighteous judgments. Then he outlined those righteous principles:

"I have been puzzled that some scriptures command us not to judge and others instruct us that we should judge and even tell us how to do it. But as I have studied these passages I have become convinced that these seemingly contradictory directions are consistent when we view them with the perspective of eternity. The key is to understand that there are two kinds of judging: final judgments, which we are forbidden to make, and intermediate judgments, which we are directed to make, but upon righteous principles. . . .

"*First,* a righteous judgment must, by definition, be intermediate. . . .

"*Second,* a righteous judgment will be guided by the Spirit of the Lord, not by anger, revenge, jealousy, or self-interest. . . .

"*Third,* to be righteous, an intermediate judgment must be within our stewardship. . . .

"*Fourth,* we should, if possible, refrain from judging until we have adequate knowledge of the facts" ("'Judge Not' and Judging," *Ensign,* Aug. 1999, 7, 9–10).

3 Nephi 14:7–8. Asking through Prayer

• President James E. Faust bore testimony of the gift and privilege we each have of access to our Heavenly Father through prayer: "Access to our Creator through our Savior is surely one of the great privileges and blessings of our lives. . . . No earthly authority can separate us from direct access to our Creator. There can never be a mechanical or electronic failure when we pray. There is no limit on the number of times or how long we can pray each day. There is no quota of how many needs we wish to pray for in each prayer. We do not need to go through secretaries or make an appointment to reach the throne of grace. He is reachable at any time and any place" (in Conference Report, Apr. 2002, 67; or *Ensign,* May 2002, 59).

3 Nephi 14:12. The Golden Rule

• Elder Russell M. Nelson quoted the Golden Rule and gave these comments:

"[Jesus] taught the Golden Rule, saying, 'All things whatsoever ye would that men should do to you, do ye even so to them' [Matthew 7:12]. This principle is found in nearly every major religion. Others such as Confucius and Aristotle have also taught it. After all, the gospel did not begin with the birth of the Babe in Bethlehem. It is everlasting. It was proclaimed in the beginning to Adam and Eve. Portions of the gospel have been preserved in many cultures. Even heathen mythologies have been enriched by fragments of truth from earlier dispensations.

"Wherever it is found and however it is expressed, the Golden Rule encompasses the moral code of the kingdom of God. It forbids interference by one with the rights of another. It is equally binding upon nations, associations, and individuals. With compassion and forbearance, it replaces the retaliatory reactions of 'an eye for an eye, and a tooth for a tooth' [Matthew 5:38]. If we were to stay on that old and unproductive path, we would be but blind and toothless" (in Conference Report, Oct. 2002, 41–42; or *Ensign,* Nov. 2002, 39).

---

3 NEPHI 14:15–20

What does the symbolism in these verses teach us about those who claim to be prophets?

---

3 Nephi 14:15. "Beware of False Prophets"

• Elder M. Russell Ballard of the Quorum of the Twelve Apostles warned against those who teach or publish false doctrine: "Let us beware of false prophets and false teachers, both men and women, who are self-appointed declarers of the doctrines of the Church and who seek to spread their false gospel and attract followers by sponsoring symposia, books, and journals whose contents challenge fundamental doctrines of the Church. Beware of those who speak and publish in opposition to God's true prophets and who actively proselyte others with reckless disregard for the eternal well-being of those whom they seduce. . . . They 'set themselves up for a light unto the world, that they may get gain and praise of the world; but they seek not the welfare of Zion' (2 Nephi 26:29)" (in Conference Report, Oct. 1999, 78; or *Ensign,* Nov. 1999, 63).

Points to Ponder

• What difference does it make to do a good deed willingly versus doing the same deed reluctantly?

• Analyze your motives to determine whether or not you are seeking "first the kingdom of God" (3 Nephi 13:33).

Suggested Assignments

• Paraphrase as many of the Beatitudes as you can remember. Then check 3 Nephi 12:3–12 to see how you did.

• What do you need to do to more fully deny yourself of unrighteous thoughts and desires? Write out a plan on how to accomplish it.

Introduction

In the time of Moses the children of Israel were stiffnecked and hard of heart. As a result, they lost the privilege of living the fulness of the higher law (see Mosiah 13:29–31). Instead, along with portions of the higher law that they were still allowed to live, the law of Moses (the lesser law) was added to help them come to Christ (see D&C 84:18–27). After His Resurrection, Jesus Christ taught the Nephites that the law of Moses was fulfilled in Him (see 3 Nephi 12:17–18). He taught that "old things had passed away" (3 Nephi 15:2–4) and that He is "the law, and the light" to follow (3 Nephi 15:9).

As you read 3 Nephi 15–17, notice the difference between the unbelieving Jews and the teachable Nephites. Contrast truths the Savior withheld from those at Jerusalem with the remarkable revelation given in the Americas. Observe that comprehending His teachings requires faith, pondering, and prayer. You will realize the tremendous worth of paying that price as you read about the indescribable joy experienced by these more faithful disciples and the miraculous experiences of their believing children.

Commentary

3 Nephi 15:1–10. Jesus Christ Gave and Fulfilled the Law of Moses

• Earlier Book of Mormon prophets taught that the law of Moses would eventually be fulfilled. Nephi, Jacob, and Abinadi all prepared their people to eventually accept the ending of the law of Moses. Elder Jeffrey R. Holland of the Quorum of the Twelve Apostles identified the reasons the Nephites were able to give up the old law and embrace the new:

"Clearly the Nephite congregation understood this more readily than did the Jewish world, partly because the Nephite prophets had been so careful to teach the transitional nature of the law. Abinadi had said, 'It is expedient that ye should keep the law of Moses *as yet;* but I say unto you, that the time shall come when *it shall no more be expedient to keep the law of Moses.'* [Mosiah 13:27.] In that same spirit Nephi emphasized, 'We speak concerning the law that our children may know the deadness of the law; and they, by knowing the deadness of the law, may look forward unto that life which is in Christ, and know for what end the law was given. *And after the law is fulfilled in Christ, that they need not harden their hearts against him when the law ought to be done away.'* [2 Nephi 25:27; italics added.]

"That kind of teaching—a caution against hardening one's heart against Christ in ignorant defense of the law of Moses—could have served (and saved) so many living in the Old World then and living throughout the world now" (*Christ and the New Covenant* [1997], 156–57).

3 Nephi 15:2–8. The Law of Moses and the Higher Law

• Jesus said that "old things had passed away, and that all things had become new" (3 Nephi 15:3). Elder Jeffrey R. Holland explained: "It is crucial to understand that the law of Moses was overlaid upon, and thereby included, many basic parts of the gospel of Jesus Christ, which had existed before it. It was never intended to be something apart or separated from, and certainly not something antagonistic to, the gospel of Jesus Christ. . . . Its purpose was never to have been different from the higher law. Both were to bring people to Christ" (*Christ and the New Covenant,* 147). Thus Jesus could say, "For behold, the covenant which I have made with my people is not all fulfilled; but the law which was given unto Moses hath an end in me" (3 Nephi 15:8).

For more information regarding the Nephites and the law of Moses, see commentary for Mosiah 13:27–35 (p. 152).

3 Nephi 15:5–8. The Covenant Is Not All Fulfilled

• For a discussion of what Jesus meant when He said, "I do not destroy the prophets" (3 Nephi 15:6), see commentary for 3 Nephi 12:17–20, 46–47 (p. 305).

What did Jesus mean when He said, "The covenant which I have made with my people is not all fulfilled"? (3 Nephi 15:8). Jehovah made a covenant with Abraham anciently. Abraham was promised (1) eternal posterity, (2) a land that would eventually be the celestial kingdom, and (3) God's priesthood power. These promises were also made to Abraham's descendants (see D&C 132:30–31) and will be fulfilled in the future.

3 Nephi 15:11–13. "This Is the Land of Your Inheritance"

• Each of the twelve tribes of Israel was assigned an area of land for their inheritance in the land of Canaan. In addition to what they received in the Holy Land, the descendants of Joseph were also promised the land of the Americas as part of their inheritance. The Savior told the twelve Nephite disciples that they and their people were "a remnant of the house of Joseph" (3 Nephi 15:12) and "this is the land of your inheritance" (v. 13).

• Elder Orson F. Whitney (1855–1931) of the Quorum of the Twelve Apostles described the land of inheritance as follows: "Another name for America, authorized by the Book of Mormon, is the Land of Joseph, referred to by the Patriarch Jacob in blessing his twelve sons (Gen. 49:22–26), and by the Prophet Moses in his farewell benediction upon the twelve tribes of Israel (Deut. 33:13–15). Jacob's allusion to Joseph as 'a fruitful bough by a well, whose branches run over the wall, was fulfilled in the migration of Lehi and his companions from Asia to America over the Pacific Ocean. It is hardly necessary to add, that one of the main features of these western continents are those mighty mountain ranges, the Andes and the Rockies, well termed by the Hebrew Patriarch 'the everlasting hills,' nature's depositories for 'the precious things of the earth'—gold, silver, and other minerals—and for 'the precious things of heaven'—the sacred records already discovered and others that are yet to come forth" ("The Book of Mormon: Historical and Prophetic Phases," *Improvement Era,* Sept. 1927, 944–45).

3 Nephi 15:17. "One Shepherd"

• Jesus Christ is often called the Good Shepherd (see D&C 50:44; John 10:7–18; Alma 5:38–60; Helaman 7:18). The metaphor of the shepherd and his relationship to his sheep connotes personal care and concern. One modern commentator spoke of the personal care involved in the work of the shepherd:

"By day and by night the shepherd is always with his sheep. . . . This was necessary on account of the exposed nature of the land, and the presence of danger from wild animals and robbers. One of the most familiar and beautiful sights of the East is that of the shepherd leading his sheep to the pasture. . . . He depends upon the sheep to follow, and they in turn expect him never to leave them. . . .

". . . As he is always with them, and so deeply interested in them, the shepherd comes to know his sheep very intimately. . . . One day a missionary, meeting a shepherd on one of the wildest parts of the Lebanon, asked him various questions about his sheep, and among others if he counted them every night. On answering that he did not, he was asked how he knew if they were all there or not. His reply was, 'Master, if you were to put a cloth over my eyes, and bring me any sheep and only let me put my hands on its face, I could tell in a moment if it was mine or not'" (George M. Mackie, *Bible Manners and Customs* [n.d.], 33, 35).

• Elder Neal A. Maxwell (1926–2004) of the Quorum of the Twelve Apostles, speaking about this personal care said:

"Jesus is so personal in His shepherding and tutoring! . . .

". . . Jesus knows and cares for each individual; He watches carefully over the seemingly smallest of things" (*That Ye May Believe* [1992], 204–5).

---

3 NEPHI 15:18

What is the relationship between belief and understanding? How does this apply to your study of the gospel?

---

3 Nephi 16:1–3. Other Sheep

• Verses 1–3 of 3 Nephi 16 make it clear that there are "other sheep" besides the Nephites and that the Savior planned to visit them. We are told in 3 Nephi 17:4 that these other sheep are the "lost tribes of Israel." The Good Shepherd watches over all His flocks, caring for them as needed.

3 Nephi 16:3–13. The Gathering of Israel

• For more information on the gathering of Israel, refer to "The Gathering of Israel" in the appendix (p. 416).

3 Nephi 16:4–7. The Book of Mormon Will Bring Us to a Knowledge of Christ

• President Boyd K. Packer, President of the Quorum of the Twelve Apostles, explained that a major purpose of the Book of Mormon is to help bring us to a knowledge of Jesus as the Christ:

"The central purpose of the Book of Mormon is its testament of Jesus Christ. Of more than 6,000 verses in the Book of Mormon, far more than half refer directly to Him.

"So, 'we talk of Christ, we rejoice in Christ, we preach of Christ, we prophesy of Christ, and we write according to our prophecies, that our children may know to what source they may look for a remission of their sins' (2 Nephi 25:26)" (in Conference Report, Apr. 2005, 8; or *Ensign,* May 2005, 8–9).

3 Nephi 16:4–13. Who Are the Gentiles?

• The majority of references in the Book of Mormon to the word *gentile* are references to anyone who is not a Jew. A Jew was anyone who was a descendant of Judah and anyone from the land of Jerusalem—like the children of Lehi. President Joseph Fielding Smith (1876–1972) explained that by this definition many Gentiles did have the blood of Israel: "In this Dispensation of the Fulness of Times, the gospel came first to the Gentiles and then is to go to the Jews. [See D&C 19:27.] However, the Gentiles who receive the gospel are in the greater part, Gentiles who have the blood of Israel in their veins" (*Answers to Gospel Questions*, comp. Joseph Fielding Smith Jr., 5 vols. [1957–66], 4:39).

Elder Bruce R. McConkie (1915–85) of the Quorum of the Twelve Apostles described this as well: "We have heretofore identified the Jews as both the nationals of the kingdom of Judah and as their lineal descendants, all this without reference to tribal affiliation. And we have said, within this usage of terms, that all other people are Gentiles, including the lost and scattered remnants of the kingdom of Israel in whose veins the precious blood of him whose name was Israel does in fact flow. Thus Joseph Smith, of the tribe of Ephraim, the chief and foremost tribe of Israel itself, was the Gentile by whose hand the Book of Mormon came forth, and the members of The Church of Jesus Christ of Latter-day Saints, who have the gospel and who are of Israel by blood descent, are the Gentiles who carry salvation to the Lamanites and to the Jews" (*The Millennial Messiah* [1982], 233).

3 Nephi 17:1–3. "Ponder upon the Things Which I Have Said"

• Some students of the gospel may feel that simply reading the scriptures or listening to the words of the prophets is adequate. The Savior, however, directed the Nephites to not only listen to His words but to "go ye unto your homes, and ponder upon the things which I have said" (3 Nephi 17:3). This, He taught, would help them understand and prepare their "minds for the morrow" when He would return (v. 3). This is in harmony with other passages of scriptures that command us to ponder what we read, see, and hear. Moroni listed pondering as one of the essential features in gaining a testimony of the Book of Mormon (see Moroni 10:3). Nephi told his readers, "My soul delighteth in the things of the Lord; and my heart pondereth continually upon the things which I have seen and heard" (2 Nephi 4:16).

• President Marion G. Romney (1897–1988) of the First Presidency described the power of pondering:

"As I have read the scriptures, I have been challenged by the word *ponder,* so frequently used in the Book of Mormon. The dictionary says that *ponder* means 'to weigh mentally, think deeply about, deliberate, meditate.' . . .

"*Pondering* is, in my feeling, a form of prayer. It has, at least, been an approach to the Spirit of the Lord on many occasions. Nephi tells us of one such occasion:

"'For it came to pass,' he wrote, 'after I had desired to know the things that my father had seen, and believing that the Lord was able to make them known unto me, as I sat *pondering* in mine heart I was caught away in the Spirit of the Lord, yea, into an exceeding high mountain. . . .' (1 Ne. 11:1. Italics added.)

"Then follows Nephi's account of the great vision he was given by the Spirit of the Lord, because he believed the words of his prophet father and had such a great desire to know more that he pondered and prayed about them" (in Conference Report, Apr. 1973, 117–18; or *Ensign,* July 1973, 90).

• Pondering the things of God helps to keep us from becoming complacent in our approach to Him. Elder Neal A. Maxwell explained the dangers of not regularly internalizing the gospel in our lives: "The worshipers at Rameumptom so ritualized their religion that they never spoke of their God 'again until they had assembled themselves together' a week later at the holy stand. (Alma 31:23.) Note the contrast in how Jesus instructed His followers on this hemisphere: [3 Nephi 17:3.] See how the Master focuses on the family—on pondering, praying, preparing together! It should not surprise us, if we routinize our religion and do not assign the highest priority to the kingdom, that our hearts and minds will quite naturally drift to other things" (*Wherefore, Ye Must Press Forward* [1977], 30–31).

> ### 3 NEPHI 17:2–3
> *What did the Savior send the Nephites home to do? What are some of the benefits that come to us as we pray and ponder?*

3 Nephi 17:4. Scattered Israel Is Not Lost unto the Father

• Although the scattered tribes of Israel are lost to the knowledge of man, they are not lost to God. He knows where they are, "for he knoweth whither he hath taken them" (3 Nephi 17:4). His knowledge of them and the Savior's visit to the lost tribes of Israel suggests the possibility that we will someday have access to other accounts of Jesus's visits to His sheep.

Elder Neal A. Maxwell observed: "Lost books are among the treasures yet to come forth. Over twenty of these are mentioned in the existing scriptures. Perhaps most startling and voluminous will be the records of the lost tribes of Israel (see 2 Nephi 29:13). We would not even know of the impending third witness for Christ except through the precious Book of Mormon, the second witness for Christ! This third set of sacred records will thus complete a triad of truth. Then, just as the Perfect Shepherd has said, 'My word also shall be gathered in one' (v. 14). There will be 'one fold and one shepherd' (1 Nephi 22:25) in a welding together of all the Christian dispensations of human history (see D&C 128:18)" (in Conference Report, Oct. 1986, 70; or *Ensign,* Nov. 1986, 52).

3 Nephi 17:5–10. Jesus Healed and Blessed the People

• Evidence of the great compassion Jesus felt for the people, His brothers and sisters, is shown in 3 Nephi 17:5–10. He asked for the sick to be brought to Him, and He healed them all. Elder Jeffrey R. Holland focused on the power of this spiritual moment: "Calling for the sick and the blind, the halt and the maimed, the leprous and the withered, those that were 'afflicted in any manner,' Christ asked that they be brought forward that he might heal them. . . . Sensing with divine insight that these people desired to behold the miracles he had performed for their brothers and sisters in Jerusalem, and recognizing instantly that their faith was sufficient for them to be healed, Christ responded to each need within the multitude, 'and he did heal them every one as they were brought forth unto him.' In response to such an outpouring of compassion and mercy, all of the congregation, the healed as well as the whole, did 'bow down at his feet, and did worship him; and as many as could come . . . did kiss his feet, insomuch that they did bathe his feet with their tears.' [3 Nephi 17:5–7, 9–10.]" (*Christ and the New Covenant,* 268–69).

3 Nephi 17:11–24. "Behold Your Little Ones"

• While serving as the general president of the Primary, Sister Michaelene P. Grassli referred to the capacity of children for spiritual experiences:

"It's significant to me that . . . the Savior gave the most sacred teachings only to the children, then loosed their tongues so they could teach the multitude. (See 3 Ne. 26:14.)

"Is it any wonder that following the Savior's visit to the Nephites, they lived in peace and righteousness for two hundred years? Because of miraculous instructions, blessings, and attention they and their children received, righteousness was perpetuated by their children's children for many generations.

"Let us not underestimate the capacity and potential power of today's children to perpetuate righteousness. No group of people in the Church is as receptive to the truth" ("Behold Your Little Ones," *Ensign,* Nov. 1992, 92–94).

• Church members in Chile had a similar experience when President Spencer W. Kimball (1895–1985) visited them: "One of the greatest expressions of love for children that I have seen occurred when I was serving as a stake president in Chile. President Spencer W. Kimball visited Chile for an area conference. Members of the Church from four countries met together in a stadium that held about fifteen thousand people. We asked President Kimball what he would like to do after the conference. His eyes full of tears, he said, 'I would like to see the children.' One of the priesthood leaders announced over the microphone that President Kimball would like to shake the hands or bless each of the children in the stadium. The people were astounded—there was a great silence. President Kimball greeted about two thousand children one by one, crying as he shook their hands or kissed them or put his hands on their heads and blessed them. The children were very reverent and looked at him and cried too. He said he'd never felt this kind of spirit in his life. It was a tremendous moment in the lives of all the Church members there" (Janet Peterson and Eduardo Ayala, "Friend to Friend," *Friend,* Mar. 1996, 6–7).

Points to Ponder

• What do you think is meant by the Savior's statement, "Behold, I am the law, and the light"? (3 Nephi 15:9).

• Why do you think Jesus Christ told the people to ponder the things that He taught and to ask Heavenly Father for understanding? Why was this process important in preparing them for His next visit?

• What importance have you placed upon understanding the covenants in the Book of Mormon?

Suggested Assignments

• Share with a friend or family member an explanation of what the "other sheep" mentioned in John 10:16 refers to.

• Discuss with a friend what it might have been like to be one of those who witnessed the marvelous miracles and events described in 3 Nephi 15–17.

Introduction

During His visit to the Nephites, the Savior instituted the sacrament and emphasized that the purpose of the sacrament is to remember Him. He promised, "If ye do always remember me ye shall have my Spirit to be with you" (3 Nephi 18:11). This same promise is part of the sacrament prayer. While you study 3 Nephi 18–19, ponder what Jesus taught about the sacrament and about prayer and how these teachings can help you deepen your discipleship of Christ so you can more fully enjoy the companionship of the Holy Ghost.

Commentary

3 Nephi 18:1–14. "This Shall Ye Do in Remembrance"

• The Savior taught that the principal purpose for taking the sacrament is to *remember* Him. We have an opportunity to concentrate on the Son of God during

the sacrament ordinance; we should not allow our thoughts to wander or be distracted. Elder Jeffrey R. Holland of the Quorum of the Twelve Apostles described several appropriate ways to remember the Lord while renewing our covenants through the sacrament:

"We could remember the Savior's premortal life and all that we know Him to have done. . . .

"We could remember the simple grandeur of His mortal birth to just a young woman. . . .

"We could remember Christ's miracles and His teachings, His healings and His help. . . .

". . . We could remember that Jesus found special joy and happiness in children and said all of us should be more like them. . . .

"We could remember that Christ called His disciples friends. . . .

"We could—and should—remember the wonderful things that have come to us in our lives and that 'all

things which are good cometh of Christ' (Moroni 7:24). . . .

"On some days we will have cause to remember the unkind treatment He received, the rejection He experienced, and the injustice . . . He endured. . . .

". . . We can remember that Jesus had to descend below all things before He could ascend above them, and that He suffered pains and afflictions and temptations of every kind that He might be filled with mercy and know how to succor His people in their infirmities" (in Conference Report, Oct. 1995, 90–91; or *Ensign,* Nov. 1995, 68–69).

3 Nephi 18:6–7. The Sacrament and the Administering of Angels

• Elder Dallin H. Oaks of the Quorum of the Twelve Apostles explained how the ministering of angels is also a part of the promises of the sacramental prayers:

"These ordinances of the Aaronic Priesthood are also vital to the ministering of angels. . . .

". . . Angelic messages can be delivered by a voice or merely by thoughts or feelings communicated to the mind. . . .

". . . Most angelic communications are felt or heard rather than seen. . . .

"In general, the blessings of spiritual companionship and communication are available only to those who are clean. . . . Through the Aaronic Priesthood ordinances of baptism and the sacrament, we are cleansed of our sins and promised that if we keep our covenants we will always have His Spirit to be with us. I believe that promise not only refers to the Holy Ghost but also to the ministering of angels, for 'angels speak by the power of the Holy Ghost; wherefore, they speak the words of Christ' (2 Nephi 32:3). So it is that those who hold the Aaronic Priesthood open the door for all Church members who worthily partake of the sacrament to enjoy the companionship of the Spirit of the Lord and the ministering of angels" (in Conference Report, Oct. 1998, 50–51; or *Ensign,* Nov. 1998, 38–39).

3 Nephi 18:16, 24. "I Have Set an Example for You"

• Elder Neal A. Maxwell (1926–2004) of the Quorum of the Twelve Apostles admonished that whatever our role, we should seek to emulate the Savior's character as much as we can:

"Each of us plays various roles in family, Church, community, business, education, and so forth. Though we have differing needs, we have in common the need to focus on all Christ's qualities, especially those which individually we most need to develop more fully. . . .

"We can, of course, stop short and merely adopt a few techniques illustrated by the Savior. But unless we emulate Him as completely as we can, we will have deprived ourselves of the great model. Moreover, our emulation is to be of both style and substance. God's love underwrites his listening, for instance. Can we conceive of a God who is a nonlistener? Or who is lacking in power? Or who is unwilling to assert Himself on an issue of principle? As we become more like Him it will take place in both attributes and actions" (*A Wonderful Flood of Light* [1990], 110).

3 Nephi 18:18. "Watch and Pray Always"

• President Henry B. Eyring of the First Presidency reflected on the importance of the commissions to "always remember him" (D&C 20:77, 79) and to "pray always" (3 Nephi 18:18):

"What does the Master mean when He warns us to 'pray always'?

"I am not wise enough to know all of His purposes in giving us a covenant to always remember Him and in His warning us to pray always lest we be overcome. But I know one. It is because He knows perfectly the powerful forces that influence us and also what it means to be human. . . .

". . . He knows what it is like to have the cares of life press in upon us. . . . And He knows how our human powers to cope are not constant. . . .

". . . As the forces around us increase in intensity, whatever spiritual strength was once sufficient will not be enough. And whatever growth in spiritual strength we once thought was possible, greater growth will be made available to us. Both the need for spiritual strength and the opportunity to acquire it will increase at rates which we underestimate at our peril. . . .

"Start with remembering Him. You will remember what you know and what you love. . . .

"The Lord hears the prayers of your heart. The feelings of your heart, of love for our Heavenly Father and for His Beloved Son, can be so constant that your prayers will ascend always" ("Always" [CES fireside for young adults, Jan. 3, 1999], 2–3, 5; see also "Always," *Ensign,* Oct. 1999, 8–10, 12).

3 Nephi 18:18. "Sift You as Wheat"

• When Jesus warned the Nephites, "Satan desireth to have you, that he may sift you as wheat" (3 Nephi 18:18), He was teaching the same message He had expressed to Peter (see Luke 22:31).

Elder Bruce R. McConkie (1915–85) of the Quorum of the Twelve Apostles explained Jesus's words: "This is an idiomatic expression which was clear to the people in that day, more so than to people in our day. In essence and thought content Jesus is saying, 'Peter, Satan wants you in his harvest. He wants to harvest your soul, and bring you into his granary, into his garner, where he will have you as his disciple.' It is the same figure that we use when we say that the field is white, already to harvest. And we go out and preach the gospel and harvest the souls of men. Well, Satan wanted Peter; he wanted to sift him as wheat or to harvest his soul" (*Sermons and Writings of Bruce R. McConkie,* ed. Mark L. McConkie [1998], 127).

3 NEPHI 18:18–21
What instructions did Jesus give here that would improve your prayers?

3 Nephi 18:21. "Pray in Your Families"

• President Gordon B. Hinckley (1910–2008) discussed the importance of family prayer: "I feel satisfied that there is no adequate substitute for the morning and evening practice of kneeling together—father, mother, and children. This, more than soft carpets, more than lovely draperies, more than cleverly balanced color schemes, is the thing that will make for better and more beautiful homes" (in Conference Report, Apr. 1963, 127).

3 Nephi 18:26–32. A Sacred Ordinance

• Notice that in 3 Nephi 18:26 the Savior ceased speaking to the multitude and turned to the leaders "whom he had chosen." His message in verses 28–29 was given to priesthood leaders as a warning against allowing the unworthy to partake of the sacrament. We learn from these verses that members of the Church should leave the responsibility of determining worthiness to partake of the sacrament to those the Lord has called to make such judgments, such as the bishop or stake president.

Minerva K. Teichert, Courtesy of BYU Museum of Art

• While serving as a member of the Seventy, Elder John H. Groberg explained what it means to partake of the sacrament worthily:

"If we desire to improve (which is to repent) and are not under priesthood restriction, then, in my opinion, we are worthy. If, however, we have no desire to improve, if we have no intention of following the guidance of the Spirit, we must ask: Are we worthy to partake, or are we making a mockery of the very purpose of the sacrament, which is to act as a catalyst for personal repentance and improvement? If we remember the Savior and all he has done and will do for us, we will improve our actions and thus come closer to him, which keeps us on the road to eternal life.

"If, however, we refuse to repent and improve, if we do not remember him and keep his commandments, then we have stopped our growth, and that is damnation to our souls.

"The sacrament is an intensely personal experience, and we are the ones who knowingly are worthy or otherwise. . . .

"As we worthily partake of the sacrament, we will sense those things we need to improve in and receive the help and determination to do so. No matter what our problems, the sacrament always gives hope.

"Most of these problems we must work out ourselves. For example, if we aren't paying our tithing, we simply determine to start doing so. But for some problems, we must see our bishop—the Spirit will let us know which" (in Conference Report, Apr. 1989, 50; or *Ensign,* May 1989, 38–39).

3 Nephi 18:36–37. Jesus Gave His Disciples "Power to Give the Holy Ghost"

• The multitude did not know what the Savior did or said when He touched His disciples and spoke to them; however, Mormon informed us that the disciples testified "that he gave them [the disciples] power to give the Holy Ghost" (3 Nephi 18:37). Moroni fulfilled his father's promise to the reader that "I will show unto you hereafter that this record is true" (3 Nephi 18:37) when he later gave an account of this event and the words Christ spoke to the twelve disciples. He further explained that when the Savior touched His disciples to give them authority, He was laying on His hands (see Moroni 2:1–3).

> **3 NEPHI 19:6–8, 16–17**
> *Why do you think kneeling when possible is an important part of prayer?*

3 Nephi 19:9. The Disciples Prayed for the Holy Ghost

• The twelve disciples, whom Jesus had chosen, prayed "that the Holy Ghost should be given unto them" (3 Nephi 19:9). Elder Bruce R. McConkie explained the meaning behind the request:

"There is . . . a difference between the gift of the Holy Ghost and the enjoyment of the gift. All saints after baptism receive the gift or right to the sanctifying power of the Spirit; only those who are worthy and who keep the commandments actually enjoy the promised reward. In practice, members of the Church enjoy the companionship of the Spirit from time to time as they manage, by obedience, to get in tune with the Infinite.

"The actual enjoyment of the gift of the Holy Ghost is a supernal gift that a man can receive in mortality. The fact of its receipt is a witness that the saints so blessed are reconciled to God and are doing the things that will assure them of eternal life in the realms ahead" (*A New Witness for the Articles of Faith* [1985], 257).

• President Heber J. Grant (1856–1945) spoke of asking God twice a day for the guidance of the Holy Spirit: "I have little or no fear for the boy or the girl, the young man or the young woman, who honestly and conscientiously supplicate God twice a day for the guidance of His Spirit. I am sure that when temptation comes they will have the strength to overcome it by the inspiration that shall be given to them. Supplicating the Lord for the guidance of His Spirit places around us a safeguard, and if we earnestly and honestly seek the guidance of the Spirit of the Lord, I can assure you that we will receive it" (*Gospel Standards* [1976], 26).

• President Marion G. Romney (1897–1988), Second Counselor in the First Presidency, stated that we can obtain and keep the Spirit by following a simple four-point program: "If you want to obtain and keep the guidance of the Spirit, you can do so by following this simple four-point program. One, pray. Pray diligently. . . . Second, study and learn the gospel. Third, live righteously; repent of your sins. . . . Fourth, give service in the Church" ("Guidance of the Holy Spirit," *Ensign,* Jan. 1980, 5).

3 Nephi 19:10–13. Baptized Anew

• President Joseph Fielding Smith (1876–1972) explained why Jesus commanded the Nephites to be baptized again:

"When Christ appeared to the Nephites on this continent, he commanded them to be baptized, although they had been baptized previously for the remission of their sins. . . . The Savior commanded Nephi and the people to be baptized again, *because he had organized anew the Church under the gospel* [see 3 Nephi 19:7–15; 26:17]. *Before that it had been organized under the law* [see 3 Nephi 9:15–22; 11:10–40; 12:18–19; 15:4–10].

". . . For the same reason Joseph Smith and those who had been baptized prior to April 6, 1830, were again baptized on the day of the organization of the Church" (*Doctrines of Salvation,* comp. Bruce R. McConkie, 3 vols. [1954–56], 2:336).

3 Nephi 19:18, 22. "They Did Pray unto Jesus"

• There is no place in scripture where we are taught to pray to Jesus. In this unique instance, however, the disciples offered prayers to the Son instead of the Father. Elder Bruce R. McConkie suggested a reason this may have occurred: "There was a special reason why this was done in this instance and on a onetime basis. Jesus had already taught them to pray in his name to the Father, which they first did. . . . Jesus was present before them as the symbol of the Father. Seeing him, it was as though they saw the Father; praying to him, it was as though they prayed to the Father. It was a special and unique situation" (*The Promised Messiah: The First Coming of Christ* [1978], 560–61). It should also be noted that the Savior specifically stated that the people were praying to Him on this occasion because, as He said, "I am with them" (3 Nephi 19:22). Furthermore, on this occasion "they did not multiply many words, for it was given unto them what they should pray" (3 Nephi 19:24).

3 Nephi 19:19–20, 27–28. "I Thank Thee"

• The scriptures give many examples of the Savior expressing thanks to His Father (see Mark 14:23; John 6:5–11; 11:33–35, 41; 1 Corinthians 11:23–24). Upon returning to visit the Nephites a second time, Jesus began His first and second prayers recorded in scripture by thanking His Father (see 3 Nephi 19:19–20, 27–28). Elder Robert D. Hales of the Quorum of the Twelve Apostles emphasized this principle:

"Prayer is an essential part of conveying appreciation to our Heavenly Father. He awaits our expressions of gratefulness each morning and night in sincere, simple prayer from our hearts for our many blessings, gifts, and talents.

"Through expression of prayerful gratitude and thanksgiving, we show our dependence upon a higher source of wisdom and knowledge—God the Father and his Son, our Lord and Savior Jesus Christ" (in Conference Report, Apr. 1992, 89; or *Ensign,* May 1992, 64).

3 Nephi 19:20–23, 29. A Prayer for Unity

• Jesus prayed to Heavenly Father for unity among His followers and also for unity among the people His followers taught (see John 17:11, 20–21). Christ also taught the principle of unity in the Doctrine and Covenants: "I say unto you, be one; and if ye are not one ye are not mine" (D&C 38:27).

Elder Jeffrey R. Holland compared Jesus Christ's prayer for unity in 3 Nephi 19:20–23 with John 17:11, 20–23:

"From the Savior's language, we see clearly it is the Holy Ghost that provides such unity, a doctrinal point not so clearly communicated in the New Testament account. Furthermore, it is significant that one of the ultimate evidences God has of our belief in Deity is that we are seen and heard praying. Christ noted this evidence on behalf of the Nephites. To the Father he said, 'Thou seest that they believe in me because thou

hearest them' [3 Nephi 19:22]. . . . It is the key to the miraculous manifestations of heaven and the personal companionship of the Holy Comforter(s)" (*Christ and the New Covenant* [1997], 280).

• Elder D. Todd Christofferson of the Quorum of the Twelve Apostles explained how we may become one with the Father and the Son:

"Jesus achieved perfect unity with the Father by submitting Himself, both flesh and spirit, to the will of the Father. The Savior's ministry was always clearly focused because there was no debilitating or distracting double-mindedness in Him. Referring to His Father, Jesus said, 'I do always those things that please him' [John 8:29]. . . .

"Surely we will not be one with God and Christ until we make Their will and interest our greatest desire. Such submissiveness is not reached in a day, but through the Holy Spirit, the Lord will tutor us if we are willing until, in process of time, it may accurately be said that He is in us as the Father is in Him. At times I tremble to consider what may be required, but I know that it is only in this perfect union that a fulness of joy can be found" (in Conference Report, Oct. 2002, 76–77; or *Ensign,* Nov. 2002, 72–73).

3 Nephi 19:24. "They Did Not Multiply Many Words"

• What does it mean to pray and "not multiply many words"? (3 Nephi 19:24). Elder Gene R. Cook of the Seventy gave the following insights:

"When the Nephite disciples were praying in the presence of Jesus, they set a good example for us all. The record says . . . 'they did not multiply many words. . . .'

"This is consistent with the commandment the Lord gave to the Jews during his mortal ministry. He said, 'When ye pray, use not vain repetitions, as the heathen do: for they think that they shall be heard for their much speaking.' (Matthew 6:7; also see 3 Nephi 13:7.)

"When we pray publicly, let us be careful to never be swept away in the desire for the honors of men, which might cause us to pray without real intent or to unnecessarily extend the length of our prayers. The same caution applies to those who pray for a mortal audience rather than simply to be heard by the Lord. We must always be careful to avoid 'flowery' prayers or prayers to impress. Surely the Lord is not pleased with such an approach, nor will he answer the prayers of one who is not focused on the Lord or who prays without real intent" (*Receiving Answers to Our Prayers* [1996], 43–44).

---

3 NEPHI 19:24–25

What appears to have happened to the disciples in these verses? Compare your answer with 3 Nephi 19:28–29 as well as Moses 1:9–11.

---

3 Nephi 19:35. Miracles Come to Those Who Have Faith

• Great miracles accompanied the Savior's visit to the Saints in Book of Mormon times—miracles of healings, angels, shining countenances, prayers too sacred to be written, and many other marvelous manifestations. Jesus declared to His disciples, "So great faith have I never seen among all the Jews; wherefore I could not show unto them so great miracles, because of their unbelief" (3 Nephi 19:35).

Do miracles occur today, or has the day of miracles ceased? Elder Dallin H. Oaks taught that miracles still occur; however, we often don't hear of them because of their sacredness:

"Why don't our talks in general conference and local meetings say more about the miracles we have seen? Most of the miracles we experience are not to be shared. Consistent with the teachings of the scriptures, we hold them sacred and share them only when the Spirit prompts us to do so. . . .

". . . Modern revelation directs that 'they shall not boast themselves of these things, neither speak them before the world; for these things are given unto you for your profit and for salvation' (D&C 84:73). Another

revelation declares, 'Remember that that which cometh from above is sacred, and must be spoken with care, and by constraint of the Spirit' (D&C 63:64). . . .

"Latter-day Saints generally follow these directions. In bearing testimonies and in our public addresses we rarely mention our most miraculous experiences, and we rarely rely on signs that the gospel is true. We usually just affirm our testimony of the truthfulness of the restored gospel and give few details on how we obtained it. Why is this? Signs *follow* those that believe. Seeking a miracle to convert someone is improper sign seeking. By the same token, it is usually inappropriate to recite miraculous circumstances to a general audience that includes people with very different levels of spiritual maturity. To a general audience, miracles will be faith-reinforcing for some but an inappropriate sign for others" ("Miracles" [CES fireside for young adults, May 7, 2000], 3, www.ldsces.org).

Points to Ponder

• How might remembering how you felt when you were baptized improve your experience the next time you partake of the sacrament?

• The disciples prayed "for that which they most desired," which was "that the Holy Ghost should be given unto them" (3 Nephi 19:9). What do you most desire? Is your desire something you include in your prayers? Why or why not?

• The Savior's countenance "did smile upon" His disciples (3 Nephi 19:25, 30). What do you think this means? What can you do to allow your countenance to smile upon others?

Suggested Assignments

• Now that you have read several scriptures and other teachings about the sacrament, develop your own plan for making the sacrament a more meaningful part of your life.

• Study the descriptions of the Savior's prayers in 3 Nephi 19:19–23, 27–29, 31–32. Ponder the principle that these descriptions teach you about improving your prayers. Record your observations and conclusions in your journal.

Introduction

The hope of all righteous parents is that their descendants will come to know God for themselves and be faithful to Him. God promised Abraham and his descendants that in the latter days their posterity would have the blessings of the gospel and would be gathered to places of safety. The Father commanded the Savior to teach these promises to the Nephites.

The principle of gathering involves more than assembling people together on certain lands. It also includes a spiritual gathering that occurs when someone comes in contact with and joins the Church. In their scattered condition, Israel lost the knowledge of their God, His gospel, the priesthood, the temple, and the truths of salvation. The Father promised, however, that He would reach out to Israel in the last days and offer them His gospel, His priesthood, the temple, and the path to eternal life. Heavenly Father wants to offer the blessings of the gospel to all of His children and is helping to bring about this latter-day gathering.

Commentary

3 Nephi 20:1. We Should Continually Pray in Our Hearts

• After their prayer had ended, the Savior gave the Nephites important counsel to keep a prayer continually in their hearts. Elder Russell M. Nelson of the Quorum of the Twelve Apostles similarly declared:

"Prophets have long told us to pray humbly and frequently. . . .

"Prayers can be offered even in silence. One can *think* a prayer, especially when words would interfere" (in Conference Report, Apr. 2003, 5; or *Ensign,* May 2003, 7).

• President Boyd K. Packer, President of the Quorum of the Twelve Apostles, taught:

"Learn to pray. Pray often. Pray in your mind, in your heart. Pray on your knees. . . .

"Prayer is *your* personal key to heaven. The lock is on your side of the veil [see Revelation 3:20]" (in Conference Report, Oct. 1994, 76–77; or *Ensign,* Nov. 1994, 59).

---

3 NEPHI 20:8–9
What does the Savior promise those who partake of the sacrament? Why is this promise so significant?

---

3 Nephi 20:8–9. The Sacramental Promise of Being Filled with the Spirit

• Concerning the blessings associated with partaking of the sacrament, Elder Dallin H. Oaks of the Quorum of the Twelve Apostles taught: "Attendance at church each week provides the opportunity to partake of the sacrament, as the Lord has commanded us (see D&C 59:9). If we act with the right preparation and attitude, partaking of the sacrament renews the cleansing effect of our baptism and qualifies us for the promise that we will always have His Spirit to be with us. A mission of that Spirit, the Holy Ghost, is to testify of the Father and the Son and to lead us into truth (see John 14:26; 2 Nephi 31:18). Testimony and truth, which are essential to our personal conversion, are the choice harvest of this weekly renewing of our covenants. In the day-to-day decisions of my life and in my personal spiritual growth, I have enjoyed the fulfillment of that promise" (in Conference Report, Apr. 2002, 38; or *Ensign,* May 2002, 34).

• Elder Oaks also counseled: "To those brothers and sisters who may have allowed themselves to become lax in this vital renewal of the covenants of the sacrament, I plead in words of the First Presidency that you 'come back and feast at the table of the Lord, and taste again the sweet and satisfying fruits of fellowship with the saints' ('An Invitation to Come Back,' *Church News,* 22 Dec. 1985, 3). Let us qualify ourselves for our Savior's promise that by partaking of the sacrament we will 'be filled' (3 Nephi 20:8; see also 3 Nephi 18:9), which means that we will be 'filled with the Spirit' (3 Nephi 20:9). That Spirit—the Holy Ghost—is our comforter, our direction finder, our communicator, our interpreter, our witness, and our purifier—our infallible guide and sanctifier for our mortal journey toward eternal life" (in Conference Report, Oct. 1996, 82; or *Ensign,* Nov. 1996, 61).

3 Nephi 20:11–13. Isaiah Wrote of the Gathering of Israel

• Jesus commanded the Nephites, as well as us, to search the words of Isaiah. As we see the fulfillment of Isaiah's prophecies, we will know that God is keeping His covenant with the house of Israel. The Bible Dictionary explains that "the bulk of Isaiah's prophecies deal with the coming of the Redeemer" ("Isaiah," 707). The scattering and the gathering of Israel are also two of Isaiah's major themes.

Teachings of the Redeemer and the gathering of Israel are closely related. God scattered Israel because they sinned and rejected Him. The Atonement, however, provides them a chance to be reconciled to God, to have their sins remitted, and to be gathered to Him both spiritually and physically.

• For more information on the gathering of Israel, refer to "The Gathering of Israel" in the appendix (p. 416).

---

3 NEPHI 20:11–13

What is the key to knowing the timing of the gathering? (see 3 Nephi 21:1–7). What role do we play in the gathering? (see D&C 88:81).

• The Savior spoke of fulfilling His Father's covenant to gather scattered Israel. Who is Israel and why were they scattered? The Lord promised Abraham that his descendants would have the gospel and the priesthood and that through them all the families of the earth would be blessed (see Abraham 2:9–11). This promise was renewed with Abraham's son Isaac (see Genesis 26:3–5), with Isaac's son Jacob (see Genesis 28:12–15), and with Jacob's descendants, the children of Israel.

Sadly, the children of Israel sinned against God and forfeited these promises. Eventually, in fulfillment of God's warnings, they were expelled from their promised land and scattered throughout the earth. However, the Lord has not forgotten them. Heavenly Father promised that they would one day be taught the gospel and gathered to lands of promise. This promise is part of the covenant He made that He would gather and teach the children of Israel.

• President Spencer W. Kimball (1895–1985) explained that by accepting the gospel covenant, we comply with the law of the gathering: "Now, the gathering of Israel consists of joining the true church and their coming to a knowledge of the true God. . . . Any person, therefore, who has accepted the restored gospel, and who now seeks to worship the Lord in his own tongue and with the Saints in the nations where he lives, has complied with the law of the gathering of Israel and is heir to all of the blessings promised the Saints in these last days" (*The Teachings of Spencer W. Kimball,* ed. Edward L. Kimball [1982], 439).

• In the early days of the Church, leaders encouraged converts to join with the Saints in central places, such as Ohio, Missouri, Illinois, and Utah. Today the Saints are instructed to build up the Church where they live. President Dieter F. Uchtdorf of the First Presidency explained:

"In our day, the Lord has seen fit to provide the blessings of the gospel, including an increased number of temples, in many parts of the world. Therefore, we wish to reiterate the long-standing counsel to members of the Church to remain in their homelands rather than immigrate to the United States. . . .

"'As members throughout the world remain in their homelands, working to build the Church in their native countries, great blessings will come to them personally and to the Church collectively'" (First Presidency letter, Dec. 1, 1999)" (in Conference Report, Oct. 2005, 106; or *Ensign,* Nov. 2005, 102).

• Elder Douglas L. Callister of the Seventy described the purposes and processes of Israel's gathering in the last days: "Our present gathering is primarily spiritual, not geographic. Christ declared that in the latter-days He would 'establish [His] church,' 'establish [His] people,' and 'establish . . . among them [His] Zion' (3 Ne. 21:22; 3 Ne. 20:21; 3 Ne. 21:1). As He establishes His Church in our day, people can be taught the gospel and be 'brought to the knowledge of the Lord their God' (3 Ne. 20:13) without leaving their homes. In contrast to the pronouncements during the early days of the restored Church, our leaders have decreed that now the gathering should take place within each land and among every tongue. Our need to be physically near large numbers of Saints is less than it was a century ago because Church magazines and satellite transmissions bridge distance and time, creating a sense of oneness throughout the entire Church. All have access to the same keys, ordinances, doctrine, and spiritual gifts" ("Book of Mormon Principles: The Gathering of the Lord's Faithful," *Ensign,* Oct. 2004, 59).

3 Nephi 20:14, 22. A Land of Inheritance

• Jesus taught the Nephites that Heavenly Father gave them the land of America as an inheritance. Lehi also had received this promise when he arrived in the promised land (see 2 Nephi 1:5). This confirmed the blessing that Jacob gave to Joseph when he said, "The blessings of thy father have prevailed above the blessings of my progenitors unto the utmost bound of the everlasting hills" (Genesis 49:26). The phrase "utmost bound of the everlasting hills" refers to the Western Hemisphere. President Joseph Fielding Smith (1876–1972) explained: "The Lord gave . . . America, as an everlasting possession to Joseph, the son of Jacob. His posterity, when cleansed from sin, and when they come forth in the resurrection, shall inherit this part of the earth. This land shall be theirs forever" (*Doctrines of Salvation,* comp. Bruce R. McConkie, 3 vols. [1954–56], 1:88).

3 Nephi 20:21–22; 21:23–29. The New Jerusalem Will Be Built in America

• Zion, the New Jerusalem, is to be a place of safety, both physically and spiritually. The Savior, in speaking of the last days, counseled us to "stand in holy places" (see D&C 45:32) and promised us safety in Zion and in her stakes (see D&C 115:6). The Savior taught

His disciples that the city of Zion, the New Jerusalem, would be "a land of peace, a city of refuge, a place of safety" in the time leading up to the Second Coming (see D&C 45:66–71).

The tenth article of faith states: "We believe in the literal gathering of Israel and in the restoration of the Ten Tribes; that Zion (the New Jerusalem) will be built upon the American continent; that Christ will reign personally upon the earth; and, that the earth will be renewed and receive its paradisiacal glory."

On another occasion, the Prophet Joseph Smith (1805–44) taught: "The building up of Zion is a cause that has interested the people of God in every age; it is a theme upon which prophets, priests and kings have dwelt with peculiar delight; . . . it is left for us to see, participate in and help to roll forward the Latter-day glory, 'the dispensation of the fullness of times. . . .' A work that is destined to bring about the destruction of the powers of darkness, the renovation of the earth, the glory of God, and the salvation of the human family" (*History of the Church,* 4:609–10).

3 Nephi 20:22. God Will Dwell in Our Midst

• While teaching the Nephites about Zion or the New Jerusalem, the Savior promised that He would "be in the midst" of His people (3 Nephi 20:22). The Lord used a similar phrase in the Doctrine and Covenants:

"But behold, verily, verily, I say unto you that mine eyes are upon you. I am in your midst and ye cannot see me;

"But the day soon cometh that ye shall see me, and know that I am; for the veil of darkness shall soon be rent, and he that is not purified shall not abide the day.

"Wherefore, gird up your loins and be prepared" (D&C 38:7–9).

The promise that God will dwell in the midst of Zion can have reference to Him being in the temple in Zion (the New Jerusalem) and that "all the pure in heart that shall come into [the temple] shall see God" (see D&C 97:16).

3 Nephi 20:23–24. "A Prophet Shall the Lord Your God Raise Up"

• In Deuteronomy 18:15 Moses prophesied that one day in the future "the Lord thy God will raise up unto thee a Prophet from the midst of thee, of thy brethren, like unto" Moses. In 3 Nephi 20:23–24 the Savior identified Himself as that Prophet. This is such a significant prophecy concerning the coming of the Messiah that it can be found in the Old Testament, New Testament, Book of Mormon, Doctrine and Covenants, and Pearl of Great Price (see Deuteronomy 18:15–19; Acts 3:22; 3 Nephi 20:23–24; D&C 133:63; Joseph Smith—History 1:40).

3 Nephi 20:25–27. Becoming Children of the Covenant

• Jesus identified the Nephites as "children of the covenant" (3 Nephi 20:26). Elder Russell M. Nelson explained what covenant the Savior was referring to and how this phrase applies to us:

"The covenant that the Lord first made with Abraham and reaffirmed with Isaac and Jacob is of transcendent significance. . . .

"We are also children of the covenant. We have received, as did they of old, the holy priesthood and the everlasting gospel. Abraham, Isaac, and Jacob are our ancestors. We are of Israel. We have the right to receive the gospel, blessings of the priesthood, and eternal life. Nations of the earth will be blessed by our efforts and by the labors of our posterity. The literal seed of Abraham and those who are gathered into his family by adoption receive these promised blessings—predicated upon acceptance of the Lord and obedience to his commandments" (in Conference Report, Apr. 1995, 42–43; or Ensign, May 1995, 33).

3 Nephi 20:29. Prophecy Concerning the Restoration of Jerusalem

• The restoration of the tribe of Judah and the city of Jerusalem appears as an important theme in Old Testament and Book of Mormon prophecy. In our dispensation, the Lord has declared:

"Let them, therefore, who are among the Gentiles flee unto Zion.

"And let them who be of Judah flee unto Jerusalem, unto the mountains of the Lord's house" (D&C 133:12–13).

Concerning the restoration of Judah, the Prophet Joseph Smith testified: "Judah must return, Jerusalem be rebuilt, and the temple, and water come out from under the temple, and the waters of the Dead Sea be healed. It will take some time to rebuild the walls of the city and the temple, &c.; and all this must be done before the Son of Man will make His appearance" (History of the Church, 5:337).

3 Nephi 20:29–33. The Jews Will Believe and Be Gathered

• On October 24, 1841, Elder Orson Hyde (1805–78) of the Quorum of the Twelve Apostles offered an apostolic prayer from the summit of the Mount of Olives on behalf of the Jewish people who were scattered throughout the world. At the time of his prayer there were few Jews living in Palestine, and the political climate was such that there  was not much hope that they would ever be allowed to gather there. Since that time a number of remarkable events have occurred as the modern country of Israel was born and became a "homeland" for the Jewish people. While it is evident that the Lord's blessings have attended this "gathering," it is clear that this is not the fulness of the gathering of the Jews that was prophesied of by the prophets in the Book of Mormon.

Elder Bruce R. McConkie (1915–85) of the Quorum of the Twelve Apostles explained that the current gathering of the Jews to their homeland is not a fulfillment of this prophecy, but a political gathering. "As all the world knows, many Jews are now gathering to Palestine, where they have their own nation and way of worship, all without reference to a belief in Christ or an acceptance of the laws and ordinances of his everlasting gospel. Is this the latter-day gathering of the Jews of which the scriptures speak? No! It is not; let there be no misunderstanding in any discerning mind on this point. This gathering of the Jews to their homeland, and their organization into a nation and a kingdom, is not the gathering promised by the prophets. It does not fulfill the ancient promises. Those who have thus assembled have not gathered into the true Church and fold of their ancient Messiah" (*The Millennial Messiah* [1982], 229).

• President Marion G. Romney (1897–1988) of the First Presidency spoke of the gathering of Judah. He read selections from the Book of Mormon that teach what the Jews must do before the Father will gather them to the land of their inheritance. From these selections we learn that when the Jews "no more turn aside their hearts against the Holy One of Israel" (1 Nephi 19:15); when they "come to the knowledge of their Redeemer" (2 Nephi 6:11); when they "shall be restored to the true church and fold of God" (2 Nephi 9:2); when they "believe in me, that I am Christ" (2 Nephi 10:7); when they believe that Christ is the Son of God and believe in the Atonement and "worship the Father in his name, with pure hearts and clean hands, and look not forward any more for another Messiah" (2 Nephi 25:16); when "the fulness of my gospel shall be preached unto them" and they "shall pray unto the Father in [the Savior's] name" (3 Nephi 20:30–31), *then* they will be gathered to Jerusalem, the land of their inheritance.

"These predictions by the Book of Mormon prophets make it perfectly clear that the restoration of the house of Israel to the lands of their inheritance will signal their acceptance of Jesus Christ as their Redeemer, to which I testify, in the name of Jesus Christ" (in Conference Report, Apr. 1981, 21; see also pp. 19–20; or *Ensign,* May 1981, 17; see also p. 16).

3 Nephi 20:35. God Will Make Bare His Holy Arm

• What is the meaning of the phrase "the Father hath made bare his holy arm"? (3 Nephi 20:35). "In ancient times, men prepared for battle by throwing their cloak away from the shoulder of their fighting arm (Ps. 74:11). At the second coming of Christ, God will make bare his arm when he shows forth his power for all to see (D&C 133:2–3)" (Donald W. Parry, Jay A. Parry, Tina M. Peterson, *Understanding Isaiah* [1998], 466).

• In our day the Lord reveals His power in the great latter-day work of the Restoration. Elder Neal A. Maxwell (1926–2004) of the Quorum of the Twelve Apostles taught that this is true today just as it was during the great events of the early days of the Church: "Now, my brethren, 'these are [your] days' (Helaman 7:9) in the history of the Church. Mark well what kind of days they will be, days when, with special visibility, the Lord will 'make bare his holy arm in the eyes of all the nations' (D&C 133:3). God will also 'hasten' His work (D&C 88:73). He will also 'shorten' the last days 'for the elect's sake' (Matthew 24:22); hence, there will be a compression of events (see Joseph Smith—Matthew 1:20). Furthermore, 'all things shall be in commotion' (D&C 88:91). Only those in the process of becoming the men and women of Christ will be able to keep their spiritual balance" (in Conference Report, Apr. 1992, 57; or *Ensign,* May 1992, 39).

3 Nephi 20:36–37. "Put on Thy Strength" and "Loose Thyself from the Bands of Thy Neck"

• Doctrine and Covenants 113 explains that the phrase "put on thy strength" means that latter-day priesthood holders will "put on the authority of the priesthood, which [they have] a right to by lineage" (D&C 113:7–8). "The bands of [thy] neck are the curses of God upon her, or the remnants of Israel in their scattered condition among the Gentiles" (D&C 113:10).

Speaking of the eventual movement toward the millennial era, Elder Bruce R. McConkie explained the Savior's words: "We have already seen that Jesus put chapter 52 of Isaiah in a millennial context. In it is found the cry: 'Awake, awake; put on thy strength, O Zion; put on thy beautiful garments, O Jerusalem, the holy city: for henceforth there shall no more come into thee the uncircumcised and the unclean.' In the day of which we speak there will be none who are unclean in the telestial sense of the word, for the wicked will be destroyed by the brightness of His coming. And there will be none who are uncircumcised, as it were, for all who seek the blessings of the Holy City will be in harmony with the plans and purposes of Him whose city it is" (*Millennial Messiah,* 315).

---

3 NEPHI 20:36–37, 41

What is the Savior's counsel for us in these verses? How can you follow that counsel?

---

3 Nephi 20:40. "How Beautiful upon the Mountains"

• Elder Jeffrey R. Holland of the Quorum of the Twelve Apostles taught that this wonderfully descriptive phrase, "how beautiful upon the mountains are the feet of

him that bringeth good tidings unto them, that publisheth peace," refers to those who spread the Lord's gospel, but that it more specifically refers to the Savior Himself: "These familiar passages, written first by Isaiah but spoken of and inspired by Jehovah himself, are often applied to anyone—especially missionaries—who bring the good tidings of the gospel and publish peace to the souls of men. There is nothing inappropriate about such an application,

but it is important to realize—as the prophet Abinadi did—that in its purest form and original sense, this psalm of appreciation applies specifically to Christ. It is he and only he who ultimately brings the good tidings of salvation. Only

through him is true, lasting peace published. To Zion, in both the old and new Jerusalems, it is Christ who declares, 'Thy God reigneth!' It is his feet upon the mountain of redemption that are beautiful' [3 Nephi 20:40]" (*Christ and the New Covenant* [1997], 286).

3 Nephi 20:41. "Be Ye Clean That Bear the Vessels of the Lord"

• Elder Jeffrey R. Holland taught what it means for priesthood holders to be clean: "As priesthood bearers, not only are we to *handle* sacred vessels and emblems of God's power—think of preparing, blessing, and passing the sacrament, for example—but we are also to *be* a sanctified instrument. Partly because of what we are to *do* but more importantly because of what we are to *be,* the prophets and apostles tell us to 'flee . . . youthful lusts' and 'call on the Lord out of a pure heart.' They tell us to be clean" (in Conference Report, Oct. 2000, 51–52; or *Ensign,* Nov. 2000, 39).

The injunction "be ye clean that bear the vessels of the Lord" (3 Nephi 20:41), given to those in ancient times who handled sacred vessels of worship, applies to modern priesthood holders as well. President Gordon B. Hinckley (1910–2008) reminded a gathering of the priesthood of this important command when he said: " 'Be ye clean that bear the vessels of the Lord' (D&C 133:5). Thus has He spoken to us in modern revelation. Be clean in body. Be clean in mind. Be clean in language. Be clean in dress and manner" (in Conference Report, Apr. 1996, 68; or *Ensign,* May 1996, 48).

President Hinckley further counseled: "A tattoo is graffiti on the temple of the body. Likewise the piercing of the body" (in Conference Report, Oct. 2000, 70; or *Ensign,* Nov. 2000, 52).

Elder M. Russell Ballard of the Quorum of the Twelve Apostles counseled young men and women "to avoid evil talk, to choose your friends wisely, to stay away from pornography and illicit drugs, to not attend evil concerts and dangerous parties, to respect your bodies and keep yourselves morally clean in every way" (in Conference Report, Apr. 2001, 86; or *Ensign,* May 2001, 66).

3 Nephi 21:1–9. The Latter-day Gathering of Israel

• Jesus told the Nephites He would give them "a sign" (3 Nephi 21:1) so they would know when the gathering of Israel had begun. He then foretold the Restoration of the gospel, the coming forth of the Book of Mormon, the establishment of a free nation in America, and the taking of the gospel to their seed (see vv. 1–7). He called the Restoration of the latter days "a great and a marvelous work" (see v. 9). In the early days of the Restoration, the Savior said "a marvelous work is about to come forth" (see D&C 4:1).

President Gordon B. Hinckley spoke of the miracle of the Restoration and of our responsibility to help move the work forward:

"This glorious gospel was ushered in with the appearance of the Father and the Son to the boy Joseph. The dawn of the dispensation of the fulness of times rose upon the world. All of the good, the beautiful, the divine of all previous dispensations was restored in this most remarkable season. . . .

"Do we really comprehend, do we understand the tremendous significance of that which we have? . . .

"We of this generation are the end harvest of all that has gone before. It is not enough to simply be known as a member of this Church. A solemn obligation rests upon us. Let us face it and work at it.

"We must live as true followers of the Christ, with charity toward all, returning good for evil, teaching by example the ways of the Lord, and accomplishing the vast service He has outlined for us" (in Conference Report, Apr. 2004, 84–85; or *Ensign,* May 2004, 83–84).

• For more information on the gathering of Israel, refer to "The Gathering of Israel" in the appendix (p. 416).

3 Nephi 22. Isaiah Used Sacred Imagery to Teach of the Gathering

• The Savior quoted Isaiah 54 in its entirety to further teach concerning the gathering of Israel. Using imagery that is common in prophetic writing, Isaiah personified Israel as a woman whose husband is the Lord. Though forsaken for a time because of wickedness, the day will come when she shall be reconciled to her "Husband" with great mercy. Using this imagery, Isaiah portrayed

beautifully the unfolding miracle of the Restoration. He promised that as the number of her children increased, her tent would need to be enlarged and her stakes strengthened to accommodate her growing family (see 3 Nephi 22:1–3). The sacred commitment of the marriage covenant is brought to mind as the Lord declared the depth of His commitment to Israel (see vv. 4–10). Israel is promised places of safety and beauty (see vv. 11–12) and protection from her enemies (see vv. 13–17).

3 Nephi 22:13. "Thy Children Shall Be Taught of the Lord"

Longin Lonczyna, © 1985 IRI

• While serving as the general president of the Primary, Sister Patricia P. Pinegar explained how 3 Nephi 22:13 is used in our day to guide us in teaching our children: "The world is not a safe place. It is not a place where children will feel peace, hope, and direction unless they are taught to love and follow the Savior. Please help them know that these great blessings can be theirs, and show them what they need to do to receive these blessings" (in Conference Report, Oct. 1999, 85; or *Ensign,* Nov. 1999, 68).

3 Nephi 22:17. "No Weapon That Is Formed against Thee Shall Prosper"

• There have always been those who have fought against the work of the Lord. As Isaiah promised, they have not prospered in their efforts against us. President Gordon B. Hinckley taught that their works would come to naught:

"As surely as this is the work of the Lord, there will be opposition. There will be those, perhaps not a few, who with the sophistry of beguiling words and clever design will spread doubt and seek to undermine the foundation on which this cause is established. They will have their brief day in the sun. They may have for a brief season the plaudits of the doubters and the skeptics and the critics. But they will fade and be forgotten as have their kind in the past.

"Meanwhile, we shall go forward, regardless of their criticism, aware of but undeterred by their statements and actions" (in Conference Report, Apr. 1994, 76; or *Ensign,* May 1994, 60).

Points to Ponder

• The Savior promised that He would gather Israel to fulfill the covenant Heavenly Father made with their fathers (see 3 Nephi 16:5, 11; 20:12–13). This is a global promise with very personal implications. What do you know about the experiences of the first convert Latter-day Saints in your extended family? What sacrifices did they make to gather with the Saints?

• When have you felt Heavenly Father reach out and touch your heart to draw you to Him?

Suggested Assignments

• Create a plan on how to make the sacrament more meaningful in your daily life. Share your plan with someone who could help you accomplish your goal.

• Make a list of at least three activities you could do to assist in the gathering of Israel in these latter days.

Introduction

During the second day of His three-day ministry, the Savior endorsed and expounded on the prophecies of Isaiah and Malachi. He observed the extent of Isaiah's prophecies as touching on "all things concerning my people which are of the house of Israel" (3 Nephi 23:2). Jesus Christ personally examined the scriptural record for accuracy and caused that the fulfillment of Samuel's prophesy of the Resurrection and the words of Malachi be included (see 3 Nephi 24:1; 26:1–2). Malachi's words declare the blessings associated with the law of tithing and the role the prophet Elijah would have during the last days in preparation for the Second Coming.

The Lord commanded each of us to search the scriptures and the prophets (see 3 Nephi 23:5). The Savior declared it is wisdom that "these scriptures . . . should be given unto future generations" (3 Nephi 26:2). Every Latter-day Saint has a duty to diligently search the scriptures. Consider what it means to diligently search the scriptures and the prophets rather than merely reading them.

Commentary

3 Nephi 23:1. "Great Are the Words of Isaiah"

• The Savior taught that the breadth of Isaiah's prophecies covered "all things concerning my people" (3 Nephi 23:2)—a remarkable magnitude of God's dealings. The Savior endorsed Isaiah's prophecies by declaring, "Great are the words of Isaiah" (3 Nephi 23:1). Chapter 22 of 3 Nephi is the last of over 20 Isaiah chapters quoted in the Book of Mormon. Notice that the Savior particularly directed His listeners to *search* the writings of the prophet Isaiah (see 3 Nephi 23:1). It is not surprising that Isaiah is quoted heavily in the Book of Mormon and in other scripture.

President Boyd K. Packer, President of the Quorum of the Twelve Apostles, emphasized the unique and important role of the prophecies of Isaiah and why the Lord preserved his words:

"Isaiah is the most quoted prophet in the New Testament. The Lord Himself quoted Isaiah seven times, the Apostles forty times more. In addition there are ninety partial quotes or paraphrases of Isaiah's words.

"Isaiah is the most quoted prophet in the Doctrine and Covenants. Sixty-six quotations from thirty-one chapters of Isaiah attest to the singular importance of this great prophet.

"All of this confirms that the Lord had a purpose in preserving Isaiah's words" (*Let Not Your Heart Be Troubled* [1991], 280).

• *Note:* For additional background on Isaiah and suggestions on how to study and understand his writings, see commentary for 1 Nephi 20–21 (p. 43) and for 2 Nephi 12–16 (p. 73).

3 Nephi 23:1–5. Search the Scriptures

• The Lord commands His Saints to search the scriptures rather than merely read them. When people *search* the scriptures they carefully examine them in an effort to discover something, or they explore thoroughly by serious inquiry and inspection. *Searching* the scriptures also indicates that we *meditate* (see Joshua 1:8), *study* (see 2 Timothy 3:15; D&C 26:1), *heed* (see 1 Nephi 15:25), and *ponder* (see 2 Nephi 4:15). In addition to the scriptures, the Savior commanded us to search the words of the prophets (see 3 Nephi 23:5).

© 1999 Bryant Livingston

---

3 NEPHI 23:1–5

What did the Lord say about Isaiah's writings? What value is there in searching the scriptures and the prophets?

• The Prophet Joseph Smith (1805–44) encouraged the Saints to search the scriptures in order to receive an independent witness of the truth and to obtain direct instructions from God: "Search the Scriptures—search the revelations which we publish, and ask your Heavenly Father, in the name of His Son Jesus Christ, to manifest the truth unto you, and if you do it with an eye single to His glory, nothing doubting, He will answer you by the power of His Holy Spirit. You will then know for yourselves and not for another. You will not then be dependent on man for the knowledge of God; nor will there be any room for speculation. No; for when men receive their instruction from Him that made them, they know how He will save them. Then again we say: Search the Scriptures, search the Prophets, and learn what portion of them belongs to you" (*History of the Church,* 1:282).

• Although searching the scriptures may be difficult at first, President Gordon B. Hinckley (1910–2008) promised that those who seriously study the scriptures will be enlightened and their spirits lifted: "I am grateful for the emphasis on reading the scriptures. I hope that for you this will become something far more enjoyable than a duty; that, rather, it will become a love affair with the word of God. I promise you that as you read, your minds will be enlightened and your spirits will be lifted. At first it may seem tedious, but that will change into a wondrous experience with thoughts and words of things divine" ("The Light within You," *Ensign,* May 1995, 99).

• President Henry B. Eyring of the First Presidency said that if we rush too quickly while reading the scriptures we are not allowing the Holy Ghost to tutor us:

"The Holy Ghost will guide what we say if we study and ponder the scriptures every day. The words of the scriptures invite the Holy Spirit. . . . With daily study of the scriptures, we can count on this blessing. . . .

"We treasure the word of God not only by reading the words of the scriptures but by studying them. We may be nourished more by pondering a few words, allowing the Holy Ghost to make them treasures to us, than by passing quickly and superficially over whole chapters of scripture" (in Conference Report, Oct. 1997, 114–15, or *Ensign,* Nov. 1997, 83–84).

3 Nephi 23:6–13. Importance of an Accurate Scriptural Record

• The accuracy and completeness of the scriptural record is vital since we rely on it to gain our understanding of God and His plan for us. Verses 6–13 in 3 Nephi 23 include the fulfillment of Samuel's prophecies about the Resurrection that had previously been missing and that the Savior asked to be included in the record.

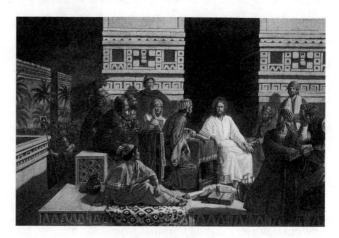

3 Nephi 24:1. "The Words Which the Father Had Given unto Malachi"

• The importance of Malachi's prophecies was emphasized by the Savior, who quoted a portion of His words to the people in America as directed by the Father (see 3 Nephi 24:1). Who was the prophet Malachi? Malachi was an Old Testament prophet who wrote and prophesied at approximately 430 B.C. *Malachi* means "my messenger," and the first part of his prophecy "is addressed to the priesthood, reproving them for their neglect of service to God. The second part (2:10–4:6) is addressed to the people, speaking against marriage outside the covenant, divorces from wives within the covenant, and neglect of tithe paying. . . . The faithful are encouraged to remain so, with the assurance that the Lord is mindful of them, and the disobedient shall fail in the day of the Lord's coming" (Bible Dictionary, "Malachi," 728). The latter part of Malachi's message declares the blessings that come from obeying the law of tithing and the special role the prophet Elijah would play in the last days in preparation for the Second Coming (see 3 Nephi 24–25).

3 Nephi 24:1. The Lord "Shall Suddenly Come to His Temple"

• Elder Dallin H. Oaks of the Quorum of the Twelve Apostles taught that one "reason for repeated reading of the scriptures is that many of the prophecies and doctrinal passages in the scriptures have multiple meanings" and "multiple fulfillments" ("Scripture Reading and Revelation," *Ensign,* Jan. 1995, 8). Such is the case with the phrase "the Lord . . . shall suddenly come to his temple" (3 Nephi 24:1). It was partially fulfilled when the Lord appeared in the Kirtland Temple on April 3, 1836, at the beginning of this dispensation (see D&C 110:1–10); it is partially fulfilled each time the Savior comes to any of His temples; it will also be partially fulfilled as part of the Second Coming when the earth will be cleansed from wickedness and become a celestial abode (see D&C 88:25). Hence, the earth will be appropriately referred to as a temple of the Lord.

3 Nephi 24:2. A Refiner's Fire and Fuller's Soap

• Malachi employed powerful symbolism by describing the Messiah's coming "like a refiner's fire, and like fuller's soap" (3 Nephi 24:2). A *refiner* is "a man who separates the precious metals from the dross with which in nature they are usually found mixed. Part of the process consists in the application of great heat, in order to bring the mass into a fluid state, hence the term 'refiner's fire'" (Bible Dictionary, "Refiner," 760).

The Savior is like a refiner. Elder Bruce R. McConkie (1915–85) of the Quorum of the Twelve Apostles explained: "His mission is to cleanse, purify, and refine the human soul so that it can return to his Father's kingdom in purity, free from dross. (3 Ne. 27:19–21.) His cleansing power 'is like a refiner's fire, . . . And he shall sit as a refiner and purifier of silver' in that great day when he comes to judge the world. (Mal. 3:2–3; 3 Ne. 24:2–3; D.&C. 128:24)" (*Mormon Doctrine,* 2nd ed. [1966], 624).

A *fuller's* "work was to cleanse garments and whiten them" through the use of soap (Bible Dictionary, "Fullers," 676). The Atonement of Jesus Christ acts like "fuller's soap" to cleanse us from our sins and prepare us to stand pure and spotless before the judgment seat.

3 Nephi 24:5. Those Who Oppress Widows and the Fatherless

• God holds us accountable for our neglect of the widows and the fatherless. President Thomas S.

Monson expressed how important widows are to the Lord and our need to minister to them:

"The word *widow* appears to have had a most significant meaning to our Lord. He cautioned his disciples to beware of the example of the scribes, who feigned righteousness by their long apparel and their lengthy prayers, but who devoured the houses of widows [see Luke 20:46–47]. . . .

"And to the Prophet Joseph Smith he directed, 'The storehouse shall be kept by the consecrations of the church; and widows and orphans shall be provided for, as also the poor' [D&C 83:6]. . . .

"There may exist an actual need for food, clothing, even shelter. Such can be supplied. Almost always there remains [a widow in need]. . . .

"Let us remember that after the funeral flowers fade, the well-wishes of friends become memories, and the prayers offered and words spoken dim in the corridors of the mind. Those who grieve frequently find themselves alone. Missed is the laughter of children, the commotion of teenagers, and the tender, loving concern of a departed companion. The clock ticks more loudly, time passes more slowly, and four walls do indeed a prison make" (in Conference Report, Oct. 1994, 90–91; or *Ensign,* Nov. 1994, 70).

> **3 NEPHI 24:8–12**
> *What blessings are promised to those who pay their tithing?*

3 Nephi 24:8–12. Tithes and Offerings

• Those who live the law of tithing show their faith in God. Obedience to this law brings the blessings stated in 3 Nephi 24:10–12. Elder Jeffrey R. Holland of the Quorum of the Twelve Apostles shared five reasons why every member of the Church, in any kind of circumstance, should obey the law of tithing:

"I . . . suggest five reasons why all of us, rich or poor, longtime member or newest convert, should faithfully pay our tithes and offerings.

"First, do so for the sake of your children. . . . Teach your children that many of the blessings of the Church are available to them because you and they give tithes and offerings to the Church. . . .

"Second, pay your tithing to rightfully claim the blessings promised those who do so. . . .

"Third, pay your tithing as a declaration that possession of material goods and the accumulation of worldly wealth are *not* the uppermost goals of your existence. . . .

"Fourth, pay your tithes and offerings out of honesty and integrity because they are God's rightful due. . . .

"This leads to a fifth reason to pay our tithes and offerings. We should pay them as a personal expression of love to a generous and merciful Father in Heaven. Through His grace, God has dealt bread to the hungry and clothing to the poor. At various times in our lives, that will include all of us, either temporally or spiritually" (in Conference Report, Oct. 2001, 39–41; or *Ensign,* Nov. 2001, 33–35).

• President Harold B. Lee (1899–1973) described one of the blessings we can receive from paying tithing: "The promise following obedience to this principle is that the windows of heaven would be open and blessings would be poured out that we would hardly be able to contain. The opening of the windows of heaven, of course, means revelation from God to him who is willing thus to sacrifice" (*The Teachings of Harold B. Lee,* ed. Clyde J. Williams [1996], 206).

• President Heber J. Grant (1856–1945) testified that God will bless those who obey the law of tithing with increased wisdom: "I bear witness—and I know that the witness I bear is true—that the men and the women who have been absolutely honest with

God, who have paid their tithing . . . , God has given them wisdom whereby they have been able to utilize the remaining nine-tenths, and it has been of greater value to them, and they have accomplished more with it than they would if they had not been honest with the Lord" (in Conference Report, Apr. 1912, 30).

• Elder Dallin H. Oaks addressed the statement some people give when faced with whether or not they will be obedient to the commandment to pay tithing:

"Some people say, 'I can't afford to pay tithing.' Those who place their faith in the Lord's promises say, 'I can't afford not to pay tithing.'

"Some time ago I was speaking to a meeting of Church leaders in a country outside of North America. As I spoke about tithing, I found myself saying something I had not intended to say. I told them the Lord was grieved that only a small fraction of the members in their nations relied on the Lord's promises and paid a full tithing. I warned that the Lord would withhold material and spiritual blessings when his covenant children were not keeping this vital commandment.

"I hope those leaders taught that principle to the members of the stakes and districts in their countries. The law of tithing and the promise of blessings to those who live it apply to the people of the Lord in every nation. I hope our members will qualify for the blessings of the Lord by paying a full tithing" (in Conference Report, Apr. 1994, 44; or *Ensign,* May 1994, 34).

3 Nephi 24:16–18. "I Make Up My Jewels"

• How do we become one of the Lord's jewels? A jewel is a precious stone measured by its intrinsic and extrinsic value in the marketplace. Malachi and other prophets used the imagery of jewels symbolically to refer to people who "feared the Lord"—those who show respect for Him, keep His ordinances, and have their names in "a book of remembrance" (3 Nephi 24:16–18; see also D&C 60:4; 101:3; Exodus 28:15–21). Thus, to become one of the Lord's jewels, you must faithfully keep the covenants associated with every ordinance regardless of worldly pressure. By doing this you show that you love the Lord, and your name will be recorded in the book of remembrance.

3 Nephi 25:1. "Neither Root Nor Branch"

• What does it mean that the "proud . . . and all that do wickedly" will be burned and left without either root or branch? (3 Nephi 25:1). This phrase refers to the theme of 3 Nephi 25. Consider your *roots* to be your parents or ancestors and your *branches* to be your children or posterity. To be united with our roots and branches, we must receive temple ordinances. The Lord said He would send Elijah before the Second Coming to restore priesthood keys that would allow families to be complete—both roots and branches. In 1836 the sealing power was restored, and it provides the way for families to be eternally linked (see D&C 110:14–16; 128:18). However, the proud and the wicked will be burned up and left without either root (ancestors) or branch (posterity), leaving them cut off from their family and the sealing blessings.

Elder Jeffrey R. Holland spoke of this idea: "Elijah restored the sealing powers whereby ordinances that were sealed on earth were also sealed in heaven. . . . Without that link no family ties would exist in the eternities, and indeed the family of man would have been left in eternity with 'neither root [ancestors] nor branch [descendants]'" (*Christ and the New Covenant* [1997], 297–98).

3 Nephi 25:2. "Calves in the Stall"

• For an explanation of "calves in the stall," see commentary for 1 Nephi 22:24 (p. 47).

> ### 3 NEPHI 25:5–6
> *Who is to come before "the great and dreadful day," and what will he do?*

3 Nephi 25:5–6. Elijah Shall Turn Hearts

• On his first visit on the evening of September 21, 1823, the angel Moroni quoted the prophecy from Malachi 4:5–6 📖 to the Prophet Joseph Smith "with a little variation from the way it reads" (Joseph Smith—History 1:36–39; see also D&C 2). This prophecy was fulfilled on April 3, 1836, in the Kirtland Temple when Elijah appeared and restored the priesthood keys to Joseph Smith and Oliver Cowdery (see D&C 110:13–16). From this first visit to the end of his ministry, the Prophet Joseph Smith continually mentioned Malachi's prophecy and the mission of Elijah.

In addition to the prophetic explanation he gave in Doctrine and Covenants 128:17–18, the Prophet Joseph Smith also taught: "Elijah was the last Prophet that held the keys of the Priesthood, and who will, before the last dispensation, restore the authority and deliver the keys of the Priesthood, in order that all the ordinances may be attended to in righteousness. It is true that the Savior had authority and power to bestow this blessing; but the sons of Levi were too prejudiced. 'And I will send Elijah the Prophet before the great and terrible day of the Lord,' etc., etc. Why send Elijah? Because he holds the keys of the authority to administer in all the ordinances of the Priesthood; and without the authority is given, the ordinances could not be administered in righteousness" (*History of the Church,* 4:211).

• The Prophet Joseph Smith also explained the meaning of the word *turn* and its application in our lives:

"The word *turn* here [in Malachi 4:5–6] should be translated *bind,* or seal. But what is the object of this important mission? or how is it to be fulfilled? The keys are to be delivered, the spirit of Elijah is to come, the Gospel to be established, the Saints of God gathered, Zion built up, and the Saints to come up as saviors on Mount Zion.

"But how are they to become saviors on Mount Zion? By building their temples, erecting their baptismal fonts, and going forth and receiving all the ordinances, baptisms, confirmations, washings, anointings, ordinations and sealing powers upon their heads, in behalf of all their progenitors who are dead, and redeem them that they may come forth in the first resurrection and be exalted to thrones of glory with them; and herein is the chain that binds the hearts of the fathers to the children, and the children to the fathers, which fulfills the mission of Elijah" (*History of the Church,* 6:184).

3 Nephi 26:2. "These Scriptures, Which Ye Had Not with You"

• Jesus Christ emphasized the importance of accurate scriptural records. In addition to the fulfillment of the prophecies of Samuel the Lamanite being added to the scriptural record (see 3 Nephi 23:7–13), the Savior followed the command of the Father to give the people in America "scriptures, which ye had not" (3 Nephi 26:2). He quoted the writings of Malachi, an Old Testament prophet who lived nearly 200 years after Lehi left Jerusalem. Malachi's teachings would not have been on the plates of brass since he lived 200 years after Lehi left Jerusalem.

3 Nephi 26:6–12. If They Believe, Then Greater Things Will Be Made Manifest

• President Spencer W. Kimball (1895–1985) taught that before obtaining greater manifestations or additional scripture we must read and believe what has already been revealed: "I have had many people ask me through the years, 'When do you think we will get the balance of the Book of Mormon records?' And I have said, 'How many in the congregation would like to read the sealed portion of the plates?' And almost always there is a 100-percent response. And then I ask the same congregation, 'How many of you have read the part that has been opened to us?' And there are many who have not read the Book of Mormon, the unsealed portion. We are quite often looking for the spectacular, the unobtainable. I have found many people who want to live the higher laws when they do not live the lower laws" (*The Teachings of Spencer W. Kimball,* ed. Edward L. Kimball [1982], 531–32).

3 Nephi 26:19. "They Taught, and Did Minister One to Another"

• This is the pattern in the Lord's Church in every dispensation: His covenant people teach one another the doctrine of the kingdom and minister to one another in the fellowship of gospel bonds, for the Lord's people comprise one great family.

Points to Ponder

• How much time and effort do you spend each week reading the scriptures in the standard works? How much of that time and effort do you think qualifies as "searching"?

• In what ways have you turned your heart to your fathers? What more can you do to assist in family history and temple work?

Suggested Assignments

• Develop a plan that will enable you to regularly *search* the scriptures and the most recent conference addresses from the current prophets.

• List the blessings mentioned in 3 Nephi 24:8–12 that have been fulfilled in your life or that you have seen fulfilled in others as a result of living the law of tithing. Write a brief paragraph explaining the purpose and blessings that come from faithfully obeying the law of tithing. Share your observation with someone.

• Collect and organize the names of some of your deceased ancestors for submission to the temple. Arrange to have the temple ordinance work done for them. If possible, participate in completing this temple work.

Introduction

Near the end of His ministry to the Nephites, the Savior explained what constituted His gospel. This block of scripture in 3 Nephi 27–30 also contains more information on translated beings (the three Nephite disciples) than anywhere else in the scriptures. Through studying chapter 28, you will better understand why the Lord chooses to translate some of His mortal servants. Finally, 3 Nephi ends with Mormon describing the Book of Mormon's role in the latter-day gathering of Israel and the Lord (through Mormon) warning the Gentiles in the latter days to repent and turn unto Him. This is a good opportunity to recommit to using the Book of Mormon in your life and in inviting others to come unto the Savior.

Commentary

3 Nephi 27:3–8. "Tell Us the Name Whereby We Shall Call This Church"

• When we become members of the Church of Jesus Christ, we take His name upon us because it is His Church. In President Gordon B. Hinckley's (1910–2008) first conference address as President of the Church, he spoke of the sacred association of the Church, its name, and its accompanying responsibilities:

"This church does not belong to its President. Its head is the Lord Jesus Christ, whose name each of us has taken upon ourselves. We are all in this great endeavor together. We are here to assist our Father in His work and His glory, 'to bring to pass the immortality and eternal life of man' (Moses 1:39). Your obligation is as serious in your sphere of responsibility as is my obligation in my sphere. No calling in this church is 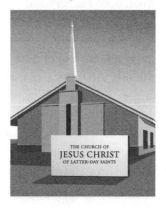 small or of little consequence. All of us in the pursuit of our duty touch the lives of others. To each of us in our respective responsibilities the Lord has said:

"'Wherefore, be faithful; stand in the office which I have appointed unto you; succor the weak, lift up the hands which hang down, and strengthen the feeble knees' (see D&C 81:5).

"'And in doing these things thou wilt do the greatest good unto thy fellow beings, and wilt promote the glory of him who is your Lord' (D&C 81:4)" (in Conference Report, Apr. 1995, 94; or *Ensign,* May 1995, 71).

• Elder James E. Talmage (1862–1933) of the Quorum of the Twelve Apostles described the logic the Lord used in answering the question by what name His Church should be called: "You will remember that after Christ had established his Church among the aboriginal peoples of this continent, when he appeared as a resurrected Being amongst them, after he had chosen and ordained twelve men to direct the affairs of the Church, there was some little disputation as to the name the Church should bear, and the Twelve, remembering the Lord's gracious promise that when they would call upon him, united in heart and purpose, they would be sure of a hearing, fasted and prayed, and He appeared again amongst them there in their council meeting in bodily presence and asked them what they would. They said, 'Lord, we will that thou wouldst tell us the name whereby we shall call this Church.' His answer, as we may render it in modern style of speech, was to this effect: Why should there be any question on so simple a matter as that? Whose church is it? Is it the church of Moses? If so, call it, of course, by the name of Moses; or if it be the church of any other man, then call it by his name, but if it be my Church, as ye say, and it is, then call it by my name" (in Conference Report, Apr. 1922, 70).

3 Nephi 27:5–6. "Take upon You the Name of Christ"

• Elder Robert D. Hales of the Quorum of the Twelve Apostles explained the relationship between taking upon us the name of Christ and the law of obedience and receiving the blessing of the companionship of the Holy Ghost:

"When we are baptized, we take upon ourselves the sacred name of Jesus Christ. Taking upon us His name is one of the most significant experiences we have in life. Yet sometimes we pass through that experience without having a full understanding.

"How many of our children—how many of us—really understand that when we were baptized, we took upon us not only the name of Christ but also the law of obedience?

"Each week in sacrament meeting we promise to remember the atoning sacrifice of our Savior as we renew our baptismal covenant. We promise to do as the Savior did—to be obedient to the Father and always keep His commandments. The blessing we receive in return is to always have His Spirit to be with us" (in Conference Report, Oct. 2000, 6; or *Ensign*, Nov. 2000, 8).

---

3 NEPHI 27:13–21

What does the Lord say are the essentials of His gospel?

---

3 Nephi 27:13–22. "This Is the Gospel Which I Have Given unto You"

• Elder Neal A. Maxwell (1926–2004) of the Quorum of the Twelve Apostles taught that the simplicity of the gospel is the very reason some people find the gospel so difficult to accept:

"There is in the Book of Mormon a statement in which the Lord says, 'Behold this is the gospel, which I have given unto you,' and then he describes his gospel. (See 3 Nephi 27:13–18.) It is a simple story of a world to which a Savior has been sent whom men may accept or reject, but who is, nevertheless, the Messiah.

"That simple story is the very thing, of course, the world cannot accept, and it is so simple that some may even be offended inwardly at times by the so-called simplicity of the gospel. . . .

". . . There are those who may share some of our beliefs and values, but for whom the restoration of the gospel is a stumblingblock they cannot get over the

top of. But to most of mankind, what we proclaim is 'foolishness'" (*For the Power Is in Them* [1970], 47–48).

The Savior Himself defined His gospel as faith, repentance, baptism, and the Holy Ghost (see 3 Nephi 27:19–20) and enduring to the end (see v. 16). He also stated that the gospel was Him coming into the world to do the Father's will and to "be lifted up upon the cross" (vv. 13–14).

3 Nephi 27:24–26. The Lord Will Judge the World out of the Books

• "Out of the books which have been written, and which shall be written, shall this people be judged, for by them shall their works be known unto men.

"And behold, all things are written by the Father" (3 Nephi 27:25–26).

President Joseph F. Smith (1838–1918) defined the role that written records will play in the Judgment:

"The Lord will make a record also and out of that shall the whole world be judged. And you men bearing the holy Priesthood—you apostles, presidents, bishops, and high priests in Zion—will be called upon to be the judges of the people. Therefore, it is expected that you shall set the standard for them to attain to, and see that they shall live according to the spirit of the gospel, do their duty, and keep the commandments of the Lord. You shall make a record of their acts. You shall record when they are baptized, when they are confirmed, and when they receive the Holy Ghost by the laying on of hands. You shall record when they come to Zion, their membership in the Church. You shall record whether they attend to their duties as priests, teachers or deacons, as elders, seventies or high priests. You shall write their works, as the Lord says here. You shall record their tithings . . . ; but we shall judge the people, first requiring them to do their duty. In order to do that, those who stand at the head must set the example" (*Gospel Doctrine*, 5th ed. [1939], 157).

3 Nephi 27:27. 📖 "What Manner of Men Ought Ye to Be?"

• Elder John M. Madsen of the Seventy focused particularly on the word *ought* in the Lord's teachings to become as He is. Elder Madsen described the Lord's words as more than an invitation, but a requirement of our covenants:

"To receive Him and know Him, we and all mankind must, as Moroni exhorts, *'come unto Christ, and be perfected in him'* (Moroni 10:32; italics added). In other words, we must come unto Christ and strive to 'become' like Him (see Dallin H. Oaks, in Conference Report, Oct. 2000, 40–44; or *Ensign,* Nov. 2000, 32–34).

"Said the risen Lord: 'What manner of men ought ye to be? Verily I say unto you, even as I am' (3 Nephi 27:27). The meaning of the word *ought,* as used in His question 'What manner of men ought ye to be?' is crucial to understanding His answer, 'Even as I am.' The word *ought* means 'to be necessary' or 'to be held or bound in duty or moral obligation' (*Noah Webster's First Edition of an American Dictionary of the English Language,* 7th ed. [1993], 'ought'; see also Luke 24:26), suggesting—and the holy scriptures, ancient and modern, confirm—that it is 'necessary,' and that we are 'bound,' as by covenant, 'to be,' as He declared, 'even as I am' (3 Nephi 27:27; see also 3 Nephi 12:48; Matthew 5:48; 1 John 3:2; Moroni 7:48)" (in Conference Report, Apr. 2002, 93; or *Ensign,* May 2002, 79).

Harry Anderson, © IRI

3 Nephi 28:1–6. Desires and Ministry of John the Beloved

• The Prophet Joseph Smith (1805–44) and Oliver Cowdery received specific revelation through the Urim and Thummim regarding the circumstances and subsequent blessings of John's request to tarry in the flesh. This information was from a "parchment" written and hidden by John himself, but apparently lost. In April 1829, Joseph's and Oliver's specific questions on this passage of the Book of Mormon resulted in the revelation recorded in Doctrine and Covenants section 7.

3 Nephi 28:9–10, 36–40. The Doctrine of Translation

• The following definitions help clarify the doctrines of translation, transfiguration, and resurrection. Notice the difference between translated beings and the more temporary state of transfiguration:

Translated beings. "Persons who are changed so that they do not experience pain or death until their resurrection to immortality" (Guide to the Scriptures, "Translated Beings").

"Many have supposed that the doctrine of translation was a doctrine whereby men were taken immediately into the presence of God, and into an eternal fullness, but this is a mistaken idea. Their place of habitation is that of the terrestrial order, and a place prepared for such characters He held in reserve to be ministering angels unto many planets, and who as yet have not entered into so great a fullness as those who are resurrected from the dead" (Joseph Smith, *History of the Church,* 4:210).

Transfiguration. "The condition of persons who are temporarily changed in appearance and nature—that is, lifted to a higher spiritual level—so that they can endure the presence and glory of heavenly beings" (Guide to the Scriptures, "Transfiguration").

Resurrection. "The reuniting of the spirit body with the physical body of flesh and bones after death. After resurrection, the spirit and body will never again be separated, and the person will become immortal" (Guide to the Scriptures, "Resurrection").

3 Nephi 29:1–4. Covenants with the Children of Israel

• Elder Jeffrey R. Holland of the Quorum of the Twelve Apostles wrote of the role the Book of Mormon plays in the fulfilling of God's covenant with respect to Israel:

"Mormon concluded his description of this majestic season [the visit of the Savior among the Nephites] . . . by testifying that when a record of [Jesus Christ's] visit would come to the Gentiles (in the form of the Book of Mormon), then all might know that the covenant and promises to Israel of the last days were 'already beginning to be fulfilled.' . . .

"God's covenant will be kept with all of his covenant people. No one will be able to 'turn the right hand of the Lord unto the left' on this matter. And the call to the Gentiles, for which Christ's visit to the Nephites published in the Book of Mormon is the ultimate latter-day declaration, is for them to claim the same covenant and promises" (*Christ and the New Covenant* [1997], 308).

> ### 3 NEPHI 29:4–7
> *How did Mormon describe the behaviors of those who reject the Lord's latter-day revelations? What will their punishment be?*

3 Nephi 29:4–8. Do Not Spurn the Words of the Lord

- In 3 Nephi 29 the words *spurn* and *hiss* are used to warn Book of Mormon readers in the latter days to not treat lightly the Lord's covenants with Israel. *Spurn* means "to reject with disdain" and *hiss* is "to express contempt or disapprobation by hissing" (*Noah Webster's First Edition of an American Dictionary of the English Language, 1828* [1967]). The use of such terms suggests that in the time of the coming forth of the Book of Mormon there will be a pronounced lack of understanding, belief, and reverence for both the reality of the Second Coming and the work of the Lord in gathering Israel (especially the tribe of Judah).

3 Nephi 30:2. Turn from Your Wicked Doings

- At the conclusion of the Savior's visit among the Nephites, Mormon returned to what was a major theme of the Lord's instructions among the people—that in the last days the Gentiles will reject the teachings of the Lord and grow rapidly in wickedness to their destruction (see 3 Nephi 16:10; 21:14–21). The writings in 3 Nephi seem to have had a profound effect upon Mormon. In his final testimony, Mormon revisited the Savior's teachings and prophecies condemning the wicked and perverse and the pollutions and hypocrisies of the last days. In the last verses of 3 Nephi, Mormon offered the only antidote to these destructive conditions—come unto Jesus Christ and have faith in Him, repent of your sins, be baptized, and be filled with the Holy Ghost "that ye may be numbered with my people who are of the house of Israel" (3 Nephi 30:2).

Points to Ponder

- Why is it important for the Church of Jesus Christ to be called by the Savior's name?

- How might you take the name of the Savior upon you more completely?

- In what ways are *translation* and *transfiguration* different? In what ways are they similar? How do *translation* and *transfiguration* differ from *resurrection*?

- Mormon identified some wicked ways. How are they manifest in the world today?

Suggested Assignments

- Make a list of some of the Savior's characteristics you consider to be most important. Take a personal inventory of your own life with regard to these characteristics and formulate a plan to better fulfill His mandate to be "even as I am" (3 Nephi 27:27).

- Read 3 Nephi 27:5 and the sacrament prayers (Moroni 4:3; 5:2). Identify the principles mentioned that will help you understand the meaning of taking Christ's name upon you.

CHAPTER 47

4 Nephi

Introduction

Fourth Nephi covers the nearly 200 years of unity and harmony following Jesus Christ's visit to the Americas. The people "were all converted unto the Lord" (4 Nephi 1:2), resulting in a society that people of all ages have dreamed of. Elder Jeffrey R. Holland of the Quorum of the Twelve Apostles observed that following Christ's visit, "His majestic teachings and ennobling spirit led to the happiest of all times, a time in which 'there were no contentions and disputations among them, and every man did deal justly one with another. And they had all things common among them; therefore there were not rich and poor, bond and free, but they were all made free, and partakers of the heavenly gift' [4 Nephi 1:2–3]. That blessed circumstance was, I suppose, achieved on only one other occasion of which we know—the city of Enoch, where 'they were of one heart and one mind, and dwelt in righteousness; and there was no poor among them' [Moses 7:18]" (in Conference Report, Apr. 1996, 40; or *Ensign,* May 1996, 30).

Tragically, the second half of 4 Nephi reveals how a righteous and happy people allowed pride and apostasy to enter their lives, bringing the eventual destruction of their society. As you study this book of scripture, seek to understand what led to the happiness of the Nephite society as well as what led to the misery and destruction of their society.

Commentary

4 Nephi 1:2. "The People Were All Converted unto the Lord"

• President Marion G. Romney (1897–1988) of the First Presidency gave the following insight regarding the meaning of true conversion:

"Webster [dictionary] says the verb, 'convert,' means 'to turn from one belief or course to another.' That 'conversion' is 'a spiritual and moral *change*. . . .' As used in the scriptures, 'converted' generally implies not merely mental acceptance of Jesus and his teachings but also a motivating faith in him and in his gospel—a faith which works a transformation, an actual *change* in one's understanding of life's meaning and in his allegiance to God—in interest, in thought, and in conduct. . . .

"In one who is wholly converted, desire for things inimical [contrary] to the gospel of Jesus Christ has actually died, and substituted therefor is a love of God with a fixed and controlling determination to keep his commandments. . . .

". . . From this it would appear that membership in the Church and conversion are not necessarily synonymous. Being converted . . . and having a

testimony are not necessarily the same thing either. A testimony comes when the Holy Ghost gives the earnest seeker a witness of the truth. A moving testimony vitalizes faith; that is, it induces repentance and obedience to the commandments. Conversion, on the other hand, is the fruit of, or the reward for, repentance and obedience" (in Conference Report, Oct. 1963, 23–24).

4 Nephi 1:2. "There Were No Contentions and Disputations among Them"

• Regarding the way members of the Church should treat others, the Lord revealed, "Every man seeking the interest of his neighbor, and doing all things with an eye single to the glory of God" (D&C 82:19).

• What would it take in today's world to build a society that did not have any contentions or disputations? President Spencer W. Kimball (1895–1985) taught how this goal can be achieved:

"First, we must eliminate the individual tendency to selfishness that snares the soul, shrinks the heart, and darkens the mind. . . .

"Second, we must cooperate completely and work in harmony one with the other. . . .

"Third, we must lay on the altar and sacrifice whatever is required by the Lord. We begin by offering a 'broken heart and a contrite spirit' [3 Nephi 9:20]" (in Conference Report, Apr. 1978, 123; or *Ensign,* May 1978, 81).

4 Nephi 1:2. "Every Man Did Deal Justly"

• Elder Sheldon F. Child of the Seventy explained what it means to "deal justly" with one another when he spoke about honesty and integrity:

"When we say we will do something, we do it.

"When we make a commitment, we honor it.

"When we are given a calling, we fulfill it.

"When we borrow something, we return it.

"When we have a financial obligation, we pay it.

"When we enter into an agreement, we keep it" (in Conference Report, Apr. 1997, 39; or *Ensign,* May 1997, 29).

• President N. Eldon Tanner (1898–1982) of the First Presidency illustrated the importance of dealing justly with others:

"A young man came to me not long ago and said, 'I made an agreement with a man that requires me to make certain payments each year. I am in arrears [behind in fulfilling financial obligations], and I can't make those payments, for if I do, it is going to cause me to lose my home. What shall I do?'

"I looked at him and said, 'Keep your agreement.'

"'Even if it costs me my home?'

"I said, 'I am not talking about your home. I am talking about your agreement; and I think your wife would rather have a husband who would keep his word . . . and have to rent a home than to have a home with a husband who will not keep his covenants and his pledges" (in Conference Report, Oct. 1966, 99).

4 Nephi 1:3. "They Had All Things Common among Them"

• One of the attributes that distinguished the Nephite people was that "they had all things common among them" (4 Nephi 1:3). President Marion G. Romney described what this phrase means and how it worked:

"This procedure [the united order] preserved in every man the right of private ownership and management of his property. . . . Each man owned his portion, which, at his option, he could alienate, keep and operate, or otherwise treat as his own. . . .

". . . He consecrated to the Church the *surplus* he produced above the needs and wants of his own family. This surplus went into a storehouse, from which stewardships were given to others, and from which the needs of the poor were supplied" (in Conference Report, Apr. 1977, 119; or *Ensign,* May 1977, 93).

President Romney also explained what leads a people to live in such a way: "When we reach the state of having the 'pure love of Christ,' our desire to serve one another will have grown to the point where we will be living fully the law of consecration. Living the law of consecration exalts the poor and humbles the rich. In the process, both are sanctified. The poor, released from the bondage and humiliating limitations of poverty, are enabled as free men to rise to their full  potential, both temporally and spiritually. The rich, by consecration and the imparting of their surplus for the benefit of the poor, *not by constraint, but willingly as an act of free will,* evidence that charity for their fellowmen characterized by Mormon as 'the pure love of Christ.' (Moro. 7:47.) This will bring both the giver and receiver to the common ground on which the Spirit of God can meet them" (in Conference Report, Oct. 1981, 132–33; or *Ensign,* Nov. 1981, 93).

• Elder Robert D. Hales of the Quorum of the Twelve Apostles explained how we are preparing to live the law of consecration: "The law of tithing prepares us to live the higher law of consecration—to dedicate and give all our time, talents, and resources to the work of the Lord. Until the day when we are required to live this higher law, we are commanded to live the law of the tithe, which is to freely give one-tenth of our income annually" (in Conference Report, Oct. 2002, 28; or *Ensign,* Nov. 2002, 27).

4 Nephi 1:5. Miracles "in the Name of Jesus"

• President Spencer W. Kimball explained that miracles are also a part of the Church today, as they have been in the past:

"We do have miracles today—beyond imagination! If all the miracles of our own lifetime were recorded, it would take many library shelves to hold the books which would contain them.

"What kinds of miracles do we have? All kinds—

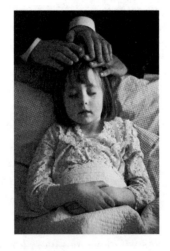

revelations, visions, tongues, healings, special guidance and direction, evil spirits cast out. Where are they recorded? In the records of the Church, in journals, in news and magazine articles and in the minds and memories of many people" (*The Teachings of Spencer W. Kimball,* ed. Edward L. Kimball [1982], 499).

4 Nephi 1:13, 15–16. "There Was No Contention among All the People"

• Elder Russell M. Nelson of the Quorum of the Twelve Apostles described the source of the great peace that was described in 4 Nephi:

"Personal peace is reached when one, in humble submissiveness, truly loves God. Heed carefully this scripture:

"'There was no contention in the land, *because of* the love of God which did dwell in the hearts of the people' (4 Nephi 1:15; italics added; see also 1:2).

"Thus, love of God should be our aim. It is the first commandment—the foundation of faith. As we develop love of God and Christ, love of family and neighbor will naturally follow. Then will we eagerly emulate Jesus. He healed. He comforted. He taught, 'Blessed are the peacemakers: for they shall be called the children of God' (Matthew 5:9; see also 3 Nephi 12:9).

"Through love of God, the pain caused by the fiery canker of contention will be extinguished from the soul. This healing begins with a personal vow: 'Let there be peace on earth, and let it begin with me' (Sy Miller and Jill Jackson, 'Let There Be Peace on Earth' [Beverly Hills, Calif.: Jan-Lee Music, 1972]). This commitment will then spread to family and friends and will bring peace to neighborhoods and nations.

"Shun contention. Seek godliness. Be enlightened by eternal truth. Be like-minded with the Lord in love and united with Him in faith. Then shall 'the peace of God, which passeth all understanding' (Philippians 4:7), be yours, to bless you and your posterity through generations yet to come" (in Conference Report, Apr. 1989, 88; or *Ensign,* May 1989, 71).

4 Nephi 1:15–17. A Zion Society

• Elder Dallin H. Oaks of the Quorum of the Twelve Apostles described the conditions described in 4 Nephi 1:15–17 as a Zion society. This ought to be what we strive for today: "In those brilliant generations that followed the appearance of the resurrected Christ in the New World, 'there were no contentions and disputations among [the people], and every man did deal justly one with another' (4 Nephi 1:2). Fourth Nephi records: 'Surely there could not be a happier people among all the people who had been created by the hand of God' (1:16). We should be striving to regain that condition. As modern revelation declares: 'Zion must increase in beauty, and in holiness' (D&C 82:14)" (in Conference Report, Oct. 1986, 28; or *Ensign,* Nov. 1986, 23). (For additional information on latter-day Zion, see commentary for 3 Nephi 20:21–22; 21:23–29 on p. 325.)

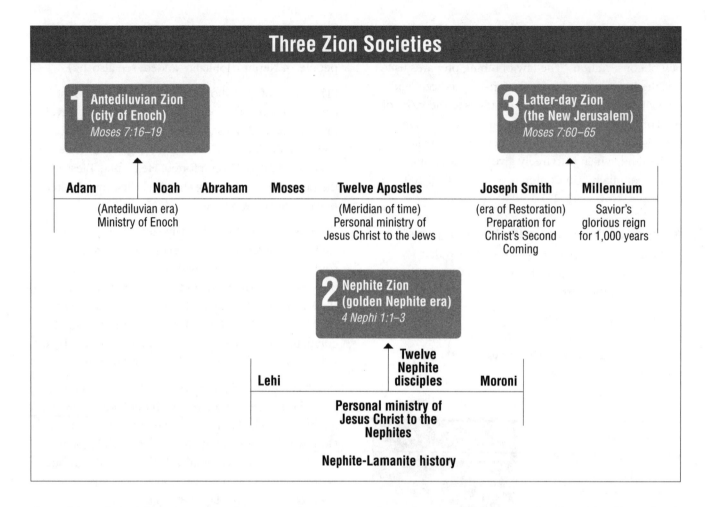

Three Zion Societies

1 Antediluvian Zion (city of Enoch)
Moses 7:16–19

3 Latter-day Zion (the New Jerusalem)
Moses 7:60–65

Adam	Noah	Abraham	Moses	Twelve Apostles	Joseph Smith	Millennium

(Antediluvian era) Ministry of Enoch

(Meridian of time) Personal ministry of Jesus Christ to the Jews

(era of Restoration) Preparation for Christ's Second Coming

Savior's glorious reign for 1,000 years

2 Nephite Zion (golden Nephite era)
4 Nephi 1:1–3

Lehi — Twelve Nephite disciples — Moroni

Personal ministry of Jesus Christ to the Nephites

Nephite-Lamanite history

4 Nephi 1:16–17. There Were No "Manner of -Ites"

• Because of the unity and peace in the land, each of the formerly distinct groups in the Book of Mormon, such as the Lamanites and the Nephites, set aside their worldly traditions and embraced as their highest priority the doctrine that they "were in one, the children of Christ, and heirs to the kingdom of God" (4 Nephi 1:17). As the gospel spreads forth to "every nation, kindred, tongue, and people" (Mosiah 16:1), one of the challenges we face as a Church is being "one," or having unity among our members. This can be challenging when so many races, cultures, and traditions are brought together.

• President James E. Faust (1920–2007) of the First Presidency taught that despite diversity of cultures, races, or traditions, unity can be developed:

"I have learned to admire, respect, and love the good people from every race, culture, and nation that I have been privileged to visit. In my experience, no race or

class seems superior to any other in spirituality and faithfulness. Those who seem less caring spiritually are those individuals—regardless of race, culture, or nationality—spoken of by the Savior in the parable of the sower who are 'choked with cares and riches and pleasures of this life, and bring no fruit to perfection' [Luke 8:14]. . . .

"As we move into more and more countries in the world, we find a rich cultural diversity in the Church. Yet everywhere there can be a 'unity of the faith' [Ephesians 4:13]. Each group brings special gifts and talents to the table of the Lord. We can all learn much of value from each other. But each of us should also voluntarily seek to enjoy all of the unifying and saving covenants, ordinances, and doctrines of the gospel of the Lord Jesus Christ.

"In the great diversity of peoples, cultures, and circumstances, we remember that all are equal before the Lord" (in Conference Report, Apr. 1995, 81–82; or *Ensign,* May 1995, 61–62).

• Elder Richard G. Scott of the Quorum of the Twelve Apostles further counseled members of the Church to set aside any cultural traditions, racial traditions, or other traditions that conflict with the teachings of Jesus Christ, because these traditions undermine the great plan of happiness:

"Your Heavenly Father assigned you to be born into a specific lineage from which you received your inheritance of race, culture, and traditions. That lineage can provide a rich heritage and great reasons to rejoice. Yet you have the responsibility to determine if there is any part of that heritage that must be discarded because it works against the Lord's plan of happiness. . . .

"I testify that you will remove barriers to happiness and find greater peace as you make your first allegiance your membership in the Church of Jesus Christ, and His teachings the foundation of your life. Where family or national traditions or customs conflict with the teachings of God, set them aside. Where traditions and customs are in harmony with His teachings, they should be cherished and followed to preserve your culture and heritage. There is one heritage that you need never change. It is that heritage that comes from your being a daughter or son of Father in Heaven. For happiness, control your life by that heritage" (in Conference Report, Apr. 1998, 112, 114; or *Ensign,* May 1998, 86–87).

4 Nephi 1:20. "There Began to Be Lamanites Again"

• Divisiveness is a result of unrighteousness. The following commentary suggests that pride is the beginning of all such divisions and the reason that some individuals "revolted from the church" and took upon themselves the name *Lamanites* (4 Nephi 1:20). "Why would it matter to a people what they were called? Why would it be so important for them to be called Lamanites? Why would a group choose to forsake the transcendent privileges of unity in order to be designated by this or that name? The answer

is simple: pride. A desire to be different. A yearning to be acknowledged. A fear of being overlooked. A craving for public notice. The righteous feel no need for attention, no desire to be praised, no inclination to demand recognition. The prideful demand their rights, even when they are wrong. The prideful feel that they must do things their way, even when that way is the wrong way. The prideful insist that they must pursue their own path, even when the road they take is wide and broad and leads to destruction" (Joseph Fielding McConkie, Robert L. Millet, and Brent L. Top, *Doctrinal Commentary on the Book of Mormon,* 4 vols. [1987–92], 4:204–5).

Jerry Thompson, © IRI

4 Nephi 1:24. "Lifted up in Pride"

• Several times in Book of Mormon history the people passed through a cycle of righteousness, prosperity, riches, pride, wickedness, destruction, humility, and righteousness again. For more information and a diagram depicting the pride cycle, refer to "The Cycle of Righteousness and Wickedness" in the appendix (p. 414).

Refer to the commentary for Helaman 3:33–34, 36; 4:12 (p. 264) and the commentary for Helaman 12:5–6 (p. 278).

---

4 NEPHI 1:24–30

As you study these verses, identify the process that ultimately led the people to deny Christ.

---

4 Nephi 1:36. "True Believers in Christ"

• Elder Neal A. Maxwell (1926–2004) of the Quorum of the Twelve Apostles spoke of the characteristics that define those who truly believe in the Savior:

"*True believers are settled in their views of Christ.* Despite their weaknesses, their spirituality is centered on the Savior, so their views of everything else are put in that precious perspective.

"*True believers gladly perform their duties in the kingdom.* These duties are usually measurable and straightforward. They include partaking worthily of the sacrament, rendering Christian service, studying the scriptures, praying, fasting, receiving ordinances, attending to family duties, paying tithes and offerings. . . .

"*True believers are humble.* They are 'meek and lowly of heart' [Moroni 7:43]. . . . They are not easily offended. They do not resist counsel. . . .

"*True believers are willing to do what Christ wants.* . . . Are we willing to let the Lord lead us into further developmental experiences? Or do we shrink back? The things which enlarge the soul inevitably involve stretching.

"*True believers have a balanced contentment.* They strike a balance between being too content and wishing for a more important role. . . .

"*True believers truly pray.* Their prayers are sincere. . . . The true believer's prayers, at least some of the time, are inspired.

"*True believers have both right conduct and right reasons for that conduct.* They are so secure in their relationship with the Lord that their goodness would continue even if nobody were watching. . . .

"*True believers rejoice in the success of others.* . . . They don't regard colleagues as competitors.

"*True believers remember that forgetting is part of forgiving.* They follow the Lord's example: 'I [will] remember [their sins] no more' (D&C 58:42). . . .

"*True believers are innocent as to sin, but not naive.* They are kind, but candid. They love their fellowmen. . . .

"*True believers are happy.* Instead of a 'woeful countenance,' true believers in Christ have a disciplined enthusiasm to work righteousness. They are serious about how they live life, but are also of good cheer" ("True Believers," *New Era,* Apr., 1994, 20–24).

4 Nephi 1:38–39. "They Did Teach Their Children That They Should Not Believe"

• Elder Russell M. Nelson counseled parents to avoid using labels that polarize or lead to the development of prejudices in their children's hearts:

"When the Nephites were truly righteous, their previous patterns of polarization vanished. 'There was no contention in the land, because of the love of God which did dwell in the hearts of the people. . . .

"Unfortunately, the sequel to that story is not a happy one. This pleasant circumstance persisted until 'a small part of the people . . . had revolted . . . and taken upon them the name of Lamanites' [4 Nephi 1:20], reviving old prejudices and teaching their children again to hate, 'even as the Lamanites were taught to hate the children of Nephi from the beginning' [4 Nephi 1:39]. And so the polarizing process began all over again.

"I hope that we may learn this important lesson and delete segregating names from our personal vocabularies. The Apostle Paul taught that 'there is neither Jew nor Greek, there is neither bond nor free, there is neither male nor female: for ye are all one in Christ Jesus' [Galatians 3:28; see also Colossians 3:11].

"Our Savior invites us 'to come unto him and partake of his goodness; and he denieth none that come unto him, black and white, bond and free, male and female; . . . all are alike unto God' [2 Ne. 26:33]" ("A More Excellent Hope," *Ensign,* Feb. 1997, 63).

4 Nephi 1:42–46. Secret Oaths and Combinations

• For further information on contention and secret works, see commentary for Helaman 1:1–21 (p. 262) and for Helaman 1–2 (p. 262).

4 Nephi 1:46. None Were Righteous Except the Disciples of Jesus

• After reading 4 Nephi 1:46 one might get the impression that the 12 disciples of Jesus and the three Nephites were the only righteous people left among the Nephites. However, Mormon left an important clarification on this point in Alma 45:13–14. According to these verses, at the end of the Book of Mormon, "the peaceable followers of Christ" (Moroni 7:3) were also referred to as disciples of Jesus.

Points to Ponder

• How would your life be different if you lived in a society similar to the one described in the first half of 4 Nephi? How can you help create this same kind of harmony and peace in your family and home?

• In the second half of 4 Nephi the people fell into a two-part pattern that led to destruction. First, pride (4 Nephi 1:24–43; see also 3 Nephi 6:28–29) and second, secret combinations (4 Nephi 1:42–46; see also 3 Nephi 6:28–29). This pattern would again appear in the book of Ether (pride in Ether 11:12–14; and secret combinations in Ether 13:15). How can you avoid making the same mistakes the Nephites made at the end of the 200 years of peace and prosperity?

Suggested Assignments

• Contention and the importance of eliminating it are emphasized in 4 Nephi. After identifying sources of contention that occur in your own life, outline a strategy of what you can do to eliminate or minimize contention in your life.

CHAPTER 48

Mormon 1–6

Introduction

Having summarized accounts of the Lord's visit among the Nephites and the 200-year era of peace that followed, Mormon reported that, starting in the 201st year, pride, disunity, and wickedness took over (see 4 Nephi 1:24–47). In the book of Mormon we read of events where he was an eyewitness. These events include the demise of the Nephite civilization. In Mormon 1–6 we can empathize with Mormon's sorrow over the destruction of his people, a destruction which came upon them because of their rejection of the Lord and His gospel. We can also resolve to avoid such calamity in our own lives.

Commentary

Mormon 1:1. "I, Mormon"

• The Prophet Joseph Smith (1805–44) taught, "The word Mormon, means literally, more good" (*History of the Church,* 5:400).

• In an overview of Mormon's life, President Gordon B. Hinckley (1910–2008) referred to the meaning associated with Mormon's name, a name that has become a reference to The Church of Jesus Christ of Latter-day Saints:

"May I remind you for a moment of the greatness and of the goodness of this man Mormon. He lived on this American continent in the fourth century after Christ. When Mormon was a boy of ten, the historian of the people, whose name was Ammaron, described him as 'a sober child, and . . . quick to observe' (Mormon 1:2). Ammaron gave him a charge that when he reached the age of twenty-four, he was to take custody of the records of the generations who had preceded him.

"The years that followed Mormon's childhood were years of terrible bloodshed for his nation, the result of a long and vicious and terrible war between those who were called Nephites and those who were called Lamanites.

"Mormon later became the leader of the armies of the Nephites and witnessed the carnage of his people, making it plain to them that their repeated defeats came because they forsook the Lord and He in turn abandoned them. . . .

"He wrote to our generation with words of warning and pleading, proclaiming with eloquence his testimony of the resurrected Christ. He warned of calamities to come if we should forsake the ways of the Lord as his own people had done.

"Knowing that his own life would soon be brought to an end, as his enemies hunted the survivors, he pleaded for our generation to walk with faith, hope, and charity, declaring, 'Charity is the pure love of Christ, and it endureth forever; and whoso is found possessed of it at the last day, it shall be well with him' (Moroni 7:47).

"Such was the goodness, the strength, the power, the faith, the prophetic heart of the prophet-leader Mormon" (in Conference Report, Oct. 1990, 69–70; or *Ensign,* Nov. 1990, 52).

Mormon 1:16. Willful Rebellion against God

• Elder Jeffrey R. Holland of the Quorum of the Twelve Apostles contrasted the spiritual maturity of Mormon with the sinful state of Mormon's people. In spite of Mormon's righteous desire, he was forbidden to preach because of the rebellious condition of his people: "The maturing Mormon, by then fifteen years of age, stood beyond the sinfulness around him and rose above the despair of his time. Consequently, he 'was visited of the Lord, and tasted and knew of the goodness of Jesus,' trying valiantly to preach to his people. But as God occasionally does when those with so much light reject it, Mormon literally had his mouth shut. He was forbidden to preach to a nation that had willfully rebelled against their God. These people had rejected the miracles and messages delivered them by the three translated Nephite disciples, who had now also been silenced in their ministry and been taken from the nation to whom they had been sent" (*Christ and the New Covenant* [1997], 318).

• While serving as a member of the Seventy, Elder Dean L. Larsen explained that rebellion against God has individual roots which, if not corrected, spread with devastating consequences:

"Historically, the drifting away from the course of life marked out by the Lord has occurred as individuals begin to make compromises with the Lord's standard. This is particularly true when the transgression is willful and no repentance occurs. Remember Mormon's description of those who turned away from the true path in his day. They did not sin in ignorance. They willfully rebelled against God. It did not occur as a universal movement. It began as individual members of the Church knowingly began to make compromises with the Lord's standard. They sought justification for their diversions in the knowledge that others were compromising as well. Those who willfully sin soon seek to establish a standard of their own with which they can feel more comfortable and which justifies their misconduct. They also seek the association of those who are willing to drift with them along this path of self-delusion.

"As the number of drifting individuals increases, their influence becomes more powerful. It might be described as the 'great and spacious building syndrome.' The drifting is the more dangerous when its adherents continue to overtly identify with and participate with the group that conforms to the Lord's way. Values and standards that were once clear become clouded and uncertain. The norm of behavior begins to reflect this beclouding of true principles. Conduct that would once have caused revulsion and alarm now becomes somewhat commonplace" ("Likening the Scriptures unto Us," in Monte S. Nyman and Charles D. Tate Jr., eds., *Alma, the Testimony of the Word* [1992], 8).

Mormon 1:19. Sorceries, Witchcrafts, and Magic

• President James E. Faust (1920–2007) of the First Presidency warned against intrigue with Satan's mysteries: "It is not good practice to become intrigued by Satan and his mysteries. No good can come from getting close to evil. Like playing with fire, it is too easy to get burned. . . . The only safe course is to keep well distanced from him and any of his wicked activities or nefarious practices. The mischief of devil worship, sorcery, casting spells, witchcraft, voodooism, black magic, and all other forms of demonism should be avoided like the plague" (in Conference Report, Oct. 1987, 40; or *Ensign,* Nov. 1987, 33).

Mormon 2:13. "The Sorrowing of the Damned"

• Elder Neal A. Maxwell (1926–2004) of the Quorum of the Twelve Apostles noted the contrast between godly sorrow and "the sorrowing of the damned": "After recognition, real *remorse* floods the soul. This is a 'godly sorrow,' not merely the 'sorrow of the world' nor the 'sorrowing of the damned' when we can no longer 'take happiness in sin' (2 Corinthians 7:10; Mormon 2:13). False remorse instead is like fondling our failings. In ritual regret, we mourn our mistakes but without mending them" (in Conference Report, Oct. 1991, 40; or *Ensign,* Nov. 1991, 31).

In contrast to the sorrowing of the damned, President Ezra Taft Benson (1899–1994) explained the nature of godly sorrow so that we might understand the sorrow that leads to cleansing repentance: "Godly sorrow is a gift of the Spirit. It is a deep realization that our actions have offended our Father and our God. It is the sharp and keen awareness that our behavior caused the Savior, He who knew no sin, even the greatest of all, to endure agony and suffering. Our sins caused Him to bleed at every pore. This very real mental and spiritual anguish is what the scriptures refer to as having 'a broken heart and a contrite spirit' (D&C 20:37). Such a spirit is the absolute prerequisite for true repentance" (*The Teachings of Ezra Taft Benson* [1988], 72).

Mormon 2:15. "The Day of Grace Was Passed"

• Elder Jeffrey R. Holland noted the chilling line in Mormon's account that time had run out for saving his people: "It is at this moment in Nephite history—just under 950 years since it had begun and just over 300 years since they had been visited by the Son of God himself—that Mormon realized the story was finished. In perhaps the most chilling line he ever wrote, Mormon asserted simply, 'I saw that the day of grace was passed with them, both temporally and spiritually.' His people had learned that most fateful of all lessons—that the Spirit of God will not always strive with man; that it is possible, collectively as well as individually, to have time run out. The day of repentance can pass, and it had passed for the Nephites. Their numbers were being 'hewn down in open rebellion against their God,' and in a metaphor almost too vivid in its moral commentary, they were being 'heaped up as dung upon the face of the land'" (*Christ and the New Covenant,* 319).

• President Spencer W. Kimball (1895–1985) described how we today might also remove ourselves from the cleansing grace of repentance: "It is true that the great principle of repentance is always available, but for the wicked and rebellious there are serious reservations to this statement. For instance, sin is intensely habit-forming and sometimes moves men to the tragic point of no return. . . . As the transgressor moves deeper and deeper in his sin, and the error is entrenched more deeply and the will to change is weakened, it becomes increasingly near-hopeless, and he skids down and down until either he does not want to climb back or he has lost the power to do so" (*The Miracle of Forgiveness* [1969], 117).

> ### MORMON 2:19
> *What do we learn from this verse that gave hope to Mormon amidst his sorrow for the wickedness of his people?*

Mormon 2:26. "We Were Left to Ourselves"

• We may not recognize and appreciate how much Heavenly Father helps us in our daily lives as we try to live faithfully. Mormon wrote that when his people became wicked they lost the strength of the Lord that had previously protected them. While serving as a member of the Seventy, Elder Ray H. Wood explained: "When a person violates any of God's commandments, if there is no repentance the Lord withdraws His protective and sustaining influence. When we lose power with God, we know of a certainty that the problem lies within us and not within God. 'I, the Lord, am bound when ye do what I say; but when ye do not what I say, ye have no promise' (D&C 82:10). Our misdeeds bring despair. They sadden and extinguish the 'perfect brightness of hope' offered by Christ (2 Nephi 31:20). Without God's help, we are left to ourselves" (in Conference Report, Apr. 1999, 54; or *Ensign,* May 1999, 40–41).

Mormon 3:8–11. Mormon Refused to Be a Commander

• In spite of Mormon leading his people for approximately 35 years, at this point he refused to lead them. Mormon must have been influenced by the abridgement he was making of the Book of Mormon. He saw Captain Moroni's and Helaman's justifiable reasons to go to war (see Alma 43:9–58:12)—defending their lands, houses, wives, children, rights, privileges, liberty, and ability to worship. He taught the people these purposes of war (see Mormon 2:23–24). After seeing the motivation the Nephites in his day had for fighting the Lamanites—to "avenge themselves" and that they "began to boast in their own strength" and that they were guilty of great "wickedness and abomination"—he temporarily refused to lead their armies (Mormon 3:9–14).

Mormon 3:9; 4:8. Boasting

• Elder Neal A. Maxwell cautioned us to recognize Heavenly Father's power instead of our own: "Before enjoying the harvests of righteous efforts, let us therefore first acknowledge God's hand. Otherwise, the rationalizations appear, and they include, 'My power and the might of mine hand hath gotten me this wealth' (Deuteronomy 8:17). Or, we 'vaunt' ourselves, as ancient Israel would have done (except for Gideon's deliberately small army), by boasting that 'mine own hand hath saved me' (Judges 7:2). Touting our own 'hand' makes it doubly hard to confess God's hand in all things (see Alma 14:11; D&C 59:21)" (in Conference Report, Apr. 2002, 43; or *Ensign,* May 2002, 37).

Mormon 3:12. "According to the Love of God Which Was in Me"

• When he was in the Presiding Bishopric, Bishop Glenn L. Pace admonished us to strive to emulate the love Mormon exhibited: "This prophet had Christlike love for a fallen people. Can we be content with loving less? We must press forward with the pure love of Christ to spread the good news of the gospel. As we do so and fight the war of good against evil, light against darkness, and truth against falsehood, we must not neglect our responsibility of dressing the wounds of those who have fallen in battle. There is no room in the kingdom for fatalism" (in Conference Report, Oct. 1990, 8; or *Ensign,* Nov. 1990, 8–9).

Mormon 3:18–22. Our Judgment

• Elder Bruce R. McConkie (1915–85) of the Quorum of the Twelve Apostles explained that others would take part in our Judgment: "The reality is that there will be a whole hierarchy of judges who, under Christ, shall judge the righteous. He alone shall issue the decrees of damnation for the wicked" (*The Millennial Messiah* [1982], 520).

The scriptures teach that there will be at least five sources who will take part on Judgment Day:

1. Ourselves (see Alma 41:7; *History of the Church,* 6:314)

2. Our bishops (see D&C 41:9; 58:14, 17–20; 64:40; 72:17)

3. Scriptures (see Revelation 20:12; 2 Nephi 25:18; 29:11; 33:14; 3 Nephi 27:25–26)

4. Apostles (see Matthew 19:27–30; 1 Nephi 12:9; 3 Nephi 27:27; Mormon 3:18; D&C 29:12)

5. Jesus Christ (see John 5:22; 3 Nephi 27:14)

• President John Taylor (1808–87) further elaborated on the role of the Apostles in our judgment: "Christ is at the head. . . . It would seem to be quite reasonable, if the twelve apostles in Jerusalem are to be the judges of the twelve tribes, and the twelve disciples on this continent are to be the judges of the descendants of Nephi, that the brother of Jared and Jared should be the judges of the Jaredites, their descendants; and, further, that the first presidency and twelve who have officiated in our age, should operate in regard to mankind in this dispensation" (*The Gospel Kingdom,* sel. G. Homer Durham [1987], 138).

Mormon 3:20–22; 5:12–14. An Admonition to Believe in Christ

• President Gordon B. Hinckley testified that the Book of Mormon is another witness for Christ: "This scripture

of the New World, is before us as an added witness of the divinity and reality of the Lord Jesus Christ, of the encompassing beneficence of His atonement, and of His coming forth from the darkness of the grave. Within these covers is found much of the sure word of prophecy concerning Him who should be born of a virgin, the Son of the Almighty God. There is a foretelling of His work among men as a living mortal. There is a declaration of His death, of the lamb without blemish who was to be sacrificed for the sins of the world. And there is an account that is moving and inspiring and true of the visit of the resurrected Christ among living men and women in the western continent. The testimony is here to handle; it is here to be read; it is here to be pondered; it is here to be prayed over with a promise that he who prays shall know by the power of the Holy Ghost of its truth and validity (see Moroni 10:3–5)" (in Conference Report, Apr. 1994, 95; or *Ensign,* May 1994, 72).

Mormon 4:23. Brief Overview of the Movements of the Plates

• Ammaron told Mormon to take the large plates of Nephi from the Hill Shim and add to them. Mormon was to leave the rest of the plates (plates of brass, small plates of Nephi, and plates of Ether) in the Hill Shim (see Mormon 1:2–4). Mormon removed the large plates, wrote a full account of the activities of his people on them, and used a selected portion of them to create his own condensed and abridged history of his people (see Mormon 2:18). Later Mormon returned to the Hill Shim and removed all of the plates (plates of brass, small plates of Nephi, plates of Ether, and all other plates) from the hill (see Mormon 4:23). Fearing that the Lamanites might destroy the records, Mormon hid the plates again—except his abridgement and the small plates of Nephi (the gold plates) in the Hill Cumorah (see Mormon 6:6). These gold plates Mormon gave to his son Moroni (see Mormon 6:6; Words of Mormon 1:1–7).

MORMON 5:12–14

What did Mormon perceive were the main purposes of his record keeping? (see also Mormon 3:20–21).

Mormon 5:16. The Spirit "Ceased to Strive with Their Fathers"

• President Harold B. Lee (1899–1973) explained that the wicked people of Mormon's time had lost not only the Holy Ghost, but the Spirit of Christ from their lives: "Mormon described some people, his people, from whom the spirit of the Lord had departed, and when I read that . . . it seems clear to me that what he was talking about was not merely the inability to have the companionship of or the gift of the Holy Ghost, but he was talking of that light of truth to which every one born into the world is entitled and will never cease

to strive with the individual unless he loses it through his own sinning" (in Conference Report, Apr. 1956, 108).

Mormon 5:17. "Once a Delightsome People"

• Mormon lamented the depraved condition of his people, who by contrast had once been "delightsome." President Gordon B. Hinckley reflected on some blessings associated with being delightsome and the requirements to achieve such a condition: "There is the great blessing of wisdom, of knowledge, even hidden treasures of knowledge. We are promised that ours shall be a delightsome land if we will walk in obedience to this law. I can interpret the word *land* as people, that those who walk in obedience shall be a delightsome people. What a marvelous condition to be a delightsome people whom others would describe as blessed!" (in Conference Report, Apr. 1982, 60; or *Ensign,* May 1982, 40).

Mormon 5:23. "In the Hands of God"

• Mormon wrote for us in the latter days, admonishing us to recognize God and His power. We are in His hands. Elder W. Craig Zwick of the Seventy explained some symbolism and blessings suggested by being in God's hands:

"Hands are one of the symbolically expressive parts of the body. In Hebrew, *yad,* the most common word for *hand,* is also used metaphorically to mean power, strength, and might (see William Wilson, *Old Testament Word Studies* [1978], 205). Thus, hands signify power and strength. . . .

"To be in the hands of God would suggest that we are not only under His watchful care but also that we are guarded and protected by His wondrous power.

"Throughout the scriptures, reference is made to the hand of the Lord. His divine assistance is evidenced over and over again. His powerful hands created worlds, and yet they were gentle enough to bless the little children. . . .

"Every one of us needs to know that we can go on in the strength of the Lord. We can put our hand in His, and we will feel His sustaining presence lift us to heights unattainable alone. . . .

". . . How do we learn to extend our hand and connect to the comfort provided by the Lord? . . .

"Here are four keys:

"Learn

"Listen

"Seek the Spirit

"Pray always

"The Lord will provide sustenance and support if we are willing to open the door and receive His hand of divine assistance. . . .

"Imagine the wounds in His hands. His weathered hands, yes, even His hands of torn flesh and physical sacrifice, give our own hands greater power and direction.

"It is the wounded Christ who leads us through our moments of difficulty. It is He who bears us up when we need more air to breathe or direction to follow or even more courage to continue.

"If we will keep the commandments of God and walk hand in hand with Him in His paths, we will go forward with faith and never feel alone" (in Conference Report, Oct. 2003, 36–38; or *Ensign,* Nov. 2003, 34–36).

MORMON 6:16–20
What insight do you gain about Mormon from these verses? How can we incorporate some of these attributes in our own lives?

Mormon 6:16–22. Don't Reject the Open Arms of Christ

• Mormon mourned the death of his unrepentant people and sorrowed that they did not change their ways before their lives ended. If they had set aside their pride and repented of their sins, Mormon taught that their reunion with the Savior would have been joyful (see Mormon 6:17).

We too must prepare ourselves to stand before the Lord at the Judgment. President James E. Faust explained:

Harry Anderson, © IRI

"We long for the ultimate blessing of the Atonement —to become one with Him, to be in His divine presence, to be called individually by name as He warmly welcomes us home with a radiant smile, beckoning us with open arms to be enfolded in His boundless love. How gloriously sublime this experience will be if we can feel worthy enough to be in His presence! The free gift of His great atoning sacrifice for each of us is the only way we can be exalted enough to stand before Him and see Him face-to-face. The overwhelming message of the Atonement is the perfect love the Savior has for each and all of us. It is a love which is full of mercy, patience, grace, equity, long-suffering, and, above all, forgiving.

"The evil influence of Satan would destroy any hope we have in overcoming our mistakes. He would have us feel that we are lost and that there is no hope. In contrast, Jesus reaches down to us to lift us up. Through our repentance and the gift of the Atonement, we can prepare to be worthy to stand in His presence" (in Conference Report, Oct. 2001, 22; or *Ensign,* Nov. 2001, 20).

Points to Ponder

• What do you think it means to be "of a sober mind"? (Mormon 1:15).

• How can you recognize the Lord's influence in your life? (see Mormon 3:3).

• What do you think it means to be "in the hands of God"? (Mormon 5:23). What can you do to qualify to enjoy more benefits from being in God's hands?

Suggested Assignments

• Write a verse-by-verse analysis of Mormon 3:17–22. Then explain to a friend or family member the important points contained in these verses.

Introduction

By studying the final testimony of Mormon and the initial writings of Moroni, you will better understand the role and purpose of the Book of Mormon. Moroni declared: "I speak unto you as if ye were present, and yet ye are not. But behold, Jesus Christ hath shown you unto me, and I know your doing" (Mormon 8:35). Moroni's prophetic vantage point allowed him to complete the Nephite record with total awareness of both the escalating wickedness and the great spiritual blessings of the dispensation of the fulness of times. In a day when some people might be inclined to abandon faith in the face of great difficulties, Moroni's words teach us to see miracles and revelations as evidence that "God is the same yesterday, today, and forever" (see Mormon 9:9). Although the spiritual and social conditions in the world may be in a state of constant change and decline, God's covenant people can have full confidence that He is eternally the same.

Commentary

Mormon 7. Counsel to the Remnant of Israel in the Latter Days

• In his final words, Mormon addressed the descendants of the Lamanites and affirmed that they are a "remnant of the house of Israel" (Mormon 7:1). Even though the Lamanites were his mortal enemies, his love for them demonstrated his spiritual maturity and the importance of the full blessings of the gospel. Consider Mormon's final testimony and counsel as if he were speaking directly to you. He taught what you *need to know* (see Mormon 7:1–7) and what you *need to do* (see Mormon 7:8–9) in order to follow "the example of our Savior" so that "it shall be well with you in the day of judgment" (Mormon 7:10).

Mormon 7:2. "Ye Are of the House of Israel"

• Mormon's message to the remnant of the Lamanites also applies to all members of the house of Israel (see commentary for Helaman 3:30 on p. 264).

Mormon 7:2, 5. Mormon's Final Plea to Believe in Christ

• Elder Jeffrey R. Holland of the Quorum of the Twelve Apostles reflected on Mormon's poignant plea to those of the latter days to believe in Christ:

"In a soliloquy of death, Mormon reached across time and space to all, especially to that 'remnant of the house of Israel' who would one day read his majestic record. Those of another time and place must learn what those lying before him had forgotten—that all must 'believe in Jesus Christ, that he is the Son of God,' that following his crucifixion in Jerusalem he had, 'by the power of the Father . . . risen again, whereby he hath gained the victory over the grave; and also in him is the sting of death swallowed up' [Mormon 7:2, 5]. . . .

"To 'believe in Christ,' especially when measured against such tragic but avoidable consequences, was Mormon's last plea and his only hope. It is the ultimate purpose of the entire book that would come to the latter-day world bearing his name" (*Christ and the New Covenant* [1997], 321–22).

Mormon 7:8–9. The Book of Mormon and the Bible Support Each Other

• The Bible testifies of the Book of Mormon, and the Book of Mormon testifies of the Bible. Mormon declared, "This [the Book of Mormon] is written for the intent that ye may believe that [the Bible]; and if ye believe that [the Bible] ye will believe this [the Book of Mormon] also" (Mormon 7:9).

President Brigham Young (1801–77) declared it impossible for someone who claimed to truly believe in the Bible to not believe in the Book of Mormon if they have seriously studied the Book of Mormon and learned its doctrines:

"No man can say that this book (laying his hand on the Bible) is true, is the word of the Lord, is the way, is the guide-board in the path, and a charter by which we may learn the will of God; and at the same time say, that the

Book of Mormon is untrue; if he has had the privilege of reading it, or of hearing it read, and learning its doctrines. There is not that person on the face of the earth who has had the privilege of learning the Gospel of Jesus Christ from these two books, who can say that one is true, and the other is false" (*Discourses of Brigham Young,* sel. John A. Widtsoe [1954], 459).

• One purpose of the Book of Mormon is to prove to the world that the Holy Bible is true (see D&C 20:11). By reading the Book of Mormon, a person's testimony of the Bible increases. President Ezra Taft Benson (1899–1994) spoke of his love for the Bible and the Book of Mormon and how both testify that Jesus is the Christ:

Greg K. Olsen, © 1990 IRI

"I love the Bible, both the Old and the New Testaments. It is a source of great truth. . . .

". . . That sacred and holy book has been of inestimable worth to the children of men. In fact, it was a passage from the Bible that inspired the Prophet Joseph Smith to go to a grove of trees near his home and kneel in prayer. What followed was the glorious vision that commenced the restoration of the fulness of the gospel of Jesus Christ to the earth. That vision also began the process of bringing forth new scripture [the Book of Mormon] to stand shoulder to shoulder with the Bible in bearing witness to a wicked world that Jesus is the Christ and that God lives and loves His children and is still intimately involved in their salvation and exaltation" (in Conference Report, Oct. 1986, 100–101; or *Ensign,* Nov. 1986, 78).

Mormon 8:1–6. Moroni

• Moroni witnessed the death of his father, Mormon, and the destruction of the entire Nephite nation. Nevertheless, his life was preserved, and he faithfully fulfilled his mission in mortality. The Lord appointed Moroni to finish writing "the sad tale of the destruction" of the Nephites (Mormon 8:3).

Before his death Moroni wrote the last part of his father's book (Mormon 8–9), abridged the Jaredite record (the book of Ether), recorded the vision of the brother of Jared in the sealed portion of the plates (see Ether 4:4–5), and also wrote his own book (the book of Moroni). Yet Moroni's mission continues in our dispensation. In modern revelation we learn that Moroni holds "the keys of the record of the stick of Ephraim" (D&C 27:5). The resurrected Moroni ministered to the Prophet Joseph Smith and tutored him several times

Walter Rane. Courtesy of Museum of Church History and Art

on his role in restoring the fulness of the gospel, including the coming forth of the Book of Mormon (see Joseph Smith—History 1:30–60; *History of the Church,* 1:9–19). Depicting Moroni's role in the Restoration, the Church has placed statues of Moroni atop most of its temples.

• Mormon 8:1–6 reveals the circumstances under which Moroni lived and helps readers understand the urgency of his message. Elder L. Tom Perry of the Quorum of the Twelve Apostles counseled us to put ourselves in the position of those who wrote the scriptures long ago. Quoting Brigham Young, Elder Perry said:

"'Do you read the Scriptures, my brethren and sisters, as though you were writing them a thousand, two thousand, or five thousand years ago? Do you read them as though you stood in the place of the men who wrote them? If you do not feel thus, it is your privilege to do so, that you may be as familiar with the spirit and meaning of the written word of God as you are with your daily walk and conversation' (*Discourses of Brigham Young,* sel. John A. Widtsoe [Salt Lake City: Deseret Book Co., 1941], p. 128). . . .

". . . Let us take Brigham Young's advice and imagine we are standing in the place where Moroni, the last of the great Nephite prophets, stood. The assignment his father gave to him to complete the record, which was entrusted to his care, was very difficult. He must have been in a state of shock as he described the total destruction of his people.

"He must have felt compelled to describe how his people had been hunted by the Lamanites until they were all destroyed. In his feeling of loneliness, he reports that his father was among those who were killed. We sense that the only thing Moroni is living for is to complete the record, as he writes, 'Therefore I will write and hide up the records in the earth; and whither I go it mattereth not' (Mormon 8:4).

"All he has is the faith that the Lord will preserve him long enough to complete the record and that someday it will be found by one chosen of the Lord. He realizes that the record will be a voice of warning to future generations of what occurs when nations like his own turn away from the teachings of the Lord. It is from the depths of his heart that Moroni cries out to those who will eventually receive the record. He wants to spare those who read his account the heartache and misery which comes from disobedience.

"He writes first to the members of the Church and then to those who have not embraced the gospel of Jesus Christ. Moroni's last words to the members of the Church are written as a voice of warning. He writes as one who sees the history of his people repeating itself in the future" (in Conference Report, Oct. 1992, 18–19; or *Ensign*, Nov. 1992, 15–16).

Mormon 8:14–18. "Blessed Be He That Shall Bring This Thing to Light"

• Mormon 8:16 refers to the Prophet Joseph Smith, who was chosen to bring the Book of Mormon to the world (see D&C 3:5–10). Many of the ancient prophets

were aware of Joseph Smith and prayed for his success to translate and publish the gold plates, thus fulfilling the purposes of God (see Mormon 8:22, 24–25; D&C 10:46). President Boyd K. Packer, President of the Quorum of the Twelve Apostles,

spoke of the role that Joseph Smith played in bringing forth the Book of Mormon:

"The truth is, simply, that he was a prophet of God—nothing more and not one whit less!

"The scriptures did not come so much from Joseph Smith as they did through him. He was a conduit through which the revelations were given. . . .

"The Prophet Joseph Smith was an unschooled farm boy. To read some of his early letters in the original shows him to be somewhat unpolished in spelling and grammar and in expression.

"That the revelations came through him in any form of literary refinement is nothing short of a miracle" (in Conference Report, Apr. 1974, 137; or *Ensign*, May 1974, 94).

Mormon 8:19–20. "Judgment Is Mine"

• Elder Dallin H. Oaks of the Quorum of the Twelve Apostles commented on the phrase "judgment is mine, saith the Lord": "I speak of the final judgment. This is that future occasion in which all of us will stand before the judgment seat of Christ to be judged according to our works (see 1 Ne. 15:33; 3 Ne. 27:15; Morm. 3:20; D&C 19:3). . . . I believe that the scriptural command to 'judge not' refers most clearly to this final judgment, as in the Book of Mormon declaration that 'man shall not . . . judge; for judgment is mine, saith the Lord' (Morm. 8:20)" ("'Judge Not' and Judging," *Ensign*, Aug. 1999, 7).

> **MORMON 8:22**
>
> How can Moroni's words in this verse strengthen us as we labor in the Lord's cause?

Mormon 8:31. Pollutions in the Last Days

• Mormon 8:31 refers to "great pollutions" in our day. While serving as a member of the Presidency of the Seventy, Elder Joe J. Christensen suggested that the great pollutants spoken of were not environmental, but primarily spiritual:

"We all hear and read a great deal these days about our polluted physical environment—acid rain, smog, toxic wastes. But . . . there is another kind of pollution that is much more dangerous—the moral and spiritual.

"In a recent conference, Elder Boyd K. Packer said, 'As we test the *moral* environment, we find the *pollution* index is spiraling upward' (in Conference Report, Apr. 1992, p. 91; or *Ensign,* May 1992, 66). The Apostle Paul foresaw 'that in the last days perilous times shall come' (2 Timothy 3:1). And speaking of the last days, the prophet Moroni declared, 'Yea, it shall come in a day when there shall be great pollutions upon the face of the earth' (Mormon 8:31).

"Sadly, the effects of this great pollution are perhaps most evident in the mass media, films, television, and popular music. Of this, Senator Robert D. Byrd said, 'If we in this nation continue to sow the images of murder, violence, drug abuse, . . . perversion, [and] pornography . . . before the eyes of millions of children, year after year and day after day, we should not be surprised if the foundations of our society rot away as if from leprosy' (in Michael Medved, *Hollywood vs. America* [New York: Harper Perennial, 1992], p. 194).

". . . In most areas of the mass media there seems to be a declaration of war against almost everything the majority treasures most: the family, religion, and patriotism. Marriage is degraded, while premarital and extramarital relations are encouraged and glamorized. Profanity and the foulest of vulgar gutter language bombard the ears of all who listen. . . . Human life itself is trivialized by the constant barrage of violence and killings" (in Conference Report, Oct. 1993, 12; or *Ensign,* Nov. 1993, 11).

Mormon 8:34–35. Written for Us Today

• President Ezra Taft Benson declared that our study of the Book of Mormon should be influenced by our knowledge that Moroni saw our day and wrote with us in mind:

"We must make the Book of Mormon a center focus of study [because] it was written for our day. The Nephites never had the book; neither did the Lamanites of ancient times. It was meant for us. Mormon wrote near the end of the Nephite civilization. Under the inspiration of God, who sees all things from the beginning, he abridged

centuries of records, choosing the stories, speeches, and events that would be most helpful to us.

"Each of the major writers of the Book of Mormon testified that he wrote for future generations. . . .

"Mormon himself said, 'Yea, I speak unto you, ye remnant of the house of Israel' (Mormon 7:1). And Moroni, the last of the inspired writers, actually saw our day and time. . . .

"If they saw our day and chose those things which would be of greatest worth to us, is not that how we should study the Book of Mormon? We should constantly ask ourselves, 'Why did the Lord inspire Mormon (or Moroni or Alma) to include that in his record? What lesson can I learn from that to help me live in this day and age?'

"And there is example after example of how that question will be answered" (in Conference Report, Oct. 1986, 5; or *Ensign,* Nov. 1986, 6).

Mormon 9:1–6. Miserable in God's Presence

• President Joseph Fielding Smith (1876–1972) explained why the unrepentant will be miserable in the presence of Jesus Christ:

"There can be no salvation without repentance. A man cannot enter into the kingdom of God in his sins. It would be a very inconsistent thing for a man to come into the presence of the Father and to dwell in God's presence in his sins. . . .

"I think there are a great many people upon the earth, many of them perhaps in the Church—at least some in the Church—who have an idea they can go through this life doing as they please, violating the commandments of the Lord and yet eventually they are going to come into his presence. They think they are going to repent, perhaps in the spirit world.

"They ought to read these words of Moroni: 'Do ye suppose that ye shall dwell with him [Christ] under a consciousness of your guilt? Do ye suppose that ye could be happy to dwell with that holy Being, when your souls are racked with a consciousness of guilt that ye have ever abused his laws?' [Mormon 9:3]" (*Doctrines of Salvation,* comp. Bruce R. McConkie, 3 vols. [1954–56], 2:195–96).

Mormon 9:3–6. "Consciousness of Your Guilt"

• President Spencer W. Kimball (1895–1985) explained why one who has sinned feels the burden of guilt and the need for repentance:

"As repentance gets under way, there must be a deep consciousness of guilt, and in that consciousness of guilt may come suffering to the mind, the spirit, and sometimes even to the body. In order to live with themselves, people who transgress must follow one or the other of two alternatives. The one is to sear their conscience or dull their sensitivity with mental tranquilizers so that their transgression may be continued. Those who choose this alternative eventually become calloused and lose their desire to repent. The other alternative is to permit remorse to lead one to total sorrow, then to repentance, and finally on to eventual forgiveness.

"Remember this, that forgiveness can never come without repentance. And repentance can never come until one has bared his soul and admitted his actions without excuses or rationalizations. He must admit to himself that he has sinned, without the slightest minimization of the offense or rationalizing of its seriousness, or without soft-pedaling its gravity. He must admit that his sin is as big as it really is and not call a pound an ounce. Those persons who choose to meet the issue and transform their lives may find repentance the harder road at first, but they will find it the infinitely more desirable path as they taste of its fruits" ("The Gospel of Repentance," *Ensign,* Oct. 1982, 4).

Mormon 9:7–8. Revelations and the Scriptures

• Elder Dallin H. Oaks explained the connection between scriptures and personal revelation:

"What makes [Latter-day Saints] different from most other Christians in the way we read and use the Bible and other scriptures is our belief in continuing revelation. For us, the scriptures are not the ultimate source of knowledge, but what precedes the ultimate source. The ultimate knowledge comes by revelation. With Moroni we affirm that he who denieth revelation 'knoweth not the gospel of Christ' (Morm. 9:8).

"The word of the Lord in the scriptures is like a lamp to guide our feet (see Ps. 119:105), and revelation is like a mighty force that increases the lamp's illumination manyfold. We encourage everyone to make careful study of the scriptures and of the prophetic teachings concerning them and to prayerfully seek personal revelation to know their meaning for themselves" ("Scripture Reading and Revelation," *Ensign,* Jan. 1995, 7).

Mormon 9:9–10. "God Is the Same Yesterday, Today, and Forever"

• Moroni declared that God is an unchangeable being who will remain "the same yesterday, today, and forever" (Mormon 9:9). Modern revelation confirms that the coming forth of the Book of Mormon proves God continues to "inspire men and call them to his holy work" in our day as He has in the past, "showing that he is the same God yesterday, today, and forever" (D&C 20:11–12).

The *Lectures on Faith* state that in order to have perfect faith in God one must have a correct idea of God's "character, perfections, and attributes" ([1985], 38). One of God's characteristics is that He will not change: "[God] changes not, neither is there variableness with him; but that he is the same from everlasting to everlasting, being the same yesterday, today, and for ever; and that his course is one eternal round, without variation" (*Lectures on Faith,* 41). Consider the blessing of knowing that God continues His holy work in our day and will always remain the same yesterday, today, and forever.

• Moroni warned us that there are those who "have imagined . . . a god who doth vary" (Mormon 9:10). Elder Neal A. Maxwell (1926–2004) of the Quorum of the Twelve Apostles taught that we could not believe or trust in a God who changes or is still learning new truths:

"The omniscience of God in the minds of some well-meaning Latter-day Saints has been qualified by the concept of 'eternal progression.' Some have wrongly assumed God's progress is related to His acquisition of additional knowledge. . . .

". . . God derives His great and continuing joy and glory by increasing and advancing His creations, and not from new intellectual experiences.

"There is a vast difference, therefore, between an omniscient God and the false notion that God is on some sort of post-doctoral fellowship, still searching for additional key truths and vital data. Were the latter so, God might, at any moment, discover some new truth not previously known to Him that would restructure, diminish, or undercut certain truths previously known by Him. Prophecy would be mere prediction. Planning assumptions pertaining to our redemption would need to be revised. Fortunately for us, however, His plan of salvation is constantly *underway*—not constantly *under revision*" (*All These Things Shall Give Thee Experience* [1979], 14–15).

MORMON 9:20

According to Moroni, why does God cease to perform miracles among men?

Mormon 9:10–26. Miracles

• Note the evidence Moroni gave that bears witness to the miracles of God—the creation of heaven and earth (see Mormon 9:17), the creation of man (see v. 17), and the scriptural testimonies of the miracles of Jesus and the Apostles (see v. 18). The "God of miracles" described by Moroni can still be found. Elder Dallin H. Oaks bore witness that many miracles happen in our day and are present in the true Church of Jesus Christ:

"Many miracles happen every day in the work of our Church and the lives of our members. Many of you have witnessed miracles, perhaps more than you realize.

"A miracle has been defined as 'a beneficial event brought about through divine power that mortals do not understand and of themselves cannot duplicate' [in Daniel H. Ludlow, ed., *Encyclopedia of Mormonism,* 5 vols. (1992), 2:908]. The idea that events are brought about through divine power is rejected by

most irreligious people and even by some who are religious. . . .

". . . Miracles worked by the power of the priesthood are always present in the true Church of Jesus Christ. The Book of Mormon teaches that 'God has provided a means that man, through faith, might work mighty miracles' (Mosiah 8:18). The 'means' provided is priesthood power (see James 5:14–15; D&C 42:43–48), and that power works miracles through faith (see Ether 12:12; Moro. 7:37)" ("Miracles," *Ensign,* June 2001, 6, 8).

• Elder Bruce R. McConkie (1915–85) spoke of why miracles sometime cease:

"Why do signs and miracles cease in certain ages? Why are they not found at all times and among all peoples? Were those of old entitled to greater blessings than those of us who now dwell on the same earth that once was theirs? Moroni answers: 'The reason why' a God of gifts and miracles 'ceaseth to do miracles among the children of men,' and to pour out his gifts upon them, 'is because that they dwindle in unbelief, and depart from the right way, and know not the God in whom they should trust.' They worship false gods whom they define in their creeds, and they no longer walk in the same paths pursued by the saints of former days.

"It is men who have changed, not God; he is the same everlastingly. All men who have the same faith and live the same law will reap the same blessings" (*A New Witness for the Articles of Faith* [1985], 367).

Mormon 9:32–34. Moroni Wrote in Reformed Egyptian

• Moroni stated that he had the ability to write in at least two languages: Hebrew and Egyptian (see Mormon 9:32–34). He noted that if the "plates had

been sufficiently large" he would have written in Hebrew; however, those who kept the record used "reformed Egyptian" due to the lack of space (vv. 32–33). Previously in the Book of Mormon, both Nephi and King Benjamin acknowledged their use of Egyptian. Nephi stated that he wrote in "the language of the Egyptians" when he engraved the small plates (1 Nephi 1:2). When speaking to his sons about the importance of the brass plates, King Benjamin noted that Lehi could read the record because he had "been taught in the language of the Egyptians" (Mosiah 1:4). Therefore, we understand that Lehi taught the gospel and Egyptian "to his children, that thereby they could teach them to their children" (Mosiah 1:4). Evidently, this pattern continued through the generations of record keepers that followed until Moroni learned the language from his father. However, Moroni's statement that he wrote in "reformed Egyptian" (Mormon 9:32) indicates that some adaptations in the use of the language had occurred over the thousand years from the time of Lehi. This could explain why Moroni concluded with the comment that "none other people knoweth our language" but that God had prepared means for the eventual interpretation and translation of the record (Mormon 9:34).

Points to Ponder

- What do you learn from the way Mormon cared about others, including his enemies? (see Mormon 7).

- Moroni spent many years alone, yet his faith and testimony brought him peace. How can your testimony help you when you feel alone in the world?

- What are some of the "spiritual pollutions" that you see on the earth today? How can you resist being tainted by them?

- What are some miracles you have witnessed in your life?

Suggested Assignments

- Study the following scriptures, looking for prophecies of the coming forth of the Book of Mormon:

Isaiah 29:4

2 Nephi 3:19–20

2 Nephi 26:16

2 Nephi 33:13

Enos 1:15–16

Mormon 8:23

Mormon 9:30

Moroni 10:27

Moses 7:62

Joseph Smith—History 1:52–53

You might make a scripture chain of these verses by turning to Isaiah 29:4 and writing "go to 2 Nephi 3:19–20" in the margin of the page next to Isaiah 29:4. Then turn to 2 Nephi 3:19–20 and write "go to 2 Nephi 26:16" in the margin next to 2 Nephi 3:19–20. Repeat this process with all of the verses. When you reach Joseph Smith—History 1:52–53, write "go to Isaiah 29:4" in the margin, linking the chain back to the beginning.

- Prepare a five- to eight-minute talk on the blessings of accepting the Book of Mormon. You might use the following questions and resources as a guide to help you create your talk:

The Blessings of Accepting the Book of Mormon

Mormon 8:12. What blessing will come to those who do not condemn or criticize the Book of Mormon?

Mormon 8:17. Why is it important to not find fault with the Book of Mormon?

Doctrine and Covenants 20:8–15. What are some truths we will know if we accept the Book of Mormon?

From your personal experience: What are some of the spiritual blessings you have received from accepting the Book of Mormon?

President Ezra Taft Benson: "I bless you with increased *understanding* of the Book of Mormon. I promise you that from this moment forward, if we will daily sup from its pages and abide by its precepts, God will pour out upon each child of Zion and the Church a blessing hitherto unknown" (in Conference Report, Apr. 1986, 100; or *Ensign,* May 1986, 78).

Introduction

The Book of Mormon is not arranged in chronological order. If it were, the book of Ether would be listed first. The Jaredite record begins approximately 2200 B.C. First Nephi begins in 600 B.C. The book of Ether covers over 1,700 years of history from 2200 B.C. down to the time of Coriantumr. We don't know exactly when Coriantumr lived, but it was somewhere between 500 and 250 B.C. The rest of the Book of Mormon from the books of 1 Nephi to Moroni covers approximately 1,000 years of history.

Following the Flood in Noah's day, many descendants of those who had been spared became wicked. One group of people attempted to build a tower "whose top may reach unto heaven" (Genesis 11:4). The story of the Jaredite nation began with the building of the Tower of Babel. The Lord dealt with the widespread wickedness by confounding the common language and by scattering the people across the face of the earth (see Ether 1:33; Genesis 11:5–8).

The brother of Jared pled with the Lord to preserve the language of his worthy friends and family. Demonstrating great faith and led by the hand of God, the brother of Jared was able to lead this group to another land. The story of this migration is filled with important principles that we can apply to our lives today. These principles include the exercise of faith to receive divine assistance and the role of prayer in accomplishing difficult tasks. As you study the life of the brother of Jared, you will learn of the blessings that come when individuals exercise strong faith.

Here is a review of the origins of the book of Ether:

- Jaredite prophets kept the history until the final Jaredite prophet named Ether (see Ether 1:6).

- Limhi's search found part of the Jaredite record—in the form of the 24 gold plates (see Mosiah 8:7–11).

- King Mosiah translated the Jaredite record (see Mosiah 28:10–17).

- Moroni abridged or edited the Jaredite record and included it before his own writings (see Ether 1:1–6).

Commentary

Ether 1:1–2. The 24 Plates Discovered

- While the people of Limhi were in bondage, King Limhi sent out an expedition of 43 men to search for the land of Zarahemla (see Mosiah 8:7; 21:25). Though unsuccessful in finding Zarahemla, the search party found a land covered with the bones and remains of a people who had been destroyed (see Mosiah 8:8). The searchers discovered a record of 24 gold plates, which they took back to King Limhi (see Mosiah 8:9–10). When Limhi's people eventually escaped from bondage (see Mosiah 22), these plates were given to King Mosiah to translate (see Mosiah 28:1–17).

Ether 1:3–4. An Account of the Creation before Moses's Day

- It is significant that the book of Ether informs us that an account of the Creation, Adam, and a history of God's children down to the time of the Tower of Babel existed well before Moses's day. This account may have become lost through apostasy and wickedness, thus necessitating a restoration of this knowledge through revelation to Moses so we might have the record today (see Moses 1:40).

Ether 1:6–32. The Jaredite Genealogy

- Ether 1 gives a genealogy of the prophet Ether. This genealogy is a rare occurrence in the Book of Mormon and is explained by the following commentary:

"Genealogies are common in the Bible. The Hebrew people took great interest in their family histories, and genealogies seem to have been carefully kept; the number in the scriptures is an index to their importance. Notice those in Genesis 5, 11, 46; Numbers 26; 1 Chronicles 1–9; read also the accounts in Ezra 9–10 which give an  indication of the importance of keeping family histories. The Book of Mormon, however, contains only one example of an extended genealogy, that found in Ether 1:6–32. It gives the genealogy of Ether, the last prophet of the Jaredite people, whose lineage is traced back twenty-nine generations or more to Jared, who left the Tower of Babel with his family at the time of the confounding of the language of the people. Aside from this example, only scattered references of genealogical interest are found" (Sidney B. Sperry, "Types of Literature in the Book of Mormon," in *Journal of Book of Mormon Studies,* vol. 21, no. 1 (1995): 117).

Ether 1:34–35. The Brother of Jared's Name

• Elder George Reynolds (1842–1909) of the Seventy related the following account, which indicates that the brother of Jared's name (see Ether 2:13) was revealed to the Prophet Joseph Smith (1805–44): "While residing in Kirtland Elder Reynolds Cahoon had a son born to him. One day when President Joseph Smith was passing his door he called the Prophet in and asked him to bless and name the baby. Joseph did so and gave the boy the name of Mahonri Moriancumer. When he had finished the blessing he laid the child on the bed, and turning to Elder Cahoon he said, the name I have given your son is the name of the brother of Jared; the Lord has just shown [or revealed] it to me. Elder William F. Cahoon, who was standing near heard the Prophet make this statement to his father; and this was the first time the name of the brother of Jared was known in the Church in this dispensation" ("The Jaredites," *Juvenile Instructor,* May 1, 1892, 282).

Ether 1:33–38. The Language of Jared and His Brother

• Ether 1:34–38 records that the Lord did not confound the language of Jared's family, his brother, and their friends at the time of the Tower of Babel. President Joseph Fielding Smith (1876–1972) taught that the Jaredites likely spoke in the language of Adam: "It is stated in the Book of Ether that Jared and his brother made the request of the Lord that their language be not changed at the time of the confusion of tongues at the Tower of Babel. Their request was granted, and they carried with them the

speech of their fathers, the Adamic language, which was powerful even in its written form, so that the things Mahonri wrote 'were mighty even . . . unto the overpowering of man to read them.' That was the kind of language Adam had and this was the language with which Enoch was able to accomplish his mighty work" (*The Way to Perfection* [1970], 69).

Ether 1:38–42. A Chosen Land

• Just as members of the house of Israel are called a chosen people—chosen to do the Lord's work—the Book of Mormon refers to the Americas as a chosen land—chosen to be the place for the Restoration of the gospel and, eventually, the New Jerusalem. Both the members of the house of Israel and the Americas have been chosen to assist Heavenly Father in spreading the gospel throughout the world.

• President Joseph Fielding Smith explained that all of North and South America is a choice land: "The Book of Mormon informs us that the whole of America, both North and South, is *a choice land above all other lands, in other words—Zion.* The Lord told the Jaredites that he would lead them to a land 'which is choice above all the lands of the earth' [Ether 1:42]" (*Doctrines of Salvation,* comp. Bruce R. McConkie, 3 vols. [1954–56], 3:73).

• President Ezra Taft Benson (1899–1994) also spoke of the Americas being chosen lands: "In 1844, the Prophet Joseph Smith made this solemn proclamation: 'The whole of America is Zion itself from north to south' (*Teachings [of the Prophet Joseph Smith],* p. 362). The Lord Himself decreed: 'This is a land which is choice above all other lands' (Ether 2:10). This nation is part of the land of Zion. This is a land dedicated by God's servants. When a Book of Mormon prophet referred to the nations of the world, this hemisphere was designated as 'good' (Jacob 5:25–26)" (*The Teachings of Ezra Taft Benson* [1988], 123).

Ether 1:43. "This Long Time Ye Have Cried unto Me"

• The Lord explained to the brother of Jared that blessings had come to his people as a result of prayers offered over a long time. Enduring obedience coupled with frequent and persistent prayers is powerful. In an 1839 discourse in Commerce, Illinois, the Prophet Joseph Smith taught: "God is not a respecter of persons, we all have the same privilege. Come to God weary him until he blesses you &c we are entitled to the same blessings" ([recorded in Willard Richards Pocket Companion, 78–79] cited in *The Words of Joseph Smith: The Contemporary Accounts of the Nauvoo Discourses of the Prophet Joseph,* comp. Andrew F. Ehat and Lyndon W. Cook [1980], 15).

• President Spencer W. Kimball (1895–1985) similarly taught that we must put great effort into our prayers and that we must pray frequently:

"Do you get answers to your prayers? If not, perhaps you did not pay the price. Do you offer a few trite words and worn-out phrases, or do you talk intimately to the Lord? Do you pray occasionally when you should be praying regularly, often, constantly? Do you offer pennies to pay heavy debts when you should give dollars to erase that obligation?

"When you pray, do you just speak, or do you also listen? Your Savior said, 'Behold, I stand at the door, and knock: if any man hear my voice, and open the door, I will come in to him, and will sup with him, and he with me.' (Rev. 3:20.)

". . . Should we ever fail to get an answer to our prayers, we must look into our lives for a reason" ("Prayer," *New Era,* Mar. 1978, 17).

Ether 2:7–12. "A Land of Promise"

• Ether 2:8–11 states what Moroni called "the everlasting decree of God" (v. 10) concerning this land of promise. Stated three or four times, this decree is that "whatsoever nation shall possess [this land] shall serve God, or they shall be swept off" (v. 9).

President Gordon B. Hinckley (1910–2008) taught that obedience is essential if the promised land is to keep its promised blessings: "Great are the promises concerning this land of America. We are told unequivocally that it 'is a choice land, and whatsoever nation shall possess it shall be free from bondage, and from captivity, and from all other nations under heaven, if they will but serve the God of the land, who is Jesus Christ' (Ether 2:12). This is the crux of the entire matter—obedience to the commandments of God" (in Conference Report, Oct. 2001, 89; or *Ensign,* Nov. 2001, 73).

Ether 2:14. The Lord Chastened the Brother of Jared

• In modern revelation the Lord taught, "Whom I love I also chasten that their sins may be forgiven, for with the chastisement I prepare a way for their deliverance in all things out of temptation, and I have loved you" (D&C 95:1). Elder Jeffrey R. Holland of the Quorum of the Twelve Apostles commented on the strength of character it takes to endure chastening: "It is difficult to imagine what a three-hour rebuke from the Lord might be like, but the brother of Jared endured it. With immediate repentance and prayer, this prophet again sought guidance for the journey they had been assigned and those who were to pursue it. God accepted his repentance and lovingly gave further direction for their crucial mission" (*Christ and the New Covenant* [1997], 15).

• Elder Neal A. Maxwell (1926–2004) of the Quorum of the Twelve Apostles explained that God loves those whom He chastens: "The Lord is truly there to chastise those whom He loves, including the spiritually preeminent. The Brother of Jared for too long had failed to pray (see Ether 2:14). Even the good can become careless without the Lord's being there to chasten. Later, the chastened Brother of Jared saw Christ! (see Ether 3:13–16)" (in Conference Report, Oct. 1987, 37; or *Ensign,* Nov. 1987, 31).

Ether 2:19–3:6. Obtaining Light Was a Growing Experience

• Elder Robert D. Hales of the Quorum of the Twelve Apostles compared the experience of the brother of Jared to our own experiences:

"These vessels had no light. This concerned the brother of Jared. He did not want his family to make their journey in darkness; and so, rather than waiting to be commanded, he took his concern to the Lord. 'And the Lord said unto the brother of Jared: What will ye that I should do that ye may have light in your vessels?' [Ether 2:23].

"The brother of Jared's answer to this question required diligent effort on his part. He climbed Mount Shelem 'and did molten out of a rock sixteen small stones' [Ether 3:1]. He then asked the Lord to touch those stones so that they would bring forth light.

Robert Barrett, © 1986 IRI

"As parents and leaders, we must remember that 'it is not meet that [the Lord] should command in all things' [D&C 58:26]. Like the brother of Jared, we must

carefully consider the needs of our family members, make a plan to meet those needs, and then take our plan to the Lord in prayer. This will require faith and effort on our part, but He will help us as we seek His assistance and do His will" (in Conference Report, Apr. 2003, 15; or *Ensign,* May 2003, 16).

• The Lord wants us to grow and learn as we make our own decisions. He also wants us to take our conclusions to Him frequently for His confirmation. When the brother of Jared asked the Lord about the matter of light for the vessels, the Lord answered with a question of His own: "What will ye that I should do that ye may have light in your vessels?" (Ether 2:23). According to President Harold B. Lee (1899–1973), the Lord's question was similar to saying the following:

"'Well, have you any good ideas? What would you suggest that we should do in order to have light?' . . .

"Then the Lord went away and left him alone. It was as though the Lord were saying to him, 'Look, I gave you a mind to think with, and I gave you agency to use it. Now you do all you can to help yourself with this problem; and then, after you've done all you can, I'll step in to help you.'"

After considering the possibilities, the brother of Jared demonstrated his great faith by asking the Lord to touch 16 stones and supply light. The Lord answered this plea and not only provided light for the vessels but gave this faithful man a vision unlike any other.

President Lee concluded: "This is the principle in action. If you want the blessing, don't just kneel down and pray about it. Prepare yourselves in every conceivable way you can in order to make yourselves worthy to receive the blessing you seek" (*Stand Ye in Holy Places* [1974], 243–44).

Ether 2:22–23. Prayer Requires Effort

• It has often been said that we should pray as if everything depends on the Lord and work as if everything depends on us. Elder Russell M. Nelson of the Quorum of the Twelve Apostles said that he has often heard President Gordon B. Hinckley say, "I don't know how to get anything done except getting on my knees and pleading for help and then getting on my feet and going to work" (in Conference Report, Oct. 1997, 18; or *Ensign,* Nov. 1997, 16).

• Elder Bruce R. McConkie (1915–85) of the Quorum of the Twelve Apostles explained that the Lord requires us to use our agency as we seek His help. Regarding the brother of Jared's experience, Elder McConkie said: "The Lord talked to him about it a little and then he said this: 'What will ye that I should do that ye may have light in your vessels?' (Ether 2:23.) In effect, 'What are you asking me for? This is something you should have solved.' And he talked a little more, and he repeated in essence the question: 'What will ye that I should prepare for you that ye may have light when ye are swallowed up in the depths of the sea?' (Ether 2:25.) In other words, 'Moriancumer, this is your problem. Why are you troubling me? I've given you your agency; you are endowed with capacity and ability. Get out and solve the problem'" ("Agency or Inspiration?" *New Era,* Jan. 1975, 40–41).

Ether 3:1–5. "Behold, O Lord, Thou Canst Do This"

• Elder Jeffrey R. Holland spoke about the childlike, simple faith that the brother of Jared showed when he said, "Behold, O Lord, thou canst do this" (Ether 3:5): "Surely God, as well as the reader, feels something very striking in the childlike innocence and fervor of this man's faith. '*Behold, O Lord, thou canst do this.*' Perhaps there is no more powerful, single line of faith spoken by man in scripture. It is almost as if he is encouraging God, emboldening him, reassuring him. Not 'Behold, O Lord, I am sure that thou canst do this.' Not 'Behold, O Lord, thou hast done many greater things than this.' However uncertain the prophet is about his own ability, he has *no* uncertainty about God's power. There is nothing here but a single, clear, bold, and assertive declaration with no hint or element of vacillation. It is encouragement to Him who needs no encouragement but who surely must have been touched by it. 'Behold, O Lord, thou canst do this'" ("Rending the Veil of Unbelief," in *Nurturing Faith through the Book of Mormon: The 24th Annual Sidney B. Sperry Symposium* [1995], 12).

> ### ETHER 3:6–16
> *Examine these verses and determine what the brother of Jared learned about the Savior from his vision. List in your notes what you learn.*

Ether 3:15. "Never Have I Showed Myself unto Man"

• Elder Jeffrey R. Holland discussed six possible explanations for Jesus's statement that He had never shown Himself to man prior to showing Himself to the brother of Jared:

"One possibility is that this is simply a comment made in the context of one dispensation and as such applies only to the people of Jared and Jaredite prophets—that Jehovah had never before revealed himself to one of their seers and revelators. . . .

"Another suggestion is that the reference to 'man' is the key to this passage, suggesting that the Lord had never revealed himself to the unsanctified, to the nonbeliever, to temporal, earthy, natural man. The implication is that only those who have put off the natural man [and are] sanctified (such as Adam, Enoch, and now the brother of Jared)—are entitled to this privilege [see D&C 67:10–11].

"Some believe that the Lord meant he had never before revealed himself to man in that degree or to that extent. This theory suggests that divine appearances to earlier prophets had not been with the same 'fulness,' that never before had the veil been lifted to give such a complete revelation of Christ's nature and being.

Robert Barrett, © 1986 IRI

"A further possibility is that this is the first time Jehovah had appeared and identified himself as Jesus Christ, the Son of God, with the interpretation of the passage being 'never have I showed myself [as Jesus Christ] unto man whom I have created.' That possibility is reinforced by one way of reading Moroni's later editorial comment: 'Having this perfect knowledge of God, he could not be kept from within the veil; therefore he saw *Jesus*.'

"Yet another interpretation of this passage is that the faith of the brother of Jared was so great he saw not only the *spirit* finger and body of the premortal Jesus (which presumably many other prophets had also seen) but also some distinctly more revealing aspect of Christ's body of flesh, blood, and bone. . . .

"A final explanation—and in terms of the brother of Jared's faith the most persuasive one—is that Christ was saying to the brother of Jared, 'Never have I showed myself unto man *in this manner, without my volition, driven solely by the faith of the beholder*.' As a rule, prophets are *invited* into the presence of the Lord, are bidden to enter his presence by him and only with his sanction. The brother of Jared, on the other hand, seems to have thrust himself through the veil, not as an unwelcome guest but perhaps technically as an uninvited one. Said Jehovah, 'Never has man come before me with such exceeding faith as thou hast; for were it not so ye could not have seen my finger. . . . Never has man believed in me as thou hast.' Obviously the Lord himself was linking unprecedented faith with this unprecedented vision. If the vision itself was not unique, then it had to be the faith and how the vision was obtained that was so unparalleled. The only way that faith could be so remarkable was its ability to take the prophet, uninvited, where others had been able to go only with God's bidding" (*Christ and the New Covenant*, 21–23).

Ether 3:23–24, 28. Two Stones of King Mosiah

• The Prophet Joseph Smith used the same Urim and Thummim that was "given to the brother of Jared upon the mount, when he talked with the Lord face to face" (D&C 17:1). President Joseph Fielding Smith wrote a brief history regarding the Urim and Thummim:

"King Mosiah possessed 'two stones which were fastened into the two rims of a bow,' called by the Nephites *Interpreters,* with which he translated the Jaredite record [Mosiah 28:11–14], and these were handed down from generation to generation *for the purposes of interpreting languages.* How Mosiah came into possession of these *two stones* or Urim and

Thummim the record does not tell us, more than to say that it was a 'gift from God' [Mosiah 21:28]. Mosiah had this *gift* or Urim and Thummim *before* the people of Limhi discovered the record of Ether. They may have been received when the 'large stone' was brought to Mosiah with engravings upon it, which he interpreted by the 'gift and power of God' [Omni 1:20–21]. They may have been given to him, or to some other prophet before his day, just as the Brother of Jared received them—from the Lord.

"That the Urim and Thummim, or two stones, given to the Brother of Jared were those in the possession of Mosiah appears evident from Book of Mormon teachings. The Brother of Jared was commanded to seal up his writings of the vision he had when Christ appeared to him, so that they could not be read by his people. . . . The Urim and Thummim were also sealed up so that they could not be used for the purpose of interpreting those sacred writings of this vision, until such time as the Lord should grant to man to interpret them. When they were to be revealed, they were to be interpreted by the aid of the *same* Urim and Thummim [Ether 3:21–28]. . . .

"Joseph Smith received with the *breastplate* and the plates of the Book of Mormon, the Urim and Thummim, which were hid up by Moroni to come forth in the last days as a means by which the ancient record might be translated, which Urim and Thummim were given to the Brother of Jared [D&C 17:1]" (*Doctrines of Salvation,* 3:223–25).

Ether 3:25; 4:1–7. The Sealed Portion of the Book of Mormon

• Moroni wrote that the brother of Jared (Moriancumer) recorded in his vision all the inhabitants of the earth from beginning to end (see Ether 3:25; see also Ether 2:13). This vision reveals "all things from the foundation of the world unto the end thereof" (2 Nephi 27:10). Moroni explained that "there never were greater things made manifest" than what the

brother of Jared saw (Ether 4:4). We know that Moroni sealed a copy of this vision with the plates he delivered to Joseph Smith (see Ether 4:5; 5:1). Moroni further informed us of the conditions the Lord indicated must exist for this sealed portion of the record to come forth. The scriptures indicate we must repent; exercise faith in the Lord, like the brother of Jared did; and become sanctified (see Ether 4:6–7).

Ether 5. Directions to the Prophet Joseph Smith

• Moroni held "the keys of the record of the stick of Ephraim" (D&C 27:5). In Ether 5, Moroni addressed the future translator of the Book of Mormon, even though nearly 14 centuries would elapse before the Prophet Joseph Smith would read his words.

Ether 5. Testimony of the Witnesses

• Ether 5:2 refers to those "that ye [Joseph Smith] may show the plates unto," specifically the Eight Witnesses. Verses 3–4 refer to "three" who would see the plates "by the power of God," which is a specific reference to the Three Witnesses of the Book of Mormon. Verse 4 also states that the word "shall stand as a testimony," showing that the Book of Mormon itself is a witness. This same verse also shows that the Godhead are witnesses of the Book of Mormon.

Ether 5:2–4 specifically refers to the Three Witnesses of the Book of Mormon. In June of 1829 the Prophet Joseph Smith received a revelation "that three special witnesses would be designated. See Ether 5:2–4; also 2 Nephi 11:3 and 27:12. Oliver Cowdery, David Whitmer, and Martin Harris were moved upon by an inspired desire to be the three special witnesses" (D&C 17 section heading). We have the testimony of the Three Witnesses in the introductory pages of the Book of Mormon. Of these Three Witnesses, Elder Dallin H. Oaks of the Quorum of the Twelve Apostles stated:

"The solemn written testimony of three witnesses to what they saw and heard—two of them simultaneously and the third almost immediately thereafter—is entitled to great weight. Indeed, we know that upon the testimony of one witness great miracles have been claimed and accepted by many religious people, and in the secular world the testimony of one witness has been deemed sufficient for weighty penalties and judgments.

"Persons experienced in evaluating testimony commonly consider a witness's opportunity to observe an event and the possibility of his bias on the subject. Where different witnesses give identical testimony about the same event, skeptics look for evidence of collusion among them or for other witnesses who could contradict them.

"Measured against all of these possible objections, the testimony of the Three Witnesses to the Book of Mormon stands forth in great strength. Each of the three had ample reason and opportunity to renounce his testimony if it had been false or to equivocate on details if any had been inaccurate. As is well known, because of disagreements or jealousies involving other leaders of the Church, each one of these three witnesses was excommunicated from The Church of Jesus Christ of Latter-day Saints by about eight years after the publication of their testimony. All three went their separate ways, with no common interest to support a collusive effort. Yet to the end of their lives—periods ranging from 12 to 50 years after their excommunications—not one of these witnesses deviated from his published testimony or said anything that cast any shadow on its truthfulness.

"Furthermore, their testimony stands uncontradicted by any other witnesses. Reject it one may, but how does one explain three men of good character uniting and persisting in this published testimony to the end of their lives in the face of great ridicule and other personal disadvantage? Like the Book of Mormon itself, there is no better explanation than is given in the testimony itself, the solemn statement of good and honest men who told what they saw. . . .

". . . Witnesses are important, and the testimony of the Three Witnesses to the Book of Mormon is impressive and reliable" (in Conference Report, Apr. 1999, 46, 49; or *Ensign,* May 1999, 35–37).

ETHER 5

What does this chapter teach about the law of witnesses and the Three Witnesses to the Book of Mormon?

Points to Ponder

- Why do you think Moroni included the abridgment of Ether in the Book of Mormon for us to read?

- Even though the brother of Jared was and is renowned for his faithfulness, why was he still chastised by the Lord? How can we apply this to our lives?

- What lessons did the brother of Jared learn regarding what the Lord expects of us when we ask Him questions?

- How can the testimonies of the Three Witnesses to the Book of Mormon strengthen your own witness?

Suggested Assignments

- Think about a problem you currently struggle with. Using the pattern the brother of Jared used to solve his dilemma, apply the same principles as you work out your own situation. How will you apply these principles to solve your problem?

- Reflect on the strength of your prayers by rating your answers to the following questions. (*Caution:* This scale is personal and should be treated confidentially.)

How Are Your Prayers?	
On a scale of 1–10, how do you rate your personal prayers? (1 being the lowest, and 10 being the highest):	
Are they sincere enough?	1 2 3 4 5 6 7 8 9 10
Are they long enough?	1 2 3 4 5 6 7 8 9 10
Are they frequent enough?	1 2 3 4 5 6 7 8 9 10
Are they supported by obedience?	1 2 3 4 5 6 7 8 9 10
Do I listen for answers after I finish speaking?	1 2 3 4 5 6 7 8 9 10
Do I commune with the Lord instead of just talking to Him?	1 2 3 4 5 6 7 8 9 10

Introduction

In Ether 6–10, Moroni told of the Jaredites' journey across the ocean to the promised land. He then summarized the reigns of several generations of kings, contrasting periods of righteousness with periods of wickedness and conflict. Moroni observed many similarities between the Jaredites and his own people, the Nephites. He described the cycle of pride, prosperity, wickedness, and repentance that he had seen in the two nations. He outlined the grave danger we put ourselves in when we allow pride and secret combinations to get control in our society. Both the Nephite and the Jaredite civilizations illustrate the truth that what we sow, we shall reap. Following the Lord brings happiness, while straying from His commandments brings strife and misery.

Commentary

Ether 6:3. "Give Light unto Men, Women, and Children"

• The Lord Jesus Christ is the source of light for our world and for our lives (see D&C 88:5–13). The Lord touched the stones the brother of Jared presented to Him "to give light unto men, women, and children" (Ether 6:3) as they crossed the ocean. The Lord also provides light to guide us through the darkness of mortality and toward the brightness of the celestial kingdom—our promised land. Our way is lit by the light of apostles and prophets, the standard works, and inspired leaders and teachers. We too can be a light—we can light the way for others when we hearken to the Lord's counsel and keep ourselves worthy of His Spirit.

Sister Ardeth G. Kapp, former Young Women general president, counseled: "You have the light within. You can shine in darkness. You can light up the world. You can help dispel the darkness. You can make a difference" (*The Joy of the Journey* [1992], 69).

Ether 6:4–9. The Jaredites Commended Themselves to the Lord

• In the context of Ether 6:4–9 the word *commend* means to entrust their care to. In other words, the Jaredites entrusted their care to God. By commending themselves to the Lord, they demonstrated their faith

Robert Barrett, © 1986 IRI

that He could and would deliver them. "The wind did never cease to blow towards the promised land while they were upon the waters" (Ether 6:8). Contrast this attitude with the attitude of Nephi's brothers as they crossed the sea with their family. When Laman and Lemuel bound Nephi, the family's compass, the Liahona, ceased to work and their boat was "driven back upon the waters for the space of four days" (1 Nephi 18:15). Both the Jaredites and Lehi's family sought to commend themselves to the Lord's care; however, some members of Lehi's family were disobedient. The contrast between these two accounts shows that we must exercise faith and keep the commandments to receive all the blessings the Lord would give us through His care.

ETHER 6:8–12

What exemplary behavior did the Jaredites show during their voyage and after their arrival that inspires your behavior?

Ether 6:9. "Sing Praises unto the Lord"

• What are the blessings of listening to and singing songs of praise? In modern revelation the Lord stated that He will bless those who delight in righteous music (see D&C 25:12 ). The First Presidency described the power of inspirational music:

"Hymns invite the Spirit of the Lord, create a feeling of reverence, unify us as members, and provide a way for us to offer praises to the Lord.

". . . Hymns move us to repentance and good works, build testimony and faith, comfort the weary, console the mourning, and inspire us to endure to the end. . . .

". . . Hymns can lift our spirits, give us courage, and move us to righteous action. They can fill our souls with heavenly thoughts and bring us a spirit of peace" (*Hymns,* ix–x).

Ether 6:12. Tender Mercies

• For additional information on the tender mercies of God, see commentary for 1 Nephi 1:20 (p. 13) and for Moroni 10:3 (p. 401).

Ether 6:17. "They Were Taught to Walk Humbly before the Lord"

• We learn that the Jaredites were taught the importance of humility. Modern revelation also teaches us the importance of humility: "Be thou humble; and the Lord thy God shall lead thee by the hand, and give thee answer to thy prayers" (D&C 112:10).

Elder Joseph B. Wirthlin (1917–2008) of the Quorum of the Twelve Apostles explained that "humility is the recognition and attitude that one must rely on the Lord's assistance to make it through this life" (in Conference Report, Oct. 2004, 110; or *Ensign,* Nov. 2004, 104).

• Bishop Richard C. Edgley of the Presiding Bishopric named humility as one of the basic characteristics of a faithful Church member:

"As I have pondered these faithful members, I am struck by two qualities they all seem to have. First, regardless of social or economic status or position, their humility leads to submissiveness to the Lord's will. And second, in spite of the difficulties and trials of life, they are able to maintain a sense of gratitude for God's blessings and life's goodness. Humility and gratitude are truly the twin characteristics of happiness. . . .

". . . In the kingdom of God, greatness begins with humility and submissiveness. These companion virtues are the first critical steps to opening the doors to the blessings of God and the power of the priesthood. It matters not who we are or how lofty our credentials appear. Humility and submissiveness to the Lord, coupled with a grateful heart, are our strength and our hope" (in Conference Report, Oct. 2003, 103–4; or *Ensign,* Nov. 2003, 98).

ETHER 6:17

What is the relationship between humility and receiving instruction and counsel from the Lord?

Ether 6:17. "Taught from on High"

• To be "taught from on high" one must keep the commandments and be worthy of the companionship and inspiration of the Holy Ghost. Elder Richard G. Scott of the Quorum of the Twelve Apostles explained the blessings of being taught by the Spirit: "When all the challenges pour down on you, you will have a quiet inner feeling of support. You will be prompted to know what to do. You can live in a world of turmoil and great challenge and be at peace. You will be inspired to *know* what to do and to have the power or capacity to do it. Remember this promise of the Lord . . . : 'Ye are to be taught from on high. Sanctify yourselves [that is, keep my commandments] and ye shall be endowed with power' (D&C 43:16)" (in Conference Report, Apr. 1991, 44; or *Ensign,* May 1991, 35).

Ether 7. Strife Entered the Kingdom

• The brother of Jared warned his people that having a king would lead them into captivity (see Ether 6:22–23), and it did. The Jaredite king Kib and later his son Shule were both taken captive by rivals. Notice how quickly the brother of Jared's prophecy was fulfilled.

A great deal of the Jaredites' history is covered in chapter 7 of the book of Ether. Moroni recorded only highlights of this history in his abridgement. He emphasized the parallels with his own people and the lessons that would be most valuable for our day.

Ether 7:6. Geographical Insight from Moroni

• Moroni gave very little information regarding the geographic relationship between the Jaredite and Nephite lands. "However, he does indicate that the 'land of Moron' of the Jaredites 'was near the land which is called Desolation by the Nephites.' (Ether 7:6.) Inasmuch as the land of Moron was the capital land of the Jaredites and the Nephite land of Desolation was north of the narrow neck of land, it is assumed that the major portion of the Jaredite civilization lived north of the narrow neck of land" (Daniel H. Ludlow, *A Companion to Your Study of the Book of Mormon* [1976], 321–22).

Ether 7:23–27. King Shule's People Heeded the Prophets' Warnings

• In His kindness and mercy, the Lord sent prophets to warn the people of Shule's kingdom. At first they reviled and mocked the prophets; however, the prophets were protected by the righteous king's proclamation. Shule's people then heeded the prophets' warnings and repented, thus avoiding the destruction that would have come as a result of their rejection of the prophets' message.

President Henry B. Eyring of the First Presidency explained why the Lord warns His children of their wickedness: "Because the Lord is kind, He calls servants to warn people of danger. That call to warn is made harder and more important by the fact that the warnings of most worth are about dangers that people don't yet think are real" (in Conference Report, Oct. 1998, 40; or *Ensign,* Nov. 1998, 32).

Ether 7:23–27; 9:28–31. Prophets and Their Messages Are Frequently Rejected

• Why do prophets often get mocked and reviled? Elder Robert D. Hales of the Quorum of the Twelve Apostles explained:

"Prophets must often warn of the consequences of violating God's laws. They do not preach that which is popular with the world. . . .

"Why do prophets proclaim unpopular commandments and call society to repentance for rejecting, modifying, and even ignoring the commandments? The reason is very simple. Upon receiving revelation, prophets have no choice but to proclaim and reaffirm that which God has given them to tell the world" (in Conference Report, Apr. 1996, 52; or *Ensign,* May 1996, 37).

• Elder L. Aldin Porter of the Presidency of the Seventy explained another reason people often reject the prophet's counsel. He explained that people erroneously believe that prophetic warnings interfere with their agency: "Some complain that when the prophets speak with clarity and firmness, they are taking our agency away. We are still free to choose. But we must accept the consequences of those decisions. The prophets do not take away our agency. They simply warn us of what the consequences of our choices will be. How foolish it is to fault the prophets for their warnings" (in Conference Report, Oct. 1999, 82; or *Ensign,* Nov. 1999, 66).

Ether 8:1–12. Secret Combinations among the Jaredites

• Moroni paused in his rapid summary of Jaredite history to recount in great detail the instituting of secret combinations among these people. Moroni did so because these organizations caused the entire downfall of both the Jaredite and the Nephite societies (see Ether 8:21); unless we repent, secret combinations will cause the downfall of society in our own time (see vv. 23–25).

Ether 8:9 indicates that the Jaredites learned about secret combinations from records that their fathers had brought with them from the old world. It is possible that these records contained an account of the earliest secret combinations (see Moses 5:29–33, 47–55). We know that the Jaredites had records of the "creation of the world, and also of Adam, and an account from that time even to the great tower" (Ether 1:3).

The plan by which Jared's daughter proposed to help secure the kingdom for her father indicates how evil persons can take advantage of human weakness. Jared's daughter was well aware of her personal beauty, as well as Akish's desire for her. In her anxiety to help her father get power and gain, she was willing to participate in an evil plot.

Ether 8:18–25. Characteristics of Secret Combinations

• See commentary for Helaman 6:18–40 (p. 271).

> ### ETHER 8:22–26
> *What warning did Moroni issue to the people of our day, and what are the consequences of heeding or ignoring that warning?*

Ether 8:25. Satan Deceives and Is "the Father of All Lies"

• Whereas the Lord is "a God of truth, and canst not lie" (Ether 3:12), Satan "was a liar from the beginning" (D&C 93:25). The Lord revealed to Moses that "Satan, yea, even the devil, [is] the father of all lies, to deceive and to blind men, and to lead them captive at his will, even as many as would not hearken unto my voice" (Moses 4:4).

Elder Dallin H. Oaks of the Quorum of the Twelve Apostles explained that Satan "and the spirits who follow him are still deceiving the world. . . . Satan's methods of deception are enticing: music, movies and other media, and the glitter of a good time.

When Satan's lies succeed in deceiving us, we become vulnerable to his power" (in Conference Report, Oct. 2004, 46; or *Ensign,* Nov. 2004, 43).

Ether 8:26. Satan's Power Can Be Thwarted by Righteousness

• In speaking of the Millennium, Nephi explained that "because of the righteousness of [God's] people, Satan has no power; . . . for they dwell in righteousness, and the Holy One of Israel reigneth" (1 Nephi 22:26). Moroni stated that one purpose of revealing Satan's tactics is to do away with evil while looking forward to the time to come when "Satan may have no power upon the  hearts of the children of men, but that they may be persuaded to do good continually" (Ether 8:26).

The Prophet Joseph Smith (1805–44) declared: "The devil has no power over us only as we permit him; the moment we revolt at anything which comes from God, the devil takes power" (*Teachings of Presidents of the Church: Joseph Smith* [2007], 214).

Ether 9. Cycles of Great Prosperity and Tragic Wickedness

• Notice in Ether 9:5–12 that the rise of secret combinations again led to the destruction of many people. Verses 15–35 show a pattern that is repeated many times throughout the Book of Mormon:

1. The people prospered exceedingly during the righteous reigns of Emer and Coriantum (see vv. 15–25).

2. The people began to join together in secret combinations and turn to wickedness under the reign of Heth (see vv. 26–27.)

3. The Lord sent prophets to warn the people of their great wickedness (see v. 28).

4. The people of Heth rejected the prophets (see v. 29).

5. The judgments of God fell upon the people (see vv. 30–33).

6. The people humbled themselves and repented, and the Lord again blessed them (see vv. 34–35).

In the midst of these cycles of prosperity and wickedness, the Jaredites demonstrated that a people can be wealthy and remain righteous. It seems that the Jaredites were able to remain in a condition of righteousness and prosperity for over 100 years (see vv. 15–25). King Emer was even righteous enough to see the Lord (see v. 22). For a diagram depicting the pride cycle, refer to "The Cycle of Righteousness and Wickedness" in the appendix (p. 414).

Ether 9:19. Jaredite Animals

• One scholar wrote about the mention of elephants among the Jaredites and the absence of any later mention of elephants among the Nephites:

"I think it quite significant that the Book of Mormon associates elephants only with the Jaredites, since there is no apparent reason why they should not have been as common in the fifth as in the fifteenth century B.C. All we know is that they became extinct in large parts of Asia somewhere between those dates, as they did likewise in the New World, to follow the Book of Mormon, leaving only the written records of men to testify of their existence."

In this same discussion on elephants, he illustrated a point taken from Marco Polo's description of his travels. In this description Marco Polo wrote about named elements unfamiliar to his native country. Hugh Nibley then applied the general principles of Polo's experience to Book of Mormon animals named in the Book of Mormon but unknown to our culture: "'They have plenty of iron, *accarum, and andanicum,*' says Marco Polo of the people of Kobian. 'Here they make mirrors of highly polished steel, of large size and very handsome.' The thing to note here is not primarily the advanced state of steelworking in Central Asia, though that as we have seen is significant, but the fact that no one knows for sure what *accarum and andanicum* are. Marco knew, of course, but since the things didn't exist in Europe there was no western word for them and so all he could do was to call them by their only names. It is just so with the *cureloms and cumoms* of Ether 9:19. These animals were unknown to the Nephites, and so Moroni leaves the words untranslated,

or else though known to the Nephites, they are out of our experience so that *our* language has no name to call them by. They were simply breeds of those 'many other kinds of animals which were useful for the food of man'" (Hugh W. Nibley, *Lehi in the Desert and the World of the Jaredites* [1952], 217–18).

Ether 10:5–8. Wickedness and Oppression of King Riplakish

• Ether 10:5–7 describes the reign of King Riplakish. His wicked reign and his fall were very similar to the reign and the fall of the wicked King Noah (see Mosiah 11). Note the following characteristics of both kings:

Riplakish (Ether 10)	Characteristics	Noah (Mosiah 11)
Verse 5	Very immoral	Verse 2
Verse 5	Taxed the people heavily	Verse 3
Verse 6	Built spacious and elaborate buildings	Verse 8
Verse 7	Glutted himself on the work of others	Verse 6
Verse 8	Was killed by his own people	Mosiah 19:20

Isaiah warned, "For the leaders of this people cause them to err" (Isaiah 9:16; 2 Nephi 19:16). The righteous King Mosiah later commanded his people not to have kings because "the sins of many people have been caused by the iniquities of their kings" (Mosiah 29:31).

Ether 10:9–34. A High Level of Civilization

• Although the record is limited, Ether 10 provides insights about the high level of civilization enjoyed by the Jaredites under King Lib. Moroni told us the following about their level of prosperity:

1. "They were exceedingly industrious, and they did buy and sell and traffic one with another, that they might get gain" (v. 22).

2. "They did work in all manner of ore, and they did make gold, and silver, and iron, and brass, and all manner of metals. . . . And they did work all manner of fine work" (v. 23).

3. They had "silks, and fine-twined linen; and they did work all manner of cloth" (v. 24).

4. "They did make all manner of tools to till the earth, both to plow and to sow, to reap and to hoe, and also to thrash" (v. 25).

5. "They did make all manner of tools with which they did work their beasts" (v. 26).

6. "They did make all manner of weapons of war. And they did work all manner of work of exceedingly curious workmanship" (v. 27).

Moroni concluded by telling us, "And never could be a people more blessed than were they" (v. 28).

Points to Ponder

• What does it mean to commend your life to the Lord as the Jaredites did on their journey to the promised land?

• What tender mercies of the Lord can you identify in your life? (see Ether 6:12).

• What safeguards are available to help you avoid being deceived by Satan?

Suggested Assignments

• Compare the journey described in Ether 6:2–12 to our journey through mortality.

• Find verses in Ether 8:13–26 that describe the dangers of secret combinations, and summarize those dangers. Then summarize the counsel Moroni gave us in those same verses.

Introduction

The book of Ether's account of the tragic destruction of a once-great nation helps us see the inevitable consequences of rejecting the prophets and the devastating results of unrestrained sin. In contrast, we also read some profound instruction on faith in Jesus Christ. The combined teachings of the prophets Ether and Moroni demonstrate that faith leads to repentance, brings about miracles, and turns personal weakness into strength. Sadly, the Jaredites refused to heed Ether's teachings and turned away from the truth that could have saved them. As you read Ether, chapters 11–15, ask yourself the question "What lessons are there in these chapters for me and the generation I live in?"

Commentary

Ether 11. The Final Stages of Jaredite Civilization

• As with the Nephites, the Jaredite society repeatedly moved through the cycle of prosperity, apostasy, judgment, repentance, prosperity, and so on. Eventually, as with the Nephites, the depths of apostasy and wickedness became increasingly fatal. (See diagram "The Cycle of Righteousness and Wickedness" in the appendix, p. 414.) Ether 11 recounts the final stages of the Jaredite cycle of apostasy. They rejected, mocked, and reviled the prophets. Though King Shule had passed a law protecting the prophets and punishing those who persecuted them (see Ether 7:23–26), a later king made it policy to execute the prophets (see Ether 11:5). Finally, the wickedness became so rampant that the prophets "mourned and withdrew from among the people" (Ether 11:13). (See commentary for Helaman 12:5–6 on p. 278).

Ether 11:2–5, 13, 20–22. They Rejected the Words of the Prophets

• The prophet Amos taught that one role of a prophet is to warn people of impending destruction (see 2 Nephi 25:9; see also Ezekiel 33:7–10). Ether 11 clearly demonstrates the consequences of not heeding prophetic warnings. Consider what President Henry B. Eyring of the First Presidency said concerning the cost of rejecting prophetic counsel and the safety that comes from heeding prophets:

"Looking for the path to safety in the counsel of prophets makes sense to those with strong faith. When a prophet speaks, those with little faith may think that they hear only a wise man giving good advice. Then if his counsel seems comfortable and reasonable, squaring with what they want to do, they take it. If it does not, they consider it either faulty advice or they see their circumstances as justifying their being an exception to the counsel. Those without faith may think that they hear only men seeking to exert influence for some selfish motive. . . .

"Every time in my life when I have chosen to delay following inspired counsel or decided that I was an exception, I came to know that I had put myself in harm's way. Every time that I have listened to the counsel of prophets, felt it confirmed in prayer, and then followed it, I have found that I moved toward safety" (in Conference Report, Apr. 1997, 32–33; or *Ensign*, May 1997, 25).

Ether 11:7–8. Natural Disasters Can Lead to Repentance

• We read that as a result of the wars, famines, pestilences, and destructions, the people began to repent of their iniquity. President Joseph F. Smith (1838–1918) helped us understand that sometimes the Lord uses natural disasters to bring about repentance in the lives of His children:

"The Latter-day Saints, though they themselves tremble because of their own wickedness and sins, believe that great judgments are coming upon the world because of iniquity; they firmly believe in the statements of the Holy Scriptures, that calamities will befall the nations as signs of the coming of Christ to judgment. They believe that God rules in the fire, the earthquake, the tidal wave, the volcanic eruption, and the storm. Him they recognize as the Master and Ruler of nature and her laws, and freely acknowledge his hand in all things. We believe that his judgments are poured out to bring mankind to a sense of his power and his purposes, that they may repent of their sins and prepare themselves for the second coming of Christ to reign in righteousness upon the earth. . . .

"We believe that these severe, natural calamities are visited upon men by the Lord for the good of his children, to quicken their devotion to others, and to bring out their better natures, that they may love and serve him" (*Gospel Doctrine,* 5th ed. [1939], 55; for additional references to the Lord using the elements of nature to speak to people who refuse to repent, see Helaman 12:3; D&C 43:21–25; 88:88–91).

Ether 12:4. "An Anchor to the Souls of Men"

• President Gordon B. Hinckley (1910–2008) taught concerning the need to center our lives on Jesus Christ: "We live in a world of uncertainty. For some, there will be great accomplishment. For others, disappointment. For some, much of rejoicing and gladness, good health, and gracious living. For others, perhaps sickness and a measure of sorrow. We do not know. But one thing we do know. Like the polar star in the heavens, regardless of  what the future holds, there stands the Redeemer of the world, the Son of God, certain and sure as the anchor of our immortal lives. He is the rock of our salvation, our strength, our comfort, the very focus of our faith" (in Conference Report, Apr. 2002, 107; or *Ensign,* May 2002, 90).

ETHER 12:4

What relationship do you see between Ether 12:4; Mormon 5:18; and Helaman 5:12? When *has your faith been like an anchor to your soul?*

Ether 12:6. "The Trial of Your Faith"

• Trials of faith do not always come in the form of adversity. Elder Richard G. Scott of the Quorum of the Twelve Apostles taught that sometimes "the trial of

[our] faith" is simply a matter of exercising our faith: "You can learn to use faith more effectively by applying this principle taught by Moroni: 'Faith is things which are hoped for and not seen; wherefore, dispute not because ye see not, for ye receive no witness until after the *trial of your faith*' [Ether 12:6; italics added]. Thus, every time you *try your faith*—that is, act in worthiness on an impression—you will receive the confirming evidence of the Spirit. Those feelings will fortify your faith. As you repeat that pattern, your faith will become stronger" (in Conference Report, Apr. 2003, 79; or *Ensign,* May 2003, 76).

• Elder Jeffrey R. Holland of the Quorum of the Twelve Apostles wrote of the various levels of faith we experience and the prerequisites for the expression of them: "Preparatory faith is formed by experiences in the past—by the known, which provides a basis for belief. But redemptive faith must often be exercised toward experiences in the future—the unknown, which provides an opportunity for the miraculous. Exacting faith, mountain-moving faith, faith like that of the brother of Jared, *precedes* the miracle and the knowledge. He had to believe *before* God spoke. He had to act *before* the ability to complete that action was apparent. He had to commit to the complete experience in advance of even the first segment of its realization. Faith is to agree unconditionally—and in advance—to whatever conditions God may require in both the near and distant future" (*Christ and the New Covenant* [1997], 18–19).

• President Gordon B. Hinckley illustrated this principle of receiving our witness "after the trial" of faith:

"Let me give you a story of a woman in São Paulo, Brazil. She worked while going to school to provide for her family. I use her own words in telling this story. She says:

"'The university in which I studied had a regulation that prohibited the students that were in debt from taking tests. For this reason, when I received my salary I would first separate the money for tithing and offerings, and the remainder was allotted for the payment of the school and other expenses.

"'I remember a time when I . . . faced serious financial difficulties. It was a Thursday when I received my salary. When I figured the monthly budget, I noticed that there wouldn't be enough to pay [both] my tithing and my university. I would have to choose between them. The bimonthly tests would start the following week, and if I didn't take them I could lose the school year. I felt great agony. . . . My heart ached. I had a painful decision before me, and I didn't know what to decide. I pondered between the two choices: to pay tithing or to risk the possibility of not obtaining the necessary credits to be approved in school.

"'This feeling consumed my soul and remained with me up to Saturday. It was then that I remembered that when I was baptized I had agreed to live the law of tithing. I had taken upon myself an obligation, not with the missionaries, but with my Heavenly Father. At that moment, the anguish started to disappear, giving place to a pleasant sensation of tranquility and determination. . . .

"'That night when I prayed, I asked the Lord to forgive me for my indecision. On Sunday, before the beginning of sacrament meeting, I contacted the bishop, and with great pleasure I paid my tithing and offerings. That was a special day. I felt happy and peaceful within myself and with Heavenly Father.

"'The next day I was in my office; I tried to find a way to be able to take the tests that would begin on Wednesday. The more I thought, the further I felt from a solution. . . .

"'The working period was ending when my employer approached and gave the last orders of the day. When he had done so, with his briefcase in his hand he bid farewell. . . . Suddenly he halted, and looking at me he asked, "How is your college?" I was surprised, and I couldn't believe what I was hearing. The only thing I could answer with a trembling voice was, "Everything is all right!" He looked thoughtfully at me and bid farewell again. . . .

"'Suddenly the secretary entered the room, saying that I was a very fortunate person! When I asked her why, she simply answered: "The employer has just said that from today on the company is going to pay fully for your college and your books. Before you leave, stop at my desk and inform me of the costs so that tomorrow I can give you the check."

"'After she left, crying and feeling very humble, I knelt exactly where I was and thanked the Lord for His generosity. I . . . said to Heavenly Father that He didn't have to bless me so much. I only needed the cost of one month's installment, and the tithing I had paid on Sunday was very small compared to the amount I was receiving! During that prayer the words recorded in Malachi came to my mind: "Prove me now herewith, saith the Lord of hosts, if I will not open you the windows of heaven, and pour you out a blessing, that there shall not be room enough to receive it" (Malachi 3:10). Up to that moment I had never felt the magnitude of the promise contained in that scripture and that this commandment was truly a witness of the love that God, our Heavenly Father, gives to His children here on earth'" (in Conference Report, Apr. 2002, 85–86; or *Ensign,* May 2002, 73–74).

> ### ETHER 12:6 📖
> *How did Alma and Amulek, Nephi and Lehi (sons of Helaman), and Ammon and his brethren demonstrate the principle taught?*

Ether 12:8–22. Faith and Miracles

• Ether 12:8–22 is filled with examples of "wonders and marvels done by faith" (chapter summary for Ether 12). The *Lectures on Faith* explain that faith is the principle of power to do miracles:

"Faith is not only the principle of action, but of power also, in all intelligent beings, whether in heaven or on earth. . . .

". . . It was by faith that the worlds were framed. God spake, chaos heard, and worlds came into order by reason of the faith there was in Him. So with man also; he spake by faith in the name of God, and the sun stood still, the moon obeyed, mountains removed, prisons fell, lions' mouths were closed, the human heart lost its enmity, fire its violence, armies their power, the sword its terror, and death its dominion; and all this by reason of the faith which was in him" ([1985], 3, 5).

Ether 12:27. 📖 Weakness, Humility, and Grace

• Weakness comes to men and women through the Fall of Adam. The physical body and mind is susceptible to disease and decay. We are subject to temptation and struggle. Each of us experiences personal weaknesses. Nevertheless, the Lord clearly teaches that as we come unto Him in humility and faith, He will help us turn weakness into strength. His grace is sufficient to make this transformation by lifting us above our own natural abilities. In a very personal way, we experience how the power of the Atonement overcomes the effects of the Fall.

Elder Neal A. Maxwell (1926–2004) of the Quorum of the Twelve Apostles spoke of how the Lord can help us overcome our weaknesses. "When we read in the scriptures of man's 'weakness,' this term includes the generic but necessary weakness inherent in the general human condition in which the flesh has such an incessant impact upon the spirit (see Ether 12:28–29). Weakness likewise includes, however, our specific, individual weaknesses, which we are expected to overcome (see D&C 66:3; Jacob 4:7). Life has a way of exposing these weaknesses" (*Lord, Increase Our Faith* [1994], 84).

Furthermore, Elder Maxwell described how recognizing our weaknesses is one way that the Lord has chosen to increase our learning:

"When we are unduly impatient with an omniscient God's timing, we really are suggesting that we know what is best. Strange, isn't it—we who wear wristwatches seek to counsel Him who oversees cosmic clocks and calendars.

"Because God wants us to come home after having become more like Him and His Son, part of this developmental process, of necessity, consists of showing unto us our weaknesses. Hence, if we have ultimate hope we will be submissive because, with His

help, those weaknesses can even become strengths (see Ether 12:27).

"It is not an easy thing, however, to be shown one's weaknesses, as these are regularly demonstrated by life's circumstances. Nevertheless, this is part of coming unto Christ, and it is a vital, if painful, part of God's plan of happiness" (in Conference Report, Oct. 1998, 79; or *Ensign,* Nov. 1998, 63).

The scriptures testify that Jesus Christ can save us from our inadequacies as well as our sins:

1. "Most gladly therefore will I rather glory in my infirmities, that the power of Christ may rest upon me" (2 Corinthians 12:9).

2. "Let us therefore come boldly unto the throne of grace, that we may obtain mercy, and find grace to help in time of need" (Hebrews 4:16).

3. "The Lord God showeth us our weakness that we may know that it is by his grace . . . that we have power to do these things" (Jacob 4:7).

4. "I know that I am nothing; as to my strength I am weak; therefore I will not boast of myself, but I will boast of my God, for in his strength I can do all things" (Alma 26:12).

5. "If ye shall deny yourselves of all ungodliness, and love God with all your might, mind and strength, then is his grace sufficient for you, that by his grace ye may be perfect in Christ" (Moroni 10:32).

Moroni taught that not only must we exercise faith in the Lord, but we must humble ourselves as well.

The book *True to the Faith* explains the meaning of true humility: "To be humble is to recognize gratefully your dependence on the Lord— to understand that you have constant need for His support. Humility is an acknowledgement that your talents and abilities are gifts from God. It is not a sign of weakness, timidity, or fear; it is an indication that you know where your true strength lies" (*True to the Faith: A Gospel Reference* [2004], 86).

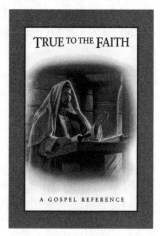

• In the Guide to the Scriptures we read that grace is "the enabling power from God that allows men and women to obtain blessings in this life and to gain eternal life and exaltation after they have exercised faith, repented, and given their best effort to keep the commandments. Such divine help or strength is given through the mercy and love of God" ("Grace").

• President Thomas S. Monson gave the following words of comfort: "Should there be anyone who feels he is too weak to change the onward and downward course of his life, or should there be those who fail to resolve to do better because of that greatest of fears, the fear of failure, there is no more comforting assurance to be had than the words of the Lord: 'My grace,' said He, 'is sufficient for all men that humble themselves before me; for if they humble themselves before me, and have faith in me, then will I make weak things become strong unto them'" (in Conference Report, Apr. 2000, 61–62; or *Ensign,* May 2000, 48).

ETHER 12:32

According to Ether 12:32; Moroni 7:40–41; and Doctrine and Covenants 138:14, what should our hope be centered in? How can you do this better?

Ether 12:33–37. This Love Is Charity

• The Savior showed the most perfect charity or sacrificial love when He gave His life and atoned for each of us. We must pray that we "may be filled with this love" so we can inherit eternal life (Moroni 7:48). Elder Marvin J. Ashton (1915–94) of the Quorum of the Twelve Apostles explained what it means to have charity:

"*Charity* is, perhaps, in many ways a misunderstood word. We often equate charity with visiting the sick, taking in casseroles to those in need, or sharing our excess with those who are less fortunate. But really, true charity is much, much more.

"Real charity is not something you give away; it is something that you acquire and make a part of

yourself. And when the virtue of charity becomes implanted in your heart, you are never the same again. It makes the thought of [putting others down] repulsive.

"Perhaps the greatest charity comes when we are kind to each other, when we don't judge or categorize someone else, when we simply give each other the benefit of the doubt or remain quiet. Charity is accepting someone's differences, weaknesses, and shortcomings; having patience with someone who has let us down; or resisting the impulse to become offended when someone doesn't handle something the way we might have hoped. Charity is refusing to take advantage of another's weakness and being willing to forgive someone who has hurt us. Charity is expecting the best of each other" (in Conference Report, Apr. 1992, 24; or *Ensign,* May 1992, 18–19).

Ether 12:41. Abide

• After spending a year in Chile, Elder Jeffrey R. Holland shared the following insight concerning the word *abide:* "'Abide in me' is an understandable and beautiful enough concept in the elegant English for the King James Bible, but *abide* is not a word we use much anymore. So I gained even more appreciation for this admonition from the Lord when I was introduced to the translation of this passage in another language. In Spanish that familiar phrase is rendered *permaneced en mi.* Like the English verb *abide, permanecer* means 'to remain, to stay,' but even [English-speakers] like me can hear the root cognate there of 'permanence.' The sense of this, then, is 'stay—but stay forever'" (in Conference Report, Apr. 2004, 32; or *Ensign,* May 2004, 32).

Ether 13:1–12. New Jerusalem

• Ether 13:1–12 describes what a great seer Ether was. Ether was shown many marvelous things by the Lord, including the establishment of a New Jerusalem prior to the Second Coming. Note what Ether said about the New Jerusalem:

1. It will be "the holy sanctuary of the Lord" (Ether 13:3).

2. It will be built on the American continent for the remnant of the seed of Joseph (see vv. 4–6).

3. It will be a holy city like the Jerusalem built unto the Lord (see vv. 8–9).

4. It will stand until the earth is celestialized (see v. 8).

5. It will be a city for the pure and righteous (see v. 10).

President Joseph Fielding Smith (1876–1972) wrote the following about the New Jerusalem:

"The prevailing notion in the world is that this [the New Jerusalem] is the city of Jerusalem, the ancient city of the Jews which in the day of regeneration will be renewed, but this is not the case. We read in the Book of Ether that the Lord revealed to him many of the same things which were seen by John. Ether, as members of the Church will know, was the last of the prophets among the Jaredites, and the Lord had revealed to him much concerning the history of the Jews and their city of Jerusalem which stood in the days of the ministry of our Savior. In his vision, in many respects similar to that given to John, Ether saw the old city of Jerusalem and also the new city which has not yet been built, and he wrote of them as follows as reported in the writings of Moroni:

"[Ether 13:2–11.] . . .

"In the day of regeneration, when all things are made new, there will be three great cities that will be holy. One will be the Jerusalem of old which shall be rebuilt according to the prophecy of Ezekiel. One will be the city of Zion, or of Enoch, which was taken from the earth when Enoch was translated and which will be restored; and the city Zion, or New Jerusalem, which is to be built by the seed of Joseph on this the American continent" (*Answers to Gospel Questions,* comp. Joseph Fielding Smith Jr., 5 vols. [1957–66], 2:103–4).

ETHER 13:1–12

What are the characteristics of the New Jerusalem listed in these verses? How can we better cultivate these same characteristics?

Ether 13:15–31. Coriantumr

• Coriantumr had devoted a great deal of time to studying "all the arts of war and all the cunning of the world" (Ether 13:16), yet he rejected the simple message of Ether, which would have brought him peace in a way that all his military skills could not.

Note the prophet Ether's promise to Coriantumr in Ether 13:20–21 as well as its fulfillment (see Ether 15:1–3, 26–32; Omni 1:20–22).

Robert Barret, © 1986 IRI

Ether 14–15. The Final Jaredite Battle

• Coriantumr and Shiz allowed all of their followers to be killed without ending the conflict. We cannot fully comprehend the horror of the final Jaredite battle in which even women and children were armed and sent to war (see Ether 15:15). This does, however, provide a graphic picture of what people become when the Spirit of the Lord withdraws and no longer strives with them (see v. 19).

Robert Barret, © 1986 IRI

Points to Ponder

- In what ways has the enabling power of the Atonement transformed your weaknesses into strengths?

- In what ways does the book of Ether serve as a warning to the nations of the earth today?

- Anger and hatred played a major role in the destruction of the Jaredites. What role do you see anger and hatred playing in the world today? How can you combat this in your own sphere of influence?

- How has your faith or spiritual resolve been tried? How did these trials of your faith bring you additional "witness" of Jesus Christ or understanding of eternal truths?

Suggested Activities

- Identify a personal shortcoming or deficiency that has come to you through mortal weakness. Using Ether 12:27 📖 as your guide, outline a strategy whereby it can be turned into a strength.

- Ponder the plea from Moroni that we "seek this Jesus of whom the prophets and apostles have written, that the grace of God the Father, and also the Lord Jesus Christ, and the Holy Ghost . . . may be and abide in you forever" (Ether 12:41). Write a short paper outlining what you can do to "seek Jesus" and to obtain "the grace of God the Father."

Introduction

After Moroni ended his abridgment of the Jaredite history (see Ether 13:1; 15:34), he presumed that he would not survive to write any additional records (see Moroni 1). However, he lived an additional 36 years after the final battle between the Lamanites and the Nephites (see Mormon 6:5; Moroni 10:1). During this time Moroni recorded additional sacred truths valuable to latter-day readers. These chapters are especially helpful for us because they contain guidelines concerning the proper administration of ordinances—especially the sacrament—and the place of the Holy Ghost in the daily administration of the Church. Moroni also highlighted the need for Church members to watch over and nourish new members who join the Church.

Commentary

Moroni 1:1–3. Moroni

• The Lord "committed the keys of the record of the stick of Ephraim" to Moroni (D&C 27:5). He thus became the principal figure in the transmission of the record to this dispensation as well as the protector of the record itself. Moroni was "the last Nephite prophet in the Book of Mormon (circa A.D. 421). Just before Mormon's death, he delivered a historical record called the plates of Mormon to his son Moroni (W of M 1:1). Moroni finished compiling the plates of Mormon. He added chapters 8 and 9 to the book of Mormon (Morm. 8:1). He abridged and included the book of Ether (Ether 1:1–2) and added his own book called the book of Moroni (Moro. 1:1–4). Moroni sealed up the plates and hid them in the hill Cumorah (Morm. 8:14; Moro. 10:2). In 1823 Moroni was sent as a resurrected being to reveal the Book of Mormon to Joseph Smith (JS—H 1:30–42, 45; D&C 27:5). He instructed the young prophet each year from 1823 to 1827 (JS—H 1:54) and finally delivered the plates to him in 1827 (JS—H 1:59). After completing the translation Joseph Smith returned the plates to Moroni" (Guide to the Scriptures, "Moroni, Son of Mormon").

Moroni 1:4. The Book of Mormon to Be of Great Worth

• The Book of Mormon plays an important part in the conversion of many people. Moroni specifically mentioned the benefit that would come to the Lamanites in the latter days as a result of the Book of Mormon. One of the earliest missionary calls in this dispensation was to Oliver Cowdery and his companions to teach the Lamanites living on the western frontier (Missouri) of early America (see D&C 28:8–10). Today the Church takes the gospel message to everyone, including the descendants of Lehi, who are scattered throughout the world.

Moroni 2:1. The Nephite "Disciples" Were Apostles

• "This book [the Book of Mormon] also tells us that our Savior made His appearance upon this continent after His resurrection; . . . that they had Apostles, Prophets, Pastors, Teachers, and Evangelists; the same order, the same priesthood, the same ordinances, gifts, powers, and blessings, as were enjoyed on the eastern continent" (Joseph Smith, *History of the Church*, 4:538).

"While in every instance the Nephite Twelve are spoken of as disciples, the fact remains that they had been endowed with divine authority to be special witnesses for Christ among their own people. Therefore, they were virtually apostles to the Nephite race" (Joseph Fielding Smith, *Doctrines of Salvation*, 3:158; see also Mormon 9:18).

Moroni 2–5. The Importance of Ordinances in the Church of Jesus Christ

• President Boyd K. Packer, President of the Quorum of the Twelve Apostles, explained why ordinances are so important: "Ordinances and covenants become our credentials for admission into His presence. To worthily receive them is the quest of a lifetime; to keep them thereafter is the challenge of mortality" (in Conference Report, Apr. 1987, 27; or *Ensign*, May 1987, 24).

President Packer also explained: "Good conduct without the ordinances of the gospel will neither redeem nor exalt mankind; covenants and the ordinances are essential" (in Conference Report, Oct. 1985, 105; or *Ensign*, Nov. 1985, 82).

• Elder Dallin H. Oaks of the Quorum of the Twelve Apostles explained the relationship that exists between our Father in Heaven, our families, and the ordinances we participate in: "The ultimate Latter-day Saint priorities are twofold: First, we seek to understand our relationship to God the Eternal Father and His Son, Jesus Christ, and to secure that relationship by obtaining their saving ordinances and by keeping our personal covenants. Second, we seek to understand our relationship to our family members and to secure those relationships by the ordinances . . . and by keeping the covenants we make. . . . These relationships, secured in the way I have explained, provide eternal blessings available in no other way. No combination of science, success, property, pride, prominence, or power can provide these eternal blessings!" (in Conference Report, Apr. 2001, 110; or *Ensign,* May 2001, 84).

MORONI 3

According to Moroni, what are the essential features in the ordination to the offices of priest and teacher?

Moroni 3:3. Ordained "to Be a Priest" or a Teacher

• President Joseph Fielding Smith (1876–1972) explained that the Nephites did not use the Aaronic Priesthood before the Savior's visit; see commentary for Jacob 1:18 (p. 115).

Moroni 3:4. Ordained "by the Power of the Holy Ghost"

• The Holy Ghost plays an important role in all priesthood ordinances. The Holy Ghost knows our hearts and actions. It is by the power of the Holy Ghost that all ordinations are ratified (see D&C 132:7). The Prophet Joseph Smith (1805–44) spoke of the role of the Holy Ghost in performing ordinations: "We believe in the gift of the Holy Ghost being enjoyed now, as much as it was in the Apostles' days; we believe that it [the gift of the Holy Ghost] is necessary to make and to organize the Priesthood, that no man can be called to fill any office in the ministry without it; we also believe in prophecy, in tongues, in visions, and in revelations, in gifts, and in healings; and that these things cannot be enjoyed without the gift of the Holy Ghost" (*History of the Church,* 5:27).

Moroni 4–5. The Sacrament

• Elder David A. Bednar of the Quorum of the Twelve Apostles spoke of the importance of partaking of the sacrament in our effort to remember our covenants:

"Through the ordinance of the sacrament we renew our baptismal covenant and can receive and retain a remission of our sins (see Mosiah 4:12, 26). In addition, we are reminded  on a weekly basis of the promise *that we may always have His Spirit to be with us.* As we then strive to keep ourselves clean and unspotted from the world, we become worthy vessels in whom the Spirit of the Lord can always dwell" (in Conference Report, Apr. 2006, 32; or *Ensign,* May 2006, 31).

MORONI 4–5

In what ways are the prayers on the bread and water similar? In what ways are they different?

Moroni 4:3. Taking upon Us the Name of Jesus Christ

• Elder Dallin H. Oaks spoke of three significant meanings that should be understood when we take the name of the Savior upon us during the sacrament:

"Our witness that we are willing to take upon us the name of Jesus Christ has several different meanings. Some of these meanings are obvious, and well within the understanding of our children. Others are only evident to those who have searched the scriptures and pondered the wonders of eternal life.

"One of the obvious meanings renews a promise we made when we were baptized. Following the scriptural pattern, persons who are baptized 'witness before the Church that they have truly repented of . . . their sins, and are willing to take upon them the name of Jesus Christ, having a determination to serve him to the end' (D&C 20:37; see also 2 Nephi 31:13; Moroni 6:3). When we partake of the sacrament, we renew this covenant and all the other covenants we made in the waters of baptism. (See Joseph Fielding Smith, *Doctrines of Salvation,* comp. Bruce R. McConkie, 3 vols. [Salt Lake City: Bookcraft, 1954–56], 2:341, 346.)

"As a second obvious meaning, we take upon us our Savior's name when we become members of The Church of Jesus Christ of Latter-day Saints. By his commandment, this church bears his name. (See D&C 115:4; 3 Nephi 27:7–8.) Every member, young and old, is a member of the 'household of God' (Ephesians 2:19). As true believers in Christ, as Christians, we have gladly taken his name upon us. (See Alma 46:15.) As King Benjamin taught his people, 'Because of the covenant which ye have made ye shall be called the children of Christ, his sons, and his daughters; for behold, this day he hath spiritually begotten you' (Mosiah 5:7; see also Alma 5:14; 36:23–26).

"We also take upon us the name of Jesus Christ whenever we publicly proclaim our belief in him. Each of us has many opportunities to proclaim our belief to friends and neighbors, fellow workers, and casual acquaintances. . . .

"A third meaning appeals to the understanding of those mature enough to know that a follower of Christ is obligated to serve him. . . . By witnessing our willingness to take upon us the name of Jesus Christ, we signify our willingness to do the work of his kingdom.

"In these three relatively obvious meanings, we see that we take upon us the name of Christ when we are baptized in his name, when we belong to his Church and profess our belief in him, and when we do the work of his kingdom" (in Conference Report, Apr. 1985, 101–2; or *Ensign,* May 1985, 80).

Moroni 4:3; 5:2. "Always Remember Him"

• President Henry B. Eyring of the First Presidency explained how easy it is to be distracted from

remembering the Lord and what we can do to remember Him more frequently:

"Those of you who have served missions may have . . . come upon your missionary journals put away in a closet in your home. You may have read and felt a shock as you remembered how hard you worked, how constantly you thought of the Savior and His sacrifice for you and for those you tried to meet and teach, and how fervently and often you prayed. The shock may have come from realizing how much the cares of life had taken you from where you once were, so close to always remembering and always praying.

"My message is a plea, a warning, and a promise: I plead with you to do with determination the simple things that will move you forward spiritually.

"Start with remembering Him. You will remember what you know and what you love. The Savior gave us the scriptures, paid for by prophets at a price we cannot measure, so that we could know Him. Lose yourself in them. Decide now to read more, and more effectively than you have ever done before" ("Always," *Ensign,* Oct. 1999, 9–10).

Moroni 6:2. "A Broken Heart and a Contrite Spirit"

• What does it mean to have "a broken heart and a contrite spirit"? President Ezra Taft Benson (1899–1994) explained that it is the same as godly sorrow, which is "a deep realization that our actions have offended our Father and our God. It is the sharp and keen awareness that our behavior caused the Savior, He who knew no sin, even the greatest of all, to endure agony and suffering. Our sins caused Him to bleed at every pore. This very real mental and spiritual anguish is what the scriptures refer to as having 'a broken heart and a contrite spirit.' (3 Ne. 9:20; Moro. 6:2; D&C 20:37; 59:8; Ps. 34:18; 51:17; Isa. 57:15.) Such a spirit is the absolute prerequisite for true repentance" ("A Mighty Change of Heart," *Ensign,* Oct. 1989, 4).

Elder Bruce D. Porter of the Seventy explained further, defining the meaning of "a broken heart and a contrite spirit":

"When our hearts are broken, we are completely open to the Spirit of God and recognize our dependence on Him for all that we have and all that we are. The sacrifice so entailed is a sacrifice of pride in all its forms. Like malleable clay in the hands of a skilled potter, the brokenhearted can be molded and shaped in the hands of the Master. . . .

". . . Those who have a broken heart and a contrite spirit are willing to do anything and everything that God asks of them, without resistance or resentment. We cease doing things our way and learn to do them God's way instead. . . .

"There is yet another dimension of a broken heart—namely, our deep gratitude for Christ's suffering on our behalf. . . . When we remember the Savior and His suffering, our hearts too will break in gratitude for the Anointed One.

"As we make the sacrifice to Him of all that we have and all that we are, the Lord will fill our hearts with peace. He will 'bind up the brokenhearted' (Isaiah 61:1) and grace our lives with the love of God" (in Conference Report, Oct. 2007, 32–33; or *Ensign,* Nov. 2007, 32).

Mormon 6:3. "A Determination to Serve"

• President Thomas S. Monson discussed the attitude that all of us must have when we are baptized and called to Church service: "Though exaltation is a

personal matter, and while individuals are saved not as a group but indeed as individuals, yet one cannot live in a vacuum. Membership in the Church calls forth a determination to serve. A position of responsibility may not be of recognized importance, nor may the reward be broadly known. Service, to be acceptable to the Savior, must come from willing minds, ready hands, and pledged hearts" (in Conference Report, Apr. 1994, 80; or *Ensign,* May 1994, 62).

Moroni 6:4. "Nourished by the Good Word of God"

• That which is "wrought upon" is impacted or influenced. In Moroni 6:4 the phrase is symbolic and

has reference to what occurs when the Spirit works on and changes a convert. The atoning sacrifice of Christ makes the remission of our sins possible, but it is through the cleansing power of the Holy Ghost—the baptism of fire—that sins are actually purged or removed (see 2 Nephi 31:17; Alma 13:12; 3 Nephi 27:20). It is also through the workings of the Holy Ghost that we gain the enabling power of the Atonement to help us become faithful Latter-day Saints.

• President Gordon B. Hinckley (1910–2008) told of a personal experience demonstrating how important it is that we take care of those who are newly converted:

"Every convert must be 'nourished by the good word of God' (Moro. 6:4). It is imperative that he or she become affiliated with a priesthood quorum or the Relief Society, the Young Women, the Young Men, the Sunday School, or the Primary. He or she must be encouraged to come to sacrament meeting to partake of the sacrament, to renew the covenants made at the time of baptism.

"Not long ago, I listened to a man and woman who spoke in my home ward. This man had served in many capacities in the Church, including that of bishop. Their most recent assignment was to fellowship a single mother and her children. He stated that it was the most joyful of all his Church experiences.

"This young woman was full of questions. She was filled with fear and anxiety. She did not wish to make a mistake, to say anything that was out of line that might embarrass her or cause others to laugh. Patiently this man and his wife brought the family to church, sat with them, put a shield around them, as it were, against anything that might happen to embarrass them. They spent one evening a week with them at their home, teaching them further concerning the gospel and answering their many questions. They led that little family along as a shepherd leads his sheep. Eventually, circumstances dictated that they move to another city. 'But,' he stated, 'we still correspond with that woman. We feel a great appreciation for her. She is now firmly grounded in the Church, and we have no fear concerning her. What a joy it has been to work with her.'

"I am convinced that we will lose but very, very few of those who come into the Church if we take better care of them" ("Find the Lambs, Feed the Sheep," *Ensign,* May 1999, 108–9).

• Elder Jeffrey R. Holland of the Quorum of the Twelve Apostles noted the universal responsibility for keeping our fellow members "in the right way": "Inspired instruction in the home and in the Church helps provide this crucial element of nourishing by the good word of God. . . . Surely the opportunity to magnify that call exists everywhere. The need for it is everlasting. Fathers, mothers, siblings, friends, missionaries, home and visiting teachers, priesthood and auxiliary leaders, classroom instructors—each is, in his or her own way, 'come from God' for our schooling and our salvation. In this Church it is virtually impossible to find anyone who is *not* a guide of one kind or another to his or her fellow members of the flock" (in Conference Report, Apr. 1998, 30–31; or *Ensign,* May 1998, 25).

Moroni 6:4. "The Author and the Finisher of Their Faith"

• The word *author* is defined as "one who produces, creates, or brings into being" (*Noah Webster's First Edition of an American Dictionary of the English Language, 1828* [1967]). In our fallen state, we must look to the Savior for the acquisition and development of faith. Hence, the fourth article of faith specifies as the first principle of the gospel "Faith in the Lord Jesus Christ."

The word *finisher* has several meanings that apply to the Savior's role in our process of developing faith. First, "one who finishes; one who completely performs." We can trust the Lord to completely perform His role as we continue to strive to become more like Him. Second, "one who completes or perfects" (*Noah Webster's First Edition*). As we do our best to keep our covenants, it is through His grace that we can finally reach perfection, the ultimate goal in our journey of faith. A definition associated with *finish* is "to polish to the degree of excellence intended" (*Noah Webster's First Edition*). When we come to the Lord in faith as His sons and daughters, He will help us become our best.

• President Henry B. Eyring discussed the central role of the Savior in our redemption. He added his testimony to Moroni's that Jesus is "'the author and the finisher of their faith' [Moroni 6:4]. It is the Savior who made possible our being purified through His Atonement and our obedience to His commandments. And it is the Savior who will nourish those who go down in faith into the waters of baptism and receive the gift of the Holy Ghost. When they always remember Him, and when they continue in childlike obedience, it is He who will assure that they have His Spirit always to be with them" (in Conference Report, Oct. 1997, 116; or *Ensign,* Nov. 1997, 84).

Moroni 6:5. Meet Together Often

• Elder Joseph B. Wirthlin (1917–2008) of the Quorum of the Twelve Apostles reminded us of the fellowship that exists in the worldwide Church. He noted the sacrifices of members of the Church to fulfill the important mandate to meet together often:

"One of the many benefits of membership in the Church is that of companionship with the Saints. During the time of my assignment in Europe, we held memorable stake conferences for the military servicemen in Germany. Many of our good brothers and sisters drove long distances to attend the meetings. A number of them arrived the night before and slept on the floor of the cultural hall. No matter the sacrifice, they came with glad hearts seeking the companionship of fellow Latter-day Saints and the chance to be instructed and edified by Church leaders. When we come together, we are 'no more strangers and foreigners, but fellowcitizens with the saints, and of the household of God' [Ephesians 2:19].

"Ours is the commandment and the blessing to 'meet together oft, to fast and to pray, and to speak one with another concerning the welfare of [our] souls' [Moroni 6:5]. In general conferences and in other Church meetings around the world, we come together seeking companionship—the good company of brothers and sisters in the gospel and the comfort of sweet communion with the Spirit of God. In our worship services, the presence of that Spirit fills our hearts with love for God and for our fellow Saints" (in Conference Report, Oct. 1997, 41–42; or *Ensign,* Nov. 1997, 32).

Moroni 6:7. "There Should Be No Iniquity among Them"

• King Benjamin explained that a person's name is blotted out only by transgression (see Mosiah 1:12). Alma warned that the names of the wicked "shall not be mingled with the names of my people" (Alma 5:57). There comes a time when each person who commits serious iniquities must repent or that person is not worthy of the Lord's presence or membership in the kingdom. Unrepentant members can lose their membership through Church disciplinary action. (For more information about the kinds of sins that require Church discipline, see commentary for Mosiah 26:32–36 on p. 164.)

MORONI 6:7–8

In what ways was Church discipline exercised during Book of Mormon times?

Moroni 6:9. "After the Manner of the Workings of the Spirit"

• Elder David B. Haight (1906–2004) of the Quorum of the Twelve Apostles spoke of the importance of invoking the Spirit in our meetings:

"The singular tragedy of the Nephite decline as recorded by Mormon in the Book of Mormon was the loss of the Holy Ghost and the spiritual gifts. Wisdom and inspiration dictated that Moroni include in his closing record the instructions by his father, Mormon, on the

ordinations, the sacrament, and practices of the Church. Noteworthy is this testimony about their meetings:

"'Their meetings were conducted by the church after the manner of the workings of the Spirit, and by the power of the Holy Ghost; for as the power of the Holy Ghost led them whether to preach, or to exhort, or to pray, or to supplicate, or to sing, even so it was done.' (Moro. 6:9.)

"That is the spirit that can and should characterize our worship and our sacrament meetings.

"A sister remarked to me after one such spiritual meeting, 'I don't recall all that was said—but I remember how we felt as we sang the closing hymn and bowed our heads in prayer'" ("Remembering the Savior's Atonement," *Ensign,* Apr. 1988, 13).

Points to Ponder

• How often do you think of the covenants you have made with God? What covenants do you remember *often?* Why should you remember all of your covenants often?

• Why do you think we are commanded to meet together frequently in the Church? What blessings come to you and others for meeting together often?

• Why is it important that we conduct our meetings after the manner of the workings of the Spirit?

Suggested Assignments

• Read the sacrament prayers on the bread and then on the water (see Moroni 4–5). As you read, make it personal to you by substituting the personal pronouns *I* and *me* for the third person pronouns *we, they,* and *them.* Think about how this changes the meaning of the sacrament prayers for you.

• Consider how many times in the scripture block Moroni challenged us to take the name of Jesus Christ upon ourselves and remember Him. Record in your personal journal several ways you might bring your life closer to your Savior.

Introduction

Here we read Mormon's powerful sermon as recorded by his son Moroni. Previous to Moroni 7, Mormon's scriptural work consisted primarily of abridging other prophets' writings. Here we read Mormon's powerful sermon that he gave to a righteous group of Church members (see Moroni 7:2–3). Mormon taught Saints who lived in a spiritually deteriorating society how to draw closer to God. This discourse emphasizes the need for proper motivation or intent in our actions, how to discern between good and evil, and the important relationship between faith, hope, and charity.

Commentary

Moroni 7:2–3. "The Rest of the Lord"

• The scriptures often speak of "the rest of the Lord." After quoting Moroni 7:3, President Joseph F. Smith (1838–1918) wrote:

"This is a very significant passage. The rest here referred to is not physical rest, for there is no such thing as physical rest in the Church of Jesus Christ. Reference is made to the spiritual rest and peace which are born from a settled conviction of the truth in the minds of men. We may thus enter into the rest of the Lord today, by coming to an understanding of the truths of the gospel. . . . Not all need to seek this rest, for there are many who now possess it, whose minds have become satisfied, and who have set their eyes upon the mark of their high calling with an invincible determination in their hearts to be steadfast in the truth, and who are treading in humility and righteousness the path marked out for the Saints who are complacent followers of Jesus Christ. . . .

"I thank our Father that I have come to a knowledge of this truth, that I know that Jesus is the Christ, in whom alone there is rest and salvation. As God lives, they are deceived who follow men and their philosophies; but happy are they who enter into the rest of the peaceable followers of Christ, obtaining sufficient hope from this time henceforth until they shall rest with him in heaven" (*Gospel Doctrine,* 5th ed. [1939], 126, 128).

> **MORONI 7:3–4**
>
> *What does it mean to be a "peaceable follower" of Christ and to have a "peaceable walk"? (see also D&C 19:23).*

Moroni 7:6–9. "With Real Intent"

• Elder Dallin H. Oaks of the Quorum of the Twelve Apostles taught that all people have numerous opportunities to give the gift of service to their fellowmen and that their motives in serving are all-important:

"Numerous scriptures teach that our Heavenly Father knows our thoughts and the intents of our heart. (See D&C 6:16; Mosiah 24:12; Alma 18:32.) The prophet [Mormon] taught that if our works are to be credited for good, they must be done for the right reasons. . . .

". . . Scriptures make clear that in order to purify our service in the Church and to our fellowmen, it is necessary to consider not only *how* we serve, but also *why* we serve.

"People serve one another for different reasons, and some reasons are better than others. . . . We should all strive to serve for the reasons that are highest and best.

". . . By way of illustration, and without pretending to be exhaustive, I will suggest six reasons. I will discuss these in ascending order from the lesser to the greater reasons for service.

"[1] Some may serve for hope of earthly reward. . . .

"[2] Another reason for service— . . . to obtain good companionship. . . .

"[3] Some may serve out of fear of punishment. . . .

"[4] Other persons may serve out of a sense of duty or out of loyalty to friends or family or traditions. . . .

"[5] One such higher reason for service is the hope of an eternal reward. . . .

"[6] . . . The highest reason of all. . . . Charity. . . .

". . . It is not enough to serve God with all of our *might and strength.* He who looks into our hearts and knows our minds demands more than this. In order to stand blameless before God at the last day, we must also serve him with all our *heart and mind.*

"Service with all of our heart and mind is a high challenge for all of us. Such service must be free of selfish ambition. It must be motivated only by the pure love of Christ" (in Conference Report, Oct. 1984, 13–16; or *Ensign,* Nov. 1984, 12–15).

• President Marion G. Romney (1897–1988) of the First Presidency shared the following personal experience regarding the importance of pure motives for doing righteous things:

"About a quarter of a century ago Sister Romney and I moved into a ward in which they were just beginning to build a meetinghouse. The size of the contribution the bishop thought I ought to contribute rather staggered me. I thought it was at least twice as much as he should have asked. However, I had just been called to a rather high Church position, so I couldn't very well [say no]. Therefore, I said, 'Well, I will pay it, Bishop, but I will have to pay it in installments because I don't have the money.' And so I began to pay. And I paid and paid until I was down to about the last three payments, when, as is my habit, I was reading The Book of Mormon, and came to the scripture which said:

"'. . . If a man . . . giveth a gift . . . grudgingly; wherefore it is counted unto him the same as if he had retained the gift; wherefore he is counted evil before God.' (Moroni 7:8.)

"This shocked me because I was out about a thousand dollars. Well, I went on and paid the three installments I had promised to pay, and then I paid several more installments to convince the Lord that I had done it with the right attitude" ("Mother Eve, a Worthy Exemplar," *Relief Society Magazine,* Feb. 1968, 84–85).

• President Henry B. Eyring of the First Presidency taught that praying with real intent includes a willingness to obey whatever instructions come from

the Lord: "The young Joseph Smith showed us how to pray that way. He believed in the promise he read in the book of James. He went to the grove with faith that his prayer would be answered. He wanted to know which church to join. He was submissive enough to be ready to do whatever he was told to do. So he prayed, as we must, already committed to obey" (in Conference Report, Oct. 2003, 95; or *Ensign,* Nov. 2003, 90).

Moroni 7:12–19. 📖 The Light of Christ

• The Bible Dictionary provides the following explanation:

"The light of Christ is just what the words imply: enlightenment, knowledge, and an uplifting, ennobling, preserving influence that comes upon mankind because of Jesus Christ. For instance, Christ is 'the true light that lighteth every man that cometh into the world' (D&C 93:2; John 1:9). The light of Christ fills the 'immensity of space' and is the means by which Christ is able to be 'in all things, and is through all things, and is round about all things.' It 'giveth life to all things' and is 'the law by which all things are governed.' It is also 'the light that quickeneth' man's understanding (see D&C 88:6–13, 41). In this manner, the light of Christ is related to man's conscience and tells him right from wrong (see Moro. 7:12–19).

"The light of Christ should not be confused with the personage of the Holy Ghost, for the light of Christ is not a personage at all. Its influence is preliminary to and preparatory to one's receiving the Holy Ghost. The light of Christ will lead the honest soul who 'hearkeneth to the voice' to find the true gospel and the true Church and thereby receive the Holy Ghost (see D&C 84:46–48)" ("Light of Christ," 725; see also Guide to the Scriptures, "Light of Christ"; *True to the Faith: A Gospel Reference* [2004], 96).

• "Conscience is a manifestation of the Light of Christ, enabling us to judge good from evil" (*True to the Faith,* 96). The "Spirit of Christ" (Moroni 7:16) and the "light of Christ" (vv. 18–19) are scriptural phrases that are often used synonymously.

President Boyd K. Packer, President of the Quorum of the Twelve Apostles, testified that this light is a gift that will help us discern between good and evil:

"Regardless of whether this inner light, this knowledge of right and wrong, is called the Light of Christ, moral sense, or conscience, it can direct us to moderate our actions—unless, that is, we subdue it or silence it. . . .

"Every man, woman, and child of every nation, creed, or color—everyone, no matter where they live or what they believe or what they do—has within them the imperishable Light of Christ" ("The Light of Christ," *Ensign,* Apr. 2005, 8, 10).

• President Joseph Fielding Smith (1876–1972) identified some differences between the Holy Ghost and the Light of Christ:

"The Holy Ghost should not be confused with the Spirit which fills the immensity of space and which is everywhere present. This other Spirit is impersonal and has no size, nor dimension; it proceeds forth from the presence of the Father and the Son and is in all things. We should speak of the Holy Ghost as a personage as 'he' and this other Spirit as 'it,' although when we speak of the power or gift of the Holy Ghost we may properly say 'it.'

"The Holy Ghost, as we are taught in our modern revelation, is the third member in the Godhead and a personage of Spirit. These terms are used synonymously: Spirit of God, Spirit of the Lord, Spirit of Truth, Holy Spirit, Comforter; all having reference to the Holy Ghost. The same terms largely are used in relation to the Spirit of Jesus Christ, also called the Light of Truth, Light of Christ, Spirit of God, and Spirit of the Lord; and yet they are separate and distinct things. We have a great deal of confusion because we have not kept that clearly in our minds" (*Doctrines of Salvation,* comp. Bruce R. McConkie, 3 vols. [1954–56], 1:49–50).

• God's inspiration through the Light of Christ is not limited to the members of this Church only. The Light of Christ has influenced many world leaders.

"The First Presidency has stated:

"'The great religious leaders of the world such as Mohammed, Confucius, and the Reformers, as well as philosophers including Socrates, Plato, and others, received a portion of God's light. Moral truths were given to them by God to enlighten whole nations and to bring a higher level of understanding to individuals. . . .

"'We believe that God has given and will give to all peoples sufficient knowledge to help them on their way to eternal salvation' (*Statement of the First Presidency regarding God's Love for All Mankind,* 15 Feb. 1978)" (James E. Faust, in Conference Report, Apr. 1980, 15; or *Ensign,* May 1980, 12).

• Elder Robert D. Hales of the Quorum of the Twelve Apostles explained a relationship between the Light of Christ and the gift of the Holy Ghost:

"Each of us brings a light to the earth—the Light of Christ. . . .

"By using the Light of Christ to discern and choose what is right, we can be led to an even greater light: the gift of the Holy Ghost" (in Conference Report, Apr. 2002, 80; or *Ensign,* May 2002, 70).

Moroni 7:17. Inspiration from Unworthy Sources

• Satan has the ability to give false revelations to those who try to force or pressure revelation. Communication from Satan will always lead away from Christ. President Boyd K. Packer counseled us regarding these false spiritual messages:

"Be ever on guard lest you be deceived by inspiration from an unworthy source. You can be given false spiritual messages. There are counterfeit spirits just as there are counterfeit angels. (See Moro. 7:17.) Be careful lest you be deceived, for the devil may come disguised as an angel of light.

"The spiritual part of us and the emotional part of us are so closely linked that it is possible to mistake an emotional impulse for something spiritual. We occasionally find people who receive what they assume to be spiritual promptings from God, when those promptings are either centered in the emotions or are from the adversary" ("The Candle of the Lord," *Ensign,* Jan. 1983, 55–56).

Moroni 7:19–25. "Lay Hold upon Every Good Thing"

• Mormon taught that faith is the key to laying hold on every good thing (see Moroni 7:25). In explaining how to "lay hold upon every good thing" by faith, the Relief Society visiting teaching message taught:

"Building personal testimony is a matter of desire and of making choices that increase our faith and hope. As we desire to 'lay hold upon every good thing,' we of necessity choose actions that increase our faith:

"We set aside meaningful time for prayer.

"We remember and renew our covenants regularly through partaking of the sacrament and visiting the temple.

"We use the scriptures as a personal road map to guide us in our actions.

"We cultivate friendships with people who help us build our testimonies.

"We make service part of our daily routine."

("Lay Hold upon Every Good Thing," *Ensign,* Mar. 1991, 70).

• While serving in the general Primary presidency, Sister Michaelene P. Grassli said that when we do good we align ourselves with God: "We can train our spiritual senses the same way so that we can recognize our Heavenly Father's will for us. We train our spiritual senses by doing good things. We are taught to 'search diligently in the light of Christ that ye may know good from evil; and if ye will lay hold upon every good thing, and condemn it not, ye certainly will be a child of Christ.' (Moro. 7:19.)" ("Follow Him," *Ensign,* Nov. 1989, 93).

MORONI 7:22–32

How do the principles discussed in these verses help us to "lay hold upon every good thing"?

Moroni 7:29–31. Ministering Angels

• Elder Jeffrey R. Holland of the Quorum of the Twelve Apostles explained that the Book of Mormon reveals the reality of angels:

"I am convinced that one of the profound themes of the Book of Mormon is the role and prevalence and central participation of angels in the gospel story. . . .

"One of the things that will become more important in our lives the longer we live is the reality of angels, their work and their ministry. I refer here not alone to the angel Moroni but also to those more personal ministering angels who are with us and around us, empowered to help us and who do exactly that (see 3 Ne. 7:18; Moro. 7:29–32, 37; D&C 107:20). . . .

"I believe we need to speak of and believe in and bear testimony to the ministry of angels more than we sometimes do. They constitute one of God's great methods of witnessing through the veil, and no document in all this world teaches that principle so clearly and so powerfully as does the Book of Mormon" ("For a Wise Purpose," *Ensign,* Jan. 1996, 16–17).

• Elder Bruce C. Hafen of the Seventy taught that angels still continue to minister to the children of man:

"The ministry of these *unseen* angels is among the most sublime forms of interaction between heaven and earth, powerfully expressing God's concern for us and bestowing tangible assurance and spiritual sustenance upon those in great need. . . .

"When do the angels come? If we seek to be worthy, they are near us when we need them most" ("When Do the Angels Come?" *Ensign,* Apr. 1992, 12, 16).

MORONI 7:29–31

Specifically what is the mission of ministering angels?

Moroni 7:32–39. Faith in Jesus Christ

• Elder Richard G. Scott of the Quorum of the Twelve Apostles counseled us on what it means to have faith in Jesus Christ:

"To gain unshakable faith in Jesus Christ is to flood your life with brilliant light. You are no longer alone to struggle with challenges you know you cannot resolve or control yourself, for He said, '*If ye will have faith in me* ye shall have power to do whatsoever thing is *expedient in me*' (Moroni 7:33; italics added).

"If you are despondent, racked by transgression, are ill, alone, or desperately in need of comfort and support, I solemnly testify that the Lord will help you when you carefully obey the spiritual law upon which that help is predicated. He is your Father. You are His child. He loves you. He will never let you down. I know He will bless you" (in Conference Report, Oct. 1991, 118; or *Ensign,* Nov. 1991, 86).

Moroni 7:40–44. Hope

• Mormon spoke of a hope that comes from or is born of faith in Christ (see Mormon 7:40, 42). Hope, centered in the life and mission of the Lord Jesus Christ, has the power to lift us above any adversity we may face. President James E. Faust (1920–2007) of the First Presidency taught that hope brings peace into a troubled life:

"There are tremendous sources of hope beyond our own ability, learning, strength, and capacity. Among them is the gift of the Holy Ghost. Through the marvelous blessing of this member of the Godhead, we can come to 'know the truth of all things' [Moroni 10:5].

"Hope is the anchor of our souls. I know of no one who is not in need of hope—young or old, strong or weak, rich or poor. In the Book of Mormon we are exhorted, 'Wherefore, whoso believeth in God might *with surety hope* for a better world, yea, even a place at the right hand of God, which hope cometh of faith, maketh an anchor to the souls of men, which would make them sure and steadfast, always abounding in good works, being led to glorify God.' [Ether 12:4; italics added]. . . .

"Everybody in this life has challenges and difficulties. That is part of our mortal test. The reason for some of these trials cannot be readily understood except on the basis of faith and hope because there is often a larger purpose which we do not always understand. Peace comes through hope" (in Conference Report, Oct. 1999, 73; or *Ensign,* Nov. 1999, 59).

• Elder Joseph B. Wirthlin (1917–2008) of the Quorum of the Twelve Apostles taught that we can have hope, because divine assistance is always available

to us: "Even when the winds of adversity blow, our Father keeps us anchored to our hope. The Lord has promised, 'I will not leave you comfortless,' [John 14:18] and He will 'consecrate [our] afflictions for [our] gain.' [2 Nephi 2:2.] Even when our trials seem overwhelming, we can draw strength and hope from the sure promise of the Lord: 'Be not afraid nor dismayed . . . ; for the battle is not yours, but God's' [2 Chronicles 20:15]" (in Conference Report, Oct. 1998, 33; or *Ensign,* Nov. 1998, 27).

Moroni 7:43–44. "Meek, and Lowly of Heart"

• Bishop H. David Burton of the Presiding Bishopric described the virtues and process of obtaining meekness: "Meekness is vital to becoming more Christlike. Without it one cannot develop other important virtues. Mormon indicated, 'None is acceptable before God, save the meek and lowly in heart' (Moroni 7:44). Acquiring meekness is a process. We are asked to 'take up [the] cross daily' (Luke 9:23). Our lifting should not be an occasional exercise. More meekness does not translate to weakness, but 'it is the presentation of self in a posture of *kindness* and *gentleness*. It reflects certitude, strength, serenity; it reflects a healthy self-esteem and a genuine self-control' (Neal A. Maxwell, "Meekly Drenched in Destiny," in *Brigham Young University 1982–83 Fireside and Devotional Speeches* [1983], 2). More meekness will allow us to be tutored by the Spirit" (in Conference Report Oct. 2004, 104–5; or *Ensign,* Nov. 2004, 99).

Moroni 7:44. Faith, Hope, and Charity

• Elder M. Russell Ballard of the Quorum of the Twelve Apostles explained the relationship between the important truths of faith, hope, and charity:

"The Apostle Paul taught that three divine principles form a foundation upon which we can build the structure of our lives. They are faith, hope, and charity. (See 1 Corinthians 13:13.) Together they give us a base of support like the legs of a three-legged stool. Each principle is significant within itself, but each also plays an important supporting role. Each is incomplete without the others. Hope helps faith develop. Likewise, true faith gives birth to hope. When we begin to lose hope, we are faltering also in our measure of faith. The principles of faith and hope working together must be accompanied by charity, which is the greatest of all. According to Mormon, 'charity is the pure love of Christ, and it endureth forever' (Moroni 7:47). It is the perfect manifestation of our faith and hope.

"Working together, these three eternal principles will help give us the broad eternal perspective we need to face life's toughest challenges, including the prophesied ordeals of the last days. Real faith fosters hope for the future; it allows us to look beyond ourselves and our present cares. Fortified by hope, we are moved to demonstrate the pure love of Christ through daily acts of obedience and Christian service" (in Conference Report, Oct. 1992, 44; or *Ensign,* Nov. 1992, 33).

• Elder Neal A. Maxwell (1926–2004) of the Quorum of the Twelve Apostles explained how the qualities of faith, hope, and charity are completely tied to Jesus Christ:

"Unsurprisingly the triad of faith, hope, and charity, which brings us to Christ, has strong and converging linkage: faith is in the Lord Jesus Christ, hope is in His atonement, and charity is the 'pure love of Christ' (see Ether 12:28; Moroni 7:47). Each of these attributes qualifies us for the celestial kingdom (see Moroni 10:20–21; Ether 12:34). Each, first of all, requires us to be meek and lowly (see Moroni 7:39, 43).

"Faith and hope are constantly interactive and may not always be precisely distinguished or sequenced. Though not perfect knowledge either, hope's enlivened expectations are 'with surety' true (Ether 12:4; see also Romans 8:24; Hebrews 11:1; Alma 32:21). In the geometry of restored theology, hope has a greater circumference than faith. If faith increases, the perimeter of hope stretches correspondingly" (in Conference Report, Oct. 1994, 45; or *Ensign,* Nov. 1994, 35).

Moroni 7:44–48. Charity: The Pure Love of Christ

• Some view charity as something we can gain on our own through deliberate efforts and specific actions. Obtaining the love of Christ, however, requires the help and blessings of our Heavenly Father. The prophet Mormon urged us to seek charity and to "pray unto the Father with all the energy of heart"; then this love is

"bestowed upon all who are true followers of his Son, Jesus Christ" (Moroni 7:48).

Elder Robert J. Whetten of the Seventy explained: "Like faith, Christlike love is a gift of the Spirit, is granted upon the principles of personal righteousness and in accordance to our level of obedience to the laws upon which it is predicated. And like faith, love must be exercised to grow" (in Conference Report, Apr. 1999, 37; or *Ensign,* May 1999, 30).

• Elder Dallin H. Oaks described charity and what one must do to obtain it: "Charity, 'the pure love of Christ' (Moroni 7:47), is not an *act* but a *condition* or state of being. Charity is attained through a succession of acts that result in a conversion. Charity is something one becomes. Thus, as Moroni declared, 'except men shall *have* charity they cannot inherit' the place prepared for them in the mansions of the Father (Ether 12:34; italics added)" (in Conference Report, Oct. 2000, 43; or *Ensign,* Nov. 2000, 34).

• Elder Jeffrey R. Holland taught why charity is such a blessing in our lives:

"The greater definition of 'the pure love of Christ,' however, is not what we as Christians try but largely fail to demonstrate toward others but rather what Christ totally succeeded in demonstrating toward us. *True* charity has been known only once. It is shown perfectly and purely in Christ's unfailing, ultimate, and atoning love for us. It is Christ's love for us that 'suffereth long, and is kind, and envieth not.' It is his love for us that is not 'puffed up . . . , not easily provoked, thinketh no evil.' It is Christ's love for us that 'beareth all things, believeth all things, hopeth all things, endureth all things.' It is as demonstrated in Christ that 'charity never faileth.' It is that charity—his pure love for us—without which we would be nothing, hopeless, of all men and women most miserable. Truly, those found possessed of the blessings of his love at the last day—the Atonement, the Resurrection, eternal life, eternal promise—surely it shall be well with them.

"This does not in any way minimize the commandment that we are to try to acquire this kind of love for one another. . . . We should try to be more constant and unfailing, more longsuffering and kind, less envious and puffed up in our relationships with others. As

Christ lived so should we live, and as Christ loved so should we love. But the '*pure* love of Christ' Mormon spoke of is precisely that—Christ's love. With that divine gift, that redeeming bestowal, we have everything; without it we have nothing and ultimately are nothing, except in the end 'devils [and] angels to a devil.' [2 Nephi 9:9.]

"Life has its share of fears and failures. Sometimes things fall short. Sometimes people fail us, or economies or businesses or governments fail us. But one thing in time or eternity does *not* fail us—the pure love of Christ. . . .

"Thus, the miracle of Christ's charity both saves and changes us. His atoning love saves us from death and hell as well as from carnal, sensual, and devilish behavior. That redeeming love also transforms the soul, lifting it above fallen standards to something far more noble, far more holy. Wherefore, we must 'cleave unto charity'—Christ's pure love of us and our determined effort toward pure love of him and all others—for without it we are nothing, and our plan for eternal happiness is utterly wasted. Without the redeeming love of Christ in our lives, all other qualities—even virtuous qualities and exemplary good works—fall short of salvation and joy" (*Christ and the New Covenant* [1997], 336–37).

Moroni 7:48. Pray "with All the Energy of Heart"

• Moroni 7:48 teaches how charity will come to a person who is continually praying "with all the energy of heart," meaning they want it more than anything else. This fervency of prayer will bring results when praying for other issues as well. President Spencer W. Kimball (1895–1985) taught that the fervency of our

prayers will affect our families: "In our family circles, our children will learn how to talk to their Heavenly Father by listening to their parents. They will soon see how heartfelt and honest our prayers are. If our prayers are hurried, even tending to be thoughtless ritual, they will see this also. Better that we do in our families and in private as Mormon pleaded, 'Wherefore, my beloved brethren, pray unto the Father with all the energy of heart.' (Moro. 7:48.)" ("Pray Always," *Ensign,* Oct. 1981, 4).

Points to Ponder

• What are the criteria noted in Moroni 7 that help us determine what is good and what is evil?

• Why is charity the "greatest of all" gifts? (Moroni 7:46).

• What difference do your attitudes and intentions make when you give service to others?

Suggested Assignments

• Based on the attributes listed in Moroni 7:45 📖 and Mormon's plea in Moroni 7:48, write a short paragraph on what you can do to increase charity in your life.

Introduction

In a day when many followers of Christ forsake righteousness to pursue the enticements of the world, what is expected of faithful Church members? President Ezra Taft Benson (1899–1994) explained: "In the final letter recorded in the Book of Mormon from Mormon to his son Moroni, he gave counsel that applies to our day. Both father and son were seeing a whole Christian civilization fall because its people would not serve the God of the land, even Jesus Christ. Mormon wrote, 'And now, my beloved son, notwithstanding their hardness, let us labor diligently; for if we should cease to labor, we should be brought under condemnation; for we have a labor to perform whilst in this tabernacle of clay, that we may conquer the enemy of all righteousness, and rest our souls in the kingdom of God' (Moroni 9:6). You and I have a similar labor to perform now—to conquer the enemy and rest our souls in the kingdom" (in Conference Report, Oct. 1987, 104; or *Ensign*, Nov. 1987, 85).

As the Book of Mormon nears its close, it proclaims the power of the Atonement and demonstrates Mormon's faithfulness to the cause of righteousness, even while Nephites were falling rapidly into profound wickedness. Mormon's letters to his son Moroni reveal the inevitable results of sin and how becoming "past feeling" leads to indescribable wickedness. Chapters 8–9 of Moroni offer valuable insight into the importance of living according to the first principles and ordinances of the gospel.

Commentary

Moroni 8:1–8. The Baptism of Little Children Prohibited

• Moroni 8 contains a letter Moroni received from his father, Mormon, that answers the question of whether little children need baptism. Note that the source for Mormon's answers on this doctrinal question came to him directly by revelation from the Lord (see Moroni 8:7). The ordinance of baptism is "for the remission of sins" (D&C 49:13). But little children have no sins. In fact, they are not capable of committing sin, nor can Satan tempt them, as the Doctrine and Covenants explains:

"Little children are redeemed from the foundation of the world through mine Only Begotten;

"Wherefore, they cannot sin, for power is not given unto Satan to tempt little children, until they begin to become accountable before me" (D&C 29:46–47).

The Lord has set the age when accountability begins—at eight years old (see JST, Genesis 17:11; D&C 68:25). Those who baptize infants to remove original sin, or the curse of Adam, as some call it, do so without a correct understanding of God and His plan (see Moroni 8:8).

MORONI 8:3

How does this verse demonstrate a righteous father's love for his son? How does this verse provide a model for Christ-centered relationships?

Moroni 8:8. "The Law of Circumcision Is Done Away"

• God declared to Abraham, "And I will establish a covenant of circumcision with thee, and it shall be my covenant between me and thee, and thy seed after thee, in their generations; that thou mayest know for ever that children are not accountable before me until they are eight years old" (JST, Genesis 17:11). God further declared to Abraham that circumcision was "a token of the covenant betwixt me and you" (Genesis 17:11). The spirit of apostasy, however, led many people in ancient times to believe that circumcision was necessary to make male children holy.

The law of circumcision was not intended to last forever. The Savior's words were revealed to Mormon: "The law of circumcision is done away in me" (Moroni 8:8). The Doctrine and Covenants explains why the law of circumcision was ended (see D&C 74:2–7).

Moroni 8:9–15. Baptizing Little Children "Is Solemn Mockery before God"

• Mormon strongly denounced the practice of infant baptism. He declared that it was "solemn mockery before God, that ye should baptize little children" (Moroni 8:9). The Prophet Joseph Smith (1805–44) taught that infant baptism denies the character of God and the saving power of the Atonement of Jesus Christ: "The doctrine of baptizing children, or sprinkling them, or they must welter in hell, is a doctrine not true, not supported in Holy Writ, and is not consistent with the character of God. All children are redeemed by the blood of Jesus Christ, and the moment that children leave this world, they are taken to the bosom of Abraham" (*History of the Church,* 4:554).

Moroni 8:22–24. "They That Are without the Law"

• Many persons live and die and never know the law of Christ. Such persons will be taught the gospel in the spirit world. There they will have the opportunity to exercise faith and repent of their sins. Living proxies on the earth perform the needed ordinances in their behalf, and the blessings of salvation may be theirs.

© 1985 Robert Barrett

Those who are not capable of understanding the gospel are not considered accountable. They, like little children, are "alive in Christ" (Moroni 8:12; see also D&C 29:49–50).

President Joseph Fielding Smith (1876–1972) explained: "They are redeemed without baptism and will go to the celestial kingdom of God, there, we believe, to have their faculties or other deficiencies restored according to the Father's mercy and justice" (*Answers to Gospel Questions,* comp. Joseph Fielding Smith Jr., 5 vols. [1957–66], 3:21).

Moroni 8:25–26. "Meekness and Lowliness of Heart"

• Mormon described a connection between faith in Christ, repentance, baptism, the gift of the Holy Ghost, and remission of sins. He taught that with remission of sins comes meekness and lowliness of heart, or humility.

Elder Francisco J. Viñas of the Seventy described some of the characteristics of someone meek and lowly in heart: "The person who obtains meekness and lowliness of heart and who enjoys the company of the Holy Ghost will have no desire to offend or hurt others, nor will he feel affected by any offenses received from others. He will treat his spouse and children with love and respect and will have good relationships with everyone he associates with. In occupying positions of leadership in the Church, he will apply the same principles as he does in the home, showing that there is no difference *between* the person he is when within the walls of his own home and the person he is in his relationship with the members of the Church" (in Conference Report, Apr. 2004, 40; or *Ensign,* May 2004, 39–40).

MORONI 8:26

How does the remission of sins lead to feeling the Holy Ghost? How can we better keep the Holy Ghost once we obtain it?

Moroni 8:28–29. "The Spirit Hath Ceased Striving with Them"

• Elder Bruce R. McConkie (1915–85) of the Quorum of the Twelve Apostles explained that men and women will lose the companionship of the Holy Ghost if they reject the light and knowledge of the gospel: "Many choose to walk in carnal paths and go contrary to the enticings of the Spirit. It is possible to sear one's conscience to the point that the Spirit will withdraw its influence and men will no longer know or care about anything that is decent and edifying. 'For my Spirit shall not always strive with man, saith the Lord of Hosts.' (D&C 1:33.)" (*A New Witness for the Articles of Faith* [1985], 260).

Moroni 9:3–5. Anger

• Mormon wrote that the Nephites would "tremble and anger" (Moroni 9:4) against him when he spoke the word of God plainly to them. Such a response is consistent with other scriptural examples of those who had hardened their hearts to principles of righteousness. The Jaredites rejected Ether and sought to kill him (see Ether 13:22). The inhabitants of Jerusalem sought Lehi's life (see 1 Nephi 1:19–20). The unrighteous in Ammonihah were so angry that they burned the believers and all of their scriptures (see Alma 14). This response to the word of God demonstrates an advanced state of wickedness that frequently precedes total destruction of cities or societies.

• Many people in our day believe they are victims of their own anger. Elder Lynn G. Robbins of the Seventy explained that we are able to choose whether to react with anger or not:

"A cunning part of his [Satan's] strategy is to dissociate anger from agency, making us believe that we are victims of an emotion that we cannot control. We hear, 'I lost my temper.' Losing one's temper is an interesting choice of words that has become a widely used idiom. To 'lose something' implies 'not meaning to,' 'accidental,' 'involuntary,' 'not responsible'—careless perhaps but 'not responsible.'

"'He made me mad.' This is another phrase we hear, also implying lack of control or agency. This is a myth that must be debunked. No one makes us mad. Others don't make us angry. There is no force involved. Becoming angry is a conscious choice, a decision; therefore, we can make the choice not to become angry. *We* choose!

To those who say, 'But I can't help myself,' author William Wilbanks responds, 'Nonsense.'

"'Aggression, . . . suppressing the anger, talking about it, screaming and yelling,' are all learned strategies in dealing with anger. 'We *choose* the one that has proved effective for us in the past. Ever notice how seldom we lose control when frustrated by our boss, but how often we do when annoyed by friends or family?' ('The New Obscenity,' *Reader's Digest,* Dec. 1988, 24; italics added)" (in Conference Report, Apr. 1998, 105; or *Ensign,* May 1998, 80).

Moroni 9:5. The Loss of Love

• One of the tragic results of anger and wickedness is the loss of the Spirit. When this happens, the Book of Mormon clearly teaches that one loses the capacity to love others. This was the case among the wicked Nephites. This loss of love leads to such things as divorce, abuse, and abandonment, all of which are rampant problems in our day.

Elder David E. Sorensen of the Presidency of the Seventy explained how a loss of love can happen in our homes: "In much of today's popular culture, the virtues of forgiveness and kindness are belittled, while ridicule, anger, and harsh criticism are encouraged. If we are not careful, we can fall prey to these habits within our own homes and families and soon find ourselves criticizing our spouse, our  children, our extended family members. Let us not hurt the ones we love the most by selfish criticism! In our families, small arguments and petty criticisms, if allowed to go unchecked, can poison relationships and escalate into estrangements, even abuse and divorce. Instead, . . . we must 'make full haste' to reduce arguments, eliminate ridicule, do away with criticism, and remove resentment and anger. We cannot afford to let such dangerous passions ruminate—not even one day" (in Conference Report, Apr. 2003, 10; or *Ensign,* May 2003, 11–12).

MORONI 9:6

What did Mormon say would result if he and Moroni ceased "to labor"? What does that teach us about persevering through difficulties?

Moroni 9:9. Chastity and Virtue Are "Dear and Precious Above All Things"

• Mormon commented that chastity and virtue are "most dear and precious above all things" (Moroni 9:9). President Gordon B. Hinckley (1910–2008) taught the importance of maintaining chastity:

"And now just a word on the most common and most difficult of all problems for you young men and young women to handle. It is the relationship that you have one with another. You are dealing with the most powerful of human instincts. Only the will to live possibly exceeds it.

"The Lord has made us attractive one to another for a great purpose. But this very attraction becomes as a powder keg unless it is kept under control. It is beautiful when handled in the right way. It is deadly if it gets out of hand. . . .

"My dear young friends, in matters of sex you know what is right. You know when you are walking on dangerous ground, when it is so easy to stumble and slide into the pit of transgression. I plead with you to be careful, to stand safely back from the cliff of sin over which it is so easy to fall. Keep yourselves clean from the dark and disappointing evil of sexual transgression. Walk in the sunlight of that peace which comes from obedience to the commandments of the Lord.

"Now, if there be any who have stepped over the line, who may already have transgressed, is there any hope for you? Of course there is. Where there is true repentance, there will be forgiveness. That process begins with prayer. The Lord has said, 'He who has repented of his sins, the same is forgiven, and I, the Lord, remember them no more' (D&C 58:42). Share your burden with your parents if you can. And by all means, confess to your bishop, who stands ready to help you" ("A Prophet's Counsel and Prayer for Youth," *New Era,* Jan. 2001, 12–13).

• If you have been the victim of sexual abuse, be assured that you have not transgressed the law of chastity. Elder Richard G. Scott of the Quorum of the Twelve Apostles explained:

"*I solemnly testify that when another's acts of violence, perversion, or incest hurt you terribly, against your will, you are not responsible and you must not feel guilty.* You may be left scarred by abuse, but those scars need not be permanent. In the eternal plan, in the Lord's timetable, those injuries can be made right as you do your part. . . .

"If you are now or have in the past been abused, seek help now. . . .

"Talk to your bishop in confidence. His calling allows him to act as an instrument of the Lord in your behalf. He can provide a doctrinal foundation to guide you to recovery. An understanding and application of eternal law will provide the healing you require. He has the right to be inspired of the Lord in your behalf. He can use the priesthood to bless you" (in Conference Report, Apr. 1992, 44; or *Ensign,* May 1992, 32).

Moroni 9:18–20. "Past Feeling"

• Mormon described to his son Moroni the pathetic spiritual state of their people. He reminded Moroni that they were "without principle, and past feeling" (Moroni 9:20). Elder Neal A. Maxwell (1926–2004) of the Quorum of the Twelve Apostles explained that failure to respond to the promptings of the Holy Spirit and failure to keep the commandments of God can lead us to this condition:

"Our capacity to feel controls our behavior in many ways, and by inaction when our feelings prompt us to do good, we deaden that capacity to feel. It was Jesus' striking sensitivity to the needs of those about him that made it possible for him to respond in action.

"At the other end of the spiritual spectrum are individuals such as Nephi's erring brothers; Nephi noted their increasing insensitivity to things spiritual: '[God] hath spoken unto you in a still small voice, but ye were past feeling, that ye could not feel his words' [1 Nephi 17:45].

"When we become too encrusted with error, our spiritual antennae wilt and we slip beyond mortal reach. This can happen to entire civilizations. In his lamentation to his son Moroni, Mormon notes the deterioration of the Nephite society. The symptoms include a wickedness so profound that Mormon's people were described by him as being 'past feeling' [Moroni 9:20]. The Apostle Paul lamented the destructive lasciviousness of Church members in Ephesus because they had developed such insensitivity in their satiation that they were 'past feeling' [Ephesians 4:19]. A sex-saturated society cannot really feel the needs of its suffering members because, instead of developing the love that looks outward, it turns man selfishly inward. Imperviousness to the promptings of the still small voice of God will also mean that we have ears but cannot hear, not only the promptings of God, but also the pleas of men" (*A Time to Choose* [1972], 59–60).

• President Boyd K. Packer, President of the Quorum of the Twelve Apostles, warned us of a modern, growing trend that also leads to a loss of the Spirit:

"The world grows increasingly noisy. Clothing and grooming and conduct are looser and sloppier and more disheveled. Raucous music, with obscene lyrics blasted through amplifiers while lights flash psychedelic colors, characterizes the drug culture. Variations of these things are gaining wide acceptance and influence over our youth. . . .

"This trend to more noise, more excitement, more contention, less restraint, less dignity, less formality is not coincidental nor innocent nor harmless.

"The first order issued by a commander mounting a military invasion is the jamming of the channels of communication of those he intends to conquer.

"Irreverence suits the purposes of the adversary by obstructing the delicate channels of revelation in both mind and spirit" (in Conference Report, Oct. 1991, 28; or *Ensign,* Nov. 1991, 22).

Moroni 9:25. "The Hope of His Glory"

• Elder Neal A. Maxwell explained that the hope Mormon spoke of is connected with faith in the Lord Jesus Christ:

"Our everyday usage of the word *hope* includes how we 'hope' to arrive at a certain destination by a certain time. We 'hope' the world economy will improve. We 'hope' for the visit of a loved one. Such typify our sincere but proximate hopes.

"Life's disappointments often represent the debris of our failed proximate hopes. Instead, however, I speak of the crucial need for ultimate hope.

"Ultimate hope is a different matter. It is tied to Jesus and the blessings of the great Atonement, blessings resulting in the universal Resurrection and the precious opportunity provided thereby for us to practice emancipating repentance, making possible what the scriptures call 'a perfect brightness of hope' (2 Nephi 31:20).

"Moroni confirmed: 'What is it that ye shall hope for? Behold I say unto you that ye shall have hope through the atonement of Christ' (Moroni 7:40–41; see also Alma 27:28). Real hope, therefore, is not associated with things mercurial, but rather with things immortal and eternal!" (in Conference Report, Oct. 1998, 77; or *Ensign,* Nov. 1998, 61).

Moroni 9:26. The Grace of God the Father and the Lord Jesus Christ

• Mormon knew that Moroni faced overwhelming challenges due the wickedness of the Nephites. Nevertheless, Mormon also knew that Moroni could endure with the assistance of divine grace. *True to the Faith* explains that grace provides strength to persevere in the daily struggles of life:

"The word *grace,* as used in the scriptures, refers primarily to the divine help and strength we receive through the Atonement of the Lord Jesus Christ. . . .

"In addition to needing grace for your ultimate salvation, you need this enabling power every day of your life. As you draw near to your Heavenly Father in diligence, humility, and meekness, He will uplift and strengthen you through His grace" (*True to the Faith: A Gospel Reference* [2004], 77–78).

Points to Ponder

• What strong terms did Mormon use to denounce the practice of infant baptism? (see Moroni 8). Why do you think he felt so strongly?

• If the Lamanites and the Nephites were comparable in their wickedness, why were the Lamanites not destroyed as well? (see Moroni 8:27–29).

• What gradual steps mentioned by Mormon in chapters 8–9 led to the eventual depravity of the Nephites? How can we avoid apostasy and wickedness in our own lives?

Suggested Assignments

• Write a paragraph that explains the doctrinal reasons why infants do not need baptism (see Moroni 8:4–23).

• Prepare a talk or lesson on the theme "How we can endure righteously when wickedness surrounds us." Use principles and doctrines from Moroni 8–9.

Introduction

Moroni concluded his writings by discussing three important principles with his readers. The first focuses on the need to learn and have a witness of the truths found in this sacred record. The second is a charge to understand and acquire the spiritual gifts available to us. Finally, he pleads with each of us to come unto Christ and be perfected in Him.

As you conclude this study of the Book of Mormon, look for these principles. Come to know for yourself the truthfulness of the book by following Moroni's promise (see Moroni 10:3–5 ). Learn of the gifts of the Spirit and seek to develop those the Lord has given you. Finally, seek to show by your actions that you are striving daily to come unto Christ.

Remember what the Prophet Joseph Smith (1805–44) declared: "I told the brethren that the Book of Mormon was the most correct of any book on earth, and the keystone of our religion, and a man would get nearer to God by abiding by its precepts, than by any other book" (*History of the Church,* 4:461; Book of Mormon introduction).

Commentary

Moroni 10:3. "When Ye Shall Read These Things"

• Elder Gene R. Cook, while serving as a member of the Seventy, spoke of the importance of pondering God's mercy as a means to achieving greater faith and humility:

"The last five words of [Moroni 10:3] offer an important admonition—'ponder it in your hearts.' What is the antecedent of 'it'—the thing that we are to ponder? It is 'how merciful the Lord hath been unto the children of men, from the creation of Adam even down until the time that ye shall receive these things.' We are to remember how loving, how provident, how good, how forgiving our Heavenly Father has been toward us.

"What usually happens when we begin to ponder how merciful the Lord has been to mankind? To us personally? What happens when we count our blessings, or perhaps our sins for which we must ask his forgiveness, and recognize his hand in our individual lives? Is it not true that our hearts turn to the Lord in love and gratitude? Do our faith and humility increase? Yes, and that, in my judgment, is the impact of verse 3—following the counsel therein helps us to become more humble, more willing and ready to receive new information and knowledge with an open mind" ("Moroni's Promise," *Ensign,* Apr. 1994, 12).

Moroni 10:4–5.  Receiving a Testimony of the Book of Mormon

• President Boyd K. Packer, President of the Quorum of the Twelve Apostles, shared the process he went through to receive a spiritual witness of the Book of Mormon:

"When I first read the Book of Mormon from cover to cover, I read the promise that if I 'would ask God, the Eternal Father, in the name of Christ, if [the things I had read were] true; and if [I would] ask with a sincere heart, with real intent, having faith in Christ, he [would] manifest the truth of it unto [me], by the power of the Holy Ghost' (Moroni 10:4). I tried to follow those instructions as I understood them.

"If I expected a glorious manifestation to come at once as an overpowering experience, it did not happen. Nevertheless, it felt good, and I began to believe. . . .

"I learned that anyone, anywhere, could read in the Book of Mormon and receive inspiration. . . .

"My experience has been that a testimony does not burst upon us suddenly. Rather, it grows. . . .

"Do not be disappointed if you have read and reread and yet have not received a powerful witness. You may be somewhat like the disciples spoken of in the Book of Mormon who were filled with the power of God in great glory 'and they knew it not' (3 Nephi 9:20).

"Do the best you can" (in Conference Report, Apr. 2005, 5–7; or *Ensign,* May 2005, 6–8).

• Elder Bruce R. McConkie (1915–85) of the Quorum of the Twelve Apostles offered more insight into how to gain a testimony of the Book of Mormon by pondering a question while reading:

"There is another and simpler test that all who seek to know the truth might well take. It calls for us simply to read, ponder, and pray—all in the spirit of faith and with an open mind. To keep ourselves alert to the issues at hand—as we do read, ponder, and pray—we should ask ourselves a thousand times, 'Could any man have written this book?'

"And it is absolutely guaranteed that sometime between the first and thousandth time this question is asked, every sincere and genuine truth seeker will come to know by the power of the Spirit that the Book of Mormon is true, that it is the mind and will and voice of the Lord to the whole world in our day" (in Conference Report, Oct. 1983, 106; or *Ensign,* Nov. 1983, 73–74).

• President Gordon B. Hinckley (1910–2008) issued the following challenge and promise to readers of the Book of Mormon:

"I offer a challenge to members of the Church throughout the world and to our friends everywhere to read or reread the Book of Mormon. . . .

"Without reservation I promise you that if each of you will observe this simple program, regardless of how

many times you previously may have read the Book of Mormon, there will come into your lives and into your homes an added measure of the Spirit of the Lord, a strengthened resolution to walk in obedience to His commandments, and a stronger testimony of the living reality of the Son of God" ("A Testimony Vibrant and True," *Ensign,* Aug. 2005, 6).

MORONI 10:3–5
What verbs describe the actions that lead a sincere truth seeker to receive a testimony of the Book of Mormon?

Moroni 10:4. "With Real Intent"

• Elder Dallin H. Oaks of the Quorum of the Twelve Apostles commented on Moroni's promise of having "real intent": "Moroni did not promise a manifestation of the Holy Ghost to those who seek to know the truth of the Book of Mormon for hypothetical or academic reasons, even if they 'ask with a sincere heart.' The promise of Moroni is for those who are committed in their hearts to act upon the manifestation if it is received. Prayers based on any other reason have no promise because they are not made 'with real intent'" (*Pure in Heart* [1988], 19–20).

Moroni 10:8–18. Gifts of the Spirit

• Elder Bruce R. McConkie described the purposes and reasons for obtaining spiritual gifts:

"[The purpose of spiritual gifts] is to enlighten, encourage, and edify the faithful so that they will inherit peace in this life and be guided toward eternal life in the world to come. Their presence is proof of the divinity of the Lord's work; where they are not found, there the Church and kingdom of God is not. The promise is that they shall never be done away as long as the earth continues in its present state, except for unbelief (Moro. 10:19), but when the perfect day comes and the saints obtain exaltation, there will be no more need for them. As Paul expressed it, 'When that which is perfect is come, then that which is in part shall be done away.' (1 Cor. 13.)

"Faithful persons are expected to seek the gifts of the Spirit with all their hearts. They are to 'covet earnestly the best gifts' (1 Cor. 12:31; D.&C. 46:8), to 'desire spiritual gifts' (1 Cor. 14:1), 'to ask of God, who giveth liberally.' (D.&C. 46:7; Matt. 7:7–8.) To some will be given one gift; to others, another; and 'unto some it may be given to have all those gifts, that there may be a head, in order that every member may be profited thereby.' (D.&C. 46:29.)" (*Mormon Doctrine,* 2nd ed. [1966], 314).

• Elder Marvin J. Ashton (1915–94) of the Quorum of the Twelve Apostles suggested additional gifts of the Spirit "that are not always evident or noteworthy but that are very important. Among these may be your gifts—gifts not so evident but nevertheless real and valuable.

"Let us review some of these less-conspicuous gifts: the gift of asking; the gift of listening; the gift of hearing and using a still, small voice; the gift of being able to weep; the gift of avoiding contention; the gift of being agreeable; the gift of avoiding vain repetition; the gift of seeking that which is righteous; the gift of not passing judgment; the gift of looking to God for guidance; the gift of being a disciple; the gift of caring for others; the gift of being able to ponder; the gift of offering prayer; the gift of bearing a mighty testimony; and the gift of receiving the Holy Ghost" (in Conference Report, Oct. 1987, 23; or *Ensign,* Nov. 1987, 20).

• President Boyd K. Packer gave counsel concerning obtaining spiritual gifts:

"I must emphasize that the word 'gift' is of great significance, for a gift may not be demanded or it ceases to be a gift. It may only be accepted when proffered.

"Inasmuch as spiritual gifts are gifts, the conditions under which we may receive them are established by him who offers them to us. Spiritual gifts cannot be forced, for a gift is a gift. They cannot, I repeat, be forced, nor bought, nor 'earned' in the sense that we make some gesture in payment and expect them to automatically be delivered on our own terms.

"There are those who seek such gifts with such persistence that each act moves them further from them. And in that persistence and determination they place themselves in spiritual danger. Rather we are to live to be worthy of the gifts and they will come according to the will of the Lord.

"Brigham Young said something in his day that surely applies to ours:

"'There is no doubt, if a person lives according to the revelations given to God's people, he may have the Spirit of the Lord to signify to him His will, to guide his duties in his temporal as well as his spiritual exercises. I am satisfied however, that in this respect, we live far beneath our privileges.' (*Discourses of Brigham Young,* p. 32.)

"Spiritual gifts belong to the Church and their existence is one of the great and abiding testimonies of the truth of the gospel. They really are not optional with the Church. Moroni taught that if they were absent then 'awful is the state of man.' . . .

"We are to seek to be worthy to receive these gifts according to the way that the Lord has directed.

"Now, I say that again—we are to seek for spiritual gifts in the Lord's way" ("Gifts of the Spirit" [unpublished remarks at a 16-stake fireside, Brigham Young University, Jan. 4, 1987], 5–6).

Moroni 10:17–18. How Can We Experience Gifts of the Spirit?

• Elder Gene R. Cook discussed the strength of discovering and using the spiritual gifts given to each person: "One of the great processes you go through in life is to discover yourself, to find those gifts and capacities God has given you. He has given you great talents, the smallest part of which you have just begun to utilize. Trust the Lord to assist you in unlocking the door to those gifts. Some of us have created imaginary limits in our minds. There is literally a genius locked up inside each of us. Don't ever let anyone convince you otherwise" ("Trust in the Lord," in *Hope* [1988], 90–91).

• Elder Parley P. Pratt (1807–57) of the Quorum of the Twelve Apostles shared several effects of having the gifts of the Spirit in our lives: "The gift of the Holy Spirit adapts itself to all these organs or attributes. It quickens all the intellectual faculties, increases, enlarges, expands, and purifies all the natural passions and affections, and adapts them, by the gift of wisdom, to their lawful use. It inspires, develops, cultivates, and matures all the fine-toned sympathies, joys, tastes, kindred feelings, and affections of our nature. It inspires virtue, kindness, goodness, tenderness, gentleness, and charity. It develops beauty of person, form, and features. It tends to health, vigor, animation, and social feeling. It invigorates all the faculties of the physical and intellectual man. It strengthens and gives tone to the nerves. In short, it is, as it were, marrow to the bone, joy to the heart, light to the eyes, music to the ears, and life to the whole being" (*Key to the Science of Theology* [1979], 61).

Moroni 10:20–21. Faith, Hope, and Charity

• Elder Joseph B. Wirthlin (1917–2008) of the Quorum of the Twelve Apostles discussed the development of faith, hope, and charity as a step by step process:

"When we keep the Lord's commandments, faith, hope, and charity abide with us. These virtues 'distil upon [our] soul as the dews from heaven' [D&C 121:45], and we prepare ourselves to stand with confidence before our Lord and Savior, Jesus Christ, 'without blemish and without spot' [1 Peter 1:19]. . . .

"These are the virtuous, lovely, praiseworthy characteristics we seek. We all are familiar with Paul's teaching that 'charity never faileth' [1 Corinthians 13:8]. Certainly we need unfailing spiritual strength in our lives. Moroni recorded the revelation 'that faith, hope and charity bringeth [us] unto [the Lord]—the fountain of all righteousness' [Ether 12:28].

"The Church of Jesus Christ of Latter-day Saints, the restored Church of the Lord on the earth today, guides us to the Savior and helps us develop, nurture, and strengthen these divine attributes" (in Conference Report, Oct. 1998, 32; or *Ensign,* Nov. 1998, 26).

Moroni 10:22. "Despair Cometh Because of Iniquity"

• President Ezra Taft Benson (1899–1994) shared this insight regarding the need to do good to avoid despair: "In the Book of Mormon we read that 'despair cometh because of iniquity.' (Moro. 10:22.) 'When I do good I feel good,' said Abraham Lincoln, 'and when I do bad I feel bad.' Sin pulls a man down into despondency and despair. While a man may take some temporary pleasure in sin, the end result is unhappiness. 'Wickedness never was happiness.' (Alma 41:10.) Sin creates disharmony with God and is depressing to the spirit. Therefore, a man would do well to examine himself to see that he is in harmony with all of God's laws. Every law kept brings a particular blessing. Every law broken brings a particular blight. Those who are heavy-laden with despair should come unto the Lord, for his yoke is easy and his burden is light. (See Matt. 11:28–30.)" ("Do Not Despair," *Ensign,* Oct. 1986, 2).

Moroni 10:27. "Ye Shall See Me at the Bar of God"

• Several prophets felt impressed to testify to the readers of the Book of Mormon that they will see us on Judgment Day, when the Lord will witness to us of the truthfulness of their words. Others in the Book of Mormon who have made similar comments include Nephi (see 2 Nephi 33:10–14), Jacob (see Jacob 6:12–13), and Mormon (see Mormon 3:20–22).

> **MORONI 10:7–8, 18–19, 26, 30**
> *Repetition is an important teaching method used in the scriptures. What does Moroni's repetition of the word exhort instruct us to do?*

Moroni 10:31–32. "Come unto Christ, and Be Perfected in Him"

• While serving as a member of the Seventy, Elder William R. Bradford described why we should follow Moroni's closing counsel:

Dale Kilbourn, © IRI

"There is great joy and happiness in striving to live righteously. In simple terms, the plan of God for His children is that they come to this earth and do all that they can to learn and live in obedience to laws. Then, after all they can do, the redeeming work of the Savior, Jesus Christ, is sufficient to do all that they could not do for themselves. . . .

"Striving to live righteously is attempting to do all that we can in obedience. With this comes the inner peace and comfort that in doing all we can, the plan of God will be accomplished in our behalf. No other feeling in the soul of man can bring the joy and happiness than that of knowing you are doing all you can to become righteous" (in Conference Report, Oct. 1999, 110; or *Ensign,* Nov. 1999, 85–86).

• At the conclusion of general conference, President Gordon B. Hinckley referred to our need to come unto the Savior by living in such a way as to bless others: "I pray that what you have heard and seen may make a difference in your lives. I pray that each of us will be a little more kind, a little more thoughtful, a little more courteous. I pray that we will keep our tongues in check and not let anger prompt words which we would later regret. I pray that we may have the strength and the will to turn the other cheek, to walk the extra mile in lifting up the feeble knees of those in distress" (in Conference Report, Oct. 2003, 109; or *Ensign,* Nov. 2003, 103).

> ### MORONI 10:32–33
> *Moroni mentioned several things we must do to become "holy, without spot." What are they, and how will you apply them in your life?*

Moroni 10:32–33. "By the Grace of God"

• Elder M. Russell Ballard of the Quorum of the Twelve Apostles explained that good works must be accompanied by the grace of Christ: "It is only through the infinite Atonement of Jesus Christ that people can overcome the consequences of bad choices. . . . No matter how hard we work, no matter how much we obey, no matter how many good things we do in this life, it would not be enough were it not for Jesus Christ and His loving grace. On our own we cannot earn the kingdom of God—no matter what we do. Unfortunately, there are some within the Church who have become so preoccupied with performing good works that they forget that those works—as good as they may be—are hollow unless they are accompanied by a complete dependence on Christ" ("Building Bridges of Understanding," *Ensign,* June 1998, 65).

Moroni 10:34. Another Testament of Jesus Christ

• On the title page of the Book of Mormon it states that one of the purposes of the Book of Mormon is to convince "Jew and Gentile that Jesus is the Christ." As a concluding witness of this focus, consider the

following fact: Of the 6,607 total verses found in the Book of Mormon, 3,925 reference Jesus Christ's name. This means that some form of Christ's name is mentioned approximately every 1.7 verses (see Susan Ward Easton, "Names of Christ in the Book of Mormon," *Ensign,* July 1978, 60–61).

Points to Ponder

• Which gifts of the Spirit do you feel you most need at this time in your life? What can you do to develop or receive these gifts promised by your Heavenly Father?

• In what ways does Moroni 10 help you understand what it means to "come unto Christ"? (Moroni 10:30).

• In what ways has reading the Book of Mormon brought you "nearer to God"? (Book of Mormon introduction). List some of the passages that have been most meaningful to you.

• What is the relationship between the grace of Christ and our goal of perfection?

Suggested Assignments

• Set a time and a schedule to study the Book of Mormon each day either topically or sequentially.

• Reread your patriarchal blessing. Then visit with those who know you best, such as your family, and identify the spiritual gifts they can see Heavenly Father has given you. Make plans on how to develop those and other gifts you desire. (*Note:* Your patriarchal blessing is personal and sacred and is typically not shared with friends.)

APPENDIX

The following appendices explain and detail particular aspects of the Book of Mormon. Some provide a helpful visual that displays complex information in a simple format. Others offer a simple overview of a broad topic. The appendices also provide students insights, connections, patterns, and themes in the Book of Mormon:

Book of Mormon Plates and Records 407

Nephite Record Keepers 408

The Witnesses of the Book of Mormon Plates 409

Possible Route Taken by Lehi's Family 410

Book of Mormon Pages and Time Periods 411

The Stick of Judah and the Stick of Joseph 412

Flashbacks from Omni through Mosiah 413

The Cycle of Righteousness and Wickedness 414

Brief History of the Scattering of Israel 415

The Gathering of Israel 416

Book of Mormon Plates and Records

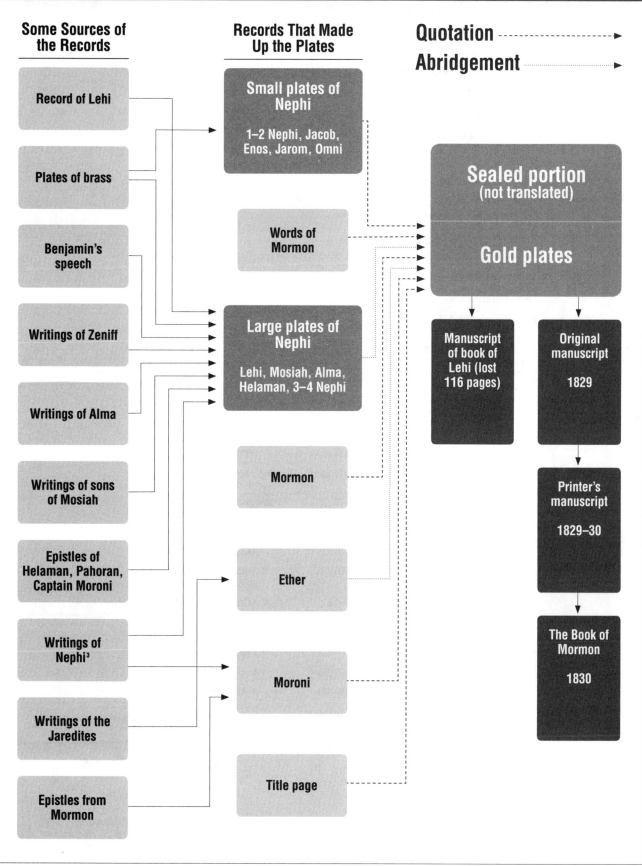

Some Sources of the Records

- Record of Lehi
- Plates of brass
- Benjamin's speech
- Writings of Zeniff
- Writings of Alma
- Writings of sons of Mosiah
- Epistles of Helaman, Pahoran, Captain Moroni
- Writings of Nephi³
- Writings of the Jaredites
- Epistles from Mormon

Records That Made Up the Plates

- Small plates of Nephi
  1–2 Nephi, Jacob, Enos, Jarom, Omni
- Words of Mormon
- Large plates of Nephi
  Lehi, Mosiah, Alma, Helaman, 3–4 Nephi
- Mormon
- Ether
- Moroni
- Title page

Quotation - - - - - ->
Abridgement ·········>

Sealed portion (not translated)

Gold plates

- Manuscript of book of Lehi (lost 116 pages)
- Original manuscript 1829
- Printer's manuscript 1829–30
- The Book of Mormon 1830

Nephite Record Keepers

Nephi
Prophet, leader, teacher, and initiator of Nephite record (1–2 Nephi)

Small plates of Nephi	Large plates of Nephi
Personal journals of prophecy and spiritual experiences	Social, political, military, and religious history

ABOUT 600 B.C. ▼ **Nephi, son of Lehi**
Prophet and author of 1–2 Nephi

▼ **Kept by the kings**

544 B.C. ▶ **Jacob, brother of Nephi**
Prophet and author of book of Jacob

▼

544–421 B.C. ▼ **Enos, son of Jacob**
Prophet and author of book of Enos

▼

420 B.C. ▼ **Jarom, son of Enos**
Prophet and author of book of Jarom

▼

361 B.C. ▼ **Omni, son of Jarom**
Nephite warrior who wrote first 3 verses of book of Omni

▼

279 B.C. ▼ **Amaron, son of Omni**
Wrote 5 verses noting the Lord's destruction of the wicked of his generation

▼

279 B.C. ▶ **Chemish, brother of Amaron**
Wrote only 1 verse

▼

▼ **Abinadom, son of Chemish**
Wrote only 2 verses

▼ **Mosiah¹**
King who united the Nephites with the Mulekites

130 B.C. ▼ **Amaleki, son of Abinadom**
Wrote 19 verses, bore fervent testimony of the Savior, and turned small plates of Nephi over to King Benjamin

○ **Benjamin, son of Mosiah¹**

130 B.C.
191–124 B.C. ▼ **Mosiah², son of Benjamin**
Last of the Nephite kings

91–72 B.C. ○ **Alma², son of Alma¹**
Prophet and first chief judge

72–56 B.C. ▼ **Helaman¹, son of Alma²**
Prophet and military leader

▶ **Shiblon, son of Alma²**

56–53 B.C. ▶ **Helaman², son of Helaman¹**

53–59 B.C. ▼ **Nephi², son of Helaman²**
Contemporary with Samuel the Lamanite

39–1 B.C. ▼ **Nephi³, son of Nephi²**
Chief Nephite disciple and Apostle of the resurrected Lord

?–A.D. 111 ▼ **Nephi⁴, son of Nephi³**

A.D. 111–194 ▼ **Amos¹, son of Nephi⁴**

A.D. 194–306 ▼ **Amos², son of Amos¹**

A.D. 306–321 ▶ **Ammaron, brother of Amos²**
Hid plates in the hill Shim in A.D. 321
Commissioned 10-year-old Mormon to continue record upon turning 24 years of age

A.D. 345–385 ○ **Mormon**
Made an abridgment of Nephite plates

The following indicate relationships:
▼ Father to son
▶ Brother to brother
○ Plates passed outside family relationships

A.D. 385–421 ▼ **Moroni, son of Mormon²**
Completed the record of his father
Added his own writings
Abridged the Jaredite record (book of Ether)
Sealed the abridged records in the Hill Cumorah

408

The Witnesses of the Book of Mormon Plates

While the Three Witnesses were not related to each other, the Eight Witnesses were very much interrelated. They were made up of the extended families of the Smiths and the Whitmers. Joseph and Emma Smith lived with the Whitmers on their farm. The Whitmers helped Joseph during the days of translation. Christian, Jacob, Peter Jr., and John Whitmer were all sons of Peter Sr. and Mary Whitmer. Hiram Page later married Catherine Whitmer, the oldest daughter of Peter Sr. and Mary Whitmer. Joseph Smith Sr., Hyrum Smith, and Samuel Smith were the father and brothers of the Prophet Joseph Smith.

The Three Witnesses

Date of Birth	Place of Birth	Age When Shown Plates	Occupation	Membership in the Church	Death
Oliver Cowdery Oct. 3, 1806	Wells, Rutland County, Vermont	23	School teacher, lawyer	Baptized May 15, 1829 Excommunicated Apr. 12, 1838. Rebaptized Oct. 1848. Died in full fellowship. Never denied his testimony concerning the Book of Mormon	Mar. 3, 1850 Richmond, Missouri
David Whitmer Jan. 7, 1805	Harrisburg, Pennsylvania	23	Farmer	Baptized June 1829 Excommunicated Apr. 13, 1838. Never returned to the Church. Never denied his testimony	Jan. 25, 1888 Richmond, Missouri
Martin Harris May 18, 1783	East-Town, Saratoga County, New York	45	Farmer	Baptized Apr. 6, 1830 Excommunicated last week of Dec. 1837. Baptized again Nov. 7, 1842. Never denied his testimony concerning the plates. Died in full fellowship	July 10, 1875 Clarkston, Utah

The Eight Witnesses

Date of Birth	Place of Birth	Age When Shown Plates	Occupation	Membership in the Church	Death
Christian Whitmer Jan. 18, 1798	Harrisburg, Pennsylvania	30	Shoemaker	Baptized Apr. 11, 1830 Always a faithful member of the Church	Nov. 27, 1835 Clay County, Missouri
Jacob Whitmer Jan. 27, 1800	Harrisburg, Pennsylvania	28	Shoemaker	Baptized Apr. 11, 1830 Apostatized 1838. Never returned to the Church. Never denied his testimony of the plates	Apr. 21, 1856 Richmond, Missouri
Peter Whitmer Jr. Sept. 27, 1809	Fayette, New York	20	Tailor, farmer	Baptized June 1829 Always a faithful member of the Church	Sept. 22, 1836 Liberty, Clay County, Missouri
John Whitmer Aug. 27, 1802	Harrisburg, Pennsylvania	27	Farmer	Baptized June 1829 Excommunicated Mar. 10, 1838. Never returned to the Church. Never denied his testimony of the plates or the Church	July 11, 1878 Far West, Missouri
Hiram Page 1800	Vermont	29	Physician, farmer	Baptized Apr. 11, 1830 Apostatized 1838. Never denied his testimony	Aug. 12, 1852 Excelsior Springs, Missouri
Joseph Smith Sr. July 12, 1771	Topsfield, Essex County, Massachusetts	58	Farmer	Baptized Apr. 6, 1830 Always a faithful member of the Church	Sept. 14, 1840 Nauvoo, Illinois
Hyrum Smith Feb. 9, 1800	Tunbridge, Vermont	28	Farmer	Baptized May 1829 Always a faithful member of the Church	June 27, 1844 Carthage, Illinois
Samuel H. Smith Mar. 13, 1806	Tunbridge, Vermont	22	Farmer	Baptized May 1829 Always a faithful member of the Church	July 30, 1844 Nauvoo, Illinois

Possible Route Taken by Lehi's Family

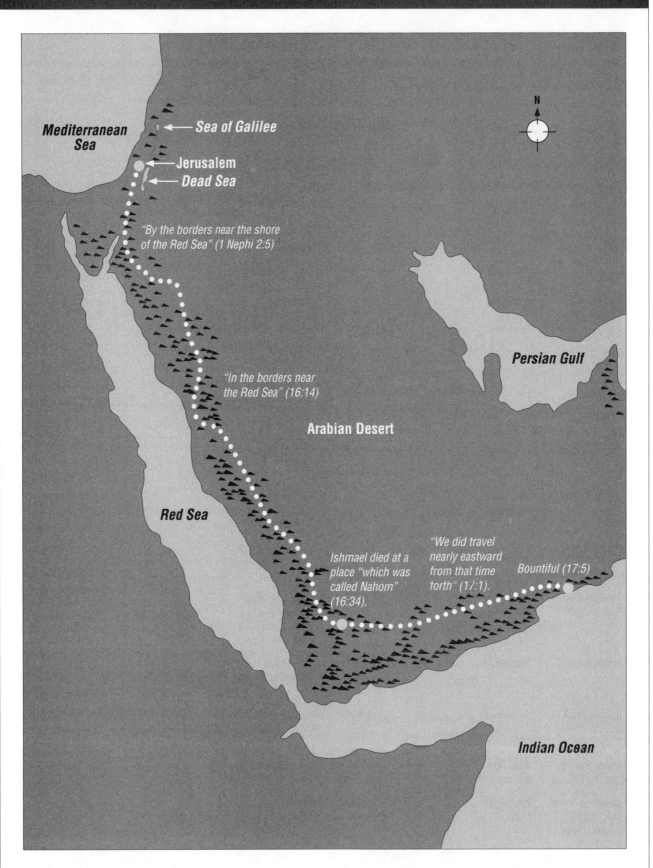

Mediterranean Sea

Sea of Galilee

Jerusalem

Dead Sea

"By the borders near the shore of the Red Sea" (1 Nephi 2:5)

N

Persian Gulf

"In the borders near the Red Sea" (16:14)

Arabian Desert

Red Sea

Ishmael died at a place "which was called Nahom" (16:34).

"We did travel nearly eastward from that time forth" (17:1).

Bountiful (17:5)

Indian Ocean

Book of Mormon Pages and Time Periods

This chart shows how many pages in the Book of Mormon correspond with each author and time period.

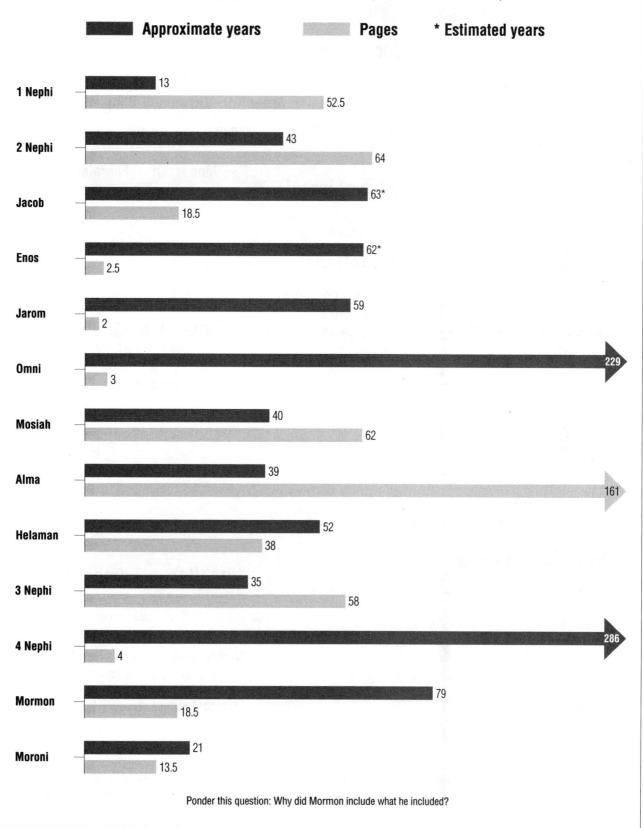

■ **Approximate years** ■ **Pages** * **Estimated years**

1 Nephi — 13 / 52.5

2 Nephi — 43 / 64

Jacob — 63* / 18.5

Enos — 62* / 2.5

Jarom — 59 / 2

Omni — 229 / 3

Mosiah — 40 / 62

Alma — 39 / 161

Helaman — 52 / 38

3 Nephi — 35 / 58

4 Nephi — 286 / 4

Mormon — 79 / 18.5

Moroni — 21 / 13.5

Ponder this question: Why did Mormon include what he included?

The Stick of Judah and the Stick of Joseph

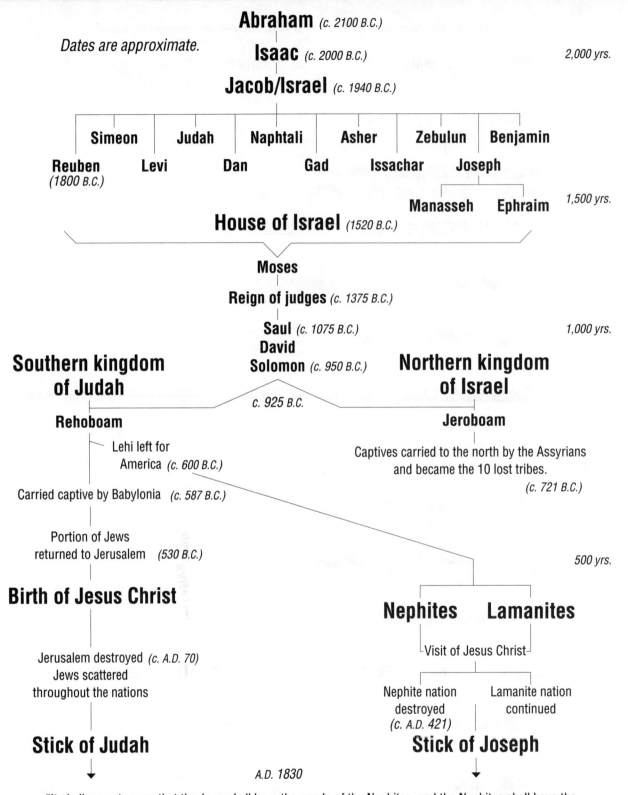

Abraham *(c. 2100 B.C.)*

Dates are approximate.

Isaac *(c. 2000 B.C.)*

2,000 yrs.

Jacob/Israel *(c. 1940 B.C.)*

Simeon **Judah** **Naphtali** **Asher** **Zebulun** **Benjamin**

Reuben **Levi** **Dan** **Gad** **Issachar** **Joseph**
(1800 B.C.)

Manasseh **Ephraim** *1,500 yrs.*

House of Israel *(1520 B.C.)*

Moses

Reign of judges *(c. 1375 B.C.)*

Saul *(c. 1075 B.C.)* *1,000 yrs.*
David
Solomon *(c. 950 B.C.)*

Southern kingdom of Judah **Northern kingdom of Israel**

c. 925 B.C.

Rehoboam **Jeroboam**

Lehi left for
America *(c. 600 B.C.)*

Captives carried to the north by the Assyrians
and became the 10 lost tribes.
(c. 721 B.C.)

Carried captive by Babylonia *(c. 587 B.C.)*

Portion of Jews
returned to Jerusalem *(530 B.C.)* *500 yrs.*

Birth of Jesus Christ

Nephites **Lamanites**

Visit of Jesus Christ

Jerusalem destroyed *(c. A.D. 70)*
Jews scattered
throughout the nations

Nephite nation
destroyed
(c. A.D. 421)

Lamanite nation
continued

Stick of Judah **Stick of Joseph**

A.D. 1830

"It shall come to pass that the Jews shall have the words of the Nephites, and the Nephites shall have the
words of the Jews; and the Nephites and the Jews shall have the words of the lost tribes of Israel; and the
lost tribes of Israel shall have the words of the Nephites and the Jews" (2 Nephi 29:13).

Flashbacks from Omni through Mosiah

To better understand the sequence of events in the books of Omni through Mosiah, review the following chart, which breaks down the books and shows the different accounts of history that are recorded during overlapping time periods.

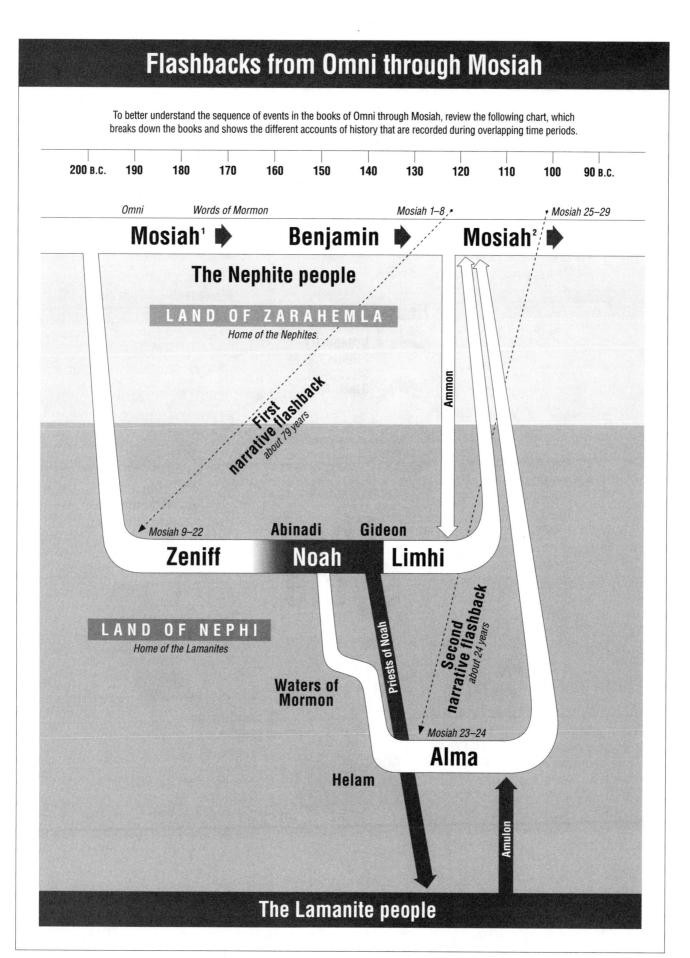

The Cycle of Righteousness and Wickedness

Book of Mormon history reveals a recurring cycle that underlies the rise and fall of nations as well as individuals. This cycle is especially clear in Helaman 3–12 and in 3 Nephi 5–9. Mormon gave a summary of this cycle in Helaman 12:2–6. Notice how the Nephites go from unrighteousness to righteousness and back to unrighteousness again in relatively short periods of time. This same tragic cycle also occurred with the Jaredite nation. The following illustration shows the cycle of righteousness and wickedness repeated throughout the books of Helaman and 3 Nephi:

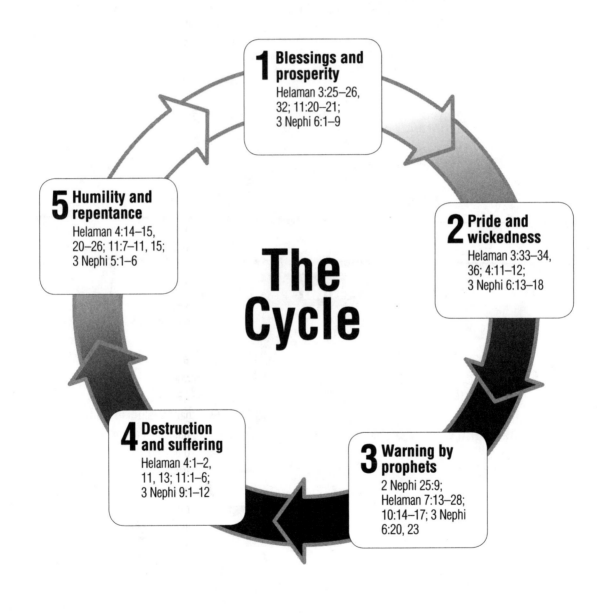

The Cycle

1 Blessings and prosperity
Helaman 3:25–26, 32; 11:20–21; 3 Nephi 6:1–9

2 Pride and wickedness
Helaman 3:33–34, 36; 4:11–12; 3 Nephi 6:13–18

3 Warning by prophets
2 Nephi 25:9; Helaman 7:13–28; 10:14–17; 3 Nephi 6:20, 23

4 Destruction and suffering
Helaman 4:1–2, 11, 13; 11:1–6; 3 Nephi 9:1–12

5 Humility and repentance
Helaman 4:14–15, 20–26; 11:7–11, 15; 3 Nephi 5:1–6

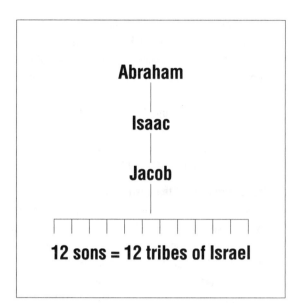

God reestablished his covenant with Abraham, his son Isaac, and his grandson Jacob. The Lord changed Jacob's name to Israel. Israel had 12 sons whose children became the 12 families or 12 tribes of Israel. Israel's family eventually survived a famine by moving from the promised land to Egypt. There they multiplied and became a great nation. After many years Moses led the children of Israel out of Egypt, and Joshua led them into the promised land. Eventually Israel divided into two nations—the northern kingdom of Israel and the southern kingdom of Judah.

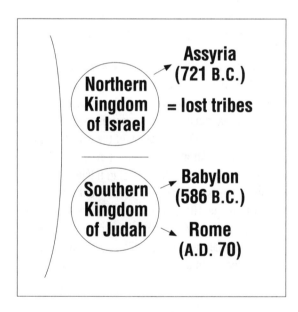

The Lord warned the children of Israel that if they turned away from Him and worshipped idols, they would be removed from the land of their inheritance. Eventually they turned from God and were conquered and carried away from the promised land. Assyria conquered the northern kingdom of Israel in 721 B.C. They eventually became known as the 10 lost tribes. Later, the southern kingdom of Judah (or the Jews) were conquered and scattered by Babylon about 587 B.C. About 70 years later, many of the Jews began to return to the land of Israel, where they remained as a nation for many generations. In A.D. 70 and again in A.D. 135, the Romans destroyed Jerusalem and scattered the Jews among all nations. Remarkably, many of the Jews maintained their identity as a people. The lost tribes, however, remained scattered throughout the world; most of them do not know that they are descendants of Israel.

The Gathering of Israel

Who Is the House of Israel?

"The house of Israel" generally refers to the descendants of Jacob, whose name was changed to Israel in the Old Testament (see Genesis 32:27–28). In the Book of Mormon the Savior expanded this definition to include not only the literal descendants of Israel (see 3 Nephi 20:25–27) but also all Gentiles who repent, are baptized, and come unto Christ (see 3 Nephi 21:6).

Israel Will Be Gathered in Fulfillment of Covenant

The gathering of Israel in the last days is a fulfillment of the covenant Jehovah made with prophets of the Old Testament (see Isaiah 11:12; Jeremiah 31:10; Ezekiel 34:12; 1 Nephi 19:15–16; Abraham 2:9–11). Jesus Christ repeated this promise in 3 Nephi 20:12–13, 29, at which time He indicated that the covenant to gather Israel was first made with Abraham as part of the Abrahamic covenant (see 2 Nephi 29:14; 3 Nephi 20:25; Abraham 2:9–11).

The Role of the Book of Mormon in the Gathering of Israel

The Savior taught in 3 Nephi 21:1–7 that the coming forth of the Book of Mormon is a sign to the entire world that the Lord has commenced to gather Israel and fulfill covenants He made to Abraham, Isaac, and Jacob (see also 3 Nephi 29:1; Ether 4:17).

Elder Russell M. Nelson of the Quorum of the Twelve Apostles taught that "the Book of Mormon is central to this work. It declares the doctrine of the gathering. It causes people to learn about Jesus Christ, to believe His gospel, and to join His Church. In fact, if there were no Book of Mormon, the promised gathering of Israel would not occur" (in Conference Report, Oct. 2006, 84; or *Ensign*, Nov. 2006, 80).

The Gathering of Israel Is Both Spiritual and Physical

The spiritual gathering of Israel occurs when someone accepts the gospel of Jesus Christ and is baptized a member of The Church of Jesus Christ of Latter-day Saints. Elder Bruce R. McConkie (1915–85) of the Quorum of the Twelve Apostles emphasized the importance of the spiritual gathering when he stated: "The spiritual gathering takes precedence over the temporal. . . . Men can be saved wherever they live, but they cannot be saved, regardless of their abode, unless they accept the gospel and come unto Christ" (*A New Witness for the Articles of Faith* [1985], 567).

Jesus Christ taught that there would eventually be two centers of gathering—the New Jerusalem and the Old Jerusalem (see 3 Nephi 20:21–22, 29). As Church membership expanded into other lands, President Spencer W. Kimball (1895–1985) taught that the gathering place today is wherever someone lives: "The gathering of Israel for Mexicans is in Mexico; in Scandinavia, for those of the northern countries; the gathering place for the Germans is in Germany; and the Polynesians, in the islands; for the Brazilians, in Brazil; for the Argentines, in Argentina" (in Conference Report, Apr. 1975, 4; or *Ensign,* May 1975, 4).

Our Responsibility to Help Gather Israel

"Being an heir to the Abrahamic covenant does not make one a 'chosen person' per se, but does signify that such are chosen to responsibly carry the gospel to all the peoples of the earth" (Bible Dictionary, "Abraham, Covenant of," 602). The promise to gather Israel is being fulfilled today as descendants of Abraham, Isaac, and Jacob bear the Lord's name, His ministry, and His priesthood to all the families of the earth, thus offering them "the blessings of the Gospel, which are the blessings of salvation, even of life eternal" (Abraham 2:11).

"It becometh every man who hath been warned to warn his neighbor" (D&C 88:81).

SUBJECT INDEX

A

Aaron
  labored for years to bring Lamanites to Christ, 168
  our dependence on Christ, 203

Aaronic Priesthood
  Nephites did not use before the Savior's visit, 383

Abominable church, 27

Abraham
  covenant God made with, 55, 264
  detail of stick of Judah and stick of Joseph, 412
  Joseph Smith's revelations teach us about, 29

Accountability
  no law, then no punishment, 68
  to the Savior for our actions, 69
  will and power control thoughts and actions, 60

Adversity
  effects of, 260
  essential part of process, 245

Afflictions
  can refine and purify, 45
  consecrate for gain, 50
  God will consecrate, 60
  see purpose of, 221
  staying faithful and grateful to the Lord through, 12

Agency
  everyone has a choice, 20
  God always acts with unfailing respect for, 53
  God's purposes will triumph without abrogating man's, 99
  had in premortal world, 192
  have will and power to control thoughts and actions, 60

Allegory of the olive trees, 122–23

Alma the Elder
  people of compared with people of Limhi, 163
  responsible for dealing with Church transgressors, 234

Alma the Younger
  challenges as high priest and chief judge, 170
  repentance of, 167

Amalickiah, 252

Amlicites
  made war against government, 170
  marked their bodies, 173–74

Ammon
  expedition to find Zeniff's colony, 146
  labored for years to bring Lamanites to Christ, 168, 200

model servant of the Lord, 198
our dependence on Christ, 203
spoke with boldness, 201
taught that only a seer could use special interpreters, 55

Angels
  call wicked to repentance, 165
  ordinances of the Aaronic Priesthood are vital to the ministering of, 317
  ministering must be in harmony with God's will, 165
  reality of their work and ministry, 194–95, 391

Anger
  best to avoid, 306
  results in loss of the Spirit, 397

Anthon, Professor Charles, 99

Anti-Christs
  counterfeit the true gospel plan, 213
  use half truths, 216

Anti-Nephi-Lehies, 205–8

Articles of Faith
  give allegiance to your sovereign and render loyal service, 248
  literal gathering of Israel, 325
  punished for our own sins, 54
  should resist temptation to lie a little, 102
  we believe in being honest, 69

Asay, Carlos E.
  all people are precious to God and should be to us, 220
  Nephi and Lehi (sons of Helaman) patterned their lives after namesakes, 268
  preachers who share saving truths always precious to converts, 154
  repeated wrongdoings form unbreakable cord, 96
  what it means to be salt of the earth, 305
  word of the Lord helps us avoid the Nephite cycle of righteousness, 223

Ashton, Marvin J.
  additional gifts of Spirit not always evident, 402–3
  choose how to respond to circumstances, 292
  obey even when we do not understand reason, 24
  real charity not something given away; something acquired, 379
  Satan tempts people to take advantage of each other, 103

Assyrians
  acted as the Lord's instrument, 84
  God's judgment on, 87

Atonement, the
  Book of Mormon bears witness of, 19
  has miraculous power that can help us change, 51

infinite in several ways, 51, 66, 138, 228–29, 405
insights about, 50, 99
should be at heart of our rejoicings, 65
understanding power of, 65–66

Ayala, Eduardo
  faithful members bless people in their homelands, 49

B

Babylon
  fall of, 90
  Isaiah foresaw destruction of, 46
  symbol for worldliness and Satan's kingdom, 46–47

Ballard, Melvin J.
  importance of repenting during mortality, 230

Ballard, M. Russell
  avoid evil practices, 328
  baptismal covenants require righteousness, 156
  bear pure testimony, 176
  be better neighbors to those not of our faith, 200
  Christ as both the Father and the Son, 153
  danger of heeding Satan's temptations, 293
  family-centered perspective helps parents, 58
  George McLaughlin prayed and fasted for branch, 199
  give heed to small and simple things, 235
  God expects us to hear and know His voice, 145
  good works must also have grace of Christ, 405
  God loves all His children equally and infinitely, 97
  Jesus suffered willingly so we might be clean, 152–53
  let us beware of false prophets and false teachers, 311
  many converted by Abinadi's testimony, 150
  no spiritual power in living by convenience, 256
  pay attention to teachings of Church leaders, 282
  performing Alma's experiment leads to conversion, 225
  plan to sin now and repent later is a trap, 266
  prayerfully set a date to have someone prepared to meet with missionaries, 168
  prayer should be yearning and show gratitude, 14
  pray for guidance in doing the Lord's work, 199–200
  priestcraft seen in those who oppose prophets, 97
  raise our voices against wicked trends, 173

relationship with faith, hope, and charity, 392

replace fear with faith, 290

responding to prophetic counsel brings safety, peace, and prosperity, 298

starting gospel conversations with friends, 201

today's secret combinations, 262

trendy dress can be unbecoming to priesthood holders, 174

value of pondering and meditating, 274

Baptism
   gate through which every soul must pass to obtain eternal life, 109
   importance of, 300

Bateman, Merrill J.
   Jesus bore our sins and experienced our deepest feelings, 153–54

Beatitudes, the
   the Savior's sermon begins with declarations, 303

Beck, Julie B.
   mothers who keep covenants have great power and influence, 258

Beckham, Janette Hales
   learning to discern teachings of Spirit, 226

Bednar, David A.
   avoid anything that offends the Spirit, 25
   coming unto Christ requires lifetime of obedience, 109
   drawing attention to self while teaching gospel is priestcraft, 171
   gift of the Holy Ghost like Liahona, 237
   grace of Christ empowers us beyond our limited capacity, 279–80
   hearer of the word must also be willing to receive by the Spirit, 111
   hold fast to the word of God, 22
   Liahona worked according to faith and diligence, 34
   like Pahoran, we can choose to not be offended, 259–60
   sacrament renews baptismal covenant, 383
   strive for baptism of Spirit, 108
   tender mercies of the Lord, 13
   words of Christ provide direction and protection, 235

Benson, Ezra Taft
   avoid being deceived by asking three questions, 128
   avoid immoral, suggestive, or pornographic influences, 239
   Book of Mormon brings men to Christ, 8, 19, 101, 285, 360
   Book of Mormon exposes enemies of Christ, 127
   Book of Mormon children were taught saving truths, 130
   Book of Mormon is keystone, 4, 7

Book of Mormon study has eternal consequences, 94

Book of Mormon teaches how to live righteously in times of war, 248, 256

born again experiences not as dramatic as in scriptures, 166

cleanse the inner vessel, 260

Columbus identified as man among Gentiles, 27–28

come unto Christ, 110

declare gospel and do it effectively, 104

despair cometh because of iniquity, 404

forefathers inspired by and fulfilled Isaiah's prophecies, 63–64

founding fathers and constitutional government necessary to Restoration, 49

godly sorrow is gift of the Spirit, 349

humility is recognition of dependence on higher power, 160–61

labor to conquer the enemy of our souls, 395

love for Bible, 355

many are developing spiritually but unable to perceive their own growth, 297

Moroni wrote with us in mind, 5

nature of godly sorrow, 233

need to plant standard of liberty among our people, 252

obedience should be our quest, not an irritant, 15

opposition provides choices, 52

picture of, 265, 286

phrase "God of Abraham, Isaac, and Jacob," 19

prepare and prevent better than repair and repent, 258–59

pride, 265

rare experience of hearing voice of Heavenly Father, 299

repentance involves more than a change of heart, 384

Satan's principal flaw, 90

Savior's visit to Nephites parallels our day, 288

scripture study important to individuals and families, 219–20

temporary nature of earthly treasures, 310

turning to fathers for blessings and counsel, 36–37

word of God gives power to resist temptation, 32

Bible. *See also* Joseph Smith Translation
   corrupted very early, 28–29
   missing plain and precious text, 28–30

Book of Mormon
   brings great personal and family blessings, 9–10
   brings stronger testimony of Son of God, 1
   demonstrates that God remembers covenant with Israel, 5
   doctrinal keystone, 7
   exposes the enemies of Christ, 127

helps discern truth from error, 8

how to recognize great worth of, 101

importance of witnesses, 10

is the great standard we are to use, 104

keystone of our religion, 4, 7, 401

leads to personal revelation, 1

most remarkable and important religious text, 4

neglecting study of has eternal consequences, 94

offers a new covenant, 7

preserved spiritual safety of Marion G. Romney, 8

rejection of is a sign of the times, 105

role in gathering of Israel in last days, 6

sealed portion of, 30–31, 366–67

study should be influenced by knowledge that Moroni saw our day, 357

substantiates miracles recorded in Old Testament, 38

teaches how to live righteously in times of war, 248

testimony of grows from a seed, 8–9

test of truth lies in reading it, 9

translation of, 134

was written for our day, 4–5

Book of Mormon Gospel Doctrine Teacher's Manual, 167

Books of Moses
   plates of brass contain, 17–18

Born again, 166–68, 234

Bradford, William R.
   joy and happiness come in righteous living, 404
   purpose of mortality to become like Heavenly Father, 245

Brandt, Edward J.
   definition of *adieu* in Jacob 7, 128–29

Brazen serpent
   children of Israel plagued, 272

Brother of Jared
   chastened by the Lord, 363
   Jesus showed Himself to, 365–66
   named Mahonri Moriancumer, 362
   received light for travel vessels, 364–65, 369
   received Urim and Thummim from the Lord, 147, 168–69, 366

Brown, Hugh B.
   each responsible for lost people we failed, 116

Burton, H. David
   meekness vital to becoming more Christlike, 392

Burton, Theodore M.
   ministering to those who are repentant, 166
   those who follow Heavenly Father appear more like Him, 179

C

Cahoon, Reynolds
son born and named Mahonri
Moriancumer, 362

Cahoon, William F., 362

Caldwell, C. Max
charity must be developed and
experienced, 158

Cannon, George Q.
taken home to God does not mean in His
immediate presence, 242

Capital punishment
1889 declaration on Church's position, 171

Captain Moroni, 248–52, 256, 407

Celestial kingdom
requires combination of divine assistance
and genuine repentance, 51
light, glory and intelligence prepared
in, 155
man needs preparation before can enter,
132
those who desire must battle every day, 211

Chains of hell
defined by Alma, 178

Charity
love is, 379
must be developed and experienced, 158
pure love of Christ, 342

Chastening, 363

Chastity
dear and precious above all things, 398
defined, 237
sexual intimacy outside marriage is sin
and forbidden by God, 119

Cherubim
figures representing heavenly creatures, 189

Child, Sheldon F.
definition of "deal justly" with one
another, 370

Chiasmus
Hebrew literary form, 232–33

Christ. *See* Jesus Christ

Christensen, Joe J.
pollutants in last days environmental and
spiritual, 356–57
pride leads to unrighteous comparisons
and our downfall, 279

Christofferson, D. Todd
become one with Father and Son, 321
justification, sanctification, and
perfection, 265
laying aside pride a first step in following
Christ, 265
offer the Lord gift of broken heart and
contrite spirit, 297

Circumcision
law of done away, 395

Columbus, Christopher
inspired of the Lord, 27–28

Come back
First Presidency invitation to, 165, 323–24
help those who strayed to the fold, 166
home to Heavenly Father, 293
it is possible to, 271

Commandments
keep and prosper, 15
keeping brings unity, 157
need for prayer and faith to obey, 15
purpose of is to bless us, 52
salvation requires more than keeping, 152
Ten given for all generations, 151
to do and some not to do, 189
ungrateful to Father and Son when
unwilling to keep, 291
violation of yields unhappiness, 282
when we violate, youth may follow, 119–20

Condie, Spencer J.
the Beatitudes lead from one to the next,
303–4
keeping covenants can strengthen
disposition to do good, 263
studying scriptures helps us face life's
decisions, 111

Confession of sins
required part of repentance process, 164

Conscience
compared to the Liahona, 237
guides our spirits, 293, 358, 396
light of Christ, 389–90
peace of, 142–43
remorse of, 246

Consecration
living the law of, 263, 342–43
storehouse kept by, 333
yielding our hearts and souls to God, 266

Constitution of United States, 47

Contention
avoid arguments and, 217, 252–53, 300
Book of Mormon lays down, 213
dissention and jeopardized the Nephite
nation, 248, 252, 399
is destructive and fostered by Satan, 194,
262, 287
no disputations and among the people,
341, 343, 346

Conversion
requires a change of heart, 179

Cook, Gene R.
discovering personal gifts of the Spirit, 403
faith in Christ will deliver us from our
bonds, 21
grace of Christ can cleanse us and assist
us in becoming perfect, 280

Nephite disciples pray without
multiplying words, 321
ponder God's mercy to achieve faith and
humility, 401

Cook, Quentin L.
definition of *Saint*, 140

Coriantumr
Jaredites' last king, 133
studied all the arts of war, 380

Correction
accept the Lord's even if it's painful, 34

Countenances
those who follow Heavenly Father appear
more like Him, 179

Covenants
essential for our eternal progression, 156
importance of, 256

Cowdery, Oliver
his witness included in 100 million copies
of Book of Mormon, 98
John the Beloved's request to tarry in the
flesh, 339
one of earliest missionaries, 382
prophecy was fulfilled when Elijah
restored priesthood keys, 335
said Joseph Smith would fulfill Isaiah's
prophecy, 99
witness of Book of Mormon plates, 10–11,
72, 367, 409

Creation
insights about, 50, 54
Joseph Smith's revelations teach us
about, 29

Crucifixion of Christ, 92, 272, 295, 354

Cultural diversity, 344

Cumorah, 352, 382, 408

Curse, the
difference between the mark and, 62, 174

Cycle of righteousness and wickedness,
223, 262, 277, 279, 293–94, 345, 369,
372–73, 375, 414

Cyrus the Great
destroyed Babylon, 46, 89

D

Dancing
the Lord approves of proper, 40

Death
spiritual and physical, 50
spiritual is second death, 120

Degrees of glory, three
D&C 76 names, 33

Destruction of the soul
defined by Joseph Fielding Smith, 50

Dew, Sheri L.
Atonement ensures we do not need to bear burdens alone, 209
connection with desire and action, 304
the Lord expects more than the world expects but He offers more, 185–86

Didier, Charles
steps to obtain a testimony, 95–96

Disobedience
blocks ties to God and erodes testimony, 49

Dissension, 252–53, 280

Doctrine and Covenants
true companion scripture to Bible and Book of Mormon, 8

Dress and appearance
grooming and manners, 173

Dunn, Loren C.
respect others' beliefs and build on common ground, 202

Dust of the earth
man must rely upon God for everything, 142

E

Edgley, Richard C.
carnal desires prevalent in today's world, 103
greatness begins with humility and submissiveness, 222–23
humility and gratitude characteristics of happiness, 370
reality of the attacks of the adversary, 102

Education
get all you can, 69

Eight Witnesses. *See* Witnesses, Eight

Enoch
city of, 341, 344, 380
Joseph Smith's revelations teach us about, 29
scriptural writings of will yet come to us, 98

Ensign
to nations, 78

Envy
opposition to God's perfect love, 180

Ephraim
detail of stick of Judah and stick of Joseph, 412
Ishmael was descendant of, 20

Euphrates River
damned to capture Babylon, 46, 89
dangerous and destructive, 84

Eyring, Henry B.
becoming as a child leads to spiritual safety, 140

central role of the Savior in our redemption, 386
Church has always been one generation away from extinction, 288
dependence upon God can fade quickly, 278
disobedience blocks ties to God and erodes testimony, 49
do temporal things well for those you serve, 201
faithful study of scriptures brings the Holy Ghost, 111
faith is a choice not an inheritance, 163
God is forgotten out of vanity, 271
God kept His promises to reach out to Lehi's covenant children, 58–59
heart drawn out to God in prayer continually, 228
humility is essential preparation for Second Coming, 76
keeping commandments brings unity, 157
the Lord calls servants to warn people of danger, 371
prayer and faith help obey commandments, 15
praying with real intent includes willingness to be obedient, 389
principles in the Lord's prayer a model to follow, 309
prompt obedience necessary to spiritual well-being, 185
prosperity leads to feelings of pride and spiritual self-sufficiency, 292
rejecting God's counsel is choosing another influence, 216
remembering the Lord, 384
remember the Savior and pray always, 318
safety in the counsel of prophets, 375
the Savior will help those who are trying to come to Him, 297
Spirit of God never generates contention, 262
study and ponder the scriptures every day, 332

F

Faith
and miracles, 377
dangers accompany seeking signs to gain, 223
includes trust in God's timing, 99
in Jesus Christ, 391
manifest by actions, 38
relationship with faith, hope, and charity, 388

Fall, the
Book of Mormon bears witness of, 19
effects of pass upon all created things, 53–54
insights about, 50
part of Heavenly Father's plan, 55
why was necessary, 54

False prophets, 311

False traditions
eternal hatred among Lamanites against Nephites, 150

Familiar spirits
spirits of dead, 85, 96

Family
raise up children unto the Lord, 19

Family proclamation
family central to plan for eternal destiny, 12, 19
marriage central to the Lord's plans for His children, 34
parents' responsibility to teach their children, 58, 143

Farrar, F. W.
description of the Savior's agonies on the cross, 139

Fasting
George McLaughlin prayed and fasted for growth of branch, 199
humbles our souls, 185

Fast offerings
how much to contribute, 118

Faust, James E.
Book of Mormon is our doctrinal keystone, 7–8
choosing right from wrong very important, 78
Christlike conduct guided by the Holy Spirit, which sanctifies us, 265
contention causes Spirit of the Lord to depart, 262
converting power of the Book of Mormon, 10
countenances of BYU students at Jerusalem Center, 179
fasting humbles our souls, 185
following Savior's example during hard times helps endure bitter cups, 299
hope brings peace into a troubled life, 392
how Fall affected Adam and Eve and posterity, 54
how Lucifer fell, 53
keep out of spiritual dead spots, 39
knowledge of the Savior comes through faith and witness of Spirit, 11
must seek for perfection now, 308
need for modern revelation, 104
need to overcome differences of culture and race, 97
no earthly authority can separate us from direct access to our Creator, 310
nurturing spiritual seeds of faith, 225
offenses that warrant Church discipline, 165
prayer is a lifeline to God, 111
premeditated repentance is a deception, 102
prepare to be worthy to stand in the Lord's presence, 353

process of establishing the Lord's Church,
172

Savior's invitation to build up the
kingdom of God, 302

scattering of Israel brought belief in God
to many nations, 126

seriousness of the sin of lying, 69

standard works are principal means of
restoring truth, 29

stand before the Savior to account for our
lives, 69

study and accept the Atonement, 143

understanding the power of the
Atonement, 65–66

unity can be developed despite diversity,
344

warned against becoming intrigued with
Satan's mysteries, 349

Yaeko Seki's family is greatest blessing in
her life, 61

Featherstone, Vaughan J.
priesthood holders need to be pure at all
times, 295
youth may break serious commandment
based on small commandment an
adult broke, 119–20

Final Judgment
justice and mercy of God will have been
so demonstrably perfect, 246
out of books, 338
see Book of Mormon prophets at the bar
of God, 404

First Presidency
1889 declaration regarding capital
punishment, 171
be judges of this dispensation, 351
counsel to Church members in military
service, 248–49, 255, 257, 259
described the power of inspirational
music, 370
discourage tattoos and piercings, 173–74
The Family: A Proclamation to the World,
12, 19, 34, 58, 143
invitation to come back, 165, 323–24
Light of Christ given to all to help toward
salvation, 390
The Living Christ: The Testimony of the
Apostles, 65, 139
Saints to build up the Church where they
live, 324
why it is of critical importance to follow,
302

First principles of gospel
Book of Mormon bears witness of, 19
requirements for all God's children, 97

First Resurrection
Christ was first person to be resurrected,
154, 243

Foreordination, 191–93

For the Strength of Youth pamphlet
choose carefully the music you listen to, 40
sexual transgressions and repentance,
237, 240
well groomed and modestly dressed, 173

Freedom of religion, 47

Fuller's soap
and refiner's fire, 333

G

Garden of Eden, 52, 54

Garden of Gethsemane, 230

Gathering, latter-day
about to be fulfilled, 89

Gathering of Israel
Isaiah taught, 329
Isaiah wrote of, 324
overview, 416

Gentiles
convincing that Jesus is the Christ, 6
frequently read about in Book of
Mormon, 31
reject the teachings of the Lord, 340

Gideon
an instrument in the hands of God, 171

Gift of the Holy Ghost
baptism of fire, 108
Christ was baptized to show that we
should receive, 107
differences between the Light of Christ
and, 390
disciples prayed for, 320
Liahona compared to, 237
living the gospel requires that we
cultivate, 25
must be received and accepted to be
enjoyed, 96
necessary to organize the priesthood, 383
not recognized as it should be, 296
Savior nourishes those who receive, 386
some members live far beneath privileges
of, 39
source of hope beyond our capacity, 392

Gifts of the Spirit, 401

God
character of, 396
great goodness of, 66
why His omniscience is necessary, 273

Godly sorrow, 233

Gold plates
brass plates led to some of the written
portions of, 16
in language of Egyptians, 136
Limhi discovered 24, 361

know truthfulness of without seeing
them, 11
Moroni directed Joseph Smith to, 29

Grace
doctrine of, 94
enabling power from God, 379
provides strength to persevere, 400
those with faith are saved from spiritual
death, 50
through faith we are justified by the
Savior's, 51

Grafting
in allegory represents groups of people,
126

Grant, Heber J.
angelic visitations ineffective on those
who will not serve the Lord, 180
blessing of paying tithing, 334
importance of witnesses to the Book of
Mormon, 10–11
picture of, 61, 334
real prosperity is growth in knowledge of
God, 61

Grassli, Michaelene P.
capacity of children for spiritual
experiences, 316
train our spiritual senses by doing good
things, 391

Gratitude
enables us to see hardships in their
earthly context, 50
and humility are twin characteristics of
happiness, 370
measure of offering to bless the poor is
measure of, 118
prayer is essential part of, 321
prayer should be filled with, 14

Great and abominable church, 27

Groberg, John H.
partake of the sacrament worthily, 319
takes faith in Christ to repent, be baptized,
or perform any ordinance, 291
trust in the Lord when making decisions,
15–16

Guilt, 207

H

Habakkuk
contemporary prophet who testified in
kingdom of Judah, 13

Hafen, Bruce C.
aspects of nourishing the word, 227
bridle passions to experience richer,
deeper love, 237
divine assistance and genuine repentance
prepare us for celestial life, 51
ministry of unseen angels, 391

Haight, David B.
  Spirit should characterize our worship and sacrament meetings, 387

Hales, Robert D.
  Atonement brings hope to righteous who face death, 211
  brother of Jared shows pattern for meeting family needs, 364
  can be a light to others, 305
  converted turn to task of bringing others to God, 131
  dealing with wayward children, 23
  feast upon words of Christ, 110
  founders of America inspired to establish religious freedom, 28
  gratitude shows our dependence on Heavenly Father and Jesus, 321
  having the Holy Ghost influences our conduct, 157
  Jesus Christ provided an example for all people, 107
  law of tithing prepares us to live law of consecration, 343
  learned from three major surgeries, 45
  process Enos went through increased his faith, 130–31
  process of experiencing change of heart, 144
  prophets must proclaim what God reveals, even if unpopular, 371
  prophets of all dispensations have willingly put their lives on the line, 155
  relationship with Light of Christ and gift of Holy Ghost, 390
  spiritual strength follows when we trust in the Lord, 85
  take hold of the scriptures, 110
  taking name of Christ is one of most significant experiences in life, 337–38
  turn to the Lord when we face trials, 36

Harris, Martin
  his witness included in 100 million copies of Book of Mormon, 98
  lost manuscript of 116 pages, 134
  visited a learned man, 99
  was witness of Book of Mormon plates, 10–11, 72, 367

Hebrew
  altered between Nephi's day and Moroni's, 12

Himni
  labored for years to bring Lamanites to Christ, 168

Hinckley, Gordon B.
  all beauty in the earth bears fingerprint of Creator, 218
  be more compassionate, 144
  blessings associated with being delightsome, 352
  Book of Mormon changes lives forever, 104–5
  Book of Mormon is another witness for Christ, 351
  Book of Mormon's truth found in reading it, 9
  Christ is the author of salvation, 66
  Christopher Columbus was inspired of the Lord, 28
  Church does not accept plural marriage, 118–19
  Church will move forward despite opposition, 329–30
  divorce is among the greatest of tragedies, 307–8
  evils of pornography, 239
  get all the education you can, 69
  go home from conference and live more righteously, 405
  happiness comes of righteousness, 61–62
  helping converts remain active, 206–7
  how to avoid being led away from the truth, 288–89
  ignorance not excuse for unacceptable behavior, 103
  impact of Restoration in history, 31
  importance of family prayer, 319
  importance of staying firm, 258
  importance of teaching by the Spirit, 111
  in world of uncertainty, Son of God is anchor, 376
  let interests range over many fields while working in profession, 64
  maintaining chastity, 398
  man overcame poor treatment by LDS associates to accept gospel, 175
  meaning associated with Mormon's name, 348
  miracle of Restoration and responsibility to move work forward, 329
  nations justified to fight under some circumstances, 250–51
  new converts need our care, 385–86
  no other act compares with Christ's Atonement, 247
  out of Zion shall go forth law, 75
  picture of, 67, 95, 402
  plead for help in overcoming pornography, 67
  prayed for U.S. and friends after 2001 attacks, 276–77
  pray on knees, then get on feet and go to work, 304
  promises to America conditioned upon obedience, 363
  promise to Book of Mormon readers, 402
  reading Book of Mormon brings stronger testimony, 1
  reading Book of Mormon can keep us spiritually sound, 9–10
  rejoice in Christ, preach of Christ, 95
  resist temptation to lie a little, 102
  Restoration's remarkable events, 93
  sacred association of Church, name, and responsibilities, 337
  serious scripture study enlightens and lifts spirits, 332
  sorrow in heaven over wars, 248
  Ten Commandments given for all generations, 151
  times when we must stand up for right and decency, 263
  use clean and virtuous language, 132–33
  warned against all forms of dishonesty, 69
  warned against tattoos and body piercing, 173–74
  warned against trusting intellect over faith, 68–69
  when sharing gospel, build on person's goodness, 202
  woman chose between tithing and school expenses, 376–77
  woman who drank coffee wanted temple recommend, 138
  work and pray for missionary opportunities, 199
  world today needs power of pure testimony, 176

Holland, Jeffrey R.
  4 Nephi reveals how righteous people came to destruction, 341
  Atonement should be at heart of our rejoicings, 65
  Book of Mormon is new covenant, 7
  Book of Mormon most remarkable and important religious text in world, 4
  Book of Mormon reveals reality of angels, 391
  Book of Mormon shows Israel's covenants being fulfilled, 339–40
  brother of Jared's response to chastening, 363
  changing what we can improves access to Atonement, 284
  Christ's love for us is true charity, 393–94
  Church members at heart of marvelous work and wonder, 30
  consequences of sexual sin and importance of chastity, 238
  day of repentance can pass, as did for Nephites, 349–50
  definition of *abide,* 379
  definition of "beautiful upon the mountains," 328
  definition of "be ye clean that bear the vessels of the Lord," 328
  definition of "plain and precious," 28
  definition of the Savior's invitation "come follow me," 296
  doctrine of Christ not complicated, 107
  dual prophecy of Immanuel, 83
  envy stands in opposition to God's perfect love, 180
  explanations for Jesus never showing Himself prior to brother of Jared, 365–66
  faith must often be exercised toward unknown future experiences, 376

five reasons to obey law of tithing, 333–34

foundation of apostles and prophets protects us, 302

God's engagement in our lives, 126

government will be upon Christ's shoulders, 85–86

importance of the Savior's titles, 86

important to study Alma 32–34 as a whole, 222

impossible for the Savior to forget us, 46

inspired instruction in home and Church nourishes us, 386

Isaiah 53 is sublime declaration of Christ, 152

Jacob 5 sketches scattering and gathering of Israel and the Atonement, 122

Jacob employed important elements of teaching, 62

Jesus Christ's prayer for unity, 321

Jesus healed and blessed people, 315–16

Korihor influenced Zoramites' false teachings, 219

law of Moses and higher law designed to bring people to Christ, 312

law of Moses brought people to Christ, 152

Mormon's final plea to believe in Christ, 354

Mormon's spiritual maturity contrasted with sinful state of Nephites, 348–49

Nephi, Jacob, and Isaiah are three Book of Mormon witnesses of Christ, 72–73

older Church members mentor younger ones, 163

olive tree a symbol of God's love, 123

parents should demonstrate faith and righteousness, 120

personal testimony is powerful response to ridicule, 217

preaching of Christ is greatest thrill, 95

prophets prepared Nephites to give up law of Moses following Atonement, 312

provision made for those who die without knowledge of gospel, 68

reality of angels' work and ministry, 194–95

result of repentance worth more than the cost, 167–68

sealing powers link us with ancestors and descendants, 335

singular sense of Christ's doctrine, 107

small plates provided greater views of gospel than 116 pages, 134–35

succor describes Christ's attention to us, 183

vanity is spiritually dangerous, 181

ways to remember the Lord while renewing sacrament covenants, 317

what newly baptized commit to do and be, 156

why Jesus retains wounds of crucifixion in His body, 299

why sexual transgression is so serious, 238

worthy priesthood holder can perform miracles in Christ's name, 295

Holy Ghost

comparison to Liahona, 34–35

continue to earn companionship of, 96

gift of is not recognized as it should be, 297

influences our conduct and solidifies our testimonies, 157

more powerful than visitation of angel, 180

speaks with a voice that is felt more than heard, 39

Homosexuality

homosexual activity a serious sin, 237

sexual stimulation can lead to acts of, 119

Honesty

seriousness of sin of lying, 218

Hope

brings peace into a troubled life, 392

relationship with faith and charity, 392–93

relationship with faith and knowledge, 224

Horses

in Western Hemisphere, 40

Hosanna

definition of, 300

House of David

definition of, 82

House of Israel, 416

Howard, F. Burton

Alma 26 strengthened his testimony of Book of Mormon, 209–10

James E. Faust story on converting power of Book of Mormon, 10

the Lord is more concerned with what a man is than with what he was, 271

Humility

acknowledgment that our talents and abilities are gifts from God, 266

definition of, 378

fortifies our dependence upon the Lord, 160–61

greatness begins with submissiveness and, 222–23

importance of, 223, 370

Hunter, Howard W.

all righteous service is equally acceptable to God, 254

can all be a little more forgiving, 210

definition of seer, 147

desire to share the gospel is natural result of personal conversion, 168

focus should be on righteousness, not recognition; on service, not status, 137

God honors human agency, 53

picture of, 137, 254

Hyde, Orson

gave apostolic prayer from Mount of Olives summit, 326

I

Immanuel

Hebrew word meaning "God is with us," 83

Infant baptism, 396

Integrity

deal justly with one another, 342

foundation for spiritual strength, 16–17

Intellect

not the only source of knowledge, 68

Interpreters. See also Urim and Thummim

seer clarifies eternal truth, 147

Isaiah

calling to prophesy, 79

circumstances during his lifetime, 44

dual nature of prophecies, 81

great are the words of, 331

guidelines for understanding, 44–45

most quoted of all prophets, 74

prophesied concerning mission of Jesus Christ, 42

reasons for difficulty in understanding, 44

reasons Nephi quoted, 43–44

wrote 100 years before Nephi's time, 72

Ishmael

descendant of Ephraim, 20

J

Jacob, son of Isaac

detail of stick of Judah and stick of Joseph, 412

house of gained covenant name of Israel, 75

Jacob, son of Nephi

saw the Redeemer, 44

Jaredites

separated from their brethren, 71

Jehovah. See Jesus Christ

Jeremiah

prophet contemporary to Lehi and Nephi, 13

quoted on plates of brass, 17

Jerusalem

definition of "born at Jerusalem," 182

destroyed, 133

expression "even to the neck" is symbolic of, 84

Nephi warned family would perish if they returned to, 20

Jesus Christ

all things typify, 73

as our Father, 144–45

Atonement of can remove our guilt, 207

can settle your individual account with justice and grant forgiveness, 131 continues to mark the path and lead the way, 22

definition of "God of Abraham, Isaac, and Jacob," 19

definition of types and shadows, 229

doctrine of is not complicated, 107

first person to be resurrected, 154

hand of is stretched out still, 87

Holy Ghost provides unity, Christ's language shows, 321

Immanuel is name for, 83

is Keeper of the Gate, 69–70

law of Moses fulfilled by, 297

Living Christ: Testimony of the Apostles, 139

miracles happen every day in the work of, 359

only one who could offer an infinite Atonement, 66

possessed merits that no other child of God could have, 52

principal figure in the Book of Mormon, 6

provided an example for all people, 107

Sabbath observance is unerring measure of our attitude toward, 158

saved only through the atoning blood of, 269

scriptures direct parents to teach faith in, 143–44

sins borne by, 153

taking upon us His name is very significant experience, 337–38

titles include Wonderful Counselor, Mighty God, Creator, Prince of Peace, 86

was and is God the Creator, 152

Jews
convincing that Jesus is the Christ, 6

frequently read about in Book of Mormon, 31

scattered, 76

Joseph Smith Translation of the Bible
helps restore many plain and precious truths, 30

Joseph, son of Jacob, given great promises concerning his posterity, 55, 71

Joseph, son of Jacob
detail of stick of, 412

given great promises concerning his posterity, 55, 71

prophesied about Joseph Smith, 56

Judah
detail of stick of, 412

kingdom of, 13, 79

Judge
out of books, 338

Judgment
bar, 112

definition of, 188–89

final and condition of our cleanliness, 66–67

Justice
mercy satisfies demands of, 51–52, 229

Justification
definition of, 51

perfection not prerequisite for, 265

K

Kapp, Ardeth G.
you can shine in darkness, 369

Kerr, W. Rolfe
words of Christ can be a personal Liahona, 110, 236

Keystone
Book of Mormon is, 4, 7, 401

Kimball, Spencer W.
abandonment of sin often requires lifestyle change, 207–8

before getting additional scripture we must believe what already revealed, 336

Church leaders call people to repentance and warn them of dangers, 132

conscience is like the Liahona, 237

death, mortal and spiritual, 284

eternal perspective helps us understand mortal suffering, 196

fervency of prayers will affect our families, 394

five essential elements of repentance, 283–84

forgiveness comes through genuine repentance, 234

gathering of Israel consists of joining the true Church, 324

given assignments in the pre-earth life, 191–92

gospel of Jesus Christ is our protection from Satan's storms, 270

hearken to those we sustain as prophets, 250

how to achieve a society with no contentions or disputations, 341

if we fail to have prayers answered, must look into our lives for a reason, 363

the Lord uses the weather to discipline His people, 277

meekness is not weakness, 304

miracles are part of the Church today, 343

need to strive for perfection, 308

New Zealanders are descendants of Hagoth, 261

picture of, 207, 219

prayers of righteous keep world from destruction, 186

scriptures have power to help us draw nearer to God, 219

sin is habit forming and can move people to the tragic point of no return, 350

some Saints want blessings without the necessary roots of discipline, 126

value of a sensitive conscience, 246–47

why one who has sinned feels burden of guilt and need for repentance, 358

King Benjamin
leader in Zarahemla, 147

King Lamoni
showed the value of service, 201

King Limhi
leader in Zarahemla, 147

people of compared with people of Alma, 159

King Noah
bondage was inevitable for his people, 159

killed by his own people, 159

was primary reason to eliminate government by kings, 150

Knowledge
relationship with hope, faith, and, 224

Kofford, Cree-L
Abinadi was and is special, 151

Korihor
philosophy of aligns with modern philosophies, 214

relied on sophistry to deceive others, 97

taught that whatsoever a man did was no crime, 214

L

Laban
Nephi commanded to kill, 16

Lake of fire and brimstone
description for the unrepentant, 127

Lamanites
cursed because of their wickedness, 62

Land
northward, 261

of inheritance, 313, 325

Language of the Egyptians
needed to study brass plates, 136

recorded on gold plates, 12

Lant, Cheryl C.
three ways to effectively read scriptures, 59

Larsen, Dean L.
how ancient Israelites went beyond the mark, 121

rebellion against God has individual roots, 349

relationship with faithfulness to the Lord and prosperity, 264

we are last laborers in the vineyard preparing for the Lord, 127

Law of Moses
fulfilled by Jesus Christ, 297, 305–6

meant to point to sacrifice of Jesus Christ, 229, 306

Lee, Harold B.
brother of Jared was showed how to pray and obtain desired blessings, 364
definition of "poor in spirit," 303
do not let self-pity or despair beckon you from the course you know is right, 299
men captained in Christ, 178
new commandments always revealed to the prophet, 16
picture of, 172, 352
pre-earth works are source of blessings in mortality, 192
priesthood offices held in this life will have effects in next world, 193
Sermon on Mount is the Lord's blueprint for perfection, 302
sin is heaviest burden, 78
spiritual significance of armor of God, 250
wicked people of Mormon's time lost Holy Ghost and the Spirit of Christ, 352

Lehi
book of, 13, 407
descendent of Manasseh, 20, 186
possible route taken by, 38, 410

Liahona
compared to conscience, 237
compared to Holy Ghost, 35
words of Christ compared to, 110
worked according to faith and diligence, 34

Light of Christ
Bible Dictionary defines, 389

Living Christ: The Testimony of the Apostles
central role of the Savior, 65
salvation comes through Jesus Christ, 139

Lost 116 manuscript pages
called the book of Lehi, 13

Lucifer. See Satan

Ludlow, Daniel H.
Book of Mormon substantiates miracles recorded in Old Testament, 38
definition of hosanna, 300
descendants of Joseph were still living in Jerusalem, 186
geographic relationship with Jaredite and Nephite lands, 371
isles of the sea means U.S., 46–47

Lund, Gerald N.
impossibility of proving there is no God, 217
Korihor has many modern-day equivalents, 213
the Savior's condescension, 25

M

Mackie, George M.
shepherd knows his sheep, 313

Madsen, John M.
what manner of men ought ye to be, 338–39

Maeser, Karl G.
snow sticks across the Alps compared to priesthood, 298

Maher-shalal-hash-baz
definition of, 84

Manasseh
detail of stick of Judah and stick of Joseph, 412
Lehi was descendant of, 20

Marriage
central to the Lord's plans for His children, 34

Marvelous work and wonder
Church members at heart of, 30
Restoration of gospel in latter days, 93

Matthews, Robert J.
Bible corrupted very early, 29
Nephi knew records would assist future generations, 94
seriousness of lying, 218

Maxwell, Neal A.
accept the Lord's correction even if it's painful, 34
adversary tries to do indirectly what we refused to let him do directly, 293
all we need to know is that God knows all, 67
being carnally minded leads to being past feeling, 218
being shown your weaknesses is part of coming unto Christ, 378
brass serpent episode points toward Christ, 272
can know the certainty of divine truths, 226
characteristics that define who truly believes in Christ, 346
children have words given to them, 224–25
Christ bore our infirmities before we bore them, 182–83
Church is not rest home for those already perfected, 260
Church members must be saintly and consecrated in conduct, 30
consecration is yielding oneself to God, 266
contrast with godly sorrow and sorrowing of damned, 349
definition of "crosses of the world," 67
definition of "take up your cross," 307
desires affect personal development and eternal blessings, 211–12
destructive consequences of infidelity, 119
dissenters become critical of the Church due to their own pride, 253
doctrinal illiteracy is significant cause of murmuring, 258

examples of hidden truths revealed by Joseph Smith, 56
faith, hope, and charity link together and bring us to Jesus Christ, 393
faith includes trust in God's timing, 99
focus on what is most important, 144
God loves those whom He chastens, 364
God's purposes will all triumph regardless of people's choice, 99
great lessons often come after difficulties, 35
hold up the shield of faith, 23
how individuals and societies become "past feeling," 398–99
if we make our religion routine, our hearts and minds will drift to other things, 315
Jesus is personal in shepherding and tutoring, 314
Jesus knew cognitively what He must do, 138–39
justice and mercy will be perfect at Final Judgment, 246
keeper of gate is Holy One of Israel, 69–70
looking beyond the mark entails looking beyond simple teachings, 121
the Lord will "make bare his holy arm in the eyes of all the nations," 327
lost books are among the treasures yet to come forth, 105
many people don't think of Christ at all, 42
miscommunications can occur even between faithful Church members, 260
must not be indifferent to wickedness in society, 169
no limit to God's knowledge, 24
parents can only give what they themselves already have, 257
personal sacrifice is willingness to put the animal in us upon the altar, 133
philosophy of ritual prodigalism is eat, drink, and be merry, 101
possible reasons for spiritual unsteadiness, 278
put off the natural man, 140
receiving answers to prayer is like opening a combination lock, 131
records of the lost tribes of Israel yet to come, 315
relationship with hope, faith, and knowledge, 224
repent frequently and regularly, 143
Satan seeks to have us disbelieve signs, 289
scriptures yet to be revealed, 98
seek to emulate the Savior's character, 318
simplicity of gospel is reason some people find it so difficult to accept, 338
those called and prepared must also prove faithful, 192
touting ourselves makes it doubly hard to confess God's hand in all things, 351
tree of life is symbol of God's love and Christ's Atonement, 22

ultimate hope tied to Jesus and
Atonement, 399
without opposition there would be no
real existence, 52
world's learned do not take Book of
Mormon seriously, 99

McConkie, Bruce R.
Alma may have been translated, 251
Atonement is infinite in scope, 228–29
Book of Mormon does not distinguish
between priests and high priests, 191
Book of Mormon's role in gathering Israel
in last days, 6
brother of Jared illustrated the need to
use our agency, 365
Christ as the Branch during Millennium, 88
conversion of the Jews, 106
Creation, Fall, and Atonement are three
pillars of eternity, 202
current gathering of Jews to homeland
is political and does not yet fulfill
prophecies in 3 Nephi 20, 326–27
definition of *anti-Christ,* 213
definition of *gentiles,* 314
definition of "great and abominable
church," 27
definition of *omnipotent,* 138
definition of *seraph,* 79
definition of "sift you as wheat," 318
definition of "top of the mountains," 74
effects of the Fall pass upon all created
things, 53–54
enjoyment of gift of the Holy Ghost is
supernal gift in mortality, 320
every nation is a gathering place for its
own people, 71
future is not all sweetness, light, and
peace, 77–78
how to become a peacemaker, 304
Immanuel both saves and condemns, 85
insights into Creation, Fall, and
Atonement, 50
Isaiah spoke of Holy One cleansing the
vineyard at Second Coming, 87
Jesus built on foundation Moses laid, 306
Joseph Smith is root of Jesse, 88
law of witnesses, 10
law governing divorce was not given to
Pharisees, 307
Lehi and Nephi's use of terms *Jews* and
Gentiles, 31
others will take part in our judgment, 351
serious study of Isaiah important for
changing and perfecting lives, 45
millennial context of the Savior's words in
Isaiah 52 and 3 Nephi 20, 327–28
miracle of being born again, 179
mysteries of God, 188
no promise of safety except for those who
love the Lord, 47
power of the Book of Mormon, 235
purposes and reasons for obtaining
spiritual gifts, 402

salvation available to all, 70
Satan to be bound by righteousness of the
people, 48
the Savior's mission is to cleanse and
purify, 333
scattering and gathering of Israel, 24
spiritual gathering precedes physical
gathering, 64
tree of knowledge of good and evil and
tree of life, 52
true doctrine of Christ, 277
unrighteousness causes the Spirit to
withdraw, 396
why miracles sometime cease, 359

McConkie, Joseph Fielding
Korihor used straw-man argument to
attack Church doctrines, 216–17
Mormon understood physical laws of
universe, 279
pride leads to divisiveness, 345

McConkie, Oscar Walter
youth may break serious commandment
based on small commandment an
adult broke, 119–20

McKay, David O.
no sin can escape retribution, 77
picture of, 77, 117
some of Lehi's children guided to Pacific
Islands, 261
what we seek above all else will largely
determine our destiny, 117

Medes
destroyed Babylon, 89

Melchizedek Priesthood
after the order of His Son, 191
all holders of were foreordained, 191
Alma noted importance of great high
priest, 194
importance of living righteously as a
holder of, 183
Nephites officiated in from days of Lehi, 62
righteous become high priests forever, 193

Mercy
satisfying the demands of justice, 51, 230,
245–46

Messiah
definition of, 70

Mickelsen, Lynn A.
baptism of fire brings cleansing from
sin, 108
similarity between cleansing through
the Atonement and washing soiled
laundry, 180

Military service, 255

Millennium
Book of Mormon will usher in, 235
children shall grow up during, 47
First Resurrection continues, 154

fulfillment of Isaiah's prophecy, 85–86
ponder conditions of, 106
Satan to be bound and have no power
during, 90, 372
two capitals for God's kingdom, 75

Millet, Robert L.
Korihor used straw-man argument to
attack Church doctrines, 216–17
Mormon understood physical laws of the
universe, 279
pride leads to divisiveness, 345

Ministering angels, 391

Miracles, 322

Missionary work
Book of Mormon teaches how to do, 101
bring good tidings and publish peace, 328
every member should do, 168
giving ourselves fully to, 158
help converted stay active, 206
permission to open Germany to, 205–6
prayerfully set a date to have someone
prepared, 168
realities of, 209–10
symbolism for Isaiah verses in 2 Nephi,
78–79

Monson, Thomas S.
blessings come from avoiding contention,
300–301
decisions have eternal consequences, 20
German Democratic Republic allows
missionaries, 205–6
importance of ministering to widows, 333
membership in the Church calls forth a
determination to serve, 385
no reason to fear failure when we serve
the Lord in faith, 184–85, 379
patriarchal blessings are like the Liahona,
237
picture of, 282, 308, 385
value of anonymous service, 308
what it means to magnify a calling,
115–16

Moriancumer, Mahonri, 362

Moroni
last Nephite prophet, 382

Morrison, Alexander B.
taking Christ's name means willing to do
whatever He requires, 204

Moses
Joseph Smith's revelations teach us
about, 29

Mothers, 257–58

Mountain of the Lord's house
America is, 74–75

Mulekites
led out of Jerusalem after Lehi's
departure, 18
separated from brethren, 71

Murmuring
cause among Church members, 258
steps leading to disobedience, 14

Mysteries of God
include saving principles of gospel, 136
to those who don't have guidance of
Spirit, 188

N

Nahom
where Ishmael died and was buried, 410

Nahum
prophet who testified in kingdom of
Judah, 13

Names blotted out
purpose of Church discipline, 164

Naphtali
lived in area of Galilee where Messiah
dwelt, 85

Natural disasters, 375–76

Natural man
definition of, 139

Nebuchadnezzar
Judah taken captive by, 76

Nehor
relied on sophistry to deceive others, 97
used priestcraft to establish religious
movement, 170

Nelson, Russell M.
Atonement is infinite in scope, 66, 229
avoid using labels that lead to prejudice,
346
callings need exclamation points, not
question marks, 15
Church members may become heirs to
the blessings of Abraham, 264
coming unto Christ leads to peace, 304
conversion leads to being born again, 179
counsel to Church members who take up
arms to defend their country, 255
Creation, Fall, and Atonement essential to
plan of salvation, 202
develop faith, keep commandments, and
repent as individuals, 266
even the Savior cannot save us in our
sins, 285
feast upon the words of Christ, 109
Golden Rule, 310–11
Holy Ghost speaks to mind and heart as
we ponder and pray, 2
importance of doctrine of the gathering, 71
infectious canker of contention, 287
information about the Book of Mormon's
translation, 5
learn gospel truths by power of Holy
Ghost, 25
love of God is the source of peace, 343
one can think a prayer, 323

path of dissent leads to real dangers, 253
people will prosper only if they obey
commandments, 15
pondering invites the Holy Ghost, 274
pray and then go to work, 364–65
readers of Book of Mormon should
concentrate on Jesus Christ, 6
the Savior loves both saints and sinners,
285
scriptures direct parents to teach faith in
Jesus Christ, 143–44
temperance can protect from aftermath of
excess, 183
why Fall was necessary, 54

Nephi
psalm of, 59
saw the Redeemer, 43

Nephite calendar systems, 288

Neum
prophecies preserved, 18
prophesied concerning mission of Jesus
Christ, 42

New Jerusalem
built in America, 325
Ether described, 379–80
out of Zion shall go forth law, 75

Nibley, Hugh
Amalekites and Zoramites head Lamanite
armies against Nephites, 249
discussion of Korihor's philosophies, 214
elephants among the Jaredites, 373
miraculous effect of Nephi's oath on
Zoram, 17
real Nephite problem was not Lamanites
but following the Lord, 256

Noah
leader in land of Lehi-Nephi, 149

Nyman, Monte S.
children in Millennium grow up without
sin, 47–48
Jesus Christ is subject of 391 of Isaiah's
425 verses, 43

O

Oaks, Dallin H.
affliction can refine and purify, 45
assurance of resurrection gives strength to
endure, 244
becoming son or daughter of Christ, 153
blessings associated with partaking of
sacrament, 323–24
caution against relying solely upon self to
determine spiritual truth, 286
charity is not an act but a condition or
state of being, 393
conditions in a Zion society, 343
connection with scriptures and personal
revelation, 358
dangers accompany seeking signs, 223–24

dangers of allowing evil into the mind, 239
definition of "born again," 167
definition of "real intent," 388–89
definition of *type,* 228
difference between sin and
transgression, 54
earth shall be full of knowledge of the
Lord, 88–89
Final Judgment is an assessment of what
we have become, 188–89
gospel teachers must not obscure
students' view of the Savior, 170–71
gratitude enables us to see hardships in
context of purpose on earth, 50
great adversities are not without some
eternal purpose or effect, 260–61
hard heart limits our spirituality, 31
have will and power to control our
thoughts and actions, 60
immortality offered through Atonement, 73
importance of being true at all times, 257
Isaiah's prophecies fulfilled, 82
judgment is the Lord's, 356
knowledge of Resurrection gives strength
to endure mortal challenges, 187
LDS belief in salvation by grace, 94–95
major earthquakes are signs of Second
Coming, 296
meaning and purpose of the gathering,
291–92
miracles happen in our day and are
present in true Church, 359
members responsible to act upon Church
leaders' admonitions, 116–17
miracles still occur, 322
ordinances secure relationships with God
and family members, 382–83
peace will come to earth after Second
Coming, 75
prepare for events preceding Second
Coming, 290
prophecies and scripture passages have
multiple meanings, 82
purpose of Church discipline, 164–65
rejecting revelation through Holy Ghost
limits learning, 188
relationship with materialism and
spirituality, 281–82
salvation does not come by keeping
commandments alone, 51, 151–52
Satan's methods of deception, 372
scripture reading creates readiness to
learn, 8
service must be motivated by love of
Jesus Christ, 388–89
sinning then repenting is devilish, 102
small voice caused hearts to burn, 298
testimony of Three Witnesses, 367
those who trust the Lord pay tithing, 334
Three Witnesses included in 100 million
copies of Book of Mormon, 98
three ways we take upon us the name of
Christ, 145

ultimate treasures on earth and in heaven are our children and our posterity, 310

vain things include property, pride, prominence, power, 278

warned against preoccupation with vain things, 181

what we have become is a result of our actions, 188–89

willingness to take upon the name of Jesus Christ, 383–84

Oaths
making of taken very seriously in Nephi's day and culture, 17

Olive tree
symbol of God's love, 123

Omner
labored for years to bring Lamanites to Christ, 168

Omniscience of God, 273

Opposition
gratitude enables us to see hardships in context of purpose on earth, 50
helps us grow stronger, 52
provides choices, 52
without there would be no real existence, 52

Ordinances
importance of, 382

Other sheep, 314

P

Pace, Glenn L.
Mormon had Christlike love for his people, 351
purpose of commandments, 22–23

Packer, Boyd K.
apply Atonement to remove guilt, 207
ask and ye shall receive, 26
baptism begins a path toward eternal life, 109
beware of promptings from the adversary, 390
blessings come to those who follow the prophets, 298
choice of life is not between fame and obscurity, but good and evil, 117
counsel concerning obtaining spiritual gifts, 403
definition of *faith*, 224
describes spiritual feelings, 132, 39
difficulty of Isaiah chapters, 72
doctrine when understood changes attitudes and behavior, 219, 277
gift of Holy Ghost not recognized as it should be, 297
God's plan gave context to Nephi's afflictions, 12
healing power of the Atonement, 142

importance of living righteously as a priesthood holder, 183

importance of patience while waiting for faith to grow, 226

irreverence obstructs delicate channels of revelation, 399

Joseph Smith's role in bringing forth Book of Mormon, 356

joy comes from following divine pattern for parenthood, 19–20

keep covenants and we will be safe, 256

knowledge of God's plan provides answers to difficult questions, 189

Light of Christ helps us discern between good and evil, 389–90

major purpose of Book of Mormon is to bring people to Christ, 314

moral pollution is spiraling upward, 357

nothing in Sodom and Gomorrah exceeded wickedness now, 98

opposition helps us grow stronger, 52

pain of conscience motivates us to seek spiritual healing by repentance, 246

pray in mind and in heart, 323

receiving a testimony of the Book of Mormon, 401

relationship with power of creation and plan of salvation, 238

revelation comes as words we feel more than hear, 39, 281

role of the prophecies of Isaiah, 331

the Savior's sacrifice allows mercy without violating justice, 245

significance of baptism, 300

speak with tongue of angels when speak by influence of Holy Ghost, 110

Spirit does not get attention by shouting or shaking, 298

spiritual disorders can cause powerful suffering, 197

studying the Book of Mormon leads to personal revelation, 1

testimony of Book of Mormon grows from a seed, 8–9

virtue of tolerance has been distorted, 169

where there is no law given, no punishment, 68

Page, Hiram
witness of Book of Mormon plates, 409

Parenthood
dealing with wayward children, 23

Parkin, Bonnie D.
covenants are expressions of the heart, 156–57

Patriarchal blessing
compared to Liahona, 237

Pearl of Great Price
scripture that contains book of Moses, 29
true companion scripture to Bible and Book of Mormon, 8

Pekah
as smoking firebrand, 82

Perry, L. Tom
Book of Mormon written for our day, 4–5
courage is necessary to choose the right over the easy and popular, 170
definition of *disciple*, 291
earth life a time of learning and testing to be worthy of eternal opportunities, 189, 245
one of greatest mysteries is why mankind fails to learn from history, 277
one purpose of earth life is to unite spirits with bodies, 189
read scriptures as though writing them, 355–56
resolve to keep covenants may lead to conversion of others, 208
rocks thrown at missionaries, 200–201
Sabbath day activities and suggestions for individuals and families, 158
story of meeting first mission companion after several years, 198
warns of preoccupation with material possessions, 23

Persecution
those who endure shall be crowned with eternal joy, 172

Perseverance
leads to success, 209

Persians
destroyed Babylon, 46

Personal revelation
connection with scriptures and, 358
studying the Book of Mormon leads to, 1

Petersen, Mark E.
Sabbath day observance reflects our appreciation of Atonement, 158

Piercing the body
President Hinckley admonished youth to keep their bodies sacred, 174

Pinegar, Patricia P.
children taught of the Lord, 329

Plan of salvation
Ammon taught Lamoni, 202
known before world created, 240–41

Plates
brass, 17–18, 407
gold, 5, 11, 98, 352, 361, 407
of Mormon (gold plates), 135, 382

Plates of Nephi
Amaleki gave small to King Benjamin, 135
first person shifts to third person in, 136
large contained secular history and record of kings, 24, 42, 113, 134, 352, 408
origin of, 17–18
small contained religious history, 24, 42, 72, 113, 133, 360, 408

why Nephi was commanded to write the small, 134

Plural marriage
Church does not accept people practicing, 119

Poelman, Ronald E.
the Lord permits the righteous to suffer consequences of evil acts by others, 195
mortality is a time to learn of opposites and choose between them, 245

Pollution
in last days, 356–57
pornography is to the mind, 239

Pondering
benefit from meditation and, 274
scriptures every day, 332
to effectively read the scriptures, 59
weigh mentally, 315

Pornography
evil monster, 67
tool of the devil, 239

Porter, Bruce D.
definition of "broken heart and contrite spirit," 384–85

Porter, L. Aldin
prophets warn but do not take away agency, 371

Pratt, Parley P.
effects of Holy Ghost upon an individual, 403
knew and comprehended Book of Mormon was true, 1

Prayer
George McLaughlin prayed and fasted for growth of branch, 199
heart drawn out to God in prayer continually, 228
the Lord's, 309
lifeline to God, 111
process Enos went through increased his faith, 130
requires effort, 364

Premortal world
children of God had agency in, 192

Pride
effect of on the Church, 264
great and spacious building, 21
many facets of characterized, 278–79
prosperity and peace can lead to, 292
sometimes called great sin of the spirit, 118

Pride cycle. See Cycle of righteousness and wickedness

Priestcraft
Nehor, 171
sin of, 96

Priesthood. See Aaronic Priesthood or Melchizedek Priesthood

Probationary state
earth life a time of learning and testing, 189

Proclamation on the family. See Family proclamation

Procrastination
thief of eternal life, 230

Prophets
result of rejecting, 20

Prosperity, 15, 61, 264, 277–79, 292, 372–73, 414

Psalm
of Nephi, 59

R

Rameumptom, 219, 228, 315

Red Sea
Lehi and his family traveled beyond, 14
map, 410

Refiner's fire, 333

Reformed Egyptian
used due to lack of space, 359
variation in language used by Lehi and Nephi, 12

Reign of the judges
Nephites adjusted their measurement of time in relation to, 169

Relief Society
every convert must be nourished, 385

Repentance
brings greater peace and joy, 60
faith leads to, 291
know conditions of, 283–84
leads us to Christ's grace, 279–80
need for faith unto repentance to receive salvation, 229–30
premeditated is a deception, 102

Rest of the Lord
definition of, 194, 388

Restoration of the gospel
America a land of liberty set apart for, 49
angel would come to earth as part of, 29
Book of Mormon confirms testimony of, 8
establishment of United States for, 28
founders of America inspired to establish religious freedom, 28
freedom of religion necessary for, 47
great and marvelous work, 30
impact of in history, 31
timetable for unfolding of, 4

Resurrection
Atonement brings to pass, 247
definition of, 187, 339

every soul born into world will receive, 50
gives us strength and perspective to endure mortal challenges, 187
timing of, 243–44

Revelation
and scriptures, 358
given to every Church member, 92
need for modern, 104
spirit of, 132

Rezin
as smoking firebrand, 82

Richards, LeGrand
mountain of the Lord's house, 74
symbolism for Isaiah verses in 2 Nephi 15, 78–79

Ricks, Stephen D.
possible meaning of name Anti-Nephi-Lehi, 207
similarities with Book of Mormon and Old Testament coronation ceremonies, 136–37

Robbins, Lynn G.
choose whether to react with anger or not, 397

Robinson, Stephen E.
great and abominable church consists of more than one entity, 27

Romney, Marion G.
being true to covenants and caring for others allows us to retain remission of sins, 175–76
be liberal in giving, 118
Book of Mormon preserved his spiritual safety, 8
conversion requires change of heart, 178
definition of true conversion, 341
gathering of Judah, 327
how to overcome giving grudgingly, 158
importance of pure motives for doing righteous things, 389
individuals who try to serve the Lord without offending the devil, 108
keep advised of the Lord's counsel, 120
living law of consecration exalts the poor and humbles the rich, 342
power of pondering, 315
reality of Satan, 103
receiving gift of Holy Ghost, 108
what pray for should be in accordance with God's will, 274

S

Sabbath day
observance, 158

Sacrament
principal purpose for taking is to remember Him, 317

promise of being filled with the Spirit, 323
renew baptismal covenant through
ordinance of, 383

Salt Lake Temple
mountain of the Lord's house, 74–75
picture of, 63, 74

Salvation
available to all men, 70
saved from both physical and spiritual
death, 50, 284–85

Samaritans
captives became known as, 82–83

Samuel the Lamanite, 281

Sanctification
means overcoming every sin and bringing
all into subjection to Christ, 193–94
of the heart, 265

Scattering of Israel
brief history of, 415
iniquity led to, 70

Scott, Richard G.
cheerfully rely on the Lord when facing
challenges in mortality, 161–62
consequences of sin, 233
continual need for cycle of conversion,
293–94
counsel to those who have been sexually
abused, 398
faith in Christ floods life with brilliant
light, 391–92
find quiet place to ponder, 274
full repentance brings forgiveness through
the Atonement, 131
God gives experiences that stimulate
growth and understanding, 35–36
lineage can provide a rich heritage, 150,
345
the Lord gives relief with divine power, 196
merits and mercy of Jesus Christ, 52
obedience yields happiness; violation of
God's commandments does not, 282
peace of conscience comes from sincere
repentance and righteous living, 142–43
quotes Spencer W. Kimball regarding five
elements of repentance, 283–84
recognizing communication from Holy
Ghost, 180–81
Redeemer provides relief from heavy
burdens, 92–93
righteous character provides foundation
of spiritual strength, 16–17
saved only through atoning blood of Jesus
Christ, 269
serious transgression requires help from
priesthood leaders, 240
sexual intimacy outside marriage is a sin
and is forbidden by God, 119
study journal can increase power of
scripture study, 199

value of having broken heart and contrite
spirit, 306
way to live in world and not be
contaminated by wickedness, 60–61
when we act on an impression, we
receive confirming evidence, 376
why we are commanded to repent, 59–60
ye are to be taught from on high, 370

Scriptures
importance of studying, 94
the Lord commands His Saints to search,
331
rod of iron, 22

Sealing power, 276

Second Coming of Christ
Babylon typifies the spiritual condition
preceding, 89
conversion of Jews following, 106
Elijah restored priesthood keys before, 335
establishment of New Jerusalem prior
to, 380
God will make bare His holy arm at, 327
Isaiah prophesied of, 76, 87
Nephi's Isaiah portions underscore major
theme of, 74, 76
only converted will remain steadfast prior
to, 288
physical upheavals signal approaching
of, 295
resurrection of righteous at, 243

Second death, 244

Secret combinations
among the Jaredites, 371–72
insights into, 262–63

Seed of Christ
how one becomes son or daughter of
Jesus, 153

Seer
definition of, 55
sees things God has hidden from world,
56, 147

Seraph
definition of, 79

Service
must be motivated by love of Jesus Christ,
388–89
spiritual value in doing temporal things
for others, 201

Sheaves
refers to converts, 209

Sherem
first anti-Christ in Book of Mormon, 127

Shiloah, waters of
symbol of Jesus Christ, 84

Signs
disbelieve the, 289
evil and adulterous generation seeks, 290
why do wicked sometimes see, 289–90

Sill, Sterling W.
characteristics of resurrected body, 187

Simmons, Dennis E.
can have peace irrespective of troubles in
the world, 258

Sin
choosing with intent to repent, 266
devilish lie that person is better off after
sinning and repenting, 102
difference between transgression and, 54
heaviest burden is, 78

Singing
the Lord approves of proper, 40

Smith, Emma
early scribe for Joseph, 5

Smith, George Albert
grandfather asked, "What have you done
with my name," 268
picture of, 268

Smith, Hyrum
prepared for missionary service, 198–99
witness of Book of Mormon plates, 409

Smith, Hyrum M.
definition of mysteries, 136

Smith, Joseph
avoid contentions and disputes with those
who do not desire truth, 217
baptism by water is but half a baptism, 108
being born again comes through
ordinances, 179
Bible's shortcomings, 104
Book of Mormon keystone of our
religion, 4, 7, 401
Book of Mormon title page is literal
translation, 4
brother of Jared's name revealed, 362
building up Zion is cause that has
interested people of every age, 325
celestial rest is of such perfection and
glory that man needs preparation, 132
chiasmus in Book of Mormon, 232
choice seer described in 2 Nephi 3, 55
comparison of discernment of true doctrine
and tasting something good, 226
definition of turn in Malachi 4 and
3 Nephi 25, 335
definition of "unpardonable sin," 238–39
devil has no power over us unless we
permit him, 372
devil sets up his kingdom in opposition to
God, 27, 277
explanation of Elijah restoring priesthood
keys, 335
felt forgotten and isolated in Liberty Jail, 85

foreordained to preside over this dispensation, 56

fundamental principles of our religion, 73

gave example of seeking a sign, 128

God is merciful to those who believe, repent, and humble themselves, 161

happiness is object and design of existence, 61

infant baptism not consistent with character of God, 396

influence of false spirit is spiritually dangerous, 218

Jehovah contemplated whole of events connected with earth, 240–41

John the Beloved's request to tarry in the flesh, 339

joining Church means we leave neutral ground, 208

learned true nature of God, 4

miracles are fruits of faith, 276

Mormon means more good, 348

Moroni ministered to, 355

nearer man approaches perfection, clearer are his views, 59

necessity of gift of Holy Ghost, 383

Nephites had same order and priesthood as Church in old world, 382

person may profit by noticing first intimation of spirit of revelation, 132

picture of, 4, 7, 78, 98, 128, 147, 238, 243

plain and precious things restored, 30

prophecies from Joseph of Egypt about, 56–57

received Urim and Thummim, 366

restoration of tribe of Judah and city of Jerusalem, 326

salvation of little children, 155

sign seekers are adulterous, 218

stem, branch, and rod quote fulfilled, 88

those ordained to calling in mortality were foreordained, 191

torment of disappointment is like a lake of fire, 127

weary God until He blesses you, 363

whatever God requires is right, 16

Smith, Joseph F.

definition of "rest of the Lord," 388

deformities will be removed in the Resurrection, 244

education of desires is important to happiness, 212

establishment of United States for Restoration of gospel, 28

Father and the Son: A Doctrinal Exposition by the First Presidency, 153

fear of death removed from Latter-day Saints, 196

the Lord uses natural disasters to bring about repentance, 375–76

members who need signs to remain steadfast walking in slippery paths, 218

people who keep commandments sustained and prospered by the Lord, 15

picture of, 128, 212

role that written records will play in Judgment, 338

those who require miracles and signs are not in good standing before God, 128

warning about teachers of false doctrine, 63

Smith, Joseph Fielding

Alma had authority to baptize, 157

Americas are Zion, 362

children of God had agency in premortal world, 192

children will be raised during Millennium without sin or temptations, 47

daughters of Zion, 77

definition of "born at Jerusalem," 182

definition of "destruction of the soul," 49–50

definition of *ensign* spoken of by Isaiah, 78

definition of "taken home to God," 242

everything in universe obeys law given unto it, except man, 279

Fall part of Heavenly Father's plan, 55

First Resurrection includes different time periods and events, 243

historical overview of interpreters in Mosiah 8, 147

Holy Ghost given to Church members so they have spirit of prophecy, 92

Holy Ghost more powerful than visitation of an angel, 180

how the word *disciple* is used in Book of Mormon, 291

Latter-day Saints are going to all parts of the world as servants in the vineyard, 129

the Lord gave America as an everlasting possession to Joseph, son of Jacob, 325

man cannot enter into kingdom of God in his sins, 357

many Gentiles did have blood of Israel, 314

may consider Jesus Christ our Father, 144–45

Nephi consecrated Jacob and Joseph to teach and direct the Nephites, 115

Nephites did not use Aaronic Priesthood before the Savior's visit, 383

Nephites officiated by virtue of Melchizedek Priesthood, 62

out of Zion shall go forth law, 75

picture of, 188, 291

procrastination is thief of eternal life, 230

salvation for little children who die before age of accountability, 396

scattering of Israel in Jacob 5, 126

sealing power, 276

simple gospel principles are mysteries to those without guidance of Spirit, 188

two nations referred to in 2 Nephi 29, 105

Urim and Thummim used by Mosiah and hid up for Joseph Smith, 366

why Jesus commanded the Nephites to be baptized again, 320

why the Lord forbade Adam to partake of the fruit, 52–53

Zenos's allegory of olive tree is one of greatest parables ever recorded, 122

Smith, Joseph Sr.

Joseph Smith named after his father, 57

witness of Book of Mormon plates, 409

Smith, Samuel H.

witness of Book of Mormon plates, 409

Snow, Erastus

importance of Ishmael's lineage, 20

Snow, Lorenzo

blessings that come through tribulation, 221

picture of, 221

Snow, Lowell M.

Jesus Christ provides constant direction, 22

Sodom and Gomorrah

world is as wicked and depraved as, 98

Sons of Mosiah

searched for key components of effective gospel study, 198

Sorensen, David E.

how loss of love can happen in homes, 397

Sorrow

godly is gift of the Spirit, 233

Sperry, Sidney B.

genealogies in the scriptures, 361–62

Spirit prison, 243

Spirit world

agency even in premortal life, 192

location of, 243

Staheli, Donald L.

need daily, fervent prayer and personal, sincere involvement with scriptures, 220

obedience to gospel principles brings happiness, 15

Steel

evidence for production of, 35, 373

Stick of Judah and stick of Joseph, 20, 105, 412

Stone, David R.

how to remove oneself from influence of the world, 181–82

Stripling warriors, 256–58

Succor

describes Christ's attention to us, 183

Syria

kingdom of, 81

T

Tabeal, son of
puppet ruler in Jerusalem, 82

Talmage, James E.
Jesus Christ is Jehovah, the Creator, 152
name the Church should bear, 337
role of knowledge in accountability, 68

Tanner, N. Eldon
rejecting the prophets brings suffering, 296
what it means to deal justly with others, 342

Tattoos
President Hinckley admonished youth to
keep their bodies sacred, 173–74

Taylor, John
God holds us responsible for those we
might have saved, 116
must be pure in heart, fear God, and keep
commandments, 26
picture of, 26, 371
who will judge us, 351

Temptations
of the devil in Lehi's dream, 21

Ten Commandments
given for all generations, 151

Tender mercies of the Lord
very personal and individualized
blessings, 13

Testimony
steps to obtain, 96
when pure, leads people to what is just,
176

Three Witnesses. *See* Witnesses, Three

Tiglath-pileser II (Pul)
Assyrian monarch, 82

Tingey, Earl C.
physical death defined by, 284

Tithing
paying shows faith in God, 333–34
prepares for higher law of consecration,
343

Title of Liberty, 252–53

Tolerance
virtue of has been distorted, 169

Tongue of angels
speak with when we speak by influence
of Holy Ghost, 110

Transfiguration
definition of, 339

Translation
definition of, 339

Transgression
difference between sin and, 54

Tree of life
symbols and interpretation of, 22

Trials
no pain suffered is wasted, 161

True to the Faith: A Gospel Reference
confession, 164
grace, 400
happiness, 245
humility, 266, 378
Light of Christ, 389
physical death, 242–43
prayer, 309
Sabbath, 158
salvation, 244

Twelve tribes of Israel, 5, 315

Type
definition of, 228

U

Uchtdorf, Dieter F.
become a disciple of Christ, 227–28
Church members should remain in their
homelands, 324

United States of America
definition of "isles of the sea," 46–47
established for Restoration of gospel, 28
founders inspired to establish religious
freedom in, 47

Unity
keeping commandments brings, 157

Unpardonable sin, 238–39

Urim and Thummim
John the Beloved's request to tarry in the
flesh, 339
seer could use special interpreters, 55
used by brother of Jared and Mosiah, hid
up for Joseph Smith, 147, 168–69, 366

V

Viñas, Francisco J.
characteristics of someone meek and
lowly in heart, 396

Voice of the people
members have a sacred obligation to
vote, 173

W

War
Book of Mormon teaches how to
righteously live in times of, 248
sometimes nations are justified and
obligated to fight, 251

Weakness, 378

Wealth
Nephites succumbed to many sins
because of, 113

Wells, Robert E.
need for faith unto repentance to receive
salvation, 229

Whetten, Robert J.
Christlike love is gift of Spirit, 393
service we render can be used to measure
depth of personal conversion, 137

Whitmer, Christian
witness of Book of Mormon plates, 409

Whitmer, David
witness of Book of Mormon plates, 10, 72,
98, 367, 409

Whitmer, Jacob
witness of Book of Mormon plates, 409

Whitmer, John
witness of Book of Mormon plates, 409

Whitmer, Peter Jr.
witness of Book of Mormon plates, 409

Whitney, Orson F.
Americas are the everlasting hills, 313
no pain or trial is wasted, 161

Widtsoe, John A.
seer is interpreter and clarifier of truth, 147

Wirthlin, Joseph B.
benefit of Church membership is
companionship with Saints, 386
companionship of Holy Ghost is a right to
be earned, 96
contention is a tool Satan uses, 262
definition of "pure in heart," 304
development of faith, hope, and charity as
a step-by-step process, 404
enduring to end requires whole heart, 109
faith is confidence in the unseen and
action that conforms to God's will, 222
fasting with prayer is powerful, 185
have hope knowing divine assistance is
always available, 392
hold firmly to rod of iron, 22
how we can know the Lord, 164
humility is recognizing the need for the
Lord's assistance, 370
things of the world can crowd out things
of the Spirit, 39
improve strength of prayers, 184
the Lord is source of living water, 89
measure of offering to bless poor is
measure of gratitude, 118
never can repay the debt owed to the
Savior, 138
prayers should be communication not
recitation, 309
sincerely following the Lord, 108

Witnesses, Eight
   Ether 5 specifically refers to, 367
   importance of, 11
   in addition to the Three Witnesses, 98
   personal information about each of, 409

Witnesses, Three
   Ether 5 specifically refers to, 367
   importance of, 10
   included in 100 million copies of Book of
      Mormon, 98
   personal information about each of, 409

Wood, Ray H.
   without repentance the Lord withdraws
      His influence, 350

Woodruff, Wilford
   having Holy Ghost more important than
      angelic visitation, 165
   Melchizedek Priesthood holders
      foreordained, 191
   picture of, 119, 165
   spoke to Jews about how to fulfill
      prophecies with the Lord's help, 93

Word of God
   having faith is a central point of
      Alma 32, 222

Workman, H. Ross
   murmuring consists of three steps, 14

Wresting the scriptures
   definition of, 194

Y

Young, Brigham
   battle unrighteousness every day, 195, 211
   cannot say Bible is true and Book of
      Mormon is untrue, 354
   difference between location of spirit
      world and God's abode, 243
   extent of the Savior's efforts to save
      mankind, 68
   Fall part of Heavenly Father's plan, 55
   forgiveness of sin results in bright
      countenance, 77
   holy desires produce corresponding
      outward works, 212
   Joseph Smith foreordained to preside over
      last dispensation, 56
   live far beneath our privileges regarding
      the Holy Ghost, 403
   picture of, 56, 354
   read scriptures as though writing them, 355
   sanctification means overcoming sin and
      making everyone subject to Christ, 193

Z

Zarahemla
   people of, 133

Zebulun
   lived in area of Galilee where Messiah
      dwelt, 85

Zedekiah
   historical context of, 13

Zeezrom
   deceitful lawyer in Ammonihah, 197

Zeniff
   leader in Zarahemla, 147
   record of, 149

Zenock
   prophecies preserved, 18
   prophesied concerning mission of Jesus
      Christ, 42

Zenos
   Hebrew prophet, 122
   prophecies preserved, 18
   prophesied concerning mission of Jesus
      Christ, 42

Zephaniah
   prophet who testified in kingdom of
      Judah, 13

Zion
   Americas are, 325, 362
   daughters of, 77
   gathering to, 291
   latter-day, 46, 63, 74
   New Jerusalem, 325, 379
   pure in heart, 26
   society, 343–44

Zoram
   miraculous effect of Nephi's oath on, 17

Zoramites
   Alma and his brethren preached to, 222
   apostate beliefs of, 220
   beliefs similar to Korihor, 218
   entered into alliance with Lamanites, 249

Zwick, W. Craig
   symbolism and blessings suggested by
      being "in the hands God," 352